SIDGWICK'S ETHICS AND
VICTORIAN MORAL PHILOSOPHY

Sidgwick's Ethics and Victorian Moral Philosophy

J. B. SCHNEEWIND

OXFORD
AT THE CLARENDON PRESS
1977

Oxford University Press, Walton Street, Oxford OX2 6DP

OXFORD LONDON GLASGOW NEW YORK
TORONTO MELBOURNE WELLINGTON CAPE TOWN
IBADAN NAIROBI DAR ES SALAAM LUSAKA ADDIS ABABA
KUALA LUMPUR SINGAPORE JAKARTA HONG KONG TOKYO
DELHI BOMBAY CALCUTTA MADRAS KARACHI

© *Oxford University Press 1977*

British Library Cataloguing in Publication Data

Schneewind, Jerome B
  Sidgwick's Ethics and Victorian Moral Philosophy.
  1. Sidgwick, Henry—Ethics
  I. Title
170'.9'24   B1649.S44

ISBN 0 19 824552 1

*Printed in Great Britain
at the University Press, Oxford
by Vivian Ridler
Printer to the University*

For

ELIZABETH

Preface

HENRY SIDGWICK's *Methods of Ethics* is an acknowledged masterpiece of moral philosophy. It is also the most important product of nineteenth-century British ethics and the main key to a full understanding of it. When I first began to study it, I found that there were no historical studies of it at all, and only one reasonably comprehensive recent philosophical discussion. This book is the result of my efforts to find answers to questions about the *Methods* which the existing literature did not supply. My main aims are philosophical. I try to show how Sidgwick's arguments and conclusions represent rational developments of the work of his predecessors, and to bring out the nature and structure of the reasoning underlying his own position. But although the book is mainly concerned with philosophical argument, it is a historical rather than a critical study. This is not because Sidgwick's work is of merely historical interest or because I can find nothing in the work to criticize. It is because it seemed necessary, before criticizing Sidgwick, to have a sound historical grasp of the problems he was trying to solve as well as a clear understanding of the solutions he offered.

Chapter 1 of this book traces Sidgwick's intellectual development, and Chapters 2 through 5 sketch the history of British ethics from the time of Reid and Bentham to the time when the *Methods* was being elaborated. While I believe that this historical material sheds considerable light on Sidgwick's thought, I know that the details will not interest everyone. Hence I have tried to make the commentary on the *Methods* which occupies Part II relatively independent of the earlier chapters. I have not tried to give a thorough critique of Sidgwick. To do so would require developing a comprehensive alternative to his own position; and even if I had one, there would not be room to present it here.

The interpretation of the *Methods* to which I have been led differs in many respects from that which seems to prevail in the literature. In particular, I find running through it a far more closely unified line of argument than is usually supposed. A comment Sidgwick makes about Aristotle's *Ethics* applies equally well to his own. 'On the whole', he says, 'there is probably no treatise so masterly . . . and containing so much close and valid thought that yet leaves on the reader's mind an impression of dispersive and incomplete work.' (*Hist.* p. 70.) An impression of dispersion and incompleteness is often left by the *Methods*. If the interpretation I offer is correct, the impression is profoundly mistaken.

My debts to the existing literature on Sidgwick are not less because of my disagreements with it. In general I have avoided explicit discussion of earlier interpretations. In one case this was not entirely possible; and so I should make it clear that, despite the many points at which I take issue with C. D. Broad's reading of Sidgwick, I owe a great deal to his pioneering analysis in *Five Types of Ethical Theory*.

In the course of writing this book I have received aid and encouragement from many institutions and people. The University of Pittsburgh allowed me a sabbatical leave in 1973–4, during which time a grant from the American Council of Learned Societies greatly facilitated my study of the Sidgwick manuscripts. Generous support from the National Endowment for the Humanities made it possible for me to continue to consult the manuscripts and the necessary books while I was working out the final form of my own book. I am most grateful to them.

I owe a more personal debt to my colleagues in the Department of Philosophy at the University of Pittsburgh, who since 1963 have allowed me to wander through the by-ways of nineteenth-century thought and have waited patiently for me to emerge with something useful. Without their support and encouragement I doubt if I should have been able to write this book. I hope they will not be disappointed by it.

I am extremely thankful for the assistance I have been given at many different libraries: at the Wren Library of Trinity College, Cambridge, where Mr. Trevor Kaye and others were extraordinarily helpful; at the Balliol College Library, the Bodleian Library, the British Museum, the Carnegie Library of Pittsburgh, Dr. Williams's Library, the Harvard University Library, and the Houghton Library at Harvard, the Princeton

University Library, and the University of Pittsburgh Library; at the Manchester College Library, Oxford, where Mrs. Katherine Swift located some important missing papers; and once again at the London Library, where the efficient and knowledgeable staff provided indispensable aid. Many others have also helped my search for Sidgwick material. I should like to thank those who told me about holdings or the absence of holdings at the University of Bristol, the Commission on Historical Manuscripts, Corpus Christi College, Oxford, Girton College, Newnham College, the New York Public Library, the Society for Psychical Research, the Tennyson Research Centre, the University of London Senate House Library, and the Yale University Library.

To the others who answered inquiries I am also grateful: Mr. William Armstrong of Sidgwick and Jackson, Mrs. Ann Baer, the Earl of Balfour, T. M. Farmiloe of Macmillan and Co., the Earl of Gainsborough, A. J. P. Kenny, David Lyons, Lady Kathleen Oldfield, Herbert M. Schueller, and P. G. Scott.

For permission to publish manuscript material, I am grateful to the Master and Fellows of Trinity College, Cambridge, to the Master and Fellows of Balliol College, and to Dr. Janine Dakyns. I should also like to thank Mrs. Peggy Dakyns for her generous hospitality while I was using the Dakyns letters.

Some of the material in Chapters 3 and 5 is derived from earlier publications of mine, in the *American Philosophical Quarterly, Supplementary Monographs* (1, 1968), in *The Monist* (vol. 58, no. 3), and in the 'Introduction' to *Mill's Ethical Writings* (Collier Books, Macmillan, 1965). I wish to thank the respective editors and publishers for permission to use this material. Part of Chapter 5 comes from a paper read at the Mill Centenary Conference in May 1973 at the University of Toronto, where I enjoyed the hospitality of John and Ann Robson and learned much from the general discussion. Annette Baier, Kurt Baier, and John Cooper discussed the papers used in Chapters 3 and 5 with me, much to my benefit.

I have had helpful conversations on various topics related to this book with Alan Donagan, Dana Scott, Wilfrid Sellars, and Wayne Sumner. W. K. Frankena and Bernard Williams read an early version of material now in Chapters 10 and 13, and their comments were very useful. Annette Baier and John Cooper read nearly the whole of the manuscript and made a large number of excellent suggestions for its improvement. I am very grateful to them. Derek Parfit read Chapter 1 and the whole of Part II at various stages of their development. The many hours I have spent going over the material with him have been of considerable value to me, and his unflagging interest and encouragement have meant more than I can say. I should promptly add that my stubbornness in rejecting much of the good advice these friends have offered leaves me alone responsible for the deficiencies, errors, and omissions which remain.

Finally I should like to thank Richard Creath, Barbara Hill, and Gail Horenstein for their assistance in bibliographical matters, and Ruth Durst, Collie Henderson, and Sarah Weisberg for their admirable typing of a difficult manuscript.

Pittsburgh and London　　　　　　　　　J. B. Schneewind
August 1975

Contents

Texts and References   xv

Introduction   1

PART I: TOWARDS *THE METHODS OF ETHICS*

1. The Development of Sidgwick's Thought   13
   - i. Sidgwick's Life   13
   - ii. Religion in the 1860s   17
   - iii. Sidgwick's Religious Development   21
   - iv. Sidgwick's Writings on Religion   26
   - v. Sidgwick's Early Ethical Views   40
   - vi. Sidgwick on Knowledge and Philosophy   52

2. Intuitionism and Common Sense   63
   - i. Reid's Ethics   64
   - ii. The Scottish School   74
   - iii. Thomas Brown   78
   - iv. Alexander Smith   81

3. The Cambridge Moralists   89
   - i. Coleridge   91
   - ii. The Coleridgeans   95
   - iii. Whewell's Ethics: The System   101
   - iv. Whewell's Ethics: The Difficulties   112
   - v. John Grote   117

4. The Early Utilitarians   122
   - i. Utility and Religion   122
   - ii. Bentham   129
   - iii. Godwin   134
   - iv. Early Criticism   140

5. The Reworking of Utilitarianism   152
   - i. Utilitarians and Rules   153
   - ii. J. S. Mill: Philosophy and Society   163
   - iii. Some Further Criticisms of Utilitarianism   166

iv. The Other Utilitarians   174
v. Mill's *Utilitarianism* and its Reception   178

PART II: *THE METHODS OF ETHICS*

6. The Aims and Scope of *The Methods of Ethics*   191
    i. The Focus on Common Sense   191
    ii. The Relation of Method to Principle   194
    iii. The Basic Methods   198
    iv. Ethics, Epistemology, and Psychology   204
    v. Ethics and Free Will   207
    vi. The Limits to Synthesis   212

7. Reason and Action   215
    i. The Basic Notion   215
    ii. Reason, Right, Ought, and Good   221
    iii. The Neutrality of Practical Concepts   226
    iv. Scepticism   229
    Appendix: The Development of I, iii and I, ix   233

8. Acts and Agents   237
    i. Martineau's Theory   237
    ii. The Religious Context of Martineau's Theory   243
    iii. Sidgwick's Criticisms: The Data   247
    iv. Sidgwick's Criticisms: The Theory   252
    v. The Outcome of the Controversy   254

9. The Examination of Common-Sense Morality   260
    i. The Role of the Examination   260
    ii. The Principles of the Examination   265
    iii. Common Sense Examined   269
    iv. The Dependence Argument   279

10. The Self-Evident Axioms   286
    i. Some Methodological Concerns   286
    ii. The Axioms Stated   290
    iii. The Source and Function of the Axioms   297
    iv. Axioms and Substantive Principles   304

11. The Transition to Utilitarianism   310
    i. Virtue and the Ultimate Good   311
    ii. Pleasure   316
    iii. Pleasure and the Ultimate Good   322

12. Utilitarianism and its Method   329
    i. Utilitarianism Stated   329
    ii. The Systematization Argument   331
    iii. The Search for a Code   336
    iv. Rules and Exceptions   340
    v. Utilitarianism and Common Sense   349

13. The Dualism of the Practical Reason   352
    i. The Viability of Egoism   353
    ii. Egoism and the Systematization Argument   358
    iii. The Axiom of Egoism   361
    iv. The Necessity of Egoism   366
    v. The Problem of the Dualism   370
    vi. The Final Uncertainty   374

PART III: AFTER THE *METHODS*

14. Sidgwick and the Later Victorians   383
    i. Evolutionism   384
    ii. Idealism: F. H. Bradley   392
    iii. Idealism: T. H. Green   401

15. Sidgwick and the History of Ethics   412
    i. Sidgwick's *History of Ethics*   412
    ii. Sidgwick in the History of Ethics   417

BIBLIOGRAPHIES

   I. Henry Sidgwick: Manuscripts and Published Writings   423
   II. (a) Checklist of Moralists, 1785–1900   433
      (b) Literature on John Stuart Mill's *Utilitarianism*,
       1861–76   441
   III. General Bibliography   444

Index   457

Texts and References

THE first edition of *The Methods of Ethics* was a closely printed volume of 473 pages. Though the book underwent innumerable alterations in subsequent editions, philosophically significant changes are the exception rather than the rule. The book grew to 509 pages, some material was cut out, a few chapter titles were altered, and the location of some material was shifted; but the number and sequence of the chapters, the topics covered, and the main conclusions remained the same. For this reason the basic text in citations is that of the final, seventh edition. Normally when this edition is cited the reader may assume that earlier editions either are no different or differ only in minor matters of wording. Occasionally this point is stressed by citations of the earlier editions. Where the alterations from edition to edition are significant, either because Sidgwick changed his views or because following the alterations helps in understanding his thought, appropriate references to those editions are given.

The texts of those of Sidgwick's other works which concern us do not vary significantly from edition to edition.

In a book like this a large number of page references must inevitably be given. They have been put into the text wherever possible, and footnotes are mostly kept for substantive material. To hold footnotes to a minimum, a system of reference involving the three bibliographies at the end of the volume is employed.

References to Sidgwick's works are uniformly made in the text. Manuscripts and books are identified by the abbreviations given in the first bibliography, which is a list of his writings. His articles are identified by giving the year and (where needed) the letter of the alphabet prefixed to the listing of the item in this bibliography. Articles that have been reprinted in collections of his own work are invariably cited by giving the page number of the collection, not the page number of the original publication. For *The Methods of Ethics* only, reference is made to specific chapters by the use of upper- and lower-case Roman numerals, without further identification, for Book- and chapter-numbers. The appropriate edition is also cited. Thus *ME* 3, p. 300 refers to page 300 of the third edition of the *Methods*; 1884b, 170 refers to page 170 of Sidgwick's article 'Green's Ethics', *Mind*, o.s. vol. ix, 1884; and I, ix refers to Book I, chapter ix, of the *Methods*.

References to other nineteenth-century moral philosophers rely heavily on the second bibliography, the first part of which is a checklist of books on ethics from 1785 to 1900. When a nineteenth-century writer is named in the text or notes and no further identification of his work is given there, this checklist will contain the missing information. A year may also be indicated to specify references in the case of prolific writers. When numerous references are made to a work, the checklist will indicate the abbreviation to be used in the text. This will also be given in a footnote when the book is discussed. The second part of the second bibliography is a list of writings on Mill's *Utilitarianism* up to 1876, for use in connection with Chapter 5, section 5.

Most of the other works referred to are identified fully in footnotes on the first occasion of reference. Any subsequent references are abbreviated. The third bibliography lists all these items and should enable the reader to locate whatever is referred to by the abbreviations. It also lists some of the many other books and articles to which I am indebted.

Introduction

SIDGWICK's *Methods of Ethics*, his best and most important work, was published in December 1874. It is a systematic treatise on moral philosophy, examining in detail a far wider range of topics than any previous book on the subject, and setting new standards of precision in wording, clarity in exposition, and care in argument. His other writings on ethics are historical and critical. The *History of Ethics*, first published as an encyclopedia article in 1878, is more comprehensive and impartial than any history that preceded it and is still widely used. In a series of essays and in lectures, some of which were published posthumously, he delivered criticisms of the two major alternatives to his own views which were elaborated during the last quarter of the century. The criticisms are detailed, incisive, and fair; and if these writings are of less enduring interest than his other ethical work, it is in part because they did their job so well.

In *The Methods of Ethics* Sidgwick aimed at bringing together the ethical views of the different schools of thought that preceded him. He succeeded at least in creating the prototype of the modern treatment of moral philosophy. The *Methods* is indeed so modern in tone and content, and so lucid in style, that it has not seemed to call for any historical or exegetical study. To write about it has for the most part been simply to write ethics. Yet if the *Methods* is an enduring work, useful to philosophers of any generation in their own investigations, it is also a mid-Victorian work, conditioned by reflection on problems and thinkers in many cases now half-forgotten or wholly unknown. The reader of the *Methods* has therefore two tasks. He needs, of course, to understand the argument of the book in its own right, not simply as a contribution toward the solution of problems in which we are interested at present. And to appreciate the achievement of the work, as well as to put himself in the best position to criticize it, he needs to see it in its historical setting.

In each of these tasks the reader of Sidgwick faces a difficulty. It has always been found hard to see any continuous and

cumulative argument in the *Methods*. The book does not have the
surface difficulties found in Kant or in Hegel, but its argument
is intricate, and the very care with which it is elaborated tends
to obscure it. An enthusiastic early reviewer, after proclaiming
that 'nothing in this book is trite', confesses that we cannot
always 'sum up the results' of the discussions, that we 'lose our
way in mazes', and that we find it 'difficult to extricate the
author's own conclusions'.[1] Other reviewers and critics have
found the same problem, and it has become common to think
that there is no over-all argument in the *Methods*. Thus Metz,
in his useful and generally perceptive history of British philosophy, says of Sidgwick that 'again and again he loses himself
in a maze of details, unable to see his way through to any clear
conclusions . . . the conclusions he did reach were rather com-
promises than genuine solutions'.[2] The most helpful discussion
of Sidgwick, and the one to which the reader is most likely to
turn for aid, is Broad's extensive and sympathetic chapter in
Five Types of Ethical Theory. Yet Broad reinforces the common
view, since he examines only selected positions defended in the
Methods and does not try to show their connection with any
unified argument. The reader is thus not encouraged to look
for more in Sidgwick than isolated insights and analyses: he
thereby misses what is central to Sidgwick's own view of his
work, and perhaps to what is most permanently valuable in it.

The difficulty facing the reader who wishes to obtain some
knowledge of the historical context of the *Methods* is of a different
kind. The history of moral philosophy up to the last part of the
eighteenth century is surveyed in many places, and is familiar to
most students of ethics. Our grasp of developments thereafter is
extremely selective. The fact that, as one writer puts it, variants
of utilitarianism 'have long dominated our philosophical tradition and continue'[3] to dominate it is reflected in our historical
as well as our analytical and constructive work. We have
studies of utilitarianism in Britain during the nineteenth century
and an extensive literature on its most influential figure, John
Stuart Mill. We have no comparable histories dealing with the
philosophical opposition to utilitarianism in the nineteenth

[1] *The Spectator*, 13 Mar. 1875, p. 342.
[2] R. Metz, *A Hundred Years of British Philosophy*, trans. Harvey *et al.*, 1938, p. 85.
[3] John Rawls, *A Theory of Justice*, Cambridge, Mass., 1971, p. 52.

century, and almost no modern studies of the philosophers who articulated it. This gap in scholarship is particularly noticeable for the period of most concern to the student of Sidgwick, the period prior to the publication of the *Methods*.

The plan of the present work is dictated by consideration of these points. In the first part we shall begin by studying the development of Sidgwick's thought up to the time when the main positions of the *Methods* were formulated, bringing out, among other things, why Sidgwick thought it important to make his philosophy a synthesis of the positions held by previous philosophers. We shall then turn to the discussions which shaped the way in which he understood those positions. A full and detailed history of ethics from Paley and Bentham is not needed, since many aspects of the rise of utilitarianism are well known. We shall concentrate on less familiar aspects of the debates and less well-known writers, particularly those needed for an understanding of Sidgwick's 'reconciliation' of opposing schools. In the second part a commentary on the main topics of the *Methods* is given, stressing the underlying argument connecting the different parts of the book. In the third and final part we shall examine briefly Sidgwick's critique of the two main ethical theories which developed after the publication of his work, showing how the systematic considerations which dominate his constructive work also run through and provide support for the criticism.

In studying Sidgwick's ethics we must in effect review British moral philosophy throughout the nineteenth century. It may therefore be useful to give some general considerations on its course before entering on detailed discussion. For purposes of philosophical study it is not wholly artificial to divide the years between the French Revolution and our own century into three periods. The first begins about the middle of the 1780s with the ethical writings of Paley, Reid, and Bentham. The second begins in the middle of the 1830s, when both John Stuart Mill and his strongest opponent, William Whewell, began publishing their ethical views. And the third begins some forty years later when, just after the death of Mill in 1873, major ethical works by Sidgwick, Bradley, and Spencer appeared. This final period we may take to end at about the start of the new century, for Sidgwick died in 1900, and in

1903, the year of Spencer's death, Moore's *Principia Ethica* was published. A few features of each of these periods must be mentioned.

During the first period there was relatively little philosophical activity in England, and the most important work was not done at the universities. In Scotland, by contrast, philosophy was already practised almost wholly in the universities. Romantic literature flourished in Britain, but it was not accompanied there by any upsurge of speculative thought of the kind that took place in Germany. For some thirty years revolution and war on the continent caused governmental repression and a general concern with immediate social and political affairs in England. Those interested in reform, including the 'philosophic radicals' or Benthamites, wrote little of what we would consider philosophy, and supporters of the *status quo* wrote proportionately less. Foremost among the latter were the religious leaders of the time. Neither Methodists nor Evangelicals were speculatively inclined, nor did they move beyond platitudinous moral teaching. Since the Church controlled the two English universities, such philosophy as was taught at them was directed at forming the minds of potential clergymen. Toward the end of our first period, a quiet and unnoticed revival of philosophical studies began at Cambridge; but elsewhere, it was generally agreed, philosophy seemed to be dead.

By this time it seemed to have died in Scotland as well. Reid, who published his lectures on ethics in 1788 when he was nearly eighty, was the last of the great eighteenth-century Scottish philosophers. He was followed at the Scottish universities by a number of disciples who presented more or less elegantly phrased versions of his views to eager Scottish students and to numbers of English gentlemen who came North for amusement when Napoleon prevented them from finishing their education with a continental grand tour. Edinburgh during our first period was indeed a centre of intellectual activity, the home of the first of the great nineteenth-century quarterly reviews and the focal point of an indigenous Scottish educational tradition in which the Scottish philosophy of common sense played a leading part. But the Scottish professoriate came to be divided by increasingly bitter religious disputes, the Scottish system of education began to come under

attack from English educators, and no philosopher of out-
standing abilities arose to continue the great tradition.⁴ Sir
William Hamilton disappointed those who in the early 1830s
expected much of him, producing mainly ill-organized erudi-
tion and badly argued metaphysics. In 1835 there appeared
a book which turned the weapons of Reid's analytical approach
against Reid's opposition to utilitarianism. Alexander Smith's
Philosophy of Morals was an excellent book, though it went
unnoticed then and has not been noticed since; but it was
also in effect an epitaph for the Scottish tradition in ethics.

Our second period begins at the time of the great flowering
of Victorian literature. The 1830s saw the death of many of
the literary and political leaders of the earlier period, and the
rise of Dickens, Tennyson, Carlyle, Browning, Macaulay,
Darwin, and many others who were to dominate the thought
and letters of the next forty years. Among them was John
Stuart Mill, who after the great political hopes and excite-
ments of the early thirties became disillusioned with active
politics and turned away from it, and from the economic,
literary, and historical essays he had been writing, toward
more purely philosophical concerns.⁵ Under the leadership of
William Whewell, philosophy continued to grow at Cambridge.
At Oxford religious controversies and religious movements
absorbed too much time and energy for philosophy to be given
anything but the dreariest routine attention until the 1860s.⁶
There was a slow increase in the amount of respectable philosophy being written, but it was largely produced by men with
other professional concerns, and it was often published in
periodicals appealing to a wide and unspecialized readership.
During the second period, however, the universities were
gradually, and not always willingly, reforming. With these
reforms there came the beginnings of academic specialization,
in other disciplines as well as in philosophy; and this, together
with the increasing concentration of philosophy in the universities, inevitably led to its professionalization.

⁴ I am indebted here to the extremely interesting book by G. E. Davie, *The
Democratic Intellect*, Edinburgh, 1961.

⁵ See Joseph Hamburger, *Intellectuals in Politics: John Stuart Mill and the Philosophic Radicals*, New Haven, 1965.

⁶ For one interesting discussion of Oxford in the nineteenth century, see John
Sparrow, *Mark Pattison and the Idea of a University*, Cambridge, 1967, pp. 64–72.

By the time our third period begins, professionalization was already well on its way, as the establishment of the first British philosophical journal, *Mind*, in 1876 makes evident. Bain in Scotland, Green at Oxford, and Sidgwick at Cambridge were among the first of a new breed of philosopher. Unclerical, independent of formal allegiance to any set creed, they saw philosophy as an academic discipline dealing with problems defined and transmitted by a group of experts who were the best available judges of proposed solutions. Herbert Spencer was the last man to write philosophy which both excited public interest and received serious attention from the academics. It is perhaps indicative that the high reputation of his evolutionism did not last his lifetime, while idealism, the revival of which was wholly the creation of the universities, persisted well into the twentieth century. Philosophy in our third period, then, came, in both Scotland and England, to be practised essentially as it is now. Not the least mark of this was its detachment. In both of the earlier periods, a concern with philosophy was usually, if not quite always, subordinate to a concern with other matters. Philosophy was used to defend religion, to support the social order, to buttress demands for political reform. The ancient ideal of the love of wisdom for its own sake seemed to have been lost. In the third period it was recovered. Philosophic ardour in the search for pure truth increased as those who practised philosophy became increasingly detached from practical affairs.

Throughout these vicissitudes certain topics of debate persisted in moral philosophy. They arose primarily from controversies between exponents and opponents of utilitarianism, and changed their form as utilitarianism changed. There were a number of changes in this doctrine over the century, but one is of prime significance here. Utilitarianism attained fame during our first period primarily as a Christian view of morality. Gradually, however, secular versions displaced religious ones and utilitarianism came to be identified as opposed to the teachings of Christianity. Opponents of the view who could at first try to argue against it on a basis of shared religious belief had eventually to show its failings, and to defend their own view, on purely rational grounds. In both phases of the debate critics of utilitarianism drew heavily upon arguments supplied by Bishop Butler. He is in fact the one thinker of the earlier eighteenth century who cannot be ignored if the moral philosophy of the nineteenth is to be understood. No other ethical writings, not even those of Paley, were so frequently reprinted during the century. In the themes of his *Sermons* and his 'Dissertation on Virtue' we find most of the topics which will concern us.

Butler's great merit, to his nineteenth-century admirers, was that he made clear the basic facts about man and God which had to be accounted for by any adequate moral philosophy. He was taken by many to have given a decisive refutation of psychological egoism. In doing so, they thought, he proved the existence of a multiplicity of basic kinds of human motivation. We have direct desires and impulses. We are also moved by rational principles of action, by a reasonable concern for the good generally both of ourselves and of others. We have further a conscience, a voice within us which claims authority over all other practical principles. The significance of this complexity was plain to an age in which it was assumed that every original part of nature was made by God for an evident purpose. The rational principles were meant to guide our actions. What, then, do they tell us to do? Here Butler was not quite so clear. In the *Sermons* he seemed to think that we should usually follow the dictates of self-love, which coincide with those of benevolence and of conscience, and that should there be a conflict we ought to obey conscience. In the 'Dissertation', however, in an argument directed against the principle of benevolence but applying also to the principle of self-love, he pointed out instances of justice and veracity in which he thought it plain that consideration of consequences ought not to be our sole guide. The explanation of this, he implied, is that while God's goal may possibly be man's greatest happiness, it does not follow that men are entitled to make happiness their own direct aim. Our faculties are too weak, our knowledge too limited, to allow us to see what will be for the best on the whole. We are to follow the rules God gives us through our consciences, and to leave the consequences to him.

Despite his conviction that morality cannot be created by arbitrary acts of divine will, Butler in his ethical theory was heavily dependent on religious assumptions. His belief that benevolence, self-love, and conscience provide reasonable and authoritative principles of action, which the morality of the plain man embodies, rested on the Christian assumption that they were implanted in us by an undeceiving deity for the express purpose of guiding our actions. What if that were not their origin—if some psychological theory of their genesis should prove true? And how would one proceed if one had to support their authority without any such argument? Without religious assurance, again, how could one be sure that benevolence and self-love will always lead us to the same acts? And if they do not, and are both rational principles of action, what becomes of the rationality of the plain man's beliefs about what he ought to do? Yet the rationality of those beliefs needs to be granted if Butler's objections to utilitarianism are to have much force. It must be emphasized that Butler did not deny that the principle of benevolence, or a utilitarian concern for happiness, ought to play a part in morals: he only denied that it could properly be taken as the sole principle of morality. This denial was so effectively challenged during the nineteenth century that the Butlerians felt it to be their major task to find some way of showing that there are moral limits to the applicability of the principle of utility. But if their arguments were to be effective against mainly secular opponents, they would have to be based solely on reason. The Butlerians had thus to go beyond Butler in providing an account of the rationality of what they claimed were the fundamental moral principles. In doing this they had to counter the utilitarian claim that the utilitarian principle and it alone represented practical rationality. In addition, the utilitarians claimed that only a moral code which conformed to their one principle could be a reasonable morality. The plain man's morality, they held, could not simply be presumed to be rational. More likely it was in need of reform, and for this the utilitarian principle provided— what they claimed the Butlerians could not provide—a rational method. The Butlerians in reply had not only to counter charges of conservatism springing from their reluctance to lay down a sweeping principle of moral reform; more basically they had to show how the morality of common sense might be rational, even if it embodied not just one but a plurality of independent principles. The controversy over morality thus moved inevitably into a controversy over the nature and limits of practical rationality.

British moral philosophy in the nineteenth century centred on the attempt to determine whether or not there is a rational basis for setting moral limits to the principle of utility. To many the justifiability of such limits seemed evident so long as the religious underpinnings were not in doubt; to others it seemed equally evident even without such foundations. Yet there were numbers who thought that belief in moral limits to utility was only a result of superstition, or bad education, or outmoded philosophy, to be explained away, not to be made the heart of an ethical theory or a moral code. The profound controversies over this issue no doubt reflected, and in some ways entered into, changes and struggles in the social, political, and economic life of nineteenth-century Britain. Our concern with them must, however, be restricted to their appearance in philosophical form. We shall turn to the details after we examine the way in which these and other issues affected Sidgwick's early intellectual life.

PART I

TOWARDS *THE METHODS OF ETHICS*

I

The Development of Sidgwick's Thought

THE main source of information about Sidgwick's life is the biography written by his brother and his wife.[1] It is on the whole an excellent book, not quite as reticent as many Victorian lives of great men, though considerably less outspoken on financial, sexual, and psychological matters than recent biographies tend to be. Such material does not usually shed much light on philosophic thought, however, and its absence is perhaps not to be regretted. What is regrettable is the brevity of the sections dealing with Sidgwick's early thought. In the present chapter an attempt is made to supplement what the biography presents to us on this topic, and to spell out more fully what went into the making of the *Methods*. We shall find, by way of a conclusion, that Sidgwick's mature views on religion, morality, and philosophic methods were substantially formed well before the actual writing of the book. The details of his development are of considerable interest in their own right.

i. *Sidgwick's Life*

Henry Sidgwick's entire lifetime fell within the reign of Queen Victoria. He was born on 31 May 1838, just a little less than one year after she came to the throne, and he died on 28 August 1900, about half a year before she did. Both of his parents were from the North of England. His father, one of several sons of a well-to-do cotton manufacturer, attended Trinity College, Cambridge, graduating in 1829. He became a clergyman of the Church of England, and in 1836 was appointed master of the grammar-school in Skipton, Yorkshire.

---

[1] *Henry Sidgwick, A Memoir*, by A(rthur) S(idgwick) and E(leanor) M. S(idgwick), London, 1906. This is cited throughout as '*Mem.*' The available manuscripts do not add much to the facts supplied by the *Memoir*, but a number of other books and articles are useful, among them those listed in Bibliography III by A. C. Benson, E. F. Benson, Horatio Brown, James Bryce, J. R. M. Butler, B. A. Clough, H. A. L. Fisher, Alan Gauld, E. E. C. Jones, F. W. H. Myers, Lord Rayleigh, and Barbara Stephen.

He died in 1841. His widow and four surviving children, after several moves, settled near Bristol. In 1852 Henry was sent to Rugby School. The following year his mother moved the rest of the family to Rugby. Henry lived at home until October 1855 when he went up to his father's college at Cambridge. After a brilliant undergraduate career he became a Fellow of Trinity in October 1859, and began what turned out to be a lifetime of teaching at Cambridge. In 1869 he resigned his Fellowship because of his religious doubts. Subscription to the thirty-nine articles of the Church of England was required by law for tenure of the Fellowship, and Sidgwick by this time felt that he could no longer honestly subscribe. He was promptly appointed to a special position which did not require sub-scription; and after the law requiring subscription was changed he was reappointed a Fellow. He hoped to be elected to the Knightbridge Professorship of Moral Philosophy in 1872, upon the death of the incumbent F. D. Maurice, but the Revd. T. R. Birks was chosen instead. Sidgwick succeeded to the chair in 1883. Except for occasional lectures, he never taught at another university. William James wanted him to come to Harvard for the year 1900, but Sidgwick was not interested in pursuing the opportunity. (Harvard, Wm. James to Sidgwick, 22 Mar. and 30 Apr. 1899.)

At the beginning of his academic career Sidgwick taught classics, which had been his main study as an undergraduate, though he was already interested in philosophy. The Moral Sciences Tripos, of which philosophy was a part, had only recently been made a pathway to a degree,[2] and advantage was soon taken of Sidgwick's growing mastery of the field. In 1865 he was examining in philosophy, and in 1867, when he

---

[2] On the history of the moral sciences tripos, see D. A. Winstanley, *Early Victorian Cambridge*, Cambridge, 1940, pp. 80–1, 208–13, and *Later Victorian Cambridge*, Cambridge, 1947, pp. 185–90. The moral sciences tripos was established in 1848 at the same time as the natural sciences tripos, but both led only to honours, not to a degree: a degree had first to be earned in classics or mathematics. Not until 1860 could a degree be earned in moral sciences alone. In 1867 history and jurisprudence were dropped from, and political philosophy added to, the moral sciences. The tripos was held in low repute until, during the 1870s, several brilliant men graduated with honours in it and moved into desirable fellowships. For further discussion of the history of philosophy at Cambridge see Sheldon Rothblatt, *The Revolution of the Dons*, London, 1968, esp. Ch. 4. For a Victorian attack on Cambridge philosophy instruction, see C. M. Ingleby, *The Revival of Philosophy at Cambridge*, Cambridge, 1870.

was allowed to change the scope of his duties permanently away from classics, he began teaching the subject. For the first few years he taught primarily moral philosophy and mental philosophy. In 1874 he added political philosophy and in 1879 political economy, though he did not thereafter teach the latter very often. He repeatedly gave lectures on ethics and the history of ethics, and on metaphysical and epistemological texts and problems. In 1886 he began offering courses on law and on legislation. Other courses on subjects allied to politics recur in the following years. But there was no year, and almost no term, in which some course on ethics was not offered. (TCC, Add. MS. b. 89/9.)

Sidgwick's interests were by no means confined to the subjects he regularly taught. He was widely read in literature, particularly poetry, for which he had an exceptional memory and a fine appreciation. One of his early essays was a brilliant pioneering appreciation of A. H. Clough,[3] whose poetry seemed to him, in the sixties at any rate, more expressive of his inmost thoughts than that of any other writer. In later years he lectured on Shakespeare at Newnham College. He studied German with great thoroughness, spending several summers in the country and developing a facility in its language and an acquaintance with its thought which were both rare in English academic circles at the time. In his early years as a tutor he studied Hebrew and Arabic and became deeply versed in the biblical scholarship of the day. His later correspondence shows an enduring interest in the intricacies of day-to-day politics. And he developed early in life a fascination with stories and reports of apparitions, ghosts, premonitions, and similar phenomena, which grew to be one of the major occupations of his later years.

By modern standards his writings are extremely varied. After finishing *The Methods of Ethics*, he wrote a history of ethics which first appeared as a long article in the great ninth edition of the *Encyclopaedia Britannica* in 1878, and was issued as a book in 1886. His *Principles of Political Economy* was finished

[3] The *Times Literary Supplement*, 12 Jan. 1973, in a review of a collection of essays on Clough, calls Sidgwick's essay a 'masterly piece' which 'must rank as a great critical essay by any standards', and rates it as the finest of the sixty reprinted essays, which range up to 1920. Sidgwick's view of Clough is discussed by D. G. James, *Henry Sidgwick*, London, 1970, Ch. III.

in 1883, and his *Elements of Politics* in 1891. He was an active contributor to *Mind* from its inception in 1876, and he wrote occasionally for other periodicals on economics, history, and politics. He also published a series of addresses and papers in the *Proceedings* of the Society for Psychical Research. Lectures on metaphysics and epistemology, as well as a book on political history, were published posthumously.

Sidgwick lived in Trinity College until his marriage in 1876 to Eleanor Mildred Balfour, sister of his former pupil Arthur James Balfour. But he was at no time a recluse scholar. There is wide testimony to his personal warmth and charm, to his brilliant conversational wit, and, especially from the later years, to his wisdom. He was an active academic reformer, his most important achievement being the foundation of Newnham College, the first home of higher education for women in Cambridge. To this he devoted considerable amounts of time, money, and effort. In 1880 he and his wife, who had no children, moved into one of the Newnham College buildings; and in 1892 Mrs. Sidgwick became the second Principal, succeeding Anne Jemima Clough. Sidgwick was always active in a number of associations of an academic or a charitable nature, and he served on several governmental commissions of inquiry. The main concern of his later years, apart from his teaching and writing, was the Society for Psychical Research. It was founded in 1882, with Sidgwick as its first president. He served many years in that office, directing, with his wife, many of its projects, participating in numerous investigations of mediums, and giving generously of time and money to the work of the group. In addition to all this he was a tireless campaigner in university politics, working for the growth of scientific studies and other disciplines then new to the academic world.

Toward the end of his life he came into contact with a new generation of philosophers. He knew McTaggart, and he knew Russell. In September of 1895 he wrote to James Ward about Russell's dissertation: 'both Whitehead and I have looked through it', he said; 'We think it decidedly able.' (TCC, Add. MS. c. 100/97A.) G. E. Moore attended some of his lectures and thought him dull. We do not know much about what Sidgwick thought of Moore, but in a letter of 1900 he comments on a report that Moore has brought out a book:

Moore! I did not know he had published any *Elements of Ethics*, I have no doubt they will be acute. So far as I have seen his work, his *acumen*—which is remarkable in degree—is in excess of his *insight*. (Dakyns, 3 Feb. 1900.)

ii. *Religion in the 1860s*

Sidgwick's central concern during his early years was religion, and the thought embodied in *The Methods of Ethics* developed in part as a major aspect of this concern. He was far from idiosyncratic in his preoccupation with these matters. We tend to think of the Victorian period as one during which religious faith was seriously challenged in Britain; but this, while true, is by no means the whole truth. Certainly there were major challenges on the intellectual level to the traditional Christian doctrines. In addition the growth of unbelief among the working classes seemed to Victorians of other classes to be a major problem; and the difficulties of providing churches and clergy for the expanding and shifting population of the rapidly growing cities were enormous. Along with the difficulties, however, there were massive efforts to overcome them. Victorians produced and read defences of religion and sermons in astonishing numbers. Victorians both lay and clerical debated ecclesiastical matters with an intensity of interest and a fullness of knowledge which have seldom been matched. Victorian church-building was of extraordinary extent. 'For churchmen', writes one authority, 'the years in the middle of the nineteenth century were years of spiritual revival. During this time more of the clergy and laity saw their religion in clearer outline and allowed its dogmas to exercise a more direct control over their lives than had possibly been the case since 1700.'[4] The great days of the late-eighteenth-century revival of personal and emotional religion that created Methodism outside the Church of England and the Evangelical party within it were over, but the rigidity concerning public worship, personal morals, and private

---

[4] G. Kitson Clark, *Churchmen and the Condition of England, 1832–1885*, 1973, p. xvii. Owen Chadwick, *The Victorian Church*, Part I, 1966, Part II, 1970, also stresses the strength of religion in the Victorian era. For a good bibliographical survey, see Claude Welch, *Protestant Thought in the Nineteenth Century*, vol. I, 1972, Ch. I. The second chapter of J. B. Schneewind, *Backgrounds of English Victorian Literature*, 1970, gives a brief review of the situation of religion and of the religious thought of the period.

enjoyments which was one legacy of that movement was at its strongest. The High Church party, transformed by the Oxford Movement and still suffering from public suspicion caused by the defection of its great leader John Henry Newman to the Roman Catholic church, was largely absorbed by the work of revivifying the traditions and improving the worship of their institution. In neither of these, which were the two main divisions of the established religion, nor indeed in most of the dissenting sects, was there much willingness to face the problems posed by recent intellectual developments. The Evangelicals distrusted reason, the High Churchmen ignored science, and a fundamentalism about the Bible which had not been dominant in earlier centuries became so during the nineteenth. The Protestant religion was incorporated into the laws, the institutions, and the feelings of the nation; and the majority was not inclined to think well of anyone so unrespectable as to doubt it.

Yet within the decade during which Sidgwick's thought was forming, serious difficulties with their religion were forced upon the public. In 1859 Darwin's *Origin of Species* was published, causing a shock to many orthodox believers which is too well known to need reviewing here. Darwin said nothing in his book about man, except that he thought the hypothesis of evolution through natural selection would shed light on him. Within a year or two, however, T. H. Huxley was telling enthralled audiences that 'the structural differences which separate Man from the Gorilla and the Chimpanzee are not so great as those which separate the Gorilla from the lower apes'.[5] Geologists, led by Lyell, had for three decades been saying that the earth was very much older than the Bible would lead us to believe. In 1863, prodded by Darwin, Lyell gave the weight of his considerable authority to the conclusion that man too was of vastly greater antiquity than was usually allowed. If biologists and geologists came to such views, could the Bible be relied upon? In the mid-sixties anthropological writings by E. B. Tylor and others proposed hypotheses to the effect that religion originated in the crude and confused thought of savages. Was Christianity another case in point—or could one still think that it had its origin in a unique divine revelation? W. E. H. Lecky's

---

[5] T. H. Huxley, *Man's Place in Nature*, 1900, pp. 143–4; from an essay published in 1863.

enormously popular history of *The Rise and Influence of the Spirit of Rationalism in Europe* (1865) suggested to many that reason might sweep away Protestant Christianity as it had already vanquished so many beliefs now admitted to be mere superstitions. And Herbert Spencer's *First Principles* (1862) seemed to draw together the cumulative weight of all of modern science and of pure reason to show that we can know nothing of the ultimate nature of the world and that mute if perhaps reverent ignoring of the Unknowable—coupled with busy attention to more manageable matters—is the inevitable and proper outcome of cosmic as well as of human history. Science, in short, in these years, came to be thought to be in opposition to religion. It had not been thought to be so as little as twenty or thirty years earlier; but now the public was being asked to choose whether it would decide upon its beliefs in a scientific way or in some other.

There were those within the ranks of firm believers who thought this a false dilemma. But they were often held to pose more of a danger to religion than agnostics or scientific unbelievers or militant atheists, because they were willing to see an accommodation of religious doctrine to modern learning. These 'broad' churchmen sought a religion that would include as many people as possible. They did not think that every saying in the Bible was sacrosanct, or that the traditional formulations of dogma were unalterable. They were the leaders in trying to awaken British thought to the textual and interpretative Biblical scholarship which had been developing in Germany for decades, and which the other church groups ignored. They also tried to show that neither Darwinism nor any other results of scientific inquiry could harm the central truths of their faith: after all, they held, it is all God's truth. Many of them were consciously applying and expanding the thought of Coleridge, who had argued that the teaching of the Bible proves itself to us by its appeal to our moral convictions and our experiences of temptation, struggle, and weakness. Religion, in their view, had its basis in experience, like science: there could not be an ultimate conflict between them. Views like these were thrust upon the public by a volume entitled *Essays and Reviews* which was published by six clergymen and a layman in 1860. Holding a variety of beliefs, the 'seven against Christ', as they were sometimes called, were united in their concern about the increasing disparity between public avowal and private doubt in religious matters, arising from the repressive atmosphere which made it difficult for people to think over the bearings on their faith of new advances in science and learning. The time had come, they felt, to stop looking for infallible scientific truth in the Bible. Religious insight and understanding grow, and with such growth the accepted formulas of religion must alter. Mark Pattison showed that churchmen had not always held what they held in 1859. Benjamin Jowett argued that the Bible should be read like any other book: it would amply vindicate the high place it holds in our lives even if read critically. These views hardly seem notable now, but the Essayists were subjected to violent polemical attacks, and two of them were brought before ecclesiastical courts. Shortly thereafter, Bishop Colenso, distressed by the faulty arithmetic and other errors of the Old Testament, published new arguments against the theory of direct verbal inspiration of the holy writings. He was also prosecuted; but though some ecclesiastical condemnations of the outspoken clergymen resulted from the cases, the net result was to show that ultimately the secular courts would allow a fair amount of personal discretion in what was to be believed and taught by a clergyman of the established church. It was the beginning of the accommodation of the church to the advance of science and scholarship.

One of the reasons the matter seemed of such great moment was that it was widely held that in some way or other religion was the foundation of morality. This was not a speculative opinion concerning the kind of rational support available for first principles of ethics. It was a practical belief about what was needed to control the passions and desires of human beings, and to assure social order. People feared that without religious beliefs about personal immortality and about rewards and punishments for one's conduct the decencies of civilization could not be maintained. The Comtists and, more importantly in Britain, John Stuart Mill, argued that new sanctions could be developed to take the place of the old, and that social sympathy would replace fear. Religious thinkers disagreed; and in any case more was at stake than simply the social order of this world. Certainly the church must take account of the earthly sufferings of her members. But if, as Christianity taught, man was in need of salvation, if his inner sinfulness could be removed only by divine aid, then what he did or did not do in this life was of secondary importance. Of course his works would show forth his inner state; but his eternal welfare was the issue here, and to put the problem simply in terms of earthly happiness would be to overlook this crucial point. Despite the Darwinians and the anthropologists and the Biblical critics, man must be held to be primarily a spiritual being, under divine laws, facing divine judgement, and subject to eternal penalties or rewards.

iii. *Sidgwick's Religious Development*

Sidgwick was raised in the firm orthodox Christian certainties of his age and class, and moved away from them to a view that was highly individual and deliberately tentative. It may have been as a result of this experience that he was always concerned about the relations between what had to be taken on authority and what one's own experience made evident, between what was commonly accepted as true and what a thinking person could see for himself to be true. His dissent from the consensus of his countrymen may have led him to insist on the need for individual insight into the truth of basic principles. At the same time his philosophical examination of the grounds on which one may justifiably feel confidence in one's beliefs led him to realize that this requires the agreement of others who are qualified judges. The problem was not simply a personal one for Sidgwick. In his own times he thought he saw a marked increase in disagreement, amounting to a break-up of the established social consensus. Other thinkers of the period agreed. John Stuart Mill, for example, following the lead of the Saint-Simonians, saw his era as one in which the old agreements at the foundations of social order were being eroded by critical thought. He believed it to be a law of historical change that a new era of consolidation of opinion would follow. Sidgwick too was hopeful, if less confident about laws of history. Progress in opinion might well ensue if dissent were freely expressed, and out of the chaos a new consensus might arise, based on broader experience and clearer insight instead of on outmoded authority. These are the lines of thought that we shall see running through Sidgwick's early years.

The available evidence does not allow for any detailed description of Sidgwick's upbringing. That he came from a religious household needs no saying, but there seems to be no information about the specific variety of Christianity he was taught at home. At Rugby he would probably have been taught a quite orthodox and relatively conservative version of the religion. The Headmaster at the time was E. M. Goulburn, who sympathized with the older evangelical views, and who later wrote the last defence of the orthodox doctrine of the eternal punishment of the damned. He had been installed in order to combat the spread of the broad churchmanship of the great revivifier of Rugby, Thomas Arnold,[6] but he does not appear to have mattered much in Sidgwick's development. One of Sidgwick's future opponents, however, did make a difference. Sidgwick says that while at Rugby he was originally 'possessed . . . by scholarly ambitions of success in classical scholarship', and that it was largely due to serious conversations with T. H. Green, some two years his senior, that he went to Cambridge 'with aspirations and tendencies towards something other than classical scholarship'.[7] Although Green aroused Sidgwick's interest in philosophy, the strongest personal influence on him was exercised by an older second cousin of the Sidgwick family who lived with them, the clergyman E. W. Benson. Benson married Sidgwick's sister in 1859, and after some years as Headmaster of a new school founded under royal patronage for the sons of army officers, went on to high ecclesiastical preferment, becoming eventually the Archbishop of Canterbury. He was a powerful and domineering man of deeply religious but non-sectarian temper, a 'moderate High Churchman' with 'no leanings to Puseyism nor . . . sympathy with Liberal or Broad Churchmanship'.[8] Benson's sermons at the school he later headed suggest that he taught the boys a highly moralistic version of Christianity;[9] but it seems clear that neither he nor Goulburn's Rugby did much to prepare them to cope with modern challenges to orthodox faith.

---

[6] Berdmore Compton, *Edward Meyrick Goulburn*, 1899, pp. 43, 49.

[7] Balliol, Sidgwick's reminiscences of Green. A small portion of these was printed in R. L. Nettleship's *Memoir* of Green, without attribution to Sidgwick: in Green's *Works*, Vol. III, 1891, p. xv, and in the separate edition of the *Memoir*, 1906, pp. 7–8.   [8] A. C. Benson, *The Trefoil*, 1923, p. 55.

[9] See e.g. E. W. Benson, *Boy-Life* (new edition), 1883, pp. 294, 338 f.

Sidgwick began to be confronted by these challenges at Cambridge. During the early part of his second year he was invited to join the exclusive discussion group known as the 'Apostles'. The group demanded, Sidgwick says, 'the pursuit of truth with absolute devotion and unreserve . . . Absolute candour was the only duty that the tradition of the society enforced. . . . The gravest subjects were continually debated.' And he adds, 'no part of my life at Cambridge was so real to me as the Saturday evenings on which the apostolic debates were held'. (*Mem.*, 34–5.) It was at this time, and largely through these discussions, that he freed himself from the influence of Benson, and it was this group that turned him decisively to philosophy. He tells us that he began to read J. S. Mill and Comte; no doubt he read others as well. In these early days, he says, he and his friends, influenced by Mill and Mill's version of Comte

aimed at . . . a complete revision of human relations, political, moral, and economic, in the light of science directed by comprehensive and impartial sympathy; and an unsparing reform of whatever, in the judgment of science, was pronounced to be not conducive to the general happiness. This social science must of course have historical knowledge as a basis; but, being science, it must regard the unscientific beliefs, moral or political, of past ages, as altogether wrong,—at least in respect of the method of their attainment, and the grounds on which they were accepted. (*Mem.*, 39–40.)

All this is sufficiently Comtian, but we should not attribute too much importance to Comte.[10] In a letter written to his old friend Henry Graham Dakyns in 1894, Sidgwick describes his relation to Comte's thought a little more fully: 'I never came near to accepting either dogmatic Agnosticism or the worship of the Grand Être, Humanity. Still, it tranquillized me in the midst of scepticism to feel that "After all, there is Positivism to fall back on"— meaning by "Positivism" practical direction of science and human progress.' (Dakyns, 6 Nov. 1894.) Criticism of accepted views of morality and politics, and concern for the methods by which these are reached, were not the only interests of the Apostles. They had an abiding interest in theology. They

[10] Walter Simon, *European Positivism in the Nineteenth Century*, 1963, a valuable survey to which I am indebted, overemphasizes Comte's influence on Sidgwick (p. 190).

disagreed completely on many points but accepted 'the necessity and duty of examining the evidence for historical Christianity with strict scientific impartiality'. (*Mem.*, 40.) This was a topic close to Sidgwick's heart. Prior to 1862, he says, he had not

in any way broken with the orthodox Christianity in which I had been brought up, though I had become sceptical with regard to many of its conclusions, and generally with regard to its methods of proof. Thus for several years the time that I devoted to the study of the questions of most serious concern was divided in a fitful and varying way between philosophy and theology. (*Mem.*, 36.)

As late as 20 June 1862, he told Dakyns:

I want to be orthodox and hunger after proofs: but feel therefore compelled to contemplate the chasm between me and orthodoxy in all its vastness, and even shrink from bridging it over by soft sayings as to the 'greater importance of morals etc.'—The distinctive tenets of Christianity are either *true* and final or not true and temporary. I cannot halt between two opinions . . .

And he adds that he has told his mother 'much that shocked her', but not as much as he has told Dakyns, 'simply because it is not true in relation to her . . . It is only true to a man who has felt the necessity in every investigation of carefully distinguishing what you start with from what you hope to arrive at'. (Dakyns, 20 June 1862.)

Thus quite early in Sidgwick's life there appeared three problems which were to occupy him for many years. One is the question of the way to go about the critical assessment of commonly accepted moral beliefs, with the correlative question it forces upon us: from what foundation or basis can one criticize positive morality? A second is the question of the truth or falsity of religious doctrines, whether specifically Christian or more generally theistic. Third, and connecting the other two, there is the methodological question of how one is to settle these issues: how are we to tell truth from error, whether in religious or in moral matters? Sidgwick had worked hard on the moral and the religious issues by the middle of 1862, but he felt he was making no progress. Impressed by the writings of Ernest Renan, he turned away from philosophical modes of dealing with the issues to history. Perhaps, he thought, through the study of Old Testament times, using the original languages, he might be able to resolve his questions about Christianity as a historical religion. (*Mem.*, 36–7.) It was no mere speculative interest that led him to undertake the considerable labour of learning Hebrew and Arabic. It was a practical problem of his own, which forced him to try to find some sort of answer to his questions about religion. That practical interest made it inevitable that his reflection on morality would continue along with his investigations of religion.

There is a note among the Sidgwick papers at Trinity College, Cambridge, of an essay read to the Apostles on 30 April 1864, with the title: 'Is the relaxation of morality produced by religious tests a thing to be deplored?' (TCC, Add. MS. c. 104/56.) The essay seems to have vanished, but the title is sufficiently eloquent. Sidgwick could not forget that he held his Fellowship partly because of his commitment to belief in the articles of the Church of England. As early as 1860 he was feeling serious doubts about its doctrines. 'Had a fearful struggle on Easter Sunday as to receiving the Sacrament— I must and will believe', he wrote in a private journal for that year, and he followed this with an impassioned prayer for stronger faith and a purer heart. (TCC, Add. MS. d. 68.) By autumn he had 'almost determined not to take orders'. There was a 'great gulf' between his views and those of the framers of the articles, and he thought that perhaps someone ought to make an issue out of subscription: should he be the one? (*Mem.*, 62.) Quite early he seems to have been decided as to the general basis on which a solution was to be reached. 'In no "spiritual pride" ', he wrote, in a journal of 1861, 'but with a perhaps mistaken trust in the reason that I find in me I wish to show forth in my own life the supremacy of reason.' (TCC, Add. MS. d. 70.) Reason had to resolve two issues: could he continue to subscribe the thirty-nine articles of the Church of England as indicators of what he believed, and, if not, what ought he to do about it? Specifically, ought he to resign his Fellowship? Of this specific concern, Sidgwick says:

I did my very best to decide the question methodically on general principles, but I found it very difficult, and I may say that it was while struggling with the difficulty thence arising that I went through a good deal of the thought that was ultimately systematised in *The Methods of Ethics*. (*Mem.*, 38.)

We can trace the main steps in the development of Sidgwick's religious views, and also of his ethical views; and doing so will enable us to see how early he came to conclusions he was to hold the rest of his life. There is less information about the growth of his position concerning method. But we can see that at a relatively early point he had fixed the main positions, leaving only elaboration for the future.

iv. *Sidgwick's Writings on Religion*

Sidgwick's first important published statement on religion came in an essay of 1866. Prior to that we can catch only glimpses of his thinking. The earliest public expression of his views is a letter to *The Times* on 20 February 1861 concerning the explosion of orthodox anger at the newly-appeared *Essays and Reviews*. 'Ecclesiastical censure', Sidgwick says, will not do. Full and fair discussion is needed, to benefit laity and clergy alike. These opinions have long been troubling people; and 'philosophy and history alike have taught them to seek not what is "safe" but what is true'. The replies should do more than attack and refute. They should contain, 'besides a refutation of errors, the definition, as far as possible, of the truths neglected or perverted in those errors'. Only in this way can the publication of the book be made a 'blessing to the Church'. (1861b, 64–5.)

That some truth is to be found in all of several apparently conflicting positions and that a synthesis of such 'half-truths' is necessary for intellectual progress are commonplaces of Victorian thought. Perhaps Sidgwick came to them through reading John Stuart Mill, who had incorporated them, under the influence of Coleridge, into his thinking. But it is not unlikely that Sidgwick read Coleridge himself.[11] At any rate at this early stage he seems, in rather romantic fashion, to think that the ability to reach to profound 'half-truths' is coupled with a tolerance for obscurity and uncertainty. In an essay on de Tocqueville in 1861 he criticizes his subject for his lack of these qualities:

Perhaps the most interesting element in the lives of great thinkers is their imperfect utterance of deep truths only half-grasped; their

---

[11] An important and interesting essay on Coleridge was published in the 1858 volume of *Cambridge Essays* by F. J. A. Hort, a Fellow of Trinity senior to Sidgwick,

consciousness of enveloping mystery and darkness, into which the light that shines from them throws only dim suggestive rays. We find nothing of this in Tocqueville . . . we cannot call him profound, either in character or in intellect. Earnest as he was in the search after truth, he was destitute of one power, necessary in the pursuit of the highest truth; he could not endure to doubt. (1861c, 366–7.)

This last power Sidgwick assuredly had, and kept; and though he lost his early admiration for obscurity and vagueness, he held to the thought that half-truths might fruitfully be brought into systematic unity.

Something of this outlook is to be found in an unpublished paper read to the Apostles in 1864, 'Is Prayer a Permanent Function of Humanity?' When Sidgwick began the study of Semitic languages, he apparently had some idea that he might 'get hold of some laws of religious progress' through comparative studies. (*Mem.*, 87.) In the paper on prayer, considerable weight is placed on the idea that man is a progressive being, and that changes in religious practice and belief, as well as the growth of knowledge, may be connected with a development of human nature toward a better and a higher form. Sidgwick indicates his belief in the value of some form of religious feeling, regardless of such progress. If there is to be a permanent rationale for prayer, he argues, it cannot be the view that the gods, or God, need to be propitiated: humanity has progressed beyond that stage. It might indeed be thought that the development of science, and the concomitant spread of belief in universal causation, rule out prayer; but Sidgwick says they do not. Prayer may be viewed as simply introducing a new antecedent into the causal chain. There is no doubt, Sidgwick says, that unusual effects may follow prayers for inner grace— greater self-control, for example, and consequently a more moral life. Even if exceptional persons can produce such changes by simply deciding to alter their lives, this is not open to everyone. One result is thus 'that considering prayer merely as a means to the end of morality, it will certainly be permanent, but perhaps not universal'. But there is another factor to take into account. For men pray, not only to propitiate the deity or to acquire self-control, but 'to indulge a profound abiding and imperious instinct'. Prayer is central to religious thought and feeling, and although some forms of theism may exist without it, 'it is not possible to conceive of an emotional relation existing between man and the unknown powers, without states of consciousness that are in substance prayers'. Most men now need such 'states of consciousness', Sidgwick thinks. Is this simply their weakness, or a disease 'destined to disappear in the perfected man'? He thinks not. There are indeed a few happy people who live contentedly and nobly in this world without the aid of religion; but Sidgwick cannot share their disregard of it. He would rather, he says, 'argue from the virtue and happiness that religion has produced in the unsymmetrical and weak to the still greater effects of the same kind, it might produce in the symmetrical and strong'. Actual religion is not yet pure enough to have this role of 'the crown of glory of a symmetrical nature. But', he concludes, 'I cannot believe the long elaboration of centuries to be in vain: and I look forward to a type of man combining the highest pagan with the highest mediaeval excellences.' (TCC, Add. MS. c. 96/5.)

Sidgwick continued to speculate all his life about the possible directions in which the emotional aspects of religion had developed and would develop, and about the need men would have for these feelings. (Cf. *Mem.*, 122, and 1899b.) His first extended public treatment of these topics occurs in his long review of J. R. Seeley's *Ecce Homo*. The book appeared in 1866 and was a considerable popular success, running through seven printings in a very short time. Neither scholarly nor argumentative, it is a passionate, though not to the modern reader very moving, portrayal of Christ's teaching. Seeley sees that teaching as almost wholly moral. Theological doctrines and dogmatic commitments, he thinks, are not essential for a Christian; morality is.[12] The first part of the book offers interpretations of some of the major events recorded in the Gospels; the second, considerably longer, gives a presentation of Christian morality. Sidgwick tells us that his review, written in mid-year, expressed the 'provisional conclusions' he had reached from his studies of Semitic languages and Biblical criticism, and immediately adds: 'My studies, aimed directly at a solution of the great issues between Christianity and Scepticism, had not, as I knew, led to a really decisive result,'

---

[12] J. R. Seeley, *Ecce Homo*, fifth edn., 1866, pp. 79, 82.

(*Mem.*, 37.) Deferring discussion of Seeley's ideas about Christian morality, we may look briefly first at Sidgwick's comments on his treatment of miracles and second at Sidgwick's insistence on the development of Christ's teaching after his lifetime. We must then note at somewhat greater length Sidgwick's response to Seeley's attack on philosophy.

Seeley's treatment of miracles, Sidgwick argues, is cavalier. Assuming that where all four gospels agree they are to be trusted, and taking it that Christ claimed to work miracles, Seeley says that since they were 'believed to be real, they had the same effect' as if they had been real: 'provisionally therefore we may speak of them as real'.[13] Sidgwick points out various reasons for not trusting the gospels even where they all agree— and not least among these is that they all relate miracles. Now either we treat the gospels historically, Sidgwick says, meaning by this 'according to the method applied everywhere else in history', or else we admit that miracles—events which violate or transcend the laws of nature—really occur. (1866, 4.) If the latter, we cannot draw a line and admit the truth of only a special class of reports of miracles, denying on general historical grounds that any other reports could possibly be true: we give up the historian's presupposition altogether. But if we accept the historian's presupposition, we must deal not with miracles but with stories of miracles; and it is not hard to give an account of such stories. Whichever alternative we choose, we must use it throughout. Seeley, Sidgwick thinks, has neither done this nor given any reason for rejecting such parts of the gospels as he does reject. He is even careless in applying his own principle of accepting what they all agree on, though he gives no clear alternative. (1866, 8–9.) Yet the question of miracles is the central and critical one, Sidgwick holds, for any modern interpretation of the Bible. Having said this, Sidgwick passes on to other topics, without saying whether he thinks the historian's presupposition is the one to be used or not. Yet the rest of the review plainly proceeds on that presupposition. Why did Sidgwick not defend it? Why did he not argue the impossibility of miracles?

No answer to these questions can be directly documented, but some of the letters point to the direction of Sidgwick's thought.

---

[13] *Ecce Homo*, p. 44.

In December 1866 he wrote a long letter to his close friend Roden Noel. He says:

> My history during the last five months has been chiefly the history of my philosophical thinking. Only I happened to read Lecky in the Long. You know the book—*History of Rationalism*. With the perverseness that sometimes characterises me, I took up the subject from entirely the opposite point of view to Lecky, and determined to investigate the *evidence* for mediaeval miracles. . . . The results have, I confess, astonished myself. I keep silence at present even from good words, but I dimly foresee that I shall have to entirely alter my whole view of the universe and admit the 'miraculous', as we call it, as a *permanent* element in human history and experience. You know my 'Spiritualistic' ghost-seeing tendencies. These all link on, and the Origins of all religions find themselves explained. However, as I say, I keep silence at present; I am only in the middle of my inquiries. (*Mem.*, 160.)

Sidgwick had been involved since his undergraduate days in what he sometimes called his 'ghostological' inquiries. (*Mem.*, 143.) In this he followed E. W. Benson, and was only one of many who became absorbed in the newly fashionable concern with mediums, messages from beyond, table-rapping, and materializations.[14] Sidgwick had seen these inquiries from the beginning as connected with philosophical and ethical questions. We may conjecture that by 1866 he thought it possible that his investigations, together with what he learned from the studies prompted by Lecky, had produced or would produce evidence sufficient to warrant some belief in experiences of contact with an 'unseen universe'. If so, this would have to be taken into account in any complete assessment of Gospel reports of miracles. For while psychic phenomena—to use a conveniently broad neutral term—need not be miraculous, and might be strictly governed by laws, they would probably shed light on reports of miracles. Yet they were sufficiently outside the scope of orthodox historical or scientific investigation to give one pause before bringing reference to them into a critical review. Recalling Sidgwick's hope of finding 'laws of religious development', we may also conjecture that he was beginning to view

---

[14] Alan Gauld, *The Founders of Psychical Research*, 1968, gives a useful summary of the development of psychical research during these years, pp. 70–7. He also discusses Sidgwick's work at some length.

reports of miracles of all sorts simply as part of the evidence concerning man's experience of the divine; but plainly he was not ready to say much about this line of thought.[15]

The second point of importance in Sidgwick's review of Seeley is his criticism of Seeley's assumption that Christianity was brought into the world fully grown. 'The morality of Christ', Seeley says, 'is theoretically perfect and not subject, as Mosaic morality was, to a further development.'[16] This is the attitude Sidgwick deplores. 'There is no more fruitful source of error in history', he remarks, 'than the determination to find the tree in the seed, and to attribute to the originators of important social changes detailed foresight as to the shape those changes were to assume.' We must not, as Seeley does, assume that Christ always intended to preach a world-wide religion, or to supersede the Mosaic law. We must not, in short, overlook the growth of religious and moral ideas. (1866, 15; 18–19.) The theme emerges most clearly at the end of the review. Sidgwick is objecting to Seeley's apparent desire to bind us all to the literal imitation of Christ, even in deeds which, as Seeley

---

[15] A letter written fourteen years later helps to confirm these conjectures. Sidgwick was answering an inquiry about his religious views from an old friend; and he explained that he distinguished between Christianity and Theism, and had not believed the former for years:

> not that I have any abstract objection to miracles, but because I cannot see any rational ground for treating the marvellous stories of the Gospels differently from the many other marvellous narratives which we meet with. . . . While, if I were to believe all these marvellous narratives, I should have to suppose a continual communication between an 'unseen universe' and our planet; and this would prevent the Gospel story from having anything like the unique character that it has for Christians.

So much is straightforward, supplementing the treatment of miracles in the 1866 review. But the letter continues:

> I do not make this latter supposition merely for the sake of argument; I am not inclined to oppose to this series of marvellous narratives (outside the Gospels) the sort of unhesitating disbelief that most of my orthodox friends do. In fact, I have spent a good deal of my leisure for some years in investigating ghost stories, spiritualistic phenomena, etc., etc. and I have not yet abandoned the hope of finding some residuum of truth in them. . . . Meanwhile . . . *Either* one must believe in ghosts, modern miracles, etc., *or* there can be no ground for giving credence to the Gospel story; and as I have not yet decided to do the former, I am provisionally incredulous as to the latter . . . (*Mem.*, 346–7.)

Probably in 1865 and 1866 he was somewhat less sceptical about the results of his spiritualistic investigations; and he would not have wanted to appear more certain about the Gospels than he felt.

[16] *Ecce Homo*, p. 197.

interprets them, seem to Sidgwick full of resentment and hatred. Neither this sort of imitation, nor strict obedience to 'the letter of an ordinance', is compatible, Sidgwick claims, with 'the true liberty of the spirit'.

For the spirit of moral heroes does not only live after them; it grows, it deepens, it enlarges after them. It transcends the limits of their earthly development; it overleaps the barriers that circumstances had fixed . . . it is measured not by what it did, but by what it might have done and will yet do. So we imitate our other patterns and examples in the essence, not the limitations of their virtues; so we must imitate our great pattern and example, the great originator and source of our morality. (1866, 38.)

Sidgwick must have had a strong personal sense of the need for a liberty of spirit which goes beyond the sayings and doings of a moral hero while yet rightly claiming to be true to his deepest insights. Seeley touched more than a theoretical point of disagreement here. He touched another in his attack on philosophy and philosophers.

An attack it was, though presented simply as a contrast between Christ's power and the impotence of philosophers. Seeley takes Christ to have founded a divine society whose whole mission was 'the improvement of morality'. And, he says, 'ever since the time of Socrates philosophy has occupied itself with the same problem'.

At the present day those who reject Christianity commonly represent that in advanced civilisation it gives place naturally to moral philosophy. Their belief is that the true and only method of making men good is by philosophy; and that the good influence of Christianity in past ages has been due to the truths of moral philosophy which are blended in it with superstitions which the world in its progress is leaving behind.[17]

Christ and the philosophers of old may seem similar, in that both had followers. But this similarity is trivial, for the philosophers needed followers only to spread their views, and in these days of printing do not need them. Christ's aim, however, was to build a new society, of which his followers were the first members. And there is a deeper difference between the philosopher and Christ: 'the one used reasoning and the other authority'.[18] Socrates hoped his pupils would forget him and think for

---

[17] *Ecce Homo*, pp. 89–90.   [18] *Ecce Homo*, pp. 91–3.

themselves: Christ insisted on his personal authority and on being a permanent exemplar to his followers. Hence Christianity must not be regarded as 'rudimentary or imperfect moral philosophy'. The two are totally different, and the difference may be put simply: 'philosophy hopes to cure the vices of human nature by working upon the head, and Christianity by educating the heart'.[19] Since, then, they both have the same object while differing in the means they use, we can ask which is better suited for the task. The answer plainly is Christianity. Philosophy cannot argue anyone into acting virtuously. Indeed, says Seeley, 'so far from creating good impulses, philosophy does something towards paralysing and destroying them', since emphasis on reasoning destroys the moral emotions, and solitude, which is necessary to the philosopher, 'is the death of all but the strongest virtue'. There follows a portrait of the philosopher, with 'a languid, melancholic, dull and hard temperament of virtue', who 'startles us at times by sudden immoralities into which he is betrayed by ingenuity unchecked by healthy feeling'.[20] The positive point Seely wishes to make does not depend on this portrait, which Sidgwick rightly dismisses as caricature. Virtue, Seeley holds, requires feeling, feeling raised to the pitch of enthusiasm. Christ and his divine society can stimulate this as nothing else can. We can only hope to build a virtuous society by creating what Seeley calls 'the enthusiasm of humanity'—a passionate love in each of us, shaped by Christ's example, for every man alike. We cannot build one by, or on, reasoning. Seeley thinks that history shows that Christianity has in fact worked far better than any mere theory could to produce good people.[21]

[19] *Ecce Homo*, p. 96.　　　　　　　　　　[20] *Ecce Homo*, pp. 99, 100.

[21] Cf. *Ecce Homo*, Chs. XIII–XIV. In the Preface to the later editions, Seeley reiterates his point, with special reference to the Stoics, especially Seneca. For a more temperately worded, but equally firm, comparison of the failure of Stoic philosophy to move the masses with the triumphant acceptance of Christianity, see the very interesting essay by J. B. Lightfoot in his edition of *St. Paul's Epistles to the Philippians*, 1868, especially pp. 306 ff. in the second edition, 1869. Lightfoot, ten years older than Sidgwick, was also a Fellow of Trinity; Sidgwick turned to him for advice in 1869 as to whether he should leave the Church. The contrast between pagan and Christian morals seems to have been a commonplace topic. Thus W. E. H. Lecky, *History of European Morals*, 1869, Ch. IV, the first section (Vol. II, p. 4) writes:

> The eye of the Pagan philosopher was ever fixed upon virtue, the eye of the Christian teacher upon sin. The first sought to amend men by extolling the

At the time *Ecce Homo* was published Sidgwick was devoting his energies increasingly to philosophy, particularly to moral philosophy. The earlier concern, shared with his friends in the Apostles, for a rational reconstruction of accepted social norms, was derived in part from the work of Mill and Comte. They held considerably more positive views than Seeley as to what philosophy could and must do for social reconstruction, and it was probably at them that his attack was directed. Mill, in particular, thought that philosophy must play the leading role in preparing a new intellectual synthesis to replace the decaying religious world view as the basis of social order, and that it must also, through the spreading of correct views of logic, disseminate better methods of thinking than were current, so that men could reach better opinions. Seeley's portrait of the philosopher may have been a caricature, but his attack on philosophy as a social force must have led Sidgwick to re-think his views on the matter. Sidgwick's response to Seeley is not quite the response that either Mill or Comte would have given.

To begin with, Sidgwick rejects Seeley's idea of reason, which restricts the concept 'as if it meant only logic; as if its supremacy kept the man entirely cold; as if it were impossible to feel ardour and enthusiasm for abstractions'. (1866, 27.) On the contrary: the Stoic was in fact moved to virtue by the enthusiasm he felt for the law which right reason, as he thought, showed him. In an unpublished manuscript on the Preface Seeley added to later editions of his book, Sidgwick elaborates this point a little. He criticizes Seeley's suggestion that only external sanctions enforced by public opinion or by God can keep people from immorality, and that since philosophy cannot provide these it is, in Seeley's words, 'speculative and useless'. Referring to Plato, Sidgwick says,

> The whole life of a philosopher, as he shows, is a continual education in disregarding public opinion and its sanctions—a continual revolt from 'King Nomos'. But precisely as public opinion loses its hold on him, the hold of reason increases: precisely in proportion as he deserves the name of philosopher, he does *not* resemble the man

beauty of holiness; the second, by awakening the sentiment of remorse. Each method had its excellencies and its defects. Philosophy was admirably fitted to dignify and ennoble, but altogether impotent to regenerate mankind. It did much to encourage virtue, but little or nothing to restrain vice. . . .

described by our author who 'often neglects' such moral precepts as society does not enforce. This is the ideal of a philosopher and it has sometimes (cf. Spinoza) been necessary that he should actually realize it and stand entirely alone, a law to himself. (TCC, Add. MS. c. 96/6.)[22]

The philosopher, however, is in fact scarcely ever really alone. What Sidgwick calls 'coterie-public-opinion' is there to sustain him: the Stoic would not want to be sneered at by fellow-Stoics, however little he might care for the opinion of the general public. Hence, Sidgwick concludes, Seeley's belief that philosophy leads to immorality if practised fulltime may be dismissed.

Sidgwick does not disagree so strongly with Seeley's assessment of the limits of reason in sustaining morality in the vast majority of people. Seeley's Preface, he says, 'completely refutes those who think that the beneficial influence of Stoicism on mankind is quantitatively comparable to that of Christianity. Nor do I think it exaggerates the superiority of Christianity as compared with philosophy when we regard them both as addressing themselves to ordinary people, individuals who compose "the masses".' (TCC, Add. MS. c. 96/6.) In the published review he says that he does not wish to dispute the view that 'an ordinary man, one of the masses, intellectually speaking, could only get his unlawful desires destroyed by means of a feeling of personal devotion', and so he admits that 'the effect of Christianity was incomparably greater than that of any philosophy could have been'. (1866, 28.) At the same time he rejects Seeley's sharp separation between reason and enthusiasm, as valuable social forces. 'In truth', he remarks, 'enthusiasm and reason are supplementary; neither can dispense with the other; and it is for the interest of the human race that each should keep a jealous watch on the other.' (1866, 27.)

What the role of reason is, and what the aims or hopes of philosophy might be, we shall see later. Here we may note simply that Sidgwick is not prepared to argue that philosophy by itself can be a great revivifying force for social change. He does not hold, as Hobbes seems to have held, that men are

---

[22] See *Ecce Homo*, Preface, xiii. Sidgwick and Seeley were friends, and Sidgwick showed this MS. to Seeley, who wrote some comments on it.

rational enough to see—if a philosopher demonstrates it to them—that a strong sovereign is a necessity for a viable social order. He does not appeal, with Bentham and James Mill, to the power of proper education to bring men to see the truths philosophers prove and to conduct their lives accordingly. He does not hint at any grand theory of history which will make inevitable the replacement of religion by rationally based morality. He does not introduce, as John Stuart Mill did, a sociological theory which would enable him to argue that philosophical theories will diffuse, through a middle-level 'clerisy' or intellectual class, and become the commonplaces of the common man. He grants that feeling, not reason, authority, not individual insight, are the mainstays of adherence to the accepted social morality. The philosopher, even untrammelled by concern for public opinion, may well be a good man himself. But his theories will not have the force that comes from the mighty emotional appeal of someone like Christ; and this suggests that Sidgwick has come to think that that 'complete revision of human relations . . . in the light of science directed by comprehensive and impartial sympathy' for which he and his friends had hoped would not be the achievement of philosophy. We may have here the first indications of that deprecation or at least limitation of philosophy toward which Sidgwick pointed in the first sentence of the Preface to the first edition of the *Methods*, when he called ethics 'trite'. (*ME* 7, v.)

In 1867 Sidgwick published an attack on Matthew Arnold, 'The Prophet of Culture'. Plainly irked by the condescending manner of the lecture which became the first chapter of *Culture and Anarchy*, Sidgwick wrote with a passion and a lively irony which are all too rare in his other works. He begins his essay by noting the importance of keeping in mind the distinction between an ideal state of society and its actual state when one is involved in evaluating various aspects of human life. Arnold, he charges, is simply muddled about this, sometimes praising ideal culture in contrast to actual religion as if he were praising actual culture, and seldom striving to understand ideal religion. (1867b, 42 ff.) The result is among other things a hopelessly inadequate conception of religion. Arnold sees it as 'a sort of spiritual police', keeping our animal nature in order. He says nothing, Sidgwick complains, of the way religion aids our emotional nature and our deepest feelings, nothing of its attempt to answer those 'indefinite but inevitable questions about the world and human destiny into which the eternal metaphysical problems form themselves in minds of rudimentary development', nothing of the involvement of religion in actual human psychology: 'how the moral growth of men and nations, while profoundly influenced and controlled by the formulae of traditional religions, is yet obedient to laws of its own and . . . modifies these formulae.' (1867b, 47.) Arnold is, in short, uncultured, even Philistine, about religion. (1867b, 49, 55.) He has moreover failed to note the faults of culture. Culture lacks the energy and enthusiasm of religion, and is too refined to move men to action. Instead of pointing up the conflict between culture and enthusiasm, it would be better, Sidgwick thinks, to see how each can aid the other. For 'culture, like all spiritual gifts, can only be propagated by enthusiasm', and enthusiasm needs to be enlightened if fanaticism is to be avoided. (1867b, 53–5.) Sidgwick's doubts about the truth of religious doctrines were, as we shall see, far graver by 1867 than they had been earlier. But the Arnold essay shows that he has not moved to a simplistic rejection of religion. He is rather trying to find a way of balancing the ideal demands of critical reason with the complex social and personal values of existing religious feeling. The same attitude pervades the *Methods* as regards the relations between critical reason and the accepted morality of one's society.

Two uncollected letters from John Stuart Mill to Sidgwick[23] —the only evidence of direct contact between the two—give us reason to believe that by the middle of 1867 Sidgwick's doubts about religion had become overwhelming. In July Sidgwick wrote asking Mill what he thought about the moral obligations resulting from religious tests and subscription to articles of belief. Mill replied, expressing sympathy with the difficulties Sidgwick raised, and agreeing to read an essay Sidgwick offered to send him on the subject. This essay must have been a draft of 'The Ethics of Conformity and Subscription', which Sidgwick published in 1870. We do not know what form the essay was in when he sent it to Mill; but it must have been in a fairly polished state before Sidgwick would have thought it

23 Published in the *Mill Newsletter*, vol. IX, no. 2, Summer 1974, pp. 9–11.

worthy of Mill's attention. On 26 November Mill wrote again, apologizing for having taken so long to read Sidgwick's paper, which he praised highly for its fairness and clarity. 'I agree with you', he said,

in thinking that an ethical theory—a fixed moral principle, or set of principles—respecting the bindingness of the obligation of a test, would be very desirable. But it seems to me that such fixed principles cannot be laid down for the case of Tests by itself; that the question requires to be taken up at an earlier stage, and dealt with as part of the much larger question. What, on the principles of a morality founded on the general good, are the limits to the obligation of veracity?

Without going into this general question, Mill adds, there would be little he himself could say; and in the essay the discussion of Tests seems to him to have been taken as far as it can go when treated by itself as Sidgwick has treated it. (TCC, Add. MS. c. 94/132, 133.) We shall discuss the 1870 version of this essay in the next section. But the fact that Sidgwick had gone as far with it as this correspondence shows he had indicates that he had in effect resolved the first of his problems—are the doctrines of religion true?—and was turning to the second—what he ought to do, since he could not accept the articles of the Church.

The final piece of evidence to be considered on Sidgwick's early views about religion is a letter he published in the *Pall Mall Gazette* on 6 January 1870 concerning clerical engagements—the commitments the clergyman makes in being ordained and serving as a minister. The letter is primarily a plea for clearer legal and judicial pronouncements on the exact limits to the deviations in belief to be allowed clergymen who do not accept in a literal sense all the doctrines and formularies of the established Church. Its details do not concern us. But Sidgwick illustrates his main point with a discussion of an issue he felt to be especially important: the question of the inspiration of the Bible. He outlines three possible views of inspiration. The first is the 'simple scripturalist' view: the Bible may contain mistakes on historical matters, but not serious ones; its scientific errors occur only when avoiding them would have required a miraculous revelation of scientific truth; and the important historical claims, and 'absolutely all the statements on moral and theological subjects in the Bible are true'. The second view, held by 'historical scripturalists', is that 'the theology of the Bible is final and authoritative'. We can increase our grasp of theological truth by coming to a better appreciation of what the Bible says, but only in this way. It is only the theological and moral claims of the Bible which are thus authoritative: the rest of it may contain error. 'They hold, therefore, that even the theology of the Bible will not be rightly understood if infallibility be rigidly claimed for all its theological statements; that to read it rightly we must read it historically, as the record of a gradually developed revelation; that the views of God and duty expressed . . . are not only imperfect but mixed with error . . . one-sided and unguarded statement. . . .' Modern readers, on this view, must try to reconcile the Biblical writers, synthesizing the truth grasped in fragments by each of them and harmonizing where apparent conflicts occur. (1870a, 9.)

The third view Sidgwick calls 'Rationalism', and his account of it must be given in full:

The Rationalist holds that the theology of the Bible has, and always will have, a unique interest for mankind, but unique only as the interest of Greek philosophy is unique, because it is the fountain from which the main stream of thought upon the subject is derived; so that not only must it always be presupposed and referred to by religious thinkers, but must also possess for them what M. Renan calls the 'charme des origines'. He holds too, that no sound developments of later thought are likely to deviate from the main lines laid down in the Bible, and that the more important part of religious truth (what may fairly be called the true religion) was discovered or revealed before the first century of Christianity was closed. But he holds that no explanation, even of these truths by the Biblical writers is to be regarded as authoritative; that the process of development which the Historical Scripturalist traces between the earlier and later of them has continued since, and will continue, and that we cannot forecast its limits; and that even where the doctrine of the Bible, taken as a whole, is clear, an appeal lies always open to the common sense, common reason, and combined experience of the religious portion of mankind.

The first view certainly, and the second perhaps, may be admitted by the Church of England, Sidgwick says, but not the third, which is a 'development amounting to a revolution'. And he adds: 'I incline myself to the view that I have termed Rationalism, and conceive that the thought of civilized Europe is moving rapidly in its direction, and that it must inevitably spread and prevail.' He is thus more decided and more outspoken than he was in 1866; and the tenor of thought here made clear was to be his for the remainder of his life. There is quite possibly a good deal in experience, particularly religious experience, that goes beyond the 'normal'; and the Bible may well contain records, however overlaid with factual and interpretative error, of experience pointing toward a theistic view of the universe. But these records are not conclusive proof that such an interpretation is the best one, and still less are they authoritative proofs of specifically Christian doctrine in theology or morality. They are no more final than the reasons Plato or Aristotle gave for believing in the divine order of the universe, though they may well be particularly rich in what they hold of religious experience, just as the Greek writings have proven to be particularly rich in philosophical suggestions. The final test—so far as any test is final—must always be our own reason, working with whatever we can learn of human experience. Progress is always possible in our understanding of the universe; but only by using rational procedures can we tell whether we have made progress, or have merely changed our minds. (1870a, 9.)

v. *Sidgwick's Early Ethical Views*

Sidgwick's views on ethics were developing along with his views on religion. In an autobiographical statement first published in 1901 he outlines the growth of his position in moral philosophy. The statement is central to our knowledge of his early thought; but as it is sketchy, and gives no dates, it needs to be supplemented from other available evidence. In the *Memoir* we are told that the *Methods* was written after Sidgwick resigned from his Fellowship in 1869. (*Mem.*, 204.) This must, however, refer to the actual composition of the book, for it can be shown that his distinctive views had been reached well before that time. In fact the evidence suggests that his ethical theory was worked out at least in outline and probably in some of the important details by 1867, i.e. by about the same time as his religious views seem to have reached their mature state. One of the main pieces of evidence for this claim is the fact that Sidgwick had drafted his pamphlet on the ethics of subscription and conformity by this time, as we have just seen. The other evidence is best reviewed in conjunction with the autobiographical statement.

Sidgwick begins by contrasting the thought of John Stuart Mill and William Whewell. The latter's book, prescribed for undergraduate study at Cambridge, where Whewell was Master of Sidgwick's college, gave him the impression that the intuitionists, of whom Whewell was a leading representative, were loose and vague in stating definitions and giving axioms. Mill's utilitarianism presented an alternative to the common-sense moral rules in which he had been brought up but which he now saw as 'external and arbitrary . . . and . . . to some extent doubtful and confused'. Thus the first system he accepted was Mill's; but because he could see no reason, on Mill's view, why one ought to sacrifice one's own happiness to that of others, he was 'forced to recognize the need of a fundamental ethical intuition'. (*ME* 7, xv–xvi.)

All this must have been fairly early. Whewell's work would probably have been familiar to him during his student days, even though he was not a philosophy student then: at any rate we find him using the technical terminology playfully in a letter to his sister in 1859. And utilitarianism was certainly on his mind well before Mill published his most famous exposition of the doctrine. Sidgwick tried at first to connect the utilitarian ethic with his religious beliefs. Thus in a journal entry for 17 March 1860 he wrote:

As to the 'Great Happ' theory I am softened to it: it is perhaps only a philosophico-logico-practical representation of 'Love is the fulfilling of the law'—But (1) we must take care to consider the soul's happiness and (2) we must not discard the props which we have in our conceptions, imperfect tho' they be of Truth, Justice, etc. (Purity, Reverence, etc. are parts of the ideal which Love will teach us to mould others to). (TCC, Add. MS. d. 68.)

This seems to be the earliest statement by Sidgwick of an inclination towards utilitarianism, and it is noteworthy that it already shows his concern to make that doctrine include the virtues as commonly listed by intuitionists. The journal immediately passes to an expression of religious doubt, and hope for relief from it. In August of the following year he wrote his friend Dakyns that the deep problem concerning him is 'the great one of reconciling my religious instinct with my growing conviction that both individual and social morality ought to be placed on an inductive basis'. (*Mem.*, 68.) Later in 1861, as Mill's *Utilitarianism* was appearing in instalments in *Fraser's Magazine*, Sidgwick was thinking about problems suggested by Comte and trying to connect his new and still tentative convictions with his old religious ones. 'The strongest conviction I have', he wrote in October,

is a belief in what Comte calls 'altruisme': the cardinal doctrine, it seems to me, of Jesus of Nazareth. I do not penetrate into my innermost feelings: it may be that my philanthropy has its root in selfishness: I may be convinced that the only means of securing my own happiness is to pursue that of my fellow-creatures: but surely if this profound and enlightened selfishness be a vice, and I sometimes fear that it is, in me, no other regimen could be applied to it than that suggested by itself, namely, devotion to society. Whether a Comtist or not I feel as if I should never swerve from my cardinal maxim, which is also his. 'L'amour pour principe' 'Le progres pour but' . . . (TCC, Add. MS. d. 70.)

Later in the same manuscript journal there are comments on other themes of interest: 'Love is to Comte the Ruler, while Conscience is to Butler (Conscience is only the reason applied to moral questions, and surely Reason cannot be a motive, only a regulative power).' There is also a very suggestive note about Whewell's doctrine of the moral sense: the doctrine, he says, when stripped of 'the last relics and rags of primaeval realism, may be found to express a valuable truth': but he does not himself say what that truth is, and the page peters out in inconclusive jottings about Whewell's doctrine of the five virtues. In a letter written in December there is an indication that he had begun thinking about a problem he was not soon to solve: 'I am quite necessarian now: but I preserve my Christianity by a dodge. . . . Miracles are explained by abstruse biological laws. Necessarianism is very jolly and quite the reverse of enervating. Only', he adds, a little surprisingly, 'Positivism I *cannot* stand.' (Dakyns, 1 Dec. 1861; part in *Mem.*, 71.)

In the 1901 autobiographical statement Sidgwick tells us that after accepting Mill's ethical theory he turned to the problem of selfishness posed by Mill's psychology, and realized from trying to solve it that an intuition was required to complete the utilitarian position. We can see this in his letters. He wrote in March 1862 to Dakyns that the problems of ethics are taking a more definite form. 'I am revolving a Theory of Ethics, which I think might appear in the form of essays; I think I see a reconciliation between the moral sense and utilitarian theories. I am reading Comte too again', he adds. 'I cannot swallow his Religion of Humanity, and yet his arguments as to the necessity of Religion of some sort have great weight with me.' (*Mem.*, 75–6.) And a letter in April carries the discussion a little further:

> I have not . . . advanced much in my 'Reconciliation of Ethical Systems'. . . . You will understand my position on this subject if you compare Bain with Comte. Bain is the only thoroughly honest Utilitarian philosopher I know, and he allows self-sacrifice . . . to constitute a 'glorious paradox', whereas Comte and all practical utilitarians exalt the same sentiments into the Supreme Rule of life. These are the views I am trying to reconcile. (*Mem.*, 77–8.)

Sidgwick says in the autobiography that 'in this state of mind [he] read Kant's Ethics again' and was much more favourably impressed than he had been. (*ME* 7, xvii.) A fair amount of time may have elapsed, however, between his initial worries about self-interest, intuition, and utilitarianism, and his study of Kant. We do not find references to Kant in the correspondence of this period, but it is plain that Sidgwick was making progress with his moral philosophy. Thus in December he wrote to Dakyns expressing doubt as to the utility of his studies of Semitic languages, and saying that as a result of this doubt he was 'falling back (in my innermost core) into philosophy, and spinning around and round on the old point of "Personal God", "Living Will", and other Theistic phrases'. He goes on to say that because he has a strong 'instinct' for 'mystical beliefs' (by which he seems to mean unprovable religious convictions) he is

> gradually developing my intuitive theories . . . You know I want intuitions for Morality; at least one (of Love) is required to supplement the utilitarian morality, and I do not see why, if we are to have one, we may not have others. I have worked away vigorously

at the selfish morality, but I cannot persuade myself, except by trusting intuition, that Christian self-sacrifice is really a happier life than classical insouciance. . . .

. . . You see, I still hunger and thirst after orthodoxy: but I am, I trust, firm not to barter my intellectual birthright for a mess of mystical pottage. (*Mem.*, 89–90).

This shows more of English religion than of Kantian philosophy, but it does make it plain that by the end of 1862 Sidgwick had come a long way toward shaping the outlines of his mature moral philosophy. The reconciling of utilitarianism with intuitionism by showing that the former requires an intuition at its base, and the bringing of egoism into line with the synthesis thus obtained, are already the main poles of his thought. That intuition is connected with 'mysticism'—with traditional, authority-based, faith—is still bothersome; and the problem of egoism is even more deeply troubling. 'I must write out my views on morals', he says in June 1863, 'as they are reaching a remarkable definiteness as far as they go.' (*Mem.*, 97.) But at least one of the problems would not get solved. About a year later he complains

I cannot get my moral sense right. I have been setting to work on a book that was to be called 'Eudaemonism Restated': and just when I have demonstrated on paper the absolute preferability of complete self-devotion, I find myself disbelieving it—or at least disbelieving it to be demonstrable. I will hope for any amount of religious and moral development, but I will not stir a finger to compress the world into a system, and it does not at present seem as if it was going to harmonise itself without compression. (*Mem.*, 107–8.)

Egoism continued to concern him, on personal as well as on philosophical grounds. In a letter late in 1865 he tells Dakyns:

The hard shell of Epicureanism (in the best sense I hope) has grown round me: I feel sometimes as if it was an extraneous adjunct—but I could not live without it now probably. I believe in a selfish ethics and in politics founded on selfishness well understood. (Dakyns, 7 Nov. 1865; continued, *Mem.*, 134.)

He continues, saying 'I think I shall try and write on Ethics in the course of next year. At present I am enlarging my mind in strict subjection to the Moral Science Tripos' (*Mem.*, 134) for which, as was noted, he began examining during the year.

This last remark suggests that Sidgwick set himself a stiff course of reading in the classics of moral philosophy, and a letter to Roden Noel shows that he had read a good deal of Kant prior to the middle of 1866. (*Mem.*, 151.) We may therefore conjecture that it was during 1865 and early 1866 that Sidgwick read Kant again with new understanding and, as he says in the autobiographical statement, studied Butler, and found in the works of More and Clarke the axiom he thought he required for his utilitarianism. (*ME* 7, xviii–xix.) But we must also take account of the review of Seeley's *Ecce Homo*, of which the autobiography says nothing.

Though the larger part of *Ecce Homo* is given over to exposition of an interpretation of Christ's moral and political doctrine, the purely ethical view Seeley attributes to him is not complicated. Christ made morality positive, not negative as it had been with the Jews, demanding a warm emotional love from each toward all others. Seeley treats this as equivalent to altruism or perhaps to utilitarianism. 'Christ', he says in his Preface, 'merges all virtue in beneficence.' He was concerned to relieve the sufferings of others, indifferent to his own. He promises men happiness if they will whole-heartedly and self-forgetfully devote themselves to doing good to others. In enjoining men to love others, Christ gave his followers a 'universal test by which they might discover what it was right and what it was wrong to do'. Hence no written code was needed by Christians. They were in a position to criticize all such codes, for 'they had in their own breasts an inexhaustible spring of morality'.[24] Without following the details into which Seeley takes this reading of the gospels, we can see that his view is close to the position Sidgwick was attracted to when he thought Comtian altruism the cardinal doctrine of Jesus. It is also, of course, reminiscent of the claim made by John Stuart Mill, that 'in the golden rule of Jesus of Nazareth, we read the complete spirit of the ethics of utility'.[25] It is all the more striking, therefore, that Sidgwick rejects this view of Christ's teaching.

His objections are partly due to the fact that here as elsewhere Seeley ignores historical development. 'The truth seems to be', he says, 'that in the simple and grand conception that

[24] For these points see *Ecce Homo*, e.g. pp. xvi, 116 ff. 122–3, 166, 181.
[25] *Utilitarianism*, Ch. II (*Collected Works*, Vol. X, p. 218).

Jesus formed of man's position and value in the universe, all the subsequent development of Christianity is implicity contained: but the evolution of this conception was gradual.' (1866, 23.) For instance, Jesus put faith above love, and it was not, Sidgwick thinks, until Paul that the order was reversed. More importantly, Christ was not a philanthropist or a Benthamite, and what he teaches is not so much the enthusiasm of humanity as 'the readiness to sacrifice all, not for humanity, but for the good cause, for the right', for that virtue of which philanthrophy is only a part. (1866, 19–20.) Nor is Christ's teaching noticeably more positive than that of Jewish morality. Christ tried to purify and extend the existing Jewish morality. He did not have to teach entirely new moral notions. The older account of Christian morality, as 'internalising and universalising what had before been too external and too limited', is better than Seeley's account. (1866, 21.) And Christ's particular part in this work is to be specified fairly carefully:

> The one thing important to Jesus in man was a principle so general that faith, love, and moral energy seem only different sides of it. It was the ultimate coincidence, or rather, if we may use a Coleridgean word, *indifference* of religion and morality. It was 'the single eye', the *rightness*, of a man's heart before God. It was faith in the conflict with baser and narrower impulses, love when it became emotion, moral energy as it took effect on the will. (1866, 23.)

Making this principle central, Sidgwick thinks, has four consequences in Christ's teaching. First, it deepens the importance of obligation. It implies that no outwardly right act can be produced 'except through the medium of right inward impulse', and it requires each man to aim at perfection. Second, properly understood, it leads to the view that 'the degree in which a man possesses this inner rightness of heart fixes his rank in the Kingdom of God at any time'. Neither external position, nor good works if the spirit in which they are done is faulty, are of any account. Third, when morality is 'made to depend on the state of the heart' the ceremonial law loses its importance. And finally, 'if man's position in the universe, or more religiously, in the sight of God, depends on his rightness of heart', then anyone may enter the Kingdom of God—a conclusion, Sidgwick thinks, drawn fully and explicitly only by Paul, though present in Jesus' thought. (1866, 23–6.)

By the middle of 1866, Sidgwick had concluded that he could not take Christ to have taught utilitarianism; and if all the later development of Christianity is implicit in Christ's teaching, he could not even take utilitarianism to represent completely the true development of that teaching. Yet he himself seems to have been moving closer to a definite commitment to utilitarian principles. There is evidence to suggest that he thought of himself as a utilitarian by the early part of 1867. The evidence comes from notes taken by Alfred Marshall (TCC, Add. MS. c. 104/65) of some meetings of the Grote Society, an informal philosophical discussion group named in honour of John Grote, around whom, when he was Knightbridge Professor of Moral Philosophy, it formed. At the meeting of 5 February, Marshall says, Sidgwick 'read a long and general sketch of various systems of morality. I. Absolute Right. II. Make yourself noble. III. Make yourself happy. IV. Increase the general happiness.' This seems to be an early version of the division of methods which Sidgwick eventually presented in the *Methods*; and during the discussion, Marshall reports, Sidgwick 'committed himself to the statement that without appreciating the effect of our actions on the happiness of ourselves or of others we could have no idea of right or wrong'. Sidgwick also criticized Bain's views on the relations between pleasure and desire. From the meeting of 19 February Marshall reports that 'Sidgwick believes in Utilitarianism and positively refused to sign any report of the sub-syndicate on which he is [a committee selecting books to be set for the Moral Sciences Tripos] unless Mill and Bentham were to be recommended.' The full significance of this stand is brought out in part of the report on the meeting of 29 May: 'S. committed himself as he had done once before to the statement that his principle with regard to selecting books for the Tripos was that someone should be able "to lay his hand upon his heart and say this represents more nearly what I think and feel than any other book on the subject".'

Sidgwick tells us in the 1901 autobiographical statement that after he had taken what he needed from Kant, Butler, and Clarke, he 'had to read Aristotle again'. Perhaps this was made necessary by the task of selecting books for the Tripos, perhaps by general preparation for teaching ethics in the autumn of

1867. At any rate it occurred to him to emulate Aristotle's examination of the common-sense morality of his society, for this, he thought, would help him to answer the question 'whether I had or not a system of moral intuitions'. The outcome, however, was 'to bring out . . . the difference between the maxims of Common Sense Morality (even the strongest and strictest, e.g. Veracity and Good Faith) and the intuitions I had already attained', i.e. the Kantian principle of universalizability and Clarke's principle of love or benevolence. (*ME* 7, xx.) It is significant that the instances he gives of common-sense maxims which on examination failed to be adequately clear and precise are the maxims which are central to his essay on 'The Ethics of Conformity and Subscription' of which, as has been shown, he sent a draft to Mill some time after the middle of 1867. Since this essay gives the fullest account of the reasoning which led Sidgwick to resign his Fellowship, and since that reasoning was by his own account so closely related to the development of his systematic views of morality, we must examine the essay in some detail.[26]

The issue as Sidgwick sees it is a purely moral one: what is the duty of the progressive members of a religious community to the rest, with regard to the expression of dissenting opinions? The issue is not to be discussed as a theological one, but 'on the neutral ground of ethics'. (*ECS*, 5–6.) And it is particularly important in this matter, he warns his readers, to avoid confusing the ideal and the actual. We must not expect the particular religious group of which we are members to become suddenly just what it ought to be: history shows that it probably will not do so. Hence the question is: supposing that religious

---

[26] The bibliography of Sidgwick's writings appended to the *Memoir* says that 'the substance of this pamphlet is repeated in the article on "The Ethics of Religious Conformity" in 1895'. That article in turn was reprinted by Sidgwick in his *Practical Ethics*, 1898. While this allows us to conclude that he continued to hold the views he first published in 1870, there are substantial changes of wording in the later version, which in particular is far more outspokenly utilitarian than the earlier. On the circumstances of the publication of the original pamphlet, cf. *Mem.*, 189 f., and also the unpublished letters to E. Enfield in Dr. Williams's Library, London. The issues to which Sidgwick addressed himself were being fairly widely discussed at this time. For a brief historical discussion, cf. G. Kitson Clarke, *Churchmen*, pp. 316–18. Clarke refers to one W. L. Clay who wrote an essay 'On Clerical Liberty of Thought and Speech', published in a volume edited by himself, *Essays on Church Policy*, 1868. Clay's essay is not far removed in spirit from Sidgwick's.

organizations such as the Church of England stay much as they are, what ought a member to do on coming to disagree with some of the group's doctrines? (*ECS*, 7–9.) Modern conditions of thought both enable and require us to reopen the question. Dissent suffers far fewer social penalties than it formerly did, and there is far more genuine tolerance of difference of opinion than formerly, especially wherever 'first principles and methods are as yet indeterminate, and where therefore persons of equal intelligence, sincerity, and application, are continually led to the most profoundly different conclusions'. (*ECS*, 12.)[27] This moderate and cultured temper, Sidgwick thinks, is a great advantage to religion and should be maintained. The strongest reason for it, as well as for reopening the question of conformity, is 'the increasing predominance of positive science as an element in our highest intellectual culture'. If theology is to win real assent for its conclusions, it must in our times work under the same conditions as science. It must seek the unconstrained agreement of thinkers working freely and independently. We can therefore make the problem more precise: given the need for free inquiry and for tolerance of differing views; given also that in fact there is increasing diversity of religious opinion among thoughtful people; how are Protestants to combine for worship and religious teaching? What terms are they to set for lay membership and for holding clerical office? (*ECS*, 13–16.)

Sidgwick canvasses a number of possible conditions for lay membership in a congregation, and finds none of them quite satisfactory. While he does not think all questions of conformity should be settled by the individual's 'instinct and sentiment', he concludes that as concerns the participation in worship of those who do not fully agree with the tenets of the group 'not only is there no definite rule laid down by the common understanding, but the effect of public worship on the worshipper is so complex and various that it would be very inexpedient to lay down such a rule'. (*ECS*, 23.) The more pressing question concerns what is required of a minister. Unlike the laity, who only hear the formulas of the church asserted and who remain silent, the clergyman must utter them.

[27] There is a brilliant passage on the modern temper in the essay on Clough, 1869c, 60.

Should he then be strictly truthful? Sidgwick gives the reason for asserting this position with a certain amount of personal warmth:

> There is no danger to religion which an earnest person more deplores and dreads than that there should insinuate itself into his religious exercises a sense of their shadowiness and unreality: a feeling that the view of the universe which they are framed to suit is not precisely that which his innermost self actually takes . . . (*ECS*, 27.)

But the cost of maintaining this strict requirement is very great. For, first, no human institution is perfect, and it is inevitable that the formularies of any church will have faults offensive to some of its ministers; and second, change in formularies is from time to time inevitable for reasons unconnected with doctrinal problems, and if so the minister is likely to be, and ought to be, in advance of his congregation. We must therefore choose, Sidgwick thinks, between two evils: loss of veracity or absolute unchangeability. His view is that we must allow some insincerity. The evil of doing so can be lessened if we make quite clear the maximum that will be permitted, and also if we encourage open avowal of dissent. No precise rule governing allowable amounts of dissent can be stated, but the issue should be discussed since 'it is only in this way that we can neutralize and dispel at once the special sophistries that tempt, and the singular scruples that beset, an individual thinker shaping his conduct in solitude'. (*ECS*, 30–1.)

Sidgwick finally discusses the extent to which the minister's formal subscription to the doctrines places special obligations on him. Stressing the need for clarity and definiteness in the law, he argues that a very strict interpretation of clerical engagements would be intolerable to a well-educated clergy. For supposing a precise credal definition to be reached, we would have to suppose that we could teach those training for the ministry to believe exactly what it says, and then never to think again, lest they change their minds. 'No one will venture to be ordained', he comments, 'except those who are too fanatical or too stupid to doubt that they will always believe exactly what they believed at twenty-three.' (*ECS*, 38.) This cannot be accepted: let us therefore, Sidgwick urges, relax clerical engagements and let us do so openly. Only so, he concludes, can we move 'towards harmonizing the inevitable conditions of a national ministry with the inexorable demands of theological thought'. (*ECS*, 40.)

There are three points to which attention may be drawn in this essay. First, Sidgwick insists on answering questions about actual practice in terms of realistic appraisals of the facts and the probabilities. He does not sketch an ideal church in an ideal society and ask how we can obtain guidance from considering it. This mode of approach, which we have already seen suggested in the essay on Arnold, is further developed in the *Methods*, where it is crucial to Sidgwick's views on the method the utilitarian will use. Second, Sidgwick fails to find any clear common-sense maxims which both relate specifically to the ethical issue concerning him and direct us to a definite solution to it. There is a duty of veracity; there are duties of fidelity to one's chosen church; but there is no principle of similar scope which tells us what to do when these two sets of duties come into conflict. Nor is there any commonly accepted rule about the duties of worshippers concerning religious truthfulness. In these findings we have examples of the failings of common-sense morality which were to be displayed in a far greater range of maxims in the detailed examination given that morality in Book III of the *Methods*. Third, the difficulties are resolved, in each case, by an appeal to what is expedient or useful or least harmful—by an appeal, in short, to some form of the utilitarian principle. No argument is given for the principle, which in fact is not even stated explicitly. It is as if Sidgwick worked on the assumption that such difficulties would naturally be resolved by appeal to the principle, so that solutions deriving from it will win general assent. And this point too—that in hard cases common sense appeals to utilitarian thinking— foreshadows a view developed at length in the *Methods*.

Religious doubt and moral philosophy were, then, intertwined in Sidgwick's thought during the years of its greatest development, from about 1857 to 1867. The main points of his ethical system became more firmly fixed in his mind as his religious beliefs grew weaker, and he seems to have come to fairly definite conclusions about both at the same time. His decision to resign his Fellowship, prompted by his ultimate dissent from the articles, was determined on utilitarian grounds.

'It is my painful conviction', he wrote to Mrs. Clough shortly after his resignation, 'that the prevailing lax subscription is not perfectly conscientious in the case of many subscribers: and that those who subscribe laxly from the highest motives are responsible for the degradation of moral and religious feeling that others suffer. It would require very clear and evident gain of some other kind to induce me to undergo this responsibility. And such gain I do not see.' (*Mem.*, 200–1.)

We must turn now to another aspect of Sidgwick's thought which developed relatively early and remained roughly the same throughout his life: his views on the nature of philosophy and the criteria of truth, and the bearing of these views on proper philosophical method.

vi. *Sidgwick on Knowledge and Philosophy*

Sidgwick's views on knowledge and on the nature of philosophy must have been developing while his religious and moral beliefs were elaborated, but there is much less evidence about their growth. The treatment of science and of the need for free discussion in the essay on the ethics of conformity suggests that Sidgwick was clear on a basic position by the time that essay was written; and there is in the 1867 essay on 'The Theory of Classical Education' a definition of philosophy as 'the sustained effort, if it be no more than an effort, to frame a complete and reasoned synthesis of the facts of the universe' (1867c, 316) which encapsulates his mature view of philosophy. There is therefore good, if not conclusive, reason to conjecture that by the time his positions on ethics and on religion had reached approximately their fully developed forms his understanding of knowledge and of the nature of philosophy had done so as well. His first published essay on these topics is an article of 1871 on 'Verification of Beliefs', but most of his writing on them is later than the publication of the *Methods*. There is, however, an unpublished essay apparently written rather earlier, probably in 1870, which presents a full account of Sidgwick's views on the nature of philosophy. 'We are impelled to science by a desire to get knowledge,' he wrote in an aphorism of 1870, 'to Philosophy by dissatisfaction with the knowledge we have got.' (TCC, Add. MS. d. 71.) The essay entitled 'Is Philosophy the Germ or the Crown of Science?' expands this remark.

Science, Sidgwick says, in the current sense of the term, seems to deal 'with some special department of fact clearly marked off and separated from other departments', but Philosophy seems not to do this, and so is perhaps 'knowledge of things in general'. This accords with the practice of those usually called philosophers, who 'had always a view of the whole'. But as it would hardly do to contrast the two by saying that science deals with what we know and philosophy with what we do not, perhaps we should take philosophy as systematizing the sciences, as the sciences systematize special departments of fact. Better still, to conform to the history of philosophy and so to include 'those excursions into the unknown and the half known' which it has always involved, philosophy might be said to aim at 'systematic knowledge of things in general'. This definition explains why we speak of 'natural philosophy' or 'philosophy of art', since each of these systematizes material already developed by other disciplines, e.g. mechanics or criticism. Philosophy cannot duplicate the work of the special disciplines, but beginning where they leave off and 'taking the fundamental principles beyond which each science as such does not attempt to go, must endeavour to combine them into a rational system'. (TCC, Add. MS. c. 95.)

Is it possible to do this? Sidgwick admits that there is no science, 'admitted by the common opinion of mankind, having a determinate method, and embodied in and handed on by a class of experts who agree in the main, however much they may differ in minor points', which aims at systematizing all the others. Although the impulse to work at philosophy is still strong, there are now many philosophies and no philosophy, just as once there were many geographies and no geography. 'If Philosophy is the Crown of Science, it must be allowed that science is not yet crowned.' None the less this 'clear idea of the aims and scope of philosophy' will help us to get rid of erroneous notions of what the enterprise is about. The whole aim of philosophy has been ignored, because it has come to be thought—Sidgwick here says he is attacking notions current at Cambridge, among other places—that philosophy deals especially with 'mind': hence the notion of 'mental philosophy', at once pleonastic on its own grounds and misleading on any others. Things were clearer in the time of Thales when it was evident at least that philosophy was an effort at general systematization.

When we consider writings from ancient times, however, we find a difficulty in drawing any clear distinction between philosophy and science. And here, Sidgwick says, we can properly consider a different view of philosophy. It is held by some that the goal of a system can never be reached, and that philosophy is valuable—if at all—only instrumentally, as intellectual training, or more importantly as generating through its misbegotten hypotheses significant scientific discoveries. Granting that philosophy has done this, and discussing a number of cases from Thales to Hegel, Sidgwick then asks if this function of philosophy is now outmoded. Philosophy, aiming at system, has indeed been a 'central vital force which causes new sciences to bud on the tree of knowledge'—but do we need it any more? Do we not have enough basic concepts, cannot knowledge now develop from 'gradual correction and modification' of what we already have, rather than spring from 'the fulminous flash of an active intellect'? Sidgwick rejects this conclusion, claiming that to argue for it is to 'abandon just the basis of experience' on which it might rest. If someone is simply not interested in 'solving the universe', well and good. But if he tells us that we ought not to try, we must ask 'by what empirical argument he proves that this crisis in the history of thought has been reached: that the endeavour to grasp the golden robe of complete Wisdom will no longer as of old leave even a fragment thereof in our hands'. More basically, Sidgwick suggests that philosophy cannot really perform its 'germinal function' if that is taken as its only function.

The supreme effort from which alone any partial discovery of the kind described can come, cannot be made without a hope of the supreme attainment that transcends all partial discoveries. Therefore in this as in other matters just from the most practical point of view, for the winning of just the most definitely measurable results, we must pursue the ideal: though the face of the ideal is 'evermore unseen/and fixed upon the far sea line'. (TCC, Add. MS. c. 95.)[28]

The belief that philosophy should aim at a complete systematization of the knowledge acquired in the special disciplines, which

[28] The quotation is from Tennyson's 'The Voyager': Sidgwick was fond of it and used it several times in his later writings.

may well have been suggested to Sidgwick by his reading of Comte, finds its fullest expression in the late lectures published as *Philosophy, Its Scope and Relations*. But it was articulated, as we can see, as early as 1867, and it underlies all of Sidgwick's philosophical writings.

If the problem of synthesizing the principles of all our knowledge into one coherent whole is the distinctively philosophical problem, the obtaining of general agreement on particular claims to knowledge is a problem for every discipline, and one on which Sidgwick puts considerable emphasis. Lack of agreement is in general, he thinks, a sign of lack of knowledge. This is why we cannot claim to know philosophy as we now know geography, and the same situation had once plagued what we now think of as the sciences. As he wrote in an early aphorism,

> Socrates was the first critical philosopher: the first thinker who divided the unknown into the knowable and the unknowable. Physical causes he placed in the latter category: for when he questioned of these one answered one thing and one another, each according to his fancy, and there was no prospect of agreement. (TCC, Add. MS. d. 71.)

Scientists have now learned how to obtain widespread assent to their conclusions, and scientific authority is consequently the prototype of acceptable authority. We have seen that Sidgwick thought the only way theologians would begin to command public respect for their conclusions would be for them to come to them in ways similar to those used by scientists, that is, by conducting their inquiries in a free and critical spirit. As early as 1866 he expressed the opinion that this was the only way to reach agreement on religious doctrine. (*Mem.*, 150.) But agreement, though a sign that knowledge has been attained, is no more than a sign. For there may all too easily be agreement on errors. Sidgwick turned more directly to the problem of sorting out error from truth in his 1871 essay on 'Verification of Beliefs'.[29]

The essay begins with a consideration of scepticism, to which we may be led, Sidgwick says, by noting that some of

[29] A version of this paper was read to the Metaphysical Society on 27 April 1870. Though the text differs considerably from the published one—it includes, among other things, strong criticism of Kant's epistemology—the main points are the same.

the beliefs we have held confidently have turned out to be mistaken. This suggests general doubt: since some of the beliefs I was sure of were wrong, what prevents all of them from being so? (1871h, 582.) Sidgwick thinks that although scepticism as a general doctrine cannot be refuted, it cannot be defended by rational argument either. 'As soon as scepticism attempts to justify itself, it inevitably limits itself; as it assumes the truth of certain premises and the validity of some method of inference.' And if we start from the existence of error in parts of our set of beliefs and infer by analogy that there may be error in all, we must keep in mind that the conviction of error in one belief can be 'no more certain than the conviction of truth elsewhere'. (1871h, 583.) The sceptic relies on a weak analogy: all our beliefs are analogous to the ones that turn out false, in that we believe them. But if we can find a sub-class of our beliefs which by appropriate criteria of truth and error never contains any erroneous beliefs, then we shall be able to say not only that scepticism cannot be proven, but also that it can be positively rejected at least from one class of beliefs. For we may be able to show that beliefs in the sub-class possess not only the weak general characteristic of being held to be true but additional characteristics not possessed by beliefs that have turned out false. The important point then, as Sidgwick sees it, is to determine the criteria of truth and error. We must ask 'how to verify beliefs, originally certain, if their certainty be called in question on general grounds', i.e. challenged by some variety of general scepticism.

Sidgwick proceeds by distinguishing two types of certainty, discursive and intuitive. The first of these, he says, 'is apprehended by contemplating the belief not alone, but in connexion with other certain beliefs'. This type of certainty it is the business of logic to deal with. But discursive certainty presupposes intuitive certainty, and it is there that the central issue is to be found. Is there an 'intuitive criterion' for this sort of certainty, a criterion which requires that we consider only the beliefs in question, by themselves? Referring to, but correcting, Descartes, Sidgwick says that this criterion would tell us to accept judgements which seem intuitively certain 'if the notions connected in them are found on reflection to be clear and distinct'. (1871h, 584.) Now this criterion does help to eliminate some error, but it still lets some in, since notions which appear simple and clear, and judgements which appear 'irresistible' at one time, do not appear so at others. Hence the intuitive criterion cannot be absolutely relied upon, although, Sidgwick says, 'all our conclusions in the science of form and number are originally guaranteed by no other'. (1871h, 585.)

It is irrelevant to bring in here, as empiricists do, considerations about the origins of our abstract ideas. 'Intuitive' is to be contrasted with 'discursive' rather than with 'innate'; and to call judgements 'intuitive' is only to say 'that our certainty of their truth is at present obtained by contemplating them alone, and not in connection with any other propositions'. Even so, empiricists would reject the Cartesian criterion, because they hold that the certainty of general propositions must rest entirely on the certainty of particular ones. The Cartesian criterion is indeed applicable to particular as well as to universal judgements, and allows—what the plain man also thinks—that we can be equally certain of judgements of both types. But the empiricist proposes to remove the apparent grounds for scepticism about universal judgements by appeal to induction from particular ones. Why does he take this view? It is true, as Mill points out, that intuitions of universal judgements often turn out to have led us into error, and Sidgwick admits that 'we cannot hope to get an intuitive criterion in so perfect a form as entirely to exclude' that possibility. But even if we are more likely to err about universal than about particular judgements, it is not clear that empiricism will help. (1871h, 585-7.) Sidgwick gives two reasons for saying this. First, it is evident that we can err in making particular judgements. Disagreements among empiricists, some of whom are materialists while others think we cognize only mental phenomena, to say nothing of commonplace errors of perception, force this conclusion on us. Second, it is impossible to see how the empiricist 'can establish upon his foundation the conclusions of science'. To Sidgwick it seems absolutely clear that 'individual premises, however manipulated, cannot establish a universal conclusion'. Even Mill, appearances to the contrary notwithstanding, does not really think they can. (1871h, 588-9.) Mill's inductive logic is essentially a method of making less general inductive propositions as certain as the principle of the uniformity of nature (which is itself, Sidgwick thinks, only hypothetical); and to make them so an inference is needed. The argument is always of the form: 'A must invariably accompany or follow B, as otherwise the principle of the uniformity of nature would not be universally true.' But this, Sidgwick points out, requires 'an inference of universal import', and such inferences are only knowable by intuition.

Sidgwick concludes 'that a logical intuition relating to universal fact, is admitted by the Empiricist. . . . But, if we are allowed the power of seeing universal truth in the single department of logic, on what ground is our natural claim to a similar faculty in other departments rejected?' The empiricist has failed to show us that we must not use the Cartesian criterion, and has even been compelled to admit general intuitions to complete his own theory. But his emphasis on inductive verification comes from a correct insight. Induction is one mode of discursive verification, and discursive verification is a necessary supplement to intuitive.

If we cannot attain absolute completeness of certitude in respect either of universal or of individual intuitions . . . our conviction of either is strengthened by perceiving a harmony between them. Only we need not limit this confirmative force to the relation between particular and general beliefs. One may say generally that as the intuitive verification cannot be made entirely trustworthy, it requires to be supplemented by a discursive verification—which consists generally in ascertaining the harmony between the proposition regarded as intuitively certain and other propositions belonging to the same department of fact . . . (1871h, 590.)

There is one more piece of evidence about Sidgwick's early views on knowledge, and it usefully fills out the sketch of a position just given. James Ward, the editor of the posthumous collection of Sidgwick's writings entitled *Lectures on the Philosophy of Kant*, included in that volume the article 'Criteria of Truth and Error' originally published in *Mind* in 1900. The article, as he points out in his Preface, is incomplete, and he appends to it what he describes as 'portions of two lectures which show the lines on which the author intended to complete it. These lectures', he adds, 'were themselves an amplification of a paper read to the Metaphysical Society and afterwards published in the *Contemporary Review* (July 1871).' (*LPK*, vi.) The paper referred to is, of course, the one we have just discussed; and Ward's remark consequently gives us grounds for treating the substance of the material he printed as coming from the same period of Sidgwick's life, even if the wording comes from some later time.

The points made are to some extent the same as those in the published article. Remarking that neither empiricism nor rationalism has given us a 'simple infallible criterion for the kind of knowledge which is to be taken as the ultimately valid basis of all else that is commonly taken for knowledge', Sidgwick goes on to say that both of them have none the less provided useful tests for guarding against error. To rationalism we owe the 'Intuitive Verification', which consists in assuring oneself by careful examination 'of the self-evidence of what appears self-evident'. It may be applied to particular as well as to universal judgements. (*LPK*, 461.) To empiricism we owe the 'Discursive Verification', which consists in 'contemplating the belief that appears intuitively certain along with other beliefs which may possibly be found to conflict with it'. (*LPK*, 462.) We should especially try to relate universal propositions which seem self-evident to the particular propositions they include. The intuitive verification stresses clarity, precision, and distinctness, while the discursive stresses the need for system and coherence. (*LPK*, 463.) A new point is now added, as Sidgwick introduces a third type of verification, the 'Social or Oecumenical Verification'. We find conflict of opinion among thinkers of historically different periods, he says, and also among thinkers of the same period, concerning apparently intuitive propositions. It is tempting to dismiss whoever fails to intuit what one intuits oneself as simply blind and mistaken. But, says Sidgwick,

a philosophic mind cannot do this, unless it can prove independently that the conflicting intuitor has an inferior faculty of envisaging truth in general, or this kind of truth; one who cannot do this must reasonably submit to a loss of confidence in any intuition of his own that thus is found to conflict with another's. (*LPK*, 464.)

Hence general agreement is a necessary condition of justifiable certainty in one's intuitive beliefs.

Sidgwick puts these three points in a slightly different light by saying that each of the types of verification corresponds to ways in which men have been convinced of error. Each involves a conflict of judgement and judgement:

> conflict between a judgment first formed and the view of this judgment taken by the same mind on subsequent reconsideration; conflict between two different judgments, or the implications of two partially different judgments formed by the same mind under different conditions; and finally, conflict between the judgments of different minds. (*LPK*, 466.)

Using the intuitive verification before assenting finally to an apparently self-evident proposition, we may forestall the first danger; using the discursive verification, we may forestall the second; and using the social verification, the third. 'I do not put these on a par', Sidgwick comments; 'the second is of special and pre-eminent importance. For the ideal aim of philosophy is systematisation. . . . But the special characteristic of *my* philosophy is to keep the importance of the others in view.' (*LPK*, 466–7.)[30]

It is interesting to note that in settling on a view giving priority to individual insight and the attainment of systematic coherence in one's own thought, while yet attributing great importance to obtaining the agreement of others, Sidgwick took a position which makes possible a coherent account of both his own personal heterodoxy and his belief in the great social utility of religious consensus. After all, the consensus that arises out of sound independent thought is the best sort of

[30] For an earlier consideration of the relations between sensations, reason, and general assent as modes of obtaining certainty, see J. D. Morell, *On the Philosophical Tendencies of the Age*, 1848. Morell's solution involves systematization in a logical manner of material derived through intuition. He takes the power of intuition to be common to all men, to reveal aspects of the spiritual nature of the universe, and to require progressive clarification of its deliverances. A much more sophisticated view of how belief is to be strengthened was put forward by the logician John Venn, a long-time friend of Sidgwick's and a fellow member of the Grote Society, in his Hulsean Lectures for 1869, *On Some of the Characteristics of Belief, Scientific and Religious*, 1870. Venn's views are very similar to Sidgwick's on the topics of the need for consensus of independent thinkers, the importance of systematization, and the unavailability of final truths or infallible criteria; but Venn was defending religion. At about this period C. S. Peirce was publishing his views on the attainment of certainty in our beliefs, which have some important resemblances to the views of Sidgwick and Venn. But there is no reason to suppose that Sidgwick knew anything of Peirce.

consensus, even if the disagreements through which one must go on the way to it are painful. Whatever the significance of this parallel may be, there are three important points to note about these early methodological positions. First, we have seen how Sidgwick hesitated about building a philosophy on intuitions, because he felt that intuitions were 'mystical' and not fully rational. The argument showing that a need for intuitions can be demonstrated even in so non-mystical a subject as logic seems to have freed him from this worry. It enabled him to detach intuitionism from what we shall see was its traditional alliance with religious doctrine and to consider whether intuitions are needed to account for morality purely on epistemological grounds, without fearing that in appealing to intuitions he might be committing himself to some objectionable substantive outlook or some irrational procedure. Second, his methodological conclusions reinforce, if they are not the source of, his view of the nature of philosophy. The synthesis which philosophy tries to achieve requires relating intuitively certain basic propositions to less general propositions already taken as constituting our knowledge of some special area, and the finding of some coherent way of relating these basic propositions to one another. Philosophy is thus itself the application of the intuitive and discursive tests at the most general level, and the ecumenical test is bound to be applied to any claim to have obtained a satisfactory result. Finally, *The Methods of Ethics* itself is constructed with these conclusions as its methodological presuppositions. They help to explain why Sidgwick felt, as he says in the autobiographical statement, that he 'ought' to examine common sense morality before deciding whether or not he had a system of moral intuitions (*ME* 7, xx), and why this examination plays so large a part within the *Methods*, not just as preparation for writing it. They underlie his appeals to intuition as well as the criteria for testing intuitions which he uses; they are behind his attempts to show that other philosophers agree with him about the self-evident principles he claims to have found; and his statement that the discursive verification is the most important one is reflected in the fact that the main line of argument in the *Methods* is an attempt to show how the apparently self-evident axioms are involved in the systematization of our moral knowledge.

2

Intuitionism and Common Sense

INTUITIONISM in Britain from the end of the eighteenth century to the time of Sidgwick was expounded by a number of philosophers who cannot easily be put into tidy classes. During the first period, up to the middle of the 1830s, Scottish intuitionism was the dominant variety.[1] It was unified not only by the nationality of its expositors but also by their common concern with the doctrines of Thomas Reid and by their complete ignorance of Kant. During the second period a number of different versions of intuitionism appeared, some of them showing varying degrees of Kantian influence. Of these the most fully developed was that taught at Cambridge by William Whewell. In the history of nineteenth-century ethical intuitionism Reid and he are the two central figures. Although Whewell acknowledged no debt to Reid and did not discuss his views, he did put Reid's works on the list of books set for the Moral Sciences Tripos.[2] It is highly probable that Sidgwick studied them with some care at a fairly early stage of his development. In the first edition of the *Methods* he made some criticisms of Reid's moral philosophy (e.g. *ME*1, 318), and his early writings on epistemology suggest a common-sense approach to its problems which he was later happy to associate with Reid. (Cf. 1895a.) His own ethical position incorporates much of the substance of Reid's and some of the methodology of Whewell's. In the present chapter, therefore, we shall discuss

[1] On Scottish philosophy generally, see James McCosh, *The Scottish Philosophy*, 1875, and S. A. Grave, *The Scottish Philosophy of Common Sense*, Oxford, 1960. For Reid, see also D. D. Raphael, *The Moral Sense*, Oxford, 1947, Ch. V. References to Reid are to the page-numbers of Hamilton's edition of the *Works* (1846–63), 9th edn., 1895, abbreviated as *R*.

The similarities between Reid's moral philosophy and that sketched by Richard Hooker in Book I of the *Laws of an Ecclesiastical Polity* are striking, and deserve exploration.

[2] A list of the set books is given in an appendix to the second edition of Whewell's *History*, pp. 279 ff. The list includes, in addition to Hamilton's edition of Reid, ethical writings by Clarke, Butler, Stewart, Paley, Whewell, Kant, and Fichte.

Reid's moral philosophy and some of the problems it raises, and shall trace, briefly, the history of the Scottish school to its end in the remarkable work of Alexander Smith. In the next chapter Whewell's ethics will be examined in the context of the views of his Cambridge predecessors and colleagues.

i. *Reid's Ethics*

Reid greatly admired Butler, and thought his 'Dissertation on Virtue' the finest essay on moral philosophy ever published. (*R.*, p. 32.) His own work carried the Butlerian combination of religion, epistemology, and ethics into an extended argument against Hume's scepticism, empiricism, and utilitarianism. As a result he was more concerned than Butler to display the rationality of morals and to relate it to an explicit theory of knowledge. Religious belief was no less vital to him than to Butler, but it was somewhat less in evidence.

Reid's epistemology depends on the view that there are self-evident general truths which can be grasped by intuition and which provide the foundations of knowledge. The view is supported by a familiar argument to prove that 'all knowledge got by reasoning must be built upon first principles'. In reasoning, Reid says, any proposition either rests on another or is self-evident. If it rests on another, the same alternative holds of its support; and 'we cannot go back in this track to infinity'. The regress stops when we find truths which support others and themselves need no support. Reid is of course aware that disagreements arise about allegedly self-evident truths, and that these pose a problem. He asks whether there is any 'mark or criterion, whereby first principles that are truly such may be distinguished from those that assume the character without a just title', and makes two suggestions in reply. (*R.*, p. 435.) First, the inconsistency of an apparently self-evident truth either with another such truth or with plain facts tells against the claim to self-evidence. Second, the 'consent of ages and nations, of the learned and unlearned, ought to have great authority' in settling such questions, because 'every man is a competent judge' of self-evidence. (*R.*, pp. 439–41.) In a discussion of specifically moral first principles, Reid warns us further to avoid merely analytic truths, since these will be of no use in determining specific duties. (*R.*, p. 479.) Despite the difficulties in the way of finding self-evident first principles of morals, Reid is confident that it can be done. 'Virtue is the business of all men', he holds, and so 'the first principles of it are written in their hearts.' (*R.*, p. 481.) Yet men must have 'ripe faculties' before they can perceive these truths, and moral education is a necessity. 'There are truths', Reid remarks, 'both speculative and moral, which a man left to himself would never discover; yet, when they are fairly laid before him he owns and adopts them, not barely upon the authority of his teacher, but upon their own intrinsic evidence, and perhaps wonders that he could be so blind as not to see them before.' (*R.*, p. 596.) It is this fact also that gives its utility to moral philosophy.

In his discussion of moral psychology, Reid begins to move well beyond Butler. He holds, like Butler, that our native powers were given us by the Creator for definite purposes; and like Butler he refuses to accept any simplifying reduction of the number of basic motivations. He discusses several kinds of 'principle of action', pointing out how most of them are directed to some object or end other than the agent's own good and hence are in a sense disinterested. His main concern, however, is to show, against Hume, that rationality in action is not confined simply to the determination of means. Reason determines ends as well. He tries to support this view by arguing that there are some ends which could not even be conceived without the use of reason, and that once these ends are formulated they do in fact generate leading principles of action, properly called 'rational principles'. There are just two such ends: one's good on the whole, and one's duty. (*R.*, pp. 579–80.)

The concept of one's good on the whole is introduced by consideration of particular goods. 'Whatever makes a man more happy, or more perfect, is good', Reid says, though he offers no defence of it. Early in life our desires are of limited scope and duration, and we are unmindful of past and future. As we grow older we learn to 'correct our first notions of good and ill, and form the conception of what is good or ill upon the whole', an abstract notion of what brings more good than harm even when all its consequences are balanced. This concept plainly requires rational thought; and Reid holds that an intelligent being necessarily desires what is good and is averse to what is 'ill'. (*R.*, pp. 580–1.) He is at pains to distinguish this desire from the affections and passions having specific objects. Such desires are contingent (*R.*, pp. 583–4), but the desire for good on the whole results from the whole constitution of our nature. He concludes that Hume has made his opposition to allowing that reason determines ends plausible only by changing the sense of the term 'passion' so as to include within its scope what is usually called 'reason'. (*R.*, p. 581.) Thus where Butler treats the principle of self-love as a paradigm of the authority of one active principle over others, Reid takes the principle of pursuing one's good on the whole as a model of the rationality of a principle. Since the principle gives 'the conception of a *right* and a *wrong* in human conduct, at least of a *wise* and a *foolish*', it allows for self-approval and self-condemnation. But it has serious defects if taken as the sole principle guiding our action. Men have difficulty in applying it directly, and few are wise or knowledgeable enough to do so. It would lead us directly to prudence, temperance, and fortitude, and indirectly to 'justice, humanity, and all the social virtues', and thus to 'a kind of virtue'. But it does not produce 'the noblest kind': the man who loves virtue and would follow it at whatever cost to himself is 'the perfect man', while he who pursues only his own good is in comparison 'mean and despicable'. (*R.*, p. 585.) Moreover, its guidance is far less clear than that given us by the principle of duty. We can hardly fail to know our duty, but can easily miss our own good on the whole. Hence we will be happier if we leave our happiness to the Creator while we pursue virtue. (*R.*, p. 586.)

The conception of duty, Reid says, is 'too simple to admit of a logical definition', and it may be for this reason that he gives less of a positive account of why it is a peculiarly rational concept than he gives of the concept of one's good on the whole. He is emphatic in denying that the notion of duty can be resolved into the notion of interest. The notion can only be explained by giving its synonyms, such as 'ought', 'fair', and 'approvable'. One may add that it is tied to our sense of worth or merit, that it is universally present in mature human beings, and that it applies only to agents possessed of reason and will, and then only to acts within the sphere of the agent's natural powers. (*R.*, pp. 586–7.) Beyond this, Reid's support for the claim that duty is a distinctively rational concept comes from his criticisms of Hume's view that moral approval and disapproval are only matters of feeling. Reid links this position with Hume's general attempt to reduce all our apparent knowledge of things beyond ourselves to knowledge of our sensations. He combats it in part by appealing to careful introspection: feeling is plainly one sort of thing, judgement another, and we can observe, when we feel approval or esteem of someone, that our having the feeling is different from, and dependent on, our judgement as to the qualities of the person esteemed. (*R.*, pp. 672–3.) Reid then presents an argument of some interest. On Hume's view, the two sentences, 'Such a man did well' and 'Such a man's conduct gave me a very agreeable feeling', must mean exactly the same thing. There are two reasons, Reid says, why this is a mistake. First, there is no grammatical rule which allows the equivalence: one sentence ascribes a property to an agent and says nothing about the speaker, the other sentence 'testifies a fact concerning the speaker'. Second, we treat a denial of the two sentences differently. To contradict the first is not rude or unmannerly, since the denial merely expresses a difference of opinion which would not offend a reasonable man. But to contradict the second would be very rude. No one can be in error about his feelings: so to contradict one who utters the second sentence is as much as to accuse him of lying. (*R.*, p. 673.) Reid adds, finally, a consideration drawn from the existence in all languages of distinct and intelligible expressions both for judgements of merit and for feelings of approval. Hume's reduction of one to the other implies, he thinks, that plain men have been speaking nonsense in all ages—an untenable conclusion altogether.

Reid does not object to speaking of a moral 'sense' which teaches us what in particular is our duty, and does not think this militates against the rationality of particular judgements, because he thinks that sensing, properly understood, includes judging. He points out the similarity of sensing in the two realms of fact and morals by saying that just as the external senses are the sources of first principles from which we obtain truths about the material world, so 'the truths immediately testified by our moral faculty are the first principles of all moral reasoning, from which all our knowledge of duty must be deduced'. (*R.*, p. 590.) As in all other cases, so here, all reasoning must start from first principles. If anyone denies all such principles, we cannot argue him into particular conclusions. For instance, suppose we try to prove monogamy right, by arguing that the balance of advantage to family and society favours it: 'if a man does not perceive that he ought to regard the good of society, and the good of his wife and children, the reasoning can have no effect upon him.' The point is generalized in Reid's comments on Hume's famous passage objecting to arguments which move from premises about what is the case to conclusions about what ought to be. Hume demands first, Reid says, an explanation of the word 'ought': but no one who speaks English really requires it, and to think otherwise is to deny the intelligibility of the commonest language. Hume asks next for an account of how 'ought' conclusions can be deduced from premises not containing the notion. And this, says Reid, is to ask for what does not exist. The first principles of morals are self-evident, not deductions at all; 'and moral truths that are not self-evident, are deduced not from relations quite different from them, but from the first principles of morals.' (*R.*, p. 675.)

Reid's further discussion of the moral faculty or conscience has less to do with demonstrating its rationality than with spelling out its position as the authoritative guide of our actions. The supremacy of conscience is not capable of proof. It is self-evident. Yet Reid does not simply leave it at that. Conscience, which belongs only to man and is not found in animals, is, he holds, a natural and original part of the human constitution —a claim he would presumably support by appeal to the simplicity and irreducibility of the basic notion involved in moral judgements. With all our original powers, 'the intention for which they are given is written in legible characters upon the face of them', and the characteristics of conscience show plainly what God meant its role to be. Conscience judges every action. It looks, not just backward as some have supposed, but forward also. Conscience acts quickly: we can rarely act so 'precipitately' that we are not aware of the moral quality of what we are about to do. Conscience prescribes the limits to every passion, affection, and appetite. Not being tied to specific contexts of action, it can deal with any case in which decisions must be made or motives and actions judged. Thus its natural scope and facility suit it to be a guide; and we know that it naturally acts as one. Whenever we transgress its dictates, we condemn ourselves. Even if other principles are stronger, we accept the judgement of conscience as to our guilt or merit. These points all help to make plain that conscience is as Reid, using the old phrase, says, 'the candle of the Lord set up within us' to control our actions, sometimes in concurrence with other active principles, sometimes in opposition to them. (*R.*, pp. 597–8.)

This of course promptly raises the question, which Butler never clearly resolved, of the relation between conscience and that regard to one's good on the whole which is so important a rational principle. What are we to do if our conscience and our regard to our own good come into conflict? Though the disinterested love of virtue is our noblest principle, no active impulse given us by God ought to be eradicated. How then are disputes to be adjudicated? Reid's reply is that the problem is 'merely imaginary'. There cannot be a conflict between conscience and prudence, for 'while the world is under a wise and benevolent administration, it is impossible, that any man should in the issue be a loser by doing his duty'. (*R.*, p. 598.) But suppose a man is an atheist, and is so misguided as to think that virtue and his own happiness call him in different directions? His case, Reid admits, is 'without a remedy'. He will act against a leading principle of his nature whatever he does, and so he is 'reduced to this miserable dilemma, whether it be best to be a fool or a knave'. And the conclusion Reid draws from this is that it shows the strong connection between morality and religion.

Reid turns at this point to a discussion of the liberty of the agent, a matter on which we may be brief, though he is not. Liberty of the will, which renders its possessor liable to judgements of merit and demerit, is power over the decisions made by the will. It presupposes a conception of alternative actions and some power of rational judgement, since without the ability to weigh reasons for and against acting, liberty would be pointless. (*R.*, pp. 599 ff.) To show that men are free in this sense, Reid offers three arguments. The first is that all men naturally have a conviction that they are free, 'a conviction so early, so universal, and so necessary in most of our rational operations' that it must be part of our original constitution and so must come from our Creator. (*R.*, p. 616.) For 'the genuine dictate of our natural faculties is the voice of God', just as much as other, more external, revelations are. Belief in our liberty is implied, Reid thinks, in voluntary exertion, deliberation, resolution, self-reproach, shame, and remorse. It is as fundamental as beliefs in the existence of material objects or other persons, in the past or in our own identity; and like these beliefs, though it cannot readily be accounted for, it is not weakened by sceptical arguments. (*R.*, pp. 617–18.) The second argument is that liberty is presupposed by the existence and reality of moral distinctions. Since their reality cannot sensibly be questioned, neither can the existence of liberty. (*R.*, pp. 620–1.) The third argument is drawn from the possibility of making prudent plans. We have not only the intellectual ability to conceive plans of action but power to carry them out as envisaged, a power which implies control over our decisions. (*R.*, p. 622.) Reid devotes much effort to critical analysis of arguments in support of necessitarianism, but we need not follow him in doing so. We turn instead to his discussion of the specific principles of morality.

The principles founded on the two rational ends do not, by themselves, tell us what to do in any specific case. The principle of pursuing one's own good on the whole only tells us to look to the future as well as the present, and to weigh costs against benefits, while the principle of conscience only tells us to do our duty. Content for the former is generated by consideration of our desires, that for the latter comes from the 'more particular' self-evident principles of morality, which are presented in Reid's final essay.

Reid gives three groups of self-evident principles. The first contains six propositions which are rather indications of the presuppositions and range of moral judgements than sources of their content. They are these: (1) some acts deserve praise, others blame, in different degrees; (2) only voluntary acts deserve either; (3) what is unavoidable deserves neither; (4) omissions as well as actions may be blameworthy; (5) we ought to be as well-informed as possible about our duty; and (6) we ought to try as hard as we can to do our duty. (*R.*, p. 637.)

With the second group we get the substantive self-evident principles. There are five of them. The first is, that 'we ought to prefer a greater good, though more distant, to a less; and a less evil to a greater'. It would be dictated by a regard to our own good even if we had no conscience, and action from it is prudence, not virtue. The second is, that 'as far as the intention of nature appears in the constitution of man, we ought to comply with that intention and to act agreeably to it'. This principle presupposes Reid's religious assumption of the divine ordering of the world and the presence of signs of the creator's intentions in all his works. The third principle concerns benevolence:

No man is born for himself only. Every man, therefore, ought to consider himself as a member of the common society of mankind, and of those subordinate societies to which he belongs, such as family, friends, neighbourhood, country and to do as much good as he can and as little hurt to the societies of which he is a member.

Reid sees this principle as leading us directly to all the social virtues, and indirectly to self-government. The reference within it to the 'subordinate societies' to which men belong is not incidental: it is directed against the supposed excessively cosmopolitan outlook fostered by utilitarian principles, and relates to a set of criticisms of utilitarianism which, as we shall see, were to become quite common. The fourth principle concerns justice:

In every case, we ought to act that part toward another, which we would judge to be right in him to act toward us, if we were in his circumstances and he in ours; or, more generally, what we approve in others, that we ought to practice in like circumstances, and what we condemn in others we ought not to do.

If there be any such thing as right and wrong in the conduct of moral agents, it must be the same to all in the same circumstances.

Reid does not stop to untangle the various elements incorporated in this statement. It represents what he thinks is the most comprehensive principle of all, covering all the rules of justice, all the details of our special duties to others, the general duties of charity and humanity, and even the duty of self-government. He points out that the principle supposes men to have the ability to distinguish right from wrong conduct, adding that they find it easier to do so when considering the case of another person than when considering their own case. The fifth and final principle is that we owe veneration and submission to God. (*R.*, pp. 638–9.)

Reid's substantive first principles articulate his Butlerian belief that benevolence is neither the whole of virtue in men nor the sole moral attribute of the deity. His objections to taking a principle of benevolence or utility as the sole first principle of morals are spelled out at some length as a part of his criticism of Hume's views on justice. We must note the main points. His first objection is that if there is, as an original part of the human constitution, a moral faculty whose judgements are different in kind from judgements of utility or agreeableness, then Hume must be mistaken in taking the latter as the foundation of morality. Such force as this argument has is derived from its implicit appeal to the assumptions that God made each original part of our nature for a definite, discoverable purpose, and that we ought to be guided by his intentions. Reid reminds us that he has argued for the existence of just such a conscience as this. If he is so far correct, he claims, then Hume is wrong, and is taking a principle common to men and animals to be the principle which should rule us, while he himself is accepting the higher principle present only in men as our ruling principle. A second general point against Hume is also made. It may well be true that everything for which we are morally meritorious is useful and that everything useful has some sort of merit, but even so merit is not the same as utility. There is a special sort of merit belonging to the moral virtues, which no one would think of attributing to other abilities, such as culinary ones, or to certain amiable characteristics such as we find in dogs, though both are useful. (*R.*, pp. 651 ff.) Reid then turns directly to Hume's view of justice. If Hume is wrong on this matter—if there is intrinsic worth in justice, and a 'natural principle in the constitution of man, by which justice is approved' (*R.*, p. 656)—then his general theory must be wrong. The discussion is complex, and only its main points can be sketched here.

Reid claims first that mature men do in fact perceive a justice or injustice in actions immediately and apart from considering utility, and are motivated by this perception. The

appeal here is to what every honest man thinks and feels: Reid
has no doubt but that the result of serious inquiry would tell
against Hume. He next argues that the sense of justice is as
natural as other feelings which Hume has allowed to be
natural—gratitude and resentment. For, he says, we have
a natural sense of injury and benefit or favour; and these
notions carry with them the notion of justice. In the remainder
of the chapter there are three arguments of major importance.
First, Reid points out that there are many kinds of case in
which we pass judgements of justice or injustice, but which
Hume ignores. Hume selects only those concerns of justice
which fit his theory best. Second, he argues that Hume's theory
leads to unacceptable results. Hume must say, he thinks, that
if there were rational and sentient creatures too weak to defend
themselves at all, they would have no rights against stronger
beings and so would not fall within the scope of any rule of
justice. We may not think this the most strikingly counter-
intuitive consequence of Hume's theory; but it is Reid's use of
it which is to be noted. 'There cannot be better evidence, that
a theory of morals . . . is false', he pronounces, 'than when it
subverts the practical rules of morals', as Hume here plainly
does. Third, he attempts to show at length that Hume's view
that justice is an artificial virtue founded on consideration of
utility does not follow from any arguments which it is plausible
to attribute to Hume, without the further assumption that
consideration of utility is the only possible way to determine the
details of what is required by justice. But this, says Reid, is
plainly false, since 'the simple rule, of not doing to his neigh-
bour what he would think wrong to be done to himself'—
which, as we saw, he considers a self-evident principle—would
yield all the rules of justice, without calling on considerations
of utility. (*R.*, p. 661.) Thus Hume's theory is too narrow to
cover all our beliefs about justice, runs counter to some of them,
and can be dispensed with in favour of a better theory.

If utility or benevolence is not, then, the sole natural principle of morals, the question arises as to the relations among the
various basic principles. Reid's last group of self-evident principles is a set which deals with questions of precedence or
order among the substantive rules. The various virtues, as
mental dispositions or principles of willing, cannot come into

conflict; but in the actual circumstances of their application, an act may be required by one and forbidden by another, as when, for instance, justice prohibits what generosity solicits. There are self-evident axioms governing these situations: 'unmerited generosity should yield to gratitude, and both to justice' is one example, and others are given, though Reid plainly does not try to present an exhaustive list. (*R.*, p. 639.)

These and the other basic axioms may be put in other words and perhaps be derived from one another, Reid says, but they cannot be derived from any principles more evident than themselves. They are at the basis of the 'best moral reasonings' of ancient and modern, heathen and Christian, authors. From them 'the whole system of moral conduct follows' quite easily. 'The path of duty is a plain path', Reid says, because everyone is required to follow it. (*R.*, p. 640.) He does not mean to disparage theory altogether. It is of some use in improving our moral judgements. But it is less important than practice, and in an important way it is dependent on the practical judgements of the plain man. Anyone who calmly and carefully attends to his conscience may know what is right and what wrong, although not everyone can do the subtle thinking needed in making and judging theories. Hence, Reid says,

wherever we find any disagreement between the practical rules of morality, which have been received in all ages, and the principles of any of the theories advanced upon this subject, the practical rules ought to be the standard by which the theory is to be corrected . . . it is both unsafe and unphilosophical to warp the practical rules, in order to make them tally with a favourite theory. (*R.*, p. 646.)

By 'Common Sense', Reid means the common or usual judgement of mankind. Here he asserts its dominance in morals, and endorses the validity of that ordinary morality which claims the *consensus gentium*.

ii. *The Scottish School*

Reid left behind him a position which combined considerable philosophical strength with a number of serious weaknesses. His followers lived from its strengths, and did only one thing to remedy its deficiencies: they put his ideas into language which, unlike his, was attractive to and readable by nineteenth-century audiences. Of his disciples the first was James Beattie, whose fame rests on his poetry and on an attack on Hume published in 1770. His lectures on the *Elements of Moral Science*, delivered during the early 1790s, showed more clearly than the previous work his dependence on Reid but did nothing to support Reid's position or his own claim to attention. The most important of the propagators of Reid's thought was clearly Dugald Stewart, whose style was praised, in contrast to Reid's, by the Edinburgh Reviewers,[3] and whose lectures, finally published in 1828, had been extremely popular for more than three decades. The Rev. Daniel Dewar, who preached in Glasgow before becoming Principal of Marischal College, Aberdeen, brought out a sober two volumes of *Elements of Moral Philosophy and Christian Ethics* in 1826, reiterating the main elements of Reid's teaching but laying far greater stress on the Christian aspects of morality and delving at length into theological concerns about predestination. Though no more original than Stewart, he had a more systematic mind, and in his rather dry way gave a not unimpressive presentation of the position. In 1833 the physician John Abercrombie published his *Philosophy of the Moral Feelings*, which is Reid's position made even more popular than Stewart had made it. Like his earlier Reidian book on the *Intellectual Powers* (1830) it went through innumerable editions; but in neither volume does he add anything of substance to what his predecessors had said. The doctrine was made still more diffuse by religious fervour in the *Sketches of Moral and Mental Philosophy* (1841) of Thomas Chalmers, the great Scottish religious leader, who lectured on ethics for many years at St. Andrews.[4] Sir William Hamilton wrote nothing on moral philosophy himself. He did, however, help spread the common-sense tradition by his edition of Reid's works, first published incompletely in 1846 and completed in 1863 after Hamilton's death, and by his edition of Stewart.

All these writers accepted the main points of Reid's ethics: the multiplicity of human motivations, the existence of rational as well as animal springs of action, the liberty of the will, the

[3] Cf., e.g., Sidney Smith, *Lectures on Moral Philosophy*, 1804–5, Lecture II; Francis Jeffrey, *Contributions to the Edinburgh Review*, 1844, Vol. IV, p. 377, cf. pp. 329–37.

[4] See the chapter on Chalmers in David Masson, *Memories of Two Cities*, Edinburgh and London, 1911.

general need for intuitively evident axioms, the agreement of mature men of all civilizations on the same set of first principles, the existence of several, irreducibly different axioms, with benevolence, justice, and veracity always figuring in the list, and the consequent rejection of utilitarianism. They all shared Reid's religious assumptions, and saw in the fact that conscience is an original and natural part of the human constitution a guarantee that God meant it to be our guide. If they did not all agree that prudence was itself a moral virtue, they were united by the firm conviction that the dictates of self-interest and those of conscience would, under God's providence, always coincide. It was a comfortable view, and one that articulated the Christian common sense of its generation exceedingly well. Aided by the elegant and easily digested writings of the Scottish philosophers, it came to be as nearly a philosophical orthodoxy as anything in Britain during our first period. The positions Reid had held were consequently prominent among those which controlled the turnings of philosophical controversy.

Certainly there were many points at which this teaching could be attacked. Its unsystematic aspect was one. What relations are there among all the many truths whose self-evidence the Reidians proclaim? Reid tells us that 'a system of morals is not like a system of geometry, where the subsequent parts derive their evidence from the preceding', but like a system of botany, where the point is to facilitate apprehension and memory rather than to give proofs. (*R.*, p. 642.) Yet he does not state all his axioms, and still less does he try to show how they serve to give order and coherence to the specific judgements of common-sense morality. His followers ignored his remarks about principles of precedence and subordination despite the fact that some of the more troublesome problems arise around just these topics. We are to care for the good of others, and Reid says that both happiness and virtue are good. Are we to promote the virtue of others as well as their happiness? And can these aims come into conflict? We are to look after the good of others and also to be just. Can these two principles give us conflicting instructions, and if so, which should take precedence, and why? And if we cannot answer these questions, do we really have a sound theory which is different from and can replace the view that benevolence is the whole of virtue, utility the only principle of morals?

These questions lead to deeper ones. The Reidians claim that the self-evident axioms are rational principles of action. One such axiom has its rationality displayed at length—the axiom requiring concern for one's own good on the whole. Rationality, in that principle, is plainly a matter of using a common measure in terms of which diverse goods can be estimated and a decision reached by weighing costs and benefits. The rationality of the other axioms is not explained. Yet an obvious explanation of it lies ready to hand: the utilitarian explanation, which simply extends to them the idea of rationality already accepted by the Reidians in their axiom of prudence, and at least partly accepted in their axiom of caring for the good of others. Why will they not accept it wholeheartedly? They claim, indeed, that to make the utilitarian principle the sole axiom would lead to conflict with common-sense beliefs on particular issues. But even if this is correct, what assurance have we of the truth or the rationality or the coherence of common-sense beliefs?

Part of the reply lies in the religious assumptions of the common-sense school. In a divinely ordered universe, these questions about conflicts arising from original principles of human nature are, like the question of a possible divergence between self-interest and duty, merely 'imaginary'. And the plain man's conscience is to be trusted, after all, because it is the voice of God. But can we be sure of that? We need not question the religious assumptions to think we might discover that conscience is not an original and natural part of the human frame. A systematic psychology might enable us to see how it originates from the action of basic laws of our nature on elements derived from sense and feeling. If so, would not the moral beliefs of the plain man be as open to criticism based on a rational theory as his other beliefs are? The Reidians may claim that conscience is shown to be original by the fact that the central concept with which it operates is unique and simple. But does not a proper theory of concept formation show that the notion of duty is really a combination of simpler elements? Indeed, if the moral faculty could be shown to be merely a generalization, due to sympathy, of the concerns generated by prudence, then its very origins would show that morality is a matter of utility. But any demonstration that the moral faculty originates in elements derived from sense and feeling shows that it does not provide a difference in principle between men and animals, and thus removes one argument against taking utility as the basis of morals.

Inside or outside the framework of religious belief, controversies springing from these issues continued, as we shall see, for years. But they stimulated no novelties among the Scottish philosophers. Stewart elaborated Reid's psychology and added objections to Paley's version of utilitarianism. He seems not to have kept informed, or not to have cared, about attacks on the foundations of his views; and neither he nor most of the other Reidians were able to do much more than deny the force of objections and reiterate the old teachings.

iii. *Thomas Brown*

One of the most widely read of the Scottish philosophers of our first period was Dr. Thomas Brown, a poet and physician as well as a younger colleague of Stewart's at Edinburgh. The lectures he read there for over a decade on the philosophy of the human mind were published in 1820, the year of his death, and frequently reprinted. He is often considered a minor member of the Scottish school. He certainly accepted much of Reid's teaching, yet his persistent attempt to use laws of associational psychology derived from Hume and Hartley to provide explanations of that multiplicity of faculties and basic concepts of which the Reidians were content to assert the existence separates him from the other members of the school.[5] Brown's *Lectures* are even more diffuse than Stewart's; their style reflects in a rather pallid way the romanticism of the era; and they are not rich in argument or insight. In one point however they call for attention. Brown, apparently alone among nineteenth-century moralists, denies that morality is a matter of reason, and claims that it rests solely on feeling.

Brown seems to have been led to this position by his epistemology. He espouses a variety of nominalism, which first leads him, in discussing morality, to the conclusion that it is mistaken to speak of right or wrong actions. Actions are nothing but

---

[5] Masson, *Memories*, pp. 97–8. References to Brown's *Lectures* are to the volume and page in the four-volume edition, Edinburgh, 1820, abbreviated *Lec. Phil.*

persons behaving in certain ways, so we should speak only of virtuous and vicious agents. He next concludes that 'virtue, as distinct from the virtuous person, is a mere name' (*Lec. Phil.* iii. 569), and it may be from this point that he moves to his distinctive doctrine. Moral judgements, he says, whether relating ostensibly to acts or to agents, 'mean nothing more than that a certain feeling of moral approbation has been excited in our minds, by the contemplation of a certain intentional production . . . of a certain amount of benefit or injury'. Although he sometimes speaks of agents or acts as having a certain 'approvableness' (e.g. *Lec. Phil.* iii. 581, 590), his objections to the moral sense doctrine of Hutcheson make it plain that he does not think of this as referring to any objective property in agents. Approvableness is just the relation between the agent and the moral feeling. 'To say, that an action excites in us this feeling, and to say, that it appears to us right, or virtuous, or conformable to duty', Brown pronounces, 'are to say precisely the same thing.' (*Lec. Phil.* iii. 590.) Brown gives no account of how we recognize the moral feeling, stripped of all objective connections. He is however sure that there is only one such feeling, and he explicates all moral terms in relation to it. The differences in our moral vocabulary arise from differences in the temporal relations between the agents who are the subjects of our moral judgements and the feelings which prompt the judgements themselves. 'To be virtuous is to act in the way' we presently feel approval of; 'to have *merit*, is to *have* acted in this way,—to feel the moral *obligation* or *duty*, is merely to think of the action and its consequences' and to feel approval at the timeless thought. Brown sees this theoretical unification of moral terminology as an argument in favour of his subjectivism. Its only other direct support comes when he points out that any merely factual characterization of a class of acts leaves open the possibility of asking why one ought to do acts so characterized. In the end a satisfactory answer to this question comes only when 'the very contemplation of the action excites in us a certain feeling of vivid approval'. (*Lec. Phil.* iii. 572–3.) Brown makes no effort to counter Reid's arguments for the rationality of moral judgements, and his criticisms of Clarke and Wollaston on this point are little more than counter-assertions. (*Lec. Phil.* iv. 17 ff.)

Brown sees that these two views of his separate him from
Reid and Stewart. In discussing the substance of morality, he
nevertheless is at one with them in spirit. He opposes any system
that reduces all obligations to one principle, he admits benevolence as one virtue among others, and he includes justice,
veracity, and a host of other virtues, making no serious effort to
reduce them to derivative positions. He attacks purely prudential systems of ethics no less than Hume's attempt to show that
utility is the measure of virtue, yet he thinks that because God
has ordered the world benevolently there is a pre-established
har ony—here he explicitly invokes Leibniz (*Lec. Phil.* iv. 57)
—between doing what is virtuous and doing what is generally
useful. His criticisms of utilitarianism are elaborations of Reid's,
and we need not follow them. But it is noteworthy that Brown
makes no effort to replace Hume's attempt to give an explanation of our moral feelings with a better one. We find ourselves
so constituted that we approve of certain things and disapprove
of others, but, he says, 'it is in vain to ask why we are so constituted', in any detail, although the general answer is plain:
God made us to have just this constitution. (*Lec. Phil.* iii. 572,
584.) This seems to imply that for Brown morality is the result
of God's having established arbitrary connections between our
moral feelings and certain states of affairs. Brown himself
emphasizes the contingency of the connection: 'Virtue . . .
cannot . . . have any universality beyond that of the minds in
which these emotions arise. We speak always, therefore, relatively to the constitution of our minds, not to what we might
have been constituted to admire if we had been created by
a different Being . . .' (*Lec. Phil.* iii. 596.) He protests that
morality is no more mutable on his view than on any other,
but his only argument for this is that we can be sure that God
will not in fact alter our nature; and this, of course, is not quite
to the point.

There were a number of other moralists during our first
period who tried to show that morality depends on the will of
God, as it does on Brown's view. Even the most enthusiastically
religious of them, Ralph Wardlaw, an important and controversial figure in Scottish circles, none the less does not go to
Brown's extreme. Wardlaw insists that because of our utterly
depraved fallen nature we cannot know what it is upon which

God rests his commands. But God's will is not 'capricious and arbitrary'. Our standard must be God's will as revealed to us, and at the same time we must be certain that God wills our duty because it is right, and does not simply make it right by his willing.[6] Jonathan Dymond, a Quaker moralist whose *Essays on the Principles of Morality* of 1829 were reprinted as late as 1880, insists also that the will of God must be our standard. He seems at times to hold that God's will constitutes rectitude, but as he expressly disclaims any intention of entering minutely into such philosophical questions one cannot attribute this view to him with certainty.[7] The proposition that morality rests on arbitrary divine decrees was repudiated expressly by almost all the Scottish moralists and by most English writers, often as a way of criticizing Paley, who was thought to be committed to it. It was even rejected by Brown's popularizer, George Payne, who, agreeing with most of the other parts of Brown's philosophy, devotes a lengthy section to criticizing him, not very effectively, on this point.[8] Brown is thus apparently as isolated in his commitment to the view that God's decrees are arbitrary as he is in his belief that morality is based on feeling. His isolation in holding the first position is a striking testimony to the strength of the Pelagian tradition in Britain. And the fact that subjectivism was unanimously taken to entail the arbitrariness of God's decrees may help to explain his isolation in holding the second position.

iv. *Alexander Smith*

The critics of Brown's subjectivism, with one exception, failed to comment on an important point which it showed about the doctrines of the Scottish philosophers: that their moral

[6] Ralph Wardlaw, *Christian Ethics* (1833), 5th edn., 1852, pp. 146 ff.

[7] Cf. Dymond, p. 15. Among others in our first period who appeal to the will of God as the criterion of morality are the Unitarian writers, John Prior Estlin, *Familiar Lectures on Moral Philosophy*, 1818, see i. 63 ff.; Lant Carpenter, in *Systematic Education*, 2nd edn., 1817, ii. 333–4, 350–61. But Estlin denies that God's will is arbitrary; and though Carpenter seems inclined to talk as if God's will is the only standard in terms of which the question can be asked, he does not positively assert its arbitrariness.

[8] George Payne, whose *Elements of Mental and Moral Science*, 1828, reached a fourth edition in 1858, tells us he mainly follows Dr. Brown, whom it is obvious he greatly admires. For his objections to Brown's moral theory see pp. 377, 475–94.

epistemology and their substantive doctrines were separable. The exception was Alexander Smith, author of *The Philosophy of Morals*, which appeared in 1835.[9] His book is plainly the best work of ethics of the Scottish school after Reid, and arguably one of the two or three finest produced in Britain between Reid and Sidgwick. It was wholly ignored on publication and has been completely forgotten since. Its importance for us is in the extent to which Smith's arguments make it clear that the essential conceptual issues in the controversy between intuitionism and utilitarianism were already present in the disagreements between the positions of Reid and Paley. The book also contains some very striking anticipations of Sidgwick.

Smith thinks there are two basic questions which a moral philosophy must answer: what is the nature of 'the mental operation by which moral distinctions are perceived', and what is the ultimate criterion of right and wrong? (*PM* I, vii, pp. 1–3.) In insisting on their separation he is doing explicitly what Brown did implicitly, denying the part of the Reidian argument against utilitarianism which rests on the existence of irreducible differences between the moral faculty and our other faculties. But Smith accepts what Brown rejects in Reid's position—the cognitivism— and rejects what Brown accepts—the opposition to utilitarianism. We shall see Smith's contribution to the theory of utilitarianism in Chapter 5. Here some aspects of his moral epistemology will be noted.

Much of Smith's work is devoted to defending the rationality of morals against Brown and earlier non-cognitivists. In the course of his criticism there occurs one of the points at which he anticipates Sidgwick. He begins with a discussion of 'the absurd consequences that would flow' from taking moral

[9] Smith wrote little else. In 1835 he published an article in *Blackwood's Magazine*, on 'The Philosophy of Poetry', which has been carefully analysed by Professor M. H. Abrams in *The Mirror and the Lamp*, 1953, pp. 149–54, where it is highly praised. Smith also wrote four articles for the *Edinburgh Review*: 'Evangelical Preaching', vol. 64, Jan. 1837; 'Douglas on the Philosophy of Mind', vol. 70, Jan. 1840; 'On Lieber's Political Ethics', vol. 73, Apr. 1841, and 'Phrenological Ethics', vol. 74, Jan. 1842. Abrams learned that Smith, who was born about 1794 and died in 1851, was educated at King's College, Aberdeen, was a schoolmaster for a while, and then, due to ill health, left teaching and served as postmaster in Banff, Scotland from 1827 until his death. On the title-page of the London Library copy of Smith's book, donated by him to the Library, Smith notes that he is the author of the article on 'Post Offices' in the seventh edition of the *Encyclopaedia Britannica*.

judgements to result solely from our feelings. His basic objection, similar to one of Reid's, is concisely stated:

if, when we pronounce an agent or action morally good, we mean, simply, that the view of such action or agent excites in the spectator an agreeable emotion, then the affirmation that such action or agent is good, does not express any thing that is true of such *agent* or *action*, but only something that is true of the *spectator*, namely, that *he* is affected after a peculiar manner by a view of a particular action. (*PM* I, p. 40.)

And this, as he goes on to show, leads to absurdities. The theory under attack is not helped, he points out, by claiming that there is an absolute quality in the act or agent which causes the feeling. For to say that there is a given quality in the act is not to say that the perception of this quality affects us agreeably: 'the question then is, which of the two, upon the hypothesis of a moral sense, is identical in meaning with this one—the action is *right*.' To take the former alternative is to give up the hypothesis, for it is to admit that it is the quality causing the feeling, not the feeling itself, which constitutes the rightness of the act. Hence the absurdities which follow from saying that 'this act is right' is synonymous with 'the spectator feels an agreeable feeling on seeing this act' are true consequences of the subjectivist or moral sense view. The absurdities may be given in Smith's own words:

that the same absolute quality may be good at one time, bad at another; or that absolute qualities of opposite kinds may both be good or both be bad at the same time. If one being is formed to behold cruelty with the agreeable, kindness with the disagreeable emotion; if another being is formed in a way the reverse of this; when the one calls cruelty good, kindness bad; when the other calls kindness good, cruelty bad; the one pronounces something absolutely true of each sort of conduct as much as the other does. Cruelty is absolutely different from kindness . . . whatever emotions may be connected with the view of each. But then cruelty is as truly good in the one way as kindness is in the other. (*PM* I, pp. 41–2.)

In spelling out the consequences of the subjectivist thesis in this manner, Smith moves a marked step beyond Reid's arguments and toward those which Sidgwick gives early in the *Methods*. Smith goes on to examine in some detail the views of

Hutcheson and Brown, showing that on their own grounds they have no effective way of turning the force of the criticisms (*PM* I, pp. 42–58), but we need not follow him.

Smith is a true Scottish intuitionist in holding that there are a number of self-evident basic axioms of morality. But his radical divergence from the school, and another of his anticipations of Sidgwick, becomes apparent from the content of his list of axioms. The first two state that it is fit that every sentient being should enjoy happiness, and unfit that any should suffer misery. The third says, at great length, that virtue deserves reward. The fourth is that 'it is fit that agents equally innocent, meritorious, or guilty, should, respectively, be equally happy or miserable, rather than unequally so'. The fifth and sixth axioms put the importance of relieving misery above the importance of creating happiness. The remaining axioms— there are seventeen concerning morals, followed by eight about the psychology of happiness—have to do with the relations among fitness, rightness, and obligation, which, on Smith's view, are not all expressive of the same idea (cf. *PM* I, pp. 5–11). There is no mention of veracity, and none of justice unless the fourth axiom is an axiom of justice; and none of the other non-utilitarian principles asserted by the Scottish school figures in the list either. Smith is in fact a utilitarian who bases his utilitarianism on intuitively evident first principles. He is aware that this is a departure from the tradition but he professes not quite to see why it should be so. 'It is singular', he writes, 'how any opposition has ever been imagined to exist between the supposition of our having a special inward sense, discriminative of right and wrong; and that of the moral goodness of actions consisting in their utility.' (*PM* II, p. 199.) He devotes a brief section to dismissing some mistaken reasons for holding that there is a real opposition (*PM* II, pp. 199–206). He does not advert to the fact that a group of religious assumptions help support the belief in this opposition. His own philosophy, despite his apparent piety, makes no use of such assumptions, and in their absence he is able to treat the claim concerning the uniqueness of the deliverances of the moral faculty as a purely epistemological point. And as such, it does not sustain the anti-utilitarian argument which Reid and the Reidians drew from it in conjunction with their religious assumptions.

There is yet a third point on which, if rather less clearly, Smith anticipates Sidgwick. It arises out of his further criticisms of subjectivism. The subjectivist tells us that 'We ought to do this' means 'we shall feel an agreeable or pleasant emotion on doing this'. Now in general, one can ask of any proposed action whether or not one ought to do it, and, more specifically, Smith says that 'of a mere emotion of pleasure . . . it can never be an absurd question to ask whether or not or why it ought to be preferred'. But on the subjectivist view, this question would be absurd. For an affirmative answer—'we ought to prefer the agreeable emotion'—would simply mean, 'it excites the agreeable emotion to excite the agreeable emotion'. But, Smith comments, 'that we ought to act so as to obtain the agreeable emotion . . . may be a true proposition or a false proposition . . . but it would not be an identical proposition'. (*PM* I, pp. 68–9.) Thus the subjectivist view cannot account for ordinary, and important, questions and answers about what we ought to do. The difficulty can, of course, be extended to any definition of moral terms in purely factual terms, but Smith's interest is in extending it to any theory which appeals to a moral sense or faculty. What are we to make of the assertion, necessary to any such view, that we ought to obey the dictates of the moral sense? Smith himself says, ingeniously, that it is a tautology though it has a use in the language none the less. It can be used to try to impel someone who knows what he ought to do, but hesitates, into doing it. It cannot be used to inform him of what in particular he ought to do. 'When we say that a man ought to perform his duty, or to do what is agreeable to conscience or the moral faculty, generally, the proposition can only be significant when used to impel; used to inform, it must be entirely tautological.' (*PM* I, p. 72.) But on the view of the moral sense school, such a proposition must be 'informative' in Smith's sense. The moral sense picks out a class of acts— those from which an agreeable emotion of a peculiar kind is derived—and tells us to do them. But there is a general objection to this:

If we define or describe the moral faculty in any other way, than merely as the faculty by which we perceive that we ought to do some things, avoid others,—that is, if we define or describe it in any way, in which the affirmation, that we ought to gratify the moral sense will be anything more than an identical proposition, we inevitably lay ourselves open to this question,—why ought we to obey the moral faculty? This must always, in such a case, be a question of real meaning, and a question to which no satisfactory answer can be given. (*PM* I, pp. 77–8.)

Smith himself defines the moral faculty simply as 'the faculty by which we perceive that we ought to do some things, and to avoid others' (*PM* I, p. 78). This makes no claims about the moral faculty except that it perceives something true. And as the only idea we have of reason is that it enables us to obtain truth, we may say that reason is the moral faculty, without falling into the problem that besets the moral sense theory.

There is more to this than an objection to Hutcheson and subjectivism: it is the basis of Smith's complaint that Reid and Stewart are superficial in their dealings with the claim that morality is rational. Smith accuses them of wavering between treating morality seriously as a matter of reason and treating it as resting on a special faculty. They seem to think, Smith says, that a being might be able to reason about non-moral topics and yet have no moral beliefs; but at the same time they say the moral faculty is rational. Smith holds that reason is a unity, and that a rational being, aware of the existence of other sentient beings, would inevitably see that those sentients ought not to suffer. (*PM* I, pp. 36–7.) This is not, he says, just a matter of what name we give to the source of our moral judgements. If the special faculty to which Reid and Stewart appeal is not simply the faculty which yields truth, and if it gives substantive directives, then we need some answer to the question, why ought we to obey it? Reid and Stewart might be willing to refer to the divine origin or divine guidance of the moral faculty. We have already noted that Smith makes no such appeal to religious assumptions. He has therefore moved away from considering intuition or the moral faculty to be a power which guarantees its deliverances in some way; and in its place he tries to show that the basic axioms of morality display their rationality in themselves. It is not their source but their content which warrants their truth.

Smith's effort to show just how the axioms are intrinsically rational is not successful. There is a kind of reasoning, he says, other than deducing one proposition from another. It consists in showing from a concept employed in a proposition that the proposition is true; and it is the kind appropriately used in 'the making out of the first and primary proposition' in a chain of reasoning. (*PM* I, p. 142 n.) The relevant concept for the axioms of morality is the concept of pleasure. It is part of that concept that pleasure can exist only in sentient beings and that it must move joy, hope, and desire. A rational being, Smith adds, seeing this much of the concept, sees further 'that pleasure is a state in which a sentient being ought to be . . . that his being in a state of pleasure . . . is fit, right . . .'. (*PM* I, p. 141.) In short, Smith proposes that the basic axioms display their own rationality because they are analytic truths: 'what is, in every axiom, predicated of a certain subject, being involved in the conception we form of that subject, must be a necessary truth . . .'. (*PM* I, p. 202). He does not discuss, or even seem to be aware of, the problems that arise from taking first principles to be true by definition. But it is important not to overlook the philosophical motivation behind this unfortunate move. Smith perceives that purely factual definitions of moral notions will not provide foundations for morality, and sees also that no appeal to a special faculty as a substantive source of moral judgements can guarantee their truth, unless strong religious or metaphysical assumptions are made about the faculty. To avoid these problems while preserving the rationality of morality, he turns to definitions which involve moral terms. These would indeed enable us to derive moral principles. But Smith fails to show that there is any necessity for us to use the conceptions as he defines them, and so he fails to resolve the problem. None the less, because he saw that neither a straight-forward appeal to facts nor the invocation of an inscrutable faculty, whatever it be called, can provide a satisfactory rational basis for morality, he moved toward a way of handling the question of the foundations of ethics which was to find its nineteenth-century culmination in the work of Sidgwick.

Smith realized more clearly than anyone until Sidgwick that the irreducibility of moral concepts and judgements to non-moral concepts and judgements does not of itself preclude the possibility of a coherent utilitarian theory. If the basic concept of morality is simple and unique, then utility cannot constitute rightness: but this does not prevent it from being the sole

3

The Cambridge Moralists

IN December 1832 Adam Sedgwick, a geologist and Fellow of Trinity College, Cambridge, delivered a lengthy discourse on the curriculum at the University to his junior colleagues. His aim was to remind them that all branches of learning could and should be subservient to the religious improvement of their students, and he devoted a good deal of his time to showing how the study of philosophy at Cambridge, relying heavily on the epistemology of Locke and the ethics of the former Cambridge tutor Paley, failed in this regard. Though his criticisms of Paley were, as we shall see, commonplace, he was requested by his auditors, in a letter written by William Whewell, to publish his discourse as an aid to their own and their students' improvement. When the little book appeared, Whewell wrote to his friend Julius Hare saying that it was even better than the original spoken address, and praising also a sermon given by a young man named Thomas Rawson Birks on 'Mathematical and Moral Certitude', which had just been delivered. Birks's declamation, he said, was full of 'most profound' philosophy and its views of morality were 'pure and elevated'. Whewell added that he himself was working on 'a philosophy such as shall really give a right and wholesome turn to men's minds'.[1] These two attacks on Paley and the support given them by Whewell mark the point at which philosophy at Cambridge began its public resistance to empiricism and utilitarianism. Whewell was only one of the Cambridge philosophers involved, though the most vocal and powerful. To understand the Cambridge position we must look back to its origins in the thought of a man who was neither a teacher at Cambridge, though he had studied there, nor primarily a philosopher, though he had a considerable influence on a number of philosophers: Samuel Taylor Coleridge.

[1] I. Todhunter, *William Whewell D.D. An Account of His Writings*, 1876, ii. 149–51, 174–5.

Coleridge's thought was first represented strongly at Cambridge by Julius Hare, a classical scholar more widely read in German thought than anyone else in England, who taught as a Fellow of Trinity from 1822 to 1832. Not only was he a close friend of Whewell's,[2] he was also a teacher of F. D. Maurice, who later became related to him by marriage; and Maurice was the most important exponent of Coleridgean religious thinking in Victorian Britain. Whewell was followed as Knightbridge Professor by John Grote, who in turn was succeeded by Maurice.[3] Sidgwick knew them all, except Hare, and knew their works. Neither Whewell nor Grote was an avowed follower of Coleridge, as Maurice was, and none of them was unoriginal enough to have been simply a follower of anyone. But their views, different in important respects though they are, have significant similarities. Two themes, in particular, are of importance in their work. They are all defending a spiritual and religious, and so far as possible a specifically Christian, outlook, and they see opposition to any utilitarian interpretation of morality as part of this defence; and they are all strongly opposed to philosophical empiricism, which they see as being, among other things, at the root of anti-religious thinking. While views of this kind were not uncommon in Victorian Britain, and often showed the influence of Kant, the forms they took at Cambridge were in large part a result of the way in which Coleridge understood both Kant and the issues. It is not

---

[2] A third person of importance, though he was less interested in philosophy, was Connop Thirlwall. Referring to Thirlwall, Hare, and Whewell, the Master of Downing College, T. Worsley, wrote to Sidgwick, apparently in connection with Sidgwick's 1876 article in *Mind* on philosophy at Cambridge, that they 'might have formed a genuine philosophic triumvirate . . . Thirlwall with his depth of thought and irony should have been the Socrates, Julius Hare as a loving student and expounder the Plato, and Whewell, as indeed another maestro di color' che sanno . . . the Aristotle. This chapter in the recent history of Philosophy at Cambridge cannot be left out, constituting as it does a main part of that history.' (TCC Add. MS. c 104/71.)

On Hare, see the two 'Introductory Notices' to E. H. Plumptre's edition of Hare's *The Victory of Faith*, 1874. One notice is by Maurice, the other by Dean Stanley. One of Hare's most promising Cambridge pupils, and later his curate, was John Sterling, who became a close friend of John Stuart Mill's and helped introduce him to Coleridgean ideas, as did F. D. Maurice.

On Thirlwall, see John Connop Thirlwall, *Cannop Thirlwall*, 1936, esp. Chs. 1–5.

[3] Thomas Rawson Birks succeeded Maurice. He was an old-fashioned Evangelical in his allegiances and his theology, and did not continue the philosophical and theological tradition here discussed. Sidgwick was Birks's successor.

the least mark of this influence that the Cambridge philosophers were far more willing than the Scottish to attempt to find some unifying ground in human rationality behind the many intuitions of moral truth which, they would have agreed, we all have. Insofar as intuitionism progressed beyond the work of Reid's followers, it did so almost entirely at Cambridge; and the one notable intuitional philosopher not at Cambridge, James Martineau, was drawn into the first major exposition of his moral philosophy when he reviewed Whewell's works on ethics.[4]

i. *Coleridge*

Coleridge[5] was possessed of a boldly speculative spirit, had read a certain amount of Kant, Jacobi, and Schelling, and used their ideas freely to help in formulating his own. But as in so many other things, so also in philosophy, he saw, or thought he saw, more than he could say, and he never produced a finished system. His ideas concerning morality are even more fragmentary than his ideas on other subjects and have been less studied than his religious or epistemological views. One cannot confidently outline a moral philosophy and call it Coleridge's; but his scattered remarks suggest something of the following kind.

Coleridge's chief concern is to lay the groundwork for a defence of Christian doctrine against the advance of science and of critical examination of the Bible. His approach is to interpret the doctrines of Christianity as the best explanation available of human experience construed in a very broad sense. The doctrines themselves are not irrational. Their discovery, indeed, may have been beyond human ability, and our first grasp of them may have come with God's help. But revelation and inspiration are not to be viewed as wholly mysterious and incomprehensible processes. They are our insights, usually dim and indistinct, often partial and one-sided, into truths about the constitution of the universe; and any of us can check and test them. This view emerges most clearly in Coleridge's well-known

---

[4] Since Sidgwick discussed Martineau's position at some length in the *Methods*, presentation of his views is deferred until Ch. 8.

[5] On Coleridge's philosophy, see J. H. Muirhead, *Coleridge as Philosopher*, 1930, where Coleridge appears to be more systematic and coherent than I have found him. See also Welch, *Protestant Thought in the Nineteenth Century*, vol. i, Ch. 5: Welch gives only two pages to the ethics. For a fuller discussion see Basil Willey, *The English Moralists*, 1964, pp. 300–12,

theory of Biblical inspiration. 'In the Bible', he claims, 'there
is more that *finds* me than I have experienced in all other
books put together . . . the words of the Bible find me at
greater depths of my being; and . . . whatever finds me brings
with it an irresistible evidence of its having proceeded from the
Holy Spirit.' (*Confessions*, p. 296.) The spirit that worked in the
various writers of the books of the Bible works in us too (*Confessions*, pp. 316–17), and because it does, we can see for ourselves where they were rightly guided by it and where, being
human, they went astray. We need not take every word and
syllable as divinely given, as if God were some sort of ventri-
loquist. We can sort out the inspired from the uninspired for
ourselves, using the testimony of the ages and our own intelligence. The point at issue in considering inspiration, Coleridge
says, is this: either we hold that the Bible is inspired of God and
therefore must be accepted as true, holy, and in all parts
unquestionable; or we hold that we can see that the Bible contains more true, holy, and unquestionable wisdom than any
other book and we conclude that it is therefore inspired by
God. (*Confessions*, pp. 323 ff.) By defending the second alternative persuasively, Coleridge gave new impetus to the belief
that the essential points of religious teaching can be checked
against, and can rest on, experiential evidence.

The major part of this experiential evidence comes, on
Coleridge's view, from the conscience. The works of God in
the world, and the adaptation of means to ends, remind me of
God's existence; but they presuppose that I have the notion of
God, and this notion, Coleridge says, which is 'essential to the
human mind', is 'called forth into distinct consciousness prin-
cipally by the conscience'. (*Omn.*, pp. 429–30.) 'The one great
and binding ground of the belief of God and a hereafter is the
law of conscience', Coleridge says, and like Kant he connects
this closely with an awareness of our being morally responsible
agents possessing free wills. (*Omn.*, pp. 418, 429; cf. *Aids*, pp.
44, 91.) There are other respects in which Coleridge's view is
similar to Kant's: for example, his description of conscience
uses, at times, directly Kantian language:

That I am conscious of something within me preemptorily commanding me to do unto others as I would that they should do unto
me;—in other words a categorical . . . imperative;—that the maxim

... of my actions ... should be such as I could, without any contradiction arising therefrom, will to be the law of all moral and rational beings;—this, I say, is a fact of which I am no less conscious ... than I am of any appearance presented by my outward senses. .... knowing that consciousness of this fact is the root of all other consciousness ... we name it conscience. (*Faith*, p. 341.)

This consciousness or conscience, for Coleridge, springs from or perhaps is the Reason (in his technical sense of that term), and is neither a feeling, a sense, nor a special faculty. Its presence in all men is shown by the universality of 'the inward experience of the diversity between regret and remorse ... so long as reason continues, so long must conscience exist'. (*Faith*, p. 342.) In addition to being the core of our personal identity, and the main source of our notion of God and of our evidence for His existence, conscience is also the channel through which God communicates with us: 'The will of God is revealed to man through the conscience.' (*Faith*, p. 348.)

What conscience tells us has two characteristics of interest. First, its deliverances are of an unique kind, not reducible to or explicable in terms of the kind of information given us by any other cognitive capacity. Criticizing someone who identified the good with the pleasant and the desirable, Coleridge says:

there is an equivocation in the main word of the definition, viz., *desirable*, by means of which you assume all that ought to be proved. ... For *desirable* means either that which actually I do desire, or that which I know I ought to desire.... You preassume, I say, that Good is nothing more than a reflex idea of the mind after a survey and calculation of agreeable or delightful sensations. .... Now this I utterly deny. *I know—intuitively know*—that there is a power essential to my nature, and which constitutes it human nature, the voice of which is I ought, I should, I ought not, I should not, and that this voice is original and self-existent, not an echo of a prior voice. (*PL*, pp. 152-3.)

The uniqueness of the deliverances of conscience is plainly shown in the distinction our language makes between utility or prudence and morality:

The sum total of moral philosophy is found in this one question, Is *Good* a superfluous word,—or mere lazy synonyme for the pleasurable and its causes. ... Or the question may be. ... stated thus, Is *good* superfluous as a word exponent of a *kind*? If it be, then moral philosophy is but a subdivision of physics. If not, then the writings of Paley and all his predecessors and disciples are false and *most* pernicious. (*TT*, p. 155.)

Elsewhere Coleridge objects to Epicureanism on the grounds that a philosopher of that persuasion has no business using the words 'right' and 'obligation', because he means by them only 'power' and 'compulsion'. Only the religious man—who, presumably, admits the intuitive abilities of conscience—can use moral terms in their proper senses. (*Aids*, pp. 90–1.) The second point about the deliverances of conscience, not surprisingly, is that they are opposed to hedonism, utilitarianism, and, more generally, to consequentialism. Ethics contemplates action, Coleridge says, 'in its originating spiritual source. . . . Not the outward deed . . . not the deed as a possible object of the sense,—is the object of Ethical Science', but rather the character of the will from which the deed springs. (*Aids*, pp. 196–7.) Even if actions dictated by and done from self-love were the same as actions dictated by and done from 'Christian principle', there would be a difference—a difference 'in that, for which all actions have their whole worth and their main value,—in the agents themselves'. (*Friend*, ii. 139.)

Coleridge's anticonsequentialism is so strong that at times he denies that Paley is a moralist at all, since Paley is concerned only with outward effects of acts. (*Aids*, pp. 196–7; *C. and S.*, p. 380 n.) But this is not all he has to say about such views. Because of his conviction that our understanding of the truths first revealed through the Bible grows and develops, he holds that views long and deeply believed by a society or a profound thinker have something important to teach us: they contain some aspect of the truth we have not seen ourselves. (*Friend*, ii. 143–4.) Egoistic and utilitarian moralists—and like many others at this time, Coleridge does not distinguish the two carefully—have grasped something that needs to be included in a full understanding of morality: 'the outward object of virtue being the greatest producible sum of happiness of all men, it must needs include the object of an intelligent self-love. . . . Hence, you cannot become better (that is, more virtuous), but you will become happier . . .' (*Aids*, p. 30.) We assume that the physical world is a unity and a harmony; we must not less assume that the spiritual world of free and intelligent agents is one as well, and that true happiness for each will be the outcome of virtue. (*Aids*, pp. 40–1; 31 ff.)

On Coleridge's view the data found in our moral experience form a substantial part of the evidence to which we must appeal to test the hypotheses about the universe and our place in it which are first suggested to us by revelation and which our testing will show to be truly inspired. Part of the confirmation is provided by the very existence of unique and irreducible moral judgements: they show our distinctive place within the universe, as possessors of powers of intuition, and of free will. Another part of the confirmation is provided by the content of the deliverances of conscience: by commanding us at times to act in opposition to our animal needs and desires, and by stressing the inner worth of agents, rather than the outer values of consequences, the dictates of conscience confirm the teachings recorded in the Bible. Presumably it is fair to infer from Coleridge's view that moral experience generally will show these features and that the morality of common sense will increasingly be explicable only in terms of the religious outlook. These general points suggest themes of great importance for the Cambridge moralists who preceded Sidgwick, and for Sidgwick as well.

ii. *The Coleridgeans*

As early as 1856 a major Victorian moralist noted the influence of Coleridge at Cambridge. 'No one talks of a "Cambridge Theology",' James Martineau wrote.

There is such a thing, nevertheless;—at least there is a theology, perfectly distinct and characteristic of the age, formed by Cambridge men and born with the impress of Cambridge studies. . . . Coleridge . . . learned at Jesus College: and the men through whom chiefly his Platonic gospel has passed into the heart of our generation, Julius Hare and Frederick Maurice, acknowledged the same *alma mater*. To those who are familiar with the writings of these eminent teachers it will not appear fanciful if we trace the origin of the school to intellectual revolt against their academic text books, Locke and Paley. Empirical psychology and utilitarian ethics were the permanent objects of Coleridge's hostility . . . it was reserved for Professors Sedgwick and Whewell, at a later time, to dethrone upon the spot the two established potentates in philosophy. (*ERA* i. 224.)

The Cambridge theologians were one segment of those who came to be referred to as the 'Broad Church' group of Anglicans. Like others who were included under this name, they held a wide variety of views on most topics, and were unified mainly by their very Coleridgean beliefs that religion need not fear and should, indeed, welcome the advance of science, that the dogmatic commitments required for membership in the Church of England should be reduced to a minimum, and that the Church should try to include as many devout people as possible. Only thus, they felt, could the Church survive in an age which was bound to see an increase of scientific study of the Bible.

The liberal Anglicans,[6] at Oxford and elsewhere as well as at Cambridge, were united not only by their rejection of empiricism and utilitarianism but by a denial of the view of progress that often went along with those positions in the early decades of the nineteenth century. They neither believed in nor wished for endless improvement in man's material lot: on the purely secular level, their view of history was rather that of Vico than of Condorcet. They saw secular history as primarily a matter of nations, and they held that nations go through regular stages of growth, maturation, decay, and death. Laws of this process may be derived, they thought, from the study of history and used to give guidance for political action. The relativism and apparent determinism involved in this view of history were countered by their Christian insistence on God's providence and on the free will of men as the ultimate agent in historical change. For the other side of their denial of a materialistic kind of progress was an affirmation of the existence of spiritual and moral progress. Later ages, they claimed, begin their slow procession through the cycles of national history at

---

[6] I am indebted to Duncan Forbes, *The Liberal Anglican Idea of History*, 1952, for much of the material in this paragraph and the next. Although Forbes does not discuss Whewell, it was his book which suggested to me that it might be profitable to think of him as the philosopher and the historian of science of the Broad Church group. See also O. Chadwick, *From Bossuet to Newman*, 1957, for discussion of a different kind of view of doctrinal development.

Whewell is generally thought to have been rather conservative; but on church matters he was viewed at the time as a liberal. See Norman Gash, *Reaction and Reconstruction in English Politics*, 1965, pp. 93, 95 n. 2. For further data on his academic and religious views, see the various letters to Hare in Mrs. Stair Douglas, *Life of William Whewell*, 2nd edn., 1882, and J. Willis Clark, *Old Friends at Cambridge*, 1900, pp. 91, 106, 123–4.

a higher intellectual and ethical level than earlier ages. The agency in bringing about moral progress was at first God, whose direct revelation was decisive for all later times; but since then man's own nature has enabled him to grow in stature as a spiritual and moral being. This is the only true progress. 'Accordingly', says J. C. Hare, 'the philosophical idea of the history of the world will be, that it is to exhibit the gradual unfolding of all the faculties of man's intellectual and moral being . . . the purpose and end of the history of the world is to realize the idea of humanity.' (*Guesses*, pp. 334–5.) Hare goes on to say that we must take seriously the commandment to be perfect as God is perfect. 'These words', he remarks, 'declare that the perfect renewal of God's image in man is not a presumptuous vision . . . but an object of righteous enterprise, which we may and ought to long for and to strive after.' (*Guesses*, p. 347.) Conscience, the voice of God within us according to Hare, is a testimony to the finer original nature we had before the Fall: it is also the means by which we achieve moral knowledge. Like Coleridge, Hare connects the conscience with the reason, and denies that the conscience is utilitarian: 'when the calculating, expediential Understanding has superseded the Conscience and the Reason, the Senses soon rush out from their dens, and sweep away everything before them.' (*Guesses*, p. 80.)

Motivated in large part by their desire to accept the advances of Biblical scholarship, the liberal Anglicans developed a theory of 'accommodation', which is a central point of their theology. Many of them were historians, and the theory of accommodation is in some sort a historical view. It holds that divine revelation at any time in history is adapted to the faculties and to the stage of spiritual and moral development of the men and the nation to whom the revelation is made. They drew from this view the conclusion that much of what is in the Bible must be understood not as conveying directly and literally some central truth, but as indicating the truth in a way that could have been plainly enough understood by the relatively primitive nation to which it was revealed, and that must be recovered through historical study now. Religious insight and understanding develop as man develops; and as our insight grows, we see more and more the ways in which divine providence is at work in the universe. The same is true in the moral realm, though here the advance is slower and more painfully achieved than in the sciences of the natural realm. But the result is assured: 'Though Chaos may only have been driven out of a part of his empire as yet, that empire is undergoing a perpetual curtailment; and in the end he will be cast out of the intellectual and moral and spiritual world, as entirely as out of the material.' (*Guesses*, p. 506.) We may conclude, therefore, that for Hare and his colleagues morality, properly studied, reveals a progressive development toward a harmonious and coherent religious and spiritual standpoint; and the fact that it does is evidence of the spiritual structure of the universe.

F. D. Maurice, whose active career spanned the Professorships of both Whewell and Grote, agrees with this general outlook. There is a theology, he says, and it is clearly his own, which

supposes the Infinite to be goodness and wisdom . . . and to be guiding men by various processes, in various regions and ages, into the apprehension of that which by their constitution they were created to apprehend. The history of Moral and Metaphysical Philosophy, is, as I think, the History of this Education. (*MMP*, i. xxix; cf. *Th.E.*, p. 300.)

The knowability of God is a key point in Maurice's theology. He strongly rejects empiricism on the grounds that that doctrine is a barrier to human communication with God. 'Ever since the position was adopted . . . that there is no knowledge but that which comes to us through the senses, the idea of a communion between the Divine Word and the heart and conscience and reason of men has been of course rejected', he writes in his major early work, *The Kingdom of Christ* (1838). (*K. of C.*, i. 44–5.) He also rejects the kind of anti-empiricism represented by H. L. Mansel, which would place limits in principle on our ability to understand God. He holds that God is always and really accessible to us, and that knowledge of God is essential for all other knowledge. 'The only possible doctrine for an age of Science', he remarks in a discussion of Comtean positivism, is

that God *can* be known; that the knowledge of Him is the root of all other knowledge; that we are only capable of knowing our fellow-creatures, and of knowing the world of nature, because we are more directly related to Him than to them; because His knowledge of them is imparted in a measure to the creatures whom he has made in His image. . . . Science demands God, as its foundation. (*Epis.*, p. 344.)

At the basis of this view of the knowability of God is Maurice's fundamental conviction that God is not to be thought of as somehow distant from us, and that the kingdom of Christ is not to be envisaged as something which will come at some indefinite future date. So far as any temporal or spatial terms are appropriate to them, God and His kingdom are here and now—only we do not see them. Terms like Heaven, Hell, and Eternity refer to the way in which each of us relates to God and to every other person. Hell is wilful and sinful self-isolation from God; Heaven is our closer union with Him. (*Th.E.*, pp. 405 f.) Social order on earth, like the order of the physical world, is an image of and is sustained by the divine order which is in and of the universe now, and which includes us all. What prevents us from seeing this more fully and from realizing it more completely than we do is our own selfishness.

Is not the world God's world? Is not the order which we see, His order? . . . Assuredly, it is God's world, God's order; . . . *how* has disorder come into this order? for that it is there, we all confess. It has come from men falling in love with this order, or with some of the things in it, and setting them up and making them into gods. (*Epis.*, pp. 120–1; cf. pp. 61, 126–7.)

God is forever reaching out to us, trying to help us to understand him; and in different ages and countries, from different intellectual backgrounds, men have tried in various ways to express and to teach what they have learned of him. Maurice is a true Coleridgean in his insistence that there is something of value to be learned from the deepest views of any thinker on religious matters. Each in his own way has seen a part or an aspect of the truth. So far as each has done so, each is right: it is only their denials, Maurice teaches, that are wrong. This attitude pervades Maurice's writings and leads him always to attempt to reconcile opposing views and to search for the truth embodied in the most diverse social schemes, religious opinions, and philosophical writings, as well as in the sects and religions of the world.[7]

If selfishness is the cause of our ignorance of God's order, conscience is the means through which we most directly come to know of it. Selfishness is a deliberate and sinful[8] failure to be what God means us to be: conscience, which Maurice like Coleridge associates closely with our real self, tells each of us what he ought or ought not to be. (*Consc.*, pp. 31, 34.) Maurice dismisses questions of the origins of conscience as irrelevant to an understanding of it. It cannot be reduced to simpler elements in sense experience (*Consc.*, pp. 32, 51, 165), nor is it simply feeling or even reason. It is the voice of God speaking within us. (*Consc.*, p. 73; *Epis.*, p. 212.) Maurice takes this to mean that conscience is not an authority on its own (he thinks he is here disagreeing with Bishop Butler): rather it transmits to us God's authoritative law, which is the law of love. Conscience gives neither rules nor subsidiary laws to guide us (*Consc.*, pp. 104 ff., 113, 125), for love expresses itself in different ways in different times and places. We see in Jesus Christ the perfect paradigm of human love, and we are called on to be like him; but we can only even begin to do this through God's working within us. Our selfishness shows itself in our opposing God's guidance. It has the effect of destroying order:

no man . . . no society, can stand upon selfishness. It must stand upon the opposite of selfishness. . . . Its root must be in love. That is the one binding force. . . . So far as any family or any nation has ever been held together, it has been held by the might not of selfishness but of sacrifice. (*Epis.*, p. 264; *Soc. Mor.*, pp. 385 ff.)

Maurice is thus claiming that while conscience reveals the law of love to us, its dictates come in the form of specific judgements about specific situations. Selfishness blinds us to the presence of God and distorts, though it cannot stifle, the voice of conscience. It is hard to find anything resembling a philosophical argument in support of these views; but if Maurice is correct, then the particular judgements of conscience will show,

---

[7] See, e.g., *MMP*, i. xxx; *Th.E.*, p. 384; *K. of C.*, i. 227, ii. 88 ff.; *Soc. Mor.* throughout but especially Ch. XVIII, in which Maurice tries to show how vitally important religious lessons can be learned even from a philosopher like Hobbes; and *Epis.*, p. 93.

[8] See Frederick Maurice, *Life of Frederick Denison Maurice*, 1884, ii. 538–40.

over the ages, a developing pattern of increasing conformity to the law of love.

iii. *Whewell's Ethics: The System*

Whewell[9] had a far more philosophical mind than the other members of the liberal Anglican group at Cambridge and incomparably more scientific knowledge and ability. His chief philosophical aim was to show how science, morality, and religion could be seen to fit together in one coherent system. By making a more profound and thorough attempt to carry out this enterprise than any of the Coleridgeans made, he revealed some of the serious difficulties with the assumptions on which they worked. In particular an ambiguity in the notion of progressive revelation, latent in their thinking, came to be critically important in his own, posing a problem of which he was never fully aware and with which, consequently, he never dealt successfully. The problem is one which arises because Whewell hoped to show both that morality should be understood in terms which also apply to science, and that there is powerful support for rejecting utilitarianism.

During the 1830s Whewell was working on his important and wide-ranging *History of the Inductive Sciences*, and on the philosophy of science which, he held, could be developed only from a basis of historical knowledge. As early as 1834 he was also thinking of a moral philosophy to be developed along the same lines as a philosophy of science—and was thinking of his views as 'guesses', a term of which Hare was fond.[10] Though Whewell did not share Hare's whole-hearted admiration of Coleridge (cf. *Lec. Hist. Add.*, pp. 119–30), he agreed with the Coleridgeans on certain points. Thus in his early lectures on moral philosophy, he insists that our knowledge of God's moral attributes is to be derived, not in the fashion of Paley and Butler from seeing the pattern of rewards and punishments associated with our actions, but from reflection on our own conscience and its deliverances. (*FM*, pp. 16–21.) This theme persisted in his thinking. Yet he also holds that 'in the mode of arriving at a belief in God, and in his moral government, the procedure of

---

[9] In addition to Todhunter and Douglas, see the articles listed in Bibliography III by Butts, Donagan, Ducasse, and Schneewind (1968).
[10] See Todhunter, ii. 187–8.

one mind is not a rule for other minds', and he presents various traditional arguments for the existence of God and his providence as 'reasonings . . . which may prove the doctrines . . . to the satisfaction of these persons who require proofs of them'. (*EMP*, 461.)

Though it is thus unclear that he would have agreed with the Coleridgeans in thinking morality the most important of the starting points from which we may rationally reach conclusions about God, he was at one with them in stressing the historical development of our insight into truth—scientific, moral, and religious. 'There are scientific truths which are seen by intuition', he writes, 'but this intuition is progressive.'[11] The same is true of intuitively known moral truths. Moral concepts, he holds,

in the progress of nations, gradually become clearer and clearer among men. We may suppose that, at first, man's social and moral faculties are very imperfectly developed . . . his moral conceptions are dim and vague. . . . As the intellectual culture of the nation proceeds . . . the conceptions . . . grow clearer in men's minds . . . nor can we say to what extent this intellectual and moral progress may proceed.

The intellectual progress of individuals follows nearly the same course, in these respects, as that of nations . . . the two careers are of the same kind; a constant advance from the material to the abstract; from the particular to the general; but in what is abstract and general, advance from the dim and vague to the distinct and precise. (*EMP*, 366–7.)

In science and in moral matters our power of intuition is directed upon Ideas in the mind of God, according to Whewell,[12] and though we never fully understand those Ideas because of the immeasurable difference between the human and the divine mind, we do none the less gain some genuine knowledge of God through our knowledge of his Ideas. Hence as our knowledge of science and of morality progresses, our understanding of God progresses along with it, and in addition every new discovery gives us a new assurance of 'the Divine nature of the human mind'.[13] In these avowedly Platonistic terms, then,

[11] William Whewell, *The Philosophy of Discovery*, 1860, p. 344.
[12] Whewell, *Discovery*, pp. 359 ff.
[13] Whewell, *Discovery*, p. 374; cf. pp. 380 ff.

Whewell elaborates a basis for a view of the progress of knowledge which brings out the religious bearing of such progress. He also elaborates, in connection with his studies of science, a view of the mode in which progress is made. We must note, briefly, what his theory is.

Every science, he holds, is demarcated by certain distinctive Ideas or Conceptions: for example, mechanics involves the Idea of force. Now the Idea of an area of investigation bears a special relation to the basic axioms which hold true within that area. The axioms are elementary truths, necessarily true though not true by definition. They are self-evident necessary truths and as such can be called 'intuitive'. But it is a result of the limited powers of the human mind that what is self-evident in itself may not be immediately self-evident to us, nor be seen to be necessarily true by all men at all times. 'Truths may be self-evident when we have made a certain progress in thinking, which are not self-evident when we begin to think', because the mind needs to develop. (*LSM*, p. 38.) There are axioms, 'tacitly assumed or occasionally stated', which 'belong to all the Ideas which form the foundations of the sciences, and are constantly employed in the reasoning and speculations of those who think clearly on such subjects'.[14] The axioms may even be articulated before their necessity is clearly realized. To see the necessity of the axioms, we must attain clarity about the fundamental Idea of the science. And Whewell tells us that the criterion of having reached sufficient clarity is 'that the person shall *see* the necessity of the Axioms belonging to each Idea; shall accept them in such a manner as to perceive the cogency of the reasonings founded upon them'.[15] For instance, one has a clear idea of space if one can follow geometrical proofs and see that they are conclusive.

The development of an Idea into clarity results from our attempt to understand the Facts within the area in which the Idea is fundamental—from our attempt to see those Facts in terms of the Idea. We use our implicit apprehension of an Idea to organize some of the facts which we have observed; the observations in turn, organized in this manner, show us further aspects of the Idea and help us to a more explicit awareness of

[14] William Whewell, *Novum Organon Renovatum*, 3rd edn., 1858, p. 41.
[15] Whewell, *Organon*, p. 42.

it; and this, again, leads us to further observations and to reorganization of the data. On Whewell's view all knowledge results from this sort of interplay between Idea and Fact, between theory and observation. Though he thinks there are some significant differences between moral knowledge and scientific knowledge, he thinks it vitally important to show that progress in moral knowledge occurs in the same way as it occurs in science. The reason he thinks the matter so urgent is made clear in his writings on the history of ethics.

Whewell traces English moral philosophy back, not to the casuists of the Catholic Church, who gave detailed moral advice without any reasoning to back it up, but to the English casuists who attempted to write books of cases for a Reformed England. These men, especially Jeremy Taylor, discussed cases primarily as illustrations of the rules and principles which were their main concern: in this they took a step in the direction of systematizing morality. (*Lec. Hist.*, pp. 34–5.) The next development came as a result of the challenge Hobbes delivered to the whole traditional Christian mode of viewing morality. The challenge could be neither ignored nor easily answered. For Hobbes's system was closely allied to the new developments in science, while his traditionally minded critics were hampered by adherence to metaphysical and methodological views derived from an outworn period. In the new system of science, Whewell says, 'much was so clearly convincing, that it was impossible to resist the evidence of its truth. . . . To reconstruct moral philosophy after the ancient systems of philosophy had been shaken to their foundations by the powerful hands of Descartes and Hobbes, Bacon and Newton, was no easy task.' First of all it was necessary to clear away the encumbrances left by the older modes of philosophizing. But Hobbes's opponents, instead of doing this, tried to repair the ruins of the old systems, or to 'dwell in huts made of wrecks and fragments'. And, Whewell adds, 'such indeed has been in great measure the condition of the common structures of morals up to the present day'. (*Lec. Hist.*, p. 59.) Even those who, like Clarke (and like Locke in some of his moods), tried to construct Christian moralities modelled after mathematical systems were not truly in touch with modern developments. The views of Clarke and Locke on this point are, Whewell holds, 'remnants retained by them of a philosophy then past. . . . If Morality is still to be capable of demonstration,' he adds, 'if her distinctions are really steadfast and unchangeable,—we must seek some new source of just principles for our reasoning, some new basis of fixity and permanency.'

Of the importance of finding such a new basis Whewell has no doubts. He sees the history of moral philosophy as involving far more than academic debates over the logic or epistemology of morals. It is part of the constant struggle between the religious view of life and the secular view, between the forces of good and those of evil, between the possibilities of human salvation and the dangers of eternal damnation. There is a morality on each side of this struggle. Utilitarianism, the morality of consequences, is the ally of worldliness. Whewell always refers to it as the 'low' morality. By contrast the morality which appeals to 'principles' is the 'high' morality. The effect of the disorder and confusion which occurred when the 'high' school, having failed to incorporate modern scientific developments in its total philosophy, was forced to give way to the delusively clear and disastrously oversimplified morality of consequences is graphically described:

The reverence which, handed down by the traditions of ages of moral and religious teaching, had hitherto protected the accustomed forms of moral good, was gradually removed. Vice, and Crime, and Sin, ceased to be words that terrified the popular spectator. Virtue, and Goodness, and Purity, were no longer things which he looked up to with mute respect. He ventured to lay a sacrilegious hand even upon these hallowed shapes. . . . There was a scene like that which occurred when the barbarians of old broke into the Eternal City. At first . . . they were awed by the divine aspect of the ancient rulers and magistrates: but when once their leader had smitten one of these venerable figures with impunity, the coarse and violent mob rushed onwards, and exultingly mingled all in one common destruction. (*Lec. Hist.*, p. 101.)

We shall see that Whewell believes there to be a place, in a properly constructed morality, for consideration of consequences. It is plain, however, that he views a morality in which the utilitarian principle is the sole or supreme principle with the greatest alarm, not simply as erroneous in theory, but as potentially disastrous in practice. Like Reid, he sees hedonism as an appeal to what is most bestial and least distinctively human in man, while he thinks the morality of principles appeals to what is more nearly divine. It is for these reasons that it is so urgent on his view to find a way of restating the 'high' morality so as to enable it to withstand the criticisms delivered by the apparently more scientific adherents of the 'low' view.

No existing version of the 'high' position, Whewell thinks, is adequate to the task. Butler's is the best that has been produced, but it is altogether too vague to be still satisfactory. Butler proved, according to Whewell, the reality of 'the office' of the moral faculty. He showed that morality could be based on principles of a unique kind, and could not be based on calculation of consequences. But he left the exact nature and the limits of the moral faculty in doubt. As a result his achievement seems easily open to being superseded by those who, like the utilitarians, claim to have scientifically precise results. Of course Butler's vagueness is only what one should expect, considering where he stood in the growth of moral thought. He was doing 'that which . . . discoverers always have to do. They search at the same time for true propositions, and for precise definitions', each being dependent on the other, in the way we have already noted. 'Men go on towards moral as they go on towards physical truth', Whewell says, and he suggests that if Cumberland had been the Kepler of the 'high' morality, Butler was its Borelli or its Huygens. (*Lec. Hist.*, pp. 128–32.) The inference is not far to seek that its Newton was yet to come.

Whewell's Platonistic remarks about Ideas in the mind of God lead one to suppose that he takes intuition to be the mental perception of these Ideas. On this view of intuition, the progress made when we systematize Facts in the light of our insight into Ideas, and then increase our insight, is like the removal of an impediment to vision or an improvement in the conditions under which the Idea is seen. The Preface to the first edition of the *Elements of Morality*, of 1845, reinforces this interpretation of his view of intuition. Whewell there says that his system of morality is like a geometrical system in some respects, and his basic principles like axioms; and he naturally takes axioms to be substantive principles the truth of which must be immediately perceived. Even after admitting, in the *Lectures* of the following year, that the analogy with geometry is misleading, Whewell continues to use the same sort of argument as Reid uses to prove the need for intuitively evident first principles—the vicious regress argument—and to suggest that these principles must be 'clearly seen'. (*LSM*, pp. 32–3.) And this seems again to indicate that Whewell's view of intuition is, except for the element of 'progressiveness', like Reid's. Yet when we look at the actual uses to which the concept of intuition is put in constructing his system, we find that in many cases it resembles this passive perception of abstract entities less than it resembles some sort of Kantian activity of reason according to a rule. Whewell seems, in fact, to be working sometimes with the Reidian notion, sometimes with a more Kantian notion, of intuition, without clearly realizing the difference.

One feature of Whewell's thought in which his departure from the Reidian notion of intuition is made evident is his insistence that the moral faculty must be simply the reason. Against subjectivist views of the moral faculty Whewell offers no specific arguments. He thinks the proposition that there are moral truths can be established easily by pointing out clear cases of true moral rules. Since faculties, on his view, are only useful names for the activities we attribute to them, and since the discovery of true general rules is one of the activities we call a function of reason (*EMP*, 10, 21), no further discussion is needed. But the point is quite general. 'Feeling is not moral feeling', he says, 'if it exclude the operation of the human faculty, the Reason ... the true guide of man is Conscience, only so long as the guide of Conscience is Reason.' (*LSM*, p. 19.) In one of his rare comments on the Scottish school Whewell turns this conclusion specifically against Stewart, who makes much of an alleged moral faculty. Whewell himself does not think it 'convenient' to assume a special moral faculty; 'for we must, in determining what actions and dispositions the Moral Faculty selects for approbation and disapprobation, give reasons; and thus the Reason comes to be the Faculty which we really employ in forming such judgments.' (*EMP*, Suppl. Ch. 1, para. 24.) Whewell's position here is thus similar to Alexander Smith's. His procedure in systematizing morality brings out yet further the difference between the notion of intuition he sometimes uses, and Reid's.

It is not Whewell's intention to try to show that the detailed rules of morality can be discovered by deriving them solely from self-evident substantive axioms. Despite his sometimes misleading language, his concern is always with ordering the moral knowledge we already have. For the most part this knowledge is implicit, needing to be made explicit, in 'permanent and definite form'; and the propositions thus articulated must be shown to be 'rationally connected one with another'. (*LSM*, pp. 10–17, 20.) The construction of a system consists primarily in doing these things. In working out the substance of his system, Whewell is guided by two considerations: that there must be one supreme rule of morality, and that this rule must be a rule for human beings.

There must be one supreme rule of morality because otherwise morality could not be rational. It may be objected that the infinite regress argument in support of the existence of self-evident axioms shows at best that there must be some unproven principles but not that there can be only one such principle. A similar objection may be raised to the attempt to rest this conclusion on an argument concerning the value of inferior goals sought as means to further ends. (*EMP*, 73.)[16] Whewell's reply is suggested by remarks in the *Lectures*. A supreme rule, he indicates there, must do four things: cover all the actions of individuals, govern all the spheres of life, delimit the spheres so that they do not conflict, and assign each man's place within each sphere. (*LSM*, pp. 80–1.) We shall suggest later how these 'spheres' may be determined. Here the point Whewell makes is that because a supreme rule must be such that it can do all these things, one may argue that there can be only one such rule. If there were more than one, they might conflict, leaving us no rational way to settle the problem; and then morality would not be fully rational. This argument is very much in the mode of Bentham's arguments for the principle of utility, as we shall see, and it seems likely that Whewell hopes, by adopting it, to reply to one of the strongest challenges of the Benthamite system. 'Whenever the question, *What is my Duty?* can be asked, our Morality ought to be able to give an

---

[16] For the objection, see Martineau, *ERA*, iii. 372. The reviews, one of *EMP*, the other of *LSM*, were originally published in 1845 and 1846 in the *Prospective Review*.

answer', Whewell says. (*LSM*, p. 97.) While there is a serious question as to his persistence in holding to all the implications of this position, there is no doubt that it is the rationale behind his view that there can be only one supreme principle.

The supreme rule must be a rule for human beings. No argument is given for this, but the point is plain. We are systematizing what rationality in action requires as it applies to humans. The force of the present consideration is to raise the question: what are the conditions under which human beings can live in accordance with a supreme moral rule? Through this formulation, human nature becomes the determining factor in Whewell's systematization of morality. We start with a large number of acknowledged moral truths. We can, so Whewell claims, show that the contents of morality provide a reasonable answer to the question of how a being with a nature such as man's can live under the guidance of a supreme moral principle.

The demands of reason on us become evident through the concept which is central to all of morality, a concept which Whewell, like Reid and many earlier writers, takes to be simple and indefinable. He holds, indeed, that the systematizer must define the key terms of the moral vocabulary; but the only definitions that can be given are what he calls 'reciprocal', i.e. they explain the meaning of one moral term by using another. Like Reid he also thinks we must take it for granted that the ordinary meaning of moral terms is already known: otherwise there is no way to explain their meanings. (*LSM*, pp. 26–8, 75–6.) The moralist can only hope to make the interconnections of these terms clearer and more explicit than they are in ordinary thought, a task Whewell undertakes in the early sections of the *Elements of Morality* (71–94), where they are defined in terms of the idea of a supreme reason or supreme rule. The other fixed point through which morality is to be systematized, the psychology of our active nature, Whewell elaborates in a Butlerian manner, stressing the complexity of human motivation and its involvement with concepts and rules. We need not go into the details either of his definitions or of his psychology, but we must give at least a rough indication of his derivation of the fundamental axioms which serve as the direct principles for systematizing our moral knowledge.

The derivation procedes by considering how action to satisfy man's basic desires becomes moralized in response to the permanent demand made by man's reason. Men desire sociability, safety, possessions, and eminence, as well as the simpler pleasures and the satisfaction of animal wants. Reason, which is distinctively human, demands that we gratify all these desires in a human way, and, since 'Reason directs us to rules', this entails that we must act in rule-governed ways. The first step in doing this is the attempt to live in accordance with positive laws. Since laws, though certainly imperfect, show how man has actually tried to impose rational constraints or rules on his desires, they help us to see what in man needs regulating, and in doing this give us clues toward understanding the content of morality. We can classify actual laws as prohibiting violence, theft, the breaking of contracts, adultery, and their own violation. These five negative constraints on external behaviour point toward five categories we can use in thinking about morality. Morality, however, requires more than law. Morality requires the rationality of our inner dispositions, not only of our external habits, and it demands positive responses, not abstentions. We must accordingly enrich the legal categories as we try to understand morality. The laws show that we need to prohibit violence, and this fact points toward a moral demand that men should be not merely peaceful but positively benevolent. Benevolence is thus one of the prime virtues. It may be formulated as the principle that 'Man is to be loved as Man'. Legal prohibition of theft shows the need for a virtue governing the possession and distribution of goods, and this is Justice, the principle of which is that 'each man is to have his own'. The law shows that men must be able to rely on one another and that this will not occur spontaneously. We must therefore admit a virtue of Integrity or Truthfulness. Fourth, as the prohibition of adultery shows, men's desires for pleasure must be controlled: hence we include Purity among the moral virtues. Its principle is that 'the Lower Parts of our Nature are to be governed by the Higher'. Finally, the general need for obedience to laws leads to the virtue of Order, whose principle is that 'we must accept positive Laws as the necessary conditions of Morality'. (*LSM*, pp. 86–9; cf. *EMP*, 106–9, 118–22.) Whewell adds a principle of moral earnestness, requiring energy in moral action, and a principle of moral purpose, requiring that all things be done as 'means to moral ends' (*EMP*, 163–4), but the five main virtues of Benevolence, Justice, Truthfulness, Purity, and Order and the corresponding axioms are his basic principles. These are not to be considered as wholly separate. They fuse, as man's moral progress continues, into a love of goodness. And as axioms they constitute, Whewell says, the Supreme Rule of morality: 'the Rule of Human Action is expressed by saying Be benevolent, be just, be true, be pure, be orderly. To be this in our actions, is to act rightly.' (*LSM*, p. 89.)

Whewell's next step is to show, in some detail, how commonplace moral rules can be systematically understood in the light of this five-fold supreme principle, and how difficulties left unresolved by the actual laws and morals of the times may be resolved by appeal to the principle. Into these matters we need not follow him, though a question or two must later be raised about some of his claims. We may note first one final point about Whewell's general theoretical approach to morality.

In various places Whewell expresses the conviction that a complete system of ethics must do justice to all the widely accepted moral opinions of mankind. In accordance with this conviction he attempts to find a place for the views of his chief antagonists, the utilitarians. He is quite prepared to admit that pleasure is good and pain bad. But they are not the only things which are good or bad, nor are they the most important. There is a distinctive moral goodness, the idea of which is quite different, and not derivable, from the idea of the goodness belonging to pleasure. This kind of goodness belongs to virtue. A dim perception of it has led mankind always to refuse to believe the measure of utility to be the measure of morality. At the same time, no one has ever succeeded in showing how a conscience or moral sense could be anything but vague and indefinite, and this accounts for the general dissatisfaction with views which appeal to them alone. We must incorporate both these points if we are to have an adequate system:

> On the one hand, the distinction of right and wrong, of moral good and evil, of virtue and vice, must be a *peculiar distinction,* different from the mere distinction of pleasure and pain . . . on the other hand, this distinction must be one *not* immediately apprehended by any peculiar sense or faculty . . . but must be a distinction

discerned by some use of the faculty of Reason which is common to all mankind. (*EMP*, Preface.)

As both sides are right about the foundations of morality—for Whewell takes the main utilitarian point to lie in its objection to a special moral faculty—so we must reconcile their claims concerning its outcome. Morality must lead to happiness. Whewell does not think we can properly support this view by arguing that production of happiness is the *criterion* of rightness. We must rather believe that action in accordance with the Supreme Rule of morality will *in fact* produce happiness for all, to the proper extent and degree. (*EMP*, 449.)

> Since Happiness is necessarily the Supreme Object of our Desires, and Duty the Supreme Rule of our actions, there can be no harmony in our being, except our Happiness coincide with our duty. . . . As moral beings, our Happiness must be found in our Moral Progress . . . we must be happy by being virtuous.

'How this is to be,' he adds 'Religion alone can fully instruct us.' He does not claim that happiness can be shown to result from doing our duty on 'merely philosophical grounds'. (*EMP*, 450.)

iv. *Whewell's Ethics: The Difficulties*

Whewell's moral philosophy is the most comprehensive system of intuitional ethics produced in Britain during the nineteenth century. Though Sidgwick makes few explicit comments on Whewell, much of the *Methods* is an implicit critique of his work. It is therefore necessary to indicate some of the serious problems which even a sympathetic critic might find with Whewell's system. There are three main points at which such difficulties become apparent: Whewell's efforts to display the rationality of the basic axioms of morals, his claim to have provided a set of principles which can answer every question about what we ought to do, and his belief that he has given a particularly strong defence of the 'high' morality, as opposed to utilitarianism, by showing that it can be based on methods like those of science.

In working out his systematization of moral knowledge, Whewell treats reason for the most part as a faculty of constructing rules. The supreme moral reason appears not as a substantive principle which we simply discover, but as the outcome of the most general action of the human ability to think rationally directed toward human behaviour and dispositions. Those 'last relics and rags of primaeval realism' to which Sidgwick objected in an early journal (see Chap. 1, p. 42) are indeed sometimes to be noticed in Whewell's thinking. He does occasionally slip into treating intuition as a power—though no doubt a rational power—of simply *seeing* some truth, whose basis or guarantee remains obscure unless obscurity is dispelled by the claim that we are seeing an eternal Idea in the mind of God. But more commonly Whewell attempts to avoid any untestable appeal to a cognizing faculty and to rest morality on propositions which are 'seen' because they plainly display their own inherent rationality. This leads him to a programme with strong resemblances to Kant's; and like Kant, Whewell runs into difficulties when he tries to work out the connection between the abstract demand that rules should govern action and the specific demands of particular rules. To take only two instances, Whewell nowhere tries to prove that our desires for sexual pleasure can be rationalized, even in connection with all our other desires and aims, only by a rigid rule of Purity, or that it is inconceivable that the social order can be regularized except in terms of the recognition of private property. This is a commonly urged difficulty with Kantian approaches to morality, and it is directly to the point here. It does not require Whewell to show that we could discover specific moral rules by deducing them from the general demand for rationality. It simply underlines the point that the elaborate strategy of moving from desires needing regulation through laws regulating external action to moralized dispositions does not make up for a failure to show the rational justification of this projected model of the historical process.

Second, Whewell is not successful in convincing us that he has found a system which can answer all our questions about what we ought to do. He does indeed try to show how his formulation of the axiom of justice enables us to criticize existing laws and how his axiom of truthfulness helps us to settle casuistical questions about promise-keeping; and it is arguable that his discussions of these points are far better than Sidgwick was prepared to allow.[17] He also examines a number of kinds of

[17] I am indebted to Alan Donagan for his comments on this matter.

cases where moral rules come into conflict, offering, usually, sensible solutions to the difficulties thus raised. When he comes to cases of necessity, where a plain moral rule must be broken to avoid final calamity to oneself or another, Whewell takes an interesting approach. He will not attempt, he says, to specify the kinds of consideration that make such transgressions excusable. The reason for drawing this limit is a moral reason. In cases like these there ought to be a struggle in the mind of the agent between the demands of morality and those of necessity. But if the moralist 'were to define, beforehand, the conditions under which lying, or homicide, or submission to lust, is the proper course; those who accepted our Rules, would, when the occasion came, take that course without the reluctance, and compunction, which are essential to make an act allowable in virtue of Necessity'. (*EMP*, 317; cf. 322.) How, then, are decisions to be reached in these hard cases? All that Whewell will say is that 'the course taken by the Actor will depend, and ought to depend, upon his state of Moral Culture', and that the effect of the decision upon the character of the actor himself ought to be considered, though probably not by the actor. (*EMP*, 324–6.) This may be correct, yet it does not help to show either that the principles Whewell enunciates dictate what we ought to do in every case or that there is good moral reason for them not to do so. Whewell has argued here that the moralist ought not to draw beforehand all the conclusions an agent might wish him to draw. He has not shown that the moral axioms would support specific conclusions in every case, even if the moralist ought not to make those conclusions evident. The question is whether the principles themselves are strong enough and comprehensive enough to entail conclusions for every possible case, not whether it is morally appropriate, supposing they are, to make the relevant inferences. Whewell's mode of treating hard cases here illustrates his occasional reversion to appeal to the concept of intuition as the ability to see what one ought to do in particular instances, a reversion which would in effect be an abandonment of the claim that the express theory should provide an answer in every case.

There are further difficulties with Whewell's claim to have provided such a theory. His one supreme principle is 'one' in only a peculiar way. It has five separate substantive axioms as its parts, and one of these, the axiom of benevolence, calls on us to promote the virtue of others as well as their happiness. (*EMP*, 418, 450.) Whewell does not discuss what we are to do if as a matter of general policy we find that the claims of justice conflict with those of benevolence, or the demand that we promote happiness conflicts with the demand that we promote virtue. He offers nothing like Reid's attempt, abortive though it was, to give an order of precedence for the various moral principles. His five axioms are all on a par: one is inclined to think Whewell sees no possibility of their coming into conflict simply as general determinants of action, and considers this only as a possibility in isolated individual cases. A possible explanation of this view is available. We have noted that Whewell thinks each area of scientific investigation is determined and delimited by the special Idea from which its axioms flow. He also speaks of the basic moral axioms as each involving an Idea (*LSM*, pp. 64–5), and he may consequently think that each moral Idea defines a 'sphere' which cannot come into any sort of general competition with the demands of other Ideas in their 'spheres'. If this were correct, it would certainly show that there are limits to the scope of the utilitarian principle, as well as removing one kind of complexity with which a complete moral theory should be able to deal. But it seems plainly false, and Whewell gives no reason to think it correct. In this connection we may note, finally, that it is striking that Whewell does not consider the principle of self-interest. He tries neither to show that we cannot regularize our behaviour wholly in terms of concern for our own good, though the admired Butler had suggested that we can, nor to say what we should do if self-interest and the dictates of other axioms should conflict on a general level. He is content with the religiously based assurance that God will see to it that such a conflict does not arise.

If on these points we cannot say that Whewell's system is much of an advance over Reid's, we find more reason for doubt when we turn to the third point, and ask how effective Whewell's mode of claiming an alliance between science and ethics is as a defence of a 'high' and anti-utilitarian morality. The difficulty can be brought out by noting a difference which Whewell indicates between the progress of knowledge in science and its progress in religion. 'In the knowledge of scientific truth,' he says,

men go on from step to step, at every step advancing to the know-ledge of a new Truth; which new Truth includes all that was true in previous knowledge, while it adds to it something more . . .

But in Revealed Truth the case is necessarily different. . . . There, the Revelation contains all the Truth; and to this Truth, succeed-ing thoughts of men cannot add, though they may develop and methodize it.

'In Science,' so he points the contrast, 'earlier views, so far as they are true, are summed up in the latest discovery. In Religion, later views are true, so far as they are derived from the original Revelation.' (*EMP*, 593.) The question we must ask is whether the 'high' morality is like a scientific theory or like a body of revealed truth. If it is like revealed truth, then its truth is unchangeable and immutable—providing the revelation is genuine. But nothing is left of the claim that the method used in supporting the 'high' morality is like the method used in science, and the morality itself cannot be used to prove the truth of the revelation on which it depends. If on the other hand moral knowledge is like scientific knowledge, and the 'high' morality the analogue of a scientific theory—and this seems, on balance, to be the view Whewell prefers—then the problems of permanence which beset any scientific theory belong also to a moral system. Is not our progress likely to be as surprising in morality as it is in science? Are we not as likely to have Copernican revolutions in the one subject as in the other? Perhaps the given state of our insight into the moral Ideas and our knowledge of the pertinent Facts has until now made it correct to say that although moral action will result in general happiness, it cannot be derived from the prin-ciple of pursuing that happiness. But tomorrow new Facts and new insights may show that we must reverse our position. We may then have to say that although moral action must be guided by rules even when the resulting acts do not in every particular case increase happiness, the moral rules themselves must ultimately by systematized and justified by the general principle of producing happiness. In short, if final knowledge of moral principles already exists, then Whewell cannot defend 'high' moral intuitionism as he has tried to defend it, by relating it to the general use of intuition in science; and if final knowledge of moral principles does not already exist, then morality is as susceptible to radical change as science itself.

v. *John Grote*

Whewell's successor, John Grote, makes little effort to deal with the problems left by Whewell's attempted synthesis. Though Grote sees moral philosophy as requiring systematic thinking, he does not suppose that the outcome must be a moral system; and he is doubtful about the value of such systems. (*Ideals*, pp. 238–9, 394.) He is also doubtful about the possibility of progress in moral philosophy. There is certainly room for bringing new factual knowledge to bear in the application of moral principles and ideals, he allows, but 'the only progress possible' when the philosopher investigates the ideals themselves 'is greater clearness of view, firmer hold in the mind of the principles it deals with, and happier expression of them'. The ideals, he says, 'are what they were in the time of Plato, and never can be different'. (*Ideals*, pp. 51–2.) Thus Whewell's attempt to draw a parallel between scientific theorizing and moral philosophizing, and thereby to defend an elaborate moral position, is without charm for Grote. What interests him, rather, is the attempt to analyse and clarify the basic concepts and problems of ethics. Philosophy, he remarks, often takes us on a long and tortuous journey to show us a simple point: the justification is that without the 'circuitous process' we usually would not be able to see what it shows us. (*Ideals*, pp. 87–8.) His own writing reflects this orientation. His books are rambling and digressive in structure, casual and meditative in style. The bulk of his main constructive work in ethics, *The Treatise on the Moral Ideals*, is taken up with analyses of various moral notions, such as benevolence, duty, honour, and truthfulness, and with discussions of pain, pleasure, happiness, and other psychological matters. They are often interesting, and they lead him sometimes to valuable critical comments on a variety of contemporary writers, but they do not add up to any readily compressible set of positions. His expressly critical work is better focussed. We shall see something of it when we come to note his main objections to J. S. Mill's utilitarianism, in Chapter 5.

Here we may sketch very briefly the suggestive, if not well developed, structure of thought lying behind Grote's otherwise unorganized reflections.

Though Grote disagrees with his Cambridge predecessors on many points, he is as insistent as any of them on the difference between moral concepts and beliefs and factual ones. Observational or 'positive' knowledge is certainly needed for morality, he holds, but what he calls the 'idea' is central to it. 'The idea of "what should be"', he says, 'lies at the heart of moral philosophy and can never be eradicated from it.' (*Ideals*, p. 18; cf. *Exam.*, pp. 162, 269, and Ch. XI.) It is a besetting error of modern ethics to try to derive knowledge of the ideal from positive knowledge alone. Grote connects our knowledge of what ought to be, or the ideal, with intuition and with reason, stressing, like his predecessors, the necessity of giving reasons in support of claims as to what ought to be. He opposes the notion that conscience can be a privileged moral faculty and treats it as a feeling. The thought that we ought to do something is the thought 'that there is *reason* why one sort of action . . . should be preferred to other sorts', just as the 'ought to be' involved in ideals 'really means that there exists reason why one . . . of these ideals is better than another'. (*Ideals*, pp. 79, 45.) Appeal to conscience as a voice within is no use: it may err, and if it is said that conscience cannot err, we need some way of showing that the voice we hear is the voice that cannot err. (*Ideals*, pp. 163, 451.) Grote gives no argument for the position that intuition of principles is needed in morality, nor does he elaborate a theory of the intuitive operation of reason. The complex epistemological reflections published in his *Exploratio Philosophica* are behind his musings on the epistemology of morals in Chapter XV of the *Treatise*, but he does not work up to explicit solutions of the problems his position seems to involve. None the less he argues that because an intuitively known ideal is necessarily involved in morality, the Benthamites themselves must be committed to one also. For all their insistence that they have purely 'positive' foundations for their ethics, they require an intuition if their interest in general happiness is to be more than a purely personal concern. If, following Bentham, they say they cannot imagine anyone denying the greatest happiness to be the all-important ideal, then, Grote says, they are 'placing the foundation of moral philosophy where . . . it ought to be placed, on . . . intuitivism.' (*Ideals*, pp. 20, 44–5.)

The effort to reconcile apparent opponents in ethics is nearly as typical of Grote as it is of the earlier Cambridge moralists. In his case the basis for reconciliation is the view that there are two fundamental aspects of human nature, the sentient and the active, and that the needs of each of these are always reflected in morality itself. (*Ideals*, pp. 1–8.) Since man as a sentient creature seeks pleasure and shuns pain, there is an important part of moral philosophy which deals with pleasures and pains as something to be enjoyed or avoided, and with the kind of value arising from pleasant or painful results of action. He calls it 'eudaemonics' and thinks the utilitarians have tried to develop it as if it were the whole of moral philosophy. But man is, in addition to being sentient, an active creature, with 'a work to do'. Pleasure and pain, from this point of view, are what should be produced and what should be prevented. Action to do these things has, however, its own kind of value, determined by the motives from which it originates and independent of the value of the results; and 'aretaics' is the name Grote gives the branch of ethics studying this kind of value and the moral laws appropriate to it. Some philosophers take it as the whole of morality, which it is not, although it is 'the principal of the two sciences' which make up ethics. (*Ideals*, pp. 72, 78 f.) In explaining it further Grote expresses the belief that action concerned with one's own good alone is not a concern of morality: morality is concerned with conflicts of interests among men and with the right distribution of happiness among persons having various claims on the agent. He gives a lengthy discussion of justice, which he presents as the main virtue concerned with the right distribution of happiness (*Ideals*, pp. 196–219), but he neither gives arguments to support his claim that aretaics generates principles independent of those generated by eudaemonics, nor discusses what might be involved in conflicts between the principle of justice and the principle of utility.

Presumably the reason why he does not discuss this latter topic is that he thinks the problem does not arise. Like Whewell he thinks that morality leads us to a point at which we feel a need for the truths religion alone can give. (*Exam.*, pp. 217–18.)

And he shares with Whewell the view that if we are to act on our moral convictions an essentially religious assumption is needed: the assumption that the moral universe is harmonious. He sees such an assumption as needed no less in theoretical than in moral matters: 'the belief that law or order, as opposed to chaos and randomness, must apply . . . to the entire of being . . . seems to me to play the same part in . . . life or the moral universe, as it does in the intellectual universe. No experience could give us this belief, but . . . intellectually, we could not think for a moment without it.' (*Ideals*, p. 373.) Applied to practice, the belief puts Grote in agreement with his intuitional predecessors. The ideas of virtue and duty cannot be resolved into the ideas of utility and happiness, but they must all point to the same courses of action. We can to some extent see that this must be so, 'because human nature is one, and is reasonable'; but

the belief which we all must more or less entertain, that they are really and entirely, upon the whole, consistent, that they coincide as to the line of action which they point out, is in fact the belief that the moral universe is *one*, and good, and the work of reason and design; a belief which . . . carries us . . . very deeply and powerfully towards ideas of religion. (*Exam.*, pp. 162–3.)

Grote also thinks we must suppose, 'in order to reason to any purpose about morals at all', that 'what we ought to do and what we wish to enjoy or have, our duties and our wants, will in the end be found in harmony with each other'. Without such a faith, Grote sees no possibility of morality. (*Exam.*, p. 349.) How would it be, he asks, 'if the different *goods* or purposes of action with our intelligence suggests to us' had no relation to each other? If that is the case, we will have

to choose whether we will do our own pleasure, or other's pleasure, . . . or the . . . rationally just, or the apparently natural, each of which things seem *good* to be done but seem also to lead us different ways: so far as this is so, there is moral chaos: there is absence of reason for acting any one way.

We must therefore have 'faith in the goodness and orderliness of the *moral* world . . . of the good that suggests itself, as what we should act for, being homogeneous, harmonious, consistent'. (*Ideals*, pp. 517–19.)

A summary of Grote's own views on moral philosophy does little to suggest the quality of the mind that becomes apparent to any reader of his more critical works—acute, probing, rather narrow and technical, keen to find flaws and mistakes. Yet if Grote was dissatisfied with most answers to philosophical questions, he never doubted that answers could be found, and that there were clues to them even in the writings he criticized most sharply. He differed in many ways from his Cambridge colleagues and predecessors, but he was profoundly committed to some of their deepest and most important convictions. When Sidgwick spoke of intuitionism, he spoke of what he knew from close personal acquaintance with one of its finest and most critical defenders. His knowledge of utilitarianism, by contrast, was derived wholly from books. The books responsible for this aspect of his education are our next concern.

4

The Early Utilitarians

MORAL philosophy is taken by the majority of those who teach and write it in the English-speaking world to be secular, in the sense that no essential appeal to religious doctrine is made in the course of expounding or supporting the tenets of a particular position. It is also taken as a matter which is primarily of interest to philosophers. It is not seen first and foremost as offering an ideological basis for political action or a pathway to personal salvation. Yet it is also thought to have practical bearings. For it is expected not only to provide a rational reconstruction of our pre-theoretical moral convictions but also to give us a way of criticizing and correcting those convictions. This way of understanding the aims and limits of moral philosophy developed, in Britain at least, out of the nineteenth-century debates between the intuitionists and the utilitarians. It was not until Sidgwick's *Methods*, which tried to reconcile these two schools, that all the characteristics of a modern treatment of ethics were fully and deliberately brought together in a single work. Sidgwick is often described as the last of the classical utilitarians. He may with as much accuracy be viewed as the first of the modern moralists.

i. *Utility and Religion*

Utilitarianism first became widely known in England through the work of William Paley. Within a few years of the publication of his theological version of the doctrine in 1785, there appeared two secular versions, one by Jeremy Bentham in 1789, the other by William Godwin in 1793. Bentham's book was almost completely ignored for decades. Godwin's received immediate acclaim, was at the centre of heated popular controversy for a few years, and then sank into an obscurity from which it has never recovered. Paley's *Moral and Political Philosophy* became a widely used textbook and was reprinted, during our first period, even more frequently than the works of Bishop

Butler. Although Paley was by no means the only exponent of religious utilitarianism during these years, we must begin by looking at his main doctrines.

The function of a system of ethics, Paley says[1] in his Preface, is 'the direction of private consciences in the general conduct of human life', and ethics itself is 'the science that teaches men their duty and the reasons of it' (I, i). Paley is more interested in teaching men their duty than in expounding the reasons for it. He gives us the latter in the first sixth of his book, in a straight-forward fashion that ignores most of the difficulties and has little use for argument. His aim is to find a corrective or supplement to the usual sources of guidance, for neither the law of honour, nor the law of the land, nor the Scriptures provide complete direction to the conscience, and the law of honour is in addition often wrong (I, ii–iv). Paley promptly turns to the 'moral sense'—but only to cast doubt on its existence (I, v). He gives a clear case of an act of appalling filial ingratitude, and asks if 'the wild boy caught some years ago in the woods of Hanover' would feel the disapproval we feel concerning this conduct. Those, he says, who maintain the existence of a moral sense or of an intuitive perception of right and wrong must say that he would; those who deny these faculties say he would not; and so we have the issue. At least we have the issue as Paley sees it: the intuitionists were to argue that this way of posing it, since it ignores the need for educating the moral faculty, is quite irrelevant. Paley thinks, on the whole, that the wild boy would not feel disapproval of ingratitude, but admits this to be only a conjecture.

The wild boy does not provide Paley's only objection to the moral sense school. In his further discussion of the topic Paley introduces themes around which debate was to centre for decades. Two points favour the claim of the moral sense, he says, the immediacy of approval or disapproval, which occur without deliberation, and the universality and uniformity of approval and disapproval 'in all ages and countries of the world'. But there are numerous arguments to set against these.

[1] All references to Paley are to his *Moral and Political Philosophy*, 1785. Since there are many different editions of this work, and since its chapters are short, references are given, in the text, by the use of Roman numerals for book and chapter or, where three numerals are given, for book, part, and chapter.

The uniformity of moral judgement is much exaggerated, and even where general approval is found, it may be accounted for more easily by the hypothesis of the association of one's idea of one's own profit with the idea of a class of acts some of whose members have been found to be to one's own benefit, than by the hypothesis of a moral sense. As for innate moral maxims, Paley thinks there cannot be any, because 'none perhaps can be assigned, which are absolutely and universally *true*; in other words, which do not bend to circumstances'. Custom, says Paley, is very apt 'to be mistaken for the order of nature', and authority, convenience, education, and general practice have a large part in making various maxims seem self-evident. Hence, he objects, a system of morality built on 'instincts' or innate principles is liable only to 'find out reasons and excuses for opinions and practices already established;—will seldom correct or reform either'. Paley himself was not a reformer; but this argument was taken up with enthusiasm by those who were. Finally, Paley asks what 'authority' a moral instinct would have. He means to inquire about the psychological ability of its dictates to compel compliance; and he points out that even if violating these dictates arouses pangs of conscience, the pangs may be borne. If the pain of doing so is outweighed by the pleasure obtained from wrong-doing then 'the moral-instinct man . . . has nothing more to say'. For if he claims that the instinct indicates the will of God and is therefore backed by divine sanctions, Paley is prepared to offer a surer way to find out what that will is than by dubious appeal to a questionable feeling. (I, v.)

Paley's definition of virtue gives the foundations of his theory. Virtue is 'the doing good to mankind in obedience to the will of God, and for the sake of everlasting happiness'. (I, vi.) The will of God, Paley explains, is what makes right acts right; doing good to mankind is the test or criterion of rightness; and the hope of eternal happiness, and the fear of eternal suffering, provide the source of the obligation to do right acts. When Paley speaks of the 'obligation' to virtue he is speaking of the motivating force which leads men to do what is virtuous. Virtue consists in doing what we are obligated to do; and to be obligated, he assumes, here following the theory sketched much earlier in the century by John Gay, is the same as to be obliged. But to be obliged to do something is to be 'urged by a violent motive resulting from the command of another': this is supported by ordinary usage, which distinguishes inducements, temptations, and persuasives, from what obliges or obligates. (II, ii.) If we try to explain the obligation to act virtuously by appealing to the fitness of things, or conformity to reason, or the promotion of the public good, we do not obtain a satisfactory answer to the question. It is still unclear what will oblige me—in other words, make me—to do what is in accordance with the fitness of things. (II, i.) When we realize that 'obligation is nothing more than an inducement of sufficient strength, and resulting . . . from the command of another', we have an answer that 'goes to the bottom of the subject, as no further questions can reasonably be asked'. God's rewards and punishments can make me do anything; and God's commands make clear what I ought to do. Prudence may be distinguished from virtue by the fact that the one considers only the goods and bads of this world, the other takes the future world into account as well. (II, iv.) No other distinctions are needed.

Paley's implicit psychology and his reduction of the notion of obligation to that of being obliged lead him very close to egoism in moral theory, but his normative principle is quite clearly not egoistic. Because God's will is the foundation of morality, we are to find out what to do by searching for his purposes, either in Scripture or by the light of nature (II, iv); and Scripture was never meant to supply a complete code. Even a cursory glance at nature suffices to show that God does not intend our misery, and that he is not indifferent to our happiness. We may therefore conclude that God wills our happiness, and that we may determine God's will by inquiring into the tendency of actions 'to promote or diminish general happiness'. (II, v.) Paley offers no other argument in support of the utilitarian principle: religion supplies the intellectual basis as well as the motivational power for morality.

In discussing the details of duty Paley is not a completely systematic user of the principle that 'whatever is expedient, is right'. (II, vi.) He is willing to rest the obligation to give money to the poor on the fact that we have a charitable impulse, since this fact about our nature directly indicates a divine intention.

He is equally willing to base this duty on a law of nature. (III, ii, v.) More frequently he argues for indirect application of the principle of expediency. In many matters, he holds, it is expedient to establish positive laws concerning some area of activity and leave all the details to them. This is his treatment of the issue of property. It is plainly God's will that the produce of the land should be used for human benefit; this requires stable possession; and only a legal system can provide adequately detailed rules for all the contingencies involved in such possession. Hence the morality of property is simply determined by the law of the land, even where the law leads to inexpediency in some cases. (III, i, iv.)

Even aside from cases covered by positive laws, Paley tends to take classes of acts or rules of action, rather than individual acts, as the primary objects of utilitarian assessment. In doing so he makes himself the forerunner of the utilitarians who were later to develop rather sophisticated versions of rule-utilitarianism; but Paley's own view, as usual, is not sophisticated. He bases his position on the claim that there is a difference between the consequences of a single act and the consequences of following a general rule, but does not attempt any analysis of the contrast. In his reasons for claiming that the utilitarian principle applies to rules rather than to acts, he gives, again without much discussion, several kinds of consideration. One is that without general rules no scheme of rewards and penalties will work, since without rules one act might be punished and an identical one rewarded. Then no one would know how to act, and, as he points out, the very notion of reward and punishment would collapse. (II, vii.) He also argues that cases where it would be disastrous if everyone acted in a given way—counterfeiting, for example, where one counterfeiter causes relatively little harm but if everyone tried it the currency system could not be maintained—provide good reason for abiding by general rules. (II, viii.) And in another place he argues that because people do, and need to, act mainly by habit, some acts are justified simply because they help maintain good habits; and among these are acting according to moral rules without trying to see if exceptions to the rule might be warranted. (I, vii, Appendix.) Paley offers no rationale for abiding by the rules which prohibit acts which are harmful only if cumulative, when we know that others will not in fact act in the untoward way, nor does he suggest that any principle other than utility is involved in any of his considerations. His move toward incorporating rules into his system seems to be a not completely articulated attempt to avoid a theory which would lead to some conclusions directly opposed to common sense.

In addition to avoiding such scandals, Paley's appeal to rules suggests one way out of a difficulty some might feel with his theology. If God's will determines the difference between right and wrong, what can it mean to say that God wills rightly? Would not this, Paley asks, be an identical proposition, and its denial not conceivable? Yet assertions about the righteousness of God's will 'are intelligible and significant'. The explanation is that once we have established rules for determining the rights and wrongs of action we think of right as referring to concurrence with a rule. We then 'go back and compare with these rules even the Divine conduct itself', despite the fact that the rules are derived from the divine will; for we overlook this at the time. (II, ix.) Paley was right in supposing that this objection would be made, and over-sanguine in thinking this reply would satisfy his critics. He does not seem, in general, to have worried much about the objections to his ethics, nor did he attempt to answer them. His silence did not hurt his sales.

No other theological utilitarian wrote anything as enduringly successful as Paley's book, but a number of writers defended ethical doctrines which were more or less similar to his and which relied as completely as his did on religious presuppositions for their support. Many of them were Unitarians, usually ministers, consciously working along the lines laid down by Hartley and Priestley, and finding in utilitarian ethics an argument against stern Calvinistic doctrines of the eternity of the punishment of the damned, then being revived by Methodists and Evangelicals.[2] In the thinking of some of them, like Dr. Thomas Cogan, there is a purely Paleyan theological utilitarianism coupled, as in Paley, with arguments against the

---

[2] On this point see Geoffrey Rowell, *Hell and the Victorians*, 1974, Ch. III. It is interesting that the Unitarians ignored the important treatise of their well-known preacher Dr. Richard Price, the *Review of the Principal Questions in Morals*, 1758, in favour of the less philosophically sophisticated work of Hartley, Priestley, and Paley. Price lived long enough to indicate his strong distaste for Paley's work in an appendix to the third edition of his *Review*, 1787.

existence of a moral sense. Others seem willing to admit the existence of a conscience or moral faculty as a mere psychological fact, but try to strip it of the significance given it by the intuitionists. To do so they appeal to Hartley's laws of the association of ideas to explain its genesis from simpler notions of pleasure and pain. They all agree with Thomas Belsham, one of the earliest and perhaps the most influential of the Unitarians during this period, that 'the only valuable end of existence is happiness' (T. Belsham, *Elements*, p. 369), and with him and Paley they are all inclined to hold that only self-interested considerations can provide the ultimate 'obligation' to virtue. Belsham has no difficulty in incorporating egoistic psychology into his philosophy, since he holds an egoistic ethic as well. Virtue, he thinks, is simply 'the tendency of an action, affection, habit, or character, to the ultimate happiness of the agent'. It is indubitable, on his view, that 'the world is governed by infinite wisdom and benevolence, and that men are destined to a future state of existence'; and given these helpful certainties we can account for the fact that benevolence is a virtue. Benevolence is simply the best means to one's own happiness. 'It is incredible', Belsham writes, 'that, under the government of God, any of his creatures should be ultimately losers by any sacrifice which they can make to the happiness of others.' Utility may therefore be taken as a criterion of virtue; and taking this in conjunction with the facts of human motivation we can see clearly that 'atheism and infidelity are inconsistent with a perfect theory of morals'. (T. Belsham, *Elements*, pp. 379–80.) William Jevons seems to be prepared to follow Belsham in his ethical egoism, but not all of the Unitarians are. Most of them, while not denying the propriety of seeking one's own good, and agreeing that divine providence assures the coincidence of self-interest and benevolence, think that the principle of general happiness ought to take precedence, if the occasion arises, over the principle of self-interest. As William Belsham puts it, benevolence provides a 'more perfect rule' of morality than self-interest because it is better calculated to produce general happiness. (W. Belsham, *Essays*, i. 286.)

There is very little resembling argument in these volumes,[3]

---

[3] Among other Unitarian writers, two who cannot be classed as utilitarians, John Prior Estlin and Lant Carpenter, also held that the principles of egoism and

unless the occasional attempt to use the laws of association to disallow claims that the moral sense has a cognitive status counts as such. The philosophical positions are crudely stated, and the practical morality spelled out in detail by Jevons and others does not rise above commonplaces. The stark and uncompromising egoism of Thomas Belsham and his few followers may bear part of the responsibility for the ease with which opponents of utilitarianism could think that doctrine indistinguishable from normative egoism.[4] What is perhaps most striking to the modern reader is the fact that although distinguished Unitarians like Dr. Southwood Smith and W. J. Fox were closely associated in practical affairs with Bentham and the Benthamites, the Unitarian philosophers see Paley, rather than Bentham, as the fountain-head of utilitarian doctrine. Bentham is mentioned only in passing by Thomas Belsham and Jevons. He is ignored by all the rest.

ii. *Bentham*

The Unitarians were not alone in ignoring Bentham's ethical writings. His *Introduction to the Principles of Morals and Legislation* in the original edition of 1789 had only a very small sale, and was not reprinted until 1823.[5] His ethical theory is ignored by most of the periodicals, and is simply not discussed in the philosophical literature. The Scottish philosophers attack Paley's version of utilitarianism, or occasionally Hume's, but never Bentham's. Mackintosh's historical *Dissertation on the*

of benevolence would coincide in their practical directions, but insisted (Ch. 2, n. 6, above) that our practical rule should be the will of God.

[4] The article on 'Philosophy, Moral', in the *British Encyclopaedia* of 1809 quotes Cogan approvingly and refers the reader indiscriminately to Hartley, Thomas Belsham, and Paley for the truth.

It was not only British opponents of utilitarianism who thought it tied to egoism. In Krug's *Allgemeines Handwörterbuch der philosophischen Wissenschaften*, 2nd edn., 1834, 'utilitarians' are said to be 'those, who judge the value or disvalue of human actions according to the mere consequences (according to the profit or harm which they themselves receive from them), and also act according to this standard. They are therefore nothing but practical egoists.' In France, Jouffroy was no clearer: he seemed to think Bentham simply disingenuous for trying to evade the horrible implications of the selfish system by substituting the principle of general good for that of the agent's own good. See T. Jouffroy, *Introduction to Ethics*, 1835, Eng. trans. 1841, vol. ii, Lecture XIV.

[5] See E. Halévy, *The Growth of Philosophic Radicalism*, 1953, pp. 27, 296; and the Introduction by the Editors of Bentham's *Introduction to the Principles of Morals and Legislation*, the Collected Works, vol. i, p. xli.

Progress of Ethical Philosophy, written for the *Encyclopaedia Britannica* in 1830 contains a long chapter entitled 'Bentham', but Bentham is hardly discussed in it, although it is admitted that no sketch of 'ethical controversy in England' would be complete without a reference to him. He is treated not as a philosopher but as the ideologist of a small and rather fanatical political group; his *Introduction* is condemned for its concealed unoriginality; and Mackintosh concludes by saying that 'the true and eminent merit of Mr. Bentham is that of a reformer of jurisprudence. He is only a moralist with a view to being a jurist.' (*Diss.*, p. 306.)[6] This is also Macaulay's view of him. In the second of three famous articles attacking the political philosophy of the Benthamites, he admits his reverence for Bentham as 'the father of the philosophy of Jurisprudence', but treats his ethics with scorn as well as indignation.[7] Bentham had a moral philosophy, and Bentham was famous, but Bentham was not famous for his philosophy. It was not until the middle of the 1830s that he began to be taken seriously as a philosopher by philosophers. For the change John Stuart Mill and William Whewell were largely responsible.

In 1833 Mill permitted the publication of an essay of his on Bentham as the anonymous appendix to a book by a friend.[8] It was very critical of Bentham but at least treated him as worthy of serious consideration. Two years later Whewell wrote a lengthy preface to a new edition of Mackintosh's *Dissertation*, in which Bentham receives calm and civil criticism, as one among the philosophers. In 1838 Mill published his major assessment of Bentham, calling him one of 'the two great seminal minds of England of their age' (the other being Coleridge) and arguing the merits of his philosophy as well as of his jurisprudence and his work as a reformer.[9] At some time after

---

[6] Blakey's *History of Moral Science*, 1833, gives Bentham barely a page.

[7] Macaulay's three articles appeared in the *Edinburgh Review* in 1829 in March, June, and October, and are reprinted in all editions of his collected essays. The second was written under the misapprehension that Bentham himself had replied to the first. The references in the text are to the second article, in the Albany edition of Macaulay's *Works*, 1913, *Essays and Biographies*, i. 373, 339 ff.

[8] E. Bulwer-Lytton, *England and the English*, 2 vols., 1833. Mill's essay is reprinted in *Mill's Ethical Writings*, ed. J. B. Schneewind, N.Y., 1965, and in vol. x of Mill's *Collected Works*, ed. Robson, 1969.

[9] Mill's view influenced Maurice's portrayal, in the *Encyclopædia Metropolitana*, 1845, ii. 673, of Paley, as only an inconsistent utilitarian and of Bentham as a far

1838 Whewell began to include lectures on Bentham in his teaching at Cambridge, and these were published in his *History* in 1852, which must be the first academic text to treat Bentham seriously as a philosopher. Mill's review of Whewell in the same year was intemperate and often inaccurate about Whewell, but the exchange between the two is the first philosophical discussion of utilitarianism in which Bentham figures importantly as a philosopher.

Since then, of course, the details of Bentham's views on ethics have come to be much discussed, and familiarity with them will be taken for granted here. He was taken to believe that 'mankind ought to act so as to produce their greatest happiness', as Macaulay summarized his first principle of morals, and to combine with this a crudely egoistic and hedonistic psychology. The combination was generally held to involve him in difficulties. Macaulay cheerfully indicated one of them:

> The word *ought*, [Bentham] tells us, has no meaning, unless it be used with reference to some interest. But the interest of a man is synonymous with his greatest happiness:—and therefore to say that a man ought to do a thing, is to say that it is for his greatest happiness to do it. And to say that mankind *ought* to act so as to produce their greatest happiness, is to say that the greatest happiness is the greatest happiness—and this is all![10]

Macaulay may have misstated Bentham's first principle of morals, though Mill understood him in the same way; and he certainly oversimplified the psychology, though it was an oversimplification to which Bentham's own careless language made him particularly liable. As Mill pointed out, Bentham did not mean to imply that all men are selfish. He only meant to give technical form to the truism that 'all persons do what they feel themselves disposed to do', and to supplement this by more detailed remarks on the varieties of actual motivation.[11]

more thorough one. Maurice still thinks of utilitarianism as primarily a political doctrine, however, and so he calls Bentham 'the completest form of utilitarian philosopher that has ever appeared' and adds 'or is likely to do so'—for he thinks new, Coleridgean, principles are soon to supersede Benthamism.

[10] Macaulay, *Works*, i. 401.

[11] For an interpretation of Bentham which differs from that given by Macaulay and Mill, see David Lyons, *In the Interest of the Governed*, Oxford, 1973. Mill's early reading of Bentham is given in his article in Bulwer-Lytton's volume, cited in n. 8 above.

But though he was not a crude egoist in psychology, Bentham thought there needed to be a considerable coincidence between what is dictated by morality and what is demanded by self-interest in a rather narrow sense, and he was widely taken to believe that this coincidence of duty and interest could only be brought about by the machinations of legislators. He may in fact have thought that there was a natural harmony of interests. It is quite clear in any case that he did not appeal to the active superintendence of a divine governor to obtain any support for belief in such a harmony. His purely secular approach to the philosophical issue, though it did not prevent him from co-operating with people who had religious beliefs, certainly kept his theory widely separated from any that they might have.

Only two points made in the *Introduction* call for some comment here, Bentham's views on proving the basic principle of morals and his criticism of all opposing positions. Bentham[12] takes for granted a view of reasoning like that accepted by Reid: 'that which is used to prove everything else', he says, 'cannot itself be proved: a chain of proofs must have their commencement somewhere.' He adds that it is 'as impossible as it is needless' to give a proof of the principle of utility. Why is it needless? Not because Bentham appeals to conscience or intuition, but because he thinks that everyone in fact 'defers' to the principle on many, if not on all, occasions, and that this gives him a way of bringing everyone to accept it. Admitting that few people take it as their sole principle, he none the less thinks that no disproof of it by argument is possible. Hence resistance to allowing it sole dominion must be prejudice, and by way of dealing with prejudices Bentham proposes a series of questions. The aim of most of them is to bring out the considerable difficulties facing anyone who tries both to abandon the utilitarian principle and to be consistent in the decisions he makes. Some of the questions bring out the peculiar position one would find oneself in if one gave up the principle altogether in matters of politics. Others raise the question of social consistency: suppose everyone gave up the principle of utility, how could one count on any sort of reliable social harmony without insisting on one's own right to decide despotically for everyone?

[12] This paragraph deals with Ch. I of Bentham's *Introduction to the Principles of Morals and Legislation*.

The point throughout the questions is to stress the need for rationality in practice, not only as involving personal consistency but also as requiring that everyone be able to use, and to know others are using, the same method of reaching decisions. The questions depend for their force on the assumption that there is no other principle which is both as widely accepted as the utilitarian principle and as well adapted as it is to function as the basic practical principle. Both the positive claim about what rationality in practice requires, and the negative claim about the unavailability of other ways of attaining it, underlie Bentham's assurance that in the principle of utility he has a standpoint from which the criticism of all accepted norms and rules may be undertaken.

Bentham's critique of 'principles adverse to that of utility'[13] is from this point of view disappointing, since it involves no serious discussion of alternatives to utilitarianism. He does indeed attack the principle of 'asceticism', the full reversal of utilitarianism, but as no one held such a view his criticisms hardly amount to much. Otherwise his attack on non-utilitarian views is essentially a reductionistic one, denying the possibility of any knowledge not derivable from sense impressions. The argument proceeds by a dichotomy. If the person who alleges possession of a moral sense, a conscience, or an intuitive faculty, does not mean to refer to some sensations or other, he is talking nonsense. If he is referring to sensations at all, he must be referring to his own sensations of liking or disliking certain acts for, by hypothesis, he is not referring to the pleasant or painful sensations others would obtain from the acts. In either case the adherent of the 'principle of sympathy and antipathy' —one of Bentham's blanket names for all opponents of utilitarianism—sets up his own decision as the final authority in morals. And whether he has no reason for deciding as he does, or uses his own likes and dislikes as his reason, his procedure is the very opposite of what is needed for a rational principle of action:

What one expects to find in a principle is something that points out some external consideration, as a means of warranting and

---

[13] This paragraph deals with Chapter II of Bentham's *Introduction*. Behind Bentham's attack there is an interesting set of doctrines concerning meaning and knowledge, not published until our own century. See C. K. Ogden, *Bentham's Theory of Fictions*, 1932.

guiding the internal sentiments of approbation and disapprobation: this expectation is but ill fulfilled by a proposition, which does neither more nor less than hold up each of those sentiments as a ground and standard for itself.

Since Bentham does not consider that there might be other principles than that of utility which satisfy this requirement, he sees the issue in simple terms. A utilitarian can use a rational and empirically testable method of determining what it is right to do in any particular case. A non-utilitarian (and ascetics do not count) cannot be anything but arbitrary in determining right and wrong. He will have not only no empirical test for moral judgements, but no rational test at all, since an appeal to intuition is tantamount to an appeal to purely personal tastes or feelings. This simplification of the issues came, largely through the influence of Mill and of Whewell, to be accepted as pointing to what was central in the debates between intuitionists and utilitarians.

iii. *Godwin*

Bentham's utilitarianism was more thorough than Paley's, but Bentham pursued its ramifications largely in the realm of social and political reform. What one might be led to by following the utilitarian principle single-mindedly to all its moral conclusions was shown to the world by William Godwin, 'the first *whole-length* broacher of the doctrine of utility', as Hazlitt called him. Godwin was led to write *Political Justice* (1793)[14] from a 'sense of the value' of a work on principles in an age of political change (*PJ*, 3), and there is no doubt that he hoped the book would produce extensive alterations in accepted systems of social, political, and moral practice. Though he seldom came up with a sensible idea for immediate reform, his

[14] All references to the *Enquiry Concerning Political Justice* will be made in the text to page numbers of the abridgement edited by K. Codell Carter, Oxford, The Clarendon Press, 1971, abbreviated as *PJ*. The abridgement contains most of the material relevant to our purposes.

I am indebted to the excellent biography by Ford K. Brown, *The Life of William Godwin*, 1926, and more especially to D. H. Monro, *Godwin's Moral Philosophy*, Oxford, 1953, which gives a far better reading of Godwin as a philosopher than Brown. The extensive bibliography of writings about Godwin compiled by Burton Ralph Pollin, *Godwin Criticism: a synoptic bibliography*, Toronto, University of Toronto Press, 1967, gives some idea of the ways in which Godwin's influence has been felt.

belief in the powers of reason, his faith in human improvability, his distrust of all government, his attack on marriage, his call for perfect sincerity between friends, and his strong views on property have enabled people of the most diverse persuasions to look upon him as a patron saint. His interest for us lies in the fact that embedded within his great political tract is the most radical application of the principle of utility that has ever been made.

Whatever the risk of oversimplifying parts of Godwin's thought, it is clear that his basic principle is utilitarian:

Morality is that system of conduct which is determined by a consideration of the greatest general good: he is entitled to the highest moral approbation whose conduct is . . . governed by views of benevolence, and made subservient to public utility . . . the only regulations which any political authority can be justly entitled to enforce, are such as are best adapted to public utility. (*PJ*, 67.)

At the same time he accepts a principle of impartiality or equity which he terms 'justice'. He equates this with the name for all moral duty, and explains it, not very helpfully, as 'that impartial treatment of every man in matters that relate to his happiness which is measured solely by a consideration of the properties of the receiver and the capacity of him that bestows. Its principle therefore, is . . . "to be no respecter of persons".' (*PJ*, 69–70.) If justice and utility are two different principles in Godwin's mind he sees no problem in holding both to be basic. Usually he treats justice simply as an alternative name for benevolence or general utility. Thus in his summary of principles he tells us that 'Justice is a principle which proposes to itself the production of the greatest sum of pleasure or happiness', and that this is 'the true standard of the conduct of one man towards another'. He offers little in the way of proof or argument to support his principle. In his discussion of good and evil he says that it is true by definition that pleasure is the sole intrinsic good and pain the sole intrinsic evil (*PJ*, 184–5). From the nature of beings such as we are, he thinks, it is obvious that 'pleasure is agreeable and pain odious, pleasure to be desired and pain to disapproved'. Because men are obviously morally equal, so that the same rule applies to everyone, Godwin infers that it is 'just and reasonable' that each of us should contribute to the benefit of others, as far as we can.

(*PJ*, 77–8.) The details of this attempt to generalize pursuit of one's own pleasure are not worked out.

Godwin's psychology is somewhat more carefully elaborated. He repudiates egoism, despite his willingness to trace our disinterested motives through Hartleyan windings to their interested origins. Though he says, with deliberate paradox, that men's opinions determine their actions (*PJ*, 42, 15), his view is that passion or desire is the ultimate source of action, operating, however, always through some belief about what is good or bad. Godwin's true rationalism is thus rather normative than descriptive. He follows Hartley in holding that our actions are fully voluntary only when done expressly for a known reason, rather than from instinct or habit; but he adds his own belief that it is vitally important that each man should be free—should think and decide for himself—in as many matters as possible. 'The conviction of a man's individual understanding', he says, 'is the only legitimate principle, imposing on him the duty of adopting any species of action.' (*PJ*, 96.) This is no merely incidental point in his thought, nor simply a version of the old doctrine that a man ought to follow his own moral judgement even if it should be mistaken. It springs from Godwin's profound passion for individual liberty and for the development of the powers of the individual, an attachment so fervent that he sometimes writes almost as if even truth were a trammel on individuality. 'Man is the ornament of the universe, only in proportion as he consults his own judgment', Godwin exclaims, and as justification he adduces that to allow someone else to dictate one's opinions makes one available as a tool of tyranny, and puts an end to one's own part in 'that happy collision of understandings, upon which the hopes of human improvement depend'. (*PJ*, 122.) One's own happiness as well as one's fullest contribution to the general happiness depend on one's thinking for oneself on every possible occasion. (*PJ*, 186–9.)

Since the basic principle of morality gives the highest reason for action, that principle ought to provide the reason for which every single action is done. Godwin is completely earnest on this point.

Morality is nothing else but that system, which teaches us to contribute upon all occasions, to the extent of our power, to the well-being and happiness of every intellectual and sensitive existence.

But there is no action of our lives, which does not in some way affect that happiness. . . . The periods, which cannot be spent in the active production of happiness, may be spent in preparation. . . . If then every one of our actions fall within the province of morals, it follows that we have no rights in relation to the selecting of them. (*PJ*, 84-5.)

This position together with Godwin's belief in the high value of doing each act for a consciously held reason seemed to many to imply that one should always act from considerations of general utility, never from affections directed at particular persons. This shocked his contemporaries, but not nearly as much as his conclusions respecting what are traditionally thought of as our special obligations to family, friends, and immediate neighbours. If one had to choose, he says, between rescuing some great benefactor of mankind—his example is Archbishop Fénelon—and rescuing a valet who happened to be one's father or brother (in the first edition the other person was a chambermaid who was one's mother), one ought plainly to rescue Fénelon. His life would result in greater happiness to the world than the valet's, and the valet's relationship to the rescuer is simply irrelevant. (*PJ*, 70-1.) Of course it may be difficult to obtain any acceptable solution to the problem posed by this sort of situation; but Godwin's paradoxical moral opinions are not confined to such cases. For instance, he argues that promising cannot create any special obligations. The only valid reason there can be for keeping a promise is that keeping it will create a greater balance of happiness than not keeping it, and this is a good reason for doing what was promised, whether the promise was made or not. (*PJ*, 103-4.) One might suppose one could make promises about actions which are otherwise, morally speaking, indifferent; but as we have seen, Godwin denies there are any such actions. Promises therefore impose no special obligations. If we must make them—and Godwin regretfully admits that in the world as it is we probably must —we should make them with general reservations about 'unforeseen and imperious circumstances', and should decide whether or not to keep them by fresh appeal to the test of general happiness. (*PJ*, 110.)

Clearly, then, Godwin has no patience with that respect for subordinate rules which plays so large a part in Paley's thought.

Such rules, Godwin explicitly says, are made necessary by our infirmities or our indolence. They are not infallible; they are valuable only so far as following them actually helps increase happiness; and it would be absurd to abide by them when examining a particular case shows that breaking them in that case would do more for happiness. (*PJ*, 155.) When Godwin applies this conclusion to truth-telling, with the remark that if a 'great and manifest evil' would arise from being truthful then the obligation to it is suspended, the outcome is hardly shocking. (*PJ*, 154–6.) The determination to appeal directly to the principle of utility leads him to rather more surprising results when he considers punishment. Only the public advantage, he says, can justify punishment. The view which sees a 'certain fitness or propriety' in inflicting pain, regardless of this advantage, rests on the belief in free will and must be dismissed. The public advantage is a sufficient as well as a necessary condition for punishing. Godwin rules out any retrospective considerations. Since it is right to inflict suffering whenever doing so will 'produce an overbalance of good', questions of innocence or guilt simply need not arise.

> An innocent man is the proper subject of punishment, if it tend to good. A guilty man is the proper subject of it under no other point of view. To punish him, upon any hypothesis, for what is past and irrecoverable, and for the consideration of that only, must be ranked among the most pernicious exhibitions of an untutored barbarism. (*PJ*, 245.)

Punishment is accordingly to be viewed simply as pain inflicted for the purpose of preventing future, greater, pain, and Godwin's discussion of punishment becomes a discussion of the uses of force and restraint in society.

Godwins holds, as does Bentham, that the motive from which an act is done constitutes an essential part of its nature, and that because the value of an act depends upon its consequences so does the value of the motive. Good motives are those which regularly produce actions leading to happiness. An agent is fully virtuous only when both his motive and his act are approvable. (*PJ*, 79–81.) While Bentham's analyses of motive, intention, disposition, and circumstance are more detailed than Godwin's, Godwin goes further than Bentham in drawing conclusions from the necessitarian assumptions both of them share. Typically he put his points in the manner most likely to offend the susceptibilities of his readers. He allows that we judge the merit of agents, but in doing so, he says, 'we are bound . . . to proceed in the same manner as in deciding the merits of inanimate substances'. (*PJ*, 83.) The obliteration of the distinction between the voluntary or moral virtues of an intelligent agent and the virtues of inanimate though useful things, a point about which even Hume, in the *Treatise*, indicates some discomfort, causes no qualms in Godwin. Man no more initiates actions than billiard balls do, on his view, though both are said to act. This is not fatalism: the fact that mind enters into the chain of causes determining human action averts that charge. It also entails that there are ways of influencing human behaviour which are not available for influencing the behaviour of other kinds of agent. The concept of virtue, Godwin allows, has been assigned to beings with minds, to describe the 'application of sentient and human capacity, and not the application of capacity in inanimate substances', but this is merely a grammatical point. Hence the denial of free will does nothing to endanger virtue. The realities of pleasure and pain remain, no matter how caused, and they are the root of the matter. Moreover, if we abandon libertarian fancies, Godwin adds, anticipating Robert Owen, we shall find ourselves in a happier temper toward ourselves as well as toward others. (*PJ*, 170–3.)

Needless to say, Godwin's conclusions do not all follow irrevocably from his moral premiss; but the fact that he gave such a radical interpretation of utilitarianism is illuminating in two respects. Historically it helps us to understand the picture of the utilitarian which we find again and again in the writings of our first period and even later—the monster of abstract rationality, basically selfish, denying the importance of family, friends, country, laws, traditions, replacing the Christian virtues of the humble heart by those of the calculating mind, reducing man to a machine for grinding out pleasures. Godwin, far more than Bentham, must be the original of these portrayals. Systematically it brings out clearly one of the major points of dispute between utilitarian and intuitionist. If morality must be rational, then in a collision between a first principle which certainly seems reasonable and that common-sense morality from which we usually draw the reasons by which we justify our actions, which is to give way? The earlier secular utilitarians had no doubt that common sense was not as reasonable as it was alleged to be. The intuitionists thought the failure was on the side of the principle.

iv. *Early Criticism*

From the time of the French Revolution to the first reform of Parliament in 1832 it seems to have been difficult for anyone in Britain to think of utilitarianism as simply a philosophical doctrine. For this there were many reasons. The secular version of it was inseparably associated in the public mind with the views of political extremists—'a Republican sect', so Macaulay described them, 'as audacious, as paradoxical, . . . as unscrupulous . . . as the French Jacobins . . . men whose minds have been put into training for violent exertion . . .'.[15] It was also associated with atheism—an association reinforced by the adherence to it of Robert Owen, who was not usually temperate in expressing his unreligious and anti-clerical views.[16] The journals dominated by the philosophical radicals frequently displayed crudely philistine attitudes toward literature and the arts, which earned them the enmity of many influential writers and contributed to the common view of them as fanatical zealots turning all their energies toward radical reform. Paley's religious utilitarianism could hardly be thought dangerous in the same way. Methodists and Evangelicals alike, however, thought him insufficiently impressed with the true experiential principles of Christianity and saw in the calculating hedonism of his ethics a reflection of the shallow worldliness of his theology. With both political and theological odium animating the objections to utilitarianism it is not surprising to find that they often seem to express more passion than their logic will sustain. We shall note the more philosophical criticisms which were commonly made.

[15] T. B. Macaulay, 'The Present Administration', *Edinburgh Review*, June 1827, p. 261. Macaulay was anxious to dissociate Whig reform policies from those of the philosophic radicals.

[16] For Owen's utilitarian attachments, see his *New View of Society* (1813), ed. G. D. H. Cole, 1963, pp. 17, 63. J. F. C. Harrison's *Quest for the New Moral World*, 1968, is of some value, but is flawed by misunderstanding of the Scottish moralists, and says little about Owenite philosophy.

The first critic to enter the field directly against Paley was the English Evangelical minister Thomas Gisborne, who, in 1790, dedicated his *Principles of Moral Philosophy*[17] to the members of the University of Cambridge in the hope that they would cease to use Paley as a textbook. He agrees with Paley that morality consists in doing the will of God, and further that God is purely benevolent; but he holds that it does not follow that our rule in life should be that of expediency. Gisborne's book is for the most part quite feeble, but this point, which may be found at least as early as Butler, has some logic behind it. It rests on the dual claim that our faculties are not adequate to enable us to find out what is for the good of the whole, and that God has given us an alternative means of discovering our duty. The latter point, in Gisborne, comes out in the assertion of a vague moral sense theory. The former gets its interest and its force from its place in a larger view, which Gisborne explains by an analogy. We may suppose the architect who designed St. Paul's Cathedral to have aimed to make the whole excellent, and may therefore conclude that each workman in building it is helping to do what is best for it. But we would not, on this account, excuse, let alone praise, a workman who argued that he himself should try to decide what would be for the best, and then built here an arch and there a dome as he thought good. He would be guilty of intolerable presumption (22–3) in thinking he could understand the whole of Wren's plan just from knowing his aim. The analogy is hardly worked out, but it plainly invokes the ancient idea of God as supervisor of a divine plan of work for the whole universe, in which each of us is given a part to play in bringing about some good. Gisborne does not doubt that God's aim is the general happiness of his creatures. His rules are based on utilitarian considerations, but for us they must be treated as absolute, because, as Gisborne says, 'a faint glimpse of particular expediency is all that can ever be attained by the wisest of men. A view of general utility is the property of God alone.' (59.) This point underlies and helps to explain the vehemence of many of the frequent objections to the pride and arrogance of utilitarians: after all, in claiming to use the principle of utility themselves, they are

---

[17] Page-references in this paragraph are to the 3rd edition of Gisborne's *Principles*, 1795.

presuming to be as God. Though the argument is sound, given its assumptions, it supposes no basic moral disagreement with utilitarianism. Its main force, consequently, is in the conclusion that men cannot make the calculations required by the principle of utility.

This is the form in which the argument is taken up by the Scottish moralists. For the most part they are content to use against Paley variations on the objections they could find Reid using against Hume. The argument from inability to know all the consequences is their main significant addition to his list. Stewart puts the point by saying that the calculations of utility are too hard for 'fallible and short-sighted' creatures like men to make, and therefore, even if it were true that God wills only our happiness, he must provide us with other, less abstract, rules of action.[18] The Scots differ from Gisborne, however, in two respects. They think that to make God's will the foundation of morals, as he and Paley do, is to make morality arbitrary; and they think it is doubtful or mistaken to say that God's sole moral attribute is benevolence. God is just and veracious as well, and therefore he wills our happiness only in so far as it accords with justice and truth. Or as Dewar puts it, God wills the happiness of his creatures only 'in connection with their moral excellency and the glory of his righteousness as well as his goodness'.[19] It must follow, on the intuitional view, that the plain man's conscience will reflect these positive moral limits to the scope of the principle of utility, a point the Scottish philosophers make by their general appeal, following Reid, to every man's ability to recognize a variety of principles as independently binding. This appeal in turn is buttressed by a general, religiously based teleology—shared, of course, with Paley—which confers a divine purpose on all the original parts of our nature. Out of the teleology there arises another source of controversy with utilitarianism.

Because we observe a number of different kinds of desires and motives in ourselves, the anti-utilitarian argument runs, we can see that we will be ignoring God's indications of his

[18] D. Stewart, *Philosophy of the Active and Moral Powers*, ed. Sir William Hamilton, 1877, vii. 231–4. Estlin, i. 78–9, and Dewar, i. 230–1, ii. 40, are among others who bring this objection.
[19] Dewar, i. 38; cf. Chalmers, p. 317; Wardlaw, pp. 159–69.

purposes if we concern ourselves only with one of them. Hence Paley's insistence on self-interest as the sole moral motive, like Godwin's insistence on benevolence, must be mistaken. Concern for self and concern for others are both shown by their original place in our nature to be fit principles for man. On the moral level, the fact that we have many immediately given moral convictions (as is made evident by the ability of children to pass moral judgements before they can reason about consequences), as well as the fact that the basic concept of morality is unique and could not have been derived from simpler perceptions, shows that our moral convictions, being original parts of our nature, are meant to be our guides. Hence, once again, there is a strong presumption against any view reducing everything to one principle.

This kind of argument leaves itself open, as has already been suggested, to a reply showing that a theoretical account of both types of apparent multiplicity can be given in a way which supports the utilitarian view. Such an answer to Stewart and Gisborne in defence of Paley was made in 1830 by Latham Wainewright, who added the accusation that the Scottish philosophers simply refuse to put forward any theory at all, and so are not really pursuing philosophy. (*Vindic.*, pp. 38–42, 98–9 n.) The most important exposition of the approach Wainewright favoured was not written to defend Paley, however, but to support secular utilitarianism. It is James Mill's psychological masterpiece, the *Analysis of the Phenomena of the Human Mind*, published in 1829. Though not primarily concerned with moral theory, Mill discusses our disinterested impulses, tracing them back in accordance with the laws of the association of ideas to basic self-interested motives. He explains the temporal immediacy of our mature judgements as resulting, not from a special faculty, but from the installation of habits through education and social conditioning. And he offers a genetic account of allegedly unique moral ideas or feelings which shows them to have developed according to the laws of association from pleasure, pain, and sense-based ideas. In giving this kind of reply to the Scottish school—in which, it may be noted, he himself had been trained—James Mill set the secular utilitarians firmly in the habit of attributing great importance to genetic accounts of disinterested motives and moral beliefs. It was a habit they kept even later, when neither they nor their opponents accepted the teleological assumptions in terms of which James Mill's theory most evidently makes sense as a reply to objections to utilitarianism and a ground of support for it. The reason for this persistence is clear. Mill's geneticism embodies a demand for explanatory simplicity in psychological and ethical theory which carries considerably more weight than the specific view Mill put forth in accordance with it. It is the counterpart, in the realm of explanation, to the demand for simple rationality in the realm of practice which Bentham articulated when he insisted on having only one basic moral principle.

Most of the other difficulties raised about Paley's views are applications of Reid's charge that utilitarianism leads to unacceptable moral consequences. A number of specific Paleyan views are involved, perhaps the most serious being the suspicion that he does not really think the teachings of Scripture take precedence of those of expediency—a charge from which Crofts and Wainewright were anxious to exonerate him[20]—but on the whole Paley's views and Paley himself were treated with respect. The same cannot be said of the prime target for moral objections, Godwin.[21]

'No work in our time gave such a blow to the philosophical mind of the country as the Celebrated Enquiry concerning Political Justice,' says Hazlitt[22] and if one is to judge from the outcry of Godwin's critics Hazlitt is correct. Godwin's friends do not seem to have written in defence of his philosophy. His enemies, though not usually philosophers, were fluent and intemperate. One or two examples must suffice. Godwin's 'savage philosophy' was the object of Robert Hall's famous and

[20] Crofts, pp. 5, 9; Wainewright, p. 7; for a similar point see also *Quarterly Review*, xxxviii, 76, 1828, p. 320, a generally hostile review reiterating all the commonplace criticisms of utilitarianism.

[21] For a full and lively account of the favourable reception of, and subsequent attacks on, Godwin's *Enquiry*, see Brown's biography, op. cit., Ch. VIII.

[22] William Hazlitt, 'Godwin', in *The Spirit of the Age*, *Works*, ed. P. P. Howe, 1930–4, vol. 11. All references to Hazlitt will be made to this edition. I have benefited from the careful study by Herschel Baker, *William Hazlitt*, 1962, and from the opening chapters of the stimulating book by Roy Park, *Hazlitt and the Spirit of the Age*, 1971. Baker thinks Hazlitt's estimates of the importance of the subjects written about in *The Spirit of the Age* extremely accurate: 'hardly any other book delineates with such precision and perception the contour of the age' (p. 435).

frequently reprinted sermon of 1799, 'Modern Infidelity', which flayed those who presume to 'innovate in the very substance of morals. . . . The curse denounced upon such as remove ancient landmarks, upon those who call good evil and evil good, put light for darkness and darkness for light . . . falls with accumulated weight upon the advocates of modern infidelity', i.e. Godwin,[23] who did not need to be named to an audience of the time. As late as 1812, when passions generally had cooled somewhat, a *Quarterly* reviewer lumps him with a 'set of speculators as wild as the old fifth-monarchy men' or those produced by the excesses of the French Revolution, and sees his proposals for reform as 'connected with the deplorable doctrines of brute materialism, blind necessity, and blank atheism, and with a system of ethics, which, attempting an impossible union between stoicism and sensuality, succeeded just so far as to deprave the morals and harden the heart'.[24] We find a more philosophical temper, though no less moral distaste, in a short pamphlet first published in 1798 by one Thomas Green, which seems to be the only substantial rational criticism of Godwin to have been produced by his contemporaries.[25]

Green devotes some pages[26] to ridiculing Godwin's belief that our motive in all our actions should be general benevolence, and some to arguing that Godwin fails, as he thinks any rationalist must fail, to give any reason in support of his first principle. He is more elaborate in showing the immorality and the impracticability of Godwin's principle. The foundation of Godwin's position, he says, is that one ought always to do all the good one can. Since the habits in which we have been raised, and the customs, laws, morals, and traditions of our society, are not the result of purely rational determinations of what will be for the best, they are all to be ignored. 'The undistinguishing proscription of all the received regulations of life, is not a remote

[23] Robert Hall, *Miscellaneous Works*, ed. O. Gregory, 1846, p. 288.

[24] *Quarterly Review*, viii, 16, 1812, p. 321.

[25] Dr. Samuel Parr preached a Spital Sermon against Godwin in 1800 and published it the next year. He objected to Godwin's view of the proper motive of moral action and thought his whole theory would lead to neglect of our duties.

[26] Thomas Green, *An Examination of the Leading Principle of the New System of Morals* (etc.), 2nd ed. 1799, to which page references in the text are made. Most of this is reprinted in D. H. Monro, *A Guide to the British Moralists*, London, 1972, pp. 198–203, 354–9. Monro uses the text of the first edition, which he dates from 1798 and which differs little from that of the second.

consequence, it is the essence, of the New System of Morals', Green writes (p. 41), and it represents what is worst about that system. Green points out that Godwin cannot accept the manœuvre, dear to Paley, of appealing to general rules; for if in some instance breaking the rule would produce more good than following it, one ought, on Godwin's view, to break it rather than be an irrational rule-worshipper. (pp. 35–8.) The upshot must be that no one will be able to trust anyone, for anyone might well think utility better served if he were to 'defraud me of my money, divulge my bosom secrets to the world, and violate . . . my partner or my child' (p. 39) than if he were to act according to the common sense rules in these matters.[27] A good man of this kind would be worse than an ordinary villain, who, evil though he may be in some ways, is at least predictable. A Godwinian would be totally unreliable. Green is anxious to show the uselessness as well as the wickedness of Godwin's view. He objects strenuously to the insistence that each man should think for himself in each case about what he should do, on the ground that it would make all action impossible. The principle of doing all the good one can is so general that to apply it, says Green, 'I must spend all my life . . . in speculation, before I could safely take the first step. . . . The rule is a most incomparable rule, but it is impossible to put it into practice.' (p. 30.)

This is clearly a variation on the charge that the rule of utility is not appropriate for such beings as we are. Its burden is not that we cannot calculate all the consequences, but that we could not reach a conclusion about what the principle requires in time to act on it: the use of the principle to guide action would prevent action. One or two other criticisms of this kind are sometimes suggested, though never very clearly or elaborately. They are usually presented by adverting to the dangers of encouraging men to think for themselves about their duties, and in some cases, as when Gisborne brings the point up against Paley (Gisborne, *Principles*, pp. 38–9), it is

[27] Brown (*Godwin*, p. 162) reports a novel of 1799 in which the hero, a complete Godwinian, 'practises seduction, parricide, incendiarism, robbery, adultery, and murder "with full harmony" to the ideas of his master. . . . Gaming, he finds, equalises property. Gratitude being banned, he seduces the wife of his protector. . . . While robbing a coach he shoots his mother, but having discarded the natural affections is not much aggrieved.'

hard to avoid the suspicion that one of its roots is the resentment of well-to-do clergy at having their poorer charges told to think about social rights and wrongs. No doubt a sense of human sinfulness and a general distrust of the plain man's powers of reasoning might well lead to doubts about how wisely exceptions would be made to accepted rules. More interestingly there are suggestions about the difficulty that would exist in forming reliable expectations concerning the behaviour of others if no one ever relied on established rules. Mackintosh, for instance (*Diss.*, p. 304), suggests both of these points very briefly in attacking Bentham.[28] But though there were perceptions of the problem posed by the high costs of using the principle of utility, the difficulties were not worked out into pointed criticisms.

Another kind of criticism of utilitarianism deals with its general view of the importance or value of human action. Godwin's provocative remarks might almost have been designed to arouse the objection, stated forcefully by Thomas Brown, that if it is solely the utility or disutility of actions which makes them right or wrong, and their agents good or bad, then the moral goodness of a person is no different in kind from the goodness possessed by an inanimate object like a chest of drawers. (*Lec. Phil.* iv. 38 ff.) And this conclusion is a *reductio ad absurdum* of utilitarian views. The distinction in kind between moral good and natural good, Brown thinks, cannot be glossed over in this way. Godwin himself had attempted to forestall the objection by pointing out that moral terms apply distinctively to rational agents who can act, in his determinist sense, freely. But this verbal manœuvre did not satisfy those who thought that in making virtue, which only man can attain, a mere means to pleasure, which men share with the beasts, the utilitarians were degrading morality.

Bentham may possibly have been on the minds of many of these critics of utilitarianism, but he was not on their lips. Macaulay charged his psychology as well as his ethics with tautology, and prophesied that the best his utilitarian principle could hope for would be to become 'a fashionable phrase

---

[28] For discussion of some philosophical issues which may underlie these criticisms, see J. L. Mackie, 'The Disutility of Act Utilitarianism', *Philosophical Quarterly*, 23, no. 92, 1973, and the literature there discussed.

among newspaper writers and members of parliament'.[29] The only person who wrote at all extensively about Bentham during our first period was Hazlitt.[30] And Hazlitt did not have a good opinion of him. Bentham has not, Hazlitt says, 'given any new or decided impulse to the human mind'. He is not a 'discoverer in legislation or morals . . . has not struck out any great leading principle or parent-truth, from which a number of others might be deduced.' He is, at best, an arranger and methodizer; he is better seen, Hazlitt suggests, as an eccentric projector, like Robert Owen.

Though Hazlitt in his early days wrote philosophical essays, in one of which he put forward some original and interesting objections to egoism, he allowed himself to be very careless in articulating his objections to Benthamism. He makes it plain that he thinks the principle of utility unsuited to creatures with the limited capacities of humans; but his objection is not simply that we cannot know the consequences of our actions, it is rather an objection to such unmitigated reliance on reason. Men cannot, or should not, be so rational. Habits, customs, and, more than anything else, sentiments are or should be the chief determinants of our actions. Hazlitt, considered a radical in his day, was no enemy of reform and certainly not a follower of Burke; but he detested methodical planning, whether for society or for works of art, thinking it cut off the spontaneous promptings of genius and deadened the sources of feeling. Conflating Bentham and Godwin, he condemns all utilitarians for demanding that we 'suspend all the natural and private affections' for logic and the good of the whole. He is horrified by the idea of using a calculus of pleasure to settle moral issues and convinced that it would lead to immoral conclusions: hardly a novel objection, though Hazlitt illustrates it strikingly. The calculus would warrant killing people to provide cadavers for medical students, he says, and he supposes Bentham would approve of slavery because the sufferings of the slaves would be more than balanced by the enjoyment derived from the sugar for tea and coffee which their labour alone can produce. Aside from these commonplace objections, Hazlitt's opposition

[29] *Works*, i. 405.
[30] This and the next paragraph are based on Hazlitt's writings in 8. 151; 11, 7 f., 14; 12, 50, 179–94, 247 ff.; 20, esp. 255–60, and also 192, 321, 376–87.

to Bentham seems to rest on what one cannot help thinking must be a wilful misunderstanding. He insists on presenting the Benthamites as opposed to the enjoyment of life. He takes their stress on utility to mean opposition to the pursuit of pleasure. These 'new Ferrets and inspectors of a Police-Philosophy', he cries, would like to keep all men at work and prevent them from being happy. Themselves miserable, cantankerous, ill-tempered cavillers and complainers, the Benthamites would like to see everyone else as wretched as they are. They oppose the arts because they themselves are unable to enjoy them. They claim that 'the Whole Duty of Man consists in his doing nothing that can give either himself or any other mortal the smallest conceivable satisfaction'. They are 'a kind of puritans in morals'.[31] They are, in short, our modern ascetics.

Hazlitt did nothing to advance the debate about utilitarianism. His curious misunderstandings of Bentham's ethics may be responsible for some of John Stuart Mill's comments in *Utilitarianism*,[32] as his disparagement of Bentham's work on method may have led Mill to stress its value in his long essay of 1838. The very enormity of his misunderstanding does suggest, however, how little Bentham's views must have been known, if Hazlitt's attacks could pass as telling.

Some of the criticisms of theological utilitarianism were answered by one or another of its exponents during our first period, and one or two volumes were devoted wholly to the defence of Paley. The rejoinders made by Wainewright are a fair specimen. He defends Paley on the moral motive by pointing out that Paley does not confine us to considering our interests in this life alone, and by reminding us that even Christ promised to reward his followers. Paley no more makes individuals judges in each case than the critics do, since Paley insists on rules which are to be followed for the most part, while his critics admit that rules have exceptions. If utility is too difficult for us to calculate, this tells against any system (such as Gisborne's or Stewart's) which inculcates prudence

---

[31] So also Macaulay in 1827 (as cited in n. 15 above): 'Philosophical pride has done for them what spiritual pride did for the Puritans in a former age: it has generated in them an aversion for the fine arts, for elegant literature . . . made them arrogant, intolerant, and impatient of all superiority.'

[32] I owe this point to Park, *Hazlitt*, who however greatly overestimates the value and originality of Hazlitt's criticisms.

and benevolence along with other virtues. Paley admits we need to be educated into knowing rules of morality, but the intuitionists or moral sense philosophers admit the need of education to develop the moral faculty. He makes similar replies to other criticisms. (*Vindic.*, pp. 6–7, 28–30, 33–5, 48–51.) No new insights, no deepening of the issues, occur. And his replies, like those of Paley's other champions, seem to have been ignored.

They were certainly ignored by the only attack on Paley to achieve much fame, Adam Sedgwick's *Discourse on the Studies of the University of Cambridge.* His criticisms, none of them original, are stated hastily and carelessly. Paley's guess about the wild boy is dismissed for reasons Stewart and others had made familiar. Paley is scolded for limiting God's moral attributes to benevolence, and ignoring his justice. Paley's rule is 'unsuitable to our nature'. It makes each man his own judge in cases of right and wrong by doing away with unalterable rules. It requires calculations we cannot make. The main objection however is to the immorality of Paley's view and indeed of any utilitarian view. 'Utilitarian philosophy and Christian ethics', he says, 'have in their principles and motives no common bond of union . . . the general acceptance of Paley's moral rule in any Christian society would inevitably debase the standard of right and wrong.' It may well flatter our pride to resolve all virtue into a single principle of considering 'worldly consequences' but it will prepare men for 'violent and ill-timed inroads on the social system, and for the perpetration of daring crimes'. And taking benevolence toward the whole creation as the basis of morality would lead to the destruction of private affections, the ignoring of special duties, the dissolution of marriage and the common bonds of social life, and the end of patriotism. (Sedgwick, pp. 39, 66, 76–8, 133.)

Discussion of Paley continued long after Sedgwick's *Discourse.* In 1835 Mill, attacking Sedgwick, criticized Paley in an attempt to separate his own variety of utilitarianism from Paley's. Alexander Smith extolled Paley's views on rules in the same year. In 1837 Whewell more or less endorsed Sedgwick's criticisms; he articulated his own quite fully in lectures which began the next year. Christopher Neville defended Paley feebly in 1839, when William Smith published a more vigorous defence of part of his doctrine. Bain edited his moral philosophy, with critical essays, in 1852; Whately edited and annotated it, and then attacked it in a strong essay in 1859; English repeated various criticisms of it in 1865; and Sidgwick's predecessor in the Knightbridge professorship, Birks, devoted several chapters of his *Modern Utilitarianism* of 1874 to reiterating all the old criticisms he could locate. But from about the middle of the 1830s it could no longer be said that Paley was the central figure in philosophical discussions of utilitarianism, as had been the case up to then. Paley's theological writings also began to decline in importance. The modes of argument and issues of significance in religious matters were changing. Increasing doubts about religion made it increasingly necessary to conduct debates about morality in terms which did not presuppose its questionable dogmas. The Coleridgeans and many others did not accept the old way of arguing to God's moral attributes from the adoption of means to ends in the natural world and from the distribution of happiness. They preferred to argue from the more specifically moral deliverances of our intuitive faculties. These changes helped make it important to show that morality, viewed by itself and independently of religion, really would sustain the religious inferences they wished to draw. The secular utilitarians were ready with a new leader to enter whole-heartedly into the discussion.

5

The Reworking of Utilitarianism

THE intuitionists took the accepted morality of the times to reflect, even if imperfectly, our common ability to grasp fundamental moral truths. Among the utilitarians those influenced by Paley had little objection to this acknowledgement of the existing code: they were never root-and-branch reformers. The position Mackintosh sketched at the end of his *Dissertation* is typical. The views of the moral sense school and those of the utilitarians, he thinks, are readily reconcilable. Since God is benevolent and wills our happiness, utility is the basic principle. But our limited capacities make it impossible for us to use it directly to guide action. The moral sentiments were given us as 'tests of morality in the moment of action', a role for which their 'quick and powerful action' suits them. The principle of utility is better fitted for use as 'the test of the sentiments and dispositions themselves'. For although we cannot calculate the consequences of individual actions, we can know 'the general tendency of every sort of action', and if we guide ourselves by the rules based on the experience of mankind, rules to which our moral sentiments attach themselves, we both avoid the absurd extremes to which utilitarians who ignore these rules are led, and have a way of improving our moral feelings. (*Diss.*, pp. 356–61.) William Godwin would have scoffed at such a view in his early days, but even Godwin changed his position, though his retractions and alterations went more or less unnoticed. In prefaces to his novels and in a dignified reply to a virulent attack on him by Dr. Parr, he showed that he had come to see the need for other motives beside rational goodwill to mankind, that he treasured the domestic affections, that he had had second thoughts about Archbishop Fénelon, and, in short, that he was willing to allow a considerable value to at least some of the commonly acknowledged maxims of morality.[1] In 1835 Whewell suggested that

[1] Parts of Godwin's reply to Parr are in Carter's abridgement of *PJ*, pp. 322–6. See also the various comments on the novels in Brown, *Godwin, passim.*

even Bentham was coming to see that rules—commonly accepted rules—of morality were essential for his theory. 'If a reverence for general maxims of morality, and a constant reference to the common precepts of virtue, take the place, in the utilitarian's mind, of the direct application of his principle,' Whewell commented hopefully, 'there will remain little difference between him and the believer in original moral distinctions; for the practical rules of the two will rarely differ.' (*Pref. M.*, p. 29.)

The younger utilitarians were not so quick to accept the suggestion.[2] An appeal to moral rules, which is far from being a reverence for common-sense maxims, might serve to turn aside two serious criticisms of their view—that we cannot actually use the utilitarian principle in particular cases to find out what to do, and that the principle leads to morally repugnant results. An appeal to rules to answer the first criticism was readily acceptable even to utilitarians bent on reform. But reference specifically to the rules of common sense as a means of answering the second criticism was not so easily incorporated into a reformist outlook. It only became a fully acknowledged part of secular utilitarian theory in the work of John Stuart Mill.

i. *Utilitarians and Rules*

The first attempt to work out with some care a mode in which the utilitarian principle could be coupled with reliance on moral rules was made by John Austin in his lectures on the *Province of Jurisprudence*, published in 1832.[3] Austin is motivated in part by opposition to the extremes to which Godwin took

---

[2] In a hostile review published in the *Edinburgh Review* in April 1804 of Bentham's *Traites de Legislation*, edited by Dumont, Francis Jeffrey says: 'The established rules and impressions of morality . . . we consider as the grand recorded result of an infinite multitude of experiments upon human feeling and fortune. . . . *General rules* of morality . . . have been suggested by a larger observation, and a longer experience, than any individual can dream of pretending to. . . . If they be founded on utility . . . it is on an utility that does not discover itself until it is accumulated. . . . Such summaries of utility, such records of uniform observation, we conceive to be the *General Rules of Morality*, by which, and by which alone, legislators or individuals can be safely directed . . . the old established morality of mankind ought upon no account to give place to a bold and rigid investigation into the *utility* of any particular act . . .' (pp. 310–12).

[3] References to *The Province of Jurisprudence Determined* are given, in the text, to the page-numbers of the edition of 1832, abbreviated as *Prov.*

the utilitarian principle: 'it was never contended or conceited by a sound, orthodox, utilitarian, that the lover should kiss his mistress with an eye to the common weal', he says dismissively (*Prov.*, p. 118), and he offers no argument against the pure act-utilitarian version of the principle. Nor does he show any interest in proving the principle. He rests his utilitarianism squarely on the will of God, treating the matter offhandedly in a purely Paleyan fashion, and moving quickly to what does interest him, the elaboration of the theory itself. In that elaboration the first important step is to insist on the necessity of general rules. The true tendency of an act, Austin holds, the sum of all its actual and probable consequences, is to be gathered by considering the effects, not of a single isolated act, but of the class of which an act is a member. 'If acts of the *class* were *generally* done or generally forborne or omitted, what would be the probable effect on the general happiness . . . ?' (*Prov.*, p. 37.) No reason is offered for insisting that this is the true tendency, but the inference drawn from the claim is important: since it is the true test, we must conclude that God's commands are general or universal. At least this is so 'for the most part'. Most of God's commands order us to do acts which, as a class, are useful. Austin seems to think that the rules are to be obeyed even if in particular instances disobeying would be more useful. His reason is that if we took them to allow exceptions, we would make too many. 'Consequently,' he says, 'where acts, considered as a class, are useful or pernicious, we must conclude that [God] enjoins or forbids them, and by a *rule* which probably is inflexible.' (*Prov.*, p. 40.) The hesitation suggested by the 'probably' is not further elaborated, and we may say therefore that Austin takes moral rules to impose obligations stronger than those which would be imposed by mere rules of thumb. He is, as Paley does not seem to have been, a genuine rule-utilitarian.

Austin thinks this point about rules enables him to answer 'the most current and specious' of the objections to utilitarianism, the claim that we cannot in particular cases know what it is most useful to do, and that we might spend endless time trying to find out, while the moment for action slipped by. (*Prov.*, pp. 41–5.) He grants that if we had to apply the principle directly, the objection would be sound. But we do not have to apply it in that way. We apply the principle only to general rules, and we determine the particulars of action by appeal to the rules. This enables us also to give proper place to the moral sentiments, for they cluster by association about the thoughts of the classes of acts specified by the moral rules. (*Prov.*, pp. 47–51.) Austin allows that there are a few very complicated cases where appeal must be made directly to utility, but thinks there are not many: by giving as an instance the possibility that rebellion might be warranted, he suggests what is needed before this mode of arguing should be invoked. (*Prov.*, pp. 53 ff.) Though in such cases the difficulties are so great that no final answer might be reached, appeal to the principle of utility would still provide a common ground on which disputing parties might try rationally to adjust their differences, and such an appeal would therefore be useful— more useful than pigheadedly sticking to abstract principles of ultimate rights, for example.

Austin's reply to the difficulty raised by the critics is of course pointless unless we can know what are the classes of actions which are useful and which, because commanded by God, are therefore our duty. Austin turns to this topic in the third lecture. He points out that if positive law and morality were what they ought to be, then sound utilitarian reasons could be given for each of the rules contained in them; but it would not follow that anyone would know all those reasons, or that any single person could have discovered all those rules. (*Prov.*, p. 63.) Specialists in the sciences take much on the authority of other specialists: ideally, the same would be true in morality. We could take the results on trust. The objection to this, he says, is that moral rules have not resulted, as scientific truths have, from unbiased and impartial inquiry. Sinister interests, customs 'deeply tinctured with barbarity', caprices of fancy, and very partial views of utility have formed them. Hence we do not have 'that concurrence or agreement of numerous and impartial inquirers' which gives authority to the sciences. (*Prov.*, pp. 65–7.) Austin simply admits the difficulty, but hopes for its gradual disappearance. Two facts give him hope. The leading principles of morality may be learned easily by the masses, and, when so learned, will enable the people themselves to correct the positive morality; and the number of those studying morality is increasing, so that more help is to be expected from experts. Political economy gives us an encouraging example of how 'the diffusion of knowledge through the great mass of the people' can work. We may expect the same progress in morality proper. (*Prov.*, pp. 85–7.) In the fourth lecture Austin ingeniously suggests that the imperfections of positive morality are exactly on a par with the imperfections, as we think them, of the rest of the universe and the rest of God's revelation to us; so that, as Butler pointed out, these imperfections provide no reason to deny that the will of God is at work here. (*Prov.*, pp. 91 f.)

There is a negative argument for his case, Austin says, because the only alternative to his view is the claim that we have a moral sense or moral feelings sufficient to guide us. All the allegedly different views of this faculty come to the same thing —that we have a felt, immediate, divinely ordained guide to action, which is not the result of education or calculation. (*Prov.*, pp. 95–6.) He finds the view quite unacceptable, since he thinks we simply do not have such feelings. We must frequently hesitate and meditate before coming to a moral conclusion, hence we do not always have immediate moral responses. And there is no great uniformity on all points of moral feeling among all men. There is some uniformity, where the common features of human nature make common utilities unmistakably clear; otherwise there is great variation. (*Prov.*, pp. 104–9.) Thus, since there is no moral sense, we must use the principle of utility. And the rest of the fourth lecture is occupied with removing two misconceptions about it: one, that thoughts of utility must always be the good man's motive, the other, that it presupposes a 'selfish' theory of psychology. Neither of these is the case, Austin argues, and it is time to stop pretending they are.

Austin's theory of rules raises, for the first time in connection with utilitarianism, the critically important question of the sociology and history of moral opinion. How does positive morality come to be formed, how can it be changed? He allows that positive morality is not now purely what it ought to be; and though it seems evident that he has no basis for claiming to know this to be the case, since to know it he would have to know what it ought to be, he supports his claim by suggesting that the sources of public opinion are extremely unlikely to produce a purely utilitarian result. At the same time, as we have noted, he hopes for better things: though rationality did not form the moral codes of the past or present, it may form those of the future. But if it is asked whether, at the moment, we generally have accurate knowledge of what we ought to do, Austin's answer must be that we probably do not, except in those cases where the common exigencies of human nature have led everyone to perceive basic utilities and disutilities. All this hardly suggests that 'reverence for general maxims of morality' and 'constant reference to the common precepts of virtue' which Whewell thought he saw arising among the utilitarians.

Whewell refers to Bentham's *Deontology* as the source of his hopes of *rapprochement*. It was a poor choice, not only because the younger philosophic radicals were embarrassed by the book and were at odds with the editor, but because it is really rather hard to find, in the chapter to which Whewell refers or anywhere else, much basis for the view that utilitarians were coming to revere common-sense morality. Bentham does indeed in that chapter—the first of the second volume—discuss some of the ordinary virtues, and make passing reference to 'foresight that lays in its stores of useful precepts with anticipating care'. (*Deon.* ii. 29.) And he says that people from the beginning of time have instinctively been led by the greatest happiness principle 'without being aware of its existence'. (*Deon.* ii. 30.) But he also says that public approbation and disapprobation are too frequently misplaced, and that 'the judgments of the public-opinion tribunal are thus sometimes in opposition with the dictates of utility . . . some of them, the mere vestiges of barbarism, make laws which resist all argument and stand unshaken on the prejudices left by feudal times'. (*Deon.* ii. 47.) In the history of morality, Bentham says, the reign of force is succeeded by the reign of fraud, and this in turn is to be succeeded by the reign of justice, by which he here means utility: but he does not suggest that we now live under the reign of justice. (*Deon.* ii. 48–9.) He seems at most to suggest that when that time arrives we may hope for a commonly accepted moral code really based on utility. He is thus even less enthusiastic about existing morality than Austin, though his view of its origins and possible reformation is very similar to Austin's.

James Mill's view of ordinary morality is somewhat different. He wrote little on morality during most of his life. The essays which established his fame as a utilitarian theorist[4] took some version of the utilitarian principle for granted but did not expound or defend it, and the brief discussions of morality in the *Analysis of the Phenomena of the Human Mind* are, as we have noted, predominantly concerned with showing how the moral feelings come to exist as results of the operation of the laws of association working on non-moral data. The publication of Mackintosh's history of ethics, however, with its curt dismissal of Bentham's moral philosophy, roused him to write a reply. The *Fragment on Mackintosh* (1835), 431 pages of sheer exasperation, is one of the most irritating and irascible works ever published. The atmosphere in it is almost paranoid; and the reader is not surprised to discover that it contains little in the way of systematic positive exposition of utilitarian doctrine. Most of it is devoted to minute dissection of Mackintosh's criticisms of utilitarian views—which were not very well placed, certainly not original, and often phrased with undue asperity—which we need not weary ourselves with following. The one topic which touches Mill to sustained exposition is the rebuttal of the charge to which Austin's doctrine of rules was also meant to be an answer: that utilitarian calculations cannot be carried out, or at least not in time for appropriate action.

Mill's response—which incidentally ignores Mackintosh's concluding remarks on the topic—has much in common with Austin's. He divides decisions into two classes: those in which 'a direct estimate of the good of the particular act is inevitable' and those in which it is not. The former concerns highly unusual acts, the latter, the vast majority, includes the usual or ordinary cases. (*Frag.*, pp. 256–7.) The latter are classified, and 'placed under general rules, universally recognized', and one acts on them as on 'pre-established decisions'. (*Frag.*, p. 163.) Mill lists the rules of prudence, temperance, justice, and fortitude as examples. Because these rules all depend on classification, they can be understood only when classification is understood. Mill

---

[4] Primarily those on education, government, and freedom of the press, written for the *Encyclopaedia Britannica*. It was the essay on government which Macaulay attacked in 1829.

holds a nominalist view of classes (expounded at length in his *Analysis*) which he summarizes for Sir James's benefit. His aim is to show that men make classes for a purpose, and that the purpose, as it concerns the classes upon which moral rules rest, is to see to it that beneficial acts are done and that harmful acts are not done. Some of these acts are such that the agent has his own reasons for doing or abstaining, others not. To control the latter group, Mill says, artificial motives have to be introduced. And this gives us the origins of the distinction between moral and immoral acts.

The acts, which it was important to other men that each individual should perform

but in which the individual had not a sufficient interest to secure the performance of them, were constituted one class. The acts, which it was important to other men that each individual should abstain from, but in regard to which he had not a personal interest sufficiently strong to secure his abstaining from them, were constituted the second class. The first class were distinguished by the name moral acts; the second, by the name immoral. (*Frag.*, p. 249.)

Then, for more particular direction, more specific rules were formed. The purpose for which the more detailed rules are formed is thus good; but, Mill allows, men have been 'cruelly defective' in working them out: 'witness the consequence—the paucity of good acts, the frequency of bad acts, which there is in the world.' (*Frag.*, p. 250.) Mill offers no explanation of why this should be so. When he comes to explain how societies formed their moral rules, he simply refers to the account of classification already given. If the distinction between acts to be praised and those to be blamed is not explained in this way, how is it to be explained? Mill says no real alternative answer to this question has ever been given. The only one he considers is the account which suggests that these rules arise from the perceptions of the moral faculty; but as he considers that faculty to be itself simply the outcome of associations around perceptions of utility, this is not an alternative to his own view—or else it is a merely verbal and ultimately non-sensical alternative. (*Frag.*, pp. 261–5; cf. p. 375.) The transmission of such rules is explained in his account of how individuals first come to learn them: children acquire habits of following the rules which are current in their own society. They obey them unreflectively, as laid down by parental and social authority, and, Mill comments, 'nearly at this point the greater part of them remain, continuing to perform moral acts and to abstain from the contrary, chiefly from the habits they have acquired, and the authority upon which they originally acted'. (*Frag.*, p. 261.) Nowhere, then, does Mill suggest an account for the 'cruelly defective' nature of our positive morality. His highly rationalistic history allows us to suppose that he might explain it by claiming that early rule-makers were ignorant of most consequences of acts, and it also suggests that his remedies would rely heavily on education.

Both Austin and Mill seem to think that the main justification for the position that action should be guided by rules is that it enables the individual to apply the principle of utility to particular cases. Alexander Smith, who regards Paley's 'development of the nature and use of general rules in morals' as 'the most important contribution the science ever received from an individual' (*PM* I, iv), does not disagree with the substance of this point, but he gives a different reason for assigning to rule-following a major role in a utilitarian morality and he elaborates interestingly on some further aspects of rule-utilitarianism.

While we can of course discuss the consequences of single acts, every proposition about what one ought to do is, Smith says, 'a general proposition', even if it takes the explicit form of a particular one. We and our hearers always separate out the circumstances in the particular case that give rise to the obligation from those that are irrelevant to it, and the particular action is then taken as 'representative of every action resembling it in those essential points'. (*PM* I, 218–19.) The axioms lying at the foundation of Smith's theory have already been noted. He takes it to follow from them that one ought to do no harm, ought to create happiness or pleasure, and ought to do this equally rather than unequally. (*PM* I, 216–17.) These inferences from the axioms tie the fitness of ends to the obligation to act—Smith is very clear that obligation is quite different from any motive impelling an agent to act—and, together with the claim about the implicit generality of all propositions concerning what one ought to do, lead Smith to conclude that 'the effect of an action is the effect of a species or class of actions, and the effect of a species or class is that from which we compute the obligation of the action'. Smith thus appeals to the universalizability of 'ought'-propositions, rather than, like Mill, to the nature of class-names, as the reason why utilitarians are to consider primarily classes of acts in their calculations. He immediately goes on to point out that in some cases no difference is made by this universalizability to the existence of obligation in particular cases. His interest is in cases where the obligation itself is affected by, or arises wholly from, the universalizability. (*PM* I, 220.)

Smith discusses three groups of cases of this kind. The first consists of actions the obligation to which arises because there is a combination of a variety of acts in one concerted plan to achieve some good. Smith thinks most of the actions performed as functions of a political community, such as defence and public works, are of this sort. (*PM* I, 220–1.) More importantly, he discusses at some length the 'ease and confidence' we enjoy when we can rely on others. He goes so far as to argue that even the wrongfulness of murder rests on this consideration. The immediate harm caused by it may be relatively small: after all, life is not always such a good thing. But the obligation to refrain from it arises from the need for peace and security, and from consideration of the alarms and terrors with which we would all live if we could not count on safety. (*PM* I, 222–3.) The second group of cases consists of those where our view of the seriousness of an obligation is affected by a factor over and above the amount of harm that is caused by its neglect in any particular case. The factor is the tendency people would naturally have to perform the harmful act, if it were not prohibited. If the tendency is considerable, the obligation is viewed as more serious. (*PM* I, 223–7.) Finally, Smith discusses briefly the way in which the knowledge that someone or other will do a beneficial act whether it is considered obligatory or not, diminishes the seriousness of the obligation to do it. (*PM* I, 224–8.) These three kinds of case illustrate the point that because in considering the obligation to act we are considering a 'species' of act, 'we are often morally obliged to perform an action which (individually) does no good, or abstain from one which (individually) does no harm'. (*PM* I, 229.)

This leads naturally to a discussion of exceptions. If the obligation to do an act arises not from its individual consequences but from its membership of an obligatory class, that obligation 'fails' if we can single out the act on account of its consequences. In doing so, we must still make a general rule; and Smith lays down the principle that in making exceptions we cannot use a method which would make every act an exception to its rule, or a method which would lose the benefits of having the original rule. (*PM* I, 229–30.) In some kinds of cases, he argues, though it may be theoretically possible to specify restricted classes of exceptions without undercutting the rule altogether, we must still not do so, even when we know that some harm results from rigidity. For ignorance and self-love often lead men to judge incorrectly of right and wrong. Hence rules about exceptions must be 'so clearly defined, and so easily understood' that there is no risk of people making too many of them. (*PM* I, 232–3.) Smith points out that there is no conceivable way of avoiding individual judgement as to the application of a rule—an interesting reply to some earlier criticisms of utilitarianism—and concludes that rules must consequently be so stated as both to avoid possibilities of abuse and 'to ensure that *concert* among numbers which is so often essential to the success of human undertakings'. (*PM* I, 235.) In making these points Smith goes beyond showing how the need for co-operation and reliability may lead to demands for stricter adherence to rules than consideration of individual cases would justify. He tries for the first time to work out utilitarian principles for the construction of such rules, as well as for classes of exceptions.

This endeavour is carried on in a complex and interesting discussion of the question of the proper description under which to consider an act when under one name it belongs to an obligatory class and under another to a forbidden class (*PM* I, 236–43), and in a further analysis of the considerations involved in determining the particular person who ought to do a beneficial act when any of a number of persons could do it. (*PM* I, 243 ff.) We cannot follow the ramifications of Smith's ingenious discussions, nor can we examine his replies to critics of utilitarianism (*PM* II, 120–98), in which appeal to rules plays an important part. We can only note that in terms of a grasp of the conceptual issues concerned in working out a coherent rule-utilitarianism, he was considerably in advance of any of his contemporaries,[5] and regret that no one ever tried to build on his work.

ii. *J. S. Mill: Philosophy and Society*

The fortunes of utilitarianism as a philosophical doctrine during the forty years following the publication of the work of Austin and Alexander Smith were determined almost entirely by the writings of John Stuart Mill. Not only did he have a position, as heir to the leadership of the philosophic radicals, from which he could command serious attention; he also possessed genuine philosophic capacity, unlike most of the Benthamites, and he acquired a clear and readable style. Mill's first important essay on ethics was his 1835 attack on Sedgwick; he included an significant chapter on morality in the *Logic* in 1843, and the discussions there of free will also bear on issues of ethics; he attacked Whewell at length in 1852; and in 1854 he drafted *Utilitarianism* which, after revision in 1859, was published in 1861. Mill's development and his views have been copiously discussed, and there is no need to review the material yet again. Still, something must be said about his position on the role of philosophy, and particularly moral philosophy, in his society and age, and about some of the criticisms of utilitarianism Mill felt himself called upon to meet. After that we shall try to show where his reworking of utilitarianism left the theory in the eyes of its critics.

Underlying Mill's many interests, shaping his aims, and influencing the ways in which he tried to achieve them, is a theory of historical change and of the conditions of social stability. Mill did not originate the theory—he learned it from the French Saint-Simonians—but he accepted it early in his career, and his understanding of the importance of moral philosophy is shaped in accordance with it.

History, on this theory, proceeds in a series of alternating periods. Although the details of the course of events in any period are unique, there are only two kinds of period, the organic and the critical. In an organic period, society is stable

---

[5] The English littérateur William Smith's *Discourse on Ethics of the School of Paley* (1839), which Mill admired, gives a clear account of the associationist theory of the moral sense, and invokes rules to explain how a conscience formed by society can none the less lead to judgements opposed to current social opinion.

and well organized; it is run by those with ability, and united by a widely accepted set of opinions. Those who make and change public opinion are a small but cohesive body—like the clergy of the Middle Ages—whose views, accepted by the masses as authoritative, provide a framework within which all particular issues may be discussed. In a critical period, by contrast, the men in power are not the men with ability, and the men who form public opinion are not agreed among themselves. Consequently the old bonds of social cohesion begin to loosen. Men start to think for themselves, refusing to accept beliefs on authority. The presuppositions of discussion are lost, and society splits ever more rapidly into factions and parties not united by any common concerns or shared viewpoints. A stable society can emerge only when a new framework of accepted beliefs re-establishes its authority.

It is clear that, on this theory, opinion plays a major role in bringing about social change and in providing social stability. Changes in fundamental beliefs make for changes in society, agreement in basic opinions is necessary for stability. Mill explains this aspect of the theory in several places[6] but nowhere with so clear an indication of its importance for moral philosophy as in an essay written in 1834. The essay is framed as a reply to criticisms made by a Frenchman, one M. Chales, of Bulwer-Lytton's *England and the English*. The point to which Mill is replying, however, is also one made by Thomas Carlyle.

'Ages of Heroism', Carlyle wrote in his 1831 essay 'Characteristics', 'are not ages of Moral Philosophy; Virtue, when it can be philosophised of, . . . is sickly and beginning to decline.' M. Chales had, in a similar vein, praised England for its lack of moral philosophy: the absence of its shows, so he said, that the English are not decadent. Mill replies[7] that the reasoning is poor and the conclusion false. It may be true that moral philosophy does not arise until a nation enters a period of decay, a 'critical' period; but this is because at such a time the people are already without a unifying doctrine. 'There never was, and never will be, a virtuous people', Mill asserts, 'where

---

[6] Cf. *The Spirit of the Age* (1831), ed. F. A. Hayek, Chicago, 1942; *System of Logic*, Bk. VI, ch. x.

[7] The quotations in the remainder of this paragraph are from Mill's 'Letter from an Englishman to a Frenchman', in the *Monthly Repository*, N.S. vol. viii, 1834, pp. 394–5.

there is not unanimity, or an agreement nearly approaching to it, in their notions of virtue.' Public immorality is worst in sceptical eras, and it is in sceptical eras, when old views are being shaken and are widely seen to be weakening, that philosophy is most likely to be 'in vogue'. Mill thinks all this is happening in Germany and in France. In England, unfortunately, he says, though all the diversities of moral opinion are present, there is no moral philosophy, 'simply because we do not philosophise upon anything'. But how, Mill asks, are we to get out of this predicament?

I wish M. Chales would point out to us how, except by the inquiries and studies which he condemns, we can ever recover from the state which he laments, how except through moral philosophy we can ever hope to arrive again at unity in our moral convictions, the necessary preliminary to any elevation of the standard of our practice. Unless, indeed, we may permit ourselves to hope for a fresh revelation from heaven . . .

The importance of a consensus on basic moral beliefs is clearly, on this view, very considerable, and the need for good moral philosophy during a critical period is as great. Carlyle, like Hazlitt, distrusted too much reliance on conscious rational thought. Mill, after a short period of submission to Carlyle's influence, reaffirmed the necessity of it. His own period, he thinks, is a critical one; and his own task, as he sees it, is to aid his times as a philosopher, not as a mystic or poet, giving a rational synthesis of beliefs, not an imaginative one. Moreover, there is no going back. The lessons of the critics of the old consensus must be absorbed, and a new set of beliefs must be developed which will be fit to serve as the basis for a new organic period.

Mill seems to have had little doubt as to the foundations on which a new social doctrine should be set. Raised a Benthamite utilitarian and an empiricist by a doctrinaire father who had lost his early religious beliefs,[8] Mill never really wavered in his

[8] See Alexander Bain, *James Mill*, 1882, pp. 88–91. Bain adds that 'Bentham never in so many words publicly avowed himself an atheist, but he was so in substance . . . As a legislator, he had to allow a place for Religion; but he made use of the Deity, as Napoleon wished to make use of the Pope, for sanctioning whatever himself chose, in the name of Utility, to prescribe. John Austin', he comments, 'followed on the same tack', but neither of the Mills did.

basic allegiances. His friendship with John Stirling and with F. D. Maurice taught him to appreciate Coleridge's point of view, and Carlyle brought other insights to him, but none of them altered his position on fundamentals. His father had early taught him the importance of sensitivity to the problem of obtaining agreement among people widely divided in their opinions, and his friendly experiences with the opponents of utilitarianism gave him a better idea of their objections to his view than the older Benthamites possessed. He was convinced he could transform the party ideology of the Benthamites into a comprehensive theory and prove that it need not be merely a source of divisive newspaper slogans but could serve as the principle of a unifying social doctrine. A reworking of utilitarian moral philosophy, showing how it could overcome objections and incorporate the main positive views of its critics, was an essential part of this programme.

iii. *Some Further Criticisms of Utilitarianism*

Carlyle, reviewing a book on German poetry of which he thought poorly, calls the author a Philistine, and adds, characteristically, 'With us, such men usually take to Politics, and become Code-makers and Utilitarians.' Like Hazlitt and Macaulay, he thinks the Benthamites despise the arts. More thoroughly and systematically than Hazlitt, he takes them to be representative of the worst aspect of the age in their reliance on external means of bringing about moral improvement, in their degrading man by making it appear that pleasure is his only proper goal, and in their atheistic refusal to see the deeper spiritual meaning of life. Ours is not a religious age, he says, analysing the 'Signs of the Times' in 1829; we no longer set an infinite value on virtue, we treat it as mere 'calculation of the profitable'. We no longer strive for internal perfection of the human soul, we look for 'external combinations and arrangements, for institutions' which will solve the problem, 'Given a world of knaves, to produce an honesty from their united actions.'[9] The demand for political reform is typical of our present reliance on mechanisms, and shows that Reid did not prevent the mechanistic philosophy of Hume from becoming

---

[9] 'Historic Survey of German Poetry' (1831), *Works*, vi. 181; 'Characteristics' (1831), *Works*, vi. 225–6; 'Signs of the Times' (1829), *Works*, v. 471–92.

dominant in Britain. We have everything backwards: 'it is the noble People that makes the noble government; rather than conversely', he says, but the philosopher of our age—Bentham —teaches, not 'the necessity and infinite worth of moral goodness' and our independence of circumstances, but that 'the strength and dignity of the mind within us is itself the creature and consequence' of circumstances. 'Practically considered, our creed is Fatalism': what wonder that we have replaced the old 'worship of the Beautiful and the Good' with 'a calculation of the profitable'.

Carlyle continues his attack on utilitarianism in many of his other works, most notably perhaps in *Sartor Resartus*, where his spokesman, passing through doubt and despair, asks whether Duty is 'no divine Messenger and Guide, but a false earthly phantasm, made up of Desire and Fear . . . ? . . . Is the heroic inspiration we name Virtue but some Passion; some bubble of the blood, bubbling in the direction others *profit* by? I know not,' he soliloquizes, 'only this I know. If what thou namest Happiness be our true aim, then are we all astray.' These gloomy thoughts occur to him when the mood of the 'Everlasting Nay' has hold of him, when the whole universe appears to him a vast soulless machine, a dismal factory in which it is appropriate that the Utilitarian 'Word monger and Motive grinder' should in his 'Logic-mill' (the pun cannot be accidental) try to 'grind out Virtue from the husks of Pleasure'. But when the deeper, truer mood of the 'Everlasting Yea' comes on him, he turns angrily away from the quest for happiness, and in a famous apostrophe to himself, exclaims, 'Foolish soul! What Act of Legislature was there that *thou* shouldst be happy? A little while ago thou hadst no right to *be* at all.' There is, he sees, in man, 'a HIGHER than Love of Happiness . . . Love not Pleasure,' he urges, 'Love God. This is the Everlasting Yea . . .' And Carlyle goes on to preach *entbehren*, 'doing without', and the doctrine of finding one's proper work and doing it, mindless of the outcome. Only so can we overcome the unreligious rationalism of the present age. In the divinely inspired promptings of the soul, especially those in which we are urged to recognize our superior and obey him, we hear the voice of God; and we are to obey it.[10]

[10] *Sartor Resartus* (1833–4), ii. 7 and 9, *Works*, iv. 110–15, 125–33.

These vast prophetic roarings impressed Carlyle's generation to an extent that may seem unaccountable to a drier philosophical mind. Fortunately we need only try to see what a philosopher might make of them if, like Mill, he were convinced that a reply, in a philosophical tone of voice, was not only possible but necessary. Looked at in this uninspired fashion, they seem to reduce to rather common objections. That virtue is treated in utilitarianism as a means, not as an end, and is thus given a degraded status; that the denial of free will emphasizes the similarity between mechanical and human action and demeans humanity; that reliance on social institutions shows more concern for earthly happiness than for perfection of soul—stripped of Carlyle's unsurpassable brilliance of statement, there seems to be little here that had not been said before. But Mill took Carlyle to be speaking for untold thousands of inarticulate people who were losing a traditional Christian belief and looking for something with which to replace it. He was anxious to prevent anti-utilitarian prepossessions from closing their minds to his views; and he shaped his presentation of his doctrine, consequently, with a number of Carlylean objections to it in mind.

He had also to ward off a number of more technical philosophical objections, vigorously propounded by Whewell. They are not always well-founded, and some of those directed at Bentham rest on misunderstandings. The better criticisms add up however to a challenge which was at least powerful enough to move Mill to try to reply.

When discussing Paley, Whewell[11] raises three points which are not quite commonplace. The first is barely suggested: the notion of 'ought' or 'obligation' is not the same as that of 'being obliged', if the latter is taken to mean 'being forced or compelled', but Paley confuses them (*Lec. Hist.*, p. 171). The other two are given a little more fully. One attacks Paley's view of the use of general rules. Whewell allows that this view removes most of the force of the criticism that utilitarianism leads to immoral results, but it does so only at serious cost to the consistency of the system. The principle that 'the consideration

---

[11] In *EMP*, Whewell gives a brief summary of objections to Paley in the Supplement, Ch. 3. Here we deal only with the criticisms published in the *History*, to which references are given in the text with the abbreviation *Lec. Hist.*

of consequences is to be applied by means of general rules' cannot, Whewell thinks, be proven within a utilitarian framework. For the principle of utility is 'the happiness resulting from each action', and on that principle moral rules should be binding only when the acts they dictate lead to happiness. 'We have no right, on such principles,' says Whewell, 'to demand for them any greater generality, any greater rigour, than we can establish by showing such a subservience' to the end. Paley in fact tends to make the following of rules itself into a separate source of justification of action. This may bring his results into line with common sense morality, but it also gives up the position that consequences alone justify acts. (*Lec. Hist.*, pp. 173–4.) As a final thrust, Whewell draws on his theory of scientific progress to point a contrast between the use of principles in the advanced sciences and the use the utilitarians claim to make of their principle. We may compare the utilitarian principle with the principle of least action in mechanics. When that principle was initially discovered, attempts were repeatedly made to calculate the motions of bodies directly from it. The attempts always failed, and no one now tries to use the principle for such calculations, although the principle is at the foundation of the science. Similarly, though it is true that right acts do produce the greatest good, no one can use such a general principle for direct calculation of the rightness of particular acts. Whewell expands this point in a passage in which, moving beyond his concern with Paley, he sketches what he hopes to be able to do when he produces his own system of morality. He outlines what he takes to be the real pattern of advance in the sciences and claims he will be able to construct his system on the same model. In effect he is challenging not just Paley but the secular utilitarians as well with the claim that their ethic is not, as they think, the sole scientific one. It represents an early, bungling, stage in the development of a science. His will be at a more advanced stage. (*Lec. Hist.*, pp. 185–9.)

The criticisms of Bentham take up the same points again, approaching them, this time, from a stress on the difficulties of making the utilitarian calculations. Whewell emphasizes the complexities of the comparisons that must be made in such calculations rather than the problems of determining the consequences of a single act. If one is tempted to lie, one must weigh the—let it be supposed—positive results of the single lie against the possible damage to a whole system of norms and expectations: this is the node of the difficulty. The Benthamite cannot consistently insist on our following the rule even though the known results of doing so are less pleasant than the known results of breaking it. And he cannot argue that there are other utilitarian reasons for following rules rigorously—for instance, that doing so helps maintain habits of virtuous action—for the Benthamite should deny that inflexible habits are valuable. The only virtuous habits, on his view, are those of being just or truthful or chaste, not always, but 'when it produces more pleasure than pain'. (*Lec. Hist.*, pp. 224–7.)

A further drawback to the utilitarian inability to avoid paradox by appeal to rules is, in Whewell's view, that the utilitarian principle cannot be used to give an explication of common-sense morality. His own conviction is that the plain man's morality is not based simply upon beliefs as to what is pleasant or painful. It recognizes other sources of right and wrong. Bentham, he points out, has never tried to show in any systematic way that this is not so. And Bentham's vehement denunciations of ordinary moral language suggest that he realizes the substance of the difficulty, and takes refuge from it in the position that ordinary morality needs reforming, not systematizing. (*Lec. Hist.*, pp. 235–40.) One may say, of course, that Bentham would hardly have considered this a serious objection. But Mill, anxious to show that utilitarianism is sympathetic to the best and wisest of human thought and is not a nest of paradoxes, needed to say something more.

There is one particular result of Benthamism which Whewell thinks so paradoxical that it is bound to lead us to recognize to what an extreme Bentham's urge for simplification has led him, and to see how utterly without foundation his view is. The fact that men are different from animals, from a moral point of view, entails, Whewell believes, that although we certainly have duties toward animals and ought not to treat them cruelly, we are not obligated to treat them as exactly on a par with people. Bentham however does and must think that their pleasures and pain are to be weighed equally with those of humans. This leads to the absurd result that 'we may sacrifice the happiness of men, provided we can in that way produce an overplus of pleasure to cats, dogs and hogs, not to say lice and fleas'. (*Lec. Hist.*, p. 237.) The problem arises first because Bentham refuses to admit any distinction of principle between human pleasure and animal pleasure, and second because he insists on deriving all moral judgements from one principle alone. Whewell himself is willing to admit that the principle of increasing human happiness is both 'universally allowed, and in some measure self-evident'. The principle of increasing all happiness, however, he thinks is neither self-evident nor generally accepted. 'If we are asked', he pronounces, 'to take this as the ground of our morality, we must at least require some reason why we should adopt such a foundation principle. No such answer is given; and thus, the whole Benthamite doctrine rests, it seems, on no visible foundation at all.' (*Lec. Hist.*, p. 238.)

If these objections—that utilitarianism leads to paradoxical and shocking moral conclusions, that it cannot escape them by appealing to inflexible rules, that it cannot systematize our pretheoretical moral convictions, that it offers no proof of its first principle and no way of using it—were not exactly novel, their reiteration was a reminder that no generally accepted answer to them had been given either. Mill's lengthy attack on Whewell elicited a careful and courteous rebuttal,[12] which made it plain that Mill had not always bothered to understand his antagonist and certainly did not turn the edge of all his criticisms. Of the many issues debated by the two, only one need be noticed here. Mill is evidently anxious to vindicate for utilitarianism the right to appeal to rules less general than the basic principle. He describes Bentham as employing the basic principle first of all to construct a group of 'secondary or middle principles, capable of serving as premises for a body of ethical doctrine not derived from existing opinions, but fitted to be their test'. Without these, Mill thinks, any universal principle is of little value. Bentham's merit is to have 'deduced a set of subordinate generalities from utility alone' and used them to test 'all particular questions'.[13] To Whewell's charge that utilities cannot be calculated, Mill replies that they can—

12 *EMP*, Supplement, Ch. 2.
13 'Dr. Whewell on Moral Philosophy' (1852), *Diss.* ii. 461.

sometimes in individual cases, always if we examine 'classes of cases', in short if we consider the consequences of everyone following set rules. But Mill does not comment on Whewell's charge that appeal to rules is inconsistent with utilitarianism, nor does he offer any basis for warranting such an appeal, not even the implicit generality of moral judgements. He goes out of his way in fact to claim that it is one of the virtues of 'utility' as a moral principle that 'a moralist can deduce from it his whole system of ethics, without calling to his assistance any foreign principle'.[14] All of these remarks suggest that on his view the utilitarian does not obtain his secondary rules by incorporating the morality of common sense. Replying to Sedgwick's claim that utility is too uncertain a guide because of the impossibility of calculating consequences, Mill says that it would indeed be uncertain if each man had to do his own calculating, but that 'everyone directs himself in morality, as in all his conduct, not by his own unaided foresight, but by the accumulated wisdom of all former ages, embodied in traditional aphorisms'. Though he is critical of the conservative tendency of the traditional wisdom, he nevertheless co-opts it as a moral ready-reckoner or 'Nautical Almanac'.[15] In a fragment of 1837 he specifically praises the aphorisms in which the wisdom of the ages is transmitted, and dismisses the criticism that they are unsystematic as beside the point. Philosophy may systematize them, he says, but 'we need not wait till this is done, before we . . . act upon them . . . . these detached truths', he adds in a striking comment, 'are at once the materials and the tests of philosophy itself; since philosophy is not called in to prove them, but may very justly be required to account for them'.[16] Mill's views on the relation between the secondary rules needed by utilitarians and the rules offered by common-sense morality were evidently not fully worked out by the time of his reply to Whewell. In any event if must have been apparent to him that the only really effective reply would be a positive account of utilitarianism. Within two years he had drafted one.

A few other contemporary criticisms may have touched Mill.[17]

---

[14] *Diss.* ii. 476–7, 497.
[15] 'Professor Sedgwick's Discourse on the Studies of the University of Cambridge', (1835) *Diss.* i. 145–7.   [16] 'Aphorisms' (1837), *Diss.* i. 207.
[17] In 1854 Dickens published *Hard Times*, a novel meant in part as an attack on the Benthamites. Although largely hitting at the *laissez-faire* economics associated,

In 1855 Frances Power Cobbe published her popularization of Kantian ethics, *An Essay on the Intuitive Morals*. Largely expository, and more enthusiastic than accurate, it devotes only a few pages to attacking utilitarianism. The main point is that the utilitarian principle is unproven, but Cobbe goes on to say that she will show that 'utilitarianism itself rest on an Intuition' (*EIM* i. 69). Her argument, when untangled from some confusion about the notion of obligation, is the old one, that a chain of reasons must have an end, and that if the end is not to be at an arbitrary point, it must be at an intuitively evident one. She does not herself think the utilitarian principle is evident; but her insistence that it could only be supported by an appeal to intuition may have given Mill one more reason to try to show how this unpalatable conclusion could be avoided.

A more influential writer than Cobbe entered the discussion when James Martineau reviewed Mill's collected *Dissertations and Discussions* in 1859.[18] Martineau devotes himself primarily to topics in logic and epistemology, and there, as in his briefer comments on ethics, he states his disagreements without much argument to support them. He appreciates Mill's efforts to find a basis for attributing value to self-development, but he thinks they fail. If morality is always to be a means to the end of happiness, there can be no foundation for attributing value to some other end which might conflict with it. One might have a taste for the other end, but that offers no grounds for saying the other end is morally authoritative. (pp. 512–17.) This is in effect Whewell's objection to the utilitarian use of secondary rules, transposed to what Martineau thinks vital, the perfection of the self or soul. Martineau goes on to complain that Mill stresses the 'outer' side of morality and neglects the 'inner': the latter is always treated as a dependent variable. (pp. 527 ff.) Even the voice of conscience is treated as a compendium of what one has heard from others, not as having its own original authority. In fact, Martineau thinks, there is no place in any utilitarian and empiricist position for truly moral

via the 'Manchester school', with Benthamism, it must have made Mill anxious to clarify the issues. See the useful discussion by Raymond Williams, 'Dickens and Social Ideas', in Michael Slater, ed., *Dickens 1970*, Chapman and Hall, 1970.

[18] Page references in this paragraph are to Martineau's review, *ERA*, vol. iii. The essay appeared in October 1859, possibly too late to affect the text of *Utilitarianism* although Mill's letters show he read it.

authority. Bentham's personal benevolence led him to identify his own happiness with the greatest happiness of the greatest number, but 'even his disciples have felt it to be one of the greatest *lacunae* of his system' that there is no 'scientific proof' moving one from his motivational doctrine to his moral principle. It is all left to the chances of an individual's tastes, which in the end leaves it within the limits of 'the selfish system'. (p. 529.) Martineau ends by regretting Mill's intemperate attitude toward the whole idea of intuitional principles. Mill thinks them necessarily reactionary in their political and social tendency: why? Is there any inherent impossibility in having a socially progressive intuitional morality? (p. 530.) It is a shrewd question, suggesting that Mill's hostility to intuitions, one of the major limitations of his purely philosophical imagination, is a result of political considerations.

iv. *The Other Utilitarians*

As *Utilitarianism* was appearing in parts in *Fraser's Magazine* during 1861, Mill wrote to the French translator of his *Representative Government* to correct a misapprehension:

> Like many of the French, you appear to be of the opinion that the *idea of Utility* is in England *the dominant Philosophy*. It is nothing of the sort. I understand that one might see in that doctrine a certain analogy with the spirit of the English nation. But in fact it is, and it has almost always been, very unpopular there. Most English writers do not only deny it, they insult it: and the school of Bentham has always been regarded (I say it with regret) as an insignificant minority.[19]

Mill, as we have seen reason to believe, was correct; but F. H. Bradley's description fifteen years later of 'modern Utilitarianism' as 'our most fashionable philosophy' (*Eth. Stud.*, p. 103) was probably not less accurate. Mill's essay was a major factor in bringing about the change. At least it would be hard to attribute it to any other account of the doctrine. None of the earlier versions had proved able to convince a large reading public that secular utilitarian morality had to be taken seriously. Before Mill's *Utilitarianism* there were only two further

[19] *The Later Letters of John Stuart Mill, 1849–1873*, ed. Francis E. Mineka and Dwight N. Lindley, Toronto & London, 1972, p. 745. Letter to Charles Dupont-White, 10 Oct. 1861, in French. My translation.

important works that might have helped to do so, though for quite different reasons neither did. One was by Herbert Spencer, the other by Alexander Bain.[20]

After the initial publication of *Utilitarianism*, Spencer wrote to its author complaining of the treatment accorded to his *Social Statics*. The book, he said, is not opposed to the utilitarian theory, as Mill had suggested in a footnote to his fifth chapter: indeed it takes happiness as the ultimate end.[21] Spencer was right, but a brief look at *Social Statics*[22] makes it all too easy to see why Mill was more anxious to disavow association with it than to claim it as the work of an ally. The book opens with an attack on the greatest happiness principle for its vagueness and its inability to yield absolutely certain and definite directives. The notion of happiness is indeterminate due to variation in human nature, Spencer says, and we are ignorant of how to attain it. Besides, the utilitarians assume that governments will always be needed in society—a mistaken generalization from one stage of progress to all (*Soc. St.*, pp. 5, 8, 13). Having thus disposed of the expediency philosophy, he turns to the moral sense position. All action to satisfy physical needs is guided by instinct, since reason is too feeble to serve that purpose. There is therefore good reason to suppose that our social needs are also served by an instinct. And so they are: the moral instinct, or moral sense. (*Soc. St.*, p. 19.) Even the Benthamite must admit the existence of such a sense. For he tells us that we ought to seek the greatest happiness and implies that everyone has an equal right to happiness; and he could only learn about the equal right from an 'innate perception' or an intuition. (*Soc. St.*, pp. 22–3.) The office of the moral sense has, however, been misunderstood even by its advocates. Its task is only 'to originate a moral axiom': the development of the details of morality is the function of reason. (*Soc. St.*, pp. 29–30.)

[20] During the 1850s the relevant writings of Hume, Hutcheson, Bentham, James Mill, and John Austin were out of print. Academic handbooks, such as they were (e.g. Jones), were all anti-utilitarian. The one other writer to develop a substantial utilitarian theory was George Ramsay, whose *Enquiry into the Principles of Human Happiness and Human Duty* (1843) presents a diffuse theological version of the doctrine, together with lengthy discussions of happiness.

[21] The letter was first published in Bain's *Mental and Moral Science*, 1868, pp. 721–2. See Ch. 14, sec. i, below.

[22] References are given in the text to page-numbers of the first edition, 1850, with the abbreviation *Soc. St.* Later editions of this work were much altered.

In setting up a code, Spencer insists, we must take no account of the present imperfections of human beings or of society. Morality is meant to be a set of rules suitable for 'the guidance of humanity in its highest conceivable perfection'. As geometers consider only perfect points and perfect lines, we must consider only perfect rules for perfect men in a perfect society. (*Soc. St.*, pp. 37–8, 55–7.) Nor is this, even in practical terms, pointless. Human nature is progressive, not constant, and society is also progressive. Evil consists in the maladaptation of the faculties of sentient beings to their surroundings; all maladaptations tend to disappear; and therefore we may conclude that evil is 'evanescent', and that perfectibility, far from being a dream, is the law of nature. (*Soc. St.*, pp. 59–64.)

It is an admitted truth, Spencer says, that God wills our happiness; and it is plain that duty just means what God wills. But even though morality and happiness are two sides of the same coin, it does not follow that we should take general happiness as our direct aim. We should determine rules of action scientifically by finding out the conditions necessary for the attainment of happiness. Spencer thinks we can find four such rules: justice, negative beneficence, positive beneficence, and self-concern. (*Soc. St.*, pp. 66–9.) He proposes to elaborate only upon justice, and his mode of deriving the rule will give a sample of his general method of proceeding. Duty means God's will, and God wills our happiness. Now our happiness comes from the exercise of our faculties; the exercise of our faculties requires us to have the freedom to exercise them; and therefore everyone must have the right to exercise them freely. Since there exist many people, each person's right to this freedom must be limited by being compatible with a like exercise by everyone else. And this is the principle of justice. (*Soc. St.*, pp. 76–8.) It is also the axiom to the truth of which the moral sense attests. (*Soc. St.*, p. 91.) It cannot be limited by any other principle, and it enables us to derive a large number of very specific moral rules. These turn out to be rules upon which a *laissez-faire* theorist of the purest sort would look with great approval, and the bulk of the book is devoted to their elucidation.

Spencer thinks that because the Benthamites as well as the moral sense philosophers must rest their views on his intuitive principle he has 'the strongest possible evidence' in favour of it, namely 'the testimony of all parties'. (*Soc. St.*, p. 94.) Yet another point in its favour is that it provides a synthesis of the hitherto conflicting views of different philosophers. (*Soc. St.*, p. 458.) His assurance of the soundness of his view is thus quite complete.

Spencer's muddled eclecticism and dogmatic eccentricity plainly made his work out of the question as a suitable popular account of utilitarianism. Bain was neither grossly muddled nor eccentric, but he did not produce a full-scale work on ethics. His most sustained positive contribution to the subject occurs in a long chapter in *The Emotions and the Will*, which was published in 1859 with Mill's aid and encouragement.[23] Much of the chapter is devoted to criticism of views opposed to utilitarianism. Whewell in particular is singled out and attacked, largely for his Platonizing assumptions about ideas and truths. Bain here uses his own interesting theory of belief to provide an alternative nominalist position which is, he thinks, in accordance with utilitarianism. He goes on to offer an explanation of observable uniformities in the moral beliefs accepted in different ages and societies, as the result of observation of obvious utilities and of the general human tendency to impose uniformity which shows itself even in unimportant matters. His point is that no appeal to a moral sense is needed to explain these uniformities, a familiar enough point in the associationist tradition; but his stress on the rational perception of utilities in explaining positive moralities may have helped Mill toward his final acceptance of common-sense morality as providing the secondary principles needed in a utilitarian theory. Though Bain proceeds to give a brief account of the principle of utility, he offers no reason in support of it; and the rest of the chapter is mainly devoted to arguing that the moral feelings are best explained as internalizations of the social judgements which we are made to accept by penalties and rewards from childhood on. Bain offers an account of how the conscience so formed can come to resist social opinion and give us independent moral feelings, but except in detail he adds nothing to the Hartleyan line exemplified in the work of James Mill, William Smith, and others.

[23] In this paragraph, Ch. XV of *The Emotions and the Will* (1859) is discussed.

v. *Mill's* Utilitarianism *and its Reception*

In his mature writings Mill made little appeal to Saint-Simonian theories, but he did not cease to think that a coherent ethic, acceptable to a wide public and with a sound philosophical basis, was vitally needed as an instrument of social progress. Thus in 1847 he urged John Austin to write 'a systematic treatise on morals', saying that 'until it is done we cannot expect much improvement in the common standard of moral judgments and sentiments'.[24] Nor did he cease to think earlier versions of utilitarianism philosophically inadequate: we find him in 1854 telling an inquirer that 'ethics as a branch of philosophy is still to be created'.[25] His own presentation of utilitarianism was undoubtedly meant in part to remove popular antipathy to and suspicion of the doctrine. It also had another purpose. He believed that the deepest aspects of public opinion are formed by the influence of the intellectuals, whose views, when unified, slowly and enduringly go to shape the social consensus. *Utilitarianism* was therefore designed also to convince the 'clerisy', including the philosophers, of the soundness of Mill's moral outlook.

This dual purpose helps us to understand both the style and the content of *Utilitarianism*. The *System of Logic* shows that he did not hesitate to write technical treatises. The importance of the *Logic* in Mill's view, however, was that it might teach sound methods of thought to the few who are authorities and who make public opinion. On moral matters everyone must do his own thinking and must have a personal grasp of the basic principles: hence the more popular form of the book on ethics. Even Mill's strong objections to all forms of intuitional moral doctrine may have had one root in the fear that the general public could not make the discrimination, which a philosopher might, between a kind of intuitionism which allows for, and a kind which excludes, improvement in moral beliefs. There is at any rate no question of Martineau's correctness in locating political and social sources of Mill's rejection of intuitionism. If the explicit statements in the essay on Whewell do not suffice to show it, the *Autobiography* makes it plain:

[24] *The Earlier Letters of John Stuart Mill, 1812–1848*, ed. Francis E. Mineka, Toronto & London, 1963, p. 511.
[25] *Later Letters*, p. 235.

The notion that truths external to the mind may be known by intuition or consciousness, independently of observation and experience, is . . . in these times, the great intellectual support of false doctrines and bad institutions. By the aid of this theory, every inveterate belief and every intense feeling, of which the origin is not remembered, is enabled to dispense with the obligation of justifying itself by reason, and is erected into its own all-sufficient voucher and justification. There never was such an instrument devised for consecrating all deep seated prejudices.

One aim of the *Logic*, Mill continues, was to deprive intuitionism in morals of the support it derives from the belief that intuitions are indispensable in mathematics and science. He recognizes that 'to deprive a mode of thought so strongly rooted in human prejudices and partialities of its mere speculative support, goes but a very little way towards overcoming it; but', he goes on, hopefully, 'prejudices can only be combatted by philosophy.'[26] In that combat *Utilitarianism* was designed to carry out several tasks. It was, to begin with, to disarm its readers' objections and to convince them that they were in large part utilitarians already. Mill's definite acceptance of common-sense morality as the source of the middle axioms needed for applying the basic principle; his distinction of higher and lower pleasures;[27] his explanation of justice in utilitarian terms; his modifications of egoistic psychology; his insistence on the importance of individual character; his attempt to show how virtue might become part of the ultimate end—all these were meant to remove the taint of paradox from the theory, and to draw in those Christians who held that the care of the soul is of more moment than the enjoyment of life. If this much could be achieved then the arguments showing that the basic principle could be supported without appeal to intuitions, and the general display of the simplicity, power, and coherence of the theory, might convince the reader that utilitarianism really was the best available rational explication of his own best convictions. And if so, then the standard the theory supplies for systematic rectification of accepted opinion might be expected to be put to work.

[26] J. S. Mill, *Autobiography*, Ch. VII, near beginning.
[27] It has been suggested that this distinction was made to enable Mill to reply to Whewell's objections about giving equal weight to the pleasures of animals: see H. B. Acton, 'Animal Pleasures', *Massachusetts Review*, vol. 21, spring 1961, pp. 541–8.

Though Mill shared the desire of his predecessors to improve common-sense morality, strategic considerations moved him away from the kind of direct attack upon it which had been common in their writings. This alteration of the expected Benthamite stance led to a noticeable change in the common understanding of utilitarian theory within a dozen years of the appearance of *Utilitarianism*. A brief review of the reception of Mill's essay will give us a good idea of the problems which were commonly thought to remain in the position he defended. The matter is of particular interest to us, because it gives a good indication of some of the main difficulties in utilitarianism which must have been known to Sidgwick when he was working out his own moral philosophy.

Published philosophical discussions of Mill's essay during the first dozen or more years following its publication were almost entirely hostile. For a year or two it received no attention at all; by the middle of the 1860s a few criticisms had appeared; and the turning-point in admission of its importance did not come until the end of the decade. It was brought about by the appearance of a book which caused more discussion of utilitarianism in the popular periodicals than the doctrine ever received again, the *History of European Morals from Augustus to Charlemagne* (1869) by the historian W. E. H. Lecky. Lecky's *History* was reviewed in all the major journals and many of the minor ones, and most of the reviewers concentrated on his massive first chapter, a lively survey of the debate between the two schools of ethics. Lecky himself was vehemently opposed to utilitarianism. His chapter is simply a compilation of all the standard criticisms of it. He ignored Mill almost completely, and so did some of the reviewers. But most even of those who sympathized with Lecky's stance were impatient with his carelessness, and a large element in their impatience was due to his failure to come to grips with what was by then increasingly accepted as the best version of the theory he was attacking—Mill's.

We cannot here cover all the criticisms that were offered of Mill during the period prior to the publication of Sidgwick's *Methods*, but a look at the comment on four main topics will suffice for our purposes.[28] We shall consider Mill's views on

---

[28] To simplify citations, a checklist of publications on Mill's *Utilitarianism* between 1861 and 1876 is given as the second part of Bibliography II.

the derivability of moral notions from non-moral ones; his so-called 'proof' of the principle of utility; his distinction between higher and lower pleasures; and his position on the use of common-sense morality as the source of the middle axioms of a utilitarian ethic.

James McCosh in 1865 offers the first objection to Mill's account of the derivation of 'the ideas involved in the words *ought, obligation, merit, demerit*', but has no argument to show it mistaken. At the least the rudiments of argument were supplied by two criticisms in the following year, and Lecky adverts to the point rather vaguely.[29] For the first full articulation of the objection we must go to John Grote. His *Examination of the Utilitarian Philosophy*, which Bain called 'the best hostile criticism of Utilitarianism that I am acquainted with',[30] was partly written in 1861 as Mill's essays were appearing in *Fraser's*. Grote had it set up for publication after the appearance of *Utilitarianism* in book form, but he lacked confidence in its value, did not publish it, kept adding to it, and left a tangled mass of manuscripts to his literary executor, who finally brought it out in 1870, four years after his death. It is of particular interest to us because there can be little doubt that Sidgwick would have heard many of the criticisms of Mill in discussion. As we have seen, Grote holds that no true ethical view can be constructed which does not recognize a sharp distinction between the ideal and the actual. To show this in Mill's terms, he asks whether Mill's principle that the promoting of happiness makes an action right can be held to be true in virtue of the meaning of the word 'right'. If this were so, Grote says, it would be hard to see why there are separate words for 'right' and its synonyms. Moreover, the utilitarian principle would not really be a proposition since it would not really join two different ideas.[31] The view that the utilitarian principle is true in virtue of the meaning of 'right' amounts to the view that language would be more truthful if actions were only distinguished from one another in terms of their relation to happiness. Since moral terms do not do this, they could be dropped from the language. But the

---

[29] McCosh, *Stewart*, p. 142; cf. McCosh, *Examination of Mill*, pp. 385–90; Bascom, pp. 442–3, 435 ff.; Mansel, pp. 364–5; Lecky, p. 34.

[30] A. Bain, *John Stuart Mill*, 1882, p. 115.

[31] Grote *Exam.*, pp. 267–8.

consequences of dropping them, Grote says, are not acceptable, for if we did, we should not be able to say why action promotive of happiness 'should be recommended rather than that which is not so: there is no other idea of rightness, goodness, valuableness, than that which belongs to itself'. Without a moral vocabulary, in short, we could neither praise nor give reasons for doing certain actions. We could only say of actions that they are what they are. But, Grote asks, 'if felicific action is better than that which is not felicific, *why* is it better'? There must, he thinks, be 'a moral preferableness of one sort of action to another', which may coincide with the promoting of happiness 'but is not, in the notion of it, the same thing'.[32]

The same sort of point is forcibly made in an essay of 1872 by W. G. Ward.[33] His first aim is to show that the idea of moral goodness is not 'complex and resolvable . . . into simpler elements', but simple. If Mill disagrees, Ward says, then he must take it that 'morally good' means neither more nor less than 'conducive to general enjoyment'. Now ideas of moral goodness and its 'correlatives' are familiar to us all. If we simply consider any of the innumerable commonplace moral propositions in which such ideas figure, we will immediately see that this definition must be wrong. For example, when someone says that man is bound to do what God commands, it is plain that he does not *mean* than man's obedience would minister to general enjoyment, even though this might also be true: the latter is simply a different proposition.

> If [Mill's] theory were true, it would be a simply tautologous proposition to say, that conduct, known by the agent as adverse to general enjoyment, is morally evil. . . . Now . . . the contradictory of a tautologous proposition is simply unmeaning.

But Mill himself would not hold that it is meaningless to say that 'some conduct, known by the agent to be adverse to general enjoyment, may be morally good'; and plainly that proposition is not meaningless. Ward goes on to point out, as Grote did, that this is a general result: 'Arguments entirely similar to those which have here been given would equally suffice to disprove any *other* analysis which might be attempted,

[32] Grote, *Exam.*, pp. 268–9, 275–6.
[33] All quotations in this paragraph are from Ward, pp. 80–7.

of the idea "morally good"; and we conclude, therefore, that this idea is simple and incapable of analysis.' Ward's next step is predictable. If 'morally good' is a simple idea, then it cannot be contained in the conclusion of a syllogism unless it is expressly included in one of the premises. Hence it cannot be the case, as Mill says it is, that all moral judgements are inferential. For if a moral judgement is a conclusion, somewhere its premises must contain the simple idea of goodness, and must therefore contain a moral judgement. The moral premiss, since it cannot be known inferentially, must be known intuitively; for if not, we are off on an infinite regress which would force us to conclude that there is no moral knowledge. But Mill holds that some moral judgements are known to be true. Hence he must admit that there are some intuitively known moral judgements.[34]

In his 1870 review of Grote's *Examination*, Rev. J. Llewellyn Davies remarks that 'the difficulty of obtaining an adequate sense for the word "ought"—of extracting the imperativeness which we associate with the idea of duty—out of the elements of the Utilitarian creed, is so obvious and familiar that no hostile critic could fail to insist upon it'.[35] Our survey of the development of intuitional thought should have made it evident why this was so. It should also lead us to expect sharp criticism of Mill's attempt to provide a rational basis for the utilitarian principle without invoking any intuitively evident principle. And this, indeed, is what we find. Those of the early critics who deal with the 'considerations' presented as capable of 'determining the intellect' to assent to the principle unanimously find them very weak. Some of the now notorious difficulties are noted quite early. R. H. Hutton claims in his 1863 review in *The Spectator* that Mill, although he has abandoned crude psychological egoism, cannot say why we ought to sacrifice our own good to that of others. He needs, Hutton thinks, 'a dictate of unresolved conscience after all to bridge over the chasm from self interest to human interest', and so his theory requires a moral faculty as much as any intuitional

---

[34] Ward had presented the same line of argument in support of ethical intuitionism in lectures he gave at the Roman Catholic training college for priests, St. Edmunds, and published as *On Nature and Grace*, 1860; see esp. pp. 48–70.

[35] Davies, 1870, p. 91.

theory does. The writer of the anonymous book against Mill of 1864 points out—for what seems to be the first time in print—the failure of the analogy between 'visible' and 'desirable', and suggests, not very clearly, that there is a 'fallacy of speech' involved in the argument.[36] The brief notice in the *North American Review* in 1865 says that the 'proof' fails since it 'shows nothing more than that each man desires *his own* happiness', and, not showing that anyone in fact desires the general happiness, gives no reason for saying that the general happiness is desirable. Nor is it shown, the reviewer writes, that 'happiness' and 'desirable' are synonymous.[37] McCosh adverts obscurely to a 'gap . . . which utilitarianism cannot fill up' between pursuing my own good and the obligation to pursue the good of others;[38] but he does not further explain the problem. During the Lecky controversy, R. H. Hutton again touches on the 'proof'. Hutton's concern here is that no basis is given for saying that equal amounts of happiness are equally desirable, regardless of who enjoys them: since each man seeks his own happiness, 'to whom is A's happiness as desirable as an equal lot of B's?'[39] Up to 1870 the other writers do not touch on the topic, and so Grote's criticism is the first full discussion of it to be published, as it was the first to be written.

Mill's general endeavour, Grote says, is in this matter as in others to base the idea on the 'ground of experience and observation'. Hence Mill tried to present his main premiss as a factual one. The premiss is that each man desires what is pleasant to him, a point, Grote remarks, which Mill 'gravely speaks of as a fact which we might possibly doubt'. The general problem with Mill's rationale for his principle is then this:

> Mr. Mill has to prove that 'happiness', as the ideal *summum bonum* of man, is the one thing which ought to regulate his conduct . . . this is not a thing that *any* observation can prove, and it is quite a vain proceeding to set observation . . . to warrant a truism and then to say that in doing so it proves a point entirely different.

Observation cannot show that man desires the desirable 'if by the desirable we mean the *ideally desirable*'; and the truism that

---

[36] Anon, *Utilitarianism Explained*, pp. 63–4.   [37] Thayer, p. 263.
[38] McCosh, *Stewart*, pp. 143–4; *Examination*, pp. 403–4.
[39] Hutton, 1869, p. 71; Mill is not explicitly mentioned.

each desires what he actually desires (and this is all that Mill's allegedly factual premiss comes to, in Grote's view) will not help prove any moral theory.[40] Moreover, even supposing that because each desires his own happiness, his own happiness is a good to him, we can hardly conclude that the happiness of the aggregate is a good to the aggregate: for the conclusion is 'unmeaning' unless the aggregate can desire or act. And if Mill had really shown that in the same way that each man's happiness is his own end, 'the aggregate happiness is an end to *each individual*', much of his philosophizing would have been unnecessary.[41] Grote is aware, unlike some later critics, that Mill does not mean to give a logically conclusive proof. Hence he does not offer further technical consideration of the details of Mill's argument. Most of his chapter is given over to broader considerations of the inadequacies of Mill's treatment of the issue, considerations resting in large part on Grote's view that human nature is as essentially active as it is sentient, so that an idea of the highest good which takes account only of the sentient aspect of it will necessarily be incomplete. But Grote's executor and editor, J. B. Mayor, with a tidier if less perceptive mind, puts into footnotes two technical points. First, there is a formal failure of analogy between 'visible' and 'desirable'; second, Mill commits the formal fallacy of composition in his attempt to move from what is desired *by each* to what is desirable *for all*.[42]

The critics' disapproval of Mill's distinction of higher and lower pleasures is almost as unanimous as their disbelief in his 'proof'. The first, eulogistic, reviewer in the *Westminster* avoids the topic altogether, but the other critics do not. Cliffe Leslie and Hutton raise questions about it; Rands hints that Mill is inconsistent for asserting it; Mansel says that to admit a distinction of kind among pleasures is to admit an independent, non-hedonistic standard; Laurie 'gladly notes' that the move takes Mill away from pure utilitarianism; even Lecky dismisses Mill here, and finds his view 'completely incompatible with utilitarian theory'; Hutton agrees with him; and Grote, too, comments that the admission of a qualitative distinction among pleasures introduces a basic incompatibility into utilitarianism. Only Mill's disciple John Morley is bold enough to defend Mill

[40] Grote, pp. 63–5.   [41] Grote, pp. 70–1.   [42] Grote, pp. 65 n., 70 n.

on the issue. He fails to see any inconsistency arising from the distinction. The *Westminster* reviewer of Grote, though trying to defend Mill, is not so brave. He thinks the qualitative distinction might be reduced to a quantitative one, but goes on to add that the recognition of qualitative differences 'has nothing in it necessarily contradicting the Utilitarian formula'—without, however, making out a case for this claim.[43]

We come, finally, to Mill's acceptance of the rules of common-sense morality as the middle axioms or secondary rules to be used by a utilitarian in applying his principle until the philosopher gives him better ones. Whewell's objection to his move goes unnoticed and unrepeated by Mill's early critics. They treat Mill's view not as raising a question of the internal consistency of utilitarianism, but as dealing with its moral substance. They see that Mill is trying to show that utilitarianism does not entail the paradoxical conclusions to which the Benthamites, to say nothing of Godwin, allowed it to lead them. A few of the critics think he fails, and repeat the old kind of charge. McCosh and Lecky do so. The Rev. Robert Watts calls Mill's doctrine 'morally pernicious' and says, anticipating Bradley, that it leads to Jesuitry. Henry Reeve, editor of the *Edinburgh Review*, blames utilitarianism generally for the increase of political corruption, the decline of commercial good faith, the loss of integrity among manufacturers, the extinction of respect for parental authority in America, the reckless rush to ruin of 'multitudes of young men of the upper classes', and the decay of female decorum.[44] But for the most part what is striking is the absence of such criticisms. Mill has not convinced his antagonists that common-sense morality can best be systematized on the utilitarian principle. Nor are they willing to accept the stronger claim made by Mill's enthusiastic *Westminster* reviewer of 1863, who thinks that 'utility is even already accepted as the only test' of human conduct.[45] But they are prepared to debate the question of the interpretation of common-sense morality, and to debate it, not as partisans in an ideological battle, nor as separated by an impassable moral

---

[43] Leslie, pp. 157–8; Rands, ii. 23–4; Mansel, p. 374; Laurie, pp. 102–3; Lecky, p. 90 n.; Hutton, 1869, pp. 79–83; Grote, Ch. III; Birks, pp. 224 f., 232 f.; Morely, pp. 535–6; Anon., *Westminster Rev.*, 1871, pp. 20–1.

[44] Watts, pp. 34–7; Reeve, p. 21. Birks, 1874, also thinks utilitarianism corrupts.

[45] Anon, *Westminster Rev.*, 1863, p. 63.

gulf from despicable opponents, but as fellow philosophers who, however critical they may be of one another, are working together to solve a common theoretical problem. Instead of treating the divergences between utilitarian conclusions and common-sense convictions as indications that the utilitarian principle makes gross immorality inescapable, they are treated as showing simply that utilitarianism fails to give a satisfactory account of certain moral beliefs which we all hold in common, and which we agree in treating in the way Mill suggests in his remarks on aphorisms—as data which must be adequately systematized by any theory if the theory is to be acceptable.

Intuitionists could carry on serious philosophical discussion only with opponents who were prepared to take common-sense morality seriously. The earlier utilitarians plainly did not meet this condition, and the interest showed by Austin and James Mill in rules was not an interest in the rules accepted already by common sense. John Stuart Mill convinced the intuitionists that he did take common sense seriously, largely because of his incorporation of it into his theory but also because of his much-mocked distinction between higher and lower pleasures. His views on this topic caused his critics to doubt his logical abilities, but persuaded them of what Thayer called his 'noble qualities of mind'. The usual explanation the critics gave of his use of the distinction was that Mill shared with every decent man certain values incompatible with the older hedonism, and was trying to adapt his theory to take them into account. Thus reassured of Mill's moral soundness, they could allow him to be earnest in granting weight to common sense moral convictions and in seeking a theory which would accommodate them. 'Whether or not happiness be the sole criterion of morality,' wrote the Rev. William Kirkus, 'Mr. Mill's conclusions are all on the right side.'[46] With the conclusions agreed upon, only the theory seemed to remain debatable.

Mill, of course, did not think the conclusions were all settled, and hoped that his principle, once accepted, would lead to significant changes in popular morality. Nor did he try to conceal this hope. But this feature of his moral philosophy did not prevent utilitarianism from being treated largely as a theoretical matter for philosophers to discuss. No doubt there was

[46] Thayer, p. 266; cf. Blackie, p. 329. Kirkus, pp. 359–60.

PART II

THE METHODS OF ETHICS

6

The Aims and Scope of *The Methods of Ethics*

SIDGWICK intended *The Methods of Ethics* to be a technical work. He aimed to treat 'ethical science' with 'the same disinterested curiosity to which chiefly we owe the great discoveries of physics', and he explicitly disavowed any desire to make the book edifying. (*ME* 7, vi.) 'It is essentially an attempt to introduce precision of thought into a subject usually treated in a too loose and popular way,' he told a friend, 'and therefore I feel cannot fail to be somewhat dry and repellent.' (*Mem.*, p. 295.) He also meant the book to be systematic. In deliberate opposition to Grote's rejection of system in moral philosophy, Sidgwick held that 'to a philosophical mind it is only a "systematic" manner of thought on such a subject that can approve itself as a "right manner" '. (1871b, 182.) If it was not intended to present a complete system of morality it was certainly meant to represent the best Sidgwick could do to satisfy 'the one impulse (as human as any) which it is the special function of the philosopher to direct and satisfy: the effort after a complete and reasoned synthesis of practical principles'. (1871e, 198.) To understand the way in which the *Methods* is systematic, we must first be clear about what it is and what it is not intended to cover and to establish.

i. *The Focus on Common Sense*

In the Preface to the first edition of the *Methods* Sidgwick tells us that his aim is to give an examination 'both expository and critical, of the different methods of obtaining reasoned convictions as to what ought to be done which are to be found—either explicit or implicit—in the moral consciousness of mankind'. Philosophers, he adds, have from time to time worked up these convictions into 'systems now historical', but his own emphasis is to be on the convictions themselves, not on the systems. He proposes to criticize the different methods 'from a neutral position' and to 'put aside temporarily' the need everyone feels to find the correct method. He is not, in other words, trying to prove that a single method used by common sense is the sole proper one, still less that some common-sense conviction is a fundamental truth. In the Preface to the second edition he expresses in several ways his regret that critics have taken him to be defending some particular moral theory or to be criticizing common-sense morality in a purely hostile way, 'from the outside'.[1] In an effort to prevent such 'misdirection of criticism' in the future, he says, he has altered the wording of passages responsible for it. This general restriction of aims is made equally clear in the text, from the first edition onwards. 'I have refrained', Sidgwick says, 'from expressly attempting any such complete and final solution of the chief ethical difficulties and controversies as would convert this exposition of various methods into the development of an harmonious system.' While he hopes the book will make clear the issues that arise in trying to construct such a system, and is therefore 'led to discuss the considerations which should . . . be decisive in determining the adoption of ethical first principles', his interest is always in 'the processes rather than the results'. (*ME* 7, pp. 13–14.)

These clear, emphatic, and reiterated statements about what is aimed at in the *Methods* indicate that it is a mistake to view the book as primarily a defence of utilitarianism. It is true, of course, that a way of supporting utilitarianism is worked out in detail in the *Methods*, and that there are places in it where Sidgwick seems to be saying quite plainly that utilitarianism is the best available ethical theory. From his other writings we know also that he thinks of himself as committed to utilitarianism, and that he assumes it in analysing specific moral and political issues. Yet it does not follow that the *Methods* itself should be taken simply as an argument for that position. We must try to understand it in a way that makes sense of its author's own explicit account of it. To do so we may begin by asking why he chooses to focus his philosophical ethics on common-sense morality. Our earlier investigations make it possible to give a brief answer.

Historically, as we have seen, common-sense morality had

[1] The criticisms to which Sidgwick refers are those by Bain, *Mind*, o.s. I, 1876; Barratt, *Mind*, o.s. II, 1877; and Bradley, *Hedonism*, 1877.

come by the middle of the 1860s to occupy a central place in the ethical controversies between the 'two schools' of the early Victorian era. Both agreed in accepting it as valid and binding, at least to some extent and on some basis. We have also seen what importance Sidgwick attached to the fact that scientists, working independently, could regularly come to agreement. Philosophers, whom he took to be the counterpart in questions of ethics to scientists, had come to no agreements on theoretical issues, but they seemed to be willing to treat common-sense morality as providing the data against which their theories might be tested. To begin at this point would therefore be to begin with the nearest thing to uncontested matters in ethics. Sidgwick's methodological views support the conclusion thus suggested by historical developments. A complete rational system requires intuitively evident starting-points. Now the dictates of common-sense morality are taken by many, including some philosophers, to be self-evident. It is therefore possible that they provide what is needed, and this possibility must be scrutinized. The ecumenical test, requiring that a theory should elicit wide agreement among those competent to judge it, leads us to the same conclusion. Common-sense morality contains the dictates accepted by 'that portion of mankind which combines adequate intellectual enlightenment with a serious concern for morality'. (*ME* 7, p. 215.) Those who accept it are competent judges, and a theory which generates the conclusions they already accept will naturally obtain a large measure of general assent.[2] The third methodological requirement, internal consistency, in effect serves to pose the problem with which Sidgwick is mainly concerned: to what extent can common-sense morality be systematized on a self-evident basis? A sound and useful answer to this question, he holds, requires that we investigate primarily the methods involved in common-sense morality rather than its specific judgements.

[2] Sidgwick believes there are some radical differences within common-sense morality itself, arising from differences concerning a metaphysical issue. These are discussed in section v of this chapter. He never contemplates the possibility that such differences might arise from social position and be correlated with social class. There seems to be no indication that Sidgwick was aware of, let alone paid any attention to, the kind of criticism a Marxist might give of his assumption that a social consensus is possible in a class society.

ii. *The Relation of Method to Principle*

Sidgwick takes science to provide a paradigm of how to obtain sure progress in knowledge. The methods by which science has achieved this status had been discussed and analysed by many philosophers, not least by Whewell and Mill. Sidgwick particularly admires Mill's main work on method, the *System of Logic*. It was here, he says, that Mill showed his real originality. He took up the task of reconciling the older Aristotelian logic with the Baconian logic which developed as modern science broke away from the dominance of Aristotle. 'It required a rare combination of philosophic insight and comprehensive scientific culture even to conceive definitely the task which Mill set himself', Sidgwick comments, 'and which he at least so far achieved as to revolutionize the study of logic in England.' (1873c, 193.) Mill also suggested that the utilitarian principle provides a method for obtaining rational settlement of moral disagreements, but Sidgwick does not have a high opinion of Mill's work in ethics. Nor does he think Whewell has given us a method where Mill failed. Is it possible to find a rational method which yields agreement on moral matters as reliably as the methods of science generate agreement elsewhere? An interest in this question is one of Sidgwick's reasons for concentrating on method. There are other reasons as well, which emerge from an understanding of what he means when he speaks of 'methods of ethics'. He is, however, not as clear on this topic as one must wish he had been. His statements about what a method is are so scattered and so apparently diverse that one careful critic has accused him of being seriously inconsistent on the matter.[3] The situation, however, is not quite as bad as that.

Sidgwick tells us that a method is a 'rational procedure by which we determine what individual human beings "ought"— or what it is "right" for them—to do'. (*ME* 7, p. 1.) He nowhere gives a similarly general account of what a principle is, and as he frequently speaks of methods 'taking' principles, it may seem that he does not clearly distinguish them. Yet it is not hard to see what he has in mind. Roughly speaking, a principle asserts

[3] Marcus G. Singer, 'The Many Methods of Sidgwick's Ethics', *The Monist*, vol. 58, no. 3, July 1974.

that some property which acts may or may not possess is an ultimate reason for the rightness of acts. A method is a regular practice of using some property of acts as the property from whose presence or absence one infers that specific acts are or are not right. Since a principle says nothing about a procedure for reaching conclusions about the rightness of specific acts, and a method says nothing about the ultimate reason justifying the use of the property through which such conclusions are reached, each plainly requires the other. At times it seems as if Sidgwick has no fixed idea of a systematic relation between principle and method. But we shall find that there is such an idea if we follow his thought on two points. One has to do with the nature of the relation supposed to hold between a method and the principle to which it relates: is this a contingent relation, or a necessary one? The other has to do with the nature of the connection between the rightness of particular acts and the property which we use, in a method, as the indicator of rightness: is the property only a test or sign of the act's being right, or is it a property which makes the act right?

Some of the remarks in I, vi, where principles and methods are discussed are misleading. After comment on a variety of principles and methods apparently used by the plain man, Sidgwick says: 'we find that almost any method may be connected with almost any ultimate reason by means of some—often plausible—assumption.' (*ME* 7, p. 83.) In the first edition this was preceded by the comment that 'we seem to find . . . that there is no necessary connexion between the Method and the Ultimate Reason in any ethical system'. (*ME* 1, p. 64.) But here, as so often in Sidgwick's writings, what we 'seem to find' does not give the substance of his own view. An important passage, added in the second edition gives us the vital clue. His treatise, Sidgwick says, is concerned 'with the critical exposition of the different "methods" . . . which are logically connected with the different ultimate reasons widely accepted'. (*ME* 7, p. 78.) The methods to be considered, he is saying, must be connected with principles 'logically' and so not by means of some, even plausible, assumption; and the principles or reasons to be considered must be ultimate, really different from one another, and widely accepted. By restricting the reasons or principles to ultimate ones, Sidgwick shows that he intends to consider principles which purport to give not mere signs or criteria of rightness, but properties which make right acts right. Postponing consideration of the way in which one principle or method is seen to be really different from another to the next section, we must try to clarify further the distinction between methods which are logically connected with an ultimate principle and methods which are connected in some other way—indirectly connected, as we shall say.

An ultimate principle gives some property or feature of acts which makes them right. A method logically connected to an ultimate principle is one which uses the right-making characteristic itself as the property to be identified by the moral agent in the process of making decisions. In an indirectly connected method the agent identifies right acts by means of a property which is not the right-making property, and which is connected with that property by means of a contingent proposition. The property used in an indirectly connected method we may call a 'criterial' property. Now a further complication arises because either a right-making property or a criterial property may be too abstract to enable the plain man to use it in deciding what he ought to do. If so, then some methodical way of identifying the acts possessing the property will be needed. Such a further step in specifying a usable method will involve factual assumptions connecting a readily identifiable property with the more remote right-making property or the criterial property. For instance, suppose we hold as an ultimate principle that what makes right acts right is their producing general happiness. We might also believe that increasing individual freedom of choice is a necessary and sufficient condition of increasing general happiness, and that it is easier to find out if an act does the former than to find out if it does the latter. Then we might adopt a method based on the former property as our method of deciding what we ought to do. Of course the same sort of specifying procedure might be carried out with an indirectly connected method. Yet the basic difference between the two kinds of method is not removed even when such specification occurs. For if we use a method logically connected with a principle, further specification of the method is still specification of how to identify the presence of a right-making characteristic; while if we use an indirectly connected method, further specification of the method is specification of how to identify the presence of a mere mark or sign of rightness.

Sidgwick discusses briefly a variety of kinds of principles, and methods linked to them in different ways and by different assumptions, but he is centrally concerned only with methods logically connected to ultimate principles. He is prepared to examine various possible specifications of such methods into more readily or reliably applicable procedures—for instance, allegedly scientific measures of pleasantness—but always as ways of obtaining improved indicators of the presence or absence of a basic right-making characteristic. Indirectly connected methods and specifications of them are brought up only to be dismissed.

The point underlying the restriction to logically connected methods is also one of the points behind Sidgwick's general concern with the methods rather than the specific contents of common-sense morality. There is obviously much disagreement among men on specific moral judgements, but much of it springs from divergence in factual belief. It would of course be pointless to try to systematize moral beliefs in so far as they rest on contradictory factual assumptions. By concentrating on methods we simply eliminate all the problems arising from disagreement on factual matters. And by insisting on the restriction to logically connected methods, we specifically eliminate some serious problems which might arise over very general assertions—perhaps factual, perhaps religious, perhaps metaphysical—the truth of which it is not within the province of ethics as such to settle. We deal with methods, in other words, because in doing so we deal with the rational determinant of moral judgements which is, aside from ultimate principles themselves, the most purely moral. We therefore give ourselves the best hope of finding out to what extent the distinctively moral aspect of common-sense morality can be systematized.

For the sake of clarity the discussion so far has been conducted as if a method could involve only one ultimate principle. Though Sidgwick himself sometimes talks as if he accepts this assumption, it is plain from the latter sections of his work that he does not. A method may involve several principles, provided that the different right-making properties indicated by them do not compel the method to yield conflicting results in particular cases.

iii. *The Basic Methods*

Sidgwick investigates in detail only three methods of ethics—egoistic hedonism, universalistic hedonism or utilitarianism, and intuitionism. These are intended to be specific methods, not general categories into which some or possibly all ethical theories must fall.[4] Moreover it should be borne in mind that Sidgwick views it as ultimately an unsatisfactory division of methods. The suggestion carried by the names of the methods, that one of them is selected because of the way in which it tells us to arrive at knowledge of our duties while the others are selected because of substantive principles determining our duties, does not imply confusion on his part. It indicates a problem deeply rooted in the work of his predecessors and contemporaries which he himself attempts to resolve in the course of the *Methods*. Yet to say this is not to say that his selection of methods for discussion is satisfactory. It is easy to see how the three methods are related to philosophical positions of importance to British thinkers of the Victorian period. It is less easy to understand why Sidgwick thinks they provide adequate coverage of the theoretical possibilities. His remarks on this matter are not always clear.

One of Sidgwick's firmest convictions is that common-sense morality embodies different ultimate principles and different methods. (*ME* 7, p. 6.) He offers no explanation of this fact, he simply takes it as setting a basic problem. If the commonly used methods and principles come into conflict with one another, they cannot all continue to be accepted by rational beings. We must therefore ask how far they can be brought into systematic unity. To reply, we must first extract some clearly stated methods from the 'mixture of different methods, more or less disguised under ambiguities of language' which most people use. It is 'natural methods rationalised' or, we might say, ideal types of methods, which are to be examined as 'alternatives between which—so far as they cannot be recon-

---

[4] As C. D. Broad, *Five Types*, pp. 206–7, seems to think. This is probably in part a result of Broad's rather careless account of what Sidgwick takes a method to be, p. 148.

ciled—the human mind is necessarily forced to choose, when it attempts to frame a complete synthesis of practical maxims and to act in a perfectly consistent manner'. (*ME* 7, p. 12.)

There are several conditions to be met by the idealized methods Sidgwick will examine. First, as we have noted, he considers only methods related to principles which are widely held to be both ultimate and reasonable. This eliminates a large number of methods whose principles involve ends frequently held as ultimate but not widely thought to be reasonable, such as fame. Second, a proposed ultimate principle must generate a logically connected method which is usable, and, third, the method must be really different from other methods. Otherwise neither the principle nor its method can be considered. Three things which may feature in principles plainly meet these conditions: happiness, human perfection, and conformity to the demands of duty as such, as these are indicated by common terms like 'justice' and 'veracity'. In I, vi (which did not reach its final form until the fifth edition), Sidgwick suggests, in terms reminding us of one of John Grote's views, a reason why these three concepts seem to provide ultimate principles. They reflect the basic distinction between the human being as an enduring entity—with perfection as the ultimate reason—and the human as having a nature which is both sentient and active—with happiness and duty, respectively, as the appropriate ultimate reasons. (*ME* 7, p. 78, added in *ME* 2.) Similarly, other basic concepts may seem to suggest other possible ultimate reasons. The ideas of God, nature, and self, point toward obeying God, following nature, or realizing self, as moral principles. Sidgwick's objections to considering them show the meaning of his insistence that the methods to be examined must be not only rational and usable but also different from one another. If a principle asserts obedience to God to be the ultimate right-making property, the method logically connected with it must enable us to ascertain his commands. To use an 'external' revelation for this purpose, Sidgwick says, is to move outside the limits of ethics, because only other disciplines could show it to be reasonable to accept such a revelation. If we rely on internal revelation, like the Coleridgeans, it is difficult to see how this differs from a direct reliance on reason. And since an appeal to reason to determine God's commands

usually turns out to be an appeal either to intuitively apprehended rules or to considerations of happiness, the notion of
obeying God plainly fails to generate a method really different
from the three already set for examination. Sidgwick treats following nature and realizing self as candidates for a basic right-
making characteristic, in the same way. The details are forceful
and clear, and need no special comment. (*ME* 7, pp. 79–83.)

So far there is little to object to in Sidgwick's construction
of idealized methods. Questions arise when he tries to explain
how the three ultimate reasons he thinks worthy of attention
are connected with the methods he proposes to examine. There
do not seem to be any serious problems about the treatment
of happiness. He claims that it is widely thought that acting for
one's own happiness on the whole is reasonable, and so is
acting for general happiness, and thus he easily generates the
methods of egoism and utilitarianism. (*ME* 7, p. 9.) But perfection is not treated as generating its own logically connected
method. Sidgwick ties it to the intuitional method, for reasons
which are not immediately clear. Before we try to explain the
connection we must ask whether he even has a clear notion of
intuitional method.

Sidgwick gives various accounts of intuitionism, distinguishing three 'phases' of the method and suggesting that the
term itself may be used in a wider or a narrower sense. The
phases of the method are said to be, first, 'perceptional intuitionism', in which it is claimed that particular acts present
themselves to us immediately as right to do; second, 'dogmatic
intuitionism', in which it is claimed that certain classes of
acts are intuitively seen to be right; and third, 'philosophical
intuitionism', in which a small number of extremely broad
principles are seen to be intuitively valid. (*ME* 7, pp. 100–2.)
The third phase seems to be the same as intuitionism in the
broader sense of the term. In its narrower sense, the term
refers to a method of ethics which presupposes that 'we have
the power of seeing clearly that certain kinds of actions are
right and reasonable in themselves apart from their consequences' (*ME* 7, p. 200); in the wider sense what is presupposed
is only that 'the practically ultimate end of moral actions' is
'their conformity to certain rules or dictates of Duty unconditionally prescribed'. (*ME* 7, p. 96; cf. 201.) The latter is

a broader sense because it does not exclude dictates requiring actions precisely because of their consequences. Sidgwick's introduction of this wider sense of 'intuitionism' has the important function of enabling him to separate two aspects of the historical position which intuitionists, as we have seen, did not usually clearly distinguish: the epistemological aspect, the claim that some moral rules can be known immediately or non-inferentially, and the moral aspect, the claim that there are some binding rules requiring acts because of their own character and not on account of—indeed, regardless of—their consequences. The separation of aspects of the historical position is indispensable for Sidgwick's own suggestions about the reconciliation of intuitionism and utilitarianism. Confusion arises, however, because Sidgwick does not clearly present one single ultimate principle as involved in all three phases of intuitionism, and because by distinguishing senses of the term itself he suggests a greater difference between the third phase and the other two than there actually is. What induces him to separate the third phase is that it does not provide a usable method like the other methods he proposes to examine. But there is good reason for calling the third phase 'intuitional' none the less, a reason which becomes apparent when it is noticed that all three phases are logically connected to the principle that what makes right acts right is their conformity to unconditionally binding dictates of reason. (*ME* 7, p. 3.) The difference among the phases is a function of difference in the scope of the dictate believed to be intuitively given as a binding rational precept. In both perceptional and dogmatic intuitionism the dictates allegedly given by intuition are specific enough to enable the logically connected method to lead to definite decisions about particular acts. In the third phase, as we shall see, the dictates alleged to be intuitively given are not specific enough, by themselves, to lead to definite decisions about particular acts. Normally a principle which could not generate a stronger method would be dismissed. We must follow Sidgwick in postponing for some time, until Chapter 10, the explanation of his view of the role this type of intuition plays in morality. (*ME* 7, p. 102.) Here we can only say that the third phase of intuitional method is never taken by him to be, like the first two, a candidate for being a usable daily procedure for making moral decisions. It is brought in to make possible one kind of solution to the theoretical problems of synthesizing basic moral beliefs. This is one reason why Sidgwick suggests that it should take a different sense of the term 'intuitional'. Yet it is clearly enough connected with the other two phases of the intuitional method to deserve its nomenclatural link with them.

Sidgwick does not in fact examine perceptional intuitionism in any detail, since he thinks it is obviously unsatisfactory, even to the plain man, as a final position. It is dogmatic intuitionism which receives his detailed scrutiny. One difficulty in understanding this method is in seeing why Sidgwick links it, not to the general principle that what makes right acts right is their conformity to unconditionally binding precepts of reason, but to the goal of human perfection or excellence.

Sidgwick's explanation hinges on his view that the largest element in human perfection is generally agreed to be the moral element. Moral excellence, he continues, is generally agreed to be excellence in the performance of one's duties; and so the method to be studied in association with the apparently self-evident aim of human perfection is the intuitional method. (*ME* 7, pp. 9–11.) Now the intuitional method is originally introduced, in I, i, to show that Sidgwick is taking account of the fact that not everyone sees morality as a matter of producing or aiming at some end or goal. Many people take what we might now call a deontological view of morality, 'according to which conduct is held to be right when conformed to certain precepts or principles of Duty'. (*ME* 7, p. 3). Perfection, on the other hand, is presented as an end or goal at which it seems intrinsically reasonable to aim. It is unfortunate, therefore, that to obtain a method from it Sidgwick ties it to deontological intuitionism instead of allowing it to generate a non-hedonistic teleological method. This either suggests that the value of perfection is reducible to or explicable in terms of the value of the acts that a morally excellent person does or would do, a claim not all perfectionists would accept; or else it suggests that intuitionism is after all a teleological theory, with the production or exemplification of moral excellence as its end. In neither case does Sidgwick seem to allow for coverage of as full a range of common-sense opinions as he wants. What leads to this situation?

Part of the answer is suggested by a passage from the first edition:

> We have used the term 'Intuitional' to denote the method which recognises rightness as a quality inherent in actions independently of their conduciveness to any end. With this method we have agreed to associate that which aims at the perfection of the individual as the ultimate end: because of this Perfection moral excellences have commonly been regarded as at least the chief constituent: and these moral excellences can only be defined as dispositions and habits that tend to right or virtuous action, the rightness or virtuousness being intuitively ascertained. There are, no doubt, important differences between this method and what is commonly known as Intuitive Morality: but their general co-incidence may perhaps justify us in regarding the former as merely a phase or variety of the latter. (*ME* 1, p. 80; replaced in *ME* 3.)

Now Sidgwick asserts, through all the editions, that since dispositions are not directly knowable, they 'can only be definitely conceived by reference to the volitions and feelings in which they are manifested'; and he thinks this makes it impossible to regard dispositions as 'primary objects of intuitive moral judgments'. (*ME* 7, p. 201.) Perfectionism cannot generate a logically connected method which is really different from the method of dogmatic intuitionism, because it cannot provide anything really different to have intuitions about. The argument here rests on a dubious and undefended reductionistic view of dispositions; but it is not in fact Sidgwick's only argument for refusing to give separate status to a perfectionist principle. In III, xiv, he provides a careful examination of such a position as part of the argument to show that the ultimate good is pleasure. While he reiterates the difficulty arising from the reductionist view of dispositions, he brings up other problems as well, as we shall see, and he concludes from considering them that 'the ethical method which takes Perfection, as distinct from Happiness, to be the whole or chief part of ultimate good', is unsatisfactory. (*ME* 1, p. 378.) Thus he does in effect consider the possibility of a fourth method, one involving a non-hedonistic teleological principle; and he need not, therefore, have linked dogmatic intuitionism as a method to perfection as an end. Had he not done so, it would have been clearer than it is that the dogmatic intuitionism he examines is a deontological, not a covertly teleological, method. He might also have been forced into a deeper examination of this deontological method by the need to find some other principle with which to connect it.

iv. *Ethics, Epistemology, and Psychology*

In I, iii, Sidgwick presents arguments to show that the basic concept involved in morality is simple and unique, and therefore not reducible to any concept used in the descriptive sciences and disciplines. From this position, which we shall discuss in the next chapter, he takes it to follow that the basic principles of morality cannot be deduced from propositions derived from other areas of study. But there are quite different ways in which non-ethical propositions might be necessary for the construction of a rational synthesis of our moral beliefs, and one of the aims of the *Methods* is to determine whether and where this is so. From the first edition through the last Sidgwick expresses his interest in what he calls 'the very important question whether ethical science can be constructed on an independent basis; or whether it is forced to borrow a fundamental and indispensable premiss from Theology or some similar source'. (*ME* 7, p. 507; *ME* 1, p. 470.) Sidgwick's ways of handling problems seem as if they were designed according to a policy of keeping the non-ethical commitments of moral philosophy to an absolute minimum. Such a policy might arise from the methodological principle of aiming at general agreement, since the fewer the extra-moral involvements of a theory, the fewer the opportunities it provides for dissent. Whether they were consciously designed to do so or not, Sidgwick's procedures and arguments generally—though certainly not always—lead him to think that the moral philosopher is not required to say much, if anything, about non-moral issues. We have already noted, for instance, that by examining the methods rather than the specific judgements of ordinary morality, Sidgwick by-passes innumerable factual issues. His insistence on dealing with methods logically connected to their principles and on considering only principles purporting to give ultimate right-making properties, has the same effect. Some of the other points at which analogous conclusions are reached may now be considered briefly.

We may begin with certain matters of epistemology. There are two issues which Sidgwick dismisses in the Preface to the first edition of the *Methods* as irrelevant: the issue of 'the Origin of the Moral Faculty' and that of 'the nature of the object of ethical knowledge'. Like anyone who engages in reasoning on ethical questions, he says, he assumes 'that there is something under any given circumstances which it is right or reasonable to do, and that this may be known'. If this is granted then further enquiries into the epistemology of ethics would be neutral with respect to the moral concerns at the heart of Sidgwick's work. He does occasionally speak, especially in the earlier editions, of 'qualities' of rightness or goodness, but this is not to be construed as implying a theory of the sort later put forth by Moore or Ross about the ontological status of what is known when we know that an act is right or good. Any theory Sidgwick has on this matter remains implicit.

The objections to bringing in considerations of origins are made quite explicit. Among Sidgwick's predecessors it was the associationists who showed most interest in the origins of ideas. Against them, he points out a faulty analogy in J. S. Mill's idea of mental chemistry. In the case of real chemistry we can, in the case of mental chemistry we cannot, detect the elements in the compounds and resolve the compounds back into the elements. Sidgwick also points out that even if our basic moral concept is a development from simpler and earlier concepts, it does not follow that the concept 'has not really the simplicity which it appears to have when we now reflect upon it', so that even in terms of an argument at the psychological level associationism fails to establish a pertinent point. (*ME* 7, p. 32 and n.) Sidgwick's own arguments move beyond the psychological level, though as we shall see they continue to involve it. In criticizing those who thought the question of the original or derived nature of a faculty a matter of significance for philosophy, he delivers objections pertinent to both pre-evolutionary and evolutionary views. The claim, in both cases, he says, is that if a faculty can be shown to be 'original' it is thereby shown to be trustworthy, while if it is shown to be 'derived' doubt is cast on its deliverances. Sidgwick points out a serious internal difficulty with this view (*ME* 7, pp. 212–13), and goes on to make a general point of rather more significance. Because, as he has by this time argued, the fundamental concept of ethics is unique and simple, and because the propositions of ethics 'relate to matter fundamentally different from that with which physical science or psychology deals', moral judgements cannot be inconsistent with the results of any such science. 'They can only be shown to involve error', he says, 'by being shown to contradict each other'. This cannot lead to general sceptical conclusions about them. (*ME* 7, p. 213.) And if we should find serious contradictions among ethical beliefs when these have originally presented themselves to us as self-evident, we will remain in a state of doubt about them even if it is shown that they are 'original'. (*ME* 7, p. 214.) In short, moral judgements can be neither supported nor attacked by theories of their origin, and no detailed discussion of such theories is needed. By Sidgwick's time, geneticism had had a long reign in English thought; in the form of evolutionism it was to dominate many of its thinkers for still longer; but well before F. H. Bradley's famous ejection of psychologism from logic, Sidgwick had seen plainly that questions of origin are irrelevant to claims about the logical status of concepts and the truth or falsity of moral judgements.

We turn now to questions of what may be called very broadly moral psychology. Sidgwick discusses a number of topics here—psychological egoism, the moving power of reason, free will—and in each case he tries to show that only very minimal claims as to the facts must be made by the moral philosopher, though false or exaggerated claims must, of course, be rejected.

Psychological egoism is criticized in detail in the well-known fourth chapter of Book I. The rejection of the theory, and some of the criticisms Sidgwick makes of it, were commonplace among his intuitionistic predecessors. The arguments have been reviewed many times since then, and need not be gone over again. We should, however, note the way in which on Sidgwick's view the subject is pertinent to ethics at all. (On this matter we may disregard the extensive changes made in the chapter for the second edition.) His concern is caused by the charge, sometimes made by critics of utilitarianism, that psychological egoism commits one to ethical egoism. This is a mistake, Sidgwick thinks, for two reasons. It overlooks the possibility that one's beliefs about what is right or wrong, determined quite independently of beliefs about what will be pleasurable to oneself, might be major determinants of pleasure or pain. More importantly, it fails to realize that 'a psychological law invariably realised in my conduct does not admit of being conceived as "a precept" or "dictate" of reason', or in other words as an ethical principle, because such a principle 'must be a rule from which I am conscious that it is possible to deviate'. (*ME* 7, p. 41.) Psychological egoism would neither prove nor disprove ethical egoism. It would simply make it inapplicable. Indeed if psychological egoism, and by implication any similar monistic motivational theory, were true, no ethical principle would be applicable. For it would be quite unreasonable, Sidgwick thinks, to hold to a principle dictating actions which were psychologically impossible, and pointless to have one dictating the inevitable. 'The question of duty', he says, 'is never raised except when we are conscious of a conflict of impulses and wish to know which to follow.' (*ME* 7, p. 81.) Once it is established or allowed that we act from a multiplicity of impulses, Sidgwick's interest in psychological detail ends. It is not essential for the moral philosopher to know what the impulses are which may come into conflict, so long as he knows that no one of them necessarily always prevents the others from affecting us.

Not the least of our active impulses, on Sidgwick's view, is that which represents the motive power of reason. His treatment of it is characteristic. As we shall see in the next chapter, he defends the view that there is such a power or motivating force, connected with rational judgements about what we ought to do. But he does not think it important to determine precisely the 'emotional characteristics of the impulse that prompts us to obey the dictates of Reason' (*ME* 7, p. 39), nor does he raise any metaphysical questions about how reason can be practical. He stops with the bare minimum needed for moral philosophy.

v. *Ethics and Free Will*

Sidgwick's unwillingness to encumber ethical theory with controversial non-moral positions is nowhere more strikingly displayed than in his claim that the issue of free will and determinism is simply irrelevant to most moral matters. The chapter in which this claim is argued (I, v) underwent considerable revision, even as late as the fifth edition. However, the main line of argument is basically the same in all the editions, so that the significance of the alterations is easily apparent.

Sidgwick begins with a clarification of the issue. We cannot, he says, identify free action either with disinterested action or with rational action as such. The discussion of psychological egoism has shown the existence of disinterested acts even at an instinctive level which no one claims is within the realm of free choice. And the identification of free action with rational action, which is the special line the Kantians take, seems to Sidgwick to involve confusion of two senses of 'freedom'. (*ME* 7, p. 57.) We sometimes speak of a man being a slave to his passions or dominated by his desires, and in contrast with this we may speak of acting freely when someone has resisted these impulses in order to do what seems rational. Sidgwick, who quotes Whewell asserting this, does not deny it, but he adds that we also find situations in which the dictation of reason seems external and feels like servitude or slavery. (*ME* 7, p. 58 and n. 2; *ME* 1, pp. 44–5.) From this he infers that there is no conclusive empirical ground for taking either the reason or the passions to represent a 'real' self. And though there may be a sense in which we speak of a man as free when and because he acts rationally, we also say at times that a man acted quite freely in doing something irrational. In opposition to Kant, Sidgwick holds that the sense of 'freedom' which concerns the libertarian is this second sense, in which a man may be just as free when he acts wrongly or irrationally as he is when he acts rightly or rationally. This sense of the term is needed to preserve the connection between freedom and responsibility. (See esp. 1888a.) If we may say that we are slaves to our passions when we act wrongly, we must also 'admit that our slavery is self-chosen'. This, at least, is what our experience seems to show us. And the question of free will is whether it is true that one who wilfully chooses to act wrongly could have chosen to act rightly, even if 'the antecedents of his volition, external and internal', had been just what they were. (*ME* 7, pp. 58–9.) Is my volition completely determined by the qualities of my past self, including its inherited as well as its acquired characteristics; or is it always possible that I might choose 'to act in the manner that I now judge to be reasonable and right' regardless of my past? (*ME* 7, pp. 61–2.)

Sidgwick then gives the arguments on either side. The determinist appeals to the whole force of the sciences, and to the continuing increase of the range of scientific inquiry, all implying determinist assumptions. He points out that we explain the actions of others in causal terms, and that social life relies completely on the predictability of human action. He notes, finally, that even if some decision of our own is made deliberately and with the feeling of freedom, when the act is past we naturally view it as no less explicable in causal terms than the acts of others. (*ME* 7, pp. 63–4.) The libertarian sets against this 'formidable array of cumulative evidence' only what Sidgwick calls 'the immediate affirmation of consciousness in the moment of deliberate action': when I am deciding what to do, I cannot think the outcome predetermined. My sense of freedom might really be illusory; but to see that it is so when I am choosing would be to alter my whole concept of what I call 'my action'. Hence the affirmation of consciousness is not just a report of a feeling. It is connected with a central part of the common sense understanding of the world. For this reason the issue between determinism and libertarianism is not to be settled easily. Sidgwick confesses that he himself cannot settle it. (*ME* 7, pp. 65–6; *ME* 1, p. 51.)

The next step is to show that the issue has only limited significance for morality. Sidgwick proposes to do this by showing that resolving it would for the most part make no difference to our view of the rationality of actions. It would not affect, first, one's view of the ends it would be reasonable to pursue. Happiness is plainly a rational aim regardless of one's belief in liberty; and Sidgwick thinks that neither perfection nor the virtues as we understand them presuppose possession of free will. Moreover, 'if Excellence is in itself admirable and desirable, it surely remains so whether any individual's approximation to it is entirely determined . . . or not'. (*ME* 7, p. 68.) Second, the resolution of the issue would not in general affect the rationality of using various means. If we only consider means whose reliability is established on scientific grounds, the point is clear. An act causing a given result will cause it whether the act itself is determined or free. It is only if we hold the theological view which makes the reward of virtue depend on free choice of virtuous acts that we should think the question of means affected by the issue. In that case determinism would undermine the belief that virtuous acts are means to the reasonable end of one's own good. (*ME* 7, p. 69.) But this is a matter beyond Sidgwick's scope. Of course in so far as freedom of will implies the unpredictability of human action, we might find that libertarianism leads us to rely somewhat less than determinism would on the actions of others. But we could not make any specific corrections of our expectations on this ground alone, and would simply have to live with a somewhat greater level of uncertainty than we now live with about human acts in general. (*ME* 7, p. 70.)

Are there, then, any issues of importance touched by the free will problem? If so, they involve retrospective moral judgements. Remorse, so far as it 'implies self-blame irremovably fixed on the self blamed', Sidgwick says, 'must tend to vanish from the mind of a convinced Determinist'. (*ME* 7, p. 71.) But this is of no great practical moment, since a determinist with a keen love of goodness might dislike his own shortcomings so much that his dislike had the same effects as remorse is alleged to have by libertarians. More importantly, questions of punishment and reward, and of merit and demerit, seem to hinge on the outcome of the debate. The usual retributive view of punishment involves belief in free will, as do ordinary ideas of responsibility and of desert. Now the determinist can give these notions a meaning which is clear and definite and which is moreover, from a utilitarian point of view, the only suitable meaning. He abandons retributive and retrospective aspects of the terms, and ties them to benefits to be derived from encouraging or discouraging acts. To say, for example, that someone is responsible for some act is on this view to say that fear of punishment could have deterred him from doing it; and similar accounts of other apparently retrospective terms can be given and a determinist analogue of libertarian views on all this part of morality constructed. In fact, Sidgwick argues later, such a determinist interpretation of these concepts is more easily incorporated into all our other specific practical judgements than a libertarian interpretation. Hence the effect of determinism even on our ideas of what it is reasonable to do about punishment and reward is negligible. (*ME* 7, pp. 71–2.) For moral purposes the issue does not need to be settled.

This, then, is the general line of argument followed in all the editions. In the earlier editions, it is, first, more strongly suggested that libertarianism is the view embedded in common sense; and, second, the determinist is allowed to argue that common sense is changing in this respect, and coming closer to a determinist view. On the first point, Sidgwick says, up to the fourth edition, that the libertarian view 'is the natural and primary view of the matter: that, on the Determinist theory, "ought", "responsibility", "desert", and similar terms, have to be used, if at all, in new significations: and that the conception of Freedom is, so to say, the pivot upon which our moral sentiments naturally play.' (*ME* 1, p. 50; *ME* 2, p. 54; *ME* 3, pp. 62–3, where Freedom is called the 'hidden pivot'; *ME* 4, pp. 65–6, where 'ought' is dropped from the list of terms.) In the fifth edition Sidgwick still implies that the established use of terms in ordinary language presupposes libertarianism, and adds that ' "responsibility", "desert", and similar terms have to be used, if at all, in new significations by Determinists'. (*ME* 5, pp. 71–2.) This is not denied in the final version but there is less stress on the verbal revisionism implied by determinism. (*ME* 7, p. 71.) As to the second point, up to the fifth edition the determinist allows that on his view punishment becomes deterrent and ceases to be retributive, but he is given the suggestion that 'this is the more practical view, and the one towards which civilization—quite apart from the Free-will controversy—seems to tend'. (*ME* 1, p. 50; *ME* 4, p. 66.) From the fifth edition onward this point is not made in the chapter on free will, though it is not clear why. Sidgwick continued to believe in the possibility of the kind of change in commonly used concepts which the determinist proposes. We shall turn shortly to the significance of this point. First we must ask how successful Sidgwick is in neutralizing the free will issue for moral philosophy.

Sidgwick never attempts to dismiss the free will issue as illusory (cf. *ME* 1, p. 46; *ME* 2, p. 50), only as irrelevant. Granted that it is a real problem, are his arguments for its unimportance convincing? The answer will depend on our view of his assumption that the important aspects of morality are those concerned with decisions about what is to be done, and that retrospective judgements, those essential to feelings of remorse and guilt and to assessments of responsibility, merit, and blameworthiness, are of little moment except in so far as they are logically tied to some set of prospective judgements. The fact that the focus of Sidgwick's investigation of morality is on methods of determining what is right for a person to do makes it clear how deeply he is committed to an approach which makes prospective judgements about actions more important than retrospective judgements about persons. We shall discuss this point again in Chapter 8. Here we may note that if retrospective judgements about persons were taken as centrally important, it would seem less clear that the free will issue may rightly be dismissed as affecting only peripheral matters. Sidgwick's view that the belief in perfection as a reasonable ultimate end is independent of any conclusions about free will is after all not unchallengeable. Many of those who take perfection or moral virtue as the highest good would think it extremely misleading to claim, as Sidgwick does, that 'the manifestations of courage, temperance, and justice do not become less admirable because we can trace their antecedents in a happy balance of inherited dispositions developed by careful education'. (*ME* 7, p. 68.) Not *less* admirable, perhaps, they might reply; but if the suggestion about inheritance and education points to strict determinism, then, surely, admirable in a different way—as we admire straight noses and golden hair, not as we admire honesty under severe temptation. Sidgwick's own remarks on the ways in which the common moral vocabulary would alter if determinism came to dominate public opinion may well seem to be a clear admission of their point. If so, the argument for the relative unimportance of the free will issue in moral matters rests on an assumption which begs the question.

vi. *The Limits to Synthesis*

Sidgwick's *Methods*, it is well known, ends with what its author takes to be a problem which can only be resolved by the truth of a metaphysical or theological proposition asserting the moral order of the universe. He himself sees no way to prove any such proposition, and it is easy to suppose that this is what keeps him from thinking he can provide a complete synthesis of the rational methods and principles in common-sense morality. The discussion of free will points to two other considerations which also go to prevent the working out of a final system of ethics. One is that the issue of free will leads to systematic differences of opinion on moral issues, yet it cannot be resolved by moral philosophy. Because of the nature of the disagreements to which the free-will issue leads, any system-atization of common sense must omit a significant aspect of its moral convictions; and because the issue lies outside the scope of moral philosophy, it reveals another point, in addition to that indicated by the question of moral order, at which ethical theory fails to be an independent science. The second difficulty in the construction of a complete synthesis springs from the belief in moral progress which is clearly indicated in the discussion of free will.

There can be no doubt that Sidgwick thinks common sense morality is improving. (cf. *Mem.*, p. 243.) Study of the history of morality, he says, leads him 'to regard the current civilised morality of the present age as merely a stage in a long process of development, in which the human mind has . . . been gradually moving towards a truer apprehension of what ought to be. We do not find merely change . . . we see progress . . .' (*GSM*, pp. 351–2.) The 'different views of the ultimate reason-ableness of conduct' (*ME* 7, p. 6) which Sidgwick thinks are embedded in common-sense morality are, as his remarks on free will show, partly differences in the concepts through which morality is structured, and progress must consist to some extent in conceptual change. It also consists, Sidgwick thinks, in movement out of 'error, confusion, and uncertainty' resulting from 'wider experience, fuller knowledge, more extended and refined sympathies'. There is no reason to suppose the develop-ment complete. We should therefore presume that there are deficiencies in our own morality similar to those we find in the moralities of the past. The construction of a system of morality would help in removing the deficiencies (*GSM*, pp. 351–2), and, he suggests in a late paper, might even be instrumental in changing public opinion. (1898, pp. 606–7.) Sidgwick also has no apparent doubts as to the direction of progress. Utilitarianism, he says, is 'that to which we can now see that human development has been always tending'; it is 'the adult and not the germinal form of Morality'. (*ME* 7, pp. 456–7; *ME* 1, p. 427; cf. *ME* 7, p. 281; 1887, pp. 33–4.)[5]

A complete synthesis of rational principles and methods is desirable but not attainable—at least not yet. The problem of moral order in the universe, and to a much lesser extent the problem of free will, prevent it. More interestingly the existence of progress in morality suggests the possibility that no synthesis can be final and definitive. After all, it never is in science, and science provides the model Sidgwick thinks moral philosophy should emulate. Sidgwick never fully worked out this implication of his belief in moral progress, and did not discuss the problems it raises. But it is quite in accordance with the belief that he should view his own contribution to solving the problems of ethics as exemplary and tentative rather than complete and permanent.

---

[5] Rowell, *Hell*, attributes a certain amount of influence, in bringing about a decline in popular belief in the punishment of the wicked in Hell, to Benthamite arguments as to the uselessness of eternal punishment and in favour of a preventive and reformative view of punishment generally: see p. 13.

7

Reason and Action

SIDGWICK holds that morality involves an 'elementary concept' which is unique to it and which cannot be defined. It follows, he thinks, that the basic premisses of ethical reasoning cannot be deduced from non-ethical premisses. Methodological tests of the foundations of ethical reasoning are available but 'the premisses of our reasoning . . . must, if not methodological, be purely ethical: that is, they must contain, implicitly or explicitly, the elementary notion signified by the term "ought"; otherwise there is no rational transition possible to a proposition that does affirm "what ought to be".' (1879a, 107.) It was, of course, neither original nor unusual on Sidgwick's part to declare the fundamental concept of morality indefinable or to draw this conclusion from the declaration. But his own version of the view is in some respects different from, and is more carefully elaborated than, analogous views among his intuitional predecessors. It differs also from similar views held by later philosophers. Hence, although Sidgwick's arguments and conclusions on this point are perhaps the best known part of the *Methods*, we must review them here at least briefly. The two main chapters concerning the topic are I, iii and ix. A great many changes were made between the first and second edition versions of them, and some of the details of the changes are discussed in the appendix to this chapter.

i. *The Basic Notion*

The idea Sidgwick takes to be unique and essentially different from ideas representing what is, is not simply the idea for which we use the word 'ought', or the idea for which we use 'right' or 'duty', but a fundamental notion common to all these. Throughout I, iii, he uses a variety of terms in discussing the issue, and in the rhetorical question he asks summarizing the problem he does not attempt to complete the list: 'What definition can we give of "ought", "right", and other terms expressing the same fundamental notion?' His answer, of course, is that 'the notion which these terms have in common is too elementary to admit of any formal definition'. (*ME* 7, p. 32.) In his initial arguments concerning this notion Sidgwick aims to show three things: first, that the notion is essentially different from notions representing what is the case; second, that it is simple and indefinable; and third, that it makes propositions in which it is an essential term subject to rational considerations. In examining Sidgwick's arguments we must try to see just how they support these three points, and to what extent or in what way they are meant to be proofs of them.

Sidgwick begins by pointing out that we all know what it is to feel a conflict between non-rational desires and reason, as, for instance, when we want another piece of cake but think it would be unwise to take it, or when spitefulness tempts us to do something we see to be unfair. (*ME* 7, p. 23.) In cases like these we commonly think our desires are 'irrational': they prompt us to 'volitions opposed to our deliberate judgments'. Now common sense assumes, Sidgwick says, that right acts or acts we ought to do are reasonable or rational and that simply recognizing the rationality of an act gives us a motive for doing it, a motive which is quite different from other desires or inclinations. It is however sometimes held by philosophers that this is not the case, and that action is always motivated by some non-rational desire. Practical judgements are thought to be either expressions of desires or inclinations or else factual judgements containing information to which our desires lead us to react favourably or unfavourably. It is not disputed, in other words, that we do control our actions in accordance with our 'deliberate judgements'. But while common sense takes them to be determined by rational considerations, the contrary opinion is that they are, or only work through, desires and feelings. (*ME* 7, pp. 24–5.) Which view is correct?

With the issue posed in this manner, Sidgwick is in a position to hold that his first point is simply accepted by all parties. Deliberate judgements about what we ought to do are different from other judgements in that they provide explicit direction of action. An assertion like 'He wants to do so-and-so but thinks it would be unwise' is agreed to be a commonplace possibility.

The question is about one of its components. If the common-sense view is correct there is control of action by reason, if the philosophers are correct the control is by feeling, but in either case the uniqueness of judgements of right, because of their tie with action, is accepted.

Sidgwick's mode of arguing for his second point, the simplicity of the 'common notion', is to try to bring the reader to recognize a set of distinctions among ideas which might easily be mistaken one for another. Once the distinctions are made, he thinks, the reader will be able to pick out the idea which is involved in moral terms and to see that it is simple. The first distinction, introduced in I, i, is that between the notion of something which is right as a means to some end, and something which is right or which ought to be done regardless of any reference to an end. In I, iii, he brings the distinction forcibly home by noting that if we confine ourselves to the former interpretation of 'right', certain judgements which are meaningful if we use terms as they are used in ordinary discourse become self-contradictory or absurd. For example, taking 'right' to mean only 'efficiently productive of desired results', we could not coherently claim—as we plainly can—that it is right to act justly regardless of the results of doing so. The point is not simply that the proposed definition is inadequate, but also that in seeing its inadequacy we are led to see that we have an idea different from the idea of 'being an effective means'. (*ME* 7, p. 26.) This notion, Sidgwick claims, turns up in everyone's thought at some point. In the intuitionist's mind it turns up in the recognition of categorically binding prescriptions. In the mind of the utilitarian it comes out in the thought of the goal of general happiness: he may treat everything else as a means, but he must think that pursuit of that end is unconditionally prescribed. The egoist can also find the concept. Men do not always pursue their own greatest good, and he thinks they ought—in this sense—to do so. (*ME* 7, p. 7.) Sidgwick claims that even someone who refuses to accept any ultimate goal as rational can find this concept in his thought. For even such a person will find himself thinking that if someone happens to adopt a goal, then he simply ought to take the appropriate steps to reach it; and in thinking this he is not just thinking that those are the steps which would lead to the goal. (*ME* 7, p. 37.) In each case introspection reveals the presence of a notion which may resemble others but is still distinct from them.

Similar treatment is given to accounts of the ideas of duty and right which confuse them with ideas of compulsion or the avoidance of threatened pain. There is an element of truth in such accounts but they do not accurately represent 'the special ethical use' of the terms. No matter what sort of sanction ethical terms are supposed to involve, we can construct meaningful judgements contrasting what we ought to do with what we might suffer for doing. This is clearest, perhaps, when we find ourselves at odds with public opinion, for then we have a 'crucial experience' which shows that the idea of duty is not the same to us as the idea of what others will disapprove of our not doing. Even if we think of the sanctions as pains to be inflicted by God to make us obey his laws, we can see that 'ought' is not equivalent to 'will be punished by God unless', since we think that the judgement that one ought to do a certain act is part of the reason for believing that God will punish us if we do not. (*ME* 7, pp. 29–31.) Sidgwick also uses the time-honoured appeal to the belief that God is just. This must mean, he points out, not merely that God will punish or reward us in various ways but also that it is right for him to do so, and to say that it is right cannot, in this case, mean that God is bound under threat of penalties to do so. (*ME* 7, p. 31.)

All these arguments are instances of traditional intuitionist objections to reductionist definitions of moral terms. In Sidgwick's chapter they do two things. They serve, first, as strict logical objections to proposed definitions. But to criticize a finite, and indeed very small, set of proposed definitions would not prove that no such definition could be correct. Sidgwick does not think it would. The second function of the arguments is to bring home that we have a positive notion which is not articulated by those definitions and which would not be articulated by others of the same kind. This is why, after dismissing associationistic accounts of our ideas as irrelevant, he says that 'a psychologist must accept as elementary what introspection carefully performed declares to be so; and, using this criterion, I find that the notion we have been examining, as it now exists in our thought, cannot be resolved into any more simple notions'. (*ME* 7, p. 32.) This is also why he says he has 'been trying to exhibit' the basic notion (*ME* 7, p. 35)—a quite precise account of the procedure.[1] At this stage he is simply pointing out a fact—that we have such-and-such an idea—without offering either explanation or justification of it.

If we are agreed about the uniqueness and simplicity of the basic notion, we have still to settle the third point, the involvement of the notion with reason. A simple notion which is different in kind from others because it is tied to the control of action might not be a notion which requires that judgements essentially using it be decided upon by rational methods. 'I ought to do so-and-so' might mean something like 'I have a feeling of approval of my doing so-and-so'. In considering this possibility,[2] Sidgwick first appeals to a logical matter. He points out that on the theory in question both of two contradictory moral judgements could be true, since each half of the contradiction could be asserted by a different speaker, and there is no logical difficulty about different speakers having different feelings. Then 'we should have two coexistent facts stated in two mutually contradictory propositions', and Sidgwick thinks it obvious that this reduces the theory to absurdity. (*ME* 7, p. 27.) Both Reid and Alexander Smith used analogous arguments against subjectivism, but this seems to be the first time the point is made as Sidgwick makes it, by showing that the position implies what our ordinary use of language would treat as an absurdity. Sidgwick does not expand on the argument or apply it to the case where the fact supposedly stated by a moral judgement is the existence of moral feelings in more than one person or in all people; but the form of the argument is clear and its further application obvious. Sidgwick also does not anticipate the complex rejoinders which were to be developed by emotivists. He is willing to accept the obvious grammar of ordinary sentences expressing moral judgements as indicating the nature of their content, and to rest his argument on that base.

[1] For a similar methodological view see Bertrand Russell, *Principles of Mathematics* (1903), 1956, pp. 129–30.

[2] The theory, as we have seen in Ch. 2, sec. iii, was held by Thomas Brown as well as by Hume.

Sidgwick thinks the subjectivist might reply that we sometimes make claims which are phrased in objective language but which we are willing to rephrase as simple reports of our own feelings if the objective-sounding claim is challenged, and that in altering the language we are not making any change in the substance of what we say. The subjectivist thinks morality belongs in this class. Now Sidgwick is willing to grant that there are some apparently objective judgements of which all this is true. But morality is in quite a different category. The reason involves the nature of moral feeling:

> The peculiar emotion of moral approbation is, in my experience, inseparably bound up with the conviction, implicit or explicit, that the conduct approved is 'really' right—i.e. that it cannot, without error, be disapproved by any other mind. If I give up this conviction... I may no doubt still retain a sentiment prompting to the conduct in question, or ... a sentiment of repugnance to the opposite conduct: but this sentiment will no longer have the special quality of 'moral sentiment' strictly so called. (*ME* 7, p. 27.)

Sidgwick gives some cases where we may experience this for ourselves. We sometimes come to judge that we ought to act in a way in which we have always previously thought we ought not to act. We may still feel a distaste, due to the persistence of the feeling which involved the old judgement, for acting as we now think we ought; but the feeling will differ 'in kind and degree' from the feeling we had when judgement supported sentiment. The mere repugnance we might call a 'quasi-moral' feeling; the newer, reason-supported, aversion is a 'moral' one. The same point holds even if the feeling in question is augmented by a sympathy with the feelings of others. We can think our way to a new moral position, opposed to the feelings of the whole society as well as to our own habitual ones. Then, Sidgwick says, we have again a 'crucial experiment proving the existence in us of moral sentiments' which are different from even complex quasi-moral feelings. In short, when the rationality implied in the objective form of moral judgements is given up, a feeling that goes with the judgement changes. To retreat to a subjective claim is to change the substance of the assertion, not merely to rephrase it. Hence moral judgements are not, as the subjectivist suggests, in the same class as those in which a change from an objective to a subjective form does not change the content.

Sidgwick's rejection of subjectivism raises more questions than it answers. His criticisms involve a heavy reliance on introspection as a source of information about concepts. They assume that the grammatical forms of ordinary language can tell us something important about the nature of what we talk about. They put forward the important idea that some experiences classed as feelings necessarily involve certain kinds of rational belief. None of these points is explicitly discussed, let alone defended. Part of the reason may be Sidgwick's general reluctance to tie his ethics to theories concerning non-ethical points. More important is the fact that this is only a first step in the treatment of the main issue. Sidgwick is here concerned to establish a fact or two about the data which a satisfactory theory must systematize. The subjectivism he dismisses is treated as making a rather crude error about it. The defence of the rationality of morality in I, iii, is meant only to show that common sense moral concepts are *prima facie* such as to make judgements using them subject to rational criticism and support. It is not meant as a final reply to scepticism. Sidgwick does not ignore scepticism, as we shall see shortly. His dealings with it are complex, and involve much more than a discussion of moral concepts.

ii. *Reason, Right, Ought, and Good*

The basic simple notion can be made clearer, Sidgwick says, though it cannot be defined, by bringing out its relation to 'other notions with which it is connected in ordinary thought'. (*ME* 7, p. 33.) His remarks on these notions show that he sees them as systematically linked to the basic concept and definable in terms of it. They also give a good indication of what the basic notion itself is. It is, roughly, the notion of a demand made by reason on action, or, more generally, the notion of a requirement which our own rationality presents to our desires and volitions. This is indicated in several passages in which Sidgwick treats the notions of rightness and rationality in action as equivalent (e.g. *ME* 7, pp. 5, 77, 344; *GSM*, p. 326). It also emerges in his analysis of the concept of goodness, which, as we shall see, is defined in terms of the demands of reason on desire. The systematization of moral concepts which is thus brought about reflects a view of Sidgwick's to which he adverts briefly in explaining why happiness and duty provide basic principles of morals. This is the view, which we have already noted earlier, that there are two morally significant aspects of human nature, sentience and activity. We can now see that some moral concepts embody the demands of our reason mainly on the active aspect of our nature, some its demands particularly on the sentient side. The basic notion itself is not, as it might be for Whewell, a platonic entity visible to our mental gaze; it is not an introspectively discoverable mental entity; it is not a concept derived from perception of a unique non-natural property. It is the constraint imposed by reason, which in matters of theory is familiar enough through the laws of logic, as it bears on activity and sentience.

The terms 'ought', 'right', and 'duty' are used primarily in connection with the demands of reason on action. This is borne out by the fact that there is a special ethical or moral sense of 'ought' which must be distinguished from a broader sense of the term. In 'the narrowest ethical sense', 'ought' implies 'can'. It is in this sense, which is the sense Sidgwick mainly uses, that the term carries to judgements using it the special rational impulse to action which has already been mentioned. (*ME* 7, pp. 33–4.) The broader sense, used in wistful judgements such as 'There ought to be more sunny days in Spring' does not carry the implication of ability. It is more like the notion of what is desirable, and is akin to 'good'. Significantly, Sidgwick says that good actions, like many other good things, 'are not implied to be in our power in the same strict sense as "right" actions'. (*ME* 7, p. 113.) Some of the action-oriented terms, as we have seen when discussing psychological egoism, presuppose an agent who is not always and necessarily moved by the special impulse connected with practical rational judgements. For 'ought' and 'obligation' at least, though not for 'right', Sidgwick takes the Kantian view that potential or actual conflict between what reason requires and what some non-rational passion inclines the agent to do, is a requisite. Of a being, such as God, not subject to these conflicts, we could at most say that his actions are 'reasonable' or 'right'. (*ME* 7, p. 35; cf. p. 217.) Finally, another feature which 'right' shares with 'ought' and 'duty' brings out again their close connection with the active side of our nature. A judgement that an act ought to be done or is right implies 'an authoritative prescription to do it'. A judgement that an act is good does not imply such a directive, since an attribution of goodness is comparative and raises the possibility of obtaining a greater good than the act in question would yield. (*ME* 7, p. 106.)

The concept of 'good' seems to be linked to the sentient and desiring side of our nature as 'ought' and 'right' are to its active aspect. This explains why Sidgwick's account of the meaning of 'good' is developed by criticism of definitions of the concept in terms of pleasure and desire. He begins by pointing out difficulties in the position that 'good' means simply 'conducive to pleasure'. When we compare things in respect of their goodness, he says, we compare them in terms of a pertinent comparison class, not simply as means to pleasure. Not all the kinds of pleasure we get from wine, for instance—such as the pleasure of slaking thirst—go to show that it is good as wine. Goodness of conduct may therefore also involve more than productiveness of pleasure. Second, we generally admit that there are people of good taste or judgement who can tell good from bad in various classes of things. We do not assume that they judge solely on the basis of the pleasure they obtain. They judge, rather, on the basis of 'a universally valid standard'; and while anyone who disagrees with them because he gets more pleasure from something than they do will not be mistaken about the amount of pleasure he gets, he will or certainly may be mistaken about the goodness. (*ME* 7, pp. 107–8.) Thus even in judging instrumental good—the plausible case—no support is given to the idea that 'good' just means 'conducive to pleasure'. Sidgwick adds that the noun 'good' cannot be taken to mean 'pleasant' by anyone who holds that it is significant and not tautological to claim that pleasure is the good or ultimate. And surely, he urges, the meaning does not change from the noun to the adjective. (*ME* 7, p. 109.)

A more positive move towards a definition begins with consideration of the possibility that 'good' means 'object of desire'. To simplify matters, Sidgwick says, he begins with consideration of what a man desires for its own sake and for himself alone. He rejects the simple equation of 'good' with 'desired' on the ground that it allows no room for something essential to the concept, the possibility of comparing the degrees of different goods. (*ME* 7, p. 110; cf. 106.) Can we then equate 'good' with a notion of 'desirable' as meaning 'what would be desired if one could obtain it and also had a perfect forecast of what having it would be like'? No, for not only does this limit our judgements of good to what is within our reach, it also overlooks the fact that there are some things which we desire and do not regret having obtained, but which destroy certain desires; while if we had fostered those desires and gratified them instead, they would have led us to what we would now admit to be greater goods. We might try to allow for this by saying that one's own good on the whole is what one would *now* desire if one could foresee all the consequences of obtaining it. This would give precision to the rather vague meanings of 'good' and 'desirable' in ordinary discourse, though it is so complicated that it would be paradoxical to say that it is 'what we commonly *mean* when we talk of a man's "good on the whole" '. But it is rejected as a definition because, although it recognizes a kind of normative element in the concept, it reduces that element to matters of fact and includes no genuine dictate of reason. It is more in accordance with common sense, Sidgwick urges, to recognize that there is a rational dictate to aim at what is taken to be one's own good. Since common sense keeps this element of authoritative dictation 'merely implicit or latent', Sidgwick defines the concept of 'my ultimate good on the whole' as 'what I would desire if my desires were in harmony with reason and I were considering myself alone'. And then, by removing the restriction to one person, he obtains a definition of 'ultimate good on the whole' as 'what one would desire if one's desires were in harmony with reason and one took oneself to have an equal concern for all existence'. (*ME* 7, p. 112.)

In moving to his final definition of 'own good', Sidgwick is not simply taking the tentative complex account already developed—that a man's own future good on the whole is 'what he would now desire if all the consequences of all the different lines of conduct open to him were accurately foreseen and adequately realised in imagination at the present time'—and adding to it the recognition that there is a rational dictate to aim at this 'if in any case a conflicting desire urges the will in an opposite direction'. (*ME* 7, pp. 111–12.) No doubt he has it in mind that something like this 'hypothetical composition of impulsive forces' would be involved in determining what it is to have one's desires in harmony with reason; and he certainly takes this kind of knowledge and appreciation of future consequences to be vital to rationality. Yet the final definition of 'own good' does not give the same privileged status as the previous one to the agent's desires at the present point of time, that is, at the moment of assessment or choice. It removes the restriction to what would be desired *at a given moment*, just as the definition of 'good on the whole' removes the restriction to what would be desired *by a given person*. The final account of 'own good' thus eliminates the possibility that a particular decision about what is good might be influenced by the desires one merely happened to have at the present moment in a way which would not be reasonable if one took into account all one's future desires. Similarly the final account of 'ultimate good' eliminates the possibility of introducing irrationality by considering the desires of only one person.

'Good, on my view,' Sidgwick says elsewhere, 'is what it is reasonable to seek to keep, or aim at getting; and Evil is what it is reasonable to seek to get rid of and avoid.' (*GSM*, p. 331.) The notion of what it is reasonable to seek, or to aim at getting, helps to bring out the connection between the concept of 'good' and the concept of 'right' or 'what it is reasonable to do'. Judgements of right, we have seen, involve a definite precept to perform acts judged right, and imply that we have the ability to do them. Judgements of good, being comparative, do not entail a definite dictate, and imply nothing about our abilities. Sidgwick does not indicate that there are any other significant differences between the meanings of 'right' and 'good'. We need therefore only say that the right act is, on his view, the best act which it is possible for the agent to do, to make clear the way in which the same basic notion is involved in both concepts. In the first two editions this is precisely what Sidgwick says. 'Though conduct on the whole wrong may have a certain goodness, the right conduct must always be best, or at least the best that is in our power', he writes in the first edition; and in the second, 'though wrong conduct may be judged to have a certain kind of goodness, right conduct must always be "best" . . . or, more strictly, . . . it must be "best in our power" . . .' (*ME* 1, p. 99; *ME* 2, p. 100.)

The concepts of goodness and rightness then represent differentiations of the demands of our own rationality as it applies to our sentient and our active powers. Seeing this helps give us a better understanding of what Sidgwick takes the basic indefinable notion of practical rationality to be. It is what is common to the notions of a reason to desire, a reason to seek or aim at, a reason to decide or choose, a reason to do; it does not involve an authoritative prescription to act where there is barely reason to desire something, or even where there is fairly strong reason, but only where there is stronger reason to desire one thing than to desire anything else, and that one thing is within our powers. At this point it becomes the through-and-through 'ought' or 'right' of definite dictates claiming to give authoritative guidance to our conduct. If any 'meta-ethical' answer to the question of the nature of the object of moral judgements is implicit in Sidgwick's position, it is that moral judgements embody the fact that we are reasonable beings who feel and act. In judging what is right or good, we are following out the implications of our rationality for the practical aspects of our nature.

Many objections might be made to Sidgwick's views about the basic concept of practical rationality and about the ways he relates it to the less fundamental concepts in whose meaning he thinks it is the common element. It will be more profitable, however, to pass them by in favour of commenting on the relation of his views here to some further aspects of his thought.

iii. *The Neutrality of Practical Concepts*

A satisfactory account of the meanings of key moral terms must be acceptable, Sidgwick thinks, to people with widely different moral views. Substantive issues cannot properly be settled by definitions. For example, the notion that terms such as 'ought' and 'right' have in common is

the same in different ethical systems: different systems give different answers to the fundamental question, 'what is right', but not, there-fore, a different meaning to the question. The Utilitarian . . . affirms that 'what is right' in any particular case is what is most conducive to the general happiness; but he does not—or ought not to—mean by the word 'right' anything different from what an anti-utilitarian moralist would mean by it. (1889f, p. 480.)

Sidgwick does not discuss how this demand for neutrality in practical concepts is to accommodate the fact that different positions on the issue of free will lead to using certain practical terms in different senses. Perhaps this is because he believes that the moral differences involved are slight and are disappearing. In other respects it is clearer that neutrality is preserved in his account of the meaning of moral terms.

The definition given of 'good' allows for degrees of desirability, since it is a concept which must be used in making comparisons; but it leaves it open whether what it is reasonable to desire, for its own sake, is to be found in the consequences of acts, in the characteristics of acts themselves, in characteristics of the agents, or in some combination of these. Thus, Sidgwick can say, both those who take the good to be virtue and those who take it to be pleasure may agree that the good is what it is reasonable to desire or aim at. There is also room, as far as the definition is concerned, for anyone who wishes to claim that the good is to be found in beauty, regardless of whether it is created by humans or not. Sidgwick is aware of the tradition which makes a distinction of kind between 'moral good' and 'natural good', assigning virtue to the first category and pleasure to the second (cf. *ME* 7, p. 479); and his definition is designed to bring out a way in which the two can be seen as species of one general kind. 'In modern languages', he comments in the first edition, 'the term "Good" as applied to conduct has distinctly the specific meaning of "morally excellent". It seems however legitimate, and convenient for our present purpose, to consider this only as a special application of the fundamental notion of "Good" = "intrinsically preferable or desirable".' (*ME* 1, p. 93; cf. also *ME* 1, pp. 96, 210, 441–2.) Sidgwick thinks the ideas of natural and of moral good are contained in common-sense morality 'undistinguished and therefore unharmonised'. (*ME* 7, pp. 239–40.) His account of 'good' enables us to distinguish them and so to raise clearly the question of their harmony. The account is thus similar to Kant's account of 'good', in allowing us to speak univocally of the goodness of virtue and the goodness of happiness as well as of the goodness of means and the goodness of ends. It differs, clearly, in stressing rational desire rather than rational willing or choice as the determinant of goodness. But the careful refusal to allow any actual desire to count simply by definition as a specific determinant of good leaves his definition purely formal.

The formalist approach is also evident in his account of 'right' and 'ought'. These terms imply that a judgement using them gives a definite directive to act, but imply nothing about what directive is given. They imply that the directive given is a reasonable one, but imply nothing about what the reason for it is. Sidgwick is aware, for instance, that many people do not consider purely self-interested considerations to be 'moral' reasons for actions, but he himself does not use the term 'moral' in such a limited way. His concern is with the methods by which we obtain ultimate rational direction for action. He does not think that the question of the content of the principles involved in such methods can be settled by simple linguistic considerations. If what is 'moral' must by definition involve concern for the good of others and not only concern for the good of the agent, then, Sidgwick would say, it may well turn out that principles which are 'moral' in this sense are not the principles underlying the most important or finally authoritative rational methods for guiding action. The point is to determine how we are to decide what it is ultimately reasonable to do, regardless of whether the ultimately reasonable is called 'moral' or not. He is consequently not willing to say that the very meaning of 'ought', even its narrower ethical meaning, rules out the possibility that self-interested considerations may support moral judgements.

One question that may arise about the neutrality of ethical terms on his account springs from his assertion that the right act must be the best act within the agent's power.[3] It may seem that this definition must bias his account of morality in favour of a consequentialist position, whether egoistic or universalistic, and against a purely deontological position. But it does not do so. It is clear from the purely formal nature of the definition of 'good' that the goodness which is maximized when

[3] I have benefited from the discussion of some of the issues here in Bernard Williams, 'A Critique of Utilitarianism', in *Utilitarianism For and Against*, by J. J. C. Smart and Bernard Williams, 1973, esp. pp. 86–9.

the right act is done is not necessarily the goodness of consequences. Moreover, the definitions neither say nor imply
anything about how the presence of goodness and rightness is
to be determined. They leave open both the possibility that
we may determine the rightness of acts by using some measure
of comparative goodness to tell which of the acts the agent
can do is best or produces the most good, and the possibility
that we may determine the rightness of acts by using some
non-comparative indicator of duty (such as a direct dictate of
God), and then infer that this must be the act by doing which
we do what is best. The definitions, finally, do not say whether
rightness is a characteristic that makes things good, or goodness
a characteristic that makes things right. Sidgwick does eventually arrive at a position on this particular point, but it is only
by means of a lengthy attempt to systematize our common-sense
moral judgements. The only point settled by the definitions of
'right' and 'good' is that rightness necessarily involves maximizing goodness to the extent the agent is able to do so. The
definitions are neutral enough to accommodate both sides in
the utilitarian–intuitionist controversy.

iv. *Scepticism*

In doing moral philosophy, then, we are concerned with what
it is reasonable to desire, to seek, and to do. Sidgwick has little
to say about reason as such, and what little he says he puts
in commonplace terms. To say that moral judgements are
dictates of reason, he points out, is not to say that they are
given by 'the dictation of reason' or obtained by conscious
reasoning (*ME* 7, p. 345)—he is no Godwinian—but only that
they bear the characteristic marks of judgements which are
subject to rational support and critique. They can be con-
tradicted, their truth or falsity is objective in the sense that
what any one person thinks, if he thinks correctly, cannot be
denied without error by others, and reasons for and against
them can be given. (*ME* 7, pp. 33–4.) This holds as much for
judgements about particular acts as for those about general
principles. The operations of reason are on Sidgwick's view
typically carried out not at the level of particular judgements,
which are usually assigned to a perceptual faculty or a sense,
but at higher levels of generality. In matters of morality the

difference of degree of generality is unimportant because particular moral judgements are taken to be generalizable. The moral truth contained in a judgement about a single act, Sidgwick says, 'is implicitly conceived to be intrinsically universal, though particular in our first apprehension of it' (*ME* 7, p. 34), and this is another ground for assigning morality to the realm or faculty of reason. Sidgwick takes reasoning to involve both inferential and non-inferential or intuitive processes. In Chapter 9 we shall discuss in more detail what he thinks is required for a proposition to serve as a reason for a moral judgement. We shall see that he does not think that there is any special or specifically moral kind of reasoning.

What strikes the modern reader, then, is not anything original or singular about Sidgwick's view of reason or reasoning, but the apparent assurance with which, after the very few arguments already discussed, he takes it that moral judgements can be fully rational. He simply spends no time discussing relativism or scepticism as such in the *Methods*, though some examination of them occurs in later writings. Such confident rationalism seems to belong to the Victorian age, which, however troubled it may have been with religious doubt, does not appear to have been nearly as troubled as later periods by various forms of doubt about the reasonableness of morality. Sidgwick saw quite early that there is a valid kind of relativism, and that some people might confuse this with the kind which is thought to militate against the rationality and objectivity of morals. Duties are indeed relative to the circumstances and personal conditions of agents, but the variation here is itself based on objective principles and does not show them to be impossible. 'My ideal', he wrote in 1871 to his friend Roden Noel,

is a law infinitely constraining and yet infinitely flexible, not prescribing perhaps for any two men the same conduct, and yet the same law, because recognised by all as objective, and always varying on rational and therefore general grounds, 'the same', as Cicero says, 'for you and for me, here and at Athens, now and for ever'. (*Mem.*, p. 243.)

Relativism as a sceptical view arising from the variation or moral opinion from age to age and from society to society, however, Sidgwick is quite prepared to dismiss. He admits the variation but is undisturbed by any legitimate inferences to be drawn from it. Differences of factual belief and differences in the extent of sympathetic appreciation of the feelings of others are sufficient to account for many of the differences we find in particular moral judgements. (See *GSM*, pp. 226–7.) Sidgwick might also have applied to arguments based on cultural difference what he says about sceptical arguments from the genesis of moral beliefs: once the distinction is drawn between commonly accepted maxims which are not really self-evident and basic axioms which are, it is not clear that data concerning variation in moral opinion have any bearing on the matter. For they do not tend to discredit the latter, and the former have in any event no claim to be taken as absolutely true. We shall see, when in Chapter 11 we come to examine the method Sidgwick thinks the utilitarian should use, that he as a utilitarian would be prepared to grant a substantial measure of validity to the existing code of any society, on utilitarian grounds; but this is not admitting a kind of variation in morals which leads to scepticism.

We have already discussed the analysis of scepticism on which Sidgwick bases his treatment of it, in Chapter 1. Complete scepticism, he holds, cannot be supported by rational argument. In so far as the discovery of error among our firm beliefs creates a presumption that any or all of our beliefs may be erroneous, the presumption may be rebutted by identifying a clear subclass of beliefs within which no error has been found. The full justification for positively rejecting scepticism, rather than ignoring it, depends on finding such a subclass of beliefs. Hence for Sidgwick the full justification of the claim that morality is rational requires finding a class of moral beliefs of this kind. And to do this, in turn, requires the systematic reconstruction of our common-sense morality, showing how its methods can be based on self-evident axioms which are consistent with one another and which elicit general agreement. We have noted that Sidgwick disavows the intention of presenting such a system in the *Methods*. He makes it clear, however, that if such a complete systematization of morality cannot, in principle at least, be obtained, then a form of scepticism is the upshot. Contemplating the situation he would be in if he were forced to admit an irremovable contradiction in the apparently self-evident principles which could serve to systematize common-sense morality, he says he would be forced to abandon—not morality, which habit and sympathy would keep strong in him, but—the idea of rationalizing morality fully. Supposing then that a case were to arise in which the contradictory principles were inescapably involved, 'practical reason, being divided against itself, would cease to be a motive on either side: the conflict would be decided by the comparative preponderance of one or other of two groups of non-rational impulses'. He does not of course say that the appearance of a basic contradiction would prove the truth of moral scepticism. But reason could not be effectively practical under the supposed conditions, and hence, Sidgwick says in an apt term, he would 'lapse to the position which many utilitarians since Hume have avowedly held—that ultimate ends are determined by feeling, not by reason'. (1889f, p. 485; cf. *ME* 1, p. 472; *ME* 7, p. 508.)

In so far as the arguments for the rationality of moral judgements depend either upon ordinary language or upon introspection, they are, as Sidgwick would agree, inconclusive. Common sense, as he repeatedly tells us, is not a final court of appeal. Its evidence is only one part of what must be considered. Paradigm cases of what we actually say or think are not decisive, for, as we have seen in the case of terms that presuppose some strong theory of free will, what we say and think may change. Introspection can be erroneous. And that ability to grasp simple concepts and obtain basic propositions which Sidgwick calls 'intuition' is never held to be incapable of error. By calling it 'intuition', Sidgwick says, he does not 'mean to prejudge the question of its ultimate validity, when philosophically considered'. (*ME* 7, p. 211; cf. p. 342, n. 2.) Language and introspection as well as common-sense beliefs and intuitions provide evidence which must all be fitted into a coherent system before we can have anything which approaches being a finally reliable view. The possibility of linking all our ethical concepts through one common basic notion is therefore itself part of the argument to show that practical judgements are within the domain of reason.[4]

---

[4] This important point explains Sidgwick's occasional expressions of doubt about the irreducibility and simplicity of the basic notion of ethics. At one place he says

Appendix. The Development of I, iii, and I, ix

In the first edition of the *Methods* the views which we have been examining are far less fully developed than they came to be. Neither the distinctive arguments in support of the rationality of moral judgements nor the definition of 'good' as 'what is reasonably desired' are presented. Sidgwick tries in I, i, to isolate a special sense of 'ought', the sense which comes plainly to mind when we think of 'an end *absolutely* prescribed by reason' (*ME* 1, p. 8), and he rejects simplistic forms of relativism while admitting a form which is compatible with the basic objectivity of morality. Nowhere does he say much about a fundamental moral notion, except in a footnote to I, viii, which, to a reader of the later editions, suggests a great deal:

> I may remind the reader that I use the terms 'right' and 'reasonable', and the equivalent phrase 'what ought to be' [done or aimed at], to express a notion so fundamental that it does not seem possible to define it in the ordinary way: but only in the manner in which I have tried to make it clear in c. 1 of this book, by distinguishing it from other notions with which it is liable to be confunded. (*ME* 1, p. 80 n.)

Later in III, i, Sidgwick remarks on the difference between admittedly subjective judgements of taste and moral judgements (*ME* 1, p. 183), but the point is not systematically explored.

The connection between reason and morality is discussed briefly in I, iii. Sidgwick points out that mental 'faculties' are known only from their effects. Hence it is important to be precise about what is claimed about mental phenomena in the claim to locate their source in one or another faculty. When we say that moral distinctions are apprehended by reason, he holds, we are saying simply that there is such a thing as moral truth or error, and that 'two conflicting judgments as to what ought to be done cannot both be true and sound'. He explicitly

that possibly 'ought' and 'is', which are co-ordinate simple notions, may 'prove capable of being arranged in some system of rational evolution; but . . . no such system has as yet been constructed, and . . . therefore the notions are now and for us ultimate'. (1889f., p. 480.) A similar point is made in a later paper (1892c), some of which is used in *Phil.*, p. 235.

The question of moral scepticism in Sidgwick is discussed briefly again in Ch. 15.

refuses to try to prove this. He says that it must be assumed by all who make moral judgements; and since he is only examining methods of reasoning used generally, he does not need to prove what no one disputes. (*ME* 1, p. 23.) He does argue against those who, by appealing to a moral sense, think they have filled the need for objective truth or rationality in morals. A sense gives us feelings but cannot attribute to some of them the supremacy which is claimed by morality. If a sense is understood not as giving feelings but as informing us of something which must be admitted by everyone, then the quarrel about sense or reason in ethics can be dropped; for Sidgwick is prepared to agree that emotion always accompanies the deliverances of the moral faculty. (*ME* 1, p. 24.)

To clarify the role of reason, Sidgwick distinguishes between a 'categorically imperative' function of reason and a function in which it dictates means to ends, with no assumption that the end itself is rational. (*ME* 1, pp. 24–5.) Here what reason does is to 'introduce consistency into our conduct', since it tells us that once we have adopted an end and seen what is the means to it we are inconsistent if we do not use the means. 'One meaning of "irrational" as applied to conduct is "inconsistent",' Sidgwick says, and he goes on to distinguish two levels of inconsistency and irrationality. If our impulses are not harmonized by any conscious thought they may not in fact conflict, yet conduct resulting from them is in his view irrational because it is 'absolutely unsystematised and in that sense inconsistent'. (*ME* 1, p. 25.) If the impulses conflict because, having reached a certain degree of generality, they are no longer merely momentary, we have a second grade of irrationality. One who acts reasonably, Sidgwick says, 'acts by general rules or notions', and thinks a desire unreasonable either if it conflicts with one of them or if it cannot be subsumed under one of them, i.e. 'when no general grounds can be stated for it'. As if this were not a sufficiently strong requirement for rationality, Sidgwick continues:

But again, general rules and maxims may in their turn be found mutually inconsistent, in either sense: and here too conduct appears to us irrational or at least imperfectly rational, not only if the maxims upon which it is professedly based conflict with and contradict one another, but also if they cannot be bound together and firmly concatenated by means of some one fundamental principle. For practical reason does not seem to be thoroughly realised until a perfect order, harmony, and unity of system is introduced into all our actions. (*ME* 1, pp. 25–6.)

This passage does not occur after the first edition and it is not replaced by any equally explicit and strong statement of the conditions of rationality. But it gives us an important insight into Sidgwick's thinking, showing clearly the ideal of practical rationality which always haunted him. This ideal sets the standard against which common sense morality is to be tried and found wanting.

Sidgwick immediately points out that while it is possible for conduct to satisfy certain 'formal' conditions of rationality by thorough subordination to the needs of some end, such conduct is not fully rational unless the end is itself rational. Reason, therefore, he concludes, in addition to judging means–ends relations and the consistency of maxims, determines 'the ultimate ends and true first principles of action'. He simply assumes that it is 'an intuitive operation of the practical reason' which is involved in doing this. (*ME* 1, p. 26.)

The second question discussed in I, iii, is whether reason can be a spring of action. The view laid down is that there is a 'certain desire or impulse to do' whatever is seen to be reasonable, and that this is 'generally admitted'. (*ME* 1, p. 28.) This rather Pickwickian way of making reason a spring of action is dropped in the second edition and replaced, a little hesitantly, by the final view, or more precisely, the final refusal to adopt a view, which was discussed in Chapter 6.

In I, ix, Sidgwick discusses the relations of 'right' and 'good'. Up to this point, he says, emphasis has been placed on the former notion, which seems unavoidable in discussing the guidance of action. 'We may perhaps say,' he comments, 'that this notion of "ought", when once it has been developed, is a necessary form of our moral apprehension, just as space is now a necessary form of our sense perception.' (*ME* 1, p. 93; *ME* 2, p. 94; not in *ME* 3.) We might however make the good central rather than the right, and concentrate on what we are attracted to rather than what we are directed to. At this point Sidgwick notes the two differences between 'right' and 'good' which we have discussed above and remarks on the fact that the concept of 'good' essentially admits of degrees. How then do we estimate degrees of goodness? Sidgwick argues, for the most part as in the final edition, that the standard of goodness is not simply pleasure. He suggests that we estimate the degree of goodness of things of any given kind by 'such simple ultimate intuitions' as those by which we judge comparable aspects of physical objects. Without giving general consideration to the comparison of goods of different kinds, he comments only on the comparison of the right and the good. This is, he thinks, a 'purely formal' difference: 'their practical prescriptions are never found to conflict.' (*ME* 1, p. 99.) The remainder of the chapter is devoted (as it continues to be in later editions) to discussion of the relation of what is ultimately good to human consciousness.

In the second edition almost all the discussion of moral concepts is concentrated in I, iii. Here the arguments in support of the objectivity and rationality of moral judgements are introduced (*ME* 2, pp. 25 ff.) and a rudimentary form of the analysis of the concept of intrinsic goodness is also given. (*ME* 2, pp. 32–3.) I, ix is not essentially altered.

The third edition contains extensive changes in I, iii. Sidgwick is less tentative about the position concerning the irreducibility of moral to non-moral judgements and about the motive power of reason, though he adds little to the arguments. A discussion of the distinction between 'objective' and 'subjective' rightness, added in *ME* 2, is moved to another chapter, and the analysis of the concept of intrinsic good moved to its final place in I, ix. This analysis is there given in what is, in the main, its final form, though later editions contain numerous verbal changes.

The arguments in support of the intuitional view of moral concepts and the position on the interconnections of these concepts were not, then, fully articulated until a decade after the first publication of the *Methods*. But the germs of most of the later points are present in the earliest version and none of the changes amounts to a radical departure from its positions.

8

Acts and Agents

SIDGWICK wrote more frequently about James Martineau's views than about those of any of his other contemporaries except Herbert Spencer. Spencer got more attention in the late lectures, but more consideration of Martineau went into the making of the *Methods*, which, from the first edition on, contained a chapter devoted largely to criticism of him—a degree of attention accorded no other philosopher. Yet Martineau is now even more completely forgotten by philosophers than Spencer. To understand Sidgwick's controversy with him, we shall therefore have to begin with some account of his position. A few facts about him are pertinent. Martineau, who was born in 1805 and died in 1900, was the greatest leader of the Unitarians in Victorian England. In 1845 and 1846 he published two long, careful reviews of Whewell's ethical writings, and it was from these that Sidgwick first learned Martineau's own theory. Although the positive aspects of the theory were only sketched in outline in the reviews, Martineau thought well enough of Sidgwick's criticisms to feel he had to deal with them when he finally came to publish a full account of his moral philosophy in *Types of Ethical Theory* (1885). Martineau's philosophy was shaped by his reaction against the associationistic and utilitarian views of the earlier Unitarian writers and was firmly fixed by the times of the reviews of Whewell. Later developments in ethics did not alter his thinking. He is thus a pre-Sidgwickian intuitionist, despite the accident of the late appearance of his major work in ethics.

i. *Martineau's Theory*

Martineau's philosophy is unabashedly a defence of religious doctrine, and his version of religion is Christian. Like the Cambridge Coleridgeans, he holds that we need not rely solely on a miraculous revelation for knowledge of God and his purposes. God reveals himself to all men through various aspects of experience. All men have immediate and intuitively evident beliefs in an external world, an enduring self, and a moral order. No philosophical arguments, not even Kant's, Martineau holds, have given any good reason to doubt these deliverances of consciousness, and from them we may be led to a religious understanding of the universe and of our lives. The world outside us is studied by the sciences, which can tell us only of sequences of phenomena. But because each of us is an active, willing agent, we have the idea of a kind of causation which is independent of sequence and regularity, and which is free. Through this idea of ourselves we come to see the universe as an expression of a will like our own, but infinite. Science confirms this belief by its discovery of regularity in outer phenomena, while the moral aspects of God, by far the most important aspects, are revealed through our intuitions of the moral order. Philosophy, Martineau holds, is the interpretation of the basic intuitions through which God reveals himself in experience.

The basic fact within the realm of morality is that we have a tendency to approve and disapprove, or to pass judgements of right and wrong.[1] In interpreting this fact, Martineau's first step is to claim that the objects of moral judgement are 'persons exclusively and not things'. (*TET*, p. 21.) Actions are judged, but only in so far as they are 'personal phenomena', not as physical happenings. 'It follows', Martineau thinks, 'that what we judge is always the inner spring of an action, as distinguished from its outward operation.' (*TET*, p. 24.) He puts a great deal of weight on this point, which he takes to be self-evident. 'It is a characteristic of the Christian ethics, and finds its most solemn expression in the Sermon on the Mount', he says, and comments that 'it is directly opposed to the maxim that the only value of good affections is for the production of good actions'. The emphasis on springs of action connects Martineau's view with the doctrine of justification by faith. In making it central, he says, 'we touch upon an essential distinction between the Christian and the Utilitarian ethics; and confidently claim for the former the verdict of our moral consciousness.' (*TET*, pp. 26–7.)

---

[1] All references to Martineau are to *Types of Ethical Theory* (1885), 3rd edn., 1891, vol. ii, abbreviated in the text as *TET*. Pagination seems to be the same as that in the second edition, which Sidgwick used.

Martineau begins the elaboration of his theory by distinguishing between spontaneous and voluntary acts. A voluntary act involves the presence of at least two different impulses to action, a conscious comparison between them, and a choice of one of them, while a spontaneous act involves only the presence of one impulse, followed by action. (*TET*, pp. 33 ff.) The impulses present prior to voluntary action must involve 'simultaneous possibilities' of action: the impulses themselves must be 'co-present', and action on either of them must be really possible to the agent. (*TET*, pp. 37–8.) This last point leads Martineau to think that liberty of choice is vitally important to morality: 'either free-will is a fact, or moral judgment a delusion.' (*TET*, p. 41.) Now moral judgement is not passed on spontaneous acts, but only on voluntary acts; and the basic form of moral judgement, in Martineau's view, is the assessment of one spring of action as higher in value than another one simultaneously present and conflicting with it in the direction its impulse would give to practise. The measure used in judging one spring higher than another is not pleasure, but 'Moral Worth'; and Martineau thinks he can claim the authority of Sidgwick for taking this as a basic moral notion which is unique and unanalysable. (*TET*, pp. 46–7.) Though the basic concept is simple, we can work out a systematic scale of values because whenever a pair of impulses presents itself to a moral agent, it is immediately clear to him which is of greater moral worth. As the agent experiences more and more pairs of impulses, he will have more and more 'resources . . . for forming an entire scale of principles, exhibiting the gradations of ethical rank'. This scale will never be complete, but we can always improve on what we have. (*TET*, p. 48.) Martineau takes it that a principle or impulse of higher worth ought to be followed out into action rather than one of lower worth, and he is therefore led to define conscience as our own 'critical perception . . . of the relative authority of our several principles of action'. To have conscience working within us we do not need explicit knowledge of the ranking of motives. We need only 'implicit knowledge', which Martineau describes as 'a feeling, true to the real relations of duty, that this is worthier than that'. (*TET*, pp. 54–8.) The assumptions sketched here enable us, Martineau thinks, to account for variation in moral opinion among men, despite their common ability to intuit rankings on a universally valid scale of value. Different men have different ranges of experience of the springs of action. Hence they tend to compare some given impulse with quite different impulses, and, not noticing that their judgement result from different comparisons, they think they value the impulse differently. But further experience will reconcile their views. (*TET*, pp. 61–2.)

The value of motives on the scale is the fundamental determinant of right action. 'Every action is right', Martineau says, 'which, in presence of a lower principle, follows a higher: every action is wrong, which, in presence of a higher principle, follows a lower.' (*TET*, p. 270.) But consideration of the motives alone is not sufficient to tell us precisely which action to do. Once conscience has told the agent which is the worthier motive, it is up to his reason to determine the act which in the circumstances best expresses that motive. To do this the agent must consider consequences and must calculate the best means for realizing the motive. But the choice made on these grounds, Martineau holds, is not the distinctively moral choice. It is a rational choice, or as he sometimes says, a prudential choice. Error in making it is not moral error and is not condemned in the same way or the same terms as the error of choosing to act on the less worthy of one's motives. (*TET*, pp. 232–5, 275.)

The hierarchy of motives is involved in determining merit and virtue as well as rightness. To understand judgements of merit we must consider prudence first. Prudence is our concern for the effects of action on us, rather than for their origins within us. Impulses to act have natural degrees of strength as well as degrees of relative worth, and they may be ranked according to strength. Martineau gives an oddly un-Butlerian account of living prudently. It is, he says, gratifying impulses 'in the order of their eagerness' or strength. For this reason the prudential scale of impulses, unlike the moral scale, will vary from man to man. Prudence varies like fancy, morality is universal like reason. (*TET*, pp. 74–7.) Merit is a resultant of both aspects of impulses, their strength and their worth. For it depends on the resistance put up against a strong desire by one who sees that he ought to act on another, worthier, impulse. Since the strength of motives varies, what is meritorious or disgraceful varies also. (*TET*, pp. 80–2.) There is a related distinction between merit and virtue, since someone who must struggle to do his duty is less virtuous, but more meritorious, than one to whom following the higher impulse is always easy. Both merit and virtue presuppose genuine freedom of choice. (*TET*, p. 87.) So, indeed, does every moral concept: it must be at least conceivable that a holy being should deviate from the right course if such a being is to be said to be doing his duty. (*TET*, pp. 95–8.)

What, then, is the nature of the authority possessed by the higher over the lower of any pair of active impulses? The 'feeling' of authority, as he often refers to it, is in its nature simple and admits of 'little analysis', but as it is often confused with other feelings we can clarify it by seeing the errors of certain philosophers. Bentham's view is first dismissed. The moral sense is not just an '*ipse dixit*', a private feeling to which each individual happens to assent. Quite the contrary: to sense the authority of an impulse is to sense something higher than oneself. And since each of us is a person, that which is higher than we can only be another person, 'greater and higher and of deeper insight'. Not surprisingly Martineau identifies this person as God. (*TET*, pp. 99, 104–5.) The moral faculty, he tells us, is 'the communion of God's life and guiding love entering and abiding with an apprehensive capacity in myself'. Because we are able to move from moral awareness to religious consciousness, we see that we cannot take the authority of conscience to be merely subjective, nor can we treat it simply 'as that of Reason "impersonally conceived"; for that which is real in the universal Archetype of all Mind cannot be either an abstraction or an accidental phenomenon of human individuality'. (*TET*, p. 105.) Martineau also rejects Paley's account of moral authority, which reduces it to hopes and fears of future rewards and punishments (*TET*, pp. 111–13), but his positive comments here and later shed little further light on his own view.

The substance of Martineau's ethical system is given in a lengthy analysis of motives, which is aimed at constructing an explicit scale of their comparative moral worth. He distinguishes primary principles, which are 'essentially disinterested' and lead us to seek certain types of external objects or states of affairs, from secondary principles whose aim is always some state of ourselves (*TET*, p. 167), and he analyses each of them. The principles combine to create complex passions and impulses which sometimes appear, on introspection, to be simple (*TET*, pp. 182 ff.), and some of these complex springs of action are also discussed. The distinction between passions directed at external states of affairs and those directed at one's own condition clearly derives from Butler, as does Martineau's insistence that prudence and conscience are not themselves separate active impulses: 'each exercises simply a judicial function, and on grounds peculiar to itself, arbitrates among their pretensions, and sets free some one of them from the hesitation imposed by the importunity of the others. . . . Prudence is evidently confined altogether to the secondary principles; while Conscience has a discriminating voice over the whole.' (*TET*, p. 186.) The outcome of his discussions is the table of springs of action (*TET*, p. 266) which Sidgwick reproduces in III, xii. We shall note some of its details when we come to consider Sidgwick's criticisms of it.

On Martineau's view, then, the human being has a free moral personality, and as such is capable of possessing the highest and most important kind of value which the universe can contain. In making the goodness of the moral agent basic, and defining right action in terms of the choices a good man would make, Martineau is reflecting in the logic of his theory—in what he refers to as the 'order of derivation' of the concepts (*TET*, p. 56)—the order of importance he sees in its objects. His view is constructed in deliberate opposition to that of the utilitarian, who takes as his basic concept the idea of the goodness of states of affairs which have value quite independently of how they are brought into existence. The notions of the goodness of a human agent and the rightness of action are then explained in terms of potential or actual production of these states of affairs. To Martineau, here repeating a similar criticism made by earlier opponents of utilitarianism, this is tantamount to viewing personality, the unique free bearer of the highest value, as a mere instrument for the production of a lower kind of good. This direct inversion of what Martineau sees as the moral order of the universe is reflected in the inversion of the proper conceptual order in the moral theory of utilitarianism. The mistaken logic of the utilitarian theory and its moral wrongheadedness, he suggests, are not in the end separable.

ii. *The Religious Context of Martineau's Theory*

Martineau's view, though expounded at length and with fervour, is not richly supported with argument, and it is tempting to dismiss it as eccentric. If we ask instead why it seemed so obvious to him as not to need much proof, we may find a standpoint from which his view is more intelligible, and Sidgwick's concern with it more comprehensible.

We get a clue as to where to begin from Martineau's emphasis on consideration of motives rather than consequences, and his insistence that this is required in order to obtain an account of the distinctively moral kind of evaluation. Questions of the worth of an agent's motives arise more naturally when we are assessing merit and demerit, praiseworthiness or culpability, than when we are trying to reach a decision about what act ought to be done next. If we look at Martineau's various positions in this light, it becomes clear that the guiding thought in all of them is that retrospective moral judgements are to be taken as paradigmatic for all of morality. He himself makes this quite explicit when he contrasts his own view with that of James Mill. On Mill's view, he says, the moral sentiments are 'a prospective artifice for extracting serviceable conduct which needs a bonus to produce it. In mine, they are a retrospective verdict of "well done!" or "ill done!" on conduct already put forth.' (*TET*, p. 347.) If Martineau's distinctive positions can be defended at all, it is by taking them as arising always from consideration of what we can be held responsible for in moral assessments of past actions.[2]

When we are morally assessing an agent we tend to discount things that it was not within his power to control. That we do so, it is plausible to say, is a distinctive mark of a moral assessment of an agent. We do not discount such things so widely in other sorts of assessments of agents. A temporary lack of ability

---

[2] There are passages in T. H. Green's *Prolegomena to Ethics* which show his strong interest in retrospective contexts, but Green does not confine morality to them. See *Prol. E.*, paragraphs 291–2.

may be overlooked, but if, for instance, it is simply beyond a man's power ever to run a mile in under six minutes, then he is just no good—for the track team. The one kind of assessment of a person in which even his permanent disabilities are ignored, it may seem, is the moral kind. His circumstances too are discounted wholly in moral assessment, but not so completely, and sometimes not at all, in other types of evaluation. We can put the difference between moral and other kinds of assessment in another way. In moral assessment, we may say, it must be entirely up to the agent whether or not he gets a high rating; in other kinds it is not.

If we press this point further we can see how Martineau might have been led to the view that the object of moral intuition is the comparative worth of motives. Plainly the consequences of actions are not wholly up to the agent. One can appeal to familiar instances of the failure of well-meant attempts to do good and to the familiar judgements we make on such failures to show that common sense does not hold people responsible for such results. One could then generalize this to the conclusion that results are not the object of moral judgement. A similar line of thought can easily lead to excluding the act itself, as distinct from the results, particularly if one is inclined to identify the act with the bodily movements of the agent who does it. And Martineau is inclined to do this, since he estimates the intention and the motive, as mental events, separately from the action. He holds that 'intellectual' errors— mistakes of fact or computation—are not thought by common sense to be blameworthy. 'The choice of means by which to carry out the workings of a spring of conduct', he says, 'can be made only by consideration of consequences. This subsidiary rule, however, must be regarded as rather of an intellectual than of a moral nature; for if a man err in its application, he will be mistaken only, and will not be a proper object of disapprobation.' (*TET*, p. 275.) Now to form intentions is to calculate, on the basis of what we know or believe, how best to realize a given goal or aim. In so far as intentions depend on such 'intellectual' points they do not make us worthy of moral praise or blame, and so they are not the prime object of moral judgement. What then is left?

We cannot, for Martineau, simply answer, 'Motive'. That

a given motive is present and operative in one—a desire for a certain object or situation—is not something which by itself is entirely up to the agent. One cannot be held responsible for it. And it is for this reason that Martineau says that cases where only one motive is present are not cases where moral judgements can apply. It is only where there is more than one that the critical situation arises. As we have seen, Martineau thinks it is entirely up to the agent which of two simultaneously present motives he will act upon. It is not up to him to determine which two are present. He is no more to blame if heredity has endowed him with propensities to irascibility, gluttony, and sloth, than he is if he was born into disease, poverty, and corruption. He no more makes the psychological situation he finds within himself—allowing for the need for long range attempts at self-improvement—than he makes the world around him. What he can always do, Martineau holds, is to make the best of his situation, or, more precisely, make the better of it, by choosing to act from the better of two competing motives. But if this is the only thing about which distinctively moral judgements can be passed, then for morality to be possible at all, the character of his own motives must be clear to each agent and the relative value of any pair of motives must be unmistakeably evident.

The logic behind Martineau's position, then, is the logic of counting as truly moral only what is considered as such in retrospective assessments of agents. The question is why he should have been so concerned about this particular aspect of morality. The answer, it may be supposed, lies in his deeply felt religious beliefs. He repeatedly accuses all utilitarian views of being opposed to religion, and he thinks of his own position as the only thorough-going alternative to them. And it is not hard to see how a morality built within a general framework of Christian presuppositions might well make consideration of the worth of agents central, and relegate consequences and rules determining the rightness of acts to a secondary place. 'Who may say', writes a commonplace preacher of the period, 'that the objects contemplated by the Divine Mind were not the discipline and moral trial of the men, while the course of action adopted or the thing done has (irrespective of such discipline and trial) been a matter of secondary importance, or of no importance at all?'[3] One central strand of Christian thought holds that union with God, the ultimate end of human life, can be achieved only by those who are pure in spirit, and takes this to mean that moral goodness is in some way a condition of salvation. Such goodness is within the reach of all men. It does not depend on special knowledge, on natural abilities which are distributed unequally by a stepmotherly nature, on worldly wealth or position. It depends only on our trying as hard as we can to live as we ought—to pattern ourselves after the perfect exemplar whom God has sent us as a guide. The effects of our actions matter less than our striving for goodness. Our life is meant to be a time of trial and probation. Since God is looking after the world, and after us, the outcome of our efforts is in his hands. At the last judgement we will be asked, not what we actually accomplished, but what we hoped and tried to do. The last judgement, on this interpretation, is a moral judgement.

Christianity, which one is inclined at times to think contains every possible position, contains a long tradition of thought opposed to this moralistic view of salvation. In the anti-moralistic interpretation, the gift of divine grace, which is the one thing needful for salvation, must come before any worthwhile or deserving human choice or action is even possible. The position denying the possibility of man's meriting grace by his own volition, stressing the human depravity resulting from Adam's fall, and underlining the mysteriousness and incomprehensibility of God's redeeming action, was influential in the earlier part of the nineteenth century among Methodists and Evangelicals, though it had fewer articulate exponents later in the century. It was repugnant to the early Unitarians, who opposed the Calvinistic Christianity of their contemporaries, and Martineau was at one with them on this point. The general tendency of his philosophical ethics is plainly congruent with the religious stress of a moralistic Christian outlook. We may therefore see in his religion an explanation of his assumption that the paradigm judgements of morality are retrospective judgements, and of his consequent attempt to construct an entire theory on this basis.

[3] Edward Arthur Smedly, *A Treatise on Moral Evidence*, Cambridge, 1850, pp. xiii–xiv.

Martineau's position has on the face of it little to recommend it and Sidgwick's discussion, though certainly making a number of sound criticisms, seems to do little to advance the construction of his own theory. Yet the basic disagreement between the two is of some significance for an understanding of Sidgwick. It is a disagreement over the issue of whether what is central to a moral theory is consideration of the goodness or badness of the character of moral agents, or consideration of the rightness or wrongness of the acts moral agents perform. We have already seen that Sidgwick assumes the correctness of the second alternative in his attempt to show that the free will issue is irrelevant to ethics. Martineau offered the only philosophically serious attempt to defend the first alternative— sketched, we have noticed, by Coleridge—in Britain during the Victorian era. This may help to explain why Sidgwick devoted so much attention to his work. Most contemporary moral philosophers seem to assume that if either position is correct, it is obviously Sidgwick's. Sidgwick did not think the matter entirely obvious; and such interest as the controversy still has for us hinges on the fact that the criticisms of Martineau show some of the reasons Sidgwick has for the position he takes.

iii. *Sidgwick's Criticisms: the Data*

Sidgwick accepts neither Martineau's claim that the conscience of every man 'tells the same story', nor his belief that the sense of duty gives us irresistible evidence of the existence of a personal authority rightly ruling us. (1887, p. 31; *GSM*, pp. 322–5.) His main disagreement, however, is with the view that moral judgement of motives must be taken as basic in ethics. This, Sidgwick holds, is not simply a plain and obvious matter of fact. Comparison of motives is not the present normal form of moral judgements, and there is no reason to suppose it the original form in the development either of the individual or of the race. Martineau's position must therefore be judged as a theory is judged, in terms of its ability to account for the data and to meet the other requirements which theories must meet. (*ME* 7, pp. 364–5.) In the next section we shall examine why Sidgwick thinks it fails to meet these requirements. Here we shall look at his consideration of the data. To see how he brings out the errors of the view that moral judgements are in fact mainly concerned with motives, we must touch briefly on some aspects of his moral psychology. Matters are simplified by the fact that Martineau seems to work with ideas of the meanings of 'intention' and 'motive' which are very close to Sidgwick's. Martineau discusses these terms only incidentally. (*TET*, pp. 272 f., 294 f.) Sidgwick gives a fuller account.

The intention of an act, Sidgwick holds, is the agent's 'volition or choice of realising the effects as foreseen' of bodily movements he can control. Under 'foreseen effects' we must include all the foreseen effects, whether or not the agent desired them; for even if he did not want certain things to occur, or wanted them not to occur, if he chose to do something knowing they would occur he is held responsible for them. Sidgwick thinks this is in accordance with the ordinary use of the term 'intention'.[4] (*ME* 7, pp. 201–2.) 'Motive', by contrast, is defined in terms of desired effects. Sidgwick thinks the word is ambiguous in ordinary discourse. It means either 'foreseen consequences so far as the agent desired them' or else 'the desire of such consequences' (*ME* 7, p. 202; cf. p. 362); and for the purposes of his discussion of Martineau, Sidgwick proposes to take the second sense. He therefore thinks of motives as 'the desires of particular results, believed to be attainable as consequences of our voluntary acts, by which desires we are stimulated to will those acts'. (*ME* 7, p. 363.) In addition, a motive, as a felt desire, seems in Sidgwick's view no less than in Martineau's, to be directly available to introspection. In the first edition Sidgwick explicitly contrasts motives, which are said to be 'known to us directly by introspection', with dispositions, which, as we have noted, are knowable only through their effects (*ME* 1, p. 179); and although this clear statement disappears after the second edition, the treatment of dispositions and motives in the final version still supposes the view it expresses.

What, then, are our ordinary moral judgements about?

---

4 In the first edition Sidgwick defines 'action' as 'the effects as he [the agent] foresaw them in the act of willing, the intended effects, or briefly, the *intention*'. And he contrasts this with the 'motive', which is 'the conscious impulse to action, whether desire or aversion, which can be introspectively ascertained'. (*ME* 1, p. 179.) Though the view that the action just is the intention was less evident after the first edition, the general points in Sidgwick's position remained the same throughout the editions.

Sidgwick tries to clarify the issue by pointing out that everyone agrees that 'the moral judgements which we pass on actions relate primarily to intentional actions regarded as intentional'. It is not, in other words, acts simply as changes in the positions of human bodies, on which we pass moral judgements. (*ME* 7, p. 201.) He seems to think that because we only judge acts 'presumed to be intentional' we need no further discussion of the way moral judgement relates to acts and to intentions. There is rather more of an issue about motives. Sidgwick agrees that we sometimes do judge motives. It is commonly agreed, for example, that acts may be made better or worse by the presence of various motives. It may also be held that the intention of an act can be wrong while the motive is good, as in the case of a man committing perjury to save the life of a parent. 'Such judgments are, in fact, continually passed in common moral discourse', Sidgwick says (*ME* 7, p. 202), but what they indicate is that an act may be judged to be right or wrong independently of any judgement of the motive. To bring out another aspect of our ordinary thought on this matter, Sidgwick considers a case in which a man does what duty prescribes, but does it from a plainly bad motive: for instance, he prosecutes someone he really thinks guilty of a crime but does so purely from malice. Admitting that the prosecutor ought to get rid of his malice, and so agreeing that his intention is not wholly right unless it includes some effort to do so, Sidgwick says that it is plain that we cannot always control strong feelings. This is particularly difficult if we are in any case going to do the act to which the feeling prompts us. But 'if that act be clearly a duty which no one else can so properly perform, it would be absurd to say that we ought to omit it because we cannot altogether exclude an objectionable motive'. (*ME* 7, pp. 202–3.) Common sense holds, in short, that moral judgements about actions can be determined independently of judgements about motives, and that the former cannot ordinarily be overridden by the latter. In the first edition Sidgwick makes the point by saying simply that common sense thinks we must not do a bad act from a good motive. (*ME* 1, p. 179; cf. *GSM*, pp. 334–5.)

Ordinary judgements of rightness are about intentional acts, not about motives, then, and Sidgwick thinks that although we

do pass judgements about what an agent ought to do concerning his own motives we are mainly interested in intentions
about external effects. (*ME* 7, p. 204.) To bring this out, he
considers the Stoic or Kantian view, that 'the moral value of
our conduct depends upon the degree to which we are actuated
by . . . the desire or free choice of doing what is right as such'.
He is partly concerned to point out the paradox which arises
if one combines this view, as some philosophers have, with the
belief that being virtuous is the best means toward the attainment of one's own happiness. If one knows this, it is impossible,
he thinks, for anyone to 'exclude from his motives a regard for
his own interest', and so the knowledge that virtue is rewarded
would prevent the acquisition of virtue, a view Sidgwick thinks
untenable. (*ME* 7, pp. 204–5.) More importantly, he points out
that those who hold that the motive of duty for duty's sake is
a necessary condition of right action would not usually claim
that it is also a sufficient condition. They would admit that
a man who acts from a pure desire to act rightly might 'have
a wrong judgment as to the particulars of his duty, and therefore, in another sense, may act wrongly'. Hence if one takes it
as a necessary condition of right action that the motive is the
love of duty, one must distinguish two kinds of rightness,
which have been called 'formal' and 'material', though Sidgwick indicates his own distaste for these terms. (*ME* 7, p. 206.)
Formal rightness is present whenever the agent is moved by
the pure moral motive, material rightness when in addition
'he intends the right particular effects'. (*ME* 7, p. 207.) But
material rightness is plainly what presents problems to the
plain man, even when he is quite willing to do his duty; and it
is therefore our primary concern. (*ME* 7, p. 207; cf. *ME* 1,
p. 181.)

Another aspect of this complex issue points toward the same
conclusion. Those who distinguish formal from material rightness imply, Sidgwick says, that when someone is formally right
he has both a belief that his act is right and a desire to do it as
right. But someone may have the belief while doing the act
from some other motive, although it is not possible to do an
act from the desire to do what is right without the belief that
it is right. Now moralists of this school, like everyone else,
would agree that it is more important for the agent to think his

act is right than to be moved by the pure moral motive. For it is generally accepted that an act cannot be completely right if the agent does it believing it to be wrong. Once again, the centrality of rightness of acts is made clear. (*ME* 7, p. 207.)

This point in turn raises another question. Suppose someone who is moved by the purest moral motive is mistaken about what is objectively right. We might ask whether in such a case it would be better for him to do what is objectively wrong, but right in terms of his subjective convictions, or whether he should do what is objectively right even against his convictions. In dealing with this question Sidgwick makes an important point. The question can arise only in quite unusual circumstances. No agent, thinking about what he himself ought to do, 'can distinguish what he believes to be right from what really is so' (*ME* 7, p. 207), and therefore the question cannot be raised in a standard deliberative situation. It can only arise if one person is aware that another, holding firm but mistaken moral convictions, is about to act on those convictions. Then, if it is not possible to lead him to alter his opinions, the first person might wonder whether it would be worse to bring him to act against his convictions (e.g. by a bribe) or to let him proceed on his objectively wrong way. Common sense, Sidgwick thinks, would regard subjective rightness as more important than objective in most cases of this sort, though not if the damage that would result from preventing the wrong act were very great. (*ME* 7, p. 208; cf. *GSM*, pp. 332–3.) But the very fact that it is only in these special circumstances, not generally, that this kind of question can arise, shows that for the most part the plain man is concerned with objective rightness, and not with subjective rightness or what the agent merely thinks is right. The latter, Sidgwick suggests, is a matter connected with our concern for the agent's moral character. The former is tied directly to our primary concern for what ought to be done.

One further point of interest is added. Kant, says Sidgwick, 'seems to have held that all particular rules of duty can be deduced from the one fundamental rule' that we should act as if the maxim of our action were by our will to become a universal law of nature. Sidgwick agrees that universalizability is a necessary condition of rightness but holds that it is not sufficient. In fact, he says, we often find equally conscientious persons in disagreement as to what ought to be done in a given case, although each could sincerely will his own maxim to be a universal law. If we say both are right, we 'obliterate altogether the distinction between subjective and objective rightness' and allow that except for mistakes of fact whatever anyone thinks right is right. But this is 'in flagrant conflict with common sense'. It would also make it pointless to set up a clear and precise moral code, since the whole point of such a code is to help us reach agreements about what ought to be done. (*ME* 7, pp. 209–10.) Kant sometimes presents his basic law as if, like Martineau, he derived it from generalizing the principle which guides our retrospective judgements of agents to cover our prospective judgements of acts as well. Sidgwick's criticism may or may not rest on a defensible reading of Kant. In either case it indicates clearly that on his own view there is a point to judgements about the objective and material rightness of acts which is different from, and independent of, our concern with the moral character of agents.

iv. *Sidgwick's Criticisms: the Theory*

If these considerations show that judgement of the moral value of motives is not as a matter of fact the normal or most prevalent form of moral judgement, and that it is also not accepted as always the most important or overriding form, the point Martineau must prove is that by taking judgements of motive as basic, a theory results which 'approves itself . . . by the systematic clearness and mutual consistency of the results' to which it leads different people, and 'by its freedom from the puzzles and difficulties' to which other methods are subject. (*ME* 7, p. 365.) A whole series of problems with Martineau's theory shows, Sidgwick thinks, that it does not meet these tests.

The criticisms of Martineau are presented after Sidgwick has completed his own examination of common-sense morality, in the course of which he brings out in detail how impossible it is to extract from it completely clear and precise rules of right action on which everyone agrees. This result is used in one of the first objections to Martineau. Impulses towards moral goals, such as truth or frankness or justice, are 'observable as distinct and independent impulses' in people who have been properly raised. But their existence poses a dilemma for any theory like Martineau's. To exclude them from the hierarchical list of motives is to omit a major class of motives. To include them threatens the theory with inability to yield a way of making decisions which improves on common sense rules of objective rightness. If someone decides to act on a moral motive rather than on some other motive, seen to be lower, he must still determine what specific act to do. If the 'objects' of the moral impulses are thought of in common sense terms, the Martineauvian theory will duplicate all the difficulties Sidgwick has already found in common-sense morality. On the other hand, if the 'object' of a moral sentiment is conceived in clear and simple terms then the Martineauvian view is likely to forfeit consensus about the relative value of that motive *vis-à-vis* the others. Either way Martineau's view offers no gain over common sense. (*ME* 7, pp. 365-6.)

Suppose, then, that the moral sentiments, and self-love, which some philosophers have taken to be one of them, are excluded from the scale of motives. Sidgwick thinks we still cannot set up a scale which will elicit the general assent of competent judges, for several reasons. There are indeed some easy agreements—for instance, bodily appetites are generally thought to have less value than benevolent affections—but the difficulty of getting beyond them is considerable. 'For example, when we compare personal affections with the ideal of knowledge or of beauty, or the passion for the ideal in any form, much doubt and divergence of opinion become manifest.' (*ME* 7, p. 367.) Next, in actual cases complexity of motive, not simplicity, is the rule; and this raises a basic issue of principle. Suppose that, as will generally be the case, a complex motive contains both higher and lower motives as its elements, and that the compound impels us in one direction while another motive intermediate in value between the elements of the compound moves us in another. How on Martineau's view are we to decide? More generally, Sidgwick thinks it impossible to draw up a ranking of motives such that it is always desirable to act from the higher rather than the lower. The reason is that the natural motives each have 'proper spheres', within which common sense thinks they should operate. If a motive which is usually thought to be 'higher' threatens to intervene where a lower one is appropriate, common sense thinks it ought not. (*ME* 7, p. 370.) Thus 'a regard to health is higher than appetite for pleasant food', but we do not therefore think that we ought to choose our food always and exclusively 'from sanitary calculations'. (*GSM*, p. 356.) Sidgwick makes no further use of the notion of the proper sphere of motives, and we may therefore pass it by without noting some of the questions it raises, and some of the replies Martineau might make to his use of it. For Sidgwick's final argument against Martineau is meant to show that the scale of motives is in any event unimportant.

When one is involved in a case of conflict between motives, he says, it may begin simply as a struggle between the two that happen to be present in one. But it would not be settled simply in the terms posed by the two motives whose opposed promptings initiate deliberation. Putting himself in the position of trying to settle a deliberative question by appeal to motives, Sidgwick says that other, higher, motives would inevitably be drawn in: 'If a serious question of conduct is raised, I cannot conceive myself deciding it morally by any comparison of motives below the highest: . . . the question must inevitably be carried into the court of whatever motive we regard as supremely regulative.' (*ME* 7, p. 372.) Suppose someone has injured me deliberately, and I could harm him in retaliation. Resentment prompts me to do so, compassion may urge me to forgive him. If because of the conflict I deliberate, I would not, Sidgwick says, stop at comparing these two motives. 'I should certainly go on to the consideration whether the immediate evil of the pain I was proposing to inflict is or is not outweighed by its ulterior good effect in teaching him not to offend again.' (*GSM*, p. 360.) Here, of course, Sidgwick appeals to the utilitarian principle, but his point is to show that *some* highest motive must determine the decision in any really serious case. If so the highest motive is not limited in its scope by any of the subordinate ones, and the whole complex scale is unimportant once it enables us to determine which motive is the highest.

v. *The Outcome of the Controversy*

Martineau replied at some length to these criticisms and others made by Sidgwick, who in turn discussed some of his replies. We need not follow all the windings of their argument.

Sidgwick's criticisms are generally telling, Martineau's defences generally uninteresting. His main retort to Sidgwick is, however, worth considering.

Toward the beginning of his answer to Sidgwick, Martineau says that the provision in our nature for determining moral judgements of character is not adequate by itself for answering questions of applied ethics. Ethics 'have two sides—a Rationale within the mind, and a Criterion out of it: the one, a law of character, the other, a law of conduct', and both are needed for reaching complete judgements about what to do. It is not hard 'to show that if with the first alone we attack the problems of the second, we find ourselves in "a nest of paradoxes" ', but this is just the line Sidgwick takes. (*TET*, p. 279.) Martineau reminds us that he himself points out whenever he discusses a complex motive 'that its best concrete application cannot be determined without consulting the canon of consequences', which is the rational canon outside the mind. (*TET*, p. 281.) On his view this is not the distinctively moral canon, but it is none the less needed. And Sidgwick consistently fails to notice his view on this point.

> Throughout his criticism Professor Sidgwick has lost sight of the place which I expressly reserve for his utilitarian canon of consequences, and has argued as if I proposed to work out a code of morals from intuitive data. He does not notice the fact that I only give *priority* to the canon of obligation proper, and contend that consequences to the general happiness can carry no obligation, unless the altruistic affections are in their nature invested with authority over impulses that conflict with them; so that we must go to the scale of impulses before we proceed to the reckoning of consequences. (*TET*, p. 300.)

Martineau charges in effect that all the criticisms which rest on the point that the scale of motives by itself is inadequate for the guidance of conduct are beside the point. They criticize his ethical theory for failing to do what it explicitly professes not to do, while ignoring the part of the theory from which answers to questions of conduct could properly be derived.

Sidgwick does not directly reply to this charge. The nearest he comes to doing so is a suggestion that he disagrees with Martineau's view of the moral status of 'intellectual error'. We have already seen that Martineau thinks mistakes of fact and calculation not morally culpable. He even urges that the terms 'right' and 'wrong' as applied to them have a different meaning than they have when applied to moral decisions. (*TET*, pp. 55–6.) Sidgwick says that our common moral sentiment toward a moral fanatic—for instance, a nihilist who knowingly kills innocent bystanders by dynamiting the emperor's train—is one of *moral* disapproval, and in this it differs from our feelings toward an intellectual fanatic, such as a circle-squarer or maker of perpetual motion machines. (*GSM*, p. 334.) By saying that Martineau has overlooked this point, Sidgwick implies that the nihilist has made an intellectual error and is none the less morally condemned for it. But his language here is curiously evasive. People who can distinguish between the agent and his act and who can disapprove the act while recognizing the agent's 'rectitude of purpose', he says, 'ought . . . to make this distinction'; but the plain man cannot do so. Now surely to say this is to say only that the plain man is not clear-headed about the issue. It does not show Martineau to be mistaken. No more does Sidgwick's other comment do so. When we consider such appalling acts as the nihilist's, or as Torquemada torturing heretics for the good of their souls, he says, we can recognize that subjectively they are done from the best of motives, but common sense still 'does not hesitate to pronounce them profoundly bad. Does Martineau', Sidgwick asks rhetorically, 'wish that these acts should cease to be regarded with moral aversion?' (*GSM*, pp. 334–5.) The bearing of this is unclear. On the one hand Sidgwick is not asserting that mistake of fact is as much a ground of moral blameworthiness as deliberate choice of known wrong. On the other hand Martineau could argue on a number of his own grounds that acts like these should be regarded as 'profoundly bad'. Sidgwick's comments seem merely to reiterate the existence of a distinction between subjective and objective rightness, without coming to grips with Martineau's claim that only the subjectively right is a matter of distinctively moral concern. Martineau's important thesis that 'intellectual' matters, including consideration of consequences, are irrelevant to morality as such, is not touched.

The error in Martineau's theory can none the less be put briefly. If he had limited his thesis to cases in which retrospective judgements of agents are at issue, he would have had something of a foundation in common-sense morality for his denial of the importance of the objective situation. We do, in such contexts, excuse certain kinds of errors of fact or reasoning, and we then determine the agent's personal moral standing independently of the way the situation actually was. Martineau's error lies in assuming that the same limitation of what is morally relevant holds in every context of moral inquiry. In fact the limitation holds at best (and it would require great care to state it precisely) in contexts where we are assessing moral agents on the basis of what they have already done. What an agent ought, morally speaking, to take into account when he is making a decision is not limited by what an assessment of his merit or his praiseworthiness will be based on afterwards. In a context calling for a decision, he must hold that there is an objectively right act which his deliberations can enable him to discover, and he must consider many facts as morally relevant to discovering it. Otherwise he cannot think in a morally appropriate manner. What is morally relevant in his situation cannot be simply his own motives. The distinction Martineau draws between a canon of motives and a canon of consequences is not the distinction between the morally significant and the merely intellectual. It is a distinction relating to a difference between the point of evaluating agents and the point of determining the rightness of acts.

Sidgwick is not as clear on this matter as could be desired. To the question whether moral judgements of rightness are about the external results of actions or their inner origins he, like Martineau, assumes that there must be a single answer which will be appropriate for both the context in which we are trying to reach decisions about future acts, and the context in which we are evaluating agents on the basis of what they have already done. This is why he sometimes seems to identify the act with the intention, and why he holds that 'it is always the choice or intention, and not its actual result, that is approved or disapproved'. (*GSM*, p. 337.) He does not seem to see that for moral purposes the distinction between act and intention is primarily of use in retrospective contexts, and that in prospective contexts we cannot start with an existing set of intentions from among which we identify the right one, but must form intentions by considering what will actually result from the various courses of action open to us. Sidgwick does not question this underlying assumption of Martineau's because he shares it. Yet his criticisms of Martineau's theory are not beside the point, even when they presuppose that an adequate account of the consideration of 'external effects of action' is a proper part of ethics and not merely part of a 'separate and subsequent investigation'. (*GSM*, p. 337.) Only an unduly constricted view of morality could lead to the opposite view.

We have suggested that Martineau's religious position may have helped to lead him to take such a constricted view. A framework of Christian assumptions enables one to attribute a special kind of point to assessment of moral character, a point entirely independent of the daily, practical, forward-looking need we have to be able to distinguish good people from bad ones. One can also see how with Christian assumptions it might seem reasonable for a man to consider the external consequences of his acts much less important than their effects on the one soul which, as Martineau stresses (*TET*, pp. 126–8), God has given into his own special care. Yet the religious assumptions do not force Martineau's position upon him. He could consistently alter his view so as to remove the narrow focus on the evaluation of agents and include a theory of rules of action. He could take rules to be derived from the study of the actions good men have done, and to be needed in the process of forming the moral character of the young, as well as for the moral progress of the race. But if this kind of alteration would make his position on what is included in morality more inclusive and less paradoxical, it would only leave it more readily open to the main point of Sidgwick's line of criticism: that the appeal to a scale of relative values of motives provides no independent and rational method for determining what acts are to be done. Martineau himself agrees that 'for the estimate of Conduct' the appeal to motives must be supplemented by appeal to 'the canon of Consequences'. (*TET*, p. 276.) Neither in his extremely unconvincing attempt to reply to Sidgwick's argument that in serious cases appeal to the scale of motives reduces to appeal to the highest motive (*TET*, pp. 298–300), nor anywhere else, does Martineau offer any substantive principle other than the 'canon of consequences' which can enable us to determine the details of right conduct. He does not, indeed, tell us that the canon of consequences instructs us to consider only pleasure and pain. But he does not tell us what else it instructs us to consider. Once he admits that determination of the specific action which is to be done as right is properly a moral matter, he comes very close to accepting a utilitarian principle as basic to his theory. His only alternative would be to fall back on unsystematized common sense, and hope that within its rules he would find some way of limiting the scope of the principle of utility. Sidgwick's lengthy examination of common-sense morality is meant to show, among other things, that that would be a forlorn hope.

9

The Examination of Common-Sense Morality

THERE are four different discussions of the substance of common sense morality in the *Methods of Ethics*. It is reviewed briefly in connection with egoism in Book II, in much more detail in connection with utilitarianism in Book IV, and most fully in Book III, which devotes one long chapter to a critique of common sense in relation to intuitionism and nine chapters to preparations for this critique. Our present concern is with the two discussions in Book III. The attention to detail, the nicety of discrimination, and the breadth of perspective displayed there in the consideration of ordinary moral concepts and maxims make these chapters among the most enduringly valuable of Sidgwick's contributions to ethics. No abstract can do justice to their richness, and nothing short of a separate volume could contain an assessment of their many conclusions. Our aim in dealing with them must be quite limited. We must pay a certain amount of attention to Sidgwick's specific analyses of moral rules, since his conclusions about them establish the main features of common-sense morality which any ethical theory must be able to explain, and are therefore of importance for the discussion of utilitarianism and, to a lesser extent, of egoism. But we must concern ourselves primarily with the role played by the detailed examination of common-sense morality in the over-all argument of the *Methods*. For it is here, perhaps more than elsewhere, that it may seem hardest to find and follow such a line of argument.

i. *The Role of the Examination*

The reasons for Sidgwick's focus on common sense have already been noted in a general way in Chapter 6. His position on the more specific issue of the role of common sense opinions in proving a first principle must now be discussed. It may be thought that Sidgwick is mistaken in giving common-sense morality a part in this task at all. 'Common moral opinions have in themselves no probative force whatever in moral philosophy', writes R. M. Hare: actual moral judgements can only help us to check 'anthropological theories about what, in general, people think one ought to do, not moral principles about what one ought to do'.[1] Sidgwick seems to disagree with this. He holds, as we have seen, that common-sense morality provides the detailed material which a philosophical ethic must systematize, and he thinks that if a philosopher is 'in any important point... in flagrant conflict with common-sense', his theory will be rejected. (*ME* 7, p. 373.) To what extent, then, does Sidgwick attribute 'probative force' to existing moral beliefs? And what is his basis for attributing such force to them?

In the course of our historical discussions we have seen how the intuitionists before Sidgwick would have replied to the questions raised by Hare's dictum. The plain man, they held, has the ability to recognize his duty or to apprehend the principles of right action, and this ability is shown in the fact that commonly accepted moral belief—'received opinion', in the useful phrase revived by Hare—is for the most part, and in so far as it is not distorted by factual error, true. By the time of John Stuart Mill, secular utilitarianism was also working its way toward an answer to the questions. Received opinion is the record of men's lengthy experience of what makes for happiness and what makes for misery, and as such, though it is in many ways vitiated by superstition and error, it contributes to our knowledge of right and wrong. Either of these rationales for attributing probative force to received moral opinion requires, of course, to be shown to be correct, but such demonstrations need not proceed without any recourse at all to received opinion. For instance, if received opinion should turn out, on examination, to have all the marks of a body of rational and veridical beliefs, organized around a plurality of basic principles, this would go to confirm the intuitionist hypothesis. In such a case, the examination of common-sense morality would help us to come to see the truth of, and would enable us to support, a position about morality which itself explains why received opinion

---

[1] R. M. Hare, 'The Argument from Received Opinion', in *Essays on Philosophical Method*, London, Macmillan, 1971, p. 122; review of John Rawls, *A Theory of Justice*, *Philosophical Quarterly*, 1973, p. 148. See also Peter Singer, 'Sidgwick and Reflective Equilibrium', *The Monist*, 1974, pp. 492–507.

possesses the probative force we attribute to it. A similar mode of argument may be available to the utilitarian.

Sidgwick's own view of the probative force of received opinion is neither that of his intuitionist predecessors nor that of John Stuart Mill. At the outset of investigation, common-sense morality represents to Sidgwick simply what the plain man, and the philosopher himself at this point, thinks he knows, or does not doubt, about what he ought to do and about what is good. It is therefore reasonable to start from these beliefs; but Sidgwick's final position on the extent to which common-sense morality is sound, and on the reason for its being sound, emerges only gradually from his criticism of the claims of both the earlier intuitionists and the earlier utilitarians. The examination of utilitarian claims, particularly those by Mill, and Sidgwick's alternative position, will occupy us in Chapter 12. The critique of common-sense morality in Book III is undertaken as a way of testing not only Sidgwick's own pre-theoretical convictions but also the claims of the form of intuitionism he thinks is most important—dogmatic intuitionism, which holds that we have non-inferential knowledge of a set of definite rules or principles each directing us to do acts of a clearly demarcated class or kind. Dogmatic intuitionists hold that received opinion has probative force to a high degree and to a great extent: Sidgwick's critique of received opinion is intended to show that their view must be mistaken. This negative conclusion points us, moreover, toward a positive view of the true probative force of common-sense morality, as well as toward other important conclusions. Our main task in the present chapter is to outline the argument which underlies the details of the critique of common-sense morality and to show just what its outcomes are.

The structure of the argument is outlined in IV, ii. Although the outline comes after Book III, it is Sidgwick's only presentation of the place of the examination of common-sense morality in the over-all argument of the *Methods*. Since Sidgwick explicitly tells us that one part of the complex argument he sketches here has already been carried out in Book III (*ME* 7, p. 422), we can and indeed must use his statement as the guide to our interpretation of the relevant parts of that book. The programmatic statement in IV, ii, is couched in terms of the way a utilitarian might try to reason an egoist or an intuitionist into accepting the utilitarian principle. Here, as in several other places in the *Methods*, such as the discussion of the axioms in III, xiii, and the concluding chapter, Sidgwick seems to abandon his stance of neutrality and to argue in his own voice for utilitarianism. We shall follow him in carrying on our discussion largely in terms of utilitarianism, and we shall here also ignore the discussion of egoism. But the points to be made need not be confined to utilitarianism.

Sidgwick brings out two difficulties with the idea of proving a first principle at all. The first involves a traditional problem. If a proof, he says, must be 'a process which exhibits the principle in question as an inference from premisses upon which it remains dependent for its certainty', then a proof of a first principle is logically impossible. A principle which is first is by definition the source of the certainty of any other propositions within its domain, and if there are premisses upon which a principle remains dependent for its certainty, then they and not it must be first. The next difficulty involves a less commonly discussed problem. A process of reasoning must start with premisses of some sort. If we assume that the person to whom the utilitarian is trying to demonstrate his principle has intuitionistic moral beliefs, and if these are the premisses the utilitarian uses in his argument, then the argument 'must be one which establishes a conclusion actually *superior* in validity to the premisses from which it starts'. Now the notion of superior validity here introduced is not the same as the notion of superior certainty from which the first problem of proof arises. But Sidgwick promptly shows us what he means by it. If the prescriptions determined by one principle conflict with those determined by another, then, he says, one principle is superior in validity to the other when its precepts 'must be accepted as over-ruling' the precepts of the other. (*ME* 7, pp. 419–20.) 'Superior in validity to' is not, in other words, a general epistemological notion like 'better known than', it is rather the notion of superior moral authority. Plainly two principles equally certain or equally well known might have different degrees of validity in this sense. And this suggests that in Sidgwick's view there are two things required of a first moral principle: that it be at least as certain or well known as any other moral principle, and that it be superior in validity to any other.

The examination of common-sense morality bears out this suggestion. It is presented first of all as a search for principles whose certainty is not derived from anything else, i.e. for really self-evident principles, and its clearest outcome is that the principles of common-sense morality are not what we are looking for. Sidgwick then works out the principles whose certainty he really thinks is intuitively given. It is only after this that the concern for principles of superior validity is introduced and we are told that in the course of our search for self-evident principles we have already established some results of importance on this point also. Sidgwick explains the matter in this way. The intuitionist has been brought to see that a principle requiring that we maximize good is self-evidently certain, but he thinks a number of other principles are so as well. We can only address rational argument to the intuitionist if we can find a way of reasoning 'which on one hand allows the validity, to a certain extent, of the maxims' he thinks self-evident, but which also 'shows them to be not absolutely valid, but needing to be controlled and completed by some more comprehensive principle'. (*ME* 7, p. 420.) We might, in other words, turn the intuitionist into a utilitarian by showing him that his own principles call for or need a principle like the utilitarian principle which is 'superior in validity' to his own. And since a first principle must be supreme in validity as well as in certainty, this would show that his principles cannot be first principles, while the utilitarian principle whose self-evidence he has already granted can be. (*ME* 7, p. 421.)

There is thus a dual purpose underlying the examination of common-sense morality. There is first the search for really self-evident principles. This is discussed in the next two sections of this chapter, and as we shall see, its mode of procedure is quite clearly laid out by Sidgwick. Second, there is the search for a principle superior in validity to other moral principles. The procedure here is not so explicitly outlined. To find such a principle requires an investigation in two stages, which Sidgwick calls the negative and the positive stages. (*ME* 7, p. 421.) The negative stage, which uses what will be called the 'dependence' argument, is the only stage carried out in Book III. The positive stage, which uses what will be called the 'systematization' argument, occurs in IV, iii. The negative stage is intended to show the intuitionist that the principles he takes to be self-evident, such as truthfulness, 'have only a dependent and subordinate validity'. The positive stage requires the utilitarian to show 'how Utilitarianism sustains the general validity of the current moral judgments . . . and at the same time affords a principle of synthesis, and a method for binding the unconnected and occasionally conflicting principles of common moral reasoning into a complete and harmonious system'. (*ME* 7, pp. 421–2.) The systematization argument is discussed in Chapter 11. The last section of the present chapter shows how the critique of common-sense morality in Book III involves the dependence argument, since Sidgwick himself gives no detailed explanation of how it does.

ii. *The Principles of the Examination*

The examination of common-sense morality is meant to have two parts, though in fact they are not kept perfectly distinct. In the first, which occupies III, ii to III, x, Sidgwick is trying simply to clarify its contents and to state its rules as accurately and precisely as possible. In the second, which comes in III, xi, he tests the propositions thus obtained to see if they sustain the claims made for them by the theory of the dogmatic intuitionist. This order of proceeding is made necessary by the relation between ordinary morality and intuitionism as a philosophical theory. Even the plain man agrees that it is unsatisfactory to rely solely on intuitions about the rightness or wrongness of particular acts, since he is often perplexed about what he ought to do, and seeks guidance from general rules. The intuitionist philosopher thinks such general rules are present in the plain man's morality, and that they can be taken as axioms which enable us to give 'exact and scientific treatment' of the whole of morality. He does not think, however, that these axioms are always stated precisely by plain men in the course of their moral reasoning. He thinks, rather, that 'they are at least implied in these reasonings, and that when made explicit their truth is self-evident, and must be accepted at once by an intelligent and unbiassed mind'. (*ME* 7, pp. 228–9.) The plain man is not able to articulate the axioms of mathematics for himself, but he assents to them once they are formulated and the terms used in them are explained. 'Similarly, if we are not able to claim for a proposed moral axiom, in its precise form, an explicit and actual assent of "orbis terrarum", it may still be a truth men before vaguely apprehended, and which they will now unhesitatingly admit.' (*ME* 7, p. 229; cf. p. 353.) In order to have a fair test of the intuitionist's claim, therefore, we must refine common-sense formulas 'to a higher degree of precision than attaches to them in the common thought and discourse of mankind in general', and this is the task of the first and longer part of the examination of common-sense morality. (*ME* 7, p. 215; cf. 338.) Whewell makes a distinction, similar to Sidgwick's, between what he calls 'operative' principles which are implicit in men's thought and 'express' principles which are their articulated counterparts. (*EMP*, 161.) On this point, as on many others in the discussions which follow, Sidgwick has Whewell's form of intuitionism in mind.

For reasons discussed in the preceding chapter Sidgwick proposes to examine chiefly rules concerning the objective rightness of acts, and concerning their external side rather than their motives or volitions or intentions. He assumes that there is a way of talking about acts which enables us to distinguish them both from the volitions which give rise to them and from the consequences which they in turn bring about (*ME* 7, p. 97; p. 200, n. 3); and for the most part it is rules about acts so understood which concern him. Because of his definition of the subject matter of ethics, he deals mainly with acts which individuals can do as individuals, not with those, such as declaring war or proclaiming a session open, which they can only do in virtue of a role they play in some institution. As to the much-debated question whether there are intuitions of such rules, Sidgwick takes it to be a simple matter of fact inquiry. It is not a question of the validity of the allegedly intuitive rules or of their truth. It is only the question, whether one finds in one's conscious experience anything like a 'judgment or apparent perception that an act is in itself right or good'. Sidgwick thinks it would be paradoxical to deny that one finds such judgements, though introspection is not infallible and we are liable to 'confound with intuitions other states or acts of mind essentially different from them', such as strong impulses or vague sentiments. (*ME* 7, p. 211.) Sidgwick gives little attention to the question of who the people are whose apparent intuitions are to be examined, though at one point he suggests that they are those who combine 'adequate intellectual enlightenment with a serious concern for morality'. (*ME* 7, p. 215.) The reason for his lack of concern, he says, is that his conclusions are so negative that it seems hardly necessary to worry about the matter. He would have needed to define the 'experts' more carefully had his results been meant to be more positive. (*ME* 7, p. 343, n. 1.)

These points bear on the first or explicative part of the examination of common sense. The principles governing its second or critical part are spelled out at the beginning of III, xi. Sidgwick lists four criteria to be used in deciding whether an apparently self-evident proposition, of the kind reflection elicits from and articulates for common sense, is really self-evident.[2] The claim that a proposition is self-evident combines both psychological and epistemological elements, and the criteria are accordingly mixed. First, 'the terms of the proposition must be clear and precise'. (*ME* 7, p. 338.) Sidgwick seems to mean something fairly rigorous by this commonplace. He is prepared to condemn a term if it does not either definitely apply or definitely not apply to any proposed instance. A term allowing borderline cases would be imprecise. Clarity is presumably achieved when every conceptual component of a term is understood as precise. Hence if a term is complex we must be able to give a full analysis of it in

---

[2] The idea of setting up criteria for distinguishing real from merely apparent self-evident principles does not originate with Sidgwick. In Note A to his edition of Reid's *Works*, Sir William Hamilton gives a list of over a hundred philosophers who, he thinks, have accepted the philosophy of common sense. Among them are a number who give criteria of self-evidence. The most interesting set is that proposed by Buffier, the eighteenth-century Jesuit sometimes thought to have anticipated Reid. Buffier gives three criteria: the allegedly self-evident propositions should be so clear that if one tries to prove or to attack them, one can only do so by relying on propositions which are manifestly less clear and certain; they should be so universally received that those who attack them are less than one to a hundred; and they should be so strongly impressed on us that we act in accordance with them even if we do not give them our explicit verbal assent. (Hamilton's *Reid*, p. 787.) Buffier's criteria are also given by W. G. Ward in his main work on ethics, *Nature and Grace*, 1861. The tests, he says, are not subtle or profound but Buffier deserves praise for having tried to deal with the 'all-important task of providing us with tests, whereby genuine intuitions may be distinguished from spurious'. (p. 37.) Sidgwick did not know Ward's work prior to 1869 (*Mem.*, p. 221), though he did know Hamilton's *Reid*.

precise terms, while a term involving only a simple concept must be clear if it is meaningful to us at all.

Second, 'the self-evidence of the proposition must be ascertained by careful reflection'. (*ME* 7, p. 339.) In the first two editions, this condition reads, 'The principles must be really self-evident' (*ME* 1, p. 318; *ME* 2, p. 314), but the point is the same in either wording: it is to eliminate certainties arising from sources other than rational insight. We must ask ourselves if we would take the proposition in question to be certain even if we had no strong feelings about the subject it concerns; even if we did not accept the code of manners, or the customs, of our society; even if we did not agree with the laws of our society or its code of honour; and even if we did not accept what is peculiar to our age and country in the positive morality which we take to be our own. (*ME* 7, pp. 339–41.)

Third, 'the propositions accepted as self-evident must be mutually consistent'. (*ME* 7, p. 341.) This criterion is perhaps more significant for what it does not require than for the obvious condition it imposes. It does not require what Sidgwick elsewhere calls the 'discursive verification' of a first principle (see Ch. 1, pp. 58–61). It does not, that is, require the allegedly self-evident principle to be consistent with other propositions which are related to it but not self-evident. Still less is it required to display any power of systematizing such propositions. By not setting this as a requisite of self-evidence, Sidgwick makes it clear that self-evidence is solely a matter of the non-inferentially warranted certainty of the proposition in question. The requirement that a first principle of morals be able to perform the tasks indicated in Sidgwick's discussion of discursive verification arises, as we shall see, from the need for a principle which is superior in validity to other moral principles.

Fourth, Sidgwick states a condition which he connects with the traditional one of general assent, though he words it cautiously. 'Since it is implied in the very notion of Truth', he says, 'that it is essentially the same for all minds, the denial of a proposition that I have affirmed has a tendency to impair my confidence in its validity.' (*ME* 7, p. 341.) The argument behind this has been explained in the early writings (see Ch. 1, p. 59): if my position is challenged, I cannot dismiss the challenge without assuming that my apparent intuitions have a privileged status which no one else's have, and this assumption is unreasonable. We can understand why Sidgwick puts the condition in the cautious way he does if we recall that the propositions he proposes to test are refinements of the plain man's beliefs and may not obtain immediate assent. It is only after the plain man has made an effort he does not usually make (*ME* 7, p. 215) that his disagreement counts as casting doubt on the self-evidence of what seems self-evident to the philosopher.

iii. *Common Sense Examined*

Armed, then, with these four conditions, Sidgwick asks the reader to consider two questions about each of the main areas of morality: whether he can give 'a clear, precise, self-evident principle' which he is willing to use in making moral judgements in that area, and if so, whether the principle is really generally accepted 'by those whom he takes to represent Common Sense'. (*ME* 7, p. 343; added *ME* 2.) The concepts defining the areas within which we are to look for principles are taken from the ordinary terms for the virtues. Sidgwick explains this decision in the very complex and much revised discussion of the relations of the notions of virtue and duty in III, ii. The virtues, he eventually concludes, are '*to some extent* capable of being realised at will' on any given occasion and are thus differentiated from the non-moral excellences of character, although like those their acquisition and display is not wholly within our power. They require us to have certain feelings, despite Kant's opinion to the contrary, but the most important part of what they require is what is demanded in ordinary rules governing duty. By examining these rules we shall therefore be examining the main element in each virtue as well. (*ME* 7, pp. 226–8.) Sidgwick thinks the order of examination is unimportant, and takes first the virtues which are most comprehensive. In following his discussions we shall bring together the results of his second, critical, review of common sense and those of his first, primarily clarificatory, exposition.

The first virtue to be considered is wisdom, which Sidgwick takes to require 'right judgment' about ends as well as about means. He does not give it the high place among the virtues which the ancients gave it, since in his view we can obtain little guidance from considering its requirements. The attainment of truth about the proper ends of action is only voluntary to the extent that it can be assisted by our control over our fears and desires, which helps us think clearly. In this respect the concept of wisdom leads us only to minor rules about self-control. A more important difficulty arises from the fact that common sense assumes that there are several ultimately reasonable ends of action. Should they be incompatible, common sense and with it the common notion of wisdom will give us no guidance about the problems this causes. (*ME* 7, pp. 232–6.) Sidgwick allows that one or two self-evident axioms can be formulated under this heading, e.g. that it is right to act reasonably. (*ME* 7, p. 343.) But they do not take us very far. In so far as they are really self-evident, it is because they are purely tautologous and offer no guidance. They may be understood in a non-tautologous sense: the proposition that it is right to act reasonably might be taken to mean that it is right to live by the conscious and active dictation of reasoning rather than under the guidance of feeling, desire, habit, etc. But this, far from being self-evident, is denied by common sense, which holds that many activities are best left to instinct, spontaneous affection, and other non-rational impulses. Common sense may or may not be right, but its dissent shows that the rule requiring the pervasive dictation of reason is not accepted as self-evident. Only the 'insignificant' truisms are left as really self-evident axioms under the heading of wisdom. (*ME* 7, p. 345.)

Benevolence is chosen for analysis next since, Sidgwick says, in modern times it is frequently treated as an architectonic virtue, regulating and systematizing all the rest. Its general maxim is taken to be 'that we ought to love all our fellow creatures'. Sidgwick is unwilling to follow Kant and others in denying the importance of an emotional element in the love here required. Benevolence at least demands the cultivation of feelings of affection or love, as well as of the disposition to act lovingly, though of course it is not within our power to call forth a feeling at any given instant. (*ME* 7, pp. 238–9.) The acts called for by benevolence may be summed up as 'doing good'; and here the unharmonized and possibly diverse aspects of the common notion of good again call for attention. Are we to promote the virtue, or the happiness, of others, or both? Kant is mistaken, Sidgwick thinks, in supposing we cannot cultivate the virtue of others: his argument would show equally that we cannot cultivate our own. But in fact the common notion of doing good seems to involve primarily promoting the long-term happiness of others. (*ME* 7, pp. 240–1.) We must ask, then, whose happiness benevolence requires us to promote. This brings us to the distinction between benevolence as the heading for a list of intuitively evident rules and benevolence as the equivalent of the utilitarian principle. The utilitarian holds that we should aim at happiness generally, counting any one person's happiness for as much as we count any other person's, and that we only follow rules favouring some people rather than others because doing so maximises the total happiness produced. Common sense, on the contrary, holds it to be 'certain without any such deduction that we owe special dues of kindness' to special classes of people. (*ME* 7, p. 242.) This is the claim vehemently made by the critics of Godwin; and the main question in the examination of benevolence is whether common sense really does contain clear and independent rules determining the services we owe in special classes of cases.

To clarify the issues still further Sidgwick tries to distinguish the duties of benevolence from the duties of justice. The former are those arising out of relations 'where affection normally exists, and where it ought to be cultivated' (*ME* 7, p. 243), or 'the duties to which men are prompted by natural affections' (*ME* 7, p. 263), while the scope of justice does not depend on the affections. In simply specifying the details of the various kinds of benevolent duties, no consideration of justice is required, though such considerations enter when the benevolent duties of different kinds come into conflict and we try to decide which is to take priority. Even if we view benevolence generally as involving problems of the right distribution of services, thereby putting it into the class of duties of justice, we do not, Sidgwick thinks, 'get any new principle for settling any conflict that may present itself'. (*ME* 7, pp. 268–71.) Hence if we are to obtain clear and definite rules for the duties of benevolence, we must do so without appeal to the principles of justice.

Sidgwick points out that while many acts arising from

affection are clearly thought to be admirable, though not obligatory—philanthropic and patriotic acts, for example—there is considerable perplexity about what is obligatory in more personal relationships. It is on the rules determining such duties that he concentrates. Now it is not difficult, he says, to list the main headings under which these duties of benevolence fall: we ought to be kind to parents, spouse, children, show gratitude to those who have rendered us services, be helpful, in less degree, to others with whom we are in contact, aid those in distress, assist our country, etc. 'These are generally recognised claims' (*ME* 7, p. 246), but serious problems arise when we try to make them more precise. Historical variation is one factor complicating the problem, for received opinion on some of these duties—e.g. hospitality, once thought very important—has changed, and on others—e.g. inheritance—is still changing. It will not suffice to leave the determination of details to custom, for custom can only be changed, as everyone admits it should be from time to time, by the action of thoughtful individuals. And to say that custom should be followed until it is obviously inexpedient is to give up the intuitive for the utilitarian method. As Sidgwick says in an important methodological statement, 'we cannot reasonably rest the general obligation upon one principle, and determine its limits and exceptions by another. If the duties above enumerated can be referred to independent and self-evident principles, the limits of each must be implicitly given in the intuition that reveals the principle.' (*ME* 7, p. 247.)

The demand that the limits and exceptions of self-evident principles must be given in the intuition revealing the principle is crucial. It is involved not only in the remainder of the analysis of benevolence, but in all the discussions of the other virtues. The principles of wisdom are untouched by it, since they seem to have no limits or exceptions—but only because they are tautologous. As for benevolence, Sidgwick repeatedly fails to find principles satisfying this demand, though he devotes a substantial effort to trying. (*ME* 7, pp. 248–62.) There are broad and indefinite rules, but no clear and precise ones. The critical review of benevolence is therefore little different in tone from the clarificatory discussions. What he finds is that in so far as the details of the general duties of familial affection, gratitude, aid to the distressed, etc., are definite and clear, they are

determined by positive law (as in the case of the duties of marriage) or custom or other factors of the kind excluded by the
second of the four tests of true self-evidence. The details in each
case are not 'capable of being deduced from a clear and universally accepted principle'. (*ME* 7, pp. 345–9.) But perhaps,
he suggests, this is only what is to be expected where the affections
are concerned; and perhaps justice offers a more favourable
case for the intuitionist.

Sidgwick begins his chapter on justice by distinguishing
justice from the virtue of observing the law or, as Whewell calls
it, the virtue of order. Not all law-breaking is unjust, as duelling
shows; not all following of a law is just, since there may be unjust laws; and some conduct which may be just or unjust is
outside the scope of law, as the conduct of a parent toward
children. From these points Sidgwick derives indications of
what is peculiar to justice. It is especially concerned with
allotting desirable or undesirable objects or situations: the
desirable directly, the undesirable as penalties for law-breaking.
(*ME* 7, pp. 265–6.) What conditions are to be satisfied, then, in
order to achieve just distribution? Equality in the application
of laws, though a necessary, is not a sufficient, condition. Absolute equality in the treatment of all persons in all cases seems
too strong a condition. But departures from absolute equality of
treatment, while allowable, must not be arbitrary: there must be
good reason for them. The main questions about the ordinary
notion of justice, then, concern the reasons for such allowable departures from equality, and the principle or principles
from which the reasons follow. (*ME* 7, pp. 267–8.)

Sidgwick begins his search for an answer in the part of justice
outside the law. The just man, here, is plainly the impartial
man who responds to all binding claims regardless of his personal
preferences. But this, though again a necessary condition of
justice, is not sufficient. It does not help us tell which claims
are reasonable. (*ME* 7, p. 268.) Among the claims to be considered are those arising from contracts, engagements, and
agreements beyond those the law enforces. These Sidgwick
proposes to deal with in a separate chapter. Second, there are
the claims arising from the natural expectations resting on tacit
understandings, customary arrangements, and other standing
relations among people. To some extent these have already been

discussed under the heading of benevolence, and we have seen that clear and definite rules cannot be elicited concerning them. Now we see that the reason why we cannot resolve those difficulties by appealing to our idea of justice is that clarity about justice seems to presuppose clarity about these rules. (*ME* 7, pp. 270–1.) Thus although it is true that 'natural and normal' expectations must be respected if we are to be just, this rule does not give us very definite guidance in extra-legal dealings. If we appeal to it to tell us how to make the laws just, we get still less assistance. For one thing, the law is itself a major factor in shaping expectations. For another, the notion of what is 'natural' wavers too ambiguously between the actual and the ideal to be useful. This leads us to a major problem about laws. We are inclined to think that the established expectations are natural and just, but we also recognize 'an ideal system of rules of distribution which ought to exist'. Received opinion contains both a conserving element and a reforming element, which these two tendencies reflect; and the problem of 'the reconciliation between these two . . . is the chief problem of political Justice'. (*ME* 7, p. 273.) This analysis raises the question of the possibility of constructing an ideal code in terms of which the actual one can be judged. 'Are there any clear principles', Sidgwick asks, 'from which we may work out an ideally just distribution of rights and privileges, burdens and pains, among human beings as such?' (*ME* 7, p. 274.)

Sidgwick thinks no satisfactory positive answer to this question has been given. He considers first a widely held theory about the matter. It is often thought that there are certain natural rights, in the possession of which everyone should be protected, and that these form the necessary limits which just laws must observe. Sidgwick thinks this view cannot be adequately developed. Common sense alone yields neither a definitive and generally accepted list of such rights nor an intuitively evident principle for obtaining such a list. (*ME* 7, p. 274.) And the main attempt to derive them from a theory is, Sidgwick thinks, defective. The theory in question, which has been held by influential thinkers ('though now . . . antiquated', he adds in *ME* 3), asserts that natural rights all spring from the basic right to freedom from interference. Sidgwick has in mind here Spencer and the extreme *laissez-faire* school; he does not discuss Kant at all in this connection. He does not think their principle, that the equality which justice seeks is equality of freedom, is self-evident. If it worked in resolving practical problems, he would be willing to admit that his moral faculty was defective. But the principle leaves too many questions unresolved to compel him to this conclusion. For instance, the principle denies that anyone should be compelled to do anything for his own good; but we plainly think it right to interfere with the freedom of babies and idiots on this ground, while the only plausible reason for this limitation on the principle seems to be the utilitarian reason. We assume that it is permissible to limit one's own freedom by a contract which might be enforced against one's later wishes. Enforcement of this kind is not a realization of freedom; and if the principle allows self-limitations of freedom, it may allow selling oneself into slavery, surely the self-destruction of the principle. A satisfactory theory of property, with all the interference with freedom it entails, cannot be constructed from the principle. (*ME* 7, pp. 274–8.) And the principle affords no sound basis for the obligation to obey the law, since the social contract theory is radically defective. (*ME* 7, pp. 297–9, a passage placed, up to *ME* 4, with the earlier criticisms.) For these and other reasons, Sidgwick concludes that, although freedom is widely desired, and brings much happiness, it cannot serve as a basic principle for jurisprudence and does not even provide a ground for the natural rights it should cover 'except in a very forced and arbitrary manner'. (*ME* 7, p. 278.)

The second possibility for a source of an ideal code which Sidgwick examines and finds wanting is the principle common sense actually uses in modifying the notion of justice as absolute equality. He describes it as a kind of universalization of the principle of gratitude: it is the principle of rewarding people in proportion to their deserts. (*ME* 7, pp. 279–83.) Hence he asks if the principle of deserving some good is as clear and definite as for scientific purposes it needs to be. One question is whether we are to award good according to the effort made or according to the worth of the accomplishment. Here Sidgwick finds himself in a difficulty, due to his not having resolved the problem of free will. For he holds, as we saw, that the notion of being deserving, in a full sense, does involve a fairly strong notion of free choice. If such notions turn out to be unacceptable the ordinary idea of deserving will have to 'vanish'. But he argues once again that this makes little practical difference, because we cannot in practice distinguish how much of a man's contribution is due to his free choice and how much to his favourable personal endowments, including his native energy level, skills, and abilities. Thus we are forced to judge claims to reward in terms of 'the worth of the services intentionally rendered' (*ME* 7, p. 285), and to complete the analysis of the common-sense notion of justice we therefore require a measure of social worth. It must be a measure allowing comparison between various types of goods and services; and Sidgwick devotes several pages to arguing that such a measure—which, he holds, is not accurately provided by a free market economy—cannot be derived from 'analysis of our common notion of Justice', or by asking what various things and services are intrinsically worth. It can only be obtained by discovering what it costs to procure the goods and whether they are worthwhile to society at that price. This is of course a utilitarian mode of calculation, though Sidgwick does not say so. He simply concludes that we cannot construct on an intuitive basis the outlines of 'an ideally just social order in which all services are rewarded in exact proportion to their intrinsic value', and cannot find self-evident principles for calculating exact amounts of good desert. Nor does common sense suppose we can, Sidgwick adds. It sticks to justice as the carrying out of contracts and the honouring of claims arising from definite expectations, and leaves 'the general fairness of Distribution by Bargaining to take care of itself'. (*ME* 7, pp. 286–90.) Similarly complex problems arise when we try to assess the degree of punishment a criminal deserves: quite aside from the difficulties arising from trying to consider motive and intention, we cannot easily find principles for estimating the gravity of crimes. (*ME* 7, pp. 291–2.)

The critical review of common-sense beliefs about justice reiterates some of the difficulties found in the clarificatory analysis (*ME* 7, p. 349), but its main stress is on the fact that the analysis fails to come up with properly scientific axioms. We have discovered 'a whole swarm of principles', Sidgwick says, each one of which, taken alone, may easily seem self-evident: *prima facie* equality in distribution of benefits and burdens, impartiality in enforcement of laws, fulfilment of natural expectations, observance of contract, respect for freedom, requital of good and ill actions. But some of these, though clear, give only necessary, and not sufficient, conditions of what is just; and those that may come into conflict with one another 'do not certainly carry with them any intuitively ascertainable definition of their mutual boundaries and relations'. (*ME* 7, p. 350.) Thus common sense gives us a number of rough working rules of justice, but leaves us without a clear and definite principle for systematizing and harmonizing their determinations.

In his discussion of the obligation to obey the law Sidgwick's opposition to Whewell is quite marked. As the questions raised by the notion of rebellion bring out, the difficulties with the obligation are considerable. A clear principle of obedience must enable us to determine who are the rightful lawmakers and what the limits of their authority are. The claims of the past and the present, of the actual and the ideal, all call for some recognition. Since these complexities take us outside ethics proper into politics, Sidgwick deals with them only briefly, concluding that 'it is impossible to elicit from Common Sense any clear and certain intuitions as to the principles on which an ideal constitution should be constructed'. (*ME* 7, p. 299.) Even if it could be intuitively determined to whose laws obedience is due, there are so many vexed questions about the limits of obedience that 'it seems idle to maintain that there is any clear and precise axiom or first principle of Order' which is generally accepted. Of course there is wide acceptance of 'a vague general habit of obedience to laws as such', but if we try to articulate it we raise problems which can be solved only by moving away from appeals to intuition and using the utilitarian method. (*ME* 7, pp. 302–3.) These points are simply reiterated in the critical discussion. (*ME* 7, p. 352.)

Sidgwick's review of promise-keeping is interesting because it is the main case in which he allows that common sense would agree on a considerably more refined version of a rule than it is itself able to articulate. After a brief effort at showing that the foundation of the obligation to keep a promise lies not in the demand for truthfulness but in the requirement of not disappointing expectations (*ME* 7, pp. 304, 354), he points out that although the obligation is frequently taken as involving the very paradigm of an intuitively clear rule, considerable work is needed to state it accurately. He thinks none the less that 'potential universality of acceptance may . . . be fairly claimed' for even a relatively elaborate rule, requiring that the parties to a promise understand it in the same sense, that the promisee must be in a position to grant release from the promise but be unwilling to do so, and that the promise was not obtained by force or fraud. (*ME* 7, p. 311.) Beyond these conditions, however, there must be others, the need for which is indicated by problems which the rule thus clarified does not resolve, but about which no consensus exists; and so we cannot hold that there is a generally accepted rule which lays down what is to be done in every possible case. (*ME* 7, p. 354.)

The treatment of the remaining virtues is brief. Cases in which common sense is agreed that truth need not be spoken, and others in which it is perplexed, are adduced to show that veracity does not furnish an axiom. We generally require truthfulness but not always, and there are no 'self-evident secondary principles, clearly defining when it is not to be exacted'. (*ME* 7, p. 317.) Moreover, in so far as limits are generally admitted to the duty of truthfulness, they seem to be determined by utilitarian considerations, so that here, as in the case of certain questions about obedience to law and about justice, we seem to see common sense itself appealing to a most unintuitional method to resolve its problems. (*ME* 7, p. 355.) The minor virtues of liberality, temperance, courage, and humility usually presuppose determination of many other points of morals before enabling us to reach specific decisions, and have less claim to be regarded as scientific axioms. Their force is often necessarily limited by utilitarian considerations (*ME* 7, pp. 322, 355), and so do not give much help to intuitionist theory. Sexual morality is considered at some length, perhaps because Whewell gave Purity such a prominent place in his scheme of the virtues. Sidgwick argues that when we discount the effects of positive law and of custom, we find no self-evident principles in this area. Two separate goods are protected by current sexual morality—the maintenance of society, and certain types of valuable feelings—but these goals do not always call for the same actions. In any event if sexual morality is only a means to these ends, it abandons its claims to be determined by separate self-evident principles. (*ME* 7, pp. 375–9.)

iv. *The Dependence Argument*

Our search for self-evident principles has not been very successful. Those we have found are either tautologies or else fail to provide more than necessary conditions of rightness. Among the rest of the principles we have examined, some contain imprecise terms, as shown by the many cases they leave undecided, others get their precision or their certainty from law, or custom, or other non-rational sources, and almost everywhere we find that there are exceptions and limits which are not fully determinate. Sidgwick's four tests of self-evidence lead him to the conclusion that the intuitionist's claim that common sense supplies truly self-evident axioms cannot be sustained. What is the outcome of the examination of common sense in terms of the search for a principle of superior validity? How does it show that the principles of common sense have only a dependent and subordinate validity?

That the intuitional school is the champion of 'independent' morality was proclaimed by Whewell, on the ground of its claim that moral principles can be known independently of knowledge of other matters, particularly of knowledge of the consequences of acts. (*Lec. Hist.*, p. 2.) Sidgwick sees two implications of this claim to independence, which bring out its general significance both for intuitionism and for Sidgwick's attack on it. One is that each principle known by intuition conclusively determines the actual moral status, as right, wrong, or indifferent, of the acts that fall under it, and not merely their putative moral status. This is the position that such principles are absolutely valid. The other is that there is no valid principle of greater generality than the common-sense principles which pertains to and has jurisdiction over all of them. Historically speaking, it is fair to attribute both these points to the intuitional school. For although Reid had suggested that there is a rank ordering of substantive principles in cases where they lead to conflict, neither he himself nor any of the later intuitionists developed this idea; and all intuitionists insisted on the existence of a plurality of ultimate moral principles. The two points are moreover logically connected. If an intuitively evident principle does no more than determine a reason for doing the acts that fall under it and does not provide a conclusive reason for doing them, then a further step is needed to move to the conclusion that a given act is actually, not just putatively, right. If the further step does not rest on a principle, dogmatic intuitionism collapses into perceptional intuitionism. But if the move from putative to actual rightness requires a principle in addition to the common-sense principles, then that principle rather than they must be the true first principle of morals. For the extent to which common-sense principles determine actual rightness is then dependent on the additional principle. Conversely, to insist that the common-sense rules must determine actual rightness is to imply that there is no higher-order principle with authority to overrule their specific determinations.

The dependence argument is Sidgwick's attempt to show that the results of the examination of common-sense morality are incompatible with these two related claims made by intuitionism about the independence of common-sense principles. The argument presupposes, as do both Sidgwick and the intuitionists, that morality is within the domain of reason, or that the objective truth or validity of moral principles requires their rationality. Its procedure is to show that reason requires first principles of a kind which common sense does not supply. The argument is as follows.

It is conceivable that there should be rules or principles which dictate the doing of acts of a certain class except in a variety of special circumstances, and that there should be no more to be said about the exceptions than that they are called for by the rule. Such a principle might even specify that the list of exceptions is complete. If the principle could be given by intuition, then we would have a case where the 'limits' were 'given in the intuition that reveals the principle'. (*ME* 7, p. 247.) But a rule or principle of this sort, though it might dictate good manners or what is traditionally correct, could not be a rational rule or principle; and since intuition is a rational faculty, it could not be given by intuition. The reason is that there is an essential difference between what can be objectively true and reasonable to accept in the moral realm and what can be objectively true and reasonable to accept in the physical. In the former, Sidgwick says, we do not admit 'variations for which we can discover no rational explanation', though we do admit this in the latter. In the physical world we find ultimately inexplicable brute facts for which no rational account can be discovered. No matter how far back we can go in our explanations, we must accept an 'accidental or arbitrary element' at some point, e.g. that there is more matter in one portion of space than in another. But, Sidgwick says, 'within the range of our cognitions of right and wrong . . . we cannot admit a similar unexplained variation'. (*ME* 7, p. 209; *ME* 1, p. 183.) Hence common-sense moral rules, if objectively true, cannot simply list unexplained exceptions and limits, as rules determining the conventions of etiquette can. Sidgwick elsewhere suggests another approach to this point. Kant, he remarks, makes too much of the existence of what logicians call 'particular' judgements, those of the form 'Some A is B', as a clue to the basic operations of our thinking. Such judgements are made, Sidgwick agrees, and are indeed indispensible, in ordinary thought, but 'they are only required because knowledge is progressive, and only represent a stage through which it has to pass in the making'. In a scientific inquiry, when we see that some members of a class have a characteristic, we are immediately led to ask what other characteristic the members of the sub-group share. 'We then seek at once to turn the "some" into the "all" of a subclass.' (*LPK*, p. 84.) The inevitable limitations on our ability to complete this process in regard to the physical world do not hold in the moral world. In morality, since principles must be completely rational, we must be able to replace common-sense rules, which say that some acts of a given kind are right, with more precise rules which say that all acts of a given kind are right, even if the specification of the kind in the precise and universal formulation is very complex.

Now the main result of the examination of common-sense morality is, in effect, that no such improved formulations of common-sense rules can be obtained by intuition. Of course it is possible to give sharp and definite specifications of rules for each of the main areas of common-sense moral concern, but the general agreement which exists when the rules are left vague and indefinite as they are in ordinary thought does not carry over to the clear and precise revisions of them. This means that in so far as they specify a complex right-making property which exhaustively determines exceptions and limits in its own class, they do not seem self-evidently certain; and in so far as they seem self-evident, they do not fully determine the exceptions and limits which they undeniably have. If a principle could be stated in which all the exceptions and limits were determined by the right-making property, however complex, then if it were a truly self-evident principle, the exceptions and limits would not be irrational. As no such principle seems to be self-evident, the only possible explanation of the exceptions and limitations in any given common sense rule is that they are determined by some principle other than the common sense rule itself. But the intuitionist, as Sidgwick says, 'cannot reasonably rest the general obligation upon one principle, and determine its limits and exceptions by another' (*ME* 7, p. 247), because to do so is to make the 'general obligation'—that determined by the common-sense rule—into a merely putative obligation. Yet we must treat exceptions and limitations in this way or else abandon the claim that moral principles are reasonable. If morality is rational, in short, the rules taken by dogmatic intuitionism as first principles can only determine putative rightness. But first principles, it is agreed, must determine actual rightness, since otherwise the rationality of morality is incomplete. The dependence argument shows, then, that from the main result of the examination of common-sense morality, it follows that the principles the intuitionist holds have only a 'dependent and subordinate validity'. (*ME* 7, p. 422.)

There is a positive outcome of the dependence argument as well. Like the negative result it arises from considering what is required if reason is to guide our action. A clue to it is given by the fact that Sidgwick begins with common-sense morality and the assumption that its rules have at least some degree of validity. So far the features of this morality which have been used in the argument are purely formal features. No use is made of the details of its substantive content. Common-sense morality is treated simply as a good specimen of a fairly complex code in a fairly complex society. The dependence argument so far may therefore be described as showing that the rules of a moral code of this kind cannot reasonably be taken to determine actual rightness. To obtain a more positive result, we can ask what sort of first principle is required, if reason is to be practical when a code of this kind is needed to enable agents to act rationally. The very failings of common-sense rules point toward the answer. A first principle must determine actual rightness. It must be exceptionless; for exceptions could only be determined by another principle, and if every principle had exceptions and limits, then every principle would be dependent on some other, and there could be no principle capable of determining actual rightness. And since the principle in question must 'control and complete' the subordinate rules of the code so as to assure their complete rationality, it must be at least as wide-ranging in its scope as they are.

The dependence argument takes us no further, but the requirements it sets for a first principle show how it is connected with the more purely positive systematization argument. For the latter consists largely in showing how a particular first principle, the utilitarian, can 'control and complete' common-sense morality. We can see also that the dependence and systematization arguments—the negative and positive phases of the argument Sidgwick outlines in IV, ix—bring out and explain different aspects of what reason requires in addition to certainty when practical rationality involves the need for a detailed code of rules. In such circumstances reason requires that there be some principle superior in validity to all others. To show that an alleged first principle has this superiority, it must be shown that it determines the limits and exceptions to other principles, while none determine such restrictions to it. But to show this is just to show that the first principle serves to systematize and harmonize the subordinate rules. Thus the requirement that a first principle of morals must have a 'discursive verification' springs from the demands of reason no less than the requirement that it pass the tests of self-evidence, but in a different way. In matters of theoretical reason, the discursive verification is mainly needed because we can rightly assume that most of our pre-theoretical beliefs are true and can serve as tests of a principle. The corrective function of the principle is secondary. In matters of practical reason, the need for a discursive verification arises primarily from the need to be certain that we have a principle which can be used to rectify our pre-theoretical beliefs. The explicative function, which as we shall see in Chapter 11 Sidgwick thinks the utilitarian principle can certainly perform, is secondary. Thus the need for the certainty and cognitive independence of a first principle is, on Sidgwick's view, a need in any sort of rational system of knowledge. The need for a principle of superior validity and moral independence arises when a first principle of action must apply to a situation where a complex set of moral rules is required for day-to-day rational guidance of action. It is needed to guarantee that the code is, or can be made, rational throughout.

Sidgwick does not argue that it is inevitable that a code of the kind which he takes to be a practical necessity in human life must have the characteristics of common-sense morality on which the dependence argument focuses attention. To that extent, it might be thought that his reliance on common sense biases the outcome of his search for first principles. Perhaps a better code is possible, in which the separate rules are clear and precise, never leave problems which they cannot in theory resolve, and continue to seem self-evident after scrutiny. The point cannot be debated here, but in view of Hare's objection to attributing any probative force to received moral opinion, it should be noted how little Sidgwick relies on common-sense morality. So far he rests no conclusions on claims about the truth of received beliefs. His conclusions stem from formal features of the accepted morality. If his reliance on received opinion biases the outcome of his search for a substantive first principle, it does so only by biasing his idea of the formal features such a principle must have.

The utilitarian principle may have the formal characteristics Sidgwick thinks are required of a moral first principle, and it is frequently appealed to, if he is correct in his description of common-sense procedures, to do just the things such a principle must do in rectifying common sense—settle conflicts arising from the clash of common-sense rules, make more precise the limits of such rules, extend them to cover new sorts of cases, etc. Common-sense morality itself thus seems to point to the utilitarian principle as offering 'that further development of its system which . . . reflection shows to be necessary'. (*ME* 7, p. 422.) But this fact is not by itself a proof of the utilitarian principle. Other principles may have the formal features necessary in a first principle, and it is only these formal features which are established by the dependence argument. Yet the case for the utilitarian principle is at least partly made by the general examination of common-sense morality. For it shows, among other things, that the factual characteristics which are treated by common-sense moral rules as indicating rightness cannot be ultimate right-making characteristics. We shall see the significance of this elimination of possible first principles other than the utilitarian in the next chapter.

10

The Self-Evident Axioms

APPEALS to self-evidence and to what is intuitively given are not very satisfactory modes of solving basic philosophical problems. There seems to be so much disagreement about what is self-evident that any claim to have found out what really is so must arouse scepticism. More importantly, the self-evident is rarely the self-explanatory, and saying that some proposition is derived by intuition gives no explanation of anything. We need more understanding of what makes certain truths true and basic than is yielded by the blunt claim that we just see them to be so. An appeal to self-evidence too often shuts off inquiry instead of answering ultimate questions.

In the present chapter it is argued that Sidgwick, like Alexander Smith and William Whewell, is aware of these shortcomings of the appeal to intuition and tries to avoid them. Like Smith, he interprets self-evidence in terms of the basic operations of ordinary reasoning, applied to practice; but where Smith fails to avoid tautology Sidgwick is clearly aware of the danger. (*ME* 7, pp. 374–9.) Like Whewell, he takes the problem to be that of working out what the most fundamental demands of reason are, given the conditions of human life; but he is more successful than Whewell in developing a solution within this framework. Though Sidgwick himself points out the Kantian affinities of his position he is by no means simply a Kantian. He is deliberately developing a traditional mode of approach to basic axioms. In doing so, he brings out distinctly new possibilities within it.

i. *Some Methodological Concerns*

Sidgwick never thought it easy to make out a claim that any specific allegedly self-evident proposition is really self-evident. We have seen how careful he is throughout the earlier parts of the *Methods* about admitting such claims and have noted the tests such claims must pass. In a discussion published in 1879 he gives a further idea of his views on how a specifically moral first principle might be given rational support.

We need to give reasons for alleged first principles, Sidgwick says, because nearly all of them are denied by some 'respectable minority' or other, and it ought to be possible to give a reasoned account of why one accepts some and not others. Yet how can principles be 'first' if they are shown to be 'dependent for their certainty on the acceptance by the mind' of other truths? It is the old question, raised in IV, ii, but in the 1879 article a quite different sort of answer is suggested. A way out of the dilemma is given, Sidgwick thinks, by 'Aristotle's distinction between logical or natural priority in cognition and priority in the knowledge of any particular mind'. (1879a, 106.) If we use this distinction we can see that some proposition may be properly 'cognizable' just by itself, while in order that some person may come to see its truth the proposition may have to be linked by a rational process to truths already accepted by the person. Sidgwick does not explain the Aristotelian distinction at this point, but he does give a brief account of it in his lectures on Kant, in the course of trying to distinguish between logical and temporal priority. This distinction, he remarks, has often been made. As a distinction between the 'naturally prior' and the 'prior for us' it goes back to Aristotle. To make quite clear how the notion of natural or logical priority can be 'purged of all chronological suggestion' he tells us that 'what is meant by priority in a purely logical sense' is

merely that the concept (or judgment) said to be logically prior to another requires to be made explicit before and in order that the concept to which it is prior may be perfectly clear and distinct (or that the judgment may be arrived at by a perfectly cogent process of inference). In this sense the notion of a straight line is logically prior to the notion of a triangle as a figure bounded by straight lines: and Euclid's axiom relating to parallels is logically prior to his 29th proposition—it is a more elementary proposition without which the other cannot be cogently established. (*LPK*, p. 41.)

The idea of a proper order of knowledge, a concept involving both logical and epistemological elements but independent of ties to the order in which people happen to acquire their beliefs, helps to determine Sidgwick's whole idea of the structure of an ethical system and plainly underlies his search for axioms. He does not define the notion of a first principle by using the Aristotelian distinction, but it is easy to do so: a logically first principle, in some domain, is one which is needed for the full proof of other propositions within that domain, and which does not require the truth of other propositions in the domain to be known before its own is knowable.

Sidgwick thinks there are two, and only two, ways of bringing someone to see the truth of a moral principle which is logically first, starting from propositions the person already accepts. In one, we begin with an 'ethical proposition' which the person already takes to be self-evidently true. We show that it is a limited and qualified version of some simpler and wider proposition, of which it asserts only a part; and by bringing out the absence of rational basis for the limitations we lead the person to accept the wider principle as 'the real first principle'. For example, someone might take it as self-evident that one ought not to inflict pain on human beings. If we bring him to see that possession of rationality is not a sufficient basis for treating one kind of sentient being differently from another, we may lead him to see that the real self-evident principle is that one ought not to inflict pain. (1879a, 106–7.) Sidgwick uses this mode of argument in a few places in the *Methods* (e.g. *ME* pp. 7, 279), not the least important of which is the instance he himself identifies in the 1879 article: the attempt to move the egoist to accept utilitarianism. (*ME* 7, pp. 420–1, 497–8.) The other mode of supporting first principles is rather different. It relies on methodological argument, in which we start by establishing criteria for picking out true first principles from false ones, whether ethical or not, and 'then construct a strictly logical deduction' in which we apply the criteria to ethics to obtain its first principles. Conditions very similar to the four listed in the *Methods* as the tests of apparently self-evident propositions are said to be the premises for this kind of argument, and Sidgwick's familiar rationale for them is given (1879a, 108f.), though the focus here is on the rejection of genetic tests of validity. The reason Sidgwick gives for his claim that there can be only these two methods of supporting a first moral principle is, as we would expect, that if our premisses are not purely methodological they must be ethical in order to yield an ethical conclusion. (1879a, 107.)

It is plain that the methodological procedure Sidgwick outlines must be more basic than the procedure of removing limitations on a proposition already thought to be self-evident. The latter can at best leave us with a new proposition which appears self-evident and which is therefore ready to be tested by the former. No doubt this is why in the *Methods* itself the emphasis is on the methodological mode. Yet from the description of the procedure of removing limitations we obtain a useful insight into Sidgwick's thinking. If in some cases we can be brought to see what is really a first principle by removing arbitrary limitations from the scope of a moral principle, it is possible that in others we can understand a real first principle by seeing that some limitations of scope are not arbitrary, but basic and inescapable.[1]

Sidgwick's search for principles which will satisfy the conditions of the methodological argument becomes, by III, xiii, an examination of what he has called the third or 'philosophical' phase of intuitionism, in which, 'without being disposed to deny that conduct commonly judged to be right is so' we none the less look for some 'deeper explanation *why* it is so' than common sense can give. We seek principles which are 'more absolutely and undeniably true and evident' than the maxims of common-sense morality, and 'from which the current rules might be deduced' either as they stand or with only minor changes. (*ME* 7, p. 102.) Such axioms can be found, Sidgwick thinks, and so philosophical intuitionism is vindicated. But he also says that the axioms are 'of too abstract a nature, and too universal in their scope, to enable us to ascertain by immediate application of them what we ought to do in any particular case' (*ME* 7, p. 379); and the way in which they allow of a deduction of the current rules is somewhat surprising, as we shall see in Chapter 12. These two points may raise questions about the completeness of the success of philosophical intuitionism.

---

[1] Whewell, *Lec. Hist.*, p. 189, suggests a procedure very much like the removal of limitations for use in ethics.

ii. *The Axioms Stated*

There is a remarkable amount of disagreement in the literature about the number of axioms Sidgwick thinks he presents[2] as well as some disagreement about their interpretation. It is therefore necessary to proceed with care in deciding just what the axioms or first principles are, as well as what their formulations mean. Where Sidgwick is clear and explicit in identifying an axiom the fact must of course be taken into account. But he is too frequently careless in labelling propositions 'self-evident' for this to be the decisive factor. In interpreting what he says, it seems sensible to try to find the smallest number of axioms with which the work to be done by first principles can be done. Each axiom should therefore be as broad in scope as possible while having its own special and indispensable function. These guidelines lead to the conclusion that there are four self-evident axioms; but to explain fully why this is so requires explaining the function of each of them, a task which will not be finished until the egoistic principle is discussed in Chapter 13.

The text of the first edition version of III, xiii, the central discussion of the axioms, is rather strikingly different from that of the final version. Most noticeably, no axiom of prudence is presented as self-evident. When introducing egoism in that edition, Sidgwick says that he begins the examination of methods by considering it because there is wider agreement about the 'reasonableness of its fundamental principle' than there is about the principles underlying the other methods (*ME* 1, p. 107)—a statement which is rather weakened in later editions. (*ME* 7, p. 119.) We might then naturally expect that the principle of egoism would come in at least as a strong candidate for testing under the four conditions of self-evidence, and our expectation is strengthened when we find Sidgwick saying, in a footnote discussing Bentham's four dimensions of pleasure, that 'proximity is a property which it is reasonable to disregard' unless it is connected with certainty, 'for my

---

[2] F. H. Hayward, *The Ethical Philosophy of Sidgwick*, 1901, pp. 109–10, says there are three, as does Hastings Rashdall, *The Theory of Good and Evil*, 1907, i., 90, 147; J. M. E. McTaggart finds five, 'The Ethics of Henry Sidgwick', *Quarterly Review*, ccv, 1906, p. 407; Broad, *Five Types*, pp. 223–6, finds six; A. R. Lacey, 'Sidgwick's Ethical Maxims', *Philosophy*, xxxiv, 1959, p. 218, finds seven; and W. K. Frankena in his article on Sidgwick in *Encyclopedia of Morals*, ed. V. Ferm, N.Y. 1956, finds eight.

feelings a year hence should be just as important to me as my feelings next minute, if only I could make an equally sure forecast of them. Indeed this equal and impartial concern for all parts of one's conscious life is perhaps the most prominent element in the common notion of the *rational*—as opposed to the merely *impulsive*—pursuit of pleasure.' (*ME* 1, p. 113 n.) But this is as near as Sidgwick comes to asserting the self-evidence of an egoistic principle, except in a sentence on the last page of the book: 'and yet we cannot but admit, with Butler, that it is ultimately reasonable to seek one's own happiness.' (*ME* 1, p. 473.) Egoism appears in III, xiii, only to be 'suppressed'. (*ME* 1, p. 366.) The axioms of justice and benevolence are developed, in the first edition, out of discussion of passages from Clarke and Kant, 'the two thinkers who in modern times have most earnestly maintained the strictly scientific character of ethical principles'. (*ME* 1, p. 357.) In the second edition, where the chapter takes the outlines of its final form, the axiom of prudence is introduced, the criticism of egoism is moved elsewhere, and the discussions of Clarke and Kant are postponed until after the principles of justice and benevolence have been presented independently. In the course of making this change Sidgwick dropped a passage of some interest (*ME* 1, p. 360), to which attention is given below. After the second edition no philosophically important changes occurred, despite a fair amount of condensing and rearranging of the text.

Sidgwick asserts the self-evident axioms in a number of places, but even when we confine our attention to III, xiii, there are so many statements of them that it is not easy to know which to take as the best representations of the basic principles. We must therefore discuss a number of possibilities, and it will facilitate the discussion to number them. Since Sidgwick says that the axioms are concerned with justice, prudence, and benevolence, the letters J, P, and B will be used to group the various possibilities put forth for each main topic.

Justice is the first concern. Sidgwick says that earlier in the *Methods* he has asserted

J1: whatever action any of us judges to be right for himself, he implicitly judges to be right for all similar persons in similar circumstances. (*ME* 7, p. 379.)

Actually at the place to which he refers us, Sidgwick says that there is one practical rule to be derived from reflecting on 'the general notion of rightness':

> J1a: if I judge any action to be right for myself, I implicitly judge it to be right for any other person whose nature and circumstances do not differ from my own in some important respect. (*ME* 7, p. 209.)

No doubt the differences between J1 and J1a are trivial; at any rate Sidgwick tells us, in III, xiii, that the principle may be put in another way:

> J2: if a kind of conduct that is right (or wrong) for me is not right (or wrong) for some one else, it must be on the ground of some difference between the two cases, other than the fact that I and he are different persons. (*ME* 7, p. 379.)

Then he says that a corresponding principle can be put in terms of what ought to be done to, rather than by, different persons. It would presumably read:

> J2a: if it is right (or wrong) for me to be treated in a certain way, and not right (or wrong) for another to be treated in the same way, this must be on the ground of some difference between the two cases, other than the fact that I and he are different persons.

Sidgwick then discusses the Golden Rule as a special application of this principle to the case where two or more people are similarly related to each other. But even aside from this limitation, which plainly disqualifies the Golden Rule from being an axiom, the statement is imprecise. One might want another to help one in sinning and 'be willing to reciprocate'; and besides, we cannot say that one should do to others what one thinks it right they should do to oneself, because there might be significant differences in the cases. Hence, Sidgwick says, a strict statement of the self-evident principle must read:

> J3: it cannot be right for A to treat B in a manner in which it would be wrong for B to treat A, merely on the ground that they are two different individuals, and without there being any difference between the natures or circumstances of the two which can be stated as a reasonable ground of difference of treatment. (*ME* 7, p. 380.)

The principle of impartiality in the administration of positive law is given as an 'application' of this principle, but it would be a mistake to take it as a separate self-evident axiom. Sidgwick explicitly identifies J3 as the strict statement of the axiom. J3 states plainly and broadly a principle having the same general function in moral considerations as the other principles suggested as axioms of justice, and none of the others adds anything, beside limitations, not in J3. We shall therefore take J3 as the basic statement and assume that other formulations such as

J4: similar cases ought to be treated similarly (*ME* 7, pp. 386–7)

are partial or limited or abbreviated ways of putting it.

Prudence is Sidgwick's second concern. Its axiom is sometimes said to be 'that one ought to aim at one's own good'. But Sidgwick definitely rejects this way of putting it, because, he puzzlingly says, it 'does not clearly avoid' being a tautology. The reason given is that we 'may define "good" as "what one ought to aim at"', and the objection is puzzling because this definition of 'good', since it contains no restriction to aiming at things *for oneself*, would not make the suggested principle tautologous. But Sidgwick merely moves on to a different point: if we construe the good in question as the agent's good 'on the whole', the added last phrase suggests a non-tautological principle.

P1: One ought to have an impartial concern for all parts of one's conscious life. (*ME* 7, p. 381.)

And in this connection Sidgwick refers back to the footnote which in the first edition contained the main statement of the principle of prudence. In the second and third editions he immediately emphasizes that this principle is 'merely negative and regulative', like that of justice. (*ME* 2, p. 354; *ME* 3, p. 380.) He then goes on to offer a formula which brings out the central part of the notion of 'on the whole':

P2: Hereafter *as such* is to be regarded neither less nor more than Now.

Both P1 and P2 assume that differences in the certainty and quantity of the good are not in question. When this point is stressed, we get another statement, which brings out the similarity to J3 more clearly:

> P3: the mere difference of priority and posteriority in time is not a reasonable ground for having more regard to the consciousness of one moment than to that of another. (*ME* 7, p. 381.)

When this principle is applied to cases of resisting temptation, we get:

> P4: a smaller present good is not to be preferred to a greater future good.

But although Sidgwick says that in this form the assertion is self-evident (*ME* 7, p. 383), the fact that its scope is narrower than that of P3 disqualifies it from being an axiom. Since P3 is at least as general as any other formulation and brings out more clearly the aspect of practical reasoning which the axiom is meant to cover, we should consider it the best statement of the principle.

The principle of benevolence involves a complication not affecting the other axioms: it is not itself self-evident, but is deduced from two principles which are. The first is introduced as presupposing that we understand the concept of the good on the whole of a single individual. If so, we can see that it is self-evident that

> B1: The good of any one individual is of no more importance from the point of view of the universe than the good of any other.

As in the case of P3, quantitative differences and differences of certainty are discounted here. Then, with no further comment, a second axiom is given:

> B2: As a rational being I am bound to aim at good generally,— so far as it is attainable by my efforts,—not merely at a particular part of it. (*ME* 7, p. 382.)

These are the two main formulations of axioms under the heading of benevolence. Each, as we shall see, has a special function to play in practical reasoning; and in addition there are complications about B2 which will be discussed in Chapter 13. Up to the fifth edition Sidgwick does not clearly recognize that the principle of benevolence itself, since he presents it as a deduction from these two axioms, could not be given as self-evident. In that edition he makes the point quite explicit: from

B1 and B2 we 'deduce, as a necessary inference, the maxim of Benevolence in an abstract form'. (*ME* 5, p. 382; *ME* 7, p. 382.) The principle itself has essentially the same wording throughout:

> B3: Each one is morally bound to regard the good of any other individual as much as his own.

Thus although in the same chapter

> B4: I ought not to prefer my own lesser good to the greater good of another

is said to be self-evident (*ME* 7, p. 383), Sidgwick's more careful passage makes clear that it is not this, but B1 and B2, which are the intuitively given axioms.

Sidgwick points out the notion of 'good' in the axioms does not presuppose the hedonistic interpretation to be given it later (*ME* 7, p. 381), and if we keep this in mind we can see that the many other formulations he gives of self-evident axioms elsewhere in the *Methods* and in other writings are all either variations or applications of the four taken here as basic, or else incorporate the hedonistic understanding of 'good'. For instance the important formulations in the Concluding Chapter, where the conflict between egoism and utilitarianism is brought to its climax, all exemplify these points:

> J5: It is right and reasonable for me to treat others as I should think that I myself ought to be treated under similar circumstances. (*ME* 7, p. 507.)
> P5: The agent's own greatest happiness is the ultimate rational end for him. (*ME* 7, p. 497.)
> B5: It is right and reasonable for me to do what I believe to be ultimately conducive to universal Good or Happiness. (*ME* 7, p. 507.)

It is unnecessary to review all Sidgwick's statements of self-evident axioms. The main ones are listed for convenience, with an asterisk marking the fundamental versions.

Statements of Self-Evident Axioms

In III, xiii:

> J1: Whatever action any of us judges to be right for himself, he implicitly judges to be right for all similar persons in similar circumstances. (*ME* 7, p. 379.)

J1a: If I judge any action to be right for myself, I implicitly judge it to be right for any other whose nature and circumstances do not differ from my own in important respects. (*ME* 7, p. 209; cf. p. 378.)

J2: If a kind of conduct that is right (or wrong) for me is not right (or wrong) for some one else, it must be on the ground of some difference between the two cases, other than the fact that I and he are different persons. (*ME* 7, p. 379.)

J2a: If it is right (or wrong) for me to be treated in a certain way, and not right (or wrong) for another to be treated in the same way, it must be on the ground of some difference between the two cases, other than the fact that I and he are different persons. (*ME* 7, p. 379.)

*J3: It cannot be right for A to treat B in a manner in which it would be wrong for B to treat A, merely on the ground that they are two different individuals, and without there being any difference between the natures or circumstances of the two which can be stated as a reasonable ground for difference of treatment. (*ME* 7, p. 380.)

J4: Similar cases ought to be treated similarly. (*ME* 7, pp. 386–7.)

P1: One ought to have impartial concern for all parts of one's conscious life. (*ME* 7, p. 381.)

P2: Hereafter *as such* is to be regarded neither less nor more than Now. (*ME* 7, p. 381.)

*P3: Mere difference of priority and posteriority in time is not a reasonable ground for having more regard to the consciousness of one moment than to that of another. (*ME* 7, p. 381.)

P4: A smaller present good is not to be preferred to a greater future good. (*ME* 7, p. 381; cf. p. 383.)

*B1: The good of any one individual is of no more importance from the point of view of the universe than the good of any other. (*ME* 7, p. 382.)

*B2: As a rational being I am bound to aim at good generally,— so far as it is in my power,—not merely at a particular part of it. (*ME* 7, p. 382.)

B3: Each one is morally bound to regard the good of any other individual as much as his own. (*ME* 7, p. 382.)

B4: I ought not to prefer my own lesser good to the greater good of another. (*ME* 7, p. 383.)

In Concluding Chapter:

J5: It is right and reasonable for me to treat others as I should think that I myself ought to be treated under similar circumstances. (*ME* 7, p. 507.)

P5: My own greatest happiness is the rational ultimate end for me. (*ME* 7, p. 497.)

B5: It is right and reasonable for me to do what I believe to be ultimately conducive to universal Good or Happiness. (*ME* 7, p. 507.)

iii. *The Source and Function of the Axioms*

In view of the care with which Sidgwick lays out the four conditions which apparently self-evident propositions must satisfy before they can be accepted as really self-evident, it is striking that he does not apply these tests directly to the alleged axioms stated in III, xiii. The explanation is that much of the work of testing has already been done, and the rest is to be done in the remainder of the *Methods*. The key terms in each axiom, unlike the mixed descriptive-*cum*-ethical notions involved in many common-sense rules, are purely ethical terms. At their core is a simple notion, which has been carefully distinguished from other notions. To anyone who understands these terms, the notion must now be clear. The non-ethical concepts involved—concepts of action, self, other, earlier, later —are so basic that to give a critical examination of them would require a digression on other branches of philosophy. The axioms are meant to hold with no exceptions and no limitations, and therefore no question of their precision can arise in the way it arises for common-sense rules. Thus the first test has already been passed. The elimination of non-rational sources of certainty required by the second test is assured by the fact that the axioms use no terms carrying merely conventional, legal, or traditional meanings. Our certainty about propositions phrased as the axioms are cannot be derived from extra-rational sources, as might the certainty that one ought to allow a guest to precede one out of one's house. The third requirement, of mutual compatibility, and the fourth, of acceptability to common sense, are discussed at length in later chapters of the *Methods*. But while the four conditions do not figure overtly in III, xiii, there is frequent mention of 'obtaining' the self-evident axioms; and some discussion of this is called for, as it is not obvious that it exemplifies either of the two ways of supporting first principles which Sidgwick thinks are available.

Two accounts are given of how the axiom of justice is

obtained. In one, Sidgwick says it may be obtained through consideration of the ordinary meaning of the notion of rightness; in the other, he says it is 'obtained by considering the similarity of the individuals that make up a Logical Whole or Genus'. (*ME* 7, p. 380.) The two accounts are not as different as they sound. J1 and J1a are brought in through reference to the position Sidgwick thinks he has established in I, iii, that rightness is an objective feature of acts. The objectivity of rightness is essentially due to the rationality of rightness, not to taking rightness as a property or quality to be observed. Now we have seen that on Sidgwick's view, while there may be ultimately arbitrary or inexplicable facts, in morality such permanent irrationalities cannot be admitted. (*ME* 7, p. 209.) Hence from the very content of the concept of rightness we can learn that there must be a reason to do an act if the act is to be right; but it is no part of the content of the concept to assert that more than one rational agent exists. If we suppose that more than one agent exists, then J1a says that variations in rightness must be attributable to variations in whatever serves as the reason for doing the act. The reference to a 'logical whole or genus' brings out the point that the agents are here considered as identical in character and different only in number, and hence that anything which is true of any one of them is true of any other. Thus the difference of rightness cannot depend on difference of agent as such. J3 then tells us what is required by reason in a situation of which we know only that it contains more than one agent of the kind to whom practical reasons may be addressed. The axiom is obtained by considering the elementary concept of ethics as it applies within a basic, and very simple, factual situation; or, we might say, by viewing the concept under a real and fundamental limitation. But the axiom is not deduced from anything that could by itself serve as a first principle of action.

A similar pattern is followed in the case of P3. It is concerned with good; and the concept of goodness has been defined, in I, ix, as 'what is reasonable to aim at or desire'. The axiom is obtained through considering a 'Mathematical or Quantitative Whole'. Sidgwick describes the kind of whole he has in mind as one 'of which the integrant parts are realised in different parts or moments of a life'. (*ME* 7, p. 391.) Taking each axiom to concern a separate aspect of practical rationality, we consider what it is reasonable to desire, supposing there to be no more than a single individual person or life whose good is of this nature. We must take into account the temporality of existence and the presence in experience of conditions which it is reasonable to aim at or to avoid. Then P3 articulates the demand of reason under these conditions or within these limits. It simply brings out the point that it is the content of such a being's experiences, not the time at which the experiences occur, which must provide the reason for aiming at or avoiding anything.

The first axiom of benevolence, which introduces the notion of universal good, is also obtained by considering a quantitative whole. Our attention is now directed not to the multiplicity of times in a life, but to the multiplicity of lives, without consideration of time. The axiom tells us that the location of a quantity of good in one life rather than another is irrelevant to its contribution to a sum total, so long as it is conceivable for different quantities to be aggregated. As we have seen, 'good' is defined in terms of what it is reasonable to desire. Hence if some feature of an object makes it reasonable for one agent to desire it to a certain degree for himself, then if that feature is present to the same degree in an object which another is to possess, the amount of good contributed to the aggregate is the same. B1 is thus the outcome of considering the notion of what it is reasonable to aim at or desire when we take an impersonal view of the existence of a multiplicity of sentient beings, i.e. when we view them without identifying any one of them as ourselves.

Sidgwick says nothing about how he obtains B2, but we can see how a utilitarian might be led to it by a train of thought of the kind we have already seen operating. In J3 we have an axiom about what it is reasonable to do, in B1 an axiom about what it is reasonable to desire. B2 is the only axiom connecting the two notions, which are, of course, the notions of the right and the good. B2 might be obtained, then, by considering the notions, supposing the existence of a multiplicity of beings who are subject to the direction of reason, who are sentient as well as active, and who can affect the desirability of each other's experiences over time. Under these conditions rationality requires that if it is the goodness of some state of affairs which

is an agent's reason for an action, then the goodness of a precisely similar state of affairs is also a reason for action, regardless
of the ownership of what is good. B2 stresses, in other words,
the fact that it is the goodness and not its locus in a life which
is the reason for action. And here, as in the case of the other
axioms, although no one of the considerations taken alone
gives a special principle of practical rationality, taken all
together such a principle is the result. As Sidgwick points out,
B2 uses the concept of good involved in B1. We shall see that
there is another way of understanding B2 when we come to
our fuller discussion of egoism and P3 in Chapter 13.

In the first edition, commenting on Samuel Clarke's mode
of obtaining a basic principle of rational benevolence, Sidgwick
makes some observations which suggest another aspect of his
axioms. It is helpful to note this aspect, which remains important despite the textual changes.

> It must be distinctly explained that here [i.e. in the case of
> Benevolence] as in the case of Equity [i.e. Justice], we must start
> with some ethical judgment, in order that the rule may be proved:
> and, in fact, the process of reasoning is precisely similar in the two
> cases. There, an individual was supposed to judge that a certain
> kind of conduct was right and fit to be pursued towards him: and
> it was then shewn that he must necessarily conceive the same con-
> duct to be right for all other persons in precisely similar circum-
> stances: and therefore judge it right for himself, in like case, to
> adopt it towards any other person. Similarly here we are supposed
> to judge that there is something intrinsically desirable—some result
> which it would be reasonable for each individual to seek for himself,
> if he considered himself alone. Let us call this the individual's Good
> or Welfare: then what Clarke urges is, that the Good of any one
> individual cannot be *more* intrinsically desirable, *because it is his*,
> than the equal good of any other individual. So that our notion of
> Ultimate Good, at the realization of which it is evidently reasonable
> to aim, must include the Good of *every* one on the same ground that
> it includes that of *any* one. (*ME* 1, p. 360.)

Here the identity of reasoning as concerns J3 and B1,
detectable in the final text, is made explicit. The passage also
suggests that all four axioms may be viewed as obtained by
the procedure of eliminating arbitrary limitations on ethical
propositions one is prepared to assert. If someone says that some

consideration is a reason for him to do a specific act, he may be brought to see that the limitation to himself is arbitrary and unfounded: it cannot be a reason for him to act unless it would equally be a reason for anyone similar to act in the same way in relevantly similar circumstances. Thus we obtain J3. If someone asserts that it is reasonable for him to care about gratifying a desire he has now, he may be brought to see that the limitation to the present is arbitrary: it cannot be reasonable only to care about the desire which happens to be felt at the moment. And this yields P3. If somebody judges that some state of himself would be good because possessed of a certain characteristic, he may be brought to see that the limitation to himself is arbitrary: if that characteristic makes the state good, it makes it so whether it be his state or another's. We thus arrive again at B1. And finally, if someone argues that because a certain object would be good, he ought to obtain it for himself, it can be pointed out that if it is the goodness which makes it reasonable for him to act to obtain the object for himself, then the limitation to obtaining it for himself is arbitrary. He should see that goodness must be a reason for acting to bring about what is good, regardless of who will possess the good— i.e., he should see that B2 is true. In the first edition this last argument is actually presented in III, xiii, as one upshot of the axioms. Sidgwick tells us that with it we have 'evolved the suppression of Egoism, the necessary universality of view which is implied in the mere form of the objective judgment "that an end is good", just as it is in the judgment "that an action is right" '. (*ME* 1, p. 366.)

The first edition presentation suggests also that all the axioms might be worded negatively, as Sidgwick words J3 and P3 throughout the editions. B1 would then say that the locus of what is good in one life or another is not a consideration determining quantity of good, and B2 would say that the locus of good in one life or another is not a determinant of whether production of the good is a reason for action. If the axioms are all thus negative, they do not seem to be able to provide the positive content needed for the guidance of action. And the first edition presentation suggests, accordingly, that we must start our practical reasoning from particular judgements about what it is rational to do or to desire in order to obtain substantive principles. From this perspective the axioms accord with Sidgwick's general view of the role of intuition in knowledge. As we saw in Chapter 1, he argues, against the empiricists, that an appeal to intuition is a necessity in all knowledge, since without it no adequate account is possible of how we can be warranted in drawing inferences. This suggests that Sidgwick takes intuition generally to be involved in providing ultimate warrants for transitions from premisses to conclusions rather than as ultimate premisses for arguments. It is not difficult to interpret the intuitively evident moral axioms in this way. J3, for example, says that what counts as a reason for one agent counts as a reason for any agent; B1 says that what gives one person a reason to desire something for himself gives everyone an equal reason to desire it; and P3 and B2 can be explicated along the same lines. The moral axioms make these inferences not simply permissible but mandatory: they prohibit the denial of certain types of inference. This still allows them to be included among the principles of reasoning; and to call them axiomatic or intuitive is to say that they present requirements which are intrinsically reasonable, or which possess ultimate rational justification.

It is striking that all the inferences required by the axioms are generalizing inferences; and the fact raises the question of the relation of Sidgwick's axioms to Kant's basic principles. Sidgwick thought himself much indebted to Kant, and he attributed the axiom of justice, J3, particularly to him. (*ME* 7, xvii.) But there are decisive differences in the ways in which Sidgwick and Kant appeal to reason. Sidgwick does not think Kant's attempt to extract basic principles of morality from pure practical reason is successful, and he himself does not try to do so. His objections to two of Kant's main moral claims make this clear. Kant's principle of universalizability is derivable from pure practical reason; but it does not provide a sufficient as well as a necessary condition of rightness. To think, as Sidgwick believes Kant does, that it gives a sufficient condition is to think that a sincere and conscientious person could not mistakenly act wrongly; and this is an error, which is just like that of 'supposing that Formal Logic supplies a complete criterion of Truth'. (*ME* 7, pp. 209–10; cf. p. 386.) Kant's attempt to drive a substantive goal of happiness from pure reason also fails. In so far as it relies on the proposition that each man will wish for help when he himself is in trouble, it abandons pure reason, since its premiss states only a contingent fact. And what is more, a strong man might feel such a wish but reject it, thinking that the wish is unreasonable and that 'he and such as he' can profit more by adopting egoism and remaining self-reliant despite the risks. In so far as Kant's argument depends on the *a priori* requirement that we respect humanity in ourselves and others, it shows at most, Sidgwick says, that one ought to respect the purely rational aspect of others. It does not show that one ought to respect, still less to forward, their purely subjective ends. Yet it is from satisfying these that, even on Kant's view, happiness arises. (*ME* 7, pp. 389–90; in the text at greater length until *ME* 4.) In pointing out these difficulties in Kant's ethics, Sidgwick underlines his own determination to take the basic contingent conditions of human existence into account in deriving moral axioms, and his willingness to accord a place to our contingent and subjective desires. We have seen something of Sidgwick's mode of incorporating references to the basic facts of human existence in the axioms. His way of incorporating our subjective desires is discussed in the next chapter.

Sidgwick's axioms, then, have their source in our reason. They are obtained not by mental inspection of esoteric entities or qualities, but by considering what reason requires of action under the conditions set by the most basic facts of human life. They function by requiring us to generalize whenever we assign a reason for an act or a desire. It was concluded in the last chapter that the dependence argument relies on and makes explicit the demands of rationality on action when a detailed moral code is a practical necessity; the systematization argument briefly outlined in IV, ii, also centres on the demands of reason; and in the next chapter it will be argued that the question of what is ultimately good is answered by considering yet another aspect of what is needed if reason is to be practical. If these claims are correct, and if the view of the axioms which has been proposed here can be sustained by showing how it leads to a faithful and sensible reading of Sidgwick's text, then we may conclude that the central thought of the *Methods of Ethics* is that morality is the embodiment of the demands reason makes on practice under the conditions of human life, and that the problems of philosophical ethics are the problems of showing how practical reason is articulated into these demands.

iv. *Axioms and Substantive Principles*

There still remain difficulties of interpreting Sidgwick's self-evident axioms. The list of axioms given above offers a clue to the problem. Some of the formulations, notably those we have argued are the central ones, easily bear the formal and negative interpretation which has been put upon them here. Others do not. Among the formulations of the axioms of prudence and of benevolence there are some—those given in the Concluding Chapter, P5 and B5, and their counterparts in other writings (e.g. 1889f, 483), for example—which seem to give full positive statements of substantive principles of egoism and utilitarianism. Is there some account of this discrepancy in Sidgwick's own explicit claims about what is self-evident which fits in with the view of the axioms sketched above?

One point of difficulty may be removed immediately. In III, xiii, Sidgwick does not claim to have taken the development of axioms to the point at which the ultimate good can be identified as pleasure. Hence the most he claims for the axioms in that chapter is that they show some variety of maximizing consequentialism to be true. They show that the fact that an act maximizes goodness makes the act right. Intuition, when pressed, leads us so far, but whether it leads to the hedonistic or some other variety of consequentialism must be shown by 'a more indirect mode of reasoning'. (*ME* 7, pp. 388-9.) Yet Sidgwick's interpreters do not agree that even a conclusion as strong as this is warranted by the axioms Sidgwick himself presents. Some commentators allow that P3 and B3 are maximizing consequential principles: 'they simply assert that more good is always more valuable than less good', as Rashdall, not very clearly, puts it. But a different view of them is offered by Seth and Hayward. Seth argues that the principles of prudence and benevolence are, like that of justice, principles of distribution, and that 'the common mark of all' is impartiality. Hayward says that the principle of prudence tells us nothing about maximizing good: it is only a principle of the indifference of time-considerations to rational calculation, and as such is needed as much by the utilitarian as by the egoist. He also sees benevolence as merely the spatial analogue of this, requiring impartiality among different selves, or *loci* of good. In a neglected but valuable monograph Paul Bernays gives essentially the same interpretation. Broad says that the principles of prudence and benevolence serve only to rule out certain kinds of reason for action and to assert that reasons are needed. And Lacey follows in this tradition. The axioms of prudence and benevolence, he says, 'are primarily concerned with covering the "indifference of space and time" ' and do not yield premisses which lead to utilitarianism or egoism.[3]

The interpretation of the axioms in the present chapter obviously agrees in the main with the negative and formalistic reading of them which predominates in the literature. It would help to support the interpretation, however, if it could aid in showing why Sidgwick frequently takes his axioms to have established so much more than, on this reading, they really have.

Sidgwick himself, it is to be noticed, is at times aware of a difference between the axioms and some fuller statement of the principles (ignoring the hedonistic interpretation of 'good'). Thus after he has worked out the axioms he says that he has tried 'to show how in the principles of Justice, Prudence, and Rational Benevolence as commonly recognized there is at least a self-evident element, immediately cognizable by abstract intuition'. Since the element thus distinguished from the commonly recognized principles is described as dependent 'in each case on the relation which individuals and their particular ends bear as parts to their whole, and to other parts of these wholes', it is plain that by 'self-evident element' Sidgwick refers to the axioms J3, P3, B1, and B2. The distinction is further drawn upon when Sidgwick says that the more or less clear apprehension of these 'abstract truths' is 'the permanent basis of the common conviction that the fundamental precepts of morality

---

[3] Rashdall, *Theory of Good and Evil*, i, 147; James Seth, 'The Ethical System of Henry Sidgwick', *Mind*, n.s. x, 1901, p. 181; Hayward, *Ethical Philosophy*, pp. 122, 133–5; Paul Bernays, 'Das Moralprinzip bei Sidgwick und bei Kant', *Abhandlung der Fries'schen Schule*, n.f. iii. Band, 3. Heft, 1910, pp. 538–9; Broad, *Five Types*, p. 227; Lacey, 'Maxims', 220–1.

are essentially reasonable'. (*ME* 7, pp. 382–3.) For the precepts, the belief in which is asserted to be based on rational
insight, are explicitly said not to be the common-sense rules to
which the dogmatic intuitionist appeals, but to be rather the
more general and basic substantive principles such as P4 and
B4. (*ME* 7, p. 383.)

A page or two later Sidgwick seems again to use the distinction between a self-evident element and a fuller principle in
which it is an element. We have been led, he says, from dogmatic to philosophical intuitionism, for we have seen that
when we insist on axioms that really pass the tests of self-
evidence we go beyond the limited principles of the former to
principles which are not in the accepted sense 'intuitionistic'.
The axiom of prudence, P3, is 'implied in Rational Egoism as
commonly accepted', and the axiom of benevolence, B3, is
'required as a rational basis for the Utilitarian system'. (*ME* 7,
pp. 386–7.) It is doubtful whether much is to be made of the
difference between 'implied in' and 'required as a basis for'
in these remarks. In the third and fourth editions the description of the relation between P3 and rational egoism is practically identical with the description of the relation between B3
and utilitarianism: 'the axiom of Prudence . . . is the self-
evident principle on which Rational Egoism is based' (*ME* 3,
p. 388; *ME* 4, pp. 386–7), and the distinction only comes in
with the fifth edition. In any event the texts clearly suggest
a distinction between the self-evident element and the full moral
principle which common sense might recognize and which is
based on or implies what is self-evident. Why, then, is Sidgwick not thorough and consistent in recognizing the distinction?

In offering an answer to this question we shall concentrate on
utilitarianism, postponing consideration of egoism to Chapter
13. J3, the axiom of justice, does not raise the problem. It is
held to provide no more than a necessary condition of rightness,
and therefore to be no more than a formal principle, although
under certain complex conditions it may serve for the utilitarian
as a sufficient determinant of rightness. (*ME* 7, pp. 416–17;
cf. below, Ch. 11, sec. iv.)

We need, then, some line of argument which leads from B1
and B2 through B3 to the fuller principle B5 (still disregarding
the hedonistic view of the good), and which may well have

influenced Sidgwick's thinking. Three points must be added to the formal axioms if the transition is to be made. First, the axioms so far assert only the general hypothetical proposition that if the goodness an act will produce is a reason for anyone to do it, it is equally a reason for everyone to do it. It must be added that the goodness an act will produce *is* a reason to do it. Second, the axioms do not explicitly say that *maximizing* goodness is essential for rightness, and this must be added. Third, the axioms do not say that maximizing goodness is the *right-making characteristic*, not merely a sign or criterion of rightness; and this must be added. From the conclusions already reached in the *Methods* it does seem possible to work out these additions; and what is more, the reasoning follows one of the patterns Sidgwick lays down as available for giving rational support to a first principle.

To obtain the first addition, we recall that if the distinction between right and wrong applies to acts at all, then it must be possible to give reasons for some acts and against others. Then there must be ultimate reasons for and against acts, and these ultimate reasons must have certain formal features. The critique of common-sense morality in Book III has shown that none of the non-ethical characteristics usually used in specifying classes of right actions can serve as an ultimate reason. J3, being purely formal, does not give a sufficient ultimate reason. This leaves only goodness; and so far as we can tell, it can serve the purpose. It is a clear and precise concept, without the other failings which force us to rule out the non-ethical candidates for position of ultimate reason. There must be some ultimate reason, and it can only be goodness. Consequently we may move from taking the axioms to mean only that *if* goodness is a reason for action for one person it is so for all, to taking them to mean that goodness *is* a reason for action.

Why, then, are we to *maximize* goodness? This seems to follow simply from the definitions of rightness and goodness. Goodness is by definition a concept allowing of degrees or of comparability, and rightness is defined in terms of bringing about the greatest good within the agent's power. An objection to taking the axioms in this way has been put concisely by Bernays, who, after noting that B4 does not follow from B1 and B2 because 'in mere impartiality there does not yet lie the preferability of the greater to the lesser good', continues by arguing that 'one cannot validly adduce against this that in the concept of the greater good is already contained the idea that it is to be preferred; for doing this would yield a tautological explanation of the two principles [P4] and [B4] which Sidgwick expressly repudiates'.[4] Now Sidgwick certainly repudiates tautological principles, but Bernays's point is still not decisive. The definitional point that rightness is conceptually *tied* to creating maximal goodness does not yield the utilitarian principle just by itself. An ultimate principle must present a characteristic that *makes* right acts right, and the definition does not establish that maximizing goodness has this status. (See Ch. 7, sec. iii.)

What shows that maximizing goodness is what makes right acts right is, once again, the negative result of the examination of common-sense morality, that none of the purely factual properties of acts can serve as an ultimate right-making characteristic. It cannot, therefore, be the case that some factual property of acts makes them right, and that this entails that doing them must maximize goodness. It must rather be the case that bringing about the most good is what makes right acts right.

Given the definitions of 'right' and 'good' and the assumption that there are some right acts, the elimination of alternative possible ultimate right-making characteristics is the key point leading from the self-evident axioms to the conclusion that maximizing goodness is what makes right acts right. But this line of reasoning answers very closely to Sidgwick's description of a methodological derivation of a self-evident principle. It involves applying the tests which must be passed by any self-evident principle to a variety of possible ethical first principles, and eliminating all but a very few of them. It then involves using the fact that most have been eliminated to warrant not only asserting the ones still left but interpreting them in a fuller and richer sense than would be justified if there were others in addition to them. If we think of Sidgwick as sometimes blending these two uses, or two stages of use, of the methodological argument from elimination of alternatives, we can understand the confusion involved in his sometimes calling B1 and B2 self-evident, and sometimes B4 or B5.

[4] Bernays, 'Sidgwick und Kant', p. 538, n. 2.

We can, then, couple the negative and formal interpretation of B1 and B2, which shows how they stem from the demands of reason on action under certain basic conditions, with Sidgwick's own tendency to understand them as giving the more substantive foundation of utilitarianism. If P3 turns out also to have both a formal and negative aspect when taken by itself, and a more substantive force when joined to a methodological argument from elimination of alternatives, we shall have yet another reason to accept the view which has been proposed in the present chapter about the underlying thought of Sidgwick's *Methods*. Before turning to that issue, however, we shall complete the discussion of Sidgwick's views on utilitarianism which has been started here. He himself discusses egoism before going on to utilitarianism. We shall need to draw on some of his earlier analyses as we proceed to examine the remainder of the argument he constructs in favour of utilitarianism and the method he develops for utilitarians to use.

The Transition to Utilitarianism

THE critique of common-sense morality is the first step in a transition from unexamined, unsystematized, positive moral opinion toward a fully examined rational morality. It shows the need for first moral principles of a kind common sense cannot itself provide. The second step in the transition is to provide the principles. As part of that step, Sidgwick obtains basic axioms for a maximizing consequentialist ethical theory. The nature of the good which the axioms require rational agents to maximize must be determined next; and the present chapter examines the way in which this part of the transition is carried out. Confining our attention still to Sidgwick's development of the utilitarian aspect of morality, we shall see in this chapter that he tries to prove pleasure to be the good by using a series of arguments similar in important respects to those already used in criticizing common sense and in working out the axioms. To complete the transition after this is done, the first principle must be brought back into relation with the common sense from which the argument began. It must be shown to be able both to explicate and to rectify that morality—to make plain the rationality already inherent in it, and to increase the extent of its rationality. Once this is done the 'proof of Utilitarianism' will be 'as complete as it can be made'. (*ME* 7, p. 422.) To examine these final steps in the transition to a fully rational morality is the task of the next chapter.

The whole procedure exemplifies Sidgwick's basic idea of the function of thought. In the most abstract account he gives of the matter, he explicitly rejects Kant's account of the activity of thinking, and says that on his own view

the essential function of thought, in all its departments, is not primarily or mainly the binding together into a whole of elements previously separate: but rather a process by which we pass from the consciousness of a vague manifold, of which the elements are obscurely thought, and even may have a merely potential existence, to a consciousness of the same manifold as not only more connected, but also more distinct in its parts or elements, and not only more distinct but fuller. (*LPK*, pp. 92–3.)

In moral thinking, plainly, the common sense from which reflection begins is the 'vague manifold' whose elements are to be analysed into distinct parts. The axioms are one of the elements which emerge from obscurity in the process and, as we shall see, our particular desirable states of consciousness are the other. The utilitarian principle, by synthesizing these two elements, enables us to give an explication and rectification of common-sense morality through which it acquires a greater degree of connection and fullness than it previously had. And by seeing it in this way, we complete the transition from a pre-theoretical to a fully rational moral consciousness.

The central text concerning the ultimate good, III, xiv, went through a great many changes, not reaching its final form until the fifth edition. The changes involve incorporating arguments from other chapters, and expanding on various points as well as rearranging the sequence of material within the chapter. But the first edition of the *Methods* contains, somewhere or other, Sidgwick's main conclusions concerning the good; and though some texts from the earlier editions help clarify the argument, we shall here, once again, work mainly with the final version.

i. *Virtue and the Ultimate Good*

For purposes of the examination of common-sense morality, Sidgwick defined virtue in III, ii, as a relatively permanent, praiseworthy, personal quality, manifested in right and supererogatory acts and differing from other human excellences in that its manifestation in any particular case as well as its acquisition are to some extent, though not entirely, within the control of the agent. As requiring the performance of right acts, virtue was examined in Book III. The examination showed that neither the general concept of virtue nor the concepts of the special virtues provide adequately precise guidance to conduct. The discussion of virtue as an ultimate good in III, xiv, does not involve a different definition but the emphasis is on the relatively permanent qualities of character rather than on their manifestation in particular right acts. The question is whether by taking such character traits as the ultimate good to be produced by action we can obtain the guidance we did not obtain from taking them as leading us directly to clear and precise rules. Since virtue is usually thought to be the chief element in human perfection, we are thus finally given an examination of perfection as providing a fundamental principle of morality. In arguing that it fails to do so, Sidgwick is also arguing against the main alternative to the view that pleasure is the ultimate good.

The course of the argument thus far has shown that particular judgements about the rightness and wrongness of specific acts require to be justified and systematized by reference to general rules of rightness, and that these in turn call for completion and rectification by absolutely universal and exceptionless principles. In those principles, we have found, rightness is determined by ultimate goodness. It is therefore a requirement for an adequate account of the ultimate good that it must yield a definite and precise substantive content for the concept which in no way presupposes the determinateness of what is right. Sidgwick's first argument against taking virtue as the ultimate good is that it fails to meet this requirement. Virtue by definition requires the doing of what is right: if the right is indefinite so long as the good is, then to say that the good is simply virtue is to make the indefiniteness inescapable. To make the ultimate good consist in virtue, when virtue requires that the right be determinate and this in turn requires that the ultimate good be determinate, simply ends us, Sidgwick says, in a logical circle. (*ME* 7, p. 392.)

Two further objections point out some of the problems in trying to evade this difficulty. First, even if it is claimed that we need not know in detail what is right or good in order to know what the virtues are and to tell when someone has them, the difficulty remains. We might take the virtues to be intuitively discernible by 'trained insight', much as artistic ability is, and to be, like artistry, incapable of being captured in precise statements. But our ideas of the virtues, Sidgwick says, 'do not become more independent by becoming more indefinite'. They still refer, though vaguely, to some notion of good or well-being beyond themselves as the final standard. They are, in short, dependent notions. If we wonder whether someone is displaying commendable liberality or regrettable profusion, admirable courage or ridiculous foolhardiness, we make the distinction 'not by intuition' but by referring either to some maxim of duty or directly to a more definite idea of good. We have already seen that the main virtues, such as benevolence and justice, presuppose the determination of the good, and the minor virtues, like zeal and earnestness, are only praiseworthy when exemplified in pursuit of the good. Thus an analogue of perceptional intuitionism fails to show that virtue can be determinate without dependence on a prior determination of the good. Next, Sidgwick's analysis of dispositions leads him to rule out the possibility that by construing the virtues as requiring us to be of a certain character, rather than to do certain kinds of acts, we could take virtue as the ultimate good. He does not deny that it is of value for us to have one sort of character rather than another. But the value must be instrumental, not intrinsic, because character traits and disposition are only definable as tendencies to act or feel in definite ways under definite circumstances, and any such tendency, Sidgwick holds, is 'clearly not valuable in itself but for the acts and feelings in which it takes effect' or for their consequences. (*ME* 7, p. 393.)

In the fourth edition Sidgwick introduces an examination of a way in which virtue might be considered to be the ultimate good which is not open to the same charge of circularity. Here, without referring to him by name, he plainly has Kant in mind. Instead of considering the separate virtues as candidates for being the ultimate good, he says, let us consider goodness of the will as such, the determination of the will to do whatever is judged right or good. It may be said that this is really the root of all virtue, and Sidgwick agrees that if this 'subjective rightness or goodness' is taken as the ultimate good the logical difficulty previously urged loses its force. But the position is none the less unacceptable. It presupposes that there is an objective rightness, and it tells us to seek it, but it does not tell us what it is. And it seems wildly paradoxical, Sidgwick thinks, to say that right-seeking is itself the ultimate end, regardless of what effects beside future right-seeking it might have. (*ME* 7, p. 394.) In the fourth edition—and, inexplicably, only there—Sidgwick allows that it would be more plausible to hold that the good will, or moral good, is only a part of the ultimate good, and that there are other 'effects of right volition' which are also ultimate goods. In that edition he proceeds to consider this Kantian view very briefly. 'On this view Ultimate Good would be composed of a moral and a non-moral element; and a moral person as such ought to seek to produce, both in his own existence and that of others, both subjective rightness of Will and non-moral good. . . .' (*ME* 4, p. 394.) The principle thus stated has an added plausibility derived from the fact, already noticed in discussion of Martineau, that in deliberation the agent cannot take any rule 'as more authoritative than the rule of doing what he judges to be right'. Thus it seems that the principle has no exceptions or limits, and is not dependent on any other principle; and if so, it might well serve as a first principle. But—in all the editions—Sidgwick argues that this appearance of independence, as far as the element of virtue in the alleged ultimate good is concerned, is misleading. Of someone other than oneself, we may judge that he is acting in accordance with his idea of what is right and that the effects of his doing so will be bad. And we have already seen (*ME* 7, p. 208) that if the badness of the results would be very serious, common sense holds that it would be right to induce such an agent to act against his convictions of rightness. Thus there is a limit to the extent to which we think it supremely good to act according to one's moral convictions: and the limit is determined by the utilitarian principle. Here a dependence argument shows that the good will cannot be an ultimate good, for its limits are determined by the claims of another good and its own directives may be overridden in the name of that other good. In short, there is a definite order of subordination in the elements of the ultimate good Kant proposes; and the conclusion is that one of the elements, virtue, is not part of the ultimate good. Sidgwick takes this result to have a practical bearing in our attitude toward fanaticism. Unswerving devotion to the right, coupled with a mistaken idea of what is right, is something we think of not as admirable but simply as dangerous. (*ME* 7, p. 395.)

That right volition is not even part of the ultimate good also results from two further considerations of the same kind. One is that however much we may value action in accordance with the dictates of reason, we do not place unlimited value on action springing from the conscious dictation of reason, i.e. from 'the predominance of consciously moral over non-moral motives'. Some things which it is reasonable to do are done better from some motive other than the purely moral one. Hence we need to decide how far conscious moral choice should extend; and this plainly subordinates the good will to some other principle. (*ME* 7, p. 395.) Second, though we generally encourage each other to be virtuous, 'our experience includes rare and exceptional cases in which the concentration of effort or the cultivation of virtue has seemed to have effects adverse to general happiness', and in such cases we moderate our urgings toward virtue. For we think that conduciveness to happiness should be the principle on which we decide how far to cultivate virtue. (*ME* 7, p. 402.) The value of the good will is thus again seen to have its limits assigned by some other principle, and goodness of will therefore cannot be an ultimate and independently valid good-making characteristic.

If Kantian attempts to make virtue an ultimate good fail, John Stuart Mill's effort to show how a utilitarian can make virtue an ultimate good is no more successful. Sidgwick shows what it comes to, without naming Mill, when he considers the position that conscious virtuous action might be part of the ultimate good if we take the ultimate good to be desirable conscious life, and add that desirable conscious life has many components, of which virtuous action is one. To bring out his objection to the position, he compares virtuous acts with the physical processes necessary to sustain conscious life. These may undoubtedly be good as a means, and it is not impossible to say that what is good as a means is also good as an end, though Sidgwick thinks one cannot attribute both kinds of goodness to an entity in the same respect. But in fact we cannot really think the physical processes are good simply in themselves and regardless of their contribution to conscious life. It cannot be an ultimately rational end of conduct that the physical processes should continue and increase, regardless of the conscious life they sustain. What is more, Sidgwick adds, conscious life just as such cannot be a rational end. For life is sometimes so awful that if it were always like that, preserving it would be simply preserving an evil. In fact life is on the whole enjoyable for most people; but it is the enjoyable quality of consciousness, not its mere existence, which makes people think it desirable. By analogy, then, if virtuous activity is part of the ultimate good, it cannot be simply as part of conscious life, but only as part of enjoyable conscious life. After all, Sidgwick asks, do we think that a virtuous life combined with extreme pain would 'remain on the whole good for the virtuous agent'? He thinks it paradoxical to say it would, and he seems to think that this supports the conclusion that if virtue is part of ultimate good, it is so only through the enjoyableness of being conscious of one's virtue. To say this, of course, is to say that virtue is good only so far as it makes people happy. Mill wanted to say something different.

ii. *Pleasure*

Virtue, then, is not the ultimate good; it is not even a part of it. The good that limits the goodness of virtue is pleasure, and it would seem, therefore, that Sidgwick might move directly to assert that it is the sole ultimate good. His reasoning is actually more complex. It will be helpful to look at his analysis of pleasure before examining the last steps of his argument for its goodness.

Sidgwick gives a more sophisticated analysis of pleasure than the earlier hedonists. He dissociates himself first from the claim that pleasure and desire are connected by the definition of the former. He is willing to allow that pleasure is a kind of feeling which 'stimulates the will to actions tending to sustain or produce it' (*ME* 7, p. 42), but he disagrees with John Stuart Mill's rash statement that desiring something and finding it pleasant are identical, and with the rather more cautious claims of Spencer and Bain to the effect that pleasure is by definition either a feeling we 'seek to bring into consciousness and retain there' or simply the same as 'motive power'. (*ME* 7, p. 125.) He also rejects their view that pleasantness is exactly proportional to strength of desire, painfulness to aversion. Some pleasures may, in anticipation and in event, be mild, yet stir us strongly to obtain them; some feelings—Sidgwick adduces tickling—may move us strongly to avoid or remove them, without being very painful. (*ME* 7, pp. 126–7.) Should we then take the view at the other extreme, that there is an indefinable simple quality of feeling called 'pleasure' which is wholly independent of volition, in the way that the quality called 'coffee-flavoured' is? Sidgwick also rejects this idea. There is, he allows, some conceptual tie between pleasure and volition; and his own view of the tie is that it is shown if we define pleasure as feeling 'which, when experienced by intelligent beings, is at least implicitly apprehended as desirable or—in cases of comparison—preferable'. (*ME* 7, p. 127.)

Sidgwick carefully points out that 'desirable' in this definition means what it has previously been explained to mean, presumably in I, ix. It follows, though Sidgwick does not note the point, that to experience or expect a pleasant feeling is to have at least the impetus to preserve or attain the feeling that is given by the special motive connected with the judgement that something is reasonably to be done or desired. But if the definition thus resolves the problem of the connection between pleasure and desire, it lays Sidgwick open to another problem, one brought out by the charge, made by Bradley and others, that on his view pleasure is good by definition. If this charge is correct, then he is also open to the charge that he allows experience to dictate what is good, since the pleasantness or painfulness of feelings is simply given in experience.[1] The first charge denies the ethical neutrality of his definition either of 'pleasure' or of 'good', the second denies that he is consistent in maintaining that 'experience can at most tell us that all men always do seek pleasure as their ultimate end' (though it does not in fact show this to be so) but 'cannot tell us that anyone ought to seek it'. (*ME* 7, p. 98.) If these charges are sound they indicate serious deficiencies in Sidgwick's thought. But, though the wording of some passages in the first edition is no doubt incautious, and may give some countenance to the charges, by the third edition Sidgwick makes it reasonably clear that they do not hold.

He does so in the course of explaining why even a strongly anti-hedonistic Stoic could accept his definition of pleasure. A moralist of this persuasion should admit, Sidgwick thinks, that we do experience certain feelings as pleasant, and that experiencing feeling as pleasant involves judging it to be

[1] See Stephen L. Darwall, 'Pleasure as Ultimate Good in Sidgwick's Ethics', *The Monist*, vol. 58, no. 3, 1974, pp. 475–89, a paper to which I am indebted for much stimulation despite my disagreement with its main contentions.

intrinsically desirable. But the Stoic should add that 'sound philosophy shows the illusoriness of such judgements'. (*ME* 7, p. 129; added, *ME* 3, p. 126.) The Stoics, he says elsewhere, 'held that what we call passion is a morbid and disorderly condition of the rational soul, involving erroneous judgment as to what is to be sought or shunned. . . . the truly wise man . . . will . . . be conscious of the solicitations of physical appetite; but he will not be misled into supposing that its object is really a good. . . .' (*Hist.*, p. 73.) In other words, we might say when we experience pleasure that we are having a feeling which presents itself as intrinsically desirable, in much the way that an optical illusion involves an experience which presents itself as veridical. But we can still think that the judgement we are tempted to make is false. What makes the feeling pleasure is simply that it presents itself as intrinsically desirable, not that the judgement which the feeling tempts us to make is true. It is not impossible that each of us should have feelings which tempt us into making false judgements of value, just as we all have experiences which tempt us into making false judgements of fact. Thus if the Stoic's position is even conceivable, Sidgwick's definitions are not question-begging, and experience does not directly compel us to admit that pleasure is really an intrinsic good.

There is an important element of truth in the notion that Sidgwick takes experience to show us what is good, even though it does not reveal any inconsistency in his thinking. Judgements of pleasure are the analogues, under the concept of goodness, of the judgements of the rightness of specific acts which the perceptional intuitionist takes to be adequate for moral guidance. These two classes of particular judgement provide the possible starting-points for the generalizing inferences warranted by the basic moral axioms. Sidgwick's objections to Kant make amply clear his belief that generalization alone is not an adequate test of initial judgements of rightness. This point is embodied in the axioms concerning rightness, J3 and B2, which show that definite determination of the right depends upon the prior determination of the intrinsically good. Our experiences of pleasure serve as the basis for the determination of the good. In giving them this status, Sidgwick takes into account what he thinks Kant fails to incorporate into his theory

—the contingent desires and satisfactions of each person. For it is just a contingent fact that some sort of feeling presents itself to us as intrinsically desirable. That one thing and not another gives us pleasure is not a determination of reason. It simply arises from the way things and we happen to be.

This is not, however, all there is to be said about the goodness of pleasure. No apparent intuition is necessarily correct, on Sidgwick's view, and the apparently intuitive judgements that certain feelings are intrinsically good might be either mistaken, or, if correct, inferential rather than intuitive. This is the final position held by our apparently intuitive judgements about the rightness of specific acts; but Sidgwick's theory requires that the apparently intuitive judgements of goodness should turn out to be real intuitions. And it is easy to see how the argument should go, though he does not develop it. Each intuition of the goodness of a feeling is clear, since it applies a simple concept to an introspectively given feeling, and each is precise, since it applies only to that feeling at that time. Next, since, as Sidgwick says in a footnote (*ME* 7, p. 398 n. 2), one cannot be mistaken in thinking a feeling is a pleasure, one cannot be wrong in thinking that it is self-evidence, rather than custom or tradition, that leads to one's certainty about the goodness of pleasure. Third, judgements about goods of this kind cannot fail to be consistent with one another. We may judge one experience more of a good than another but this does not entail that the lesser is not good at all; and what leads one person to judge it good in this way may be judged differently by another, but it does not follow that either is mistaken about the goodness of his own experience, which is the crucial point. These judgements, finally, obtain an assent as nearly universal as intuitive judgements ever obtain, since most people—with the Stoic philosopher as perhaps the only dissenter—think that pleasure is a real intrinsic good, whether they think there are others or not.

Our judgements of the goodness of pleasure thus pass the tests of intuitive certainty which all apparent intuitions must pass. But as we have seen in discussing the dependence argument, certainty is not enough. The arguments against the intrinsic and ultimate goodness of virtue show that Sidgwick thinks it possible that the kind of goodness derived from one characteristic may have its force as a reason for desiring and acting overridden when the goodness derived from some other characteristic comes into competition with it. If this occurs with any kind of goodness, then it is not ultimate goodness. Sidgwick's theory that pleasure is the ultimate good thus depends crucially upon the proposition that there is no good-making characteristic which takes precedence of the goodness of pleasure. The negative claim operates in conjunction with the intuition in establishing the ultimacy of the hedonistic good, as it does in establishing the supremacy of the consequentialist axioms. Only here, it should be noted, we have not just one axiom—that pleasure is intrinsically good—but as many self-evident propositions as there are experiences of pleasure.

Pleasure must have certain other characteristics if it is to be the ultimate good. Since goodness is the concept through which comparisons of value may be made, its substantive content must allow for such comparisons. Sidgwick approaches the question of the comparability and measurability of pleasures through the needs common to egoistic and universalistic hedonism. In each theory we are directed to seek a 'greatest possible' happiness, either our own or everyone's. The most precise interpretation of happiness, Sidgwick argues (*ME* 7, p. 120), is that which takes it to mean simply 'the greatest attainable surplus of pleasure over pain', using these terms as widely as possible. Then the fundamental assumption needed for hedonistic calculation is that pleasures and pains are commensurable, or have 'determinate quantitative relations to each other' (*ME* 7, p. 123), so that they can be thought of as elements in a total which is to be maximized. It follows, first, that intensity and duration of pleasure and pain must be capable of offsetting each other, with a shorter but more intense pain equalling a longer and fainter one. Next, we must assume that there is a perfectly neutral state of feeling— a 'hedonistic zero'—which divides pleasure from pain, the latter being simply the negative of the former. (*ME* 7, pp. 123–5.) Third, pleasures and pains must be homogeneous throughout. On methodological grounds Mill's distinction of kinds of pleasures must be rejected. (*ME* 7, p. 128.) And finally the determinate degrees possessed by pleasure and pain must be knowable. Sidgwick adds that if any sort of hedonism is to be of practical interest, we must assume that men can deliberately increase pleasure and decrease pain. (*ME* 7, pp. 129–30.) Are all these assumptions acceptable? On the answer to this question depends the workability of utilitarianism no less than of egoism.

Sidgwick's consideration of this question occupies II, iii, a chapter which reached its final form only in the third edition. It opens with replies to some objections to hedonism raised by T. H. Green (first appearing as a note in *ME* 2), which need not be considered until later, in Chapter 14, as they do not bear on the main topic—the possibility that hedonistic calculations simply cannot be performed. The egoists' difficulties here focus on obtaining accurate ideas of the intensity of pleasures. For the possessor of a pleasure cannot be mistaken about whether an experience is pleasant or not, and presumably estimates of duration even of private states are not problematic. Of course for the utilitarian the difficulties of interpersonal comparison also arise, but these again must be concerned with comparisons of intensity. Now there is no doubt, Sidgwick says, that we do compare pleasures in respect of intensity. The question is whether our comparisons are not far cruder than hedonism requires, and also subject to illusions we cannot correct. (*ME* 7, p. 140.) Can we know the comparative intensities of pleasures we feel at different times? When we try to find out, one pleasure is usually 'a representation, not an actual feeling'; and it is very difficult, Sidgwick thinks, to imagine a pleasure accurately enough to obtain a precise estimate of what its magnitude will be when it is actual. (*ME* 7, pp. 141 ff.) After considerable elaboration of the difficulties of hedonistic comparison Sidgwick concludes that two of the main assumptions of hedonism cannot be given very strong support. That pleasures and pains have definite degrees of magnitude is 'an *a priori* assumption, incapable of positive empirical verification', though not refuted by experience either; and that such degrees, if they exist, can be known by a neutral mind, with each pleasure and pain assigned a definite distance from the zero-point, is 'at best an ideal to which we can never tell how closely we approximate'. (*ME* 7, p. 146.)

These difficulties relate to estimating the intensity of past pleasures and pains. Projection into the future is even more uncertain, since one's own consistency over time is questionable. The experience of others, Sidgwick thinks, is of relatively little use because of difference among temperaments. (*ME* 7, pp. 147–9.) He concludes that there are standing reasons for serious doubt about the accuracy of hedonistic calculation when it is carried out by the ordinary methods we all use, the 'empirical reflective' methods, though, he says, he continues to use it despite its failings. (*ME* 7, p. 150.) But the question naturally arises whether the ordinary method can be replaced by a better, scientific, method. The answer is negative. We need not follow the careful detail into which Sidgwick pursues the issue in II, iv, II, v, and II, vi, where he examines common-sense aphorisms, moral rules, and a number of theories put forth by his contemporaries about pleasure, as sources of guidance to the hedonist. He finds all of them failing in one way or another, leaving us with no choice but to use the ordinary 'empirical reflective' method of estimating amounts of pleasure. He thereby lays the ground for avoiding one frequent criticism of utilitarianism, best put, perhaps, by Little:

> The conflict, which one may go through, between thinking that utilitarianism is nonsensical and thinking that there must be something in it, results, from the endeavour to make it too precise. So long as it remains vague and imprecise, and avoids the use of mathematical operations and concepts such as 'adding' and 'sums total', there is something in it; but it becomes nonsensical if it is pushed too hard in the attempt to make it an exact scientific sort of doctrine.[2]

Sidgwick would object to this only that it goes too far. That the calculations must be vague and imprecise does not entail, as Little's remark suggests, that no summative calculations can be performed at all. Rough estimates of quantity are still estimates of quantity; and though rough, they may suffice for the main purposes of the utilitarian.[3]

iii. *Pleasure and Ultimate Good*

At the very end of Book I Sidgwick 'confidently' says that 'if there be any good other than Happiness to be sought by man,

[2] I. M. D. Little, *A Critique of Welfare Economics*, 2nd edn., 1957, London, p. 55.
[3] See Amartya K. Sen, *Collective Choice and Social Welfare*, 1970, pp. 99 ff. and 103–4, for a defence of a view along these lines.

as an ultimate practical end, it can only be the Goodness, Perfection, or Excellence of Human Existence'. (*ME* 7, p. 115.) In III, xiv, it becomes clear that the main component other than virtuous action which is included in the notion of the perfection or excellence of human existence, is human involvement with certain non-hedonistic or, as Sidgwick calls them, 'ideal' goods, such as knowledge of truth and contemplation of beauty. To complete the argument for pleasure as the ultimate good, it is necessary to show that these states of mind, good though they may be, are yet not intrinsically good. Assuming, then, for reasons which will shortly be discussed, that the ultimate good must lie within the realm of 'desirable consciousness', Sidgwick first gives his reasons for narrowing desirable consciousness down to pleasure; he next explains, in the hope of removing them, the common objections to taking pleasure as the sole ultimate good; and he finally presents a general description of the problems which a substantive concept of ultimate good must help solve, claiming that pleasure can serve this purpose, and expressing doubt that any alternative concept can.

Sidgwick begins, then, by remarking that to allow ultimate good to be some form of desirable consciousness is not yet to allow that it must be happiness or pleasure. Pleasure is the kind of desirable consciousness whose desirability—once it has been shown that pleasure *is* desirable—is 'directly cognisable by the sentient individual at the time of feeling it', so that he cannot be mistaken about its goodness in any particular case. But there are other good states of mind which do not share this particular feature, for instance cognitions of truths and appreciations of beauty. There are two elements involved in such non-hedonic or ideal goods. There is the consciousness itself, and there is an objective relation to something outside it. The distinction is necessary because an apparent cognition of something may turn out to have been an error, or an apparent appreciation of beauty no more than a contemplation of mere prettiness. Hence we cannot know by introspection alone whether we are having an ideally good state of mind, as we can know by introspection that we are having a hedonically good one. (*ME* 7, p. 398.) Now it is sometimes held that the ideally good states of mind are ultimately or intrinsically good; and it seems that these goods may come into competition with the hedonic good. One might prefer knowing the truth, however painful, to relying on pleasant fictions; one might prefer the arduous contemplation of the highest art to the greater pleasure drawn from less beautiful creations. We must therefore ask whether the ideal goods really are intrinsically good. In doing so we must separate their two elements. Does the goodness arise from the state of consciousness itself—a state describable as, e.g., 'cognising that so-and-so is true'; or does it arise from the objective relation of the mind to something else—the relation which must hold if the apparent cognition is to be real knowledge of a truth?

Sidgwick thinks the consciousness itself, and alone, does not have intrinsic value. We do, he allows, sometimes think such states of mind are valuable though not immediately pleasant. But in such cases, one of two explanations holds. Sometimes it is future effects, foreseen as arising from the present state of mind, which we think good. And sometimes it is the objective relation of the mind to something else. In the former case, the value of the state of consciousness is instrumental, not intrinsic. In the latter, what we are valuing is not, strictly speaking, a state of consciousness at all, and so not something which can be intrinsically good. (*ME* 7, pp. 398–9.)

Sidgwick is not content with this victory, if such it is, because it seems merely verbal. Why not say that 'conscious life' includes the objective relations implied in states of knowing truth, contemplating beauty, etc.? Then we could consider such knowings and contemplatings as part of ultimate good, along, of course, with pleasure. And rational benevolence would then require us to pursue not only universal happiness but also these ideal goods for everyone alike. (*ME* 7, p. 400.)

Against this possibility Sidgwick appeals both to intuition and to common sense. He thinks the reader's intuition will agree with his own (cf. *ME* 1, p. 371) that 'these objective relations of the conscious subject, when distinguished from the consciousness accompanying and resulting from them, are not ultimately and intrinsically desirable; any more', Sidgwick significantly adds, 'than material or other objects are, when considered apart from any relation to conscious existence'. (*ME* 7, pp. 400–1.) The addition is significant because it shows that Sidgwick is here returning to the same source of assurance as that on which he relies at the end of Book I, when he tells us that nothing is intrinsically good 'out of relation to human existence, or at least to some consciousness or feeling'. (*ME* 7, p. 113.) Knowledge and beauty are the cases he there adduces to bring this out: it seems clear to him that it could not be reasonable to aim at producing beauty except as something to be contemplated, or pursuing knowledge except as it forwards happiness or perfection. Sidgwick does not contemplate the possibility that it might be thought desirable to preserve nature in its original state regardless of the consciousness of the sentient beings involved in it.[4] But he would presumably say that such a goal could be reasonable for us only if the activity of working toward it were part of human excellence or if doing so were to increase the well-being of sentient creatures. It is on the same principle, of denying that anything wholly outside consciousness can be part of ultimate good, that Sidgwick denies that the objective relations involved in the conscious states of knowing truth and contemplating beauty can be of intrinsic value in themselves.

Leaving aside the vexed question[5] of the tenability of the distinction Sidgwick uses here between the conscious state of knowing and the objective relation involved in it, we must ask the broader question: what is the status of Sidgwick's apparent negative principle about what cannot count as part of ultimate good? Is it a general principle, different from the axioms obtained in III, xiii, but on a par with them? Since Sidgwick does not explicitly answer this question, any attempt to do so must involve some conjecture; but there are textual clues to help.

Sidgwick's basic thought here seems to be that there is no self-evident principle enabling us to connect ultimate good out of all relation to consciousness with human action. Theology or ontology might conceivably enlighten us about a cosmic goodness 'to the realization of which the whole process of the world . . . is somehow a means', but this is insufficient. Ethics is concerned only with the good for man. (*Hist.*, p. 2.) Unless the cosmic goodness is something we ought to try to increase—

---

4 See the interesting views of Stuart Hampshire, in *Morality and Pessimism*, 1972.
5 See F. H. Bradley, *Hedonism*, pp. 92 ff.

and theologians generally, Sidgwick points out, do not think men can really give necessary aid to God (*ME* 7, p. 115)—it is irrelevant to ethics. Moreover if the universe is already wholly good, in the sense in which it is implied to be in the creation story in Genesis, its goodness in this sense is also irrelevant. For practical purposes we have to think that 'some parts of the universe' are 'less good than they might be'. Sidgwick then adds that 'we do not seem to have any ground for drawing such a distinction between different portions of the non-sentient universe, considered in themselves and out of relation to conscious or sentient beings'. (*ME* 7, p. 113, n. 2, which is part of the text until *ME* 4.) There does not seem to be any self-evident, independent principle about the relative goodness of different parts or conditions of the non-sentient universe, taken in isolation. When we come to consider the impingement of the non-sentient on the sentient parts of the universe, however, we do have such a principle—the utilitarian principle. Sidgwick's idea seems to be that in an appropriate context the superiority of the validity of this principle to that of any principle establishing non-sentient good would be clear. Then if a choice had to be made between increasing the well-being of some sentient creature, not necessarily human, and (let us say) allowing the dead planets to maintain their crystalline structures intact, as part of the natural order, we should see that it is reasonable to prefer the former. This point is suggested by Sidgwick's remarks about ideal goods. Admitting the existence of preferences for these goods over pleasure, he says we can only justify the preferences by linking them to the happiness of sentient beings. (*ME* 7, p. 401.) In the first edition the point is put more emphatically: if a preference for an ideal good leads to conflict with happiness, 'we cannot maintain the rationality' of the preference. (*ME* 1, p. 372.)

We may conclude, then, that Sidgwick is not appealing to an additional intuition to exclude the intrinsic goodness of things or states of affairs out of relation to all consciousness, but is asserting only that he finds no self-evident practical principle asserting their goodness. He thinks, moreover, that he can give an account of the goodness of the ideal goods which goes at least some way toward showing it to be a result of utilitarian considerations. This is in effect what he tries to do in his appeal to common sense against the belief in the intrinsic goodness of ideal goods. He admits that he will not obtain a complete consensus in such an appeal, because of the very claim he is contesting. But on the other side must be put the fact, as Sidgwick at any rate sees it, that common sense actually values ideal goods in proportion to the degree to which they aid sentient well-being or hedonic good. (*ME* 7, pp. 401–2.) It is, as he says later, 'unconsciously utilitarian in its practical determination of those very elements in the notion of Ultimate Good or Wellbeing which at first sight least admit of a hedonistic interpretation'. (*ME* 7, pp. 453–4.) The ideal goods are instrumental goods.

Sidgwick's attempt to remove general misconceptions about hedonism is a further part of his appeal to common sense. He holds, as has been noted, that the principles the philosopher proposes need not meet with immediate acceptance by the plain man. They may need explanation and clarification, and this is what he offers (*ME* 7, pp. 402–6), on four points. First, the term 'pleasure' is usually used in a rather narrow sense, while he intends it in a very broad sense, not restricted to coarse and sensual enjoyments. Second, common sense is so far right that hedonism itself requires individuals, for their own pleasure, to pursue other things besides pleasure and to cultivate disinterested desires. Third, common sense takes 'the pursuit of pleasure' to be the pursuit by each of his own pleasure. But this is not the only reasonable possibility. Universal happiness is a rational goal, and it is not open to the objections of paltriness that lie against selfish pleasure. Finally, universal happiness, like individual pleasure, may be best attained indirectly. The benevolent agent should have other conscious aims beside the aim of the well-being of others: he should take the ideal goods as rational ends, not directly, but indirectly. Thus the common-sense objections to hedonism, when they do not rest on misunderstanding, involve points which hedonism can accept and explain. The objections become part of the theory.

One last important consideration is adduced. The utilitarian can offer a 'final criterion of the comparative value of the different objects of men's enthusiastic pursuit, and of the limits within which each may legitimately engross the attention of mankind'. Can those who object to utilitarianism do the same? They cannot do so by appealing directly to principles of right action, since all such principles have been shown to require the prior determination of the good. In specifying the problems that must be resoluble through a determination of the good, Sidgwick reiterates an important point of Bentham's: the ultimate good must not only enable us to compare the various ideal goods among themselves, it must also allow us to rank them in relation to happiness—unless one proposes, paradoxically, to deny that happiness is an ultimate good. This is no matter of mere theoretical interest, Sidgwick insists, for we have a 'practical need' to decide whether we should pursue one ideal good rather than another, and to decide 'how far we should follow any of these lines of endeavour, when we foresee among its consequences the pains of human or other sentient beings'. And so he asks, 'if we are not to systematise human activities by taking Universal Happiness as their common end, on what other principles are we to systematise them?' (ME 7, pp. 406–7.) Reason requires a systematic ordering of human activities; the hedonistic theory of ultimate good allows such an ordering; and there is no other view of the ultimate good that does. The hedonistic interpretation of ultimate good is therefore required by practical rationality. We have finally obtained the complete utilitarian principle.

12

Utilitarianism and its Method

INTUITIONISM, rigorously pressed, yields utilitarianism: so Sidgwick says, apparently forgetting egoism and abandoning his neutral stance. (*ME* 7, p. 388.) In terms of the programme of proof outlined in IV, ii, we have been shown that the basic principle of utilitarianism is self-evidently certain, that (passing by egoism once more) no other substantive principle is, and that common-sense morality, or any code like it, requires for its own completion that there be an overriding first principle with certain formal features, which the utilitarian principle has. To complete the programme it must be shown that the utilitarian principle can be used to explain and to rectify our common-sense convictions. In doing this, Sidgwick gives his only full account of the positive relations between a true first principle and the rough data from which reflection begins. He thus shows us what he thinks, finally, of the probative force of received moral opinion.

The unparalleled amount of meticulous attention and ingenious inventiveness bestowed on utilitarian theory in the last decades by economists and political scientists as well as by philosophers has naturally made much of Sidgwick's account of the doctrine outmoded. In the present chapter, therefore, the focus is primarily on the way in which Sidgwick's development of the theory shows how he would complete a systematic morality. Yet the connoisseur of the craftsmanship of utilitarianism will find in Sidgwick's chapters, particularly those on method, interesting anticipations of many of the themes and techniques of more modern discussions.

i. *Utilitarianism Stated*

The utilitarian principle is that the conduct which is objectively right is that which will produce the greatest amount of happiness on the whole. (*ME* 7, p. 411.) Happiness is specified as it was for the egoist, in terms of surplus of pleasure over pain, and the assumptions needed for calculations by the egoist are also needed by the utilitarian. In a backward look at an old objection, Sidgwick stresses that he is talking of a standard of rightness, not about a motive to action. (*ME* 7, p. 413.) He explicitly includes the pleasures and pains of animals among those to be calculated. And he touches on two other serious problems, future generations and world population. The former he treats as a question of certainty, since the time at which someone exists cannot affect the value of his happiness. (*ME* 7, p. 414.) The latter he discusses a little more fully. He does not think that the utilitarian is to consider the average happiness per person for any given size of population and then aim at the population where the average will be largest. He is to aim, rather, at the largest total happiness, and to urge a limit to the population only at the point at which the product of the number of sentients times the average happiness begins to decrease. (*ME* 7, p. 415.)

Sidgwick makes one further comment bearing on distribution at this point. Utilitarians, he says, have ignored the problem arising from the fact that there are different possible ways of distributing the same amount of good. Admittedly it is improbable that any two distributions will carry the same balance of pleasure and pain, and so the question may not be a serious one in theory. But because of the difficulties and uncertainties of actual hedonistic calculation, there are probably many cases where so far as we know the balance of pleasure and pain is the same in all available ways of distribution; and then the question becomes a practical one. The utilitarian principle itself, Sidgwick points out, does not tell us in such cases whether one or another mode of distribution is better. (Cf. *ME* 1, pp. 239–40.) In such circumstances we must simply distribute happiness equally. This alone does not call for any special justification since, as we saw in discussing the basic axioms, 'it must be reasonable to treat any one man in the same way as any other, if there be no reason apparent for treating him differently'. (*ME* 7, p. 417.) In short, the utilitarian takes his principle as dictating that good should be distributed so as to maximise it, and appeals to the principle of equal treatment only where all quantitative questions have been settled first.

ii. *The Systematization Argument*

The systematization argument is needed to show that utilitarianism answers to Sidgwick's general idea of what a proper theory should be and do, but it has other functions as well. The dependence argument shows that a first principle must have no limits or exceptions set by another principle, and that the force of the reasons supplied by an ultimate good must never be superseded by the force of reasons based on some other kind of good. The systematization argument is meant to show that the utilitarian principle not only can but actually does meet these requirements. Now the many charges, a part of whose history we have surveyed, that utilitarianism leads to shocking and paradoxical results are in effect claims that although the principle of rational benevolence is admittedly one of the principles of morals, it can only be accepted with restrictions and limitations on its scope. The systematization argument serves to show that so far as this claim is true, it does not provide any reason against taking the utilitarian principle as the basis of morality. For it offers an alternative explanation of the restrictions and limits on the utilitarian principle—the explanation that they are self-imposed, not imposed by some other principle.

Both the explanatory and the rectificatory powers of the utilitarian principle are adverted to in the outline of the main points of the systematization argument given in IV, iii. On the one side, Sidgwick thinks it can be shown to support, in a general way, current moral rules, their exceptions and limits, and the usual view of their relative importance. It also explains certain oddities in ordinary moral thought, the existence of considerable diversity of moral opinion on some matters, and the discrepancies between moral codes in different ages and countries, by showing that there are understandable differences of opinion on what is useful underlying these disagreements. On the other side, the utilitarian principle enables us to give precision to troublingly vague ordinary rules, and to give it in terms most people can accept. The principle is, moreover, actually appealed to in such cases for guidance, as it is in cases when conflicts arise between the dictates of equally important rules and when there is disagreement over the interpretation of a rule. (*ME* 7, pp. 425–6.) The argument thus brings together two aspects which, Sidgwick points out, utilitarianism has historically had: the explanatory side which Hume presented, and the critical and reforming side which Bentham made dominant. (*ME* 7, pp. 423-4; cf. 1872d, 251.) To show the full rectificatory power of the principle requires, naturally, moving beyond consideration of the principle itself to consideration of the method grounded on it. Since the task of the systematization argument is to support the principle, not to develop the method, the discussion of the explanatory power of the principle is given first.

The utilitarian's aim here, Sidgwick says, is only to show that 'some manifest felicific tendency' is possessed by accepted rules. It is neither to claim that common-sense morality is already perfectly utilitarian, nor to argue that it has been derived from calculation of utilities. Up to now common sense has been 'unconsciously utilitarian': the theorist must show that it is natural to move from the implicit rationality of received opinion to his 'scientifically complete and systematically reflective form' of regulating conduct—a transition, the utilitarian holds, which is the culmination of the whole historical progress of morality.[1] (*ME* 7, pp. 424-5.) Sidgwick sees the transition in very Whewellian terms, as resembling the change made in a special practical discipline when a technical method based on a scientific theory replaces 'trained instinct and empirical rules'. (*ME* 7, p. 425.) Just as on Whewell's model of scientific advance the theorist does not discover the data he organizes but brings them into unity under his principle, so here the utilitarian shows how the main rules accepted by common sense are unified by his principles. Only thereafter does he generate a method for dealing with unresolved issues.

Sidgwick touches first on a traditional objection to utilitarianism, one which Lecky had stressed: that since utilitarianism makes virtue depend on productivity of happiness, it treats moral virtues as no different in kind from the excellences of tools and other material things. The failure of this objection is rapidly established. The moral virtues, Sidgwick says, involve the exercise of powers which are to some extent controllable

---

[1] If common sense is 'unconsciously utilitarian', the fact helps to show that the utilitarian principle meets the third of Buffier's tests of self-evidence—that the principle is so strongly impressed on us that we act in accordance with it even if we do not give it our explicit assent. See Ch. 9, n. 2, p. 267.

by the agent. The main cause of their not being exercised is lack of motive, and moral judgement can, up to a point, supply this lack, either by the agent himself judging an act right and so finding himself with the rational impetus to action, or by others putting moral pressure on him. (*ME* 7, p. 426.) The utilitarian can also accept the distinction between the worth of a disposition or character trait and that of an act. A particular act having harmful effects may display a character trait generally having good ones, and the utilitarian will deplore the one but not the other. Sidgwick points out that 'praiseworthy' means, to the utilitarian, 'useful to praise', not 'productive of good results'. Traits likely to be exercised whether praised or not are not praiseworthy, even if they are useful. (*ME* 7, p. 428.) With these distinctions the utilitarian can give an account of the differences between useful human, or other, qualities, and moral virtues, which both corresponds to the main points of the pre-theoretical distinctions and enables us to go beyond them to resolve certain problems—such as that of the relation of merit to effort—which seem far less soluble if we remain at the common sense level. (*ME* 7, p. 429.)

One main objection to utilitarianism was that it made for the neglect of the special relations in which people stand to one another and the duties arising from and giving form to these relations—the duties of benevolence, in Sidgwick's discussion in Book III. Sidgwick has no difficulty in showing how the utilitarian can deflect this kind of criticism. He offers several lines of argument to show that the natural affections should be cherished and developed, the services normally expected in connection with them considered as duties, and active benevolence generally directed toward those more limited groups about whom we can know something and to whom we can effectively be of help, rather than diffused as a general 'enthusiasm for humanity'. (*ME* 7, pp. 430–8.) Thus the utilitarian can argue that although the common view of the duties of benevolence is '*prima facie* opposed to the impartial universality' of the utilitarian principle, it is 'really maintained by a well-considered application of the principle'. (*ME* 7, p. 439.)

In his discussion of justice, Sidgwick accepts the main point Hume tries to establish. Hume has too restricted a view of justice, he says, since he confines it to obedience to law; but as far as he goes, he is correct in taking it to be obvious that obedience is vital as a source of happiness in a society, so vital that 'even where particular laws are clearly injurious it is usually expedient to observe them' regardless of penalties for disobedience. Sidgwick goes on to raise a question which common sense asks and Hume leaves unanswered: when is it permissible to disobey bad laws? He suggests that the answer is determined by utilitarian considerations, though he does not give any analyses of notions such as civil disobedience to show this, and his own further views on how the question should be answered come out only through his later discussion of the method of utilitarianism. (*ME* 7, p. 440.)

Most of Sidgwick's attention is taken up with the key problem left unresolved by the axiom of justice. The axiom rules out arbitrary inequality, without completely determining what counts as arbitrary: hence the question of principles for determining allowable inequalities still needs an answer. Sidgwick first makes several points about positive facts which rightly determine inequalities. Since freedom of action is an important source of social benefit and of people's own enjoyments, it is expedient to allow actual individual preferences to count as grounds for differential treatment of individuals, and to count one's own unreasoned impulses as reasons for acting. (*ME* 7, p. 442.) Next, existing normal expectations must be given weight, though here the need to alter expectations whose preservation leads to injustice must also be kept in mind. Generally speaking, reliance on the actions of others is a major source of happiness and so carries much weight. When expectations are based on definite engagements, Sidgwick holds, 'there is scarcely any advantage that can counterbalance the harm done by violating them'. There are however some exceptional cases. Sidgwick adduces some complexities concerned with promising to illustrate, claiming that obvious utilitarian considerations here command general agreement. (*ME* 7, pp. 443–4.) With expectations based on less definite undertakings, we find a major area in which the precision utilitarianism can provide helpfully replaces the vagueness of common sense. Sidgwick then turns to the ideal aspect of justice, which common sense takes to involve the principle of rewarding men according to their deserts. This is quite in accordance with utilitarianism, Sidgwick thinks, though some differences in detail may arise if a purely prospective scale of rewards is used instead of the less precise scale used by common sense. (*ME* 7, p. 446.) When differences in desert either do not exist or cannot be taken into account for practical reasons, the utilitarian falls back on strict equality. He can justify this, of course, by appeal to an intuitive principle, but Sidgwick adds that distributing means to happiness equally (in these cases) is itself likely to be the most fruitful mode of distribution, since men 'have a disinterested aversion to unreason' and an aversion to any sort of unjustified inferiority, especially to unreasonable inferiority, and both feelings are gratified by equality. (*ME* 7, p. 447.)

Utilitarianism, in short, sustains common sense on broad issues of justice in obedience to law and with respect to definite commitments, as it sustains it on the principle involved in ideal justice. In addition it gives us a way of resolving the conflicts between justice determined by existing facts and justice as demanded by the ideal. Common sense itself cannot resolve this conflict: it is 'permanently latent in the very core of Common Sense', as the analysis of the ordinary notion has made evident. The utilitarian, however, has a common measure for balancing off the otherwise incommensurable elements in the problem, and uses them as guides to utilities. (*ME* 7, p. 448.)

The chapter giving the explanatory side of the systematization argument contains a number of interpretations of other common-sense moral convictions, the details of which need not be repeated here. The chapter as a whole is the first really thorough and comprehensive attempt to reply in detail to the major moral objections commonly urged against utilitarianism on the grounds of the allegedly paradoxical or counter-intuitive results to which it leads. The mode of procedure Sidgwick uses is not, of course, original. Like John Stuart Mill and Alexander Smith, to mention no earlier precedents, he relies on the possibility of giving utilitarian reasons for following rules which are considerably narrower in scope than the utilitarian principle itself. He then appeals to obvious general facts about what is useful to show that the main rules of common sense have 'some manifest felicific tendency'. This shows that the utilitarian can establish a *prima facie* counterpart to every major common-sense rule. Broad-scope counter-examples are thus eliminated, and the limits on the utilitarian principle shown to be self-limitations. As for more particular cases, the utilitarian, not claiming a perfect coincidence between the conclusions of his principle and common sense, may be prepared to argue that common sense is in error. In discussing how and when he is to do that, Sidgwick, in addition to describing the method of utilitarianism, completes his account of the relation between the utilitarian principle and the rules of received opinion.

iii. *The Search for a Code*

The discussion of the method of utilitarianism proceeds on the assumption that the basic principle can only be actually applied through the medium of a fairly detailed and specific set of directives or rules. Sidgwick does not argue for the assumption. Perhaps the need for predictability in human conduct and the difficulties of hedonistic calculation aggravated by the limits of time, intelligence, and sympathy under which we all operate in making decisions, are so obvious that there is no need to argue for it. (Cf. *ME* 7, pp. 460–1, 464.) In any event Sidgwick directs his attention instead to the questions of locating or constructing the kind of code utilitarianism requires the plain man to use, and of determining just how the code is to be used. If up to now he has been showing the intuitionist how he is compelled by his own premises and procedures to go on to be a utilitarian, he turns at this point to show the utilitarian how his own principle prevents him from diverging very far from the results the intuitionist originally wished to defend.

Though the early Benthamites were forced to take up the Paleyan view that rules are a practical necessity even for a utilitarian, it was not until John Stuart Mill that utilitarianism definitely took the further step of identifying the rules already current in the accepted morality as the rules needed by utilitarian theory. Sidgwick agrees with Mill that common-sense rules are to be used by the utilitarian in determining what acts are right, but he disagrees with Mill's reasons for taking this view, and gives a strikingly different set of reasons of his own.

In the first two editions of the *Methods* Sidgwick makes explicit an objection to Mill's position which is only implied in the later editions. Mill holds that we can take common-sense rules to give us the beliefs of mankind about what makes for happiness. Not so, Sidgwick replies, 'the "rules of morality" recognised by "the multitude" are certainly not recognised as involving beliefs as to the effect of actions on happiness. They present themselves as the expression of an immediate preference for certain kinds of conduct', and we cannot reduce moral preferences to beliefs about effects on happiness, any more than we can reduce gastronomic preferences to beliefs about effects on health. (*ME* 1, p. 430, *ME* 2, pp. 425–6.) This indication of Mill's failure to accord a proper place to the categorial difference between moral judgements and statements of fact is replaced, from the third edition on, with the remark that people distinguish what they think morally right from what they think useful, and often come to opposed conclusions on these two matters. (*ME* 7, pp. 466–7.) The point is the same in either case. Mill's reconciliation of intuitional and utilitarian views of common-sense rules is at best a theory, not a plain appeal to fact. Sidgwick's arguments against it as a theory remain substantially unaltered throughout the editions. His general point is that although common-sense morality is unconsciously utilitarian and expresses to a large extent 'the results of human experience as to the effects of actions', we cannot simply take it over as the best available guide to attainment of general happiness (*ME* 7, p. 463), any more than the egoist could accept it as the best guide to his end. Several reasons are given for this conclusion. In the earlier stages of the development of morality more sympathy was given to the motives of the agent than a perfectly utilitarian accounting would allow, and this, together with ignorance, error, and the distorting effects of undue respect for social rank and for religious and secular authority, would tend to result in less than perfectly utilitarian rules. Appeal to evolutionary theory is no help here. The struggle for existence would not ensure a perfect morality because an imperfect morality would be only one factor among others in determining survival, and probably not the most important; and in any case it is not evident that what is maximally preservative is also maximally felicific. In conditions of rapid social change, a code once preservative and felicific may endure after it has lost its greatest utility. We see this in other societies and must suspect it in our own. Finally, where there is substantial minority opinion on moral issues we cannot simply accept the majority view. Majority opinion may be suitable only for the majority of men, and it might be generally beneficial to have special rules for special groups of people. (*ME* 7, pp. 463–6.)

Without relying on precise, large-scale utilitarian calculations, these arguments manage to produce definite reasons for holding it extremely unlikely that the rules of positive morality are the rules a utilitarian would, ideally, recommend. It seems, therefore, that the utilitarian must examine them thoroughly to see just how far they are suitable from his point of view. How far have the many points just indicated led common-sense morality to differ from 'a perfectly Utilitarian code of morality'? (*ME* 7, p. 467.)

Sidgwick copes with this question by arguing that it is doubtful if it can be answered. There are considerable difficulties in the way of constructing a 'perfect utilitarian code' in the detail and precision needed to make the comparison the question requires, and in using it in a practical manner. It is not the traditional problems of hedonistic calculation which Sidgwick sees at the root of the difficulty. It is a question concerning the nature of the people for whom the code is to be constructed.

Sidgwick's position here rests on a rejection of one of John Stuart Mill's fundamental beliefs. Mill thought that we could discover basic laws of psychology governing individual thought and feeling and could derive laws of sociology from them. He was aware that individual behaviour is profoundly influenced by the whole complex set of causes which we refer to as the historical development of society—indeed, Sidgwick remarks, this was a lesson Mill, following Comte, was largely responsible for teaching to England in mid-century—but he argued that because society is an aggregate of individuals and their actions, social laws must be reducible to laws of individual behaviour. Sidgwick urges that this is mistaken. Mill's central assumption, that we have some way of knowing what men would be like outside of any society, is false, at least as far as the more important aspects of life are concerned. Elementary processes of sensation, desire, and psychological association are perhaps independent of social influence, but if we contemplate any of the processes of thought that involve language, or any of the more refined and complex emotions, and endeavour to ascertain the causes of their actual characteristics, we are inevitably carried from the study of the mere individual into the study of the society of which he is a member. The current beliefs, the prevailing sentiments, in a given society at a given time, are no doubt beliefs and sentiments of a certain aggregate of individuals: but we have generally speaking no means of tracing and explaining their development and diffusion in the consciousnesses of the great mass of individuals who entertain them: for the purposes of our cognition, they must be treated as social facts. (1886b, 212–13; cf. *Phil.*, pp. 153 f., 158 f.)

The acceptance of 'social facts' and the complexities implied in them underlies Sidgwick's treatment of the question of an ideal code of morality. Although human nature is no doubt fixed in its most general features, he says, there is still considerable variability in the modes of thought and feeling, in the type of social structure, and in the culture in which this nature is found realized. Hence it seems 'absurd to lay down a set of ideal Utilitarian rules for mankind generally'. Now one is tempted to reply that perhaps the basic rules might be derived from the basic common features of human nature; and in fact Sidgwick does not precisely deny that this would be possible. His objection is that it would not give us a code specific and precise enough to be any improvement over, and so to be useful in testing, what we already have. Common-sense morality, it has been shown in IV, iii, is already generally utilitarian. The question therefore is whether we can construct a better code than the one common sense already has—better not only as being more purely determined by correct utilitarian calculation, but also as containing more detail and as leading to fewer hard cases and unanswerable questions. Sidgwick therefore drops the question of constructing a universal code, and asks about working one out for one's own time and country. Here, he says, we meet a dilemma. Our fellow citizens have a definite moral code. If we take it into account, it is not clear how we are to think of them as needing a whole new one. And if we leave it out of account, and construct a morality for e.g. the average Englishman minus morality, we are working with an idea of a person 'so purely hypothetical, that it is not clear what practical purpose can be served by constructing a system of moral rules for the community of such beings'. (*ME* 7, p. 468.) Suppose one had such a code: what could be done with it? It might be directly usable if giving a scientific proof of it would assure its immediate acceptance, and the rapid adaptation of moral feelings and habits to it. But as positive morality did not arise out of rational considerations alone, it will not be shaped by them alone in future, and these conditions cannot be met. Would not such a perfect code give us at least a clear goal to aim at, and so a proper test of existing rules? Sidgwick has two objections to this. First, men may simply not be able to live up to an abstractly perfect code, and in that case setting it up as the goal may do more harm than good. (*ME* 7, p. 469; cf. pp. 481–2.) Second, men's capacities for intellectual and emotional change are considerable, and are moreover to some extent open to deliberate direction. Changes of these kinds obviously have important bearings on rules for obtaining happiness. Now we cannot assume that men's habits of feelings and the limits to their knowledge are constant, unless we consider only the relatively short run; and if we consider only the relatively short run, we must admit that moral beliefs and habits of feeling are themselves as unchangeable as non-moral ones. Hence the utility of a perfect code in the short run is very doubtful, while if we consider the long run, it is far from evident that such a code can be constructed. (*ME* 7, pp. 469–73.)

The utilitarian must therefore adopt a method of piecemeal criticism and reconstruction, starting 'with the existing social order, and the existing morality as part of that order'. (*ME* 7, p. 474.) He will concern himself mostly with minor and relatively short-range changes, as being the only ones he will usually be able to recommend on a reliable factual basis. For the most part, the utilitarian must accept the rules of common-sense morality as being the nearest he can get to the kind of code made necessary by men's lack of knowledge and by the exigencies of practice.

iv. *Rules and Exceptions*

The central position Sidgwick assigns to rules in the utilitarian's method raises the question of whether the version of the theory he works out should be considered a 'rule-utilitarian' version. The distinction between rule-utilitarianism and act-utilitarianism is neither clear nor unambiguous, and the importance of assigning a philosopher to one side or the other not perhaps very great. Yet some features of Sidgwick's position may be brought into focus by using the distinction, if we specify it appropriately. Put crudely, the act-utilitarian takes rightness to be determined by the balance of good and bad in the consequences of each individual act; the rule-utilitarian takes it to be determined by the act's conformity to a moral rule whose justifiability in turn is determined by the consequences of its being accepted or followed. Both views concern objective rightness, and both may be taken to concern what makes right acts right, not mere signs or tokens of rightness. If the positions are construed in this way, there is no reason to think Sidgwick a rule-utilitarian. The basic axioms as well as the whole course of argument leading up to them show plainly that on his view what makes right acts right is their maximizing goodness, not their conformity to any substantive but less general rule, whatever its basis. But Sidgwick asks us always to distinguish between the principle and the method of any moral theory, and to attend especially to the method. Should we, then, take the conclusion he reaches about the role of the rules of common-sense morality in utilitarian deliberation to indicate that he is proposing a methodological rule-utilitarianism?

The question will be helpful only if we have a fairly definite test of whether an alleged rule-utilitarian is holding a position essentially different in moral terms from that held by an act-utilitarian. Let us say, therefore, that the crucial question is whether there are cases in which a moral agent ought to do what is dictated by a moral rule even though he knows that he could do some other act that would have more beneficial consequences. Then a position is a version of methodological rule-utilitarianism only if the rules to which it accords the central place in making practical determinations of rightness may well dictate actions which are less than maximally beneficial, and the procedures it constructs for making exceptions to these rules do not require exceptions to be made in every case where the rules do dictate a less than maximally beneficial action.

The explanatory side of the systematization argument shows only that the main rules of common-sense morality have some felicific tendency, not that they dictate acts more productive of happiness than any other rule would dictate. The arguments against Mill's understanding of the rules of common sense reinforce the negative aspect of this conclusion. So do Sidgwick's comments about the origins of common sense rules, which, if they show anything pertinent here, show that there is always some reason to presume that those rules are not likely to be the best conceivable from the utilitarian standpoint. And the argument leading to the conclusion that the utilitarian must use the common-sense code contains nothing to contravene this. There is thus no general reason to think that the rules which play the central part in the utilitarian's method, as Sidgwick sees it, would dictate the maximally beneficial acts. If they were to do so it would be a mere coincidence. So far, then, the method he gives the utilitarian seems to be a rule-utilitarian one.

If the utilitarian's method calls on him to start with common-sense rules, it also calls on him to improve them where he can; and Sidgwick presents his idea of the full utilitarian decision procedure as a discussion of the extent to which the individual utilitarian will try to reform received opinion. What he discusses as alternatives the utilitarian should consider may also be seen as steps in a regular procedure the utilitarian should use in a hard case, which we may take to be any case where he thinks there is reason to suppose that the act dictated by a common sense rule would probably produce less good than some other act open to him. The basic way of making estimates of this kind is the rough way provided by empirical hedonism, since, as Sidgwick has argued in II, vi, no scientific theory of the sources of pleasure offers a demonstrably better way of making them. And he rejects the effort to simplify the problem by saying, as John Stuart Mill among others says, that there is a whole realm of conduct which is immune to 'ethical dictation'. There may indeed, he thinks, be areas of conduct where the costs, in hedonistic terms, of directing action through rules supported by the usual moral sanctions are greater than the benefits (*ME* 7, p. 493), but such areas cannot be identified in any simple, sweeping way. They can be located only by utilitarian examination of all the different possible areas. This approach therefore offers no simplification of the problems of utilitarian calculation. (*ME* 7, pp. 477–8.)

There are two main ways, Sidgwick thinks, in which the utilitarian will want to reform common-sense morality. These are by substituting a new decision-guiding rule for a presently accepted one and by making a new exception to a presently accepted rule.

New decision-guiding rules are of two kinds: those that involve a direct conflict with an established rule, and those that simply add a new directive to existing rules, covering some new part of conduct. The considerations involved in deliberating about the first sort of change are, again, of two kinds. One kind concerns the consequences to the agent and those about whom he cares personally: a reformer may be unpopular and may suffer as a result of his well-meant efforts. The second, more important kind concerns reasons for thinking the new decision-guiding rule might not work out as well as expected. Here Sidgwick relies heavily on the fact that decision-guiding rules must be usable by ordinary people in ordinary situations. A rule which, viewed abstractly, might well seem fitted to produce better results than a presently accepted rule, may none the less be too complex or subtle for ordinary use; or its acceptance might require more self-control or greater emotional sensitivity than one can count on. (*ME* 7, p. 481.) Hence one condition under which it is allowable to appeal to utilitarian considerations to override the putative duty laid down by an accepted rule is that one must be able to propose a substitute rule which can actually be used by the plain man, and which would, if so used, be more productive of good consequences. If a received rule demands a less felicific act than would be demanded by some other formulable rule which, however, we cannot realistically expect everyone to be able to follow, the utilitarian cannot, so far, urge the new rule in place of the received one.

The reformer might reply that at least he would be setting the good example of following the highest principle, and this must be an additional good to set in the balance. Sidgwick thinks that on the whole this claim is not allowable, for two related reasons. 'It is easier to pull down than to build up', he says, and it is easier to weaken both society's tendency to act according to its code and one's own habits of moral action, than to replace them with tendencies or habits based on other rules. The risk is greater than the benefit proposed would warrant (*ME* 7, pp. 481–2), at least in most cases. Of course it might not be impossible, despite these points, for a proposed reform of accepted decision-guiding rules to be justified. No *a priori* or even very general estimate of the balance of considerations is available, Sidgwick thinks. Each case must be dealt with separately, but it is plain that these arguments 'constitute an important rational check upon such Utilitarian innovations on Common-Sense morality as are of the negative or destructive kind'. (*ME* 7, p. 483.)

The arguments do not seem to Sidgwick to apply with the same force if the proposed reform is a matter of adding a new rule concerning a part of conduct not previously touched by received rules. In doing this a utilitarian will after all only be adding to the recognized duty of benevolence, which common sense leaves, as Sidgwick has shown, quite indeterminate. The reformer must not, however, make a pest of himself, as this would weaken the force of his good example. And there is no reason why the previous stricture about the popular accept-ability of a new rule should not apply here. Excessively subtle and complicated benevolences may be as difficult for people to master as other excessively complicated rules. Sidgwick adds that for the most part the utilitarian will be more concerned with urging people to live up to the provisions of the accepted code than with changing the code. He will particularly single out for condemnation conduct that shows a want of public spirit and general good will, and urge a 'bracing and sharpening of the moral sentiments of society', but in all this he is simply reinforcing the accepted code. (*ME* 7, p. 484.)

Sidgwick next turns to the question of making exceptions to rules which the utilitarian does not challenge as a whole and does not propose to replace. Because common-sense rules are generally conducive to happiness, this is a larger and more important class of cases than those involving complete replace-ment of a received rule. But Sidgwick promptly points out that to allow an exception on general grounds is simply to establish a 'more complex and delicate rule, instead of one that is broader and simpler', the reason being that what brings about better consequences in one set of circumstances will do so in any relevantly similar set as well. Hence if one person can appeal to this fact as allowing him to make an exception to a rule, so can anyone else similarly situated. (*ME* 7, p. 485.) Thus this kind of exception-making is in fact the same as rule-changing, and presumably must satisfy the same conditions. If the rule with the new exception clause is too demanding or too complex to be generally used—and adding a new clause naturally adds complexity—then the utilitarian must abide by the unamended rule, unless, of course, some other basis for overriding the putative dictate of common sense can be found.

So far Sidgwick has not invoked the purely formal principle of universalizability either to support the claim that the utilitarian must accept the rules of common sense or to handle objectionable potential exceptions to those rules. There is a kind of case, however, to which this consideration is relevant. It occurs when 'the agent does not think it expedient that the rule on which he himself acts should be universally adopted, and yet maintains that his individual act is right, as producing a greater balance of pleasure over pain than any other conduct open to him would produce'. (*ME* 7, p. 486.) Sidgwick ties this kind of case to rules which on the utilitarian view are warranted by aggregative considerations: they cover acts, a single one or a few of which do not result in harm or good, while a large number do. It may be thought that with rules of this kind, 'the general observance is necessary to the well-being of the community, while yet a certain amount of non-observance is rather advantageous than otherwise'. (*ME* 7, p. 486.) Agreeing that this is possible, Sidgwick tries to show the limits within which the utilitarian must confine these exceptions. Universalizability, though requiring that any right act must be right for some class of persons, does not settle the description of the class. Sidgwick begins by pointing out that one crucial factor that may enter into such a description is the agent's belief that very few people will actually behave in the way he proposes to consider allowable for himself. There are some cases where we do allow something which is beneficial in particular cases although the general practice would be harmful, because we believe that very few people will in fact do what would be harmful if everyone did it. Sidgwick gives celibacy as an illustration. Those who wish to live a completely celibate life are allowed to do so, precisely because we can rely on a strong non-moral impulse to keep most people acting in the way which generally, though not always, leads to the best results. The more complicated cases are those in which the sentiment which keeps people acting in the generally beneficial way is itself a moral sentiment. An argument formally analogous to the argument concerning celibacy may be used to allow a few felicific exceptions where the existence of the generally felicific conformity is due to moral feelings and habits. But Sidgwick points out a special problem arising when the moral feelings are involved in this way. These sentiments presuppose the conviction that the acts to which they direct us are objectively right. If it is known that sometimes this is not the case—since just a few exceptions here and there help maximize happiness—the sentiments will be too weak for anyone to be justified in relying on them to produce the general conformity on which the beneficiality of making exceptions depends. In a society of perfectly enlightened utilitarians, Sidgwick adds, no one could make this kind of exception to any rule, since everyone would have and be aware of having the same reason for making an exception, and there would then be nothing to support the general practice. It is only because received moral opinion rests 'on a basis independent of utilitarian or any other reasonings' (*ME* 7, p. 488) and will not be much affected by a few acts of this kind, that such exceptions can be allowed. And it seems clear that exceptions of this kind will only rarely be permissible.

Three further aspects of Sidgwick's discussion of the utilitarian method may be noted. He sees a problem arising from the possibility of keeping one's moral views secret. Suppose that one has in mind a class of exceptions to a rule, on the grounds that allowing this class of exceptions would be hedonistically better than prohibiting it; but also that the use of the rule with this exception-clause in it would require more subtlety or sophistication than one can rightly expect from most people. Then, Sidgwick thinks, if one is known to advocate or act on that particular moral belief, one runs the risk of weakening public morality. It seems to him to follow that it may be right to do secretly what one could not do openly or even what one could not openly advocate. This, as he points out, is paradoxical in the eyes of common sense, and a good utilitarian will generally want to support the common belief that it cannot be right to do secretly what it would be wrong to do openly. (*ME* 7, pp. 489–90.) He will therefore want to keep secret the fact that in some few cases it is right to do secretly what it is not right to do openly. In fact the utilitarian will be led, more generally, to the conclusion that it is undesirable to have everyone calculating everything on a utilitarian basis, since the unavoidable indefiniteness of such calculations leaves scope for the wicked and the weak to construct specious excuses for their misbehaviour. (*ME* 7, p. 490.)

This point raises in turn the more general question of the significance of divergent moral beliefs in a society. If common-sense moral rules are generally to be taken as valid, what is the utilitarian to do when there are conflicting opinions each claiming that status? Sidgwick thinks that while contradictory moral beliefs cannot both be correct it may be advantageous at times to have conflicting opinions held by different social groups—one is reminded here of John Stuart Mill's passionate defence of diversity of opinion—and so it may be best that one person should commit an act, for which he is condemned by a segment of society. Sidgwick illustrates with the case of rebellion: he thinks rebellion is from time to time 'morally necessary' and also that rebellion ought always to be vigorously resisted, and severely punished if it fails. If it were not punished, rebellion would be tried too often and in circumstances where it was not justified. But this means that many must think the failed rebels not just unsuccessful but wrong. (*ME* 7, p. 491.) On the whole, however, the utilitarian will try to produce a more stable and uniform consensus on the divisive moral issue, since the harm done by not having such a consensus is considerable. Sidgwick also thinks he will probably prefer maintaining fairly strict rules to allowing more exceptions.

Finally, we may note that the utilitarian allows himself much greater divergence from established opinion in what he praises and condemns than in what he judges right and wrong. Common sense is much vaguer on the former than the latter, and since the utilitarian will mainly praise what is public-spirited beyond the ordinary, he can scarcely do much harm. (*ME* 7, pp. 493–5.)

Some aspects of the decision procedure Sidgwick lays out for the utilitarian seem to support the idea that he is proposing a methodological rule-utilitarianism. For it seems that an agent might be unable to formulate acceptable alternative rules or exception clauses where he none the less knows in a particular case that conformity to a received rule would be less than maximally felicific. The method seems then to require him to conform despite this. Yet Sidgwick expressly says that 'a Utilitarian must hold that it is always wrong for a man knowingly to do anything other than what he believes to be most conducive to Universal Happiness'. (*ME* 7, p. 492.) He must therefore hold that the use of his procedure for rectifying received moral rules does not force the utilitarian to contravene the principle requiring each act to be maximally felicific. Hence his rectificatory procedure must be taken to do two things. One is to provide a regular way of allowing for the correction of the very rough estimates of utility provided by first-order moral rules. The other is to bring to the correction of those estimates the considerable second-order utilities arising from the decision-making process itself. What makes the second-order utilities so significant is the great importance of having a usable code for daily life. We must be able to make reliable predictions about each other's conduct in moral matters, and we could not do so if each of us had to make complete utilitarian calculations of right and wrong prior to each decision. Possible alterations or exceptions, whether individual or based on either of the kinds of generalization Sidgwick sees to be operative in amending accepted rules—one due to regularity, the other to the logic of the central moral concept—are only allowed subject to the requirement of keeping the code usable. Hence some acts are allowed to pass as actually right even when their own proper consequences are less than maximally felicific. The reason is that the second-order benefits derived from using the decision-procedure which justifies doing them make up for the deficiencies in the consequences of the individual acts. It is, then, because of the moral significance of the methods of ethics that Sidgwick is not a methodological rule-utilitarian.

Whether Sidgwick is successful or not in this attempt to combine substantive and methodological considerations in this way, two things are clear. He makes more systematic and far-reaching use of the distinction between the two sources of utility than any of the earlier utilitarians, and thereby provides the basis for a far better reply than any of them gave to criticisms of utilitarianism drawn from pre-theoretical moral convictions. In doing this he strengthens the important claim of the utilitarian, that his first principle of morals has no exceptions or limits other than those it imposes on itself.

v. *Utilitarianism and Common Sense*

The final status of common-sense moral rules for the utilitarian, then, is what the dependence argument shows it must also be for the intuitionist: they possess dependent validity, the authority to determine putative rightness, but no more. The important point to notice about the utilitarian position is that the dependent validity of common-sense rules results from a methodological argument about the common-sense code as a whole. It relies on the fact that a code is a practical necessity for bringing reason to bear in daily decision-making. It does not rest on a belief that each of the rules within the code probably requires acts having optimal results. The reconciliation of utilitarianism and intuitionism therefore extends beyond first principles. For if the intuitionist holds that the rules of received opinion are independent, in the sense that they determine putative rightness regardless of the value of the consequences of the acts they dictate, there is an important sense in which the utilitarian must agree with him. The personal attitude Sidgwick urges the utilitarian to have toward these rules corresponds with their moral status in his theory. The utilitarian must avoid thinking of positive morality as something alien and irrational. Though its rules are not intrinsically reasonable, still less absolute or divine, they are not to be treated as 'purely external and conventional'. (*ME* 7, p. 475.) The utilitarian is to take them, not as forced upon him by social circumstances, but as his own reasons for action, at least in the first instance.

With the utilitarian position on the relation between received opinion and first principles now fully developed, we can draw together the different aspects of Sidgwick's complex and many-sided understanding of the place of common-sense morality in a system of ethics. Whether or not he abandons his avowedly neutral stance by adopting utilitarianism within the *Methods*, the theory itself shows what he thinks a fully articulated view on the subject must be like.

The matter can be put first in terms of the various arguments relating common sense and the utilitarian principle. The dependence argument shows that certain features of received opinion, which it would share with any equally complex code in an equally complex society, require us to go beyond its dictates to a different kind of principle. The appeal to self-evidence next yields rational principles of the kind required by the dependence argument. We then turn to see if these principles can systematize common sense. Since the first principles are obtained by a procedure not involving consideration of their systematizing power, the degree of their serviceability for this task provides an independent test of their acceptability. From the explanatory side of the systematization argument we learn that in so far as common-sense morality is already rational, the best explanation or model of its rationality is the utilitarian one. The rectificatory side of the systematization argument shows that in so far as received opinion still needs to be made rational, the best method of making it so is the utilitarian one. Thus the systematization argument is not meant to show that all our pre-theoretical moral opinions can be derived from the axioms. It is meant to show that the axioms provide an ideal or model of practical rationality which enables us to see that the kind of code we need for daily decision-making can be rational. The fact that one and the same ideal of rationality enables us to see that our actual code is to some extent rational and shows how it can have its rationality increased, provides stronger support for the ideal than any abstract argument about it could provide.

Sidgwick's position concerning common-sense morality also reflects different phases of the progress of rational thought, as he has outlined those phases (see Ch. 11, pp. 310–11). We begin with unreflective acceptance of the positive code of our age and country, taking it to provide authoritative guidance. But we naturally seek to make our action rational; and we move away from common sense because it does not show itself to be completely reasonable. Conflicting demands in particular cases force us to reflect and to seek rules which are clear and strong enough to settle our perplexities. Further reflection, made inevitable by the deficiencies of these rules, convinces us that some better rule than common sense contains—clearer, more precise, more authoritative—must exist if practice is to be rational. We find such principles implicit in our common moral concepts and beliefs. As we try to use them to guide our actions, we see that complete and thorough rationality in all the details of practice is more than it is reasonable to expect. Hence we return to common sense, not, now, with our original naïve attribution of final authority to it, but armed with a rational method for improving it. And finally, as we look back over the whole process, we can see that although we began without any way of justifying our starting-point, the truth to which we have been led entitles us to say that we were in fact no less justified in beginning with common-sense morality than the plain man is in continuing to rely on it.

13

The Dualism of the Practical Reason

UP to this point we have concentrated on Sidgwick's presentation of utilitarianism and ignored his position on rational
egoism. We can ignore it no longer. What he takes to be 'the
profoundest problem in Ethics' arises from the relations between
the fundamental principles of the two theories. (*ME* 7, p. 386
n. 4; cf. *GSM*, p. 106.) Sidgwick sometimes refers to it as the
problem of 'the Dualism of the Practical Reason', though he
confesses he is 'not particularly pleased with the phrase'
since it seems to imply a 'completeness of systematic construction' to which he does not lay claim. (1877a, 30; *ME* 2, xii;
ME 7, x; *ME* 3, pp. 401, 402 n. 1; *ME* 7, p. 404 n. 1; 1889f,
483.) The relations of egoism and utilitarianism, we saw, began
to perplex him at a very early stage of his philosophical development. The perplexity received its most striking expression in the
dramatic conclusion to the first edition of the *Methods*. When
we finally abandon the neutral stance we have so long maintained, he there says, and ask for a synthesis of methods, we see
that intuitionism and utilitarianism join together easily and
firmly. But there is still a 'fundamental opposition' between the
system which results from this synthesis and the system that
can be built on the principle of rational self-interest, and no
way of overcoming it seems available without invoking an
untestable metaphysical assertion. 'Hence', Sidgwick concludes,

the whole system of our beliefs as to the intrinsic reasonableness of
conduct must fall, without a hypothesis unverifiable by experience
reconciling the Individual with the Universal Reason, without
a belief, in some form or other, that the moral order which we see
imperfectly realized in this actual world is yet actually perfect.
If we reject this belief, we may perhaps still find in the non-moral
universe an adequate object for the Speculative Reason, capable
of being in some sense ultimately understood. But the Cosmos of
Duty is thus really reduced to a Chaos: and the prolonged effort of
the human intellect to frame a perfect ideal of rational conduct is
seen to have been foredoomed to inevitable failure. (*ME* 1, p. 473.)

Though Sidgwick reworded his conclusion, he never altered its substance or thought it less significant. Before asking how he was led to it, we must look at his account of egoism and its method.

i. *The Viability of Egoism*

Sidgwick discusses rational egoism in detail before discussing its self-evident axiom, defining the egoist in terms of his method as one who makes his decisions by determining the pleasures and pains he himself will incur from each course of action open to him, and choosing the course from which he will get for himself the greatest surplus of pleasure over pain. (*ME* 7, p. 121.) That there is something odd about calling this a method of 'ethics', Sidgwick is well aware; but he is concerned with egoism because it appears reasonable to the plain man, and he is unwilling to allow the connotations of a term in ordinary language to force him to omit consideration of any principle that might yield a rational decision procedure. There is no doubt that egoism seems reasonable. One might even take it to articulate the central strand in the ordinary idea of what it is for someone to act reasonably, a point Sidgwick puts by remarking that common sense tends to take interested actions as always *prima facie* reasonable, and to see the burden of proof as lying with those who think disinterested action is also reasonable. (*ME* 7, p. 120; cf. p. 419.) In holding that the egoistic end is ultimately reasonable, and that egoistic rationality is consequently not solely instrumental rationality, Sidgwick takes a position opposed to that taken by Kant. Where Kant seems to think the egoistic end too vague and indefinite to determine specific rational dictates, Sidgwick disagrees, and offers a detailed analysis in his discussion of egoistic method. More importantly, Kant thinks, for reasons he never makes very clear, that the egoistic end does not present itself to us as intrinsically rational and therefore as grounding categorical imperatives. Rather it supports only imperatives which we can all see to be rightly overriden by moral imperatives.[1] Sidgwick makes clear from the beginning his disagreement with Kant on this issue. Most men, he says, would find someone's refusal

---

[1] Kant, *Groundwork of the Metaphysics of Morals*, p. 47; *Critique of Practical Reason*, p. 37.

to look after his own happiness irrational, and would disapprove it. 'In other words, they would think that a man *ought* to care for his own happiness', and in this thought the "ought" is not a mere instrumental "ought": 'happiness now appears as an ultimate end, the pursuit of which . . . appears to be prescribed by reason "categorically", as Kant would say . . .' (*ME* 7, p. 7). Given Sidgwick's view that the fundamental concept of morality is simply the concept of what it is reasonable to do or desire, an examination of the paradigm of being reasonable is unavoidable.

Sidgwick's main explicit aim in considering the method the rational egoist should use is to show that he is confined to the ordinary empirical method which all of us, egoists or not, use in estimating happiness when we are making important decisions. Running through his discussions is a second theme: that egoism is neither impossible nor self-defeating. Its calculations can be carried out with sufficient accuracy for ordinary practice, and they do not show that the far-sighted egoist must abandon his principle or his method for some quite different one. Egoism, in short, is a viable and independent method, in addition to resting on a first principle which at least appears to give it a grounding in an ultimate reason.

It is, of course, not implied by the principle alone that the egoist's method must be the ordinary empirical method (*ME* 7, p. 121); and consequently the alternatives to that method are carefully examined and, one by one, dismissed. We have already followed Sidgwick's analysis and evaluation of the empirical method. Of the other possibilities, the only one we need to discuss is that which depends on the use of common-sense moral rules. The belief that following these rules is the best way to obtain personal happiness is probably held—if it is held at all—on religious grounds, Sidgwick thinks, but he intends to examine it only so far as it can be tested by purely empirical and secular considerations. For this purpose the commonly accepted notions of duty may be used. Self-regarding duties are of course favourable to the belief, so the examination is restricted to social duties. (*ME* 7, pp. 162–3.) To facilitate the examination Sidgwick uses the Benthamite notion that the pleasures and pains stemming from conformity to or violation of moral rules may be considered sanctions, and classed as either external or internal. The former include legal sanctions, the penalties imposed by legally established authorities, and social sanctions, the pleasures and pains to be derived from the good or ill will of our fellow men. The latter are the pleasures of a good conscience, the pangs of remorse, and the general effects on one's own mental condition of having or not having a virtuous disposition. The distinction of external and internal sanctions is important because positive morality changes. Any given positive moral code may be both in advance of existing legislation and not in accordance with the beliefs of the more thoughtful and insightful members of the community. In such cases the force of the external sanctions will be divided and weakened. (*ME* 7, pp. 164–5.)

Even leaving such cases aside, however, it seems unlikely to Sidgwick that external sanctions will always suffice to render immoral conduct imprudent. He considers first the legal sanction. To begin with, open crime is in general plainly unwise. It might not be unwise if it is part of a revolution which succeeds. But violent revolutions would not occur in any society composed of perfectly rational egoists, since the risks and losses involved in even temporary anarchy are too great to be taken. Sidgwick parts company with Hobbes (to whom he explicitly refers in the first edition, *ME* 1, p. 150) on the rationality of always 'seeking peace', i.e. living according to the moral code, in actual circumstances: 'the disturbance of political order may offer to a cool and skilful person, who has the art of fishing in troubled waters, opportunities of gaining wealth, fame, and power, far beyond what he could hope for in peaceful times.' (*ME* 7, p. 165.) What might be the case under certain conditions not likely to arise is, as usual, of little interest to Sidgwick. The Hobbesian belief that enlightened self-interest always leads men to the conduct demanded by common-sense morality seems to him to hold, at best, under such unlikely circumstances. It is not, he thinks, true under the circumstances that actually obtain. (Cf. *ME* 1, p. 151.) Sidgwick next considers secret crime. Here, he thinks, there are plainly cases where the risk of exposure is slight, the benefit to the criminal great, and the legal sanctions, consequently, impotent to assure that morality pays. (*ME* 7, pp. 165–6.) The point is of interest in part because it is parallel to the paradox the utilitarian must concede, that on his view it may be right to do secretly something that it would be wrong to do openly.

Will the social sanctions then make up for deficiencies in the legal ones? Sidgwick points out that secret crimes evade both sorts equally and that in revolutions, when opinions and sympathies are divided, the social sanction is less likely to be effective. (*ME* 7, pp. 166–7.) The problem is even more severe when we consider duties not sanctioned by the law and supported only by public opinion. Sidgwick here directly engages the argument that the virtues are profitable to their owner because they benefit others who will reward him for having them. No doubt, he allows, this gives the rational egoist solid reason to avoid a good deal of vice and to practice much virtue. But what is needed to win a reward from others is appearing to have the virtues rather than having them. Doing secret harm to others when it pays the agent is thus not excluded by the argument. Moreover, a mixture of certain vices with some virtues may make one useful to others too— more useful than pure virtue. And finally, if one used this basis for virtue, one would display one's virtues mainly toward those who could be useful to one—the rich and the powerful—and to others only if there were some special reason to do so. It all hardly adds up to a convincing rationale for being completely virtuous in the sense in question. As for the bad reputation attending open immorality, it need not do the immoral agent serious harm. The morality of a clique or sect is often different in some respects from the basic standards of common-sense morality; and just as a professional espionage agent expects the approval, not of society at large but of his fellow professionals, so the dissolute rake might look more to the approval of his comrades in sin than to the opinion of the ordinary man, and disregard the disapproval of the latter. (*ME* 7, pp. 167–9.)

The external sanctions, Sidgwick concludes, cannot ensure that it would be right for a rational egoist to live according to the socially accepted morality of his community. Does appeal to the internal sanctions help? Neither the heavenly pleasures and hellish pains, nor the pleasures and pains of anticipating them, are to be considered. Sidgwick considers briefly the pleasure of doing an individual act of duty, taken by itself, and the pain that follows the violation of duty. While admitting that only rough comparisons are possible, he holds that it is obvious that these sanctions alone would not always compensate for large sacrifices, e.g. loss of one's whole fortune, or one's life. (*ME* 7, pp. 170–1.) But this is not the basis on which the argument has usually been conducted. The argument usually concerns the whole kind of life which an egoist will lead if he ignores morality. This, at least, is Plato's theme. And it is Plato who is Sidgwick's chief target here. (*ME* 7, p. 171.) The problem with Plato's argument, as he sees it, is that it considers only the contrast between the moral man who leads a reasonable life with his passions under control, and the immoral man who allows his passions to dominate him. But this is not the issue. 'We are supposing the Egoist to have all his impulses under control, and are only asking how this control is to be exercised.' *Prima facie* there are cases where it would pay the egoist to repudiate the demands of morality; for these might lead him to death, or torture, or sacrifice of his health or fortune. To show that this is incorrect, it must be shown that self-government by moral principles is more in one's interest than self-government by selfish principles, despite these cases. Sidgwick's first comment gives the essence of his position: 'It can scarcely be said that our nature is such that only this anti-egoistic kind of regulation is possible; that the choice lies between this and none at all.' Thus the burden of proof is on the platonizing theorist. He must now show that 'the order kept by Self-love involves a sacrifice of pleasure on the whole, as compared with the order kept by Conscience'. But this—the external sanctions having been found insufficient—can only come about if the pleasures attending satisfaction of the moral feelings suffice to outweigh the loss they impose upon the rest of our nature.

At this point Sidgwick notes a complication. It might be argued that the rational egoist will not have any sentiments of approval or disapproval except those determined by egoistic calculations, so that the platonizing argument cannot work. But Sidgwick is not concerned with non-existent perfect egoists. He points out that special, 'quasi-moral' sentiments of preference for or aversion to certain classes of action may persist independently of our convictions about their rationality, at least for a time. Hence there may be in the egoist an analogue of independent moral sentiments, which may give the platonist his starting-point. What he must show is that it will pay the rational egoist to cultivate these quasi-moral sentiments to such a pitch of strength that they will always prevail over other impulses. Sidgwick now reminds us that on any view rational self-interest dictates its own limitation: we must not always be consciously thinking about ourselves if we are to obtain the happiest possible lives. The question is whether self-love dictates the *complete* dismissal of self-love as a conscious guide to action in favour of sentiments which it cannot consider intrinsically or directly reasonable. No, Sidgwick says, 'this abdication of self-love is not really a possible occurrence in the mind of a sane person, who still regards his own interest as the reasonable ultimate end of his actions'. (*ME* 7, p. 174.) No matter how strong his quasi-moral feelings and habits may become, if an occasion arises on which they demand an extreme sacrifice a rational man must be allowed and able to think again, and act as he thinks reason dictates in that special case. The egoist, in other words, may take the dictates of common-sense morality as affording reasons for action, but he can and sometimes must act against common-sense rules at the demand of his own first principle.

This suggests one final move the platonist might make: to argue that self-interest dictates abandoning the principle of egoism. To obtain the full joy of the moral feelings, it might be said, one must abandon oneself completely to them. These joys are so superior to those which one can obtain from moral feelings while still remaining an egoist, that egoism itself dictates working oneself up to the conviction that egoism is false. (*ME* 7, p. 174.) Sidgwick thinks this a consistent position but one which is 'opposed to the broad results of experience, so far as the great majority of mankind are concerned'. The pleasures and pains of conscience are simply not, for most people, that strong. Egoism does not counsel its own abandonment.

ii. *Egoism and the Systematization Argument*

So far, then, we have found no reason to abandon the deeply-rooted common-sense belief in the rationality of exclusive concern for one's own good. How well does the belief pass the various tests which Sidgwick has set for a properly philosophical theory of rational action? There is a self-evident axiom relating to rational egoism—just what the relation is, we shall examine in the next section of this chapter—and the axiom is of unrestricted scope and has no exceptions. Since it shares with the utilitarian axiom the features which make it possible for a principle to serve as a first principle in a rational system of conduct, the egoistic principle could be the beneficiary of the dependence argument just as much as the utilitarian principle. And when Sidgwick says that in his examination of egoism in Book II he has been 'considering "enlightened self-interest" as supplying a *prima facie* tenable principle for the systematisation of conduct' (*ME* 7, p. 199), he suggests that the egoistic principle can support a systematization argument, as the utilitarian principle does. The question then is whether it actually does systematize common sense as well as the utilitarian principle. In reviewing the evidence supplied by Sidgwick's examination of common-sense morality from the point of view of egoism in II, v—the parallel to his discussion of utilitarianism and common sense in IV, iii—several points of similarity between the two theories become apparent. The utilitarian principle may call for a limit to its own direct application in special classes of cases, as the egoistic principle does because of what Sidgwick calls 'the paradox of hedonism', that 'the impulse towards pleasure, if too predominant, defeats its own aim'. (*ME* 7, p. 48; cf. pp. 136–7.) The utilitarian diverges from common-sense moral judgement on some issues, even to the point of paradox, as the egoist does. The utilitarian does not think everyone should be a utilitarian and direct all his actions by conscious utilitarian calculation (*ME* 7, p. 490); and it may be conjectured that Sidgwick would agree that the egoist would be glad to see a society of altruists around him. Finally, as Sidgwick sees matters, common-sense rules are no more held overtly as guides to general happiness than they are as guides to individual happiness. There are thus a number of ways in which egoism is on a par with utilitarianism in systematizing ability. There are also some significant differences.

The differences may be summed up by saying that the utilitarian theory has greater explanatory power than the egoistic theory, while the egoistic decision-making procedure is more likely to yield clear and definite results than the utilitarian.

The two points are closely connected. The egoist has to make his decisions on the basis of the pleasures and pains of only one person. He can therefore hope to achieve more accurate results by considering each case separately than the utilitarian can—indeed, the accuracy attainable by such egoistic calculations is one of the limits determining the possible accuracy of utilitarian calculations—and he must benefit less from a code not designed with his special needs and sensibilities in mind. Hence the need for a code is not nearly so urgent on the egoistic view as it is on the utilitarian. While both the utilitarian and the egoist can treat common sense rules as determining only the putative rightness of acts, the egoist, having many more opportunities for overriding those dictates, gives the rules a much less important place. Sidgwick offers no such *en bloc* justification of common-sense morality from the egoistic standpoint as he gives it from the utilitarian. If egoistic rationality is the appropriate model for us to follow, there is much less question that it can be followed in daily life than there is when we take utilitarian rationality as the ideal. And correspondingly, Sidgwick does not exhort the egoist, as he urges the utilitarian, to avoid feeling alienated from the received moral code of his times. The egoist cannot, and need not, make that code into his own reasons for acting to the same degree as the utilitarian.

Sidgwick nowhere discusses in connection with egoism what he analyses in several places from the utilitarian standpoint, the rationale for judgements of praiseworthiness and blameworthiness, or for judgements of personal worth and merit. But it is not difficult to construct a plausible egoistic view along Sidgwickian lines. (Cf. 1877e, 166.) The egoist, he might say, will view such judgements as a means of encouraging the production of future good and preventing future harm, much as the utilitarian does. He will also probably praise and condemn much the same sorts of things the utilitarian does, since he will realize that his own best chance of profiting from the acts of others arises from his hope of obtaining a share in benefits not especially designed for him. And he will be aware that praise and blame are more effective if they are not seen to be meant to benefit the person praising.

There are many other important aspects of egoism which Sidgwick does not discuss, such as the connection between the axiom of justice, J3, and either the prudential axiom or the detailed judgements the egoist makes. In fact he seems to be very little concerned about the explanatory powers of egoism. Its ability to generate a decision procedure and the self-evidence of its axiom are what he thinks account for the common belief in its rationality and what lead him to give it so important a place among the methods of ethics. Yet this limitation of egoism as a theory offers a possible reason why Sidgwick described himself as being a utilitarian, in contexts where he could not explain his equal allegiance to the egoistic principle. If the two principles themselves generate decision procedures of equal strength, and if the procedures always lead to identical results, then the superior explanatory scope of the utilitarian principle would warrant adopting the utilitarian theory.

iii. *The Axiom of Egoism*

We have seen that the axiom which is said in III, xiii, to provide the self-evident element involved in rational egoism is not explicitly an axiom about maximizing good. P3 appears to do no more than deny the relevance of the time at which goods are present in a life to the degree of goodness they possess. As saying this, it is needed as much by the utilitarian as by the egoist. It is consequently not surprising that critics have generally thought that P3 does not provide a self-evident foundation for egoism, and that if Sidgwick has an axiom for the doctrine at all it must be found elsewhere. Something like P5, given in the final chapter of the book, seems a likely candidate, and Sidgwick suggests other similar possibilities. For instance in an article of 1889 he says that it is self-evident that 'it would be irrational to sacrifice any portion of my own happiness unless the sacrifice is to be somehow at some time compensated by an equivalent addition to my own happiness' (1889f, 483). This formulation obviously presupposes the hedonistic interpretation of ultimate good, and it adds complexities about compensation which have no place in a minimum statement of a basic axiom, but it agrees in essentials with P5. And since P5 would also generate the egoistic method as its logically connected method once the good is shown to be pleasure, it may seem that P5 should be taken as a separate basic axiom in addition to P3. Yet it may not be necessary to say this. From the axioms of benevolence, B1 and B2, we were able to derive a substantive utilitarian principle. This suggests that we should also be able to see how P3 is the axiom at the basis of a substantive egoistic principle. If we first work out a line of reasoning leading from P3 to a substantive egoistic principle like P5, we can then ask how well the reasoning explains Sidgwick's thinking.

It has been pointed out that each basic axiom should have a separate function in providing the grounds for practical rationality, or should represent an aspect of what is involved in practical reasoning which no other axiom represents. J3, for example, brings out what is involved when there exists more than one rational agent capable of right or wrong action, while B1 is concerned rather with the condition that there is more than one sentient or conscious being with an awareness of goods or evils. What, then, of P3? What it essentially involves is that there exists a plurality of times during which a sentient or conscious being is aware of good or evil. It is thus the axiom about what reason demands over time in one life, as B1 is the axiom about what reason demands over many lives. If, as is generally agreed, the utilitarian needs P3 to bring time, and the indifference of temporal location to quantity of good, into his theory, then B1 must be necessary to bring other lives, and the indifference of location in lives to quantity of good, into a theory. If we confine ourselves to P3 we can consider only a single life.

To develop the egoistic theory, then, we concentrate on P3 and ignore B1. We think of the goods of one sentient being as assembled under the control of P3 into an idea of that being's good on the whole. Now the crucial feature of the concept of good is that what is good provides reasons for desiring. To whom does it provide such reasons? Since we are now operating on the assumption of the existence of only one sentient being, we must form a notion of good on the whole which provides only the sentient being whose good it is with reasons for desiring. Following Sidgwick's suggestion that the egoist is concerned not with universal good but with his own good, we may call the concept so constructed the concept of own-good. If something is good in the sense of universal-good, then its goodness is a reason for any rational being to desire or aim at it; if it is good in the sense of own-good, then its goodness is a reason for only the rational being who will possess it to desire or aim at it. By limiting our attention to the axiom concerning time in one life, we obtain a concept of good on the whole which is different from the concept we obtain when we give our attention to the axiom concerning lives at a time.

The one axiom which connects rightness with goodness is B2. Up to now the concept of good which we have taken it to use is the concept of universal-good, obtained through B1. Hence we have called B2 an axiom of benevolence. But Sidgwick does not identify it in that way, despite its location in the text as part of the argument for B3, and we should no longer do so. It is plain that the concept of own-good can be used in B2 just as easily as the concept of universal-good. If own-good is used in B2 instead of universal-good, then the force of the term 'generally' in the axiom is confined to times within one life, and nothing is said about a plurality of lives. But then there is no difficulty in seeing how, following the pattern used in deriving a maximizing universalistic consequentialism from B1 and B2, we can obtain a maximizing egoistic consequentialism from P3 and B2. Like the utilitarian, the egoist agrees that there must be reasons for actions. He agrees also that the examination of common-sense morality has failed to turn up any factual characteristic which can serve as an ultimate determinant of rightness. Own-good, however, he points out, can serve as such a determinant. The maximizing aspect of the egoistic principle is brought in, as it was in the case of the utilitarian principles, through the conceptual tie between being right and being the best act within the agent's power, bearing in mind, of course, that now 'best' must mean 'maximal own-good'. Once it is clear that the egoist's basic principle is to be stated in terms of own-good, it is also clear that the egoist can call on the methodological mode of supporting a first principle just as much—or as little—as the utilitarian.

In short, if B2 is neutral as between the concept of own-good introduced by P3 and the concept of universal-good introduced by B1, then P3 and B2 together yield the basis for egoistic consequentialism, just as B1 and B2 together yield the basis for universalistic consequentialism. The egoist may be supposed to argue for the hedonistic interpretation of good in ways similar to those used by the utilitarian, and when he does so, he has a complete egoistic principle, P5, standing on the same footing as B5 has for the utilitarian.

Sidgwick is thus correct, on this reading of the argument, in taking P3 to be the self-evident element on which egoism is based, and our line of reasoning shows why. It also helps us to understand the argument Sidgwick thinks might be used against the egoist and the reply he thinks the egoist can make. In IV, ii, prior to sketching the line of reasoning to be followed by the utilitarian in converting the intuitionist, Sidgwick points out a way in which the utilitarian might try to bring the egoist to his point of view. The possibility of adducing the argument depends on how the egoist puts his position.

> When . . . the Egoist puts forward, implicitly or explicitly, the proposition that his happiness or pleasure is Good, not only *for him* but from the point of view of the Universe . . . it then becomes relevant to point out to him that *his* happiness cannot be a more important part of Good, taken universally, than the equal happiness of any other person. And thus, starting with his own principle, he may be brought to accept Universal happiness or pleasure as that which is absolutely and without qualification Good or Desirable: as an end, therefore, to which the action of a reasonable agent as such ought to be directed. (*ME* 7, pp. 420–1.)

The egoist can avoid the force of this argument, Sidgwick thinks, simply by 'declining to affirm' that 'his own greatest happiness is not merely the rational ultimate end for himself but a part of Universal Good'. (*ME* 7, pp. 497–8.) This is precisely what we should expect if the basis of the egoist's position is the concept of own-good. The egoist simply says that the good which, logically speaking, only he can enjoy is the sole determinant of what it is reasonable for him to desire or aim at. He does not say that the good which only he can enjoy determines the rationality of everyone's desires; and he does not say that the part of what is universally good which he happens to experience is the only part he or anyone else has reason to desire. He makes no assertion at all about the universally good.

In his 1879 paper on methodology Sidgwick says that the argument he constructs in the *Methods* for the utilitarian to use against the egoist relies on the method of removing an arbitrary and accidental limitation from a principle someone asserts as self-evident. (1879a, 107.) The egoist, in these terms, takes as self-evident a principle calling for the maximizing of own-good. The utilitarian tries to show him that the restriction of the good here to his own good has no basis. If he succeeds, the egoist is caught. For once he puts his principle in terms of universal good, he accepts B1, which, with B2, obligates him to pursue good in general across lives, not just over time: he 'can only evade the conviction of this obligation by denying that there is any such universal good', as Sidgwick puts the point in some editions. (*ME* 2, p. 355; *ME* 3, p. 381.)

The question then naturally arises whether the restriction to own-good is arbitrary and accidental. Sidgwick himself thinks it is not. After the third edition of the *Methods* had been published, a critic charged that the book gave no account of the basis of the rationality of egoism. Sidgwick agreed with him and allowed that such a basis ought to be given. (1889f, p. 484.) The passage in which he says he provides it was incorporated into the *Methods* from the fourth edition onwards:

It would be contrary to Common Sense to deny that the distinction between any one individual and any other is real and fundamental, and that consequently 'I' am concerned with the quality of my existence as an individual in a sense, fundamentally important, in which I am not concerned with the quality of the existence of other individuals: and this being so, I do not see how it is to be proved that this distinction is not to be taken as fundamental in determining the ultimate end of rational action for an individual. (*ME* 7, p. 498.)

The fact that Sidgwick sees the issue in these terms is a strong confirmation of the interpretation of the egoistic axiom which has been given here.[2] And the conviction that the egoist is not irrational in adopting a basic principle resting on the reality and significance of the distinction between his own consciousness

---

[2] Broad, in *Five Types*, p. 244, holds that a consistent egoism can be worked out only by abandoning the teleological view and taking an 'extreme deontological view' in which the egoist holds that it is self-evidently unfitting for one to sacrifice his own good, however little, to the greater good of another. This interpretation does not accord well with the text of the *Methods* and does not enable us to make good sense of the argument Sidgwick constructs against the egoist. Broad may have been led to his position by accepting Moore's assumption that only the notion of universal good is viable, and that the notion of own-good is internally incoherent. This assumption pervades Moore's attack on Sidgwick's account of egoism in *Principia Ethica*, pp. 99–104; but Moore never defends it.

and the consciousness belonging to others is one reason for Sidgwick's concern with the dualism of the practical reason.

iv. *The Necessity of Egoism*

The argument with which Sidgwick provides the utilitarian for use against the egoist may be viewed as a revised version of John Stuart Mill's famous attempt to show that the utilitarian principle about what is desirable for all can be supported on the basis of an appeal to what each man actually desires for himself. Sidgwick, explicitly rejecting Mill's argument (*ME* 7, pp. 387–8), suggests instead that one might move from what each man thinks is desirable for himself to the principle about what is desirable for all. But he also thinks that neither this argument nor any other can force the egoist to abandon his position completely. Egoism is not refuted or suppressed. It is a permanent aspect of the demand of rationality on action. 'I do not hold the reasonableness of aiming at happiness generally with any stronger conviction', Sidgwick insists, 'than I do that of aiming at one's own'. (*ME* 7, x.) This can only be so if the limited concept of own-good represents a permanently valid aspect of rationality in action. We must now try to see, in more precise detail than heretofore, the structural relations of the basic concepts and axioms through which this point is worked out.

The question can be clarified by using Sidgwick's notion of logical priority, discussed earlier (Ch. 10, sec. i). Since the notion applies both to concepts and to principles, it opens the way for asking whether relations of logical priority and posteriority hold between P3 and B1, or between the notions of own-good and universal good. It is quite possible, of course, that no such relations hold. One reason for taking this view must be noticed immediately.

Both the concept of own-good and that of universal-good involve the 'comparison and integration' of different particular goods. (*ME* 7, p. 382.) The axioms P3 and B1 show that there are two rational ways of comparing and integrating the particular goods over which they range. One is to compare and integrate over time, within an individual life; the other is to compare and integrate across lives. Now we might think P3 more certain than B1 because, as Sidgwick points out, common sense questions integration across lives in a way it does not question integration over time. It therefore considers utilitarianism to need a proof in a way in which it does not think egoism needs one. (*ME* 7, p. 419.) But Sidgwick says that on this point common sense is mistaken. In one of the most interesting passages of the *Methods*, he points out that in terms of certainty P3 and B1 are on a par. 'I do not see', he remarks,

why the Egoistic principle should pass unchallenged any more than the Universalistic. I do not see why the axiom of Prudence should not be questioned, when it conflicts with present inclination, on a ground similar to that on which the Egoists refuse to admit the axiom of Rational Benevolence. If the Utilitarian has to answer the question, 'Why should I sacrifice my own happiness for the greater happiness of another?' it must surely be admissible to ask the Egoist, 'Why should I sacrifice a present pleasure for a greater one in the future? Why should I concern myself about my own future feelings any more than about the feelings of other persons?' (*ME* 7, p. 418; worded a little differently in *ME* 1, p. 389.)

Each axiom requires a specific kind of departure from taking the agent's presently felt inclination or desire as the sole source of reasons for action. Once it is admitted that one of the two kinds of departure is questionable, Sidgwick indicates, then it should be admitted that the other kind is equally questionable. By implication, if one is admissible the other is equally so. And this equal certainty might be taken to show that Sidgwick thinks that P3 and B1, and the concepts of good associated with them, do not stand in relations of logical priority and posteriority.

Logical priority, as Sidgwick understands it, however, is not a matter of more or less certainty. It is a matter of the order in which concepts must be explicated and propositions proven if clarity and cogency are to be attained. If we look at the axioms with this in mind, we shall find it helpful to suppose that Sidgwick thinks P3 and its associated concept of own-good are logically prior to B1 and its concept of universal-good. This order of priority helps explain several points. For instance, it helps explain the way in which the definition of the concept of universal good is developed. Sidgwick sees the concepts of right and good as representing the demands of reason, the one on the active aspect, the other on the sentient aspect, of our nature. He begins his account of good by considering the goods of an individual, as determined by what the individual thinks desirable. The next step is to develop the notion of what is 'good on the whole' for one individual, and only after this notion is defined does he move to the concept 'good on the whole' *simpliciter*, without the limitation to ownership by one consciousness. (*ME* 7, pp. 111–13.) The same order, from the momentary goods of one individual to the universal good, is followed when the axioms are obtained. After P3 is given Sidgwick comments that in obtaining it we have been constructing a concept 'by comparison and integration of the different "goods" that succeed one another in the series of our conscious states', that is, in the time-series in a single life. In the same way, he says, we construct 'the notion of Universal Good by comparison and integration of the goods of all individual human—or sentient—existences'. (*ME* 7, p. 382.) In both cases, own-good is plainly treated as the logically prior concept, the concept which must be explained before and in order that the others may be clearly explicated.

The hypothesis of the logical priority of own-good also helps explain why Sidgwick treats the egoist as building his theory with the concept of own-good and refusing to move to the concept of universal-good, but never suggests that by parity of reasoning we can see the utilitarian as starting with the concept of universal-good and refusing to move to the concept of own-good. The concept of own-good on the whole carries the concept of integration over time with it. It is only because it does that the concept of universal-good, constructed by integrating own-goods, includes the temporal condition under which reason must be applied to practice. But without the temporal condition it is impossible to make sense of the ideas of action and of rational demands on action. Thus own-good is logically simpler than universal-good, and P3 must be presupposed if B1 is to generate a requirement of practical rationality. But B1 is not similarly indispensable to the ability of P3 to set a practical rational requirement. Action mindless of the goods of other selves is in fact possible. And it is interesting that in so far as Sidgwick contemplates the possibility of taking universal-good to be logically prior to own-good, he seems to associate it with an anti-hedonistic view. Thus in describing the state of moral philosophy in the mid-1880s, he says that the main issue seems to be whether the ultimate end is 'Happiness, an aggregate of pleasures realised in successive parts of time in the lives of individuals; or whether it is some Universal Good which is the good of each because it is the good of all, and not the good of all by the summation of the goods of individuals'. (*Phil.*, p. 219; from 1886b, 217.) The fact that the egoistic version of the empirical method of estimating amounts of pleasure and pain is presupposed when the method of utilitarianism is discussed makes it plain that Sidgwick treats the universal good as being the good of all by summation of the goods of individuals. This may not require the logical priority of own-good, but it suggests that a mode of thinking in accordance with that priority is deeply rooted in Sidgwick's work.

If own-good is logically prior to universal good, and P3 to B1, the inescapability of the egoistic aspect of practical rationality is evident. The hypothesis is moreover not incompatible with the fact that Sidgwick holds both principles to be equally certain and equally important. It is precisely their equality in these respects which involves the problem of the dualism of the practical reason. And if we ask why it is that reason displays itself in this dualistic form, Sidgwick is prepared with the only kind of answer he thinks appropriate to such a question. The dualism, he says in one edition, arises from

the inevitable twofold conception of a human individual as a whole in himself, and a part of a larger whole. There is something that it is reasonable for him to desire, when he considers himself as an independent unit, and something again which he must recognize as reasonably to be desired, when he takes the point of view of a larger whole; the former of these objects I call his own ultimate 'Good', and the latter Ultimate Good taken universally . . . (*ME* 3, p. 402.)

This passage was dropped, presumably because it is used in drawing a distinction between right and good in a way Sidgwick found unsatisfactory. Yet like the remark quoted earlier, noting the fundamental nature of the difference between the agent's relation to his own consciousness and his relation to that of others, this comment sheds light on the nature of Sidgwick's belief in the dualism of the practical reason. The dualism comes from the same kind of consideration as the axioms themselves. It represents the requirements action must satisfy if it is to be reasonable, given the most basic facts of human life. Each of us is a self-conscious possessor of a private consciousness. We are also members of a whole made up of those who impinge on one another's private consciousnesses. Under these conditions, Sidgwick thinks, reason requires us to be equally egoistic and utilitarian. Thus he is led to the difficulties he discusses in his final chapter.

v. *The Problem of the Dualism*

In the first edition of the *Methods* egoism is not given its own self-evident principle in the chapter on axioms, III, xiii, but the treatment in the final chapter of the problem arising from the dualism of the practical reason is not strikingly different from the treatment in later editions. Reference is made to the argument used in IV, ii (*ME* 7, pp. 420–1), to bring the egoist to utilitarianism; the egoist is allowed to reply that the argument does not convince him, but only proves that unless egoism and utilitarianism can be shown to coincide, 'Practical Reason is divided against itself'; and he adds that if we must choose between them, 'Egoistic Hedonism has clearly a prior claim on our assent'. (*ME* 1, p. 461.) In the second edition the last chapter presents essentially the statements of egoism and of the issue given in the final edition; and after the inclusion in the fourth edition of the passage on the basis of the rationality of egoism (*ME* 7, p. 498) there were no further philosophically important alterations.

We have obtained, Sidgwick says, a synthesis of intuitional and utilitarian outlooks: the problem is posed by egoism. Reasoning may well fail to convince the egoist to accept and act on the utilitarian principle. Can we show him that the egoistic principle itself dictates that he should act as the utilitarian principle directs? Putting the problem in these terms suggests that Sidgwick is trying to neutralize, since he cannot refute, the single-minded rational egoist. We have seen, however, that the issue is deeper than this. Egoistic and universalistic hedonism are equally rational: hence 'a harmony between the maxim of Prudence and the maxim of Rational Benevolence must somehow be demonstrated if morality is to be made completely rational'. (*ME* 7, p. 498.) Obvious facts suggest that such a harmony does not exist. The question then is whether sanctions can bring about what reason does not supply. Of course to some extent the examination of the relation between egoism and common-sense morality has already answered the question in the negative. And since utilitarian morality is rather more demanding than common-sense morality, the negative answer seems final. (*ME* 7, p. 499.) Utilitarians have sometimes thought the problem could be resolved by appeal to the great power of sympathy. The pleasures and pains we obtain through fellow-feeling, they think, will make up for deficiencies in the other sanctions. Sidgwick becomes unwontedly eloquent in agreeing that sympathetic pleasures and pains are important, but he holds that even with one's capacity for sympathy most fully developed it is still unlikely that there will be 'perfect coincidence between Utilitarian duty and self-interest'. With illustrations to bring out the divergence (*ME* 7, pp. 502–3), he concludes that one cannot show on empirical grounds that there is an 'inseparable connection' between acting as utility requires and promoting one's own happiness.

Are there, then, adequate religious grounds for such a conclusion? Sidgwick argues first that there are no good reasons why utilitarianism should not be the code sanctioned by a deity sufficiently powerful 'to make it always every one's interest to promote universal happiness to the best of his knowledge' (*ME* 7, p. 506). The question is whether there are moral grounds for believing in such a deity. If not, ethics as a rational science will be forced to depend on theology or some other discipline for one of its basic premises. It need hardly be said that Sidgwick finds no sufficient moral grounds for the assumption. Assurance of the existence of God is not given by any intuition as clear and certain as the intuitions of the moral axioms. A desire that virtue should be rewarded is no proof that it will be, and to say that in some sense it ought to be rewarded is simply to restate the problem. As for the 'Kantian resource' (*ME* 1, p. 471) of obtaining what one cannot prove by making it a postulate, Sidgwick repudiates it in very strong language: 'I am so far from feeling bound to believe for purposes of practice what I see no ground for holding as a speculative truth, that I cannot even conceive the state of mind which these words seem to describe, except as a momentary half-wilful irrationality, committed in a violent access of philosophic despair.' (*ME* 7, p. 507, n. 3; in text until *ME* 4.)

There is only one other possibility. A general investigation of method is needed, to see whether in other fields besides ethics we are forced to work with basic propositions which we cannot prove in any ordinary way and which we need in order to obtain coherence in a large body of knowledge. If so, we may perhaps be warranted in thinking such a proposition true. But Sidgwick will not venture to pronounce, in a treatise on ethics, whether we are or not. (*ME* 7, pp. 508–9.) The postulate in question, he notes, is not necessarily one which is in the traditional way religious. (*ME* 7, p. 507, n. 1.) 'I tend to the view', he wrote to his friend Symonds in 1886, 'that the question of Personality, the point on which the theist as such differs from the atheist, is of no fundamental ethical importance. The question is *what* is the order of the Cosmos, not whether it is consciously planned.' (*Mem.*, 455.) In the next section we shall review Sidgwick's later ideas on the issue he could not resolve in the *Methods*. Here we must try to clarify the issue itself.

It may seem that Sidgwick has set himself a problem which is insoluble, not just because it is particularly difficult but because of the very terms in which it is set. This is Broad's view. Sidgwick speaks of a 'fundamental contradiction' which a postulate of cosmic order would resolve (*ME* 7, p. 508), and Broad takes him at his word:

> It is surely quite plain that no such postulate would free ethics from the theoretical inconsistency which Sidgwick finds in it. There are two principles which are logically inconsistent with each other, and, on reflection each seems to Sidgwick equally self-evident. No God, however powerful and however benevolent, can alter the fact that these two principles are logically incompatible and that therefore something which seemed self-evident to Sidgwick must in fact have been false.[3]

Broad adds that the existence of an appropriate deity or cosmic order might make it a matter of indifference which principle one adopts as a practical agent, and this would be a comfort. But the theoretical problem would remain.

While this may be a possible reading of the text, it implies that Sidgwick could not see that his problem is in principle

[3] Broad, *Five Types*, p. 253.

insoluble because it arises from a plain logical contradiction. It would be preferable to find an interpretation which allows a postulate of cosmic order to be a solution to the problem and which also enables us to understand why Sidgwick thinks his axioms involve a contradiction. Now if it is assumed that there can be one and only one ultimate right-making characteristic, then there is no escape from Broad's way of construing the problem. Hence when we try to state the axioms as they are involved in the alleged contradiction—and Sidgwick does not do this in the final chapter as carefully as he should—we must avoid any wording which implies this assumption.

The formulations of the axioms given in the final chapter are P5 and B5. P5, that my own greatest happiness is the rational ultimate end for me (*ME* 7, p. 497), carries the implication that there is only one ultimate right-making characteristic. And neither it nor B5, that it is right and reasonable for me to do what I believe to be ultimately conducive to universal Good or Happiness, brings out clearly enough the distinction between own-good and universal-good which is so important in Sidgwick's thinking. Hence we must reformulate both of the axioms.

P6: Maximizing the agent's own good is an ultimate right-making characteristic.

B6: Maximizing the universal good is an ultimate right-making characteristic.

Despite their rather barbarous wording, these formulations seem to express Sidgwick's understanding of the two principles involved in the dualism of the practical reason, and they reveal its structure more plainly than his own statements do. Evidently there is no logical contradiction between them. If we take them as stating the principles involved in the fundamental problem of ethics, can we see why that problem should have seemed to Sidgwick to involve a contradiction, and yet a contradiction that could be resolved by a contingent proposition?

To answer this question we need to bear in mind the significance of the fact that we are now considering only *ultimate* right-making characteristics. For Sidgwick this means that the principles must determine actual rightness, not merely putative rightness. They must, in his phrase, be independently valid. If there is a perfect coincidence between the acts dictated by B6 and those dictated by P6, this condition is met. It is also met if some acts demanded by P6 are neutral with respect to B6, or some mandated by B6 neutral with respect to P6, and otherwise each principle directs doing the same acts as the other. Whether or not this complex state of affairs exists is plainly a contingent matter. But if, as Sidgwick has argued, it does not, then it is logically impossible for both P6 and B6 to be true. For it cannot be true that it is actually right to do an act maximizing own-good and not actually right to do it. Hence if B6 entails the wrongness of an act of which P6 entails the rightness, both principles cannot determine actual rightness. In short, unless their dictates coincide, P6 and B6 cannot, logically speaking, both be independently valid ultimate principles. Thus we have found the contradiction, removable by a factual proposition, which lies at the heart of Sidgwick's problem. The urgency of the difficulty it creates can perhaps be brought out by recalling that Sidgwick has tried throughout the *Methods* to discover what reason demands of action when applied under the most fundamental conditions of human life. What he finds at the end is that because of one such basic and undeniable fact about human life, practical reason inevitably makes contradictory demands on action. If this is not a formal contradiction within reason itself, its bearing on Sidgwick's real hope for philosophical ethics is sufficiently devastating to make it clear why he thinks his endeavour ends in failure.

vi. *The Final Uncertainty*

Sidgwick's striking position concerning the dualism of the practical reason and the problems it involves has been discussed more often than any other part of his theory. The discussions have at least made it clear that no brief and simple assessment of his various claims is possible; and none will be offered here. What has received considerably less careful attention is the extent to which Sidgwick himself, in his later years, thought he was able to come closer to a satisfactory solution to the problem of the dualism than he had come to at the end of the *Methods*.[4] One would like to know; and though the evidence

---

[4] For a discussion of Sidgwick's later religious thought, see Frank Miller Turner, *Between Science and Religion*, New Haven, Yale University Press, 1974, esp. Ch. 3. Turner relies heavily on Broad for his version of Sidgwick's ethics.

does not allow us to arrive at any very detailed answer, there is enough to give some satisfaction to our curiosity.

The issue posed by the *Methods* is in one respect metaphysical: is there a 'moral order' in the universe beyond that which we can verify through particular experiences? (*Phil.*, pp. 83–5, 87–8.) Naturally this raises epistemological questions, but on these Sidgwick's position remained as it was prior to the writing of the *Methods*. He never doubts that it is in principle possible to answer questions of this kind. More specifically, he never doubts the legitimacy of argument from facts within experience to conclusions of a metaphysical kind. An early statement of his position occurs in a review published in 1871 of a book of essays by R. H. Hutton, a prolific literary critic and popularizer of religious philosophy.

If we are to argue from the facts of man's nature ascertained by observation of his thought and feelings, to the most profound and comprehensive judgments as to the essence of the universe, its origin and end—and I agree with Mr. Hutton, in opposition to many careful thinkers, that such argument is legitimate—we must surely take extreme heed to get our psychological premises as irrefragible and our principles of inference as clear and definite, as possible. (1871g, 325.)

The idea that we might find experiential evidence to support metaphysical propositions is connected with Sidgwick's early interest in psychical research and in religious experience generally. And he did not alter the philosophical views that led to these interests. He was never persuaded by Kant's attempt to set *a priori* limits to knowledge, or by anyone else's. In a late paper he tells us that 'Theology is the result of the efforts of generations to understand the universe as manifested in the religious consciousness, just as sciences are the results of the similar effort to understand it as apprehended through sense-perception.' (1894c, 403.) Elsewhere he suggests that alongside rational theology and revelational theology there might be developed an 'empirical theology' whose object would be 'the reality dimly apprehended in the religious consciousness, which is normally inseparable from the moral consciousness' (1899b, 612–13).

The idea suggested by the possibility of empirical theology, that men have a gradually improving grasp of a reality of the sort traditional religion teaches, recalls the position of the Coleridgean moralists. God reveals himself, they held, not only in the Bible but also in experience, particularly moral experience, and so through examination of morality we can obtain some support for our belief in God. In the context of their teaching, the *Methods* must be seen as an attempt to obtain those 'irrefragible' premisses for which Sidgwick urged Hutton and others to seek, in a subject of special significance for religious truth. So viewed, the *Methods* shows that our moral experience does not sustain the religious conclusions the Coleridgeans wished to draw from it: morality is both egoistic and utilitarian rather than what they took to be distinctively Christian, and it reveals—if anything—a Chaos, not the sort of Cosmos they took it to point to, in the universe. It is moreover clear that Sidgwick never thought that any particular arguments do in fact yield firm religious conclusions, however possible it is in principle that some might do so. 'On one point', he wrote in 1887 in a journal he kept for John Addington Symonds,

J.A.S. has not caught my position; he says that he never expected much from *the* method of proof on which I have relied. But the point is that I have tried *all* methods in turn—all that I have found pointed out by any of those who have gone before me; and all in turn have failed—revelational, rational, empirical methods—there is no proof in any of them. Still, it is premature to despair, and I am quite content to go on seeking while life lasts . . . (*Mem.*, pp. 472–3.)

Sidgwick did go on seeking, and the philosophical results he reached are sketched in barest outline in his lectures on philosophy. After saying that philosophy tries to unify our knowledge both in the theoretical realm and in the practical, he urges that its 'final and most important task' is 'the problem of co-ordinating these two divisions of its subject-matter, and connecting fact and ideal in some rational and satisfactory manner' (*Phil.*, p. 30; cf. *LPK*, p. 31). Theology tries to resolve this profoundly difficult problem through the concept of 'a Being in whose righteous will what ought to be actually is', but the problem of evil as well as other difficulties makes this mode of solution seem to Sidgwick philosophically unsatisfactory. (*Phil.*, pp. 238–41.) Theology touches philosophical concerns again by offering to supply the postulate of the moral order of the universe. And Sidgwick does not entirely dismiss the offer, though he has reservations about it. 'I myself regard Theism', he says, 'as a belief which, though borne in upon the living mind through life, and essential to normal life, is not self-evident or capable of being cogently demonstrated.' (*Phil.*, p. 242; cf. 1894c, 400.) To allow a place for the belief, he suggests that we admit the existence of a special class of beliefs which are neither self-evident nor demonstrable. The principle of causality is, in his view, a member of this class. 'Our acceptance of such propositions must have a provisional character', Sidgwick says, as compared with beliefs of the other, usual, kinds, though he does not mean that we must ordinarily feel any less certain about them. At least, if a provisional proposition is accepted by other people and is consistent with other beliefs, then 'its certainty becomes to me . . . practically indistinguishable from other certainty, though I recognise philosophically the provisional character of the structure of thought to which it belongs'. (*Phil.*, p. 243.)

Once again Sidgwick admits the possibility that theistic belief may have a warranted place in our thought: the question is still whether it actually deserves that place. The two tests of consensus and consistency must of course be passed by any belief before it is warranted; and a basic truth must also help to systematize our other beliefs as well. If the theistic hypothesis does pass this last test, Sidgwick says, then we have grounds for accepting it. He also says that the grounds are like those on which we accept certain other hypotheses as scientifically sound. (1898a, pp. 607–8.) But he does not elaborate on this point, and he does not say that the theistic hypothesis does pass the test. We have already seen that the postulate needed to bring coherence into the practical realm is not necessarily a theistic one: perhaps this is the source of his hesitation. A remark in a paper read in 1899 suggests that he also thought that the theistic belief might not pass the test of eliciting a consensus among thoughtful persons. If one central area of experience to which appeal may be made by empirical theology is moral experience, then the existence of a significant number of people who do not see their morality as involving religious belief at all is worrisome. For it may well be that these people 'represent the beginnings of a more advanced stage in the development of the moral consciousness'. (1899b, 615.) They may be living proof, in other words, that the theistic belief is not 'essential to normal life' (*Phil.*, 242), and in any case their dissent would be grounds for doubting the belief.

From a purely philosophical point of view, then, Sidgwick continued to hold that a proposition affirming cosmic order is needed to make out the possibility of the complete rationality of practice. He thought he could allow a category into which such a belief would fit, along with others. But while he found some facts which he took to tell in its favour, he saw others as telling against it. He did not undertake on a large scale that investigation of the methodology of the sciences which he says, at the end of the *Methods* (*ME* 7, p. 509), might help us to a definite position about the permissibility of a postulate. And he does not seem to have concluded finally, anywhere, either that some proposition asserting moral order is warranted or that it is not.

There is another kind of consideration bearing on his position. 'I am led . . .', he says, 'to regard a belief in a Divine Being as indispensable to a normal human mind; and though I may not always keep this in mind in philosophical speculation, I was a man before I became a philosopher, and I do not forget it for long . . .' (1894c, 400.) There is no doubt that as a man rather than a philosopher Sidgwick felt that an 'indestructible and inalienable minimum of faith' is necessary to humanity and necessary to himself too, 'at least so far as the man in me is deeper than the methodical thinker'. These latter statements come from an extended comment Sidgwick wrote on Tennyson's *In Memoriam.* They occur just after he has praised the poet's refusal to allow feeling alone to lead us to religious assurance by denying the value of reason. Had the poet allowed it, Sidgwick remarks, 'we should have shaken our heads and said, "Feeling must not usurp the function of Reason. Feeling is not knowing. It is the duty of a rational being to follow truth wherever it leads".' (1897f, 303; in *Mem.*, p. 541.) The conclusion of his analysis may be taken to speak of his own condition as a man as well as of the poem:

assurance and doubt must alternate in the moral world in which we at present live, somewhat as night and day alternate in the physical world. The revealing visions come and go; when they come we *feel* that we *know*: but in the intervals we must pass through states in which all is dark, and in which we can only struggle to hold the conviction that

> . . . Power is with us in the night
> Which makes the darkness and the light,
> And dwells not in the light alone.
>
> (1897f, 304; in *Mem.*, p. 542.)

Sidgwick neither allows the philosophic mind to stifle the longings and insights of the natural man, nor permits the man's emotions to achieve gratification at the cost of reason. For maintaining such a balance between thought and feeling, between 'the philosopher' and 'the man', Sidgwick has been described as displaying a 'failure of nerve'.[5] This cheap phrase cannot illuminate the work of any serious thinker, least of all Sidgwick. His refusal to claim more for a proposition than he thought rationally warranted was the result of a carefully considered methodology, and reflects his deepest attitudes toward serious intellectual endeavour. 'I conceive the one important lesson that Philosophy and Theology have to learn from the progress of Science is the vague lesson of patience and hope', Sidgwick says; 'Science sets before us the ideal of a consensus of experts and continuity of development which we may hope to emulate in our larger and more difficult work.' (*Phil.*, p. 231.)[6] In his youth Sidgwick dedicated himself diffidently to the service of reason, in his work and in his life. His allegiance to it never wavered, even when it meant a final uncertainty about the possibility of a fully rational life.

[5] James, *Sidgwick*, p. 49.
[6] Sidgwick's work with the Society for Psychical Research illustrates this attitude especially clearly. See, e.g. 1889b, 2–3.

PART III

AFTER THE *METHODS*

14

Sidgwick and the Later Victorians

THE latter part of Sidgwick's life was largely devoted to enter-
prises other than moral philosophy, but with the enviable
energy possessed by so many of the great Victorians he found
time to give careful assessments of what he took to be the more
important developments in ethics. There were two schools of
thought to be taken into account, the evolutional and the
idealistic. They have been frequently discussed by scholars,[1]
and a full analysis of them is not needed here. We may confine
ourselves to some notice of Sidgwick's response to them. He
takes Herbert Spencer and T. H. Green as the main representa-
tives of the schools, and he sees them as presenting two types of
ethical thought moving away from his own 'in opposite directions, but agreeing in that they do not treat Ethics as a subject
that can stand alone. Spencer bases it on Science, Green on
Metaphysics.' (*GSM*, p. 1.) Sidgwick here indicates the one
key point on which the two views opposed to his were united.
In denying the independence of ethics, they claimed to have
worked out a greater unification of knowledge than he had
aimed at in trying to systematize morality alone. Such a claim
plainly called for Sidgwick's attention. Both Spencer and Green
also criticized utilitarian views similar to Sidgwick's and in
some cases attacked positions expressly adopted by him. But
they had little in common beyond this.

Evolutionism was not profoundly different from the older
utilitarianism. The evolutionists generally admitted their
utilitarian ancestry, remained secular and hedonistic, and
claimed mainly to be able to provide a more scientific proof
of the basic principle of morals and better means of deciding

---

[1] John Passmore, *A Hundred Years of Philosophy*, London, Duckworth, 1957,
Chs. II and III, together with the bibliographies, provides the best general introduction. Melvin Richter, *The Politics of Conscience: T. H. Green and his Age*, London,
Weidenfeld & Nicholson, 1964, is a good study of Green's moral and political
thought. See also A. G. N. Flew, *Evolutionary Ethics*, London, Macmillan, 1967.

upon the details of right action, than their forerunners. We shall therefore treat only briefly of Sidgwick's criticism of Spencer. Idealism constituted a more marked break with the British tradition. In many ways the idealists carried on from the intuitionists. They opposed utilitarianism and empiricism, and they used philosophy to defend a religious or 'spiritual' outlook. Their criticisms of the views they rejected, however, were novel to a certain extent, involving far more reliance on Hegelianism than had been evident in earlier British philosophy. And their positive views also claimed to bring to British ethics, if not absolute novelty, at least some vital points which it had neglected to its serious detriment. As a specimen of idealistic criticism, we shall examine Bradley's attack on Sidgwick, which contained many objections with which Green agreed. We shall then look at Sidgwick's examination of Green's positive views. For Green, though agreeing with Bradley on an Hegelian conception of the nature and limits of moral philosophy, was far more Kantian in substantive moral outlook. In Green's ethics Sidgwick saw the one serious effort made during his later years to spell out a real alternative to his own.

i. *Evolutionism*

Among Sidgwick's earliest published writings are discussions of books using or attacking evolutionary theory, one of Spencer's among them; consideration of Spencer occurs in the *Methods* from the first edition onward; Sidgwick reviewed parts of Spencer's *Principles of Ethics* as well as another considerable work of the evolutional school, Leslie Stephen's *Science of Ethics*,[2] and incorporated parts of these reviews in the *Methods*; and his posthumously published lectures include a long set on Spencer's ethics as well as some from a series on Spencer's epistemological and metaphysical views. The amount of effort he devoted to Spencer and evolution reflects the importance of these topics at the time, rather than Sidgwick's own estimate of them. From his earliest reviews onward he shows himself to be cautious, even distrustful, about evolutionary

[2] Sidgwick had a low opinion of Stephen's philosophical abilities even before the publication of *The Science of Ethics*. In 1879 he wrote to A. J. Balfour advising him not to load his title-page with quotations from Stephen, who, he said, was a philosophical littérateur with no real standing. BM, Add. MSS. 49832, fos. 24–5.

theories. Thus at one point after a critical remark or two about Darwin's own theory of the origin of the moral sense he argues that the matter is irrelevant to the concerns of the moral philosopher. (1872e, 230–1.) At another point he expresses an interesting view about the purely scientific aspect of Darwinism. The principle of the uniformity of nature, he says, requires us to hold—if we are to practise scientific biology at all—that the state of organic life at any one time bears some law-governed relation to its state at any other time. Scientists must therefore choose between *some* theory of evolution, in a very general sense, and some theory of spontaneous generation. But the latter is completely implausible as regards the higher forms of life. Darwin's theory fills in the outline of the type of evolutionary theory needed 'with, at least, some *prima facie* plausibility; and hence', Sidgwick comments, 'it has attained a greater reputation than is, perhaps, due to its intrinsic merits'. (1872k, 84; cf. 1876a, 53; 1886b, 207–8; *Phil.*, pp. 136–9.) Cautious willingness to accept the hypothesis of evolution by means of natural selection as a valuable scientific theory, coupled with scepticism as to its bearing on philosophy in general and on ethics in particular, characterized Sidgwick's attitude throughout his life.

Evolutionary theory was of importance in two ways during the latter part of the nineteenth century. On the one hand it provided a fruitful theoretical structure for biology and was extended to give stimulating indications of lines along which the developing disciplines of anthropology and sociology might move.[3] On the other hand it seemed to a wide variety of non-scientists, from poets and philosophers to the crudest popularizers for the public imagination, to provide a sweeping new world-view which was soundly based on science and which could replace the tottering conventional religious convictions of the time. On the former uses of the theory Sidgwick generally abstained from comment. His concern was with the latter. 'Current philosophical notions characteristic of the most recently accepted system or manner of thought in any age and country', he remarks dryly, 'are apt to exercise over men's minds an influence which is often in inverse ratio to the clearness with which the notions themselves are conceived, and the

[3] See especially J. W. Burrow, *Evolution and Society*, Cambridge, 1966, and J. P. Y. Peel, *Herbert Spencer, The Evolution of a Sociologist*, 1971.

evidence for the philosophical doctrines implied in their acceptance is examined and estimated'. (1876a, 52.) He had particular reason for concern with this type of evolutionism. Outside the *Methods* he unhesitatingly identified himself as a utilitarian, and it seemed to be all too easy for people to suppose that a utilitarian was necessarily an evolutionist. 'The essence of utilitarianism and the essence of Darwinism, the principle of utility and the principle of natural selection, have such strong elective affinities', wrote J. G. Schurman in 1888, 'that to effect their combination nothing was required but to bring them together. Their union establishes the high-water mark of contemporary utilitarianism.'[4] Sidgwick's critiques of evolutionary ethics are partly intended to separate precisely the two things Schurman thinks belong together. More generally, however, they are meant to bring out in detail just how serious the deficiencies of clarity and carefulness in evolutionary ethics are for their philosophical pretensions. He was not, of course, alone, in attacking attempts to draw moral or philosophical conclusions from the scientific theory of evolution. Many scientists, like T. H. Huxley, to say nothing of other philosophers, objected to the use being made of the theory. Their prime target, like his, was Spencer.

Spencer announced his conversion to general evolutionism shortly after the publication of *Social Statics*, and enunciated the law underlying his theory of the universe in an essay on 'Progress, Its Law and Cause' in 1857. Fuller exposition of the position came in *First Principles* in 1862. Everything that exists, he there argued, evolves from indefinite, incoherent homogeneity to definite, coherent, heterogeneity. The application of this law, in considerable detail, to the realms of biology, psychology, sociology, and, finally, morality, was to occupy him for the rest of his life. He published little on ethics for a number of years, though his position could be gathered from a letter of 1863 to J. S. Mill which was printed in Bain's *Mental and Moral Science* in 1868, and from occasional essays. In 1879 *The Data of Ethics*, containing the first part of his moral system, appeared: the other parts followed slowly, the work finally being completed in 1893. In the letter to Mill, to which Spencer frequently made reference later, evolutionary ethics is said to

---

[4] Jacob Gould Schurman, *The Ethical Import of Darwinism*, 1888, p. 126.

involve three points. First, Spencer agrees with the utilitarians that 'happiness is the ultimate end'. Second, he thinks there should be a strict and scientific determination of 'how and why certain modes of conduct are detrimental, and certain other modes beneficial'. The problem with utilitarianism is that it has been too crude and empirical, remaining satisfied with rough and uncoordinated observations, as astronomy did in its pre-modern phase. Spencer's moral science is meant to be the equivalent of modern theoretical astronomy, and evolutionary theory is to provide the basis for this great advance. Third, he thinks, as he did at the time he wrote *Social Statics*, that there are basic moral intuitions, but he now has a scientific theory to account for them. They 'are the results of accumulated experiences of Utility, gradually organized and inherited', but they are now independent of conscious awareness of these experiences. Experiences of utility,

organized and consolidated through all past generations of the human race, have been producing nervous modifications, which, by continued transmission and accumulation, have become in us certain faculties of moral intuition—certain emotions responding to right and wrong conduct, which have no apparent basis in the individual experiences of utility.[5]

These ideas received a certain measure of support from the fact that Darwin himself did not reject them. In *The Descent of Man*, in 1871, Darwin tried to show that 'the difference between man and the higher animals, great as it is, certainly is one of degree and not of kind'. Since the moral sense is the 'best and highest' difference between man and animal, an evolutionary account of it is suggested, in the course of which Spencer's letter to Mill is quoted with apparent approval. (Darwin, *Descent*, p. 123.) Thus with Darwin's acquiescence, evolution by means of natural selection, which Spencer claimed to have shown to be the law of all other realms of being, offered itself as the authoritative, scientific guide to individual and political action. The many political uses to which this sort of Darwinism was put cannot occupy us here, important though they were. Sidgwick, without by any means agreeing with Spencer's extremely

---

[5] A. Bain, *Mental and Moral Science*, 1868, pp. 721 f. Spencer reprinted most of this letter in *The Data of Ethics*.

individualistic *laissez-faire* outlook, chose to discuss the ethics in technical philosophical terms.

Spencer begins with an effort to establish a basic principle. Starting with the assertion that ethics is concerned with 'conduct', or action adapted to ends, he argues that as conduct evolves to higher and higher stages it displays increasing differentiation of ends and increasing sophistication in action to attain them. Three kinds of ends are central: self-preservation, preservation of one's species, and preservation of all living things. Humans reason about attaining their ends, and their conclusions are expressed in opinions about the goodness and badness of acts, which are judged, like all other things, in terms of the extent to which they fulfil their purposes. But there is a deeper notion of goodness underlying these means–ends judgements, Spencer thinks, the notion that 'life is good or bad, according as it does or does not bring a surplus of agreeable feeling' (*Princ. E.*, 10). The law of evolution makes it increasingly clear that this is the real standard in terms of which men judge actions. All other moral views must reduce to it in the end, for it is involved in the very meaning of the word 'good': 'The truth that conduct is considered by us as good or bad, according as aggregate results, to self or others or both, are pleasurable or painful, we found on examination to be involved in all the current judgments of conduct: the proof being that reversing the applications of the words creates absurdities.' (*Princ. E.*, 16; cf. 10.) Evolution has brought it about that no one can avoid taking 'desirable state of feeling' as the ultimate moral aim: 'pleasure . . . is as much a necessary form of moral intuition as space is a necessary form of intellectual intuition' (*Princ. E.*, 16).[6]

Sidgwick's objections to these views are trenchant if predictable. He points out first that Spencer is using an allegedly scientific explanation of action and opinion about action as a basis for a conclusion about how people ought to act. But no causal account can support a moral opinion unless it includes some argument to show that the causes tend to make the opinion

---

[6] In the *Methods* Sidgwick originally spoke of the notion of 'ought' as 'a necessary form of our moral apprehension, just as space is now a necessary form of our sense perceptions'. (*ME* 1, p. 93.) The passage was only deleted in *ME* 3, which appeared after Spencer's book. Was Sidgwick simply anxious to avoid any appearance of agreement with Spencer, or was there a deeper reason for this change?

true—an argument Spencer makes no effort to supply. (*GSM*, pp. 136–7.) Nor can the problem be evaded by so defining a key ethical term as to make one's principle true by definition. To do so makes the principle a tautology, and 'a tautology cannot be an ethical principle' (*GSM*, p. 145). Sidgwick does not make much of this point. It relates, he says, 'to form rather than substance', and most of his criticism is devoted to substance.

Here the difficulties are numerous. Spencer offers a variety of formulations of his basic principle and treats them as equivalent. In one form the principle asserts pleasure to be the ultimate end, in another, preservation, in yet another, maximum of life (explained as length of life times 'breadth', by which Spencer means roughly richness and variety of experience). The last two formulations Sidgwick thinks implausible. They seem to amount to a doctrine of life for life's sake, regardless of enjoyableness, which no one would accept. In fact, however, as he carefully shows, Spencer really takes the utilitarian formulation as basic. The others are meant as stating 'proximate' ends, more useful than the utilitarian end in deliberating about particular practical problems. (*GSM*, p. 179.) Yet Sidgwick has his doubts as to their utility. For example, even if Spencer's law of evolution is true, it tells us nothing about the connection at present between being highly evolved and being happy or producing happiness. 'We cannot, therefore', Sidgwick points out, 'take confidently, as middle axioms of Utilitarianism, the precepts "Be definite, be coherent, be heterogeneous".' (*GSM*, p. 165.) Sidgwick repeatedly raises the question of the justification for linking the formulas on which a practical method is based with the principle asserting the characteristic making right acts right. (*GSM*, pp. 146–7, 155, 163–6, 175–6.) The factual assumptions needed are seldom clearly stated, let alone defended. Spencer ought, for example, to refute pessimism and prove optimism if he wishes to take a formula of maximizing life as a basis for a method which the utilitarian principle can justify, but he does not do so. (*GSM*, pp. 146–8.) A similar problem emerges in Spencer's treatment of egoism and altruism. What preserves the species may harm the individual; what brings greater definite coherent heterogeneity into the life of a society, and so shows it to be more highly evolved, may bring narrowness and tedium into the lives of its members. But Spencer seems unable to separate consistently the egoistic and altruistic variants of hedonistic ethics, and so is unable to deal cogently with the problems raised by his insistence that his goal brings the two aims, individual and social, into harmony. (*GSM*, pp. 178 ff.; cf. 1882, 577–9, 583; and 1876, 64–5.)

One source of Spencer's failure to achieve clarity on these points is his insistence on taking 'absolute ethics' as his central theme. It is here that the evolutionary strain in his thought blends most clearly with the visionary strain which we have seen in the earlier *Social Statics*. He believes, as he did then, though on the basis of much longer expositions of arguments, that society is evolving inexorably toward a condition in which every person will be perfectly adapted in all his functions to the circumstances of life in society, and in which, consequently, there will be no motivation to do acts that cause any pain. Individual and social good will perfectly coincide, he thinks, as will the maintenance of life in its most definite coherent heterogeneity with the greatest enjoyment of life. The sense of duty will vanish, having outlived its usefulness. Since all this must certainly come Spencer simply sees no need for the distinctions in which Sidgwick is interested. He holds that the main task of the moralist is to develop an ethic for the perfect man in the perfect society. The moralist may then work out a 'relative' ethic for men of the present, who are necessarily imperfect in their imperfect societies. A 'relative' ethic is not a morality designed to cope with the fact that men now fail to comply with absolutely true moral principles. It is meant to be an interim ethic for a society in a transitory stage in which perfectly true and valid moral principles cannot yet govern practice and in which the only rules men can follow must be partly wrong and imperfect. This conception, and the methodology based on it, are rejected in the *Methods* on the basis of Spencer's earlier sketch of it. Sidgwick is no happier about the later version, although Spencer now is willing to allow that the moralist can properly develop a relative ethic, a task he simply dismissed in *Social Statics*. Sidgwick's main objection to it is one we have noted in discussing his arguments concerning the proper method for a utilitarian to use. A society in which it is always possible to act so as to produce pleasure and no pain—and this is Spencer's requisite for an absolute ethic—is so unlike our own that we cannot tell what the people in it will be like, still less determine the conditions under which they must act, in sufficient detail to work out the specifics of a moral code for them. (*GSM*, pp. 197 ff.) Hence we cannot spell out a code for them nor, *a fortiori*, use it to rectify our present morality. Spencer seems eventually to admit this, and to fall back on those merely empirical methods of moralizing that he had so harshly criticized the earlier utilitarians for employing. But even in this kind of moralizing, Sidgwick shows, he is not able to come up with maxims or rules which mark any advance on what everyone already knows or thinks.

It would not repay us to follow the many oddities and errors which Sidgwick points out in Spencer's minute moralizing. But it may be worth noticing the way in which the main objections he offers to Spencer's theory reflect his own systematic approach to moral philosophy. Since Spencer's basic principle is not given a proof, it is presumably to be taken as self-evident. But either it is not acceptable to most competent judges and therefore fails to meet one of the tests of intuitively evident principles; or else it is no different from the utilitarian principle. In the latter case, any support for Spencer's claim to have made important advances in ethics would have to be derived entirely from the superiority of the methods he develops for applying the principle. But the various formulas he gives for proximate goals grounding superior methods are not themselves logically connected with his basic principle. They can only be connected with it by extremely dubious factual assumptions. Even allowing such connections, the proximate principles do not clearly yield any systematization of our beliefs about what we ought to do which is superior to the systematization Sidgwick himself achieves. In particular the evolutional assumptions fail to help bring about a harmony between egoistic and altruistic rationales for action. And finally, Spencer fails to provide any special method for making decisions in cases where common sense is unclear. (*GSM*, pp. 249–50.) On Sidgwick's view of what a moral philosophy should do, it is hard to see how there could be a more complete failure. Nor did Spencer have much to say in reply. His criticisms of Sidgwick are not effective; and in the Preface to the second volume of the *Principles of Ethics* he admits sadly that the chapters giving a detailed code 'fall short of expectation. The Doctrine of Evolution has not furnished guidance to the extent I had hoped.' Most of its results, he concedes, are commonplaces of enlightened common sense. Bearing in mind his strong insistence from 1863 onwards on the superiority of evolutional method over mere empirical utilitarianism, this admits defeat indeed.

ii. *Idealism: F. H. Bradley*

Idealism in moral philosophy announced its arrival in Britain in F. H. Bradley's brilliantly written *Ethical Studies*, published in 1876. Avowing a need for a metaphysics which he could not as yet provide, Bradley stressed the critical bearing of his essays. He devoted a chapter to an attack on Kantian ethics, but his main targets were determinism, hedonism, egoism, utilitarianism, psychologism, and, indirectly, the empiricism he thought to be at their root. He hoped to purge English thought of its prejudice in favour of these doctrines which, so he thought, had sapped its strength and hindered its development for altogether too long, and to replace them with sounder and more fruitful views—Hegelian views. Understandably he gave little space to the *Methods*, which had appeared just as he must have been finishing his own work. A sharply critical note at the end of the essay on 'Pleasure for Pleasure's Sake' attacks Sidgwick's hedonism and his supposed suppression of egoism in terms which suggest that Bradley had not had time to study his opponent's book very carefully. In the following year he brought out *Mr. Sidgwick's Hedonism*, a pamphlet devoted entirely to attacking the *Methods*. It is the major effort of the idealistic school to come to grips with hedonism and consequentialism in their most recent form, and it is the only sustained criticism of the *Methods* by a thoroughly unsympathetic opponent to appear in Sidgwick's lifetime. Some discussion of it is therefore appropriate. Although Sidgwick reviewed *Ethical Studies* in *Mind*, he paid almost no overt attention to the later pamphlet. When he examined idealistic ethics at length, it was by discussing the version presented by T. H. Green, the acknowledged leader of the Oxford idealists.

Some of his remarks about Green show us how he would have replied to Bradley, and even without such clues it is not difficult to determine what he would have said to most of the criticisms. It has recently been claimed that Bradley's pamphlet 'blew Sidgwick's position . . . to pieces',[7] but this judgement is not sustained by any examination of the arguments. Bradley's objections, as we shall see, sometimes rest on positions which are only hinted at, occasionally arise from misunderstandings of what Sidgwick says, and often allow of effective reply. For these reasons the pamphlet—despite its rhetorical vigour—does not demonstrate in any clear and convincing way that there are serious deficiencies in Sidgwick's ethics. The fact is of some historical importance: Sidgwick's foremost critic failed to force him to undertake a major re-examination of his views.

Bradley begins with two sets of complaints about what he takes to be the vagueness of Sidgwick's account of reason. The first set is directed largely to the question of whether particular moral judgements or only universal judgements are functions of reason. Bradley objects to Sidgwick's claim that the former are implicitly general, and hints that Sidgwick's view of the way in which the moral end is reasonable is partly due to his lack of clarity about reason. (*Hedonism*, pp. 73–6.) The unstated point behind these complaints is the Hegelian one, that true rationality cannot be found either in abstract universals or in bare particulars but only in the concrete universal. Its application is made more directly later, when Bradley claims that pleasure can be taken as a rational end only if one accepts abstract universals as rational. In his second set of opening complaints Bradley turns against Sidgwick's view of reason as practical, pointing out the vagueness of the account in the *Methods* of how reason and desire are related in moving us to act. This is a matter on which much depends, Bradley suggests, and the view Sidgwick holds 'labours under well-known difficulties which . . . if not met, must gravely affect his thesis' (*Hedonism*, p. 78), but neither of these assertions is developed. As we have noted, Sidgwick substantially changed his view on the motivating power of reason after the first edition, perhaps in response to Bradley. Because of the indefiniteness of the objections,

[7] James, *Sidgwick*, 33.

however, it is hard to say if Bradley would have been satisfied by the changes.

The criticisms of what Bradley takes to be Sidgwick's defence of hedonism are rather more specific than the objections about reason. Bradley first charges that Sidgwick makes it true by definition that pleasure is good. He is led to this charge, despite his having noticed that Sidgwick formally treats 'desirable' as meaning 'what should be desired', by a misstatement of Sidgwick's account of pleasure. He takes Sidgwick to define it as 'desirable feeling' (*Hedonism*, p. 83), while Sidgwick actually defines it as 'the kind of feeling that we judge to be preferable'. (*ME* 1, p. 115.) Since Sidgwick makes it clear, even in the first edition, that he thinks no kind of judgement is immune from error, his position, as was noted in Chapter 11, ii, requires rational assessment of the judgement involved in the feeling of pleasure, and so does not leave him guilty of Bradley's charge.

Bradley's further objections to hedonism are far more Hegelian in nature. He says first that one cannot make the abstractions needed in order to arrange pleasant experiences in order of pleasantness, and that one cannot obtain an adequate measure of pleasures as such. Here, he allows, Sidgwick has seen the problems, though he is not content with Sidgwick's response to them. (*Hedonism*, pp. 83–4.) A more serious charge is that the very notions of a sum of pleasures and a greatest possible amount of pleasure are radically incoherent. The notion of an infinite quantity is a 'self-contradictory idea', but as that is admittedly not what Sidgwick means to say the goal is, Bradley examines the idea of a finite sum of pleasures. Like Green, who had adumbrated a similar point somewhat earlier,[8] Bradley takes it that 'if there is a realizable end, . . . there must be some time at which this end can be realized'; and since pleasures are perishing entities, so that a sum of pleasures cannot be real all at once, a sum of pleasures cannot be a real end. (*Hedonism*, p. 85; cf. *Eth. Stud.*, pp. 96 ff.) This objection to taking a sum of pleasures as the end holds no less for the individual's pleasures than mankind's. Bradley therefore moves on to consider the possibility that Sidgwick thinks the

[8] Introduction to Hume's *Treatise*, originally published 1874, in *Works*, i. 307–8, 370.

end is 'that at any time the sentient world should be having the greatest possible quantity of pleasantness'. (*Hedonism*, p. 86.) Of this too he makes short shrift. On a deterministic view of action, he says, we always have as much pleasure as was really possible; on a libertarian view the notion loses its meaning; and either way it is a fiction and not a possible ultimate end. (*Hedonism*, pp. 87–9.)

These objections depend on certain doctrines, concerning either the internality of relations, which makes certain types of abstraction illegitimate, or the concrete universal as the necessary structure of the moral end, which makes it impossible that the end should be a 'mere aggregate'. (Cf. *Hedonism*, p. 85.) Yet as neither Bradley nor Green, in presenting the objections, explains their conceptual bases, it is easy to feel sympathy with Sidgwick when he allows that he finds it hard to state the point of Green's version of them in a convincing manner. (1884b, 176.) In his response to Green he treats the criticisms simply in a common-sense way, making no effort to unearth the complexities behind them. So taken, the difficulties centring on the view that the moral end must be one which can be realized all at once reduce, he thinks, to the objection that the hedonistic good cannot be enjoyed at one time. His point in reply to this, in the *Methods*, can be put briefly. He sees nothing wrong with a good that cannot be enjoyed all at once, but must be enjoyed serially (*ME* 7, pp. 132 f.); as he puts it elsewhere, he cannot think anyone wise 'who has philosophized himself into so serious a quarrel with the conditions of human existence that he cannot be satisfied with the prospect of never-ending bliss, because its parts have to be enjoyed successively'. (1884b, 176; cf. *GSM*, pp. 107–8, 119.) His answer to the objection to the notion of a greatest possible amount of pleasure is also brief and sensible. We use the notion when we are making plans and decisions, and under the limitations imposed by our imperfect foresight of the future. In such contexts we can speak of the 'greatest possible amount' of time or of space without implying problematic notions of infinite sums. For example, we can try to live for the longest possible time. Similarly in deliberation we can consider which of the courses of action open to us will produce the greatest possible amount of enjoyment. We make our choices between courses of action about which we can see that one will produce more, another less, pleasure, and it is only in relation to such choices that the notion of 'greatest possible amount of pleasure' needs to be used. We do not need a distinct idea of some known greatest sum of pleasures, which is to be used to measure our progress. All we require for a 'practical criterion' is that we can knowingly increase the amount of pleasure brought into existence. Approval can be and is given, Sidgwick thinks, to 'this preference of more good to less, without introducing the notion of a possible maximum'. (*GSM*, pp. 111–13, 120–1.) Sidgwick is saying, in effect, that the problem presented by Bradley and Green is a spurious one.

Bradley turns, after his objections to the concept of pleasure as ultimate end, to examine Sidgwick's attempt to show that pleasure is the sole moral end. The argument, he says, begins with a step he is himself prepared to take: the claim that 'nothing is ultimately good unless it enters into relation to consciousness'. But he promptly challenges Sidgwick's right to divide what enters into consciousness into objective and subjective aspects. Then, deferring explanation of this, he attacks Sidgwick's appeal to the intuition of his readers. His point is that Sidgwick equivocates: sometimes he treats 'happiness' as meaning simply 'pleasure', sometimes as meaning 'desirable conscious life'; and while Bradley would be prepared to admit that the latter might possibly serve as a formula for the moral end, he would certainly be unwilling to allow the former. The equivocation, however unaware of it Sidgwick may be, makes his appeal to intuition unavailing, since the reader is never fairly presented, Bradley thinks, with a clear question whose answer could be decisive for hedonism. Bradley does not back up this charge by careful examination of the passages in which Sidgwick attempts to distinguish his own very broad concept of pleasure from a narrower concept in which it is taken as being simply a special kind of sensation. Instead, he turns to some objections to Sidgwick's claim that if we 'simplify the question by supposing only a single sentient conscious being in the universe', it is plain that 'nothing can be ultimately "good" for such a being except his own happiness'. (*ME* 1, p. 374; altered in *ME* 2, p. 372, to its final form, *ME* 7, p. 405.) It is the 'dogmatic individualism' assumed here to which

Bradley most sensibly objects. (*Hedonism*, pp. 93–4.) But again he does not follow up the point so as to satisfy the reader that any irreparable damage is done to Sidgwick's position when the assumption is noticed. His stress is still on Sidgwick's failure to produce a clear intuition of the ultimate goodness of pleasure, and he does not seem to have noticed that the appeal to the reader's intuition is only one part of Sidgwick's argument. Even in the first edition the main line of thought, as we have seen, is that there is need for a standard which will systematize our apparently conflicting judgements of what it is reasonable to do or to seek, and will give us a procedure for making decisions in hard cases. And one type of hard case which Sidgwick specifically notes is the kind in which external states of affairs as distinct from awareness of them are 'conceived to come . . . really and finally, into competition with Happiness'. (*ME* 1, pp. 371–2.) Sidgwick points out that in cases like this the plain man may well have conflicting apparent intuitions; and though Sidgwick thinks his own intuition clear on the hedonistic side, the aim of his further discussion is to show that the hedonistic principle can serve to rationalize apparent intuitions better than a non-hedonistic principle. Here, then, as in the subsequent very brief objection to Sidgwick's views on 'unconscious hedonism' (*Hedonism*, p. 98), Bradley mistakes one part of the argument for something meant to be conclusive by itself.

Bradley now takes up his deferred objection to Sidgwick's separation of objective and subjective in states of conscious awareness. Under this heading there are no doubt arguments which might be used to criticize Sidgwick's hedonism: the logic of the relations between pleasure and the conditions under which it is felt is more complex than Sidgwick realizes. But this is not Bradley's point. Bradley thinks the moral end is self-realization. This involves both improvement of the functions of the self and also increase in its enjoyments. If the two were separable, Bradley would prefer to increase the 'qualitative excellence' of function, even at the expense of pleasure. (*Hedonism*, pp. 96–7.) His main point however seems to be that we are not forced to make such a choice:

> We do not separate 'objective' and 'subjective': we do not say, Virtue *or* pleasure . . . we say *both.* . . . What we hold to against

every possible modification of Hedonism is that the standard and test is in higher and lower function, not in more or less pleasure. IF any one can prove that higher life means less or no surplus of pleasure, then he can fairly ask us to face the alternative . . .

But Bradley thinks Sidgwick has no right to try to make him face it. (*Hedonism*, p. 97.) One would think that if the concept of virtue is logically distinct from the concept of general happiness, as Bradley treats it as being, then it might be asked how one could be sure the two would always go together. Unless there is some unmentioned metaphysical objection to putting the question in this way, it is hard to see how Bradley's remarks amount to anything more than unwarranted dogmatism.

Bradley comments at the end of his pamphlet that the argument of Sidgwick's book as a whole has 'no value'. He 'can find no unity of principle which holds its parts together'. (*Hedonism*, p. 124.) Since he has failed to find the total argument it is no surprise that his discussion of the 'suppression of egoism' should be vitiated by his failure to see Sidgwick's over-all aim in offering it. That the 'suppression' can be evaded (*Hedonism*, p. 102) is of course one of Sidgwick's own conclusions. Bradley seems partly to see this and to see why it is so, but he does not explore the matter. Nor does he return to it in his closing remarks on the 'hedonistic moral theology' he takes to be implicit in Sidgwick's final insoluble problem. (*Hedonism*, p. 118.) Assuming that the problem arises only because Sidgwick naïvely holds that virtue ought to be rewarded, Bradley makes no effort to show that there is no dualism in the practical reason of the kind Sidgwick thinks he finds. Hence the discussion of the question of reward is beside the point, interesting though it is in its own right.

The longest single section of *Mr. Sidgwick's Hedonism* is the one attacking Sidgwick's conception of the aim of moral philosophy. The basis of the attack is given in *Ethical Studies*, in Bradley's comments on how one comes to know what one ought to do in particular cases. The plain man, he says, who 'has identified his will with the moral spirit of the community', knows intuitively what to do. He does not apply consciously formulated rules, and he needs no abstract reasoning. In particular, Bradley holds, philosophy cannot help him: 'there cannot', he says, 'be a moral philosophy which will tell us what to do, and . . . it is not the business of philosophy to do so'. (*Eth. Stud.*, pp. 196, 193 f.)

All philosophy has to do is 'to understand what is', and moral philosophy has to understand morals which exist, not to make them or give directions for making them. Such a notion is simply ludicrous. Philosophy in general has not to anticipate the discoveries of the particular sciences . . .; and ethics has not to make the world moral, but to reduce to theory the morality current in the world. (*Eth. Stud.*, p. 193.)

Like his belief that complete prediction of human action is made impossible in principle by the originality of the human spirit, Bradley's view rests on the unstated Hegelian idea that the world spirit, operating through us, moves ever onward to new stages in its development. The task of the philosophical owl that flies at twilight is to articulate the developments the world spirit has already undergone. Philosophy can no more anticipate its evolution in morality than it can in science. His position is thus at odds with Sidgwick's belief that the same principle which provides an adequate explication of the 'morality current in the world' must also provide the basis for a method of rectifying that morality.

The chief accusation Bradley has to make is that Sidgwick's view entails the conclusion that we must 'have a system of casuistry' (*Hedonism*, p. 105), and the point of the charge is that insistence on a full objective code is self-defeating. The code must be developed in such infinite detail to accommodate the objective differences between individuals that in the end it will amount, not to an objective code for all, but to a separate code for each. For either you stop codifying at some point, in which case you 'throw the code over', or else you 'attempt to get every possible complication within its clauses', in which case you are on the way to allowing so many exceptions that you no longer have a general code. (*Hedonism*, pp. 107–15.) Bradley is attacking Sidgwick here on the assumption that Sidgwick is a utilitarian. He does not, however, discuss much of what Sidgwick actually says about the utilitarian's proper method. Nor does he consider that the utilitarian would naturally reply, in answer to his general point, that there is a utilitarian limit to the amount of complication one ought to include in an explicit moral code, a limit far short of the lengths to which Bradley thinks the codifier must go. If this does not answer all of Bradley's objections, it at least suggests that they are far from being totally destructive of Sidgwick's position as regards the formulation of rules for general recognition. Bradley's more basic objection, that Sidgwick misconceives the function of philosophy, raises other problems, which will be touched on in connection with Green.

In his review of *Ethical Studies*, Sidgwick remarks that 'really penetrating criticism, especially in ethics, requires a patient effort of sympathy which Mr. Bradley has never learned to make, and a tranquility of temper which he seems incapable of maintaining' (1876c, 545). Though Bradley's attack on Sidgwick makes a few telling points, it largely illustrates the truth of this comment. Sidgwick changed some passages in the *Methods* in response to Bradley's objections—he purposely waited until the pamphlet appeared before completing his alterations for the second edition[9]—but perhaps he felt he would not maintain a proper tranquillity of temper himself if he tried a direct reply. As for Bradley's own position, Sidgwick thinks it is not worthy of much serious attention. His comment on the famous essay on 'My Station and Its Duties' shows him again relying on his own view of what an ethical theory should do. The position sketched in that essay, though it seems to be accepted by Bradley, will be unsatisfactory, Sidgwick says, to 'those who have been stimulated to ethical inquiry by the palpable inadequacy of the very common sense which is here offered as the solution of their difficulties'. The qualifications Bradley introduces in the later chapters of his book of the position sketched here remove the paradoxical character of the view. But 'it is also stripped of its apparent definiteness and completeness, and reduced to little more than a vague and barren ethical commonplace, dressed in a new metaphysical formula' (1876c, 518–19). A more determined and thorough effort to construct an idealistic alternative in ethics was made by T. H. Green, whose *Prolegomena to Ethics* has been called, by the finest of his commentators, 'the greatest

---

[9] BM Add. MSS. 551–9, fos. 10–11, letter of 30 Jan. 1877 to Macmillan, his publisher.

treatise on moral philosophy produced by the British school of Idealism'.[10]

iii. *Idealism: T. H. Green*

Green and Sidgwick had many similarities. Both from religious homes, they went to Rugby where, as we saw, they knew each other and discussed philosophy;[11] both began to question their inherited faith; both turned to philosophy in response to these questionings; both broke with convention by refusing to take clerical orders despite their pursuit of academic careers; both were involved, at their respective universities, in improving the teaching of philosophy; both were more widely read in German thought than was usual at the time. Both of them were concerned about the literal truth of the Christian doctrine, and the following passage, though in fact written by Green, might well have come from Sidgwick:

> And what strikes me as most conspicuously lacking in the best writing of Churchmen that I come across is any attempt to meet the objection that their distinctive doctrine is untrue. They are very successful in adapting it to the spirit, and showing that it will meet the wants, of the age; but they scarcely seem aware that all this makes no difference to those whose first interest is in truth.[12]

But the important similarities, one is tempted to say, end at about this point. Green seems to have been far more committed than Sidgwick to maintaining the truth of Christianity, in some form or other, under some interpretation or other. 'There can be no greater satisfaction to me', he wrote a friend and former pupil in 1872, after the latter's ordination,

> than to think that I at all helped to lay the intellectual platform for your religious life. . . . if I were only a breeder of heretics I should suspect my philosophy. If it is sound, it ought to supply intellectual formulae for the religious life whether lived by an 'orthodox'

---

[10] W. D. Lamont, *Introduction to Green's Moral Philosophy*, 1934, p. 19.

[11] Green and Sidgwick travelled on the continent together in 1862 with their friends, and were sporadically in contact thereafter. In his reminiscences of the 1862 tour Sidgwick wrote, 'I was at the time in a crude and confident stage of utilitarianism, and quite unappreciative of his [Green's] line of thought, which I believed myself justified in regarding as a blind alley . . .' (Reminiscences of T. H. Green, Green papers, Balliol.)

[12] Green in a letter to Henry Scott Holland in 1869, in Stephen Paget, *Henry Scott Holland*, 1921, p. 42.

clergyman or (let us say) a follower of Mazzini. As you know, I never dreamt of philosophy doing instead of religion. My own interest in it, I believe, is wholly religious; in the sense that it is to me . . . the reasoned intellectual expression of the effort to get to God . . . I hold that all true morality must be religious, in the sense of resting upon the consciousness of God: and that if in modern life it some-times seems to be otherwise, this is either because the consciousness of God, from the intellectual obstacles cannot express itself, or because the morality is not the highest . . .[13]

For Sidgwick, philosophy is the rational search for truth, and if Christianity turns out to possess it, so much the better for Christianity. For Green, it seems, philosophy has the task of showing that Christianity does possess the truth, and if the philosopher fails to come to that result, then it follows that he has more work to do.[14]

Green's philosophy centres on the belief that human life is the reproduction in our finite selves of the life of a self-conscious spirit, infinite and divine. Human knowledge, Green argues, is only possible because the divine spirit already holds all things together in its infinite mind and partially reproduces its comprehension in us; and man's goal is a realization of him-self in which he must try to come as close as possible to the perfection of the divine being. It is not difficult to see how this might serve as an intellectual formula for a religious life. It is harder to see it as a cogent system of philosophy. Sidgwick himself thought the metaphysics basically in-coherent (1884b, 175; *Mem.*, pp. 380, 586 n.) and beset with ambiguities and waverings at key points. These criticisms he

[13] Paget, *Holland*, pp. 65–6.

[14] Among other similarities between the two was the relative success of their books on ethics. With the printing figures given by Richter (*Green*, p. 294 n.) for Green's *Prolegomena* we may compare those, supplied very kindly by Mr. T. M. Farmiloe of Macmillan, for Sidgwick's *Methods*:

Methods	*Prolegomena*
1874: 1000	1883: 1000
1877: 1250	1885: 2000
1884: 1250	1891: 2500
1890: 1250	1899: 3000
1893: 1500	
1901: 1500	

Spencer's *First Principles* was advertised in 1893, thirty years after its publication, as being in its 'eighth thousand'.

expounded at length (*LPK*, pp. 209–66), but we shall restrict ourselves to his discussion of the ethics. Here his comments fall into four sets, dealing with four respects in which Green presents challenges to his own position. First, of course, Green bases morality on metaphysics, and claims that no other way of supporting a non-naturalistic ethic can be found. Second, he develops a psychology of action from his metaphysics which, he claims, is the only one making morality possible. Third, he argues that the moral principle he derives from his metaphysics provides a better account of morality than any other principle, a claim supported by a lengthy analysis of Greek and modern conceptions of virtue. He also offers a justification of the limits he sets on the possibility of using his principle as the foundation for a method of correcting existing morality. And finally he presents a number of criticisms of hedonistic utilitarianism, which he takes to be the main alternative to his own view.

On matters falling under this last heading we may be brief. Green's criticisms of utilitarianism are for the most part directed against an imprecise amalgam of the views of Bentham and J. S. Mill. He is particularly concerned to refute psychological egoism, returning to it again and again and claiming that it vitiates the whole utilitarian doctrine. Sidgwick attributes this partly to Green's ignorance of the fact that there were utilitarians, from Hume onward, who did not hold such a psychological view (*GSM*, pp. 104–5). In any case this limitation of his outlook, together with his failure to give careful attention to the way Sidgwick presents utilitarianism, make it unnecessary to consider Green's criticisms of ethical hedonism any further than we have already done. Green's philosophy can challenge Sidgwick's only by presenting a constructive systematization of morality better than his.

Green's claim to superiority begins with the assertion that he has unified the 'is' and the 'ought' where Sidgwick could see no way to do so. The unification has two parts. The spiritual principle or infinite self-consciousness supplies both the content of morality, and the conditions without which morality could not exist. As to the first, Green thinks his arguments prove the existence of one spiritual being as presupposed by the existence both of knowledge and of nature. This being we can at best characterize, on Green's own showing, as a mind which is self-conscious, which distinguishes its aspects from itself, and which combines these aspects into one eternal, changeless whole. Green shows no hesitation in moving without further ado to the treatment of this being as divine, and in saying that it is in virtue of the fact that 'the one divine mind gradually reproduces itself in the human soul' that 'man has definite capabilities, the realization of which . . . forms his true good'. (*Prol. E.*, 180.)[15] Sidgwick argues that it is hard to see what justifies us in thinking of the one eternal being as a mind at all, let alone a holy or divine mind. (*GSM*, pp. 13 f.; 1884b, 172.) And even if we should so conceive it, the idea seems 'barren' for ethical purposes. If all we know of it is that it distinguishes itself from itself and combines thoughts into an eternal whole, how does this provide us with an ideal capable of guiding action? Such an eternal being must be the presupposition of any sort of change in the natural world. Its existence therefore does not imply change in any particular direction, and hence nothing we should call improvement or progress. Moreover, since the eternal being is simply a knower, its existence implies nothing about the value of a good will, which Green intends to show is vital to moral goodness. There is thus, Sidgwick says, 'a great logical gap to be filled up in passing' from Green's metaphysics to his ethics, even supposing both of them to be sound. (*GSM*, p. 12.) The 'is' and the 'ought' are not yet unified.

Sidgwick adds a further point which suggests that they cannot be unified, at least not in Green's way. If the spiritual principle is an eternally complete being gradually reproducing itself in finite centres, it is hard to see any point to moral struggle and the attempt to make moral improvements in oneself, when these are taken, in Green's terms, as being the moral aspect (however that is to be understood) of the gradual reproduction of the eternal being in us. For 'there are no conceivable perfections that can be added to' the eternal mind, 'and the process of man's moral effort is surely futile if it is to end in nothing but the existence of that which exists already' (1884b, 179; cf. *ME* 7, p. 115). Sidgwick grants that a similar

---

[15] References to Green's *Prolegomena in Ethics*, ed. A. C. Bradley, Oxford, 1883, are by paragraph numbers.

problem arises from any theological point of view which is at all akin to commonly held religious beliefs. For it is hard to see how a deity could either need anything that the history of the world can bring into being, or could fail to obtain it; and it is hard to see also how a man's own efforts could meaningfully be involved. But, he says, he himself, unlike Green, draws from this collision of morality with the religious consciousness the conclusion that 'we ought not to use these theological notions' for philosophy until they can be 'purged of such palpable inconsistencies'. (1884b, 179; cf. *ME* 7, p. 79.) Green's metaphysics then not only fails to give direct support to a moral principle, it also threatens to negate one of the conditions necessary for meaningful morality. It may be added that this criticism helps us understand Sidgwick's reluctance to attempt a religious solution of the final problem in the *Methods*.

Green himself holds that free will is a necessary condition for the existence of morality, and he argues that free will can be defended only on the basis of a metaphysic like his own. The evolutionists, he says, give a plain illustration of the consequences of pure naturalism. They produce laws according to which man does behave, but they can make no sense of any 'ought', since 'to a being who is simply a result of natural forces, an injunction to conform to their laws is unmeaning'. (*Prol. E.*, 7.) Green's account of free will, which is similar to Bradley's, attempts to avoid both deterministic, Hobbesian, explanations of free action and indifferentist views which turn freedom into 'an arbitrary freak of some unaccountable power of unmotived willing'. (*Prol. E.*, 110.) If we explain behaviour as resulting from the interplay of circumstance and character, and see that character results from the action of self-consciousness upon desires arising from our animal nature, then, Green thinks, we can account for imputability, shame, remorse, and the other features of morality dependent on free will. Sidgwick's main criticism is that Green claims a greater distance between his own view and determinism than really exists. Green is, rightly in Sidgwick's opinion, trying to account for a kind of freedom which may be present equally in vicious and in virtuous action. Green says that this kind of freedom exists because animal desires do not, in humans, directly lead to action. They must first be taken up and brought together in some self-consciously constructed combination, in the realization of which the agent sees his own good. In this process some are rejected. They remain mere 'solicitations', and do not affect action. It is thus the supervention of the spiritual principle reproducing itself in finite beings which makes the difference between human freedom and animal determination. Yet how are we to explain why one finite self-distinguishing consciousness acts virtuously and another viciously? We cannot appeal to the fact, which is common to both in equal degree, that they are self-distinguishing consciousnesses. We must appeal to the 'animal base' from which arise those 'solicitations' which may or may not become full-fledged desires. But the animal base, since it is without the self-conciousness which is crucial to freedom, is entirely determined. Hence, Sidgwick says, 'determinism wins on the substantial issue'. (*GSM*, pp. 19–20.) Green's failure to give an adequate general account of the relations between the animal base of finite minds and the infinite spirit, on which Sidgwick comments elsewhere (*LPK*, pp. 244 ff.) is reflected in the collapse of his account of freedom.

Of the numerous criticisms Sidgwick makes on further points of Green's moral psychology, there are two worth notice. Green's metaphysics, together with his need for a defence of freedom, lead him to hold that in every act of willing a man's aim is some good for himself, some realization of himself in a state of affairs projected as his own good. Green strenuously denies that this good is or must be always the agent's own pleasure. A man may identify himself with, or find his good in, any coherent state of affairs, including one that involves considerable sacrifice of his animal existence. Sidgwick, of course, agrees; but he holds that 'the same analysis which shows me that I do not always aim at my own pleasure, shows me equally that I do not always aim at my own satisfaction' (*GSM*, p. 103). A second serious problem arises from the same view of the form of human willing. It seems to follow from Green's theory of volition that any mistakes in action must be due to intellectual error. For if in all voluntary action a man seeks to realize himself in what he takes to be his own good, the difference between the virtuous and the vicious man must be that the former has a better idea of where his true good lies. (*Prol. E.*, 171, 234.) Allowing that there are other aspects of Green's thought, unreconciled with this one, which do not lead to this conclusion (*GSM*, p. 41), Sidgwick still insists that the significance of the problem is considerable. Green's philosophy is alleged to give us a theory which will explicate the moral consciousness at the stage at which it has now arrived. Green thinks Christianity enabled man to make notable advances in moral insight (cf. e.g. *Prol. E.*, 266–8). Yet his wavering on whether vicious choice arises from simple mistake, and his seeming inability to explain knowing choice of sin, display, Sidgwick says, 'pagan or neo-pagan forms of ethical thought combined with Christian or post-Christian forms without any proper philosophical reconciliation' (1884b, 183).

These points, which may suffice to indicate the kind of objection Sidgwick raises about Green's varied uses of metaphysics, lead naturally to the main theme of their controversy, the ethical theme. A number of Sidgwick's objections concern what he takes to be serious internal problems with the system. For example, he argues that Green alternates between defining the good as the abidingly satisfying and defining it as the self-realizing (whether satisfaction is felt or not); that he vacillates between taking the good to involve realization of all our capacities, and taking it to involve the realization only of our moral capacities; and that while he criticizes the utilitarian for proposing an end which as a mere sum of vanishing entities is unattainable, his own end is, on his own showing, also unattainable. These weaknesses affect Green's handling of the problem of reconciling self-interest and concern for others. He seems to hold that the only true good is a good with respect to which competition is inconceivable. If so, this would resolve the problem; yet, Sidgwick says, it is not easy to make Green's idea of a non-competitive good coherent. To do so one must restrict the range of true goods so greatly that one comes into serious conflict with common sense. But if some real goods allow of unequal distribution, and if competition for them is possible, as Green's own discussion of justice seems to presuppose, then the problem of adjusting the claims of self and others is both serious and unresolved. From a different point of view, the very possibility of self-sacrifice seems, on the basis of Green's moral psychology, to be excluded. But Green seems at times (e.g. *Prol. E.*, 176) to think it called for, while at other times (cf. *Prol. E.*, 247) he seems to deny its moral necessity, on grounds which are never made entirely clear. Green's philosophy, if Sidgwick is right, thus plainly fails to meet the demand that a system of ethics must be internally clear and consistent. Sidgwick's reasons for thinking that it fails to meet the other demands placed on a moral system emerge from consideration of his remarks on Green's view of the limits to the applicability of a philosophical principle of morals to practice.

In his 'Introduction' to Hume, Green criticizes Butler for giving a circular, and therefore vacuous, account of the moral good. Butler, he says, tells us that the moral good is defined as what is approved by the faculty of approbation; 'but what it is that this "faculty" approves he never distinctly tells us. The good is what conscience approves, and conscience is what approves the good—that is the circle . . .'[16] Yet his own mature view seems to involve a similarly vacuous conception of the ultimate good. His search for a perfectly non-competitive good leads him to take human perfection, construed narrowly as moral perfection or the possession of a good will, as the moral end; and he is therefore compelled to say that the moral good is the will that wills the good will, and the good will is the will that wills the moral good. (*Prol. E.*, 172.) Like Bradley, he holds that 'man . . . cannot know what his capabilities are till they are realised'. Because of this, he argues, definitions of the moral ideal, if at all near the mark, will necessarily be open to the charge of circularity. Hedonism, indeed, avoids it, but only at the cost of denying that the perfection of man is the end. (*Prol. E.*, 194.) Admit that the end is human perfection, and one must conclude that it is 'not an illogical procedure, because it is the only procedure suited to the matter in hand, to say that the goodness of man lies in devotion to the ideal of humanity, and then that the ideal of humanity consists in the goodness of man'. Green explains further:

such an ideal, not yet realised but operating as a motive, already constitutes in man an inchoate form of that life . . . of which the completion would be the realised ideal itself. Now in relation to a nature such as ours . . . this ideal becomes . . . a categorical imperative. But when we ask ourselves what it is that this imperative

[16] Green, *Works*, i. 327.

commands to be done . . . We can then only say that the categorical imperative commands us to obey the categorical imperative . . . the basis of morality . . . is the duty of realising an ideal which cannot be adequately defined till it is realised . . . (*Prol. E.*, 196.)

For Green, then, morality depends far more fully than is at first apparent on the spiritual reality which makes the world possible for us. His confidence that man can learn what to do in particular cases rests directly on his assurance that the divine spirit is reproducing itself in us. Practical reason is for him—and in all essentials for Bradley as well—what Butler called the voice of God speaking within us, and what Whewell described as insight into moral ideas in God's mind. Because of this Green, like Bradley, resists any kind of system which assumes that we can know now, in principle at least, fully and completely what we ought to do. His metaphysically based concept of practical reason thus gives rise to a view profoundly different from Sidgwick's of the expectations we should have of a system of moral philosophy. Green never altered the conviction he expressed in 1872: 'I hold that all true morality must be religious, in the sense of resting upon the consciousness of God.'[17] This conviction displays the deepest of the ties between the older intuitionism and the moral philosophy of first-generation British idealism, and shows again why Sidgwick's severance of his use of the appeal to intuition from any reliance on such views marks one of the greatest differences between his position and theirs.

It is not surprising, therefore, to find that Sidgwick repeatedly objects to Green's view on the grounds that it provides no principle from which specific rules or judgements can be derived. He does little more, indeed, than to reiterate the objection in several contexts. Thus he points out that no way is offered of measuring and comparing the different elements of which human perfection, understood along Green's lines as including realization of our capacities in art and science, is composed: but when we have to make moral decisions, we must have some rational way of working out their relative worths. (*GSM*, pp. 46–7.) He adds that since on Green's view we always remain indefinitely far from perfection, we cannot

[17] Paget, *Holland*, pp. 65–6.

take perfection as a goal, by our approach to which we can measure the goodness of action. (*GSM*, pp. 48–9.) Later he points out that 'one of the subtlest and deepest of the impulses that prompt intellectual natures to vice is the desire for full and varied realization of capabilities, for richness of experience ...'. (*GSM*, p. 64.) Hence if the good lies in self-realization, a sinner may realize himself as much as a saint, and so no criterion for choice is derivable from Green's concept of the end. At the conclusion of his lectures on Green Sidgwick explains why he has so little to say on this vital point. Concerning Green's claim that his concept of the good does aid in making choices and criticizing existing moral beliefs, Sidgwick says that this is 'a purely dogmatic assertion unsupported by proofs. I cannot find', he adds wearily, 'any indication of the manner in which the notion of perfection supplies a *rational method* for reforming conventional morality ... If I could have found it, I would have examined it critically, but I can find nothing sufficiently definite for criticism to bite upon.' (*GSM*, 114–15.)

Nor is this the end of the matter. The idealists conceive the moral philosopher as the historian of the developing consciousness of the principles of morality; and they claim that this history can be better explained in terms of their general outlook than on any other basis. Sidgwick thinks this claim seriously mistaken, not merely because of his doubts about their metaphysics, but precisely because they will not or cannot provide a moral principle from which we can derive a rational method for reforming conventional morality. This emerges from one of his criticisms of Green. Green thinks we can obtain some guidance from the standards and the code of our own society. Though his tone in discussing this differs markedly from Bradley's, they agree in holding that the abstract demands of morality find concrete content in the institutions in which the progress of the divine spirit has thus far embodied itself. Sidgwick asks how this can be known. 'If we do not know in what fulfilment of man's capabilities consists, how are we to know how progress is made towards it?' To Green's answer, that positive law and positive morality are 'an expression of the absolute imperative to seek . . . the ideal of humanity' (*Prol. E.*, 197), Sidgwick's objection is plain. Examination of ordinary morality simply does not bear Green out. Common-sense rules do not reveal 'any reference to perfection of charac-ter as end. The evils that these rules aim at preventing are pain, and the loss of the material means of physical well-being . . . the good that they aim at distributing rightly is of the same kind.' (*GSM*, pp. 76–7.) Sidgwick can appeal to the substantial work of the *Methods* to back up this claim, or the equally anti-idealistic claim that egoism offers an adequate systematization of common-sense morality as well. And if the argument of the *Methods* was constructed with an eye to earlier attempts to show that morality rests on, and leads us to, 'the consciousness of God', its relevance to Green's version of the effort is still clear. Bradley did not even attempt to substantiate the idealists' historical claims about morality, and Sidgwick's detailed criticism of Green's discussion of Greek morality and moral philosophy shows both the inadequacies of Green's historical vision and his failure to enrol Aristotle in a consensus in his favour. But there is a point beyond particular difficulties with idealistic reconstructions of the development of morality, a point which, though Sidgwick is not fully explicit about it, follows from what he has said. Green's admission of the forward-looking impotence of his principle vitiates his view as to its retrospective strength. A moral principle too vacuous to support a method of rational criticism is necessarily too weak to sustain a method of historical explanation.

15

Sidgwick and the History of Ethics

SIDGWICK is unique among British moralists in the extent to which he uses a wide and profound knowledge of the speculations of his predecessors in the construction and explanation of his own position. The fact is partly obscured because the historical references were decreased from edition to edition of the *Methods* though never wholly eliminated. The presentation of his own axioms as developments of positions put forth by Clarke and Kant, for example, was dropped after the first edition. The most purely historical comment, which concerns the difference between ancient and modern approaches to moral philosophy, was almost fully retained through the third edition, relegated in part to a footnote in the next two, and cut to its final form only in the sixth edition. (*ME* 1, pp. 93–5; *ME* 3, pp. 120–3; *ME* 4, p. 106; *ME* 7, pp. 105–6.) The usual intent of the particular historical comments is to show that Sidgwick's own position effects a synthesis of the major aspects of the work of the great thinkers of the past, a point which is important because of his belief in the significance of a consensus of experts in establishing a flourishing and progressive discipline. But Sidgwick's knowledge of the history of ethics does more than give him an additional kind of argument in favour of his conclusions. The whole way in which the problems of ethics are viewed and treated in the *Methods* is affected by his general idea of the development of moral philosophy. For this reason we must look briefly at his sketch of that development.

i. *Sidgwick's History of Ethics*

The *Outlines of the History of Ethics for English Readers* began as the article on 'Ethics' for the ninth edition of the *Encyclopaedia Britannica* and was completed early in 1878. In expanding it for separate publication, as in revising it for later editions, Sidgwick made no essential changes, though he reworded many passages, enlarged the treatment of various minor figures such

as Bonaventura and Eckhart, and added sections on developments such as those represented by Spencer, Green, and
Schopenhauer. That the book has been found useful for a
century is one indication of its remarkable qualities. These do
not seem less when we compare it with earlier histories in
English.

A number of nineteenth-century British writers attempted to
survey the history of ethics, some in volumes devoted solely to
that aim, some in connection with more general histories of
philosophy or literature. Mackintosh, Blakey, Hallam, Morell,
and Whewell are the chief among them. Sidgwick's work is
superior to all of theirs in scope, in depth of philosophic grasp,
and, most importantly, in the mode in which the subject is
treated. None of the others deal seriously with ancient or
medieval philosophy, as Sidgwick does, and for the most part
it seems to be as much as the authors can do to outline the
main conclusions the different philosophers reached. Any
presentation, let alone analysis, of the arguments leading to
those conclusions seem beyond most of them. Whewell is an
exception. His history is shaped by his theory of scientific
knowledge, which provides the pattern he follows in presenting
the development of ethics. While he is weak in explaining the
internal structure of the thought of any given philosopher, he
at least brings out to some extent the ways in which various
positions stand in logical and not merely in chronological
relation to one another. Yet Whewell, like all the others,
writes his history with a polemical intent. His aim is to give the
support of history to the proposition that morality can best be
understood if it is systematized in a way that shows the claims
of Christianity to be true. He is more sophisticated in doing
this than Mackintosh or Blakey or Morrell, but a similarly
apologetic intent underlies their work as well. Sidgwick, by
contrast, tries to present a history which can be accepted by
readers of all persuasions. The brief systematic introduction to
the problems of ethics as well as the historical body of the work
is meant in this way. 'I aimed', he writes of the introduction,
'at giving not "my own conception", but a conception which
would be generally accepted as adequately impartial and
comprehensive by thinkers of different schools at the present
day.' (*Hist.*, p. ix.) This aim, which dictates much of the way

in which the analysis of argument is handled in the *History*, itself arises from a need whose history Sidgwick is concerned to trace.

Moral philosophy, Sidgwick thinks, began with the 'naïve and fragmentary utterances of sage precepts for conduct in which nascent moral reflection everywhere first manifests itself' (*Hist.*, p. 12). The pre-Socratics did not advance far in creating moral philosophy because they were not sufficiently critical of the accepted morality of their times. A proper moral philosophy, Sidgwick says, 'could not be satisfactorily constructed until attention had been strongly directed to the vagueness and inconsistency of the common moral opinions of mankind', and to do this properly took the genius of Socrates. (*Hist.*, p. 16.) Though the sophists began the work, it was he who took it furthest and who first grasped in its basic and permanent outline the nature and task of moral philosophy:

while he is always attacking common opinion, and showing it, from its inconsistencies, not to be knowledge, still the premises of his arguments are always taken from the common thought which he shares with his interlocutors, and the knowledge which he seeks is implicitly assumed to be something that will harmonise and not overthrow these common beliefs. (*Hist.*, p. 29.)

Sidgwick sees several strands of philosophy developing out of the work of Socrates, all attempting in various ways to harmonize the different elements of Greek belief about how to live. The main theme in all of them is the good for man, and their main question is how to bring the different goods man pursues into unity. As Sidgwick stresses in the *Methods*, at the start and for a long period thereafter the good was simply assumed to include two things we now sharply distinguish— pleasure and virtue or duty. There was not felt to be any antagonism between what is good in itself and what is good for man, and indeed for the individual man. (Cf. *ME* 1, p. 94; *ME* 7, pp. 105–6; *Hist.*, pp. 48–9, 52, 55 ff.) With the Stoics Sidgwick sees a new, and transitional, element entering Greek thought, and leading to one of the distinctive contributions of the Christian tradition. This is the stress on obedience to law. (*Hist.*, pp. 73 ff., 97 ff.) Sidgwick sees this as helping to create the modern view of morality, in which the idea of a moral code is central, rather than the idea of goodness or virtue. Christianity spread the juristic idea of morality as 'the positive law of a theocratic community, possessing a written code imposed by divine revelation', backed by explicit divine sanctions, and covering, at least implicitly, 'all occasions of life'. (*Hist.*, pp. 110–11.) Christianity also led men to emphasize different virtues from those to which the Greeks gave priority. The most important change of this kind brought by Christianity to our common moral opinions was 'the impulse given to practical beneficence . . . by the exaltation of love as the root of all virtues'. (*Hist.*, p. 121.) These new elements created new problems for those who wished to present the intellectual aspect of Christianity in systematic form. As far as its moral teaching is concerned, Sidgwick takes Ambrose, the teacher of Augustine, to be the first who gave 'an exposition of Christian duty systematized on a plan borrowed from a pre-Christian moralist' (*Hist.*, p. 133), and views the work of Albert the Great and Thomas Aquinas as completing the working out of a combination of Christian belief with the most systematic form of Greek thought, Aristotle's. (*Hist.*, p. 140.)

Unlike Whewell, Sidgwick does not see the next important phase in moral philosophy originating in the attempts of the Protestant casuists of reformed England to work out a religious ethic in terms of their own version of Christianity. (*Hist.*, pp. 154–5; cf. Whewell, *Lec. Hist.*, pp. 25 ff.) He takes it to have begun with a revival of the attempt 'to find an independent philosophical basis' for morality. The renewal of the classical endeavour was due in part to the rediscovery of classical texts and the recovery of Greek thought, but more importantly it was stimulated by the struggles between Protestants and Catholics, between reformers and counter-reformers. The old consensus disappeared: scientific as well as religious developments shattered the old framework of belief. It was only to be expected that in ethics as in natural science a demand for investigation untrammelled by any externally imposed limits would be made: 'and indeed, amid the clash of dogmatic convictions, that the multiplying divisions of Christendom exhibited after the Reformation, reflective persons would naturally be led to seek for an ethical method that—relying solely on the common reason and common moral experience

of mankind—might claim universal acceptance from all sects.'
(*Hist.*, p. 157.)

This, then, is what Sidgwick sees as the central problem of
moral philosophy in its modern period. And it is plain that his
own ethics, relying only on an absolute minimum of debatable
non-moral assertion, finding its foundations in the bearing of
common human reason on action, harmonizing our common
moral experience, and culminating in a method for settling
disputes about the goods for which men compete, is an attempt
to resolve it. His history is also constructed with this central need in mind. This is what differentiates it so markedly
from that of Whewell and the earlier British historians of
ethics. As can be seen most clearly in Whewell, they assume
that the history of moral philosophy begins with a striving
toward Christian truth which philosophy alone cannot reach,
that it continues with an elaboration of Christian truth in
terms of human rationality, and that it goes on as a protracted
defence of Christian truth against paganism, heresy, and mere
worldly indifference or selfishness. Sidgwick sees no such
difference of principle in the nature of the task of moral philosophy in its different periods. The differences among the
periods arise from the differences in the elements of common
belief the philosopher is called upon to criticize and ultimately
to systematize. Christian experience and moral teaching simply
added an element to the problem: they did not provide the
indispensable, and otherwise unattainable, clue to the solution.

Sidgwick views the history of moral philosophy predominantly internally. He does not deny that political events and
intellectual advances in other fields influence the history of
ethics. Indeed he stresses the importance of the spread of
Christianity, at one time, and the urgent need for political
stability, at another, as decisive factors in determining the
course of ethical speculation. But he devotes his attention
almost entirely to the way in which one attempt at systematization gives rise to others as omissions, exaggerations,
errors, and logical faults in earlier work come to light through
criticism and analysis. To a far greater extent than in the
writings of the earlier historians, therefore, the points at which
he ventures his own criticisms of the views of a historical figure
are points at which the criticism brings out the logic underlying

the next step in the actual historical development. Criticism simply for the sake of supporting a position he takes to be true is almost entirely absent from Sidgwick's *History*. This is one of the features of the work which has made it so enduringly useful.

ii. *Sidgwick in the History of Ethics*

If we take Sidgwick's ethics as an effort to resolve the problem he thinks is central in the history of modern moral philosophy, we can get a clear idea of the relation of his work to that of his predecessors. Though there are innumerable places where his analytical insight enables him to formulate particular issues with a clarity and fullness previously unmatched, his most profound and original contributions emerge in and from his exploration of the ways in which the requirements of reason and the constraints of actuality combine in common moral belief. Like many great philosophical ideas, his basic thought is at once simple in itself and complex in its bearings. Reason, for him, is simply the common human ability to obtain truths which everyone ought to accept and which are connected through the unique relationship of 'being a reason for' in structures containing propositions of greater and lesser generality. The constraints under which reason must operate in guiding action can be summarized in two uncontroversial assertions. First, each person is a rational and sentient being with an identity persisting over time who can to some extent control his own actions by the conclusions to which his reason leads him. Second, there are a multiplicity of such beings affecting one another. The starting-point of Sidgwick's argument is the demonstration, through reasoning and appeal to introspection, that we have a unique, irreducible concept of 'being a reason for' as it applies to action and to desire. From this concept we learn that our own ability to reason involves a unique kind of demand on both the active and the sentient aspects of our nature, the demand that our acts and desires be reasonable. Since, therefore, it must be possible to give reasons for our desires and actions, a complex argument involving the elimination of various principles which might serve as the ultimate determinant of such reasons leads to the conclusion that a maximizing consequentialist principle must be the most basic principle of rationality in practice. Further eliminative argument shows that the end set for us by this principle must be interpreted hedonistically. These arguments bring out what the essence of rationality in practice is, given the facts of human existence. Further argument shows that it is possible to embody this rationality in daily life through a code like that exemplified in ordinary moral belief. At least it is possible up to a point. In addition to problems of detail in working out a perfectly rational code, there is a problem of principle. The two propositions stating the constraints under which reason must be practical indicate that guidance is needed for beings of a dual nature. Each of us is, first, the possessor of a private consciousness and, next, a member of a community of interacting possessors of such consciousnesses. There are reasonable requirements for the possessor of the private consciousness, and there are reasonable requirements for the interacting conscious agents. But they do not coincide. This forces Sidgwick to the unhappy conclusion that the best that reason can do in coping with the actuality of human nature in the world as it exists, is to impose demands which in the end are incompatible. Sidgwick's conclusion is that the problem his historical analysis leads him to take as central to modern ethics cannot be fully resolved.

To no major historical figure does Sidgwick have closer affinities than to Bishop Butler. His reconstruction of Butler's insistence that concern for one's own good and concern for the good of others both equally embody the same sort of practical rationality is only the most noticeable of the similarities in their thought. It is more significant that Sidgwick develops Butler's methodology to a high degree of self-consciousness and completeness. One of Butler's main beliefs, presented in the second Sermon, is that moral philosophy must rely upon the contents of the moral experience of the normal human being, just as natural philosophy must rely upon their sensory experience. No general doubt can be cast upon the moral beliefs which emerge from this experience by truths drawn from other kinds of experience, nor can any proof of their reliability be based upon other kinds of truth. His reason for this view is suggested in the pregnant paragraph at the end of the 'Dissertation on Personal Identity':

It is ridiculous to attempt to prove the truth of those perceptions, whose truth we can no otherwise prove than by other perceptions of exactly the same kind with them, and which there is just the same ground to suspect; or to attempt to prove the truth of our faculties, which can no otherwise be proved, than by the use or means of those very suspected faculties themselves.

Precisely this position, with its assumption that moral concepts are not reducible to non-moral ones, underlies Sidgwick's mode of treating received moral opinion. But Sidgwick moves well beyond Butler in the thoroughness with which he works out the view that our moral beliefs are or can be rational. Where Butler refused to elaborate a theory, Sidgwick, like Whewell, holds that the development of a systematic understanding of our moral experience is the central task of ethics.

It is tempting to describe the dominant philosophical strategy which Sidgwick uses to carry out this task as a Kantian attempt to work out the sole conditions under which reason can be practical. Certainly his basic aim is similar to Kant's, but, as his many points of disagreement with Kant suggest, the Kantian aspect of his thinking needs to be defined with some care. He detaches the issue of how reason can be practical from the most distinctive aspects of Kantianism. He rejects the methodological apparatus of the 'critical philosophy', the Kantian distinction of noumenal and phenomenal standpoints, and the association of the issue with the problem of free will. He treats the question of the possibility of rationally motivated action as answerable largely in terms of commonplace facts; he does not attribute any special synthesizing powers to reason beyond those assumed in ordinary logic; and he does not take morality to provide us with support for religious beliefs. In refusing to base morality on pure reason alone, moreover, he moves decisively away from Kant, as is shown by his very un-Kantian hedonistic and teleological conclusions. These points make it clear that the Kantian strain in Sidgwick's thought is most marked in his central idea about the rationality of first principles. Substantive first principles of morality are not the most basic embodiment of practical rationality. The rationality of these principles is a consequence of requirements set by more formal principles which themselves delineate the general activity of reasoning, when the formal principles are applied in the circumstances of human life. Intuition is then explicable as the understanding a reasonable being has of the nature of his own activity as reasonable. If this is Kantianism, then it is not inaccurate to think of Sidgwick as a Kantian. For this is the basic thought which enables Sidgwick to reshape the issues of ethics as they reached him through his British predecessors.

The point can be illustrated by considering his treatment of egoism. Sidgwick goes beyond earlier philosophers in showing how a simple requirement of reason, applied to practice, amounts to a demand that each man pursue his own maximal well-being. In doing this Sidgwick uncovers the real strength of the many previous assertions that concern for one's own welfare is a duty. His philosophical interest in elucidating the problems of rational action also leads him to follow up the implications of this position more fully than his predecessors. He allows no evasions of the difficulties raised by the view that self-interest is as reasonable as concern for others. Thus he eschews the easy avoidance of the issues which was available to Butler and the many nineteenth-century Butlerians through their religious assurance of a cosmic moral order. He rejects Plato's attempt to show that for psychological reasons pure egoism is self-destructive, as well as Hobbes's attempt to show, on socio-political grounds, that enlightened self-interest leads one to adopt a set of norms which are not themselves egoistic. And he denies the Kantian assumption that the rationality of self-interest is so obviously of a lower degree of authority than that of morality that no difficulty of principle can arise. These negations, coupled with his refusal to eliminate egoism by means of a restrictive substantive definition of the concept of morality, lead him to work out more fully than any earlier philosopher the conceptual implications of taking self-interest to be one basic reasonable principle of action on a par with others.

The same understanding of the rationality of moral principles is at the root of Sidgwick's reconciliation of intuitionism and utilitarianism. The earlier utilitarians claimed that their principle simply expressed the demands of rationality on action. Yet although they showed how their principle could ground a rational decision procedure, they did not succeed in bringing out the rationality of the principle itself. Sidgwick's revision of intuitionism enables him to try to supply the deficiency. He eliminates from the intuitional position the last elements of commitment to the view, still evident in Whewell, that the rationality of morality results from our possessing a faculty which enables us to perceive accurately some external entity or property. More fully than his intuitional predecessors, Sidgwick sees that the objectivity of morality must be the consequence, not the source, of its rationality. By insisting on this he not only removes the feature of intuitionism which most repelled the utilitarians—the arbitrariness of the list of principles discovered by the moral faculty, and the consequent misuse to which appeal to such a faculty is liable—he also lays the ground for that deeper justification of the utilitarian principle which the utilitarians themselves had been unable to give. The utilitarian principle is shown to be one of the first principles to which the reasonable man is led when he considers the general requirements of reasoning as applied to the basic facts of human existence.

Finally, Sidgwick's position concerning received moral opinion owes much to his determination to trace our morality to its roots in our common ability to reason about practical matters. The key to his view is his realization that reason itself sets limits on the extent of the rationality of any actual code of morals. The extent to which a direct rational explanation of any given moral rule in an accepted code should be possible is less than the intuitionists sometimes seemed to think. It does not follow from this fact—as the utilitarians sometimes thought it did—that it is unreasonable to abide by the dictates of such a positive code. Reason itself demands that we tolerate a substantial amount of irrationality in a positive morality. But reason does not deny that we can decrease the extent of the irrationality. The intuitionist tendency to try to show that received moral opinion is quite as reasonable as it needs to be, is less reasonable than the utilitarian insistence that its rationality needs to be increased.

In reviewing thus briefly Sidgwick's advances over his predecessors, it has been necessary once again, as it has been throughout the present study, to ignore the richness of argument, the subtlety of analysis, and the wealth of minute observation, which pervade the *Methods* and give it much of its permanent value. But the importance of this aspect of the work has usually been recognized. What has been ignored is the originality, profundity, and comprehensive scope of the underlying argument of the book. If in its attention to detail as well as in its range of concern the *Methods of Ethics* challenges comparison, as no other work in moral philosophy does, with Aristotle's *Ethics*, in the depth of its understanding of practical rationality and in its architectonic coherence it rivals the work of Kant himself.

Sidgwick gave the problems of ethics the form in which they have dominated British and American moral philosophy since his time. For this reason a full critical evaluation of his views, taking into account their systematic connections with each other, would require a book to itself. He did not expect his own solutions of the problems to be final, though he hoped that future philosophers would be able to learn something from the way he went about finding them. He would have been interested in the various attempts made since his time to show the incoherence of egoism, and even more interested in the revival of the Hobbesian mode of trying to show that enlightened egoism leads one to adopt a disinterested method of decision-making. He would have been fascinated by the numerous advances made in giving precision to utilitarian theory, and in connecting it with theories of rationality derived from economics. Most of all he would have welcomed attempts to work out an alternative to utilitarianism as systematic, as comprehensive, and as powerful as he himself showed that utilitarianism could be. If one of the foundations of his own moral position was a belief about the demands of rationality, the other was the conviction that there is no alternative principle satisfying those demands as well as the utilitarian principle. To this second claim no one in his lifetime offered a cogent and compelling reply. Yet such a reply would have seemed to Sidgwick to present the most desirable kind of challenge a philosopher could want. Whether it has yet been provided or not is a matter still under discussion.

I

Henry Sidgwick: Manuscripts and Published Writings

THE following bibliography has the twofold purpose of making available a reasonably complete list of Sidgwick's works and of facilitating the references to those works within the text of the present volume. The abbreviations used for purposes of reference are therefore given along with each collection of manuscripts and with each book. If no abbreviation is given along with an entry of a collection or book, it is because no reference is made to it.

Articles are identified in the text by the year of publication and by the letter prefixed to the listing of the article when more than one was published during a given year. Many of Sidgwick's essays were reprinted in books of his, and some of his writings are in the *Memoir*. The reader should especially note that although articles are identified by year (and letter), *references to reprinted writings are made to the page-number of the volume in which they are reprinted*, and not to the original place of publication. The volume, if any, in which any item is included is indicated by the appropriate abbreviation with the listing of the item.

This bibliography is based on the excellent one in the *Memoir*, pp. 616–22. It does not include Sidgwick's printed circulars and other writings concerning Cambridge University academic issues. It also omits some of his letters to the public press, and many of his brief reports and remarks in the *Proceedings* and the *Journal* of the Society for Psychical Research.

A. MANUSCRIPTS

Trinity College, Cambridge, the Wren Library, Add. MSS. b. 68, 69, 71; c. 93–106; d. 64–71. This is the largest and most significant group of papers so far located. Abbreviation: TCC.

Letters to Henry Graham Dakyns, in possession of the Dakyns family. Nearly 200 letters, many of which were published at least in part in the *Memoir*. Abbreviation: Dakyns.

British Museum, Add. MSS. 49832, 55159. There are a few other Sidgwick MSS. in the British Museum (now British Library) as well, but none bearing on his philosophy. Abbreviation: BM.

Balliol College, the T. H. Green papers, Sidgwick's recollections of Green. Abbreviation: Balliol.

Harvard University, the Houghton Library, fMS Am 1092 v. 4. There are a few other letters as well. Abbreviation: Harvard.

In addition to these collections of which specific use is made in the text, there are others which have been examined. There are seventeen letters from Sidgwick, mostly concerning the Free Church Union, in Dr. Williams's Library, London. The Bodleian Library, Oxford, has a collection of letters to Mrs. A. H. Clough (MS. Eng. lett. e. 84), which includes the originals of those printed in the *Memoir*, a large number of personal letters from Sidgwick to his sister Mary Benson (Dep. Benson 3/10), a lengthy correspondence between Sidgwick and James Bryce largely concerned with political issues and with Sidgwick's *Elements of Politics* (MS. Bryce 15, fos. 1–225), and some other miscellaneous letters. Two or three other libraries have a few letters from Sidgwick's later years, not discussing philosophy. The papers in possession of the Society for Psychical Research are said to relate only to Sidgwick's interest in its concerns.

B. BOOKS

All Sidgwick's books were published by Macmillan, with the exception of *Practical Ethics*, which was published by Swan Sonnenschein.

The Methods of Ethics. 1st edn., 1874; 2nd edn., 1877; 3rd edn., 1884; 4th edn., 1890; 5th edn., 1893; 6th edn., 1901; 7th edn., 1907. Japanese translation, 1898; German translation, 1909. Abbreviation: *ME*, with first arabic numeral indicating the edition.

A Supplement to the First Edition of the Methods of Ethics, 1878 (contains the changes made for the second edition).

A Supplement to the Second Edition of the Methods of Ethics, 1884 (contains the changes made for the third edition).

The Principles of Political Economy. 1st edn., 1883; 2nd edn., 1887; 3rd edn., 1901. Abbreviation: *PPE*.

Outlines of the History of Ethics for English Readers. 1st edn., 1886; 2nd edn., 1888; 3rd edn., 1892; 4th edn., 1896; 5th edn., 1902; Italian translation, 1902. Abbreviation: *Hist*.

The Elements of Politics. 1st edn., 1891; 2nd edn., 1898; 4th edn., 1919.

Practical Ethics: A Collection of Addresses and Essays. 1st edn., 1898; 2nd edn., 1909. Abbreviation: *Prac. E.*

Philosophy, Its Scope and Relations: An Introductory Course of Lectures, 1902. Edited by James Ward. Abbreviation: *Phil.*

Lectures on the Ethics of T. H. Green, H. Spencer, and J. Martineau, 1902. Edited by E. E. Constance Jones. Abbreviation: *GSM.*

The Development of European Polity, 1903. Edited by Eleanor Mildred Sidgwick.

Miscellaneous Essays and Addresses, 1904. Edited by Eleanor Mildred Sidgwick and Arthur Sidgwick. Abbreviation: *Misc. E.*

Lectures on the Philosophy of Kant and other Philosophical Lectures and Essays, 1905. Edited by James Ward. Abbreviation: *LPK.*

C. ARTICLES, REVIEWS, PAMPHLETS, ETC.

Some of Sidgwick's early writings were published anonymously. His biographers say that the list of anonymous writings prior to 1870 is probably incomplete, though they doubt that the omitted items are significant. (*Mem.,* 616.) The papers read to the Metaphysical Society and the Synthetic Society are listed here, although they were not all published.

1860   'Goethe and Frederika' (verses), *Macmillan's Magazine,* Mar.; *Mem.,* 353.

1861a: 'Eton', *Macmillan's Magazine,* Feb.

     b: Letter to *The Times,* 20 Feb.; *Mem.,* 64–5.

     c: 'The Despot's Heir' (verses), *Macmillan's Magazine,* Mar.; *Mem.,* 64.

     d: Review of Ranke's *History of England, Macmillan's Magazine,* May.

     e: 'Alexis de Tocqueville', *Macmillan's Magazine,* Nov.; *Misc. E.*

1866   'Ecce Homo', *Westminster Review,* July; *Misc. E.*

1867a: 'Liberal Education', *Macmillan's Magazine,* Apr.

     b: 'The Prophet of Culture', *Macmillan's Magazine,* Aug.; *Misc. E.*

     c: 'The Theory of Classical Education', in *Essays on a Liberal Education,* ed. F. W. Farrar, Macmillan and Co.; *Misc. E.*

1869a: 'Mr. Roden Noel's Poems', *Spectator,* 13 Feb.

     b: Review of Courthope's *Ludibria Lunae, Spectator,* 7 Aug.

     c: 'Poems and Prose Remains of A. H. Clough', *Westminster Review,* Oct.; *Misc. E.*

     d: Review of Baring-Gould's *Origin and Development of Religious Belief, Cambridge University Gazette,* 15 Dec.

1870a: 'Clerical Engagements', *Pall Mall Gazette,* 6 Jan.

     b: Review of Broome's *Stranger of Seriphos, Spectator,* 19 Feb.

1870c: *The Ethics of Conformity and Subscription* (pamphlet), Williams and Norgate. Reprinted, in part only and with several textual alterations, in *Prac. E.* Abbreviation: *ECS.*

   d: 'The Verification of Beliefs', read to the Metaphysical Society, 27 Apr. See 1871h.

1871a: Review of Courthope's *Paradise of Birds, Spectator,* 18 Feb.

   b: Review of Grote's *Examination of the Utilitarian Philosophy, Cambridge University Reporter,* 8 Feb.

   c: Review of Swinburne's *Songs Before Sunrise, Cambridge University Reporter,* 22 Feb.

   d: Review of Maguire's *Essays on the Platonic Ethics, Cambridge University Reporter,* 1 Mar.

   e: Review of Grote's *Examination of the Utilitarian Philosophy, Academy,* 1 Apr.

   f: Review of Conway's *Earthly Pilgrimage, Academy,* 15 Apr.

   g: Review of Hutton's *Essays, Theological and Literary, Academy,* 1 July.

   h: 'The Verification of Beliefs', *Contemporary Review,* July; see 1870d.

   i: Review of Maguire's *Essays on the Platonic Ethics, Academy,* 15 Sept.

   j: Review of Beale's *Life Theories and their Influences on Religious Thought, Academy,* 15 Oct.

   k: Review of Lewes's *History of Philosophy, Academy,* 15 Nov.

   l: Review of Fraser's edition of *Berkeley's Works, Athenaeum,* 17 and 24 June.

1872a: Obituary notice of Prof. Trendelenburg, *Academy,* 1 Feb.

   b: Review of Zimmerman's *Samuel Clarke's Life and Doctrine, Academy,* 1 Apr.

   c: Review of Cobbe's *Darwinism in Morals, Academy,* 15 June.

   d: Review of Barzelotti's *La Morale nella filosofia positiva, Academy,* 1 July.

   e: Review of Spicker's *Die Philosophie des Grafen von Shaftesbury, Academy,* 15 Aug.

   f: Review of Mahaffy's *Kant's Critical Philosophy for English Readers, Academy,* 15 Sept.

   g: Review of Jödl's *Leben und Philosophie David Humes, Academy,* 15 Oct.

   h: Review of Leifchild's *Higher Ministry of Nature, Athenaeum,* 6 Apr.

   i: 'Lord Ormathwaite's *Astronomy and Geology Compared', Athenaeum,* 20 Apr.

   j: 'Monck's *Space and Vision', Athenaeum,* 18 May.

k: Review of Bree's *Exposition of Fallacies in the Hypothesis of Mr. Darwin*, Athenaeum, 20 July.

l: Review of Bikker and Hatton's *Ethics for Undenominational Schools*, Athenaeum, 27 July.

m: Note in reply to Bree, *Athenaeum*, 3 Aug. See 1872k.

n: 'Pleasure and Desire', *Contemporary Review*, Apr.

o: 'The Sophists, I', *Journal of Philology*, vol. iv, no. 8; *LPK*.

1873a: 'The Sophists, II', *Journal of Philology*, vol. v, no. 9; *LPK*.

b: Review of Spencer's *Principles of Psychology*, Academy, 1 Apr.

c: Obituary notice of John Stuart Mill, *Academy*, 15 May.

d: Review of Mansel's *Letters, Lectures, and Reviews*, Academy, 15 July.

e: Review of J. F. Stephen's *Liberty, Equality, Fraternity*, Academy, 1 Aug.

f: Review of Tuke's *Effect of the Mind upon the Body*, Athenaeum, 12 July.

g: Review of Spencer's *Principles of Psychology*, Spectator, 21 June.

h: Review of Cairnes's *Political Essays*, Spectator, 8 Nov.

i: 'Utilitarianism', read to Metaphysical Society, 16 Dec.

1874a: 'On a Passage in Plato's *Republic*', *Journal of Philology*, vol. v, no. 10.

b: Review of Green and Grose's Edition of Hume's *Treatise*, Academy, 30 May.

1875a: Review of Green and Grose's Edition of Hume's *Essays*, Academy, 7 Aug.

b: Review of Green and Grose's Edition of Hume, *Spectator*, 27 Mar.

c: 'The Late Professor Cairnes', *Spectator*, 31 July.

d: 'The Theory of Evolution in its Application to Practice', read to the Metaphysical Society, 13 July. See 1876a.

e: 'The Eton Dispute', *Spectator*, 27 Nov.

1876a: 'The Theory of Evolution in its Application to Practice', *Mind*, vol. i, no. 1. See 1875d.

b: 'Philosophy at Cambridge', *Mind*, vol. i, no. 2.

c: 'Bradley's Ethical Studies', *Mind*, vol. i, no. 4.

d: 'Prof. Calderwood on Intuitionism in Morals', *Mind*, vol. i, no. 4.

e: 'Idle Fellowships', *Contemporary Review*, Apr.; *Misc. E*.

1877a: 'Hedonism and Ultimate Good', *Mind*, vol. ii, no. 5.

b: Rejoinder to Bradley's Reply to 1876c, *Mind*, vol. ii, no. 7.

c: Review of Grote's *Treatise on the Moral Ideals*, Mind, vol. ii, no. 6.

1877d: Reply to Barratt on 'The Suppression of Egoism', *Mind*, vol. ii, no. 7.

    e: 'Bentham and Benthamism', *Fortnightly Review*, May; *Misc. E.*

1878a: 'The Relation of Psychogony to Metaphysics and Ethics', read to the Metaphysical Society, 15 Jan.

    b: Article 'Ethics', *Encyclopædia Britannica*, 9th edn.

    c: 'Dr. Georg von Gizycki on Hume's Ethics', *Academy*, 5 Oct.

1879a: 'The Establishment of Ethical First Principles', *Mind*, vol. iv, no. 13.

    b: 'Incoherence of Empirical Philosophy', read to the Metaphysical Society, 14 Jan. See 1882d.

    c: 'The So-called Idealism of Kant', *Mind*, vol. iv, no. 15.

    d: Review of Guyau's *La Morale d'Épicure*, *Mind*, vol. iv, no. 16.

    e: 'Economic Method', *Fortnightly Review*, Feb.

    f: 'What is Money?', *Fortnightly Review*, Apr.

    g: 'The Wages Fund Theory', *Fortnightly Review*, Sept.

1880a: 'On Historical Psychology', *Nineteenth Century*, Feb.

    b: 'Kant's Refutation of Idealism', *Mind*, vol. v, no. 17.

    c: 'The Scope of Metaphysics', read to the Metaphysical Society, 10 Feb.

    d: Review of Fouillée's *L'Idée moderne du droit*, *Mind*, vol. v, no. 17.

    e: 'Mr. Spencer's Ethical System', *Mind*, vol. v, no. 18.

1882a: Inaugural Address, Society for Psychical Research, *Proceedings, S.P.R.*, Vol. I, Part I.

    b: Address to Society for Psychical Research, *Proceedings, S.P.R.*, Vol. I, Part II.

    c: 'On the Fundamental Doctrines of Descartes', *Mind*, vol. vii, no. 27.

    d: 'Incoherence of Empirical Philosophy', *Mind*, vol. vii, no. 28. See 1879b; *LPK*.

    e: Review of L. Stephen, *The Science of Ethics*, *Mind*, vol. vii, no. 28.

1883a: 'A Criticism of the Critical Philosophy, I', *Mind*, vol. viii, no. 29.

    b: 'A Criticism of the Critical Philosophy, II', *Mind*, vol. viii, no. 31.

    c: 'Kant's View of Mathematical Premisses and Reasonings', *Mind*, vol. viii, no. 31.

    d: 'Kant's View of Mathematical Premisses and Reasonings', *Mind*, vol. viii, no. 32.

e: Address to Society for Psychical Research, *Proceedings, S.P.R.*, Vol. I, Part IV.

1884a: Address to Society for Psychical Research, *Proceedings, S.P.R.*, Vol. II, Part VI.

b: 'Green's Ethics', *Mind*, vol. ix, no. 34.

1885a: Review of Fowler's *Progressive Morality*, *Mind*, vol. x, no. 38.

b: Review of Martineau's *Types of Ethical Theory*, *Mind*, vol. x, no. 39.

c: 'The Scope and Method of Economic Science', read to British Association; *Misc. E.*

1886a: 'Dr. Martineau's Defence of *Types of Ethical Theory*', *Mind*, vol. xi, no. 41.

b: 'The Historical Method', *Mind*, vol. xi, no. 42.

c: Review of Bluntschli's *Theory of the State*, *English Historical Review*, Apr.

d: Note, 'The Possibilities of Mal-Observation', *Proceedings of the S.P.R.*, Vol. IV, Part X.

e: 'Bi-metallism (No. I): theory of international bi-metallism', *Fortnightly Review*, Oct.

f: 'Economic Socialism', *Contemporary Review*, Nov.; *Misc. E.*

1888a: 'The Kantian Conception of Free-Will', *Mind*, vol. xiii, no. 51; *ME* 7, Appendix.

b: Review of Pulszky's *Theory of Law and Civil Society*, *English Historical Review*, Oct.

c: Preface to Aschrott's *English Poor Law System*, London.

d: Address to Society for Psychical Research, *Proceedings of the S.P.R.*, Vol. V, Part XIII.

e: 'The Scope and Limits of the Work of an Ethical Society', delivered 18 May, to the Cambridge Ethical Society; *Prac. E.*

1889 a: Address to Society for Psychical Research, *Proceedings of the S.P.R.*, Vol. V, Part XIV.

b: 'Canons of Evidence in Psychical Research', *Proceedings of the S.P.R.*, Vol. VI, Part XV.

c: 'The Census of Hallucinations', *Proceedings of the S.P.R.*, Vol. VI, Part XV.

d: 'Experiments in Thought Transference' (with Mrs. E. M. Sidgwick), *Proceedings of the S.P.R.*, Vol. VI, Part XV.

e: 'Plato's Utilitarianism: a Dialogue by John Grote and Henry Sidgwick', *Classical Review*, Mar.

f: 'Some Fundamental Ethical Controversies', *Mind*, vol. xiv, no. 56.

1889g: 'Shakespeare's Methods, with special reference to *Julius Caesar* and *Coriolanus*', *Misc. E.*

   h: 'Shakespeare and the Romantic Drama, with special reference to *Macbeth*', *Misc. E.*

1890a: 'A Lecture against Lecturing', *New Review*, May; *Misc. E.*

   b: 'The Census of Hallucinations', *Proceedings of the S.P.R.*, Vol. VI, Part XVII.

   c: 'Second ad interim Report on the Census', *Proceedings of the S.P.R.*, Vol. VI, Part XVII.

   d: 'The Morality of Strife', *International Journal of Ethics*, vol. i; *Prac. E.*

1892a: 'The Feeling-Tone of Desire and Aversion', *Mind*, N.S., vol. i, no. 1.

   b: Review of Spencer's *Justice*, *Mind*, N.S., vol. i, no. 1.

   c: 'Aristotle's Classification of Forms of Government', *Classical Review*, Apr.

   d: 'Is the Distinction between "Is" and "Ought" Ultimate and Irreducible?', *Proceedings of the Aristotelian Society*, N.S., vol. i.

1893a: 'Unreasonable Action', *Mind*, N.S., vol. ii, no. 6; *Prac. E.*

   b: 'My Station and Its Duties', *International Journal of Ethics*, vol. iv; *Prac. E.*, under the title, 'The Aims and Methods of an Ethical Society'.

1894a: Note to the *Report* of the Gresham University Commission, January.

   b: 'Luxury', *International Journal of Ethics*, vol. v; *Prac. E.*

   c: 'A Dialogue on Time and Common Sense', *Mind*, N.S., vol. iii, no. 12; *LPK.*

   d: 'Political Prophecy and Sociology', *National Review*, Dec.

   e: 'The Trial Scene in the *Iliad*', *Classical Review*, Feb.

   f: 'Note on the term ἐκτημόροι or ἐκτημόριοι', *Classical Review*, July.

   g: 'Conjectures on the Constitutional History of Athens', *Classical Review*, Oct.

   h: Article, 'Economic Science and Economics', *Dictionary of Political Economy*, ed. Palgrave, vol. i.

   i: 'Report on the Census of Hallucinations', with Alice Johnson, F. W. H. Myers, Frank Podmore, and Eleanor Mildred Sidgwick, *Proceedings of the S.P.R.*, Vol. X, Part XXVI.

   j: 'Disinterested Deception', *Journal* of the Society for Psychical Research, Vol. VI.

1895a: 'The Philosophy of Common Sense', *Mind*, N.S., vol. iv, no. 14; *LPK.*

b: 'Theory and Practice', *Mind*, N.S., vol. iv, no. 15.

c: Review of Ritchie's *Natural Rights*, *Mind*, N.S., vol. iv, no. 15.

d: 'The Ethics of Religious Conformity', *International Journal of Ethics*, vol. vi; *Prac. E.*

e: 'The Economic Lessons of Socialism', *Economic Journal*, Sept.; *Misc. E.*

f: Note on the Memorandum of Sir R. Giffen to the Royal Commission on the Financial Relations of Great Britain and Ireland, *Report of the Commission*, vol. ii, Minutes of Evidence, p. 180.

g: Memorandum in Answer to Questions from the Royal Commission on Secondary Education, Report of the Commission, vol. vi, p. 243.

h: Prefatory Note to V. Solovev's *A Modern Priestess of Isis*, abridged and trans., Walter Leaf, London.

1896a: Review of Gidding's *Principles of Sociology*, *Economic Journal*, Sept.

b: 'The Ethics of Religious Conformity', *International Journal of Ethics*, vol. vii; *Prac. E.*

c: Preface to J. R. Seeley, *Introduction to Political Science*, edited by Henry Sidgwick.

1897a: 'The Pursuit of Culture as an Ideal', pamphlet; in part in *Misc. E.*

b: 'Involuntary Whispering considered in Relation to Experiments in Thought Transference', *Proceedings of the S.P.R.*, vol. XII, Part XXI.

c: 'Public Morality', read Jan. 26 to the Eranus Society; *Prac. E.*

d: 'Clerical Veracity', *Prac. E.*

e: 'The Pursuit of Culture', read to the London School of Ethics and Social Philosophy, Oct. 24; a part of 1897a; *Prac. E.*

f: Comments on Tennyson, in H. Tennyson, *Life of Tennyson*, 2 vols., i. 300–4; *Mem.*

1898a: 'Concessions and Questions for the Synthetic Society', in Maisie Ward, *The Wilfrid Wards and the Transition*, London, 1934, App. B.

b: 'On the Nature of the Evidence for Theism', read to the Synthetic Society, Feb. 25; *Mem.*, App. I.

1899a: Review of Gidding's *Elements of Sociology*, *Economic Journal*, Sept.

b: 'Authority, Scientific and Theological', read to the Synthetic Society, 24 Feb.; *Mem.*, App. I.

1899c: 'The Relation of Ethics to Sociology', *International Journal of Ethics*, vol. x; *Misc. E.*

d: Memorandum to the Royal Commission on Local Taxation, *Report of the Commission*, Memoranda, p. 99.

e: Article 'Political Economy, its Scope', *Dictionary of Political Economy*, ed. Palgrave, vol. iii.

f: Article 'Political Economy, its Method', *Dictionary of Political Economy*, ed. Palgrave, vol. iii.

g: Article 'Political Economy and Ethics', *Dictionary of Political Economy*, ed. Palgrave, vol. iii.

h: Autobiographical Note, in *Life of E. W. Benson*, by A. C. Benson, vol. i, 145–51; vol. ii, 249–55. In part in *Mem.*

1900 'Criteria of Truth and Error', *Mind*, N.S., vol. ix, no. 33; *LPK.*

1901a: 'The Philosophy of T. H. Green', *Mind*, N.S., vol. x, no. 37; *LPK.*

b: 'Prof. Sidgwick's Ethical View: an Auto-Historical Fragment', *Mind*, N.S., vol. x, no. 38; *ME* 6, Preface; references to *ME* 7.

II

THE first part of this bibliography is a checklist of books published on moral philosophy during the late eighteenth and the nineteenth centuries in Britain. It also includes some American publications. It does not cover the periodical literature and does not give full bibliographical details. Since it is also meant to facilitate references given in the text, it includes abbreviations used for books cited there and, where page-references are made to an edition other than the first, indicates the edition to which reference is made.

The second part of the bibliography records the literature about John Stuart Mill's *Utilitarianism* which appeared in the first decade or so after its publication. It includes periodical literature as well as books and parts of books, and for the sake of completeness it duplicates a few items already included in the first part of the bibliography.

Both lists are undoubtedly incomplete. I have not been able to examine all the items listed.

(a) Checklist of Moralists, 1785–1900

ABERCROMBIE, JOHN, *The Philosophy of the Moral Feelings*, 1830.

ADAMS, JASPER (American), *Elements of Moral Philosophy*, 1837.

ALEXANDER, ARCHIBALD (American), *Outlines of Moral Science*, 1852.

ALEXANDER, P. P., *Mill and Carlyle*, 1866.

—— *Moral Causation*, 1888.

ALEXANDER, SAMUEL, *Moral Order and Progress*, 1889.

ANON, *Utilitarian Catechism*, 1830.

—— *Utilitarianism Explained and Exemplified*, 1864.

ARTHUR, WILLIAM, *On the Difference Between Physical and Moral Law*, 1883.

ATKINSON, HENRY GEORGE [with H. Martineau], *Letters on the Laws of Man's Nature and Development*, 1851.

AUSTIN, J. B., *The Duties and the Rights of Man*, 1887.

AUSTIN, JOHN, *The Province of Jurisprudence Determined*, 1832. Abbreviation: *Prov.*

—— *Lectures on Jurisprudence*, ed. Sarah Austin, 3 vols., 1861–3.

BAILEY, SAMUEL, *Letters on the Philosophy of the Human Mind*, 3rd series, 1863.

BAIN, ALEXANDER, ed., *The Moral Philosophy of Paley*, 1852.

—— *The Emotions and the Will*, 1855; 4th edn. 1899.

—— *Mental and Moral Science. A Compendium . . .*, 1868.

BALLANTYNE, JOHN, *An Examination of the Human Mind*, 1828.

BARLOW, JAMES WILLIAM, *The Ultimatum of Pessimism: An Ethical Study*, 1886.

BARRATT, ALFRED, *Physical Ethics*, 1869.

BASCOM, JOHN (American), *Ethics*, 1879.

BAYNE, PETER, *The Christian Life*, 1855.

BEATTIE, JAMES, *Elements of Moral Science*, 2 vols., 1790–3.

BEESLY, E. S., *Comte as a Moral Type*, 1885.

BELSHAM, THOMAS, *Elements of Philosophy of the Human Mind and of Moral Philosophy*, 1801. Abbreviation: *Elements*.

BELSHAM, WILLIAM, *Essays, Philosophical, Moral, etc.*, 2 vols., 1799. Abbreviation: *Essays*.

BENTHAM, JEREMY, *Introduction to the Principles of Morals and Legislation*, 1789, 2nd edn. 1823.

—— *Table of the Springs of Action*, 1815.

—— *Deontology*, 2 vols., 1834. Abbreviation: *Deon.*

BENTLEY, J. C., *The Three Churches, or Outlines of Christian Morals and Politics*, 1852.

BEST, GEORGE PAYNE, *Morality and Utility*, 1887.

BIRKS, THOMAS RAWSON, *Oration of the Analogy of Mathematical and Moral Certainty*, Cambridge, 1834.

—— *The Present Importance of Moral Science, a Lecture*, 1872.

—— *The Philosophy of Human Responsibility, a Lecture*, 1872.

—— *First Principles of Moral Science*, 1873.

—— *Modern Utilitarianism*, 1874.

—— *Modern Physical Fatalism*, 1876.

BLACKIE, JOHN STUART, *Four Phases of Morals*, 1871.

—— *The Natural History of Atheism*, 1877.

BLAKEY, ROBERT, *An Essay showing the Intimate Connexion between our Notions of Moral Good and Evil, and our Conceptions of the Freedom of the Divine and Human Wills*, 1831.

—— *History of Moral Science*, 2 vols., 1833.

—— *History of the Philosophy of Mind*, 4 vols., 1848.

BLECKLEY, H., *Colloquy on the Utilitarian Theory of Morals*, 1873.

BOSANQUET, BERNARD, *The Philosophical Theory of the State*, 1889.

—— *The Civilization of Christendom*, 1893.

—— *Psychology of the Moral Self*, 1897.

BOSANQUET, S. R., *A New System of Logic, Adapted to Moral Philosophy*, 1870.

BOWNE, BORDEN P. (American), *The Principles of Ethics*, 1893.

BRADLEY, F. H., *Ethical Studies*, 1876. Abbreviation: *Eth. Stud.*; references to the 2nd edn., 1927.

—— *Mr. Sidgwick's Hedonism*, 1877. Abbreviation: *Hedonism*; references to F. H. Bradley, *Collected Essays*, Oxford, 1925, vol. i.

BRAY, CHARLES, *The Philosophy of Necessity*, 2 vols., 1841.

—— *On Force*, 1866.

—— *Psychological and Ethical Definitions*, 1879.

BROWN, THOMAS, *Lectures on the Philosophy of the Human Mind*, 4 vols., 1820. Abbreviation: *Lec. Phil.*; references by volume- and page-numbers.

BRUCE, JOHN, *Elements of the Science of Ethics*, 1786.

BUCKE, RICHARD MAURICE, *Man's Moral Nature*, 1879.

CAIRD, EDWARD, *The Social Philosophy and Religion of Comte*, Glasgow, 1885.

CAIRNS, WILLIAM, *Treatise on Moral Freedom*, 1844.

CALDERWOOD, HENRY, *Moral Philosophy, a lecture*, 1868.

—— *Handbook of Moral Philosophy*, 1872.

CARPENTER, LANT, 'Moral Philosophy', in *Systematic Education*, by W. Shepherd, J. Joyce, and Lant Carpenter, 1815.

—— *On the Will of God as the Principle of Duty* (pamphlet), 1837.

CASE, THOMAS, *Realism in Morals*, 1877.

CHALMERS, THOMAS, *Sketches of Moral and Mental Philosophy*, vol. v of *Works*, 1836–42, n.d.

CHAMPLIN, JAMES TIFT (American), *First Principles of Ethics*, 1861.

COBBE, FRANCES POWER, *An Essay on Intuitive Morals*, 2 vols., 1855; later entitled *The Theory of Intuitive Morals*. Abbreviation: *EIM*.

—— *Studies New and Old of Ethical and Social Subjects*, 1865.

—— *Darwinism in Morals and Other Essays*, 1872.

COGAN, THOMAS, *A Philosophical Treatise on the Passions*, 1800.

—— *An Ethical Treatise on the Passions*, 2 vols., 1813.

—— *Ethical Questions*, 1817.

COLERIDGE, SAMUEL TAYLOR, *The Friend*, 1818. Abbreviation: *Friend*; references to the edition by Henry Nelson Coleridge, 2 vols., London, 1863.

—— *Philosophical Lectures*, 1818–19. Abbreviation: *PL*; references to edition by Kathleen Coburn, London, 1949.

—— *Aids to Reflection*, 1825. Abbreviation: *Aids*; references to edition published by Bohn's Popular Library, London, 1913.

—— *Church and State*, 1830. Abbreviation: *C. and S.*; references to edition by Henry Nelson Coleridge, London, 1839.

—— *Table Talk*, 1835–6. Abbreviation: *TT*; references to edition by T. Ashe, London, 1896.

COLERIDGE, SAMUEL TAYLOR, *Omniana*, 1835–6. Abbreviation: *Omn.*; contained in edition of *Table Talk* cited above.

—— *Essay on Faith*, 1839. Abbreviation: *Faith*; references to edition reprinted in *Aids*, cited above.

—— *Confessions of an Inquiring Spirit*, 1840. Abbreviation: *Confessions*; references to edition reprinted in *Aids*, cited above.

COMBE, GEORGE, *Essays on the Constitution of Man*, 1827.

—— *Lectures on Moral Philosophy*, 1840.

—— *Moral and Intellectual Science*, 1848.

COOK, JOSEPH (American), *Conscience*, 1881.

COOPER, THOMAS, *Tracts, Ethical, Theological, and Political*, 1789.

CROFT, DR. GEORGE, *A Short Commentary . . . on . . . the Moral Writings of Dr. Paley and Mr. Gisborne*, 1797.

COURTNEY, WILLIAM LEONARD, *Constructive Ethics*, 1886.

D'ARCY, CHARLES, *A Short Study of Ethics*, 1895.

DARWIN, CHARLES, *The Descent of Man*, 1871. Abbreviation: *Descent*; references to 2nd edn., 1894.

DAVIDSON, WILLIAM LESLIE, *Christian Ethics*, 1899.

DAVIES, J. LLEWELLYN, *Theology and Morality*, 1873.

—— *The Christian Calling*, 1875.

DAVISON, WILLIAM THEOPHILUS, *The Christian Conscience*, 1888.

DAY, HENRY NOBLE (American), *The Science of Ethics*, 1876.

DEWAR, DANIEL, *Elements of Moral Philosophy and Christian Ethics*, 2 vols., 1826.

DOUGLAS, CHARLES, *The Ethics of John Stuart Mill*, 1897.

DYMOND, JONATHAN, *Essays on the Principles of Morality*, 2 vols., 1829. References to edn. of 1847.

EATON, JOHN R. T., *Bishop Butler and his Critics*, 1877.

EDGEWORTH, FRANCIS YSIDRO, *New and Old Methods of Ethics*, 1877.

—— *Mathematical Psychics*, 1881.

ENFIELD, WILLIAM, *Principles of Mental and Moral Philosophy*, 1809.

ENGLISH, WILLIAM WATSON, *Elementary Treatise on Moral Philosophy*, 1865.

—— *Essay on Moral Philosophy*, 1869.

ENSOR, GEORGE, *The Principles of Morality*, 1801.

ESTLIN, JOHN PRIOR, *Familiar Lectures on Moral Philosophy*, 2 vols., 1818.

FERGUSON, ADAM, *Principles of Moral and Political Science*, 1792.

FIELD, GEORGE, *Outlines of Analogical Philosophy*, 2 vols., 1839.

FITZGERALD, P. F., *The Rational, or Scientific, Ideal of Morality*, 1897.

FITZGERALD, WILLIAM, *The Connexion of Morality with Religion*. A sermon, 1851.

FLEMING, WILLIAM, *A Manual of Moral Philosophy*, 1860.

FLEMING, WILLIAM, *Students' Manual of Moral Philosophy*, 1867.

FOOTMAN, HENRY, *Ethics and Theology*, 1888.

FORSYTH, ROBERT, *The Principles of Moral Science*, 1805.

FOWLER, THOMAS, *Progressive Morality*, 1884 (see also John M. Wilson).

FOX, W. J., *Christian Morality*. Sermons. 1833.

GISBORNE, THOMAS, *The Principles of Moral Philosophy*, 1790. Abbreviation: *Principles*; references to 3rd edn., 1795.

—— *Enquiry into the Duties of Men*, 1794.

—— *Enquiry into the Duties of the Female Sex*, 1797.

—— *Sermons*, 1802, 1809.

GODWIN, WILLIAM, *Political Justice*, 1793, 2nd edn., 1796. Abbreviation: *PJ*; references to abridgement edited by K. Codell Carter, Oxford, 1971.

—— *Thoughts on Man*, 1831.

GORE, GEORGE, *The Scientific Basis of Morality*, 1899.

GRANT, ALEXANDER, *On the Nature and Origin of the Moral Ideas*, 1871.

GREEN, THOMAS, of Ipswich, *An Examination of the . . . new system of Morals . . . in Mr. Godwin . . .*, 1799.

GREEN, THOMAS HILL, *Prolegomena to Ethics*, ed. A. C. Bradley, 1883. Abbreviation: *Prol. E.*; references by paragraph number.

—— *Works*, ed. R. L. Nettleship, 3 vols., 1885–91.

GROTE, GEORGE, *Fragments on Ethical Subjects*, ed. A. Bain, 1876.

GROTE, JOHN, *An Examination of the Utilitarian Philosophy*, ed. J. B. Mayor, 1870. Abbreviation: *Exam*.

—— *A Treatise on the Moral Ideals*, ed., J. B. Mayor, 1876. Abbreviation: *Ideals*.

GUTHRIE, MALCOLM, *The Causational and Free Will Theories . . .*, 1877.

—— *On Mr. Spencer's Data of Ethics*, 1884.

HADDON, CAROLINE, *The Larger Life*, 1886.

HALLAM, HENRY, *Literature of Europe*, 1837–9, 4 vols.

HAMPDEN, R. D., *The Study of Moral Philosophy*, 1835.

HARE, JULIUS, with Augustus Hare, *Guesses at Truth*, 1838. Abbreviation: *Guesses*; references to edn. of 1897.

HARRIS, GEORGE, *Philosophical Treatise on the Nature and Constitution of Man*, 2 vols., 1876.

HICKOK, LAURENS P. (American), *A System of Moral Science*, 1853.

HIME, MAURICE CHARLES, *Morality*, 1882.

HODGSON, SHADWORTH H., *The Theory of Practice*, 2 vols., 1870.

HOPKINS, MARK (American), *Lectures on Moral Science*, 1862.

HUGHES, HENRY, *Principles of Natural and Supernatural Morals*, 2 vols., 1890.

HUMPHREY, WILLIAM, *Conscience and Law*, 1896.

HUXLEY, THOMAS H., *Evolution and Ethics*, 1894.
—— *Man's Place in Nature* (1863), 1900.
JEVONS, WILLIAM, *Systematic Morality*, 2 vols., 1827.
JONES, JOSEPH, *A Manual of Mental and Moral Philosophy*, 1838.
KIDD, JAMES, *Morality and Religion*, 1895.
KNIGHT, WILLIAM ANGUS, *The Unitarian Ethic*, 1893.
LAURIE, SIMON SOMERVILLE, *On the Philosophy of Ethics*, 1866.
—— *Notes . . . on certain British Theories of Morals*, 1869.
—— *Ethica, or, the Ethics of Reason*, 1885.
LECKY, WILLIAM E. H., *History of European Morals from Augustus to Charlemagne*, 1869.
—— *The Map of Life*, 1899.
LIEBER, FRANCIS (American), *Political Ethics*, 1839.
LILLIE, W. S., *Right and Wrong*, 1890.
LONG, GEORGE, *Essay on the Moral Nature of Man*, 1841.
—— *The Conduct of Life*, 1845.
M'CORMAC, HENRY, *The Philosophy of Human Nature*, 1837.
McCOSH, JAMES, *The Intuitions of the Mind*, 1860.
—— *An Examination of J. S. Mill's Philosophy*, 1866.
—— *Philosophical Papers*, 1868.
—— *Herbert Spencer's . . . Ethics*, 1885.
—— *Psychology: The Motive Powers*, 1887.
—— *Our Moral Nature*, 1892.
MacDOUGALL, PATRICK C., *Introductory Lecture on Moral Philosophy*, 1851.
MacKENZIE, JOHN STUART, *A Manual of Ethics*, 1893.
MACKINTOSH, SIR JAMES, *Dissertation on the Progress of Ethical Philosophy*, 1830. Abbreviation: *Diss.*
MacMILLAN, MICHAEL, *The Promotion of General Happiness*, 1890.
MacVICAR, JOHN GIBSON, *An Enquiry into Human Nature*, 1853.
MAGUIRE, THOMAS, *Essays on the Platonic Ethics*, 1870.
MALLOCK, W. H., *Is Life Worth Living?*, 1879.
MANSEL, HENRY LONGUEVILLE, *Letters, Lectures, and Reviews*, ed. Chandler, 1873.
MARTINEAU, HARRIET, *see* Atkinson, Henry George.
MARTINEAU, JAMES, *Types of Ethical Theory*, 2 vols., 1885. Abbreviation: *TET*; references to 3rd edn., 1891.
—— *Essays, Reviews and Addresses*, 4 vols., 1890. Abbreviation: *ERA*.
MAUDSLEY, HENRY, *Body and Will*, 1883.
MAURICE, F. D., *The Kingdom of Christ*, 1838. Abbreviation: *K. of C.*; references to 4th edn., 1891.
—— *Theological Essays*, 1853. Abbreviation: *Th. E.*; references to 5th edn., 1891.

MAURICE, F. D., *The Epistles of St. John*, 1857. Abbreviation: *Epis.*; references to edn. of 1881.

—— *Moral and Metaphysical Philosophy*, 2 vols., 1862. Abbreviation: *MMP*; references to edn. of 1872.

—— *The Conscience; Lectures on Casuistry*, 1868. Abbreviation: *Consc.*

—— *Lectures on Social Morality*, 1869. Abbreviation: *Soc. Mor.*

MEYRICK, FREDERICK, *God's Revelation and Man's Moral Sense*, 1856.

MILL, JAMES, *Analysis of the Phenomena of the Human Mind*, 1829. References to edn. by J. S. Mill, *et al.*, 2 vols., 1869.

—— *Fragment on Mackintosh*, 1835. Abbreviation: *Frag.*

MILL, JOHN STUART, *A System of Logic*, 1843.

—— *Dissertations and Discussions*, 1859, and later, enlarged editions. Abbreviation: *Diss.*; references to edn. of 1875.

—— *Utilitarianism*, 1861 (in periodical form), 1863 (book).

MILLS, WILLIAM, *Essays and Lectures*, 1846.

MORELL, JOHN DANIEL, *An Historical and Critical view of . . . Philosophy*, 2 vols., 1846.

MORGAN, C. LLOYD, *The Springs of Conduct*, 1885.

MUDIE, ROBERT, *Man, as a Moral and Accountable Being*, 1840.

—— *Man, in his Relations to Society*, 1840.

MUIRHEAD, J. H., *The Elements of Ethics*, 1892.

MURRAY, J. CLARK (Canadian), *An Introduction to Ethics* (A Handbook of Ethics), 1891.

NELSON, ROBERT J., *An Essay on Man's Moral Agency*, 1837.

NEVILLE, CHRISTOPHER, *A Defense of Paley's Moral Philosophy*, 1839.

OWEN, ROBERT, *A New View of Society*, 1813.

—— *The . . . New Moral World*, 1836.

PALEY, WILLIAM, *Principles of Moral and Political Philosophy*, 1786.

PAYNE, GEORGE, *Elements of Mental and Moral Science*, 1828.

PEABODY, A. P. (American), *Manual of Moral Philosophy*, 1873.

PEARSON, E., *Remarks on the Theory of Morals . . . of . . . Paley*, 1800.

—— *Annotations on the practical part of . . . Paley's Principles . . .*, 1801.

PENROSE, JOHN, *An Inquiry . . . into . . . Human Motives*, 1820.

—— *The Utilitarian Theory of Morals*, 1836.

PLATT, JAMES, *Morality*, 1878.

PLUMPTRE, C. E., *Natural Causation*, 1888.

POLLOCK, SIR FREDERICK, *Essays in Jurisprudence and Ethics*, 1882.

PRING, DANIEL, *Sketches of Intellectual and Moral Relations*, 1829.

RAMSAY, SIR GEORGE, of Banff, *An Enquiry into the Principles of Human Happiness and Human Duty*, 1843.

—— *Analysis . . . of the Emotions*, 1848.

REID, THOMAS, *Essays on the Active powers of Man*, 1789. Abbreviation: *R*; references to the edition of the *Works* by Sir William Hamilton (1846–63), 9th edn., 1895.

RICKABY, JOSEPH, *Moral Philosophy*, 1888.

ROWLAND, DAVID, *Laws of Nature the Foundation of Morals*, 1863.

ROYCE, JOSIAH (American), *Studies of Good and Evil*, 1898.

SAMSON, GEORGE W. (American), *Outlines of the History of Ethics*, 1861 (published anonymously).

SAVAGE, M. J., *The Morals of Evolution*, 1880.

SCHURMAN, JACOB GOULD (American), *The Ethical Importance of Darwinism*, 1888.

SEDGWICK, ADAM, *Discourse on the Studies of the University of Cambridge*, 1832.

SETH, JAMES, *A Study of Ethical Principles*, 1894.

SHEDDEN, THOMAS, *Three Essays on Philosophical Subjects*, 1866.

SIDGWICK, HENRY: see Bibliography I.

SIMCOX, EDITH, *Natural Law*, 1877.

SKINNER, JAMES, *A Synopsis of Moral and Ascetical Theology*, 1882.

SMITH, ALEXANDER, *The Philosophy of Morals*, 2 vols., 1835. Abbreviation: *PM*.

SMITH, SIDNEY, *Lectures on Moral Philosophy*, 1804–5.

SMITH, WILLIAM HENRY, *Discourse on Ethics of the School of Paley*, 1839.
—— *Gravenhurst*, 1862.

SMYTH, NEWMAN (American), *Christian Ethics*, 1892.

SOLLY, THOMAS, *The Will, Divine and Human*, 1856.

SPARKES, GEORGE, *Man, Considered Socially and Morally*, 1876.

SPENCER, HERBERT, *Social Statics*, 1851. Abbreviation: *Soc. St.*
—— *The Data of Ethics*, 1879.
—— *Principles of Ethics*, 1892–3. Abbreviation: *Princ. E.*; references to paragraph numbers.

STEPHEN, SIR LESLIE, *The Science of Ethics*, 1882.

STEWART, DUGALD, *Outlines of Moral Philosophy*, 1793.
—— *Philosophy of the Active and Moral Powers of Man*, 1828.

STRONG, T. B., *Christian Ethics*, 1895.

SULLIVAN, W. R. W., *Morality as a Religion*, 1898.

SULLY, JAMES, *Pessimism*, 1877.

TAYLOR, HUGH, *The Morality of Nations*, 1888.

THOMAS, W. CAVE, *The Science of Moderation*, 1867.

THORNTON, WILLIAM T., *Old-Fashioned Ethics and Common-Sense Metaphysics*, 1873.

TRAVIS, HENRY, *Moral Freedom reconciled with Causation*, 1865.
—— *Free Will and Law . . .*, 1868.
—— *The End of the Free-will Controversy*, 1875.

Vincent, George Giles, *The Moral System*: vol. i, 1841, vol. ii, 1846, Appendix, 1850.

Wace, Henry, *Christianity and Morality*, 1876.

Wainewright, Latham, *Vindication of Dr. Paley's Theory of Morals* . . ., 1830. Abbreviation: *Vindic.*

Ward, William George, *On Nature and Grace*, 1860.

Wardlaw, Ralph, *Christian Ethics*, 1833.

Wayland, Francis (American), *The Elements of Moral Science*, 1835.
—— *The Limitations of Human Responsibility*, 1838.

Wedgewood, Julia, *The Moral Ideal*, 1888.

Whately, Richard, *Dr. Paley's Works, A lecture*, 1859.
—— *Paley's Moral Philosophy, with annotations*, 1859.
—— *Introductory Lessons on Morals*, 1859.

Whedon, D. D., *The Freedom of the Will*, 1864.

Whewell, William, Preface to Sir James Mackintosh, *Dissertation on the Progress of Moral Philosophy*, edn. of 1835. Abbreviation: *Pref. M.*
—— *On the Foundations of Morals*, 1837. Abbreviation: *FM.*
—— *Elements of Morality including Polity*, 1845. Abbreviation: *EMP*; references by paragraph number to the 4th edn., 1864.
—— *Lectures on Systematic Morality*, 1846. Abbreviation: *LSM.*
—— *Lectures on the History of Moral Philosophy*, 1852. Abbreviation: *Lec. Hist.*; references to the 2nd edn., 1862, which contains some additional lectures with separate pagination, for which the abbreviation is *Lec. Hist. Add.*

Whinfield, William Henry, *Ethics of the Future*, 1876.

Wilson, John M., *Principles of Morals*, 2 vols., 1886 [with Thomas Fowler].

Woodgate, H. A., *The Study of Morals Vindicated* . . ., 1837.

(b) Literature on John Stuart Mill's *Utilitarianism*, 1861–76

Anon., review of Grote's *Examination of the Utilitarian Philosophy*, *Westminster Review*, xcv, 1871, 41–53 (pp. 20–6 of the American edition, to which references are made).
—— review of *Utilitarianism*, *Saturday Review*, 12 Oct. 1861, pp. 373–4.
—— notice of *Utilitarianism*, in 'The Magazines', *Spectator*, 5 Oct. 1861, p. 1096.
—— 'Utilitarianism and the "Saturday Review"', *Spectator*, 19 Oct. 1861, pp. 1144–6 (probably by R. H. Hutton).

ANON., review of Mill's *Utilitarianism, Westminster Review*, xxiii, 1863.
—— *Utilitarianism Explained and Exemplified in Moral and Political Government*, 1864 (attributed by Harvard Library to Charles Tennant, *fl.* 1860).

BAIN, ALEXANDER, *Mental and Moral Science*, 1868.

BASCOM, REV. JOHN, 'Utilitarianism', *The Bibliotheca Sacra*, xxiii, 1866, 435–52.

BIRKS, THOMAS RAWSON, *Modern Utilitarianism*, 1874.

BLACKIE, JOHN STUART, *Four Phases of Morals*, 1871.

BLECKLY, HENRY, *A Colloquy on the Utilitarian Theory of Morals*, 1873.

BOWNE, BORDEN P. 'Moral Intuition vs. Utilitarianism', *New Englander*, xxxii, 1873, 217–42.

BRADLEY, F. H., *Ethical Studies*, 1876; 2nd edn., 1935.

BRYCE, JAMES, review of Lecky's *History of European Morals, Quarterly Review*, vol. 128, Jan. 1870, pp. 49–81.

CALDERWOOD, HENRY, *Handbook of Moral Philosophy*, 1872.

CHURCH, R. W., review of Lecky's *History of European Morals, Macmillan's Magazine*, xx, May 1869, pp. 76–88.

DAVIES, REV. J. LLEWELLYN, 'Professor Grote on Utilitarianism', *Contemporary Review*, xv, Aug. 1870, 80–96.
—— 'Universal Morality and the Christian Theory of Duty', *Fortnightly Review*, vi, July 1869, 1–12.

GREENWELL, DORA, *Liber humanitatis*, 1875, pp. 85–117.

GROTE, JOHN, *An Examination of the Utilitarian Philosophy*, ed. J. B. Mayor, 1870.

HUTTON, R. H., review of *Utilitarianism, Spectator*, 11 Apr. 1863, pp. 1868–9.
—— 'The Latest Phase of the Utilitarian Controversy', *British Quarterly Review*, l, July 1869, 68–91.

KIRKUS, WILLIAM, 'Mr. John Stuart Mill', *Miscellaneous Essays*, 2nd Ser., 2nd edn., 1869.

LAURIE, SIMON S., *Notes Expository and Critical on Certain British Theories of Morals*, 1868.

LECKY, W. E. H., *History of European Morals from Augustus to Charlemagne*, 1869, 3rd edn., 1877, repr. 1920.

LESLIE, T. E. CLIFFE, 'Utilitarianism and the Common Good', *Macmillan's Magazine*, viii, June 1863, pp. 152–60.

LORIMER, JAMES, *The Institutes of Law*, 1872, 2nd edn., 1880.

MANSEL, HENRY L., *Letters, Lectures and Reviews*, ed. Chandler, 1873.

McCALL, WILLIAM, *The Newest Materialism*, 1873, Essay III: 'The Utilitarian Creed', dated 1863.

McCOSH, JAMES, *Outlines of Moral Philosophy by Dugald Stewart*, with . . . a supplement by James McCosh, 1865.

McCosh, James, *Examination of Mill's Philosophy*, 1866.

Morley, John, 'Mr. Lecky's First Chapter', *Fortnightly Review*, xxix, May 1869, pp. 519–38.

Newman, F. W., 'Epicureanism Ancient and Modern', *Fraser's Magazine*, vol. 84 o.s., 4 n.s., Nov. 1871, 606–17.

Rands, William Brighty, *Henry Holbeach, Student in Life and Philosophy*, vol. ii, 1865.

Reeve, Henry, review of Lecky's *History of European Morals*, *Edinburgh Review*, 130, July 1869, 36–56 (references to American edition).

Shairp, J. C., 'Moral Theories and Christian Ethics', *North British Review*, n.s. viii, Sept. 1867, 1–46.

Sidgwick, Henry, *The Methods of Ethics*, 1874.

—— 1871b and 1871e.

Stephen, James Fitzjames, 'Utilitarianism', *Pall Mall Gazette*, June 1869; reprinted in *Liberty, Equality, Fraternity*, 1873.

Stephen, Leslie (?), 'Mr. Lecky's History of European Morals', *Fraser's Magazine*, 80, Sept. 1869, 273–84. (Houghton attribution uncertain.)

Thayer, J. B., 'Mill's Dissertations and Discussions', *North American Review*, c, Jan. 1865, pp. 259–66.

Thornton, W. T., 'Anti-Utilitarianism', *Fortnightly Review*, 14, Sept. 1870, 314–37.

Ward, William George, 'Mr. Mill on the Foundation of Morality', *Dublin Review*, 1872; reprinted in *Essays on the Philosophy of Theism*, ed. Wilfrid Ward, 1884, vol. i, from which quotations are taken.

Watts, Robert, *Utilitarianism as Expounded by J. Stuart Mill, Alex. Bain, and Others*, n.d. (1868), '2nd edition revised'.

Williams, Robert, 'A Few Words on Utilitarianism', *Fraser's Magazine*, 80, Aug. 1869, pp. 248–56.

Wilson, John Matthias, and Thomas Fowler, *Principles of Morals (Introductory Chapters)*, 1886 (originally printed in 1875).

III

General Bibliography

ABRAMS, M. H., *The Mirror and the Lamp: Romantic Theory and the Critical Tradition*, Oxford University Press, New York, 1953.

ACTON, H. B., 'Animal Pleasures', *Massachusetts Review*, ii, no. 3 (Spring 1961), 541–8.

ALBEE, ERNEST, 'An Examination of Professor Sidgwick's Proof of Utilitarianism', *Philosophical Review*, x (1901), 251–60.

—— *A History of English Utilitarianism*, Sonnenschein & Co. Ltd., London; Macmillan Co., New York, 1902.

—— 'Reply to Barker', *Philosophical Review*, xi (1902), 614–16.

ANNAN, NOEL G., *Leslie Stephen: His Thought and Character in Relation to His Time*, Macgibbon & Kee, London, 1951.

ANSCHUTZ, R. P., *The Philosophy of J. S. Mill*, Oxford University Press, New York, 1953.

ANSCOMBE, G. E. M., 'Modern Moral Philosophy', *Philosophy*, xxxiii (1958), 1–19. Reprinted in *The Is–Ought Question: A Collection of Papers on the Central Problems in Moral Philosophy*, ed. W. D. Hudson, St. Martin's Press, New York, 1969.

BAIN, ALEXANDER, *Autobiography*, ed. W. L. Davidson, Longman, London, New York, and Bombay, 1904.

—— *James Mill, a Biography*, 1882.

—— *John Stuart Mill: A Criticism; with Personal Recollections*, Longman, London, 1882.

—— 'Mr. Sidgwick's Methods of Ethics', *Mind*, o.s. i (1876), 179–97.

—— *The Emotions and the Will*, 3rd edn., Longman, London, 1875. Ch. xi, secs. 9–10.

BAIN, MRS. A., 'Ethics from a Purely Practical Standpoint', *Mind*, n.s. v (1896), 327–42.

BAKER, HERSCHEL, *William Hazlitt*, Harvard University Press, Cambridge, Mass., 1962.

BARBOUR, G. F., 'Green and Sidgwick on the Community of the Good', *Philosophical Review*, xvii (1908), 149–66.

BARKER, SIR ERNEST, *Traditions of Civility; Eight Essays*, Ch. 7: 'Paley and his Political Philosophy', Cambridge University Press, Cambridge, 1948.

BARKER, HENRY, 'A Recent Criticism of Sidgwick's *Methods of Ethics*', *Philosophical Review*, xi (1902), 607–14.

BARRATT, A., 'Ethics and Politics', *Mind*, o.s. ii (1877), 425–76.

—— 'Ethics and Psychogony', *Mind*, o.s. iii (1878), 277–83.

—— 'The "Suppression" of Egoism', *Mind*, o.s. ii (1878), 167–86.

BARZELLOTTI, G., *The Ethics of Positivism* (1871), trans. Gandalfo and Olcott, C. P. Somerby, New York, 1878. Preface.

BEDAU, HUGO A., 'Justice and Classical Utilitarianism' in *Justice*, ed. Carl J. Friedrich and John W. Chapman, Atherton Press, New York, 1963, 284–305.

BENSON, ARTHUR C., 'The Leaves of the Tree: III—Henry Sidgwick', *Cornhill Magazine*, cii, N.S. xxix (July–Dec. 1910), 811–28. Reprinted in *The Leaves of the Tree; Studies in Biography*, by Arthur C. Benson, G. P. Putnam's Sons, New York and London, 1911.

—— *The Life of Edward White Benson*, Macmillan, London, New York, 1899.

—— *The Trefoil: Wellington College, Lincoln, and Truro*, John Murray, London, 1923.

BENSON, EDWARD FREDERIC, *Mother*, Hodder and Stoughton, London, 1925.

BENSON, EDWARD WHITE, *Boy-Life, Its Trials, Its Strength, Its Fullness: Sundays in Wellington College, 1859–1873*, new edn., Macmillan, London, 1883.

BERNAYS, PAUL, 'Das Moralprinzip bei Sidgwick und bei Kant', *Abhandlung der Fries'schen Schule*, N.F., iii. Band, 3. Heft (1910), 501–82. Also issued in pamphlet (Vandenhoeck & Ruprecht, Göttingen, 1910).

BLAKE, RALPH M., DUCASSE, CURT J., and MADDEN, EDWARD H., *Theories of Scientific Method: the Renaissance through the Nineteenth Century*, ed. E. H. Madden, University of Washington Press, Seattle, 1960.

BLANSHARD, BRAND, 'Sidgwick the Man', *Monist*, lviii (July 1974), 349–70.

BRADLEY, F. H., 'Mr. Sidgwick on Ethical Studies', *Mind*, o.s. ii, 1887, 122–5. Reprinted in *Collected Essays*, by F. H. Bradley, vol. ii, Clarendon Press, Oxford, 1935.

BROAD, C. D., *Five Types of Ethical Theory*, K. Paul, Trench, and Trubner, London; Harcourt, Brace, New York, 1930.

—— 'Henry Sidgwick', *Hibbert Journal*, xxxvii, no. 1 (Oct. 1938), 25–43. Reprinted in *Ethics and the History of Philosophy; Selected Essays*, by C. D. Broad, Routledge & Kegan Paul, London, 1952.

BROAD, C. D., 'Henry Sidgwick and Psychical Research'. *Proceedings of the Society for Psychical Research*, xlv (1938), 131–73. Reprinted in *Religion, Philosophy and Psychical Research: Selected Essays*, by C. D. Broad, Harcourt, Brace, New York, 1953.

—— 'Self and Others', in *Broad's Critical Essays in Moral Philosophy*, ed. David R. Cheney, Allen & Unwin, London; Humanities Press, New York, 1971.

BROWN, ALAN WILLARD, *The Metaphysical Society: Victorian Minds in Crisis, 1869–1880*, Columbia University Press, New York, 1947.

BROWN, FORD KEELER, *The Life of William Godwin*, J. M. Dent & Sons, London and Toronto, 1926.

BROWN, HORATIO R. F., ed., *Letters and Papers of John Addington Symonds*, Scribner's, New York, 1923.

BRYCE, JAMES, 'The Late Mr. Henry Sidgwick', *Nation*, lxii, no. 1839 (27 Sept. 1900), 244–6. Reprinted, slightly revised, as 'Henry Sidgwick' in *Studies in Contemporary Biography*, by J. B. Bryce, Macmillan, London, 1903.

BULWER-LYTTON, EDWARD GEORGE EARLE LYTTON, *England and the English*, 2 vols., Richard Bentley, London, 1933.

BURROW, JOHN WYON, *Evolution and Society: A Study in Victorian Social Theory*, Cambridge University Press, Cambridge, 1966.

BUTLER, JAMES RAMSEY MONTAGU, *Henry Montagu Butler: Master of Trinity College, Cambridge, 1886–1916*, London, 1925.

BUTTS, ROBERT E., 'Necessary Truth in Whewell's Theory of Science', *American Philosophical Quarterly*, ii, no. 3 (July 1965), 161–81.

CALDERWOOD, H., 'The Relation of Intuitionism to the Ethical Doctrine of Self-Realization', *Philosophical Review*, v, no. 4 (July 1896), 337–51.

CARLYLE, THOMAS, *Works*, 18 vols., Chapman & Hall, London, 1904.

CARRAU, L., 'Analyse de John Grote, *A Treatise of the Moral Ideals*', *Revue philosophique*, iv (juillet–decembre 1877), 530–7.

—— 'Moralistes anglais contemporains: M. H. Sidgwick', *Revue philosophique*, v (janvier–juin 1878), 263–80, 403–21.

CHADWICK, OWEN, *From Bossuet to Newman; The Idea of Doctrinal Development*, Cambridge University Press, London, 1957.

—— *The Victorian Church*, 2 vols., Oxford University Press, New York, 1966–70.

CLARK, JOHN WILLIS, *Old Friends at Cambridge and Elsewhere*, Macmillan & Co., London, 1900.

CLAY, WALTER LOWE, ed., *Essays on Church Policy*, Macmillan & Co., London, 1868.

CLOUGH, BLANCHE ATHENA, *A Memoir of Anne Jemima Clough*, E. Arnold, London and New York, 1897.

COMPTON, BERDMORE, *Edward Meyrick Goulburn*, John Murray, London, 1899.

DARWALL, STEPHEN, 'Pleasure as Ultimate Good in Sidgwick's Ethics', *Monist*, lviii (July 1974), 475–89.

DAVIE, GEORGE E., *The Democratic Intellect: Scotland and Her Universities in the Nineteenth Century*, Edinburgh University Press, Edinburgh, 1961.

DE QUINCEY, THOMAS, 'Sir James Macintosh', *Essays on Philosophical Writers*, vol. i, J. R. Osgood & Co., Boston, 1856.

DICEY, A. V., Review of Sidgwick's *Methods of Ethics*, *Nation*, xxii, nos. 558 and 559 (9 and 16 Mar. 1876), 162–3 and 180–1.

DICKENS, CHARLES, *Hard Times, for These Times*, Bradbury & Evans, London, 1854.

DONAGAN, ALAN, 'Whewell's *Elements of Morality*', *Journal of Philosophy*, lxxi (7 Nov. 1974), 724–36.

DOUGLAS, JANET MARY (MRS. STAIR), *The Life and Selections from the Correspondence of William Whewell*, Kegan Paul, London, 1882.

DRUMMOND, JAMES, *The Life and Letters of James Martineau* . . . [and a Survey of his Philosophical Work by C. B. Upton], Dodd, Mead, and Co., New York, 1902.

DUBOIS, PIERRE, *Le Problème moral dans la philosophie anglaise, de 1900 à 1950*, J. Vrin, Paris, 1967, 19–29, 49–52.

DUCASSE, C. J., 'Whewell's Philosophy of Scientific Discovery', *Philosophical Review*, lx (1951), 56–69, 213–34.

EDGEWORTH, F. Y., *Mathematical Psychics; An Essay on the Application of Mathematics to the Moral Sciences*, Kegan Paul, London, 1881.

—— *New and Old Methods of Ethics, or 'Physical Ethics' and 'Methods of Ethics'*, J. Parker & Co., Oxford and London, 1877.

EZORSKY, GERTRUDE, 'Unconscious Utilitarianism', *Monist*, lviii (July 1974), 468–74.

FABER, GEOFFREY C., *Jowett, a Portrait with Background*, Faber & Faber, London, 1957.

FAIRBROTHER, W. H., *The Philosophy of Thomas Hill Green*, Methuen, London, 1896.

FISHER, HERBERT ALBERT LAURENS, *Frederick William Maitland, Downing Professor of the Laws of England: A Biographical Sketch*, Cambridge University Press, Cambridge, 1910.

FLEW, A. G. N., *Evolutionary Ethics*, Macmillan, London, etc.; St. Martin's Press, New York, 1967.

FORBES, DUNCAN, *The Liberal Anglican Idea of History*, Cambridge University Press, Cambridge, 1952.

FOWLER, T., 'Professor Sidgwick on "Progressive Morality"', *Mind*, o.s. x (1885), 481–6.

FRANKENA, WILLIAM K., 'Henry Sidgwick', *Encyclopedia of Morals*, ed. Vergilius T. A. Ferm, Philosophical Library, New York, 1956; P. Owen, London, 1957.

—— 'Sidgwick and the Dualism of Practical Reason', *Monist*, lviii (July 1974), 449–67.

GASH, NORMAN, *Reaction and Reconstruction in English Politics, 1832–1852*, Clarendon Press, Oxford, 1965.

GAULD, ALAN, *The Founders of Psychical Research*, Schocken Books, New York, 1968.

GIZYCKI, GEORG VON, Review of *Methods of Ethics*, *Vierteljahrsschrift für wissenschaftliche Philosophie*, iv (1880–1), 114–26.

—— Review of *Methods of Ethics*, 3rd edn., *Vierteljahrsschrift für wissenschaftliche Philosophie*, ix, 1885–6, 104–12.

—— Review of *Methods of Ethics*, 4th edn., *International Journal of Ethics*, i, 1891, 120–1.

GRAVE, S. A., *The Scottish Philosophy of Common Sense*. Clarendon Press, Oxford, 1960.

GREEN, T. H., 'Hedonism and Ultimate Good', *Mind*, o.s. ii (1887), 266–9.

—— *Prolegomena to Ethics*, 5th edn., Clarendon Press, Oxford, 1906, 447–57.

—— *Works of Thomas Hill Green*, ed. R. L. Nettleship, 3 vols., Longman, London, 1885.

GRIFFIN-COLLART, EVELYNE, *Égalité et justice dans l'Utilitarisme* (*L'Égalité*, vol. II), Bruxelles, Établissements Émile Bruylant, 1974.

GROTE, (Mrs.) HARRIET LEWIN, *The Personal Life of George Grote*, J. Murray, London, 1873.

GROTE, JOHN, *Exploratio Philosophica: Rough Notes on Modern Intellectual Science*, 2 vols., Deighton, Bell, etc., Cambridge, Eng., 1865–1900.

GUYAU, JEAN-MARIE, *La Morale Anglaise contemporaine: Morale de l'utilité et d'évolution*, Coulommiers, Paris, 1879, 143–9.

HALEVY, ELIE, *The Growth of Philosophical Radicalism*, trans. Mary Morris, Faber & Gwyer Ltd., London, 1928; Beacon Press, Boston, 1955.

HALL, ROBERT, *The Miscellaneous Works and Remains of the Rev. Robert Hall*, ed. Olinthus Gregory, H. G. Bohn, London, 1846.

HAMBURGER, JOSEPH, *Intellectuals in Politics: John Stuart Mill and the Philosophic Radicals*, Yale Studies in Political Science, No. 14, Yale University Press, New Haven, Conn., 1965.

—— *James Mill and the Art of Revolution*, Yale University Press, New Haven, Conn., 1965.

HAMPSHIRE, STUART, *Morality and Pessimism*, Cambridge University Press, Cambridge, 1972.

HARE, JULIUS, *The Victory of Faith*, 3rd edn., ed. E. H. Plumptre, Macmillan, London, 1874.

HARE, R. M., 'The Argument from Received Opinion', *Essays on Philosophical Method*, by R. M. Hare, University of California Press, Berkeley, 1972.

—— Review of Rawls's *A Theory of Justice*, *Philosophical Quarterly*, xxiii (1973), 144–55, 241–52.

HARRISON, J. F. C., *Quest for the New Moral World: Robert Owen and the Owenites in Britain and America*, Routledge & Kegan Paul, London; Scribner's, New York, 1968.

HARTLEY, DAVID, *Observations on Man, His Frame, His Duty, and His Expectations*, 2 vols., S. Richardson for J. Leake and W. Frederick, 1749.

HAVARD, W. C., *Henry Sidgwick and Later Utilitarian Political Philosophy*. University of Florida Press, Gainesville, 1959.

HAYWARD, F. H., *The Ethical Philosophy of Sidgwick; Nine Essays, Critical and Expository*. S. Sonnenschein, London, 1901.

—— 'A Reply to E. E. Constance Jones', *International Journal of Ethics*, xi (1900–1), 360–5.

—— 'The True Significance of Sidgwick's "Ethics"', *International Journal of Ethics*, xi (1900–1), 175–87.

HAZLITT, WILLIAM, *The Complete Works of William Hazlitt*, ed. P. P. Howe, 21 vols., J. M. Dent, London and Toronto, 1930–4.

HERTZ, JOSEPH H., 'The Ethical System of James Martineau', Ph.D. dissertation, Columbia College, New York, 1894.

HIGHAM, FLORENCE, *Frederick Denison Maurice*, SCM Press, London, 1947.

HORNY, F. W., *Kurze, kritische Darstellung der Anfänge und Entwickelung der utilitarischen Moralphilosophie in England*, Hunderstund und Pries, Leipzig, 1881

HORT, F. J. A., 'Coleridge', in *Cambridge Essays, Contributed by Members of the University*, 4 vols., J. W. Parker, London, 1855–8.

HOUGHTON, WALTER EDWARDS, *The Victorian Frame of Mind, 1830–1870*, Yale University Press, New Haven, Conn., 1957.

HUTCHISON, T. W., *A Review of Economic Doctrines, 1870–1929*, Clarendon Press, Oxford, 1953, Ch. 3.

INGLEBY, C. M., *The Revival of Philosophy at Cambridge*, J. Hall and Son, Cambridge, 1870.

JAMES, DAVID GWILYM, *Henry Sidgwick: Science and Faith in Victorian England*, Oxford University Press, London, 1970.

450 *Bibliographies*

JARMAN, ARCHIE, *Dr. Gauld and Mrs. Myers*, Alcuin Press, Welwyn Garden City, 1964 (privately printed).

JEFFREY, FRANCIS, *Contributions to the Edinburgh Review*, 4 vols., Longman, London, 1844.

JONES, EMILY ELIZABETH CONSTANCE, *As I Remember*, A. & C. Black, London, 1922.

—— 'Henry Sidgwick's Philosophical Intuitionism', *Bericht über den III internationalen Kongress für Philosophie*, ed., Th. Elsenhans, C. Winter, Heidelberg, 1909, 920–7.

—— 'Mr. Hayward's Evaluation of Professor Sidgwick's Ethics', *International Journal of Ethics*, xi (1900–1), 354–60.

—— 'Practical Dualism', *Proceedings of the Aristotelean Society*, N.S. xviii (1918), 317–28.

—— 'Professor Sidgwick's Ethics', *Proceedings of the Aristotelean Society*, N.S. iv (1904), 32–52.

JOUFFROY, THEODORE S., *Introduction to Ethics, Including a Critical Survey of Moral Systems*, trans. William H. Channing, Hilliard, Gray & Co., Boston, 1841.

KANT, IMMANUEL, *Critique of Practical Reason*, trans. Lewis White Beck, Liberal Arts Press, New York, 1956.

—— *Groundwork of the Metaphysics of Morals*, trans. H. J. Paton, Harper & Row, New York, 1964.

KEYNES, JOHN MAYNARD, *Essays in Biography*, Harcourt, Brace, New York, 1933.

KIRK, K. E., *Conscience and Its Problems; An Introduction to Casuistry*, Longman, London, 1927.

KITSON CLARK, GEORGE SIDNEY ROBERTS, *Churchmen and the Condition of England, 1832–1885*, Methuen, London, 1973.

LACEY, A. R., 'Sidgwick's Ethical Maxims', *Philosophy*, xxxiv (1959), 217–28.

LAMONT, W. D., *Introduction to Green's Moral Philosophy*, Allen & Unwin, London, 1934.

LEAVIS, Q. D., 'Henry Sidgwick's Cambridge', *Scrutiny*, xv, no. 1 (Dec. 1947), 2–11.

LEWIS, H. D., 'Does the Good Will Define Its Own Content? A Study of Green's *Prolegomena*', *Ethics*, lviii (1947–8), 157–79.

LIGHTFOOT, J. B., *Saint Paul's Epistle to the Philippians*, Macmillan, London, 1868.

LINDSAY, A. D., 'Green and the Idealists', in *The Social and Political Ideas of Some Representative Thinkers of the Victorian Age*, ed. J. F. C. Hearnshaw, G. G. Harrap, London, 1933.

LITTLE, I. M. D., *A Critique of Welfare Economics*, 2nd edn., Oxford University Press, London, 1957.

LYONS, DAVID, *Forms and Limits of Utilitarianism*, Clarendon Press, Oxford, 1965.

—— *In the Interest of the Governed; A Study in Bentham's Philosophy of Utility and Law*, Clarendon Press, Oxford, 1973.

MACAULAY, THOMAS BABINGTON, 'The Present Administration', *Edinburgh Review*, June 1827, p. 261.

—— *The Works of Lord Macaulay*, Albany Edition, 12 vols., Longman, London, 1913.

MACDONALD, LAUCHLIN D., *John Grote, A Critical Estimate of His Writings*, M. Nijhoff, The Hague, 1966.

MACK, MARY P., *Jeremy Bentham*, Heinemann, London, 1962.

MACKIE, J. L., 'The Disutility of Act Utilitarianism', *Philosophical Quarterly*, xxiii (1973), 289–300.

MAGILL, ROBERT, *Der rationale Utilitarismus Sidgwicks*, A. Kämpfe, Jena, 1899.

MAGOUN, G. F., 'Recent English Thought in Ethics', *Journal of Speculative Philosophy*, xi (1877), 198–203.

MAITLAND, FREDERICK WILLIAM, *The Life and Letters of Leslie Stephen*, Duckworth, London, 1906.

MARTINEAU, JAMES, 'Professor Sidgwick on "Types of Ethical Theory"', *Mind*, o.s. x (1885), 628–39.

MASSON, DAVID, *Memories of Two Cities, Edinburgh and Aberdeen*, ed. Flora Masson, Oliphant, Anderson, Edinburgh and London, 1911.

—— *Recent British Philosophy: A Review, with Criticisms*, 3rd edn., Macmillan and Co., London, 1877.

MASTERMAN, C. F. G., 'Henry Sidgwick', *Commonwealth*, Oct. 1900. Reprinted in *In Peril of Change: Essays Written in Time of Tranquility*, T. Fisher Unwin, London, 1905.

MAURICE, FREDERICK DENISON, *The Life of Frederick Denison Maurice, Chiefly Told in His Own Letters*, C. Scribner's Sons, New York, 1884.

McADOO, H. R., *The Structure of Caroline Moral Theology*, Longman, London, 1949.

McCLAIN, FRANK M., *Maurice: Man and Moralist*, S.P.C.K., London, 1972.

McCOSH, JAMES, *The Scottish Philosophy, Biographical, Expository, Critical, from Hutcheson to Hamilton*, R. Carter and Bros., New York, 1875.

McTAGGART, J. M. ELLIS, 'The Ethics of Henry Sidgwick', *Quarterly Review*, ccv (1906), 398–419.

MELITZ, JACK, 'The Economics of Henry Sidgwick', unpub. doctoral dissertation, Princeton University, 1963.

MELITZ, JACK, 'Sidgwick's Theory of International Values', *Economic Journal*, lxxiii (1963), 431–41.

MELLONE, S. H., Review of *Lectures on the Ethics of Green, Spencer, and Martineau, International Journal of Ethics*, xiv (1903–4), 106–15.

MERZ, J. T., *A History of European Thought in the Nineteenth Century*, vol. iv, W. Blackwood & Sons, Edinburgh and London, 1914, 223–8.

METZ, RUDOLF, *A Hundred Years of British Philosophy*, trans. J. W. Harvey, T. E. Jessop, H. Sturt, ed. J. H. Muirhead, Allen & Unwin, London; Macmillan, New York, 1938.

MILL, JOHN STUART, *Autobiography*, Longman, London, 1873.

—— *Collected Works*, vols. xii–xiii: *Earlier Letters*, vols. xiv–xvii: *Later Letters*, University of Toronto Press, Toronto, 1963–72.

—— *Mill's Ethical Writings*, ed. J. B. Schneewind, Collier Books, New York, 1965.

—— *The Spirit of the Age*, with intro. essay by Frederick A. von Hayek, University of Chicago Press, Chicago, Ill., 1942.

MILNE, A. J. M., *The Social Philosophy of English Idealism*, Allen & Unwin, London, 1962.

MONCK, W. H. S., 'Kant's Theory of Mathematics', *Mind*, o.s. viii (1883), 255–8 and 576.

MONRO, D. H., *Godwin's Moral Philosophy; An Interpretation of William Godwin*, Oxford University Press, London, 1953.

—— comp., *A Guide to the British Moralists*, Fontana, London, 1972.

MOORE, G. E., *Principia Ethica*, Cambridge University Press, Cambridge, 1903.

—— Review of *Lectures on the Philosophy of Kant, and Other Philosophical Essays*, *Hibbert Journal*, iv, no. 15 (Apr. 1906), 686–92.

MORELL, J. D., *An Historical and Critical View of the Speculative Philosophy of Europe in the Nineteenth Century*, 2 vols., W. Pickering, London, 1846.

—— *On the Philosophical Tendencies of the Age; Being Four Lectures Delivered at Edinburgh and Glasgow*, J. Johnstone, London, 1848.

MOZLEY, J. R., *Clifton Memories*, J. W. Arrowsmith, Bristol, 1927.

—— 'Utilitarianism and Morality', *Quarterly Review*, cxli (Apr. 1876), 488–506.

MUIRHEAD, JOHN H., *Coleridge as Philosopher*, Allen & Unwin, London; Macmillan Co., New York, 1930.

—— *The Platonic Tradition in Anglo-Saxon Philosophy; Studies in the History of Idealism in England and America*, Allen & Unwin, London; Macmillan, New York, 1931.

MURPHY, ARTHUR EDWARD, *The Theory of Practical Reason*, ed. A. I. Melden, Open Court, LaSalle, Ill., 1965, 221 ff.

Murry, John Middelton, 'Newman and Sidgwick', in *Things to Come; Essays*, Macmillan, New York, 1928. Reprinted in *Selected Criticism, 1916–1957*, by J. M. Murry, chosen and introduced by Richard Rees, Oxford University Press, London and New York, 1960.

Myers, F. W. H., 'Henry Sidgwick', *Proceedings of the Society for Psychical Research*, xv (1900–1), 452–62. Reprinted in *Fragments of Prose and Poetry*, ed. Eveleen Myers, Longman, London, 1904.

Nesbitt, George L., *Benthamite Reviewing; The First Twelve Years of the Westminster Review, 1824–1836*, Columbia University Press, New York, 1934.

Nettleship, R. L., *Memoir of Thomas Hill Green*, Longman, London, 1906.

Newsome, David, *Bishop Wescott and the Platonic Tradition*, Cambridge University Press, London, 1969.

Ogden, C. K., *Bentham's Theory of Fictions*, Kegan Paul, Trench, Trubner, London, 1932.

Paget, Stephen, ed., *Henry Scott Holland; Memoir and Letters*, J. Murray, London, 1921.

Parfit, Derek, 'Later Selves and Moral Principles', in *Philosophy and Personal Relations*, ed. A. Montefiore, McGill Queen's University Press, Montreal, 1973; Routledge & Kegan Paul, London, 1974.

Park, Roy, *Hazlitt and the Spirit of the Age: Abstraction and Critical Theory*, Clarendon Press, Oxford, 1971.

Passmore, John A., *A Hundred Years of Philosophy*, G. Duckworth, London, 1957.

Pattison, Mark, *Memoirs*, Macmillan, London, 1885.

Peel, J. D. Y., *Herbert Spencer: The Evolution of a Sociologist*, Heinemann Educational, London, 1971.

Pollin, Burton Ralph, *Godwin Criticism: A Synoptic Bibliography*, University of Toronto Press, Toronto, 1967.

Prichard, H. A., *Moral Obligation; Essays and Lectures*, Clarendon Press, Oxford, 1949.

Prior, Arthur N., *Logic and the Basis of Ethics*, Clarendon Press, Oxford, 1949.

Pucelle, Jean, *La Nature et l'ésprit dans la philosophie de T. H. Green; La Renaissance de l'idéalisme en Angleterre au XIXᵉ Siècle*, 2 vols., Éditions Nauwelaert, Louvain, 1960–5.

Quinton, Anthony, *Utilitarian Ethics*, St. Martin's Press, New York, 1973.

Raphael, D. D., *The Moral Sense*, Oxford University Press, London, 1947.

—— 'Sidgwick on Intuitionism', *Monist*, lviii (1974), 405–19.

RASHDALL, HASTINGS, 'Can There Be a Sum of Pleasures?', *Mind*,
N.S. viii (1899), 357–82.

—— 'Professor Sidgwick on the Ethics of Religious Conformity:
A Reply', *International Journal of Ethics*, vii (1896–7), 137–67.

—— 'Professor Sidgwick's Utilitarianism', *Mind*, o.s. x (1885), 200–6.

—— *The Theory of Good and Evil; A Treatise on Moral Philosophy*,
vol. i, The Clarendon Press, Oxford, 1907.

RAWLS, JOHN, *A Theory of Justice*, The Clarendon Press, Oxford;
Harvard University Press, Cambridge, Mass., 1971.

RAYLEIGH, LORD, 'Some Recollections of Henry Sidgwick', *Proceedings of the Society for Psychical Research*, xlv (1938), 162–73.

REARDON, B. M. G., *From Coleridge to Gore: A Century of Religious
Thought in Britain*, Longman, London, 1971.

REES, DANIEL, *Contemporary English Ethics*, Leipzig, 1892, 34–40.

RICHTER, MELVIN, *The Politics of Conscience: T. H. Green and His Age*,
Weidenfeld & Nicholson, London, 1964.

ROTHBLATT, SHELDON, *The Revolution of the Dons*, Faber & Faber,
London, 1968, esp. Ch. 4, 133–54.

ROWELL, GEOFFREY, *Hell and the Victorians; A Study of Nineteenth-
Century Theological Controversies Concerning Eternal Punishment and the
Future Life*, Clarendon Press, Oxford, 1974.

SCHMITT-WENDEL, KARL, 'Kants Einfluss auf die englische Ethik',
Kantstudien, xxviii (1912), 54–61.

SCHNEEWIND, J. B., *Backgrounds of English Victorian Literature*,
Random House, New York, 1970.

—— 'First Principles and Common Sense Morality in Sidgwick's
Ethics', *Archiv für Geschichte der Philosophie*, xlv, Hft. 2 (1963), 137–56.

—— 'Henry Sidgwick', *Encyclopedia of Philosophy*, vol. 7, ed. P.
Edwards, Macmillan and The Free Press, New York; Collier
Macmillan, London, 1967, 434–6.

— 'Sidgwick and the Cambridge Moralists', *Monist*, lviii (1974),
371–404.

—— 'Whewell's Ethics', *Studies in Moral Philosophy*, American
Philosophical Quarterly Monograph Series, no. 1, ed. Nicholas
Rescher, Basil Blackwell, Oxford, 1968, 108–41.

SEELEY, (SIR) JOHN R., *Ecce Homo; A Survey of the Life and Work of
Jesus Christ*, 5th edn., Macmillan, New York, 1866.

SEN, AMARTYA K., *Collective Choice and Social Welfare*, Oliver &
Boyd, Edinburgh & London; Holden-Day, San Francisco, 1970.

SETH, JAMES, 'The Ethical System of Henry Sidgwick', *Mind*, N.S.
x (1901), 172–87.

—— 'Is Pleasure the Summum Bonum?', *International Journal of
Ethics*, vi (1895–6), 409–24.

S[IDGWICK], A[RTHUR] and E[LEANOR] M., *Henry Sidgwick; A Memoir*, Macmillan, London, 1906. Abbreviation: *Mem.*

SIDGWICK, ETHEL, Mrs. *Henry Sidgwick; A Memoir*, Sidgwick & Jackson, London, 1938.

SIMON, WALTER M., *European Positivism in the Nineteenth Century, an Essay in Intellectual History*, Cornell University Press, Ithaca, N.Y., 1963.

SINCLAIR, A. G., *Der Utilitarismus bei Sidgwick und bei Spencer*, C. Winter, Heidelberg, 1907.

SINGER, MARCUS G., 'The Many Methods of Sidgwick's Ethics', *Monist*, lviii (1974), 420–48.

SINGER, PETER, 'Sidgwick and Reflective Equilibrium', *Monist*, lviii (1974), 490–517.

SLATER, MICHAEL, ed., *Dickens 1970. Centenary Essays by Walter Allen and Others*, Chapman & Hall, London, 1970.

SMEDLEY, EDWARD ARTHUR, *A Treatise on Moral Evidence*, Cambridge, Eng., 1850.

SOMERVELL, D. C., *English Thought in the Nineteenth Century*, Methuen, London, 1929.

SORLEY, W. R., 'Henry Sidgwick', *International Journal of Ethics*, xi (1900–1), 168–74.

SPARROW, JOHN H. A., *Mark Pattison and the Idea of a University*, Cambridge University Press, London, 1967.

SPENCER, HERBERT, 'Replies to Criticisms', *Fortnightly Review*, n.s. xiv (July–Dec. 1873), 715–39. Reprinted in *Essays; Scientific, Political, and Speculative* by H. Spencer, vol. ii, D. Appleton, New York, 1891, 238–50.

—— 'Replies to Criticisms on *The Data of Ethics*', *Mind*, o.s. vi (1881), 82–98. Reprinted as an Appendix to *The Principles of Ethics*, vol. ii.

STEPHEN, BARBARA, *Emily Davies and Girton College*, Constable, London, 1927.

STEPHEN, LESLIE, 'Henry Sidgwick', *Mind*, n.s. x (1901), 1–7.

—— 'Sidgwick's *Methods of Ethics*', *Fraser's Magazine*, xci (Mar. 1875), 306–25.

STORR, VERNON F., *The Development of English Thought in the Nineteenth Century, 1800–1860*, Longman, London, 1913.

SULLY, JAMES, Review of *Methods of Ethics*, *Examiner*, nos. 3449 and 3500 (20 and 27 Feb. 1875), 216–17 and 242–4.

THIRLWALL, JOHN CONNOP, *Connop Thirlwall, Historian and Theologian*, S.P.C.K., London, 1936.

TODHUNTER, I., *William Whewell, D.D., Master of Trinity College, Cambridge; An account of His Writings with Selections from His Literary and Scientific Correspondence*, 2 vols., Macmillan, London, 1876.

TURNER, FRANK MILLER, *Between Science and Religion; The Reaction to Scientific Naturalism in Late Victorian England*, Yale University Press, New Haven, Conn., 1974.

VENN, JOHN, *On Some of the Characteristics of Belief Scientific and Religious; Being the Hulsean Lectures for 1869*, London, Cambridge, 1870.

WALSH, WILLIAM HENRY, *Hegelian Ethics*, Macmillan, London; St. Martin's Press, New York, 1969.

WARD, MAISIE, *The Wilfrid Wards and the Transition*, 2 vols., Sheed & Ward, London, 1934.

WARD, WILFRID, 'Some Characteristics of Henry Sidgwick', in *Ten Personal Studies*, Longman, London, 1908.

WATSON, JOHN, 'Hedonism and Utilitarianism', *Journal of Speculative Philosophy*, x (1876), 271–90.

WELCH, CLAUDE, *Protestant Thought in the Nineteenth Century*, vol. i, Yale University Press, New Haven, Conn., 1972.

WHEWELL, WILLIAM, *Novum Organon Renovatum, Being the Second Part of the Philosophy of the Inductive Sciences*, 3rd edn., J. W. Parker, London, 1858.

—— *On the Philosophy of Discovery, Chapters Historical and Critical; Including the Completion of the Third Edition of the Philosophy of the Inductive Sciences*, J. W. Parker, London, 1860. Abbreviation: *Discovery*.

WHITE, REGINALD JAMES, comp., *The Political Thought of Samuel Taylor Coleridge*, Jonathan Cape, London, 1938.

WHITMORE, CHARLES E., 'The Significance of John Grote', *Philosophical Review*, xxxvi (1927), 307–37.

WILLEY, BASIL, *The English Moralists*, Chatto and Windus, London; Norton, New York, 1964.

—— *Nineteenth Century Studies: Coleridge to Matthew Arnold*, Chatto and Windus, London; Columbia University Press, New York, 1949.

WILLIAMS, BERNARD, 'A Critique of Utilitarianism', *Utilitarianism; For and Against*, by J. J. C. Smart and B. Williams, Cambridge University Press, Cambridge, 1973.

WINCH, PETER, 'Universalizability of Moral Judgements', *The Monist*, xlix (1965), 196–214. Reprinted in *Ethics and Action* by Peter Winch, Routledge & Kegan Paul, London, 1972.

WINSTANLEY, D. A., *Early Victorian Cambridge*, Cambridge University Press, Cambridge, 1940.

—— *Later Victorian Cambridge*, Cambridge University Press, Cambridge, 1947.

WINTER, ERNST S. F., *Henry Sidgwick's Moralphilosophie*, L. P. H. Maass, Flensburg, 1904.

Index

NOTE

In this Index the text and footnotes are covered but titles of books cited are not included, except for the *Methods*. Sidgwick is referred to as 'S'.

Since it may assist the reader to know which chapters of Part II of this book are most likely to contain commentary on specific chapters of the *Methods*, a list is given here:

Part II	Methods of Ethics
Chapter 6	I, i, ii, iv–viii
Chapter 7	I, iii, ix
Chapter 8	III, i, xii
Chapter 9	III, ii–xi; IV, ii
Chapter 10	III, xiii
Chapter 11	II, ii–vi; III, xiv; I, ix
Chapter 12	IV, i, iii–v
Chapter 13	II, iv; III, xiii; Concluding Chapter

Abercrombie, 75
Action, S's definition, 248 n., 249, 257, 266, 297
Acton, H. B., 179 n.
Albert the Great, 415
Ambrose, 415
Animals, feelings of, 170–1, 330
'Apostles', the, 23, 25, 27, 34
Aquinas, 415
Aristotle, viii, 40, 47–8, 90 n., 194, 287, 411, 415, 422
Arnold, Matthew, 36–7, 51
Arnold, Thomas, 22
Associationism, 77, 78, 128, 129, 136, 143–4, 158–9, 163 n., 177, 205, 237
Augustine, 415
Austin, John, 153; on rules, 154–6, 158, 160, 187; moral sense, 156; positive morality, 156–7, 163, 165 n., 175 n., 178
Axioms, 41, 45, 61, 70, 76–7, 86–7, 103, 108–9, 114–15, 160, 175; S and, 231, 265–6, 279; statements, 290–5; list, 295–7; special functions, 290, 293, 294, 298, 299, 301, 304–5, 362, 363; obtained, 288–9, 297–303, 310, 361–3; relations among, 366–70, 372–4, 375, see Moral order; and

principles, 304–6, 307–9, 310, 363–4, 419; and pleasure, 318–20; and consciousness, 325–6; and distribution, 330; and common sense, 350–1; see Benevolence; Egoism, ethical; Justice

Bacon, 104, 194
Bain, A., 6, 43, 47; and Paley, 151; 165 n., 175; ethics, 177; 181, 192 n., 316, 386
Baker, H., 144 n.
Balfour, A. J., 16, 384 n.
Barratt, A., 192 n.
Basic moral notion, S on, 215–16, 217–19, 221–2, 226, 228, 232, 233, 297, 354, 417; see Right
Beattie, 75
Belsham, Thomas, 128, 129
Belsham, William, 128
Benevolence, 7–8, 45, 48, 71–2, 76, 80, 110–11, 115, 117, 128, 135, 141, 143, 145, 150, 176; S on, 270–3, 333, 344; 418; Spencer, 388, 390; axiom, 291, 294–5; obtained, 299–300; 301–2, 304–5; in utilitarianism, 306–9; and egoism, 362–4, 366–70
Benson, A. C., 22 n.
Benson, E. W., 22–3, 30

Bentham, vii, 3, 36, 46, 47, 108, 118, 122, 129–30; psychology, 131–2; on first principles, 132–3; simplifies issues, 133–4; 138, 139, 147; Hazlitt attacks, 148–9, 153; on rules, 157, 158, 167–8, 336; Whewell on, 169–71; and J. S. Mill, 171–2, 174, 175 n.; 241, 290, 328, 332, 354
Bernays, P., 305, 307–8
Birks, T. R., 14, 89, 90 n., 151, 186 n.
Blackie, J. S., 187 n.
Blakey, R., 130 n., 413
Bonaventura, 413
Borelli, 106
Bradley, F. H., 3, 174, 192 n., 206, 317, 325 n., 384, 392–3; criticizes S, 393 ff.; hedonism, 394–7; psychology, 397–8; aim, 398–400; S's response, 400, 408, 409, 410–11
Broad, C. D., viii, 2, 198 n., 290 n., 305, 365, 372–3, 374 n.
Brown, Ford K., 134 n., 144 n., 146 n., 152 n.
Brown, Thomas, epistemology, 78–9; principles, 80; religion, 81; 82, 84, 147, 219 n.
Browning, R., 5
Buffier, 267 n., 332 n.
Bulwer-Lytton, E., 130 n., 131 n., 164
Burke, E., 148
Butler, 7–8, 42, 45, 47, 63 n., 64, 65, 69, 72, 100, 101, 106, 109, 115, 123, 141, 156, 242, 291, 408–9, 418–19, 420

Carlyle, T., 5, 164–5, 166–8
Carpenter, L., 81 n., 128 n.
Chadwick, O., 17 n., 96 n.
Chales, 164–5
Chalmers, T., 75, 142 n.
Christ, Seeley on, 28, 31–3, 45–6; 36, 42, 47, 100, 149
Cicero, 230
Clark, J. Willis, 96 n.
Clarke, G. Kitson, 17 n., 48 n.
Clarke, S., 45, 47, 48, 63 n., 79, 104, 291, 300, 412
Clay, 48 n.
Clough, A. H., 15, 49 n.
Clough, Anne, 16, 52
Cobbe, Frances P., 173
Cogan, 127, 129 n.
Colenso, 20

Coleridge, 19, 26, 46, 89–90; on the Bible, 91–2; conscience, 92–4; moral view, 94–5; influence, 95–6; 97, 99, 101, 166, 237, 247
Common sense morality, 8, 35, 76, 192–3, 414–15, 418–19;
    explanation of, 36, 61, 68, 77–8, 97–8, 102, 110–11, 126, 143–4, 145, 155–7, 164–5, 170–1, 177, 186–7, 329, 331–6;
    inadequacy of, 23–4, 36, 46, 48, 51, 114, 124, 147, 155, 159–60, 171–2, 178–80, 187, 329, 331–2, 342–7, 348, 414;
    and theory, 65, 73–4, 76–7, 108, 116–17, 139–40, 152–3, 172, 179, 261–2, 265, 282–3, 284–5, 329, 336–7, 349–51, 359–60;
    S on, 21, 23–4, 36–7, 41, 48, 51, 61; centrality, 191–3; defined, 193, 265–7; complexity, 198, 210–12, 213, 227; relativity, 230–1; usual form, 247, 249; and subjective right, 251–2, 256, 314; examinations of, 260; why examined, 262, 264–5; refined, 266, 269; tests, 267–70; examined, 270–8; verdict, 279, 281–2; requires first principle, 283–5, 310–11, 329; and pleasure, 322–4, 327; and utility, 329, 331–6, 336–8, 342–7, 348, 349–51; and egoism, 354–8, 359–60; evolutionism and, 387, 391–2; Bradley and, 400
Compton, B., 22 n.
Comte, Comtism, 20, 23, 34, 42, 43, 45, 55, 98, 338
Condorcet, 96
Conscience, in Butler, 7–8; 42; in Reid, 68–70, 72, 76, 77; in Coleridge, 92–4, 95; in J. Hare, 97; in Maurice, 98, 100; in Whewell, 101, 107; in Grote, 118; in Paley, 123–4; 127–8; and Bentham, 132–3; 142, 173, 177, 183; in Martineau, 239, 241; 408; *see also* Moral sense
Crofts, 144
Cumberland, 106

Dakyns, 23, 24, 42, 43, 44
Darwall, S., 317 n.
Darwin, 5, 18–19, 385–6, 387
Davie, G. E., 5 n.

Davies, J. Ll., 183
Dependence argument, 264–5, 280–3, 287, 313–15, 319, 331, 349–51, 359
Descartes, 56, 104
Desire, and desirable, 93, 184–5, 224, 317, 366; 216, 223–6, 248, 316–17, 417
Determinism, 42, 69–70, 75, 92, 96, 136, 138–9, 147, 166–8, 206; S on, 207–12, 213, 227; 239, 242, 245, 405–6, 419
Dewar, D., 75, 142
Dickens, 5, 172 n.
Donagan, Alan, ix, 101 n., 113 n.
Douglas, 96 n., 101 n.
'Dualism of Practical Reason', *see* Moral order
Duty, 65–7, 70–1, 79, 112, 117, 132, 176, 199, 215–16, 218, 222, 250, 420
Dymond, 81

Eckhart, 413
Egoism, ethical, 42, 44, 47, 66, 69, 80, 125, 128–9, 131, 206, 228, 388–9, 420, 421; 'suppression' of, 291, 301, 366, 398; axiom, 290, 293–4; obtained; 298–9; 301–2, 304–6; 352; method, 353–4; and common sense, 354–8, 359–60; and justice, 361; axiom and principle, 361–4; argument against, 364–6; need for, 366–70; problem, 370–4; not solved, 371–2, 374–9, 407
Egoism, psychological, 7, 42, 43, 65, 77, 124–5, 128–9, 131–2, 136, 143, 159, 179, 184, 206–7, 388, 403, 406, 407
Enfield, 48 n.
English, 151
Essays and Reviews, 19, 26
Estlin, 81 n., 128 n., 142 n.
Euclid, 287
Evolutionism, 6, 383–6, 387–8, 389; *see also* Darwin

Fénelon, 137, 152
Fichte, 63 n.
Forbes, D., 96 n.
Fox, 129
Frankena, W., ix, 290 n.
Freedom, *see* Determinism

Gash, N., 96 n.
Gauld, A., 30 n.
Gay, 124

General agreement, 20, 21, 49, 51, 55, 59–62, 64, 76, 164–5, 177, 199, 268–9, 297, 310, 319, 326–7, 331, 359, 377, 413, 415–16
Gisborne, and Paley, 141–3, 146; 149
God, 19, 23, 27, 39, 46, 72, 96, 98, 101–2, 106, 113, 150–1, 167, 222, 238, 246, 258, 326, 401–2, 404;
and moral order, 7, 40, 44, 69, 76–7, 94–5, 98–9, 101, 112, 120, 128, 132, 141; S on, 212–13, 352, 371–2, 376–8; *see* Moral order;
and basis of morality, 20, 43, 65–6, 68, 70, 76, 80–1, 92–3, 100, 124–5, 127, 141–2, 152, 154, 176, 182–3, 409–10; S on, 199–200, 218, 229, 241; *see* Religion; Christ
Godwin, 122, 134; a thorough utilitarian, 135 ff.; psychology, 136; and rules, 137–8; and motive, 138–9; 143; attacked, 144–6; 147, 148, 152, 153, 186, 229, 271
Good,
concept, 83, 93–4, 111, 124, 147, 182–3, 221–3, 225–6, 227–9, 233, 235–6, 242–3, 307–8, 388;
agent's own, 65–6, 69, 70–1, 77, 119, 183–4, 223–5, 293–4, 298, 362–70, 406;
universal, 71, 76, 84, 111, 120, 124, 135, 138, 183–4, 224–5, 294–5, 299, 301, 362, 366–70, 414;
ultimate, 212, 304, 310, 312, 314, 316–18, 319–20, 322–8, 361, 364, 395–6, 407
Goulburn, 22
Grave, S., 63 n.
Green, Thomas, against Godwin, 145–6
Green, T. H., 6, 22, 243 n., 321, 383, 384, 392–3, 394, 395–6, 400; compared to S, 401–2; metaphysics, 402, 407; against utilitarianism, 403; ethics, 403–5; free will, 405–6; psychology, 406–7; S criticizes, 407–11
Grote, John, 47, 90, 98; on philosophy, 117, 121, 191; on ethics, 118–20; against J. S. Mill, 181–2, 183, 184–5, 186; 199

Halevy, 129 n.
Hall, 176–7
Hallam, H., 413

Hamburger, J., 5 n.
Hamilton, 5, 63 n., 75, 267
Hampshire, S., 325 n.
Happiness, 76, 112, 119, 124–5, 131,
 136–7, 141, 152, 167, 175–6, 199,
 200, 209, 322, 329–30, 388, 397–8
Hare, Julius, 89, 90, 95, 96 n., 97–8, 101
Hare, R. M., 261, 284
Harrison, J. F. C., 140 n.
Hartley, 78, 127, 128, 129 n., 136, 177;
 and Godwin, 165
Hayward, F. H., 290 n., 304–5
Hazlitt, on Godwin, 134, 144; against
 Bentham, 148–9; 165, 166
Hegel, 2, 54, 384, 392
History of ethics,
 S and, 29–30, 45, 49, 191, 412,
  413–17;
 Whewell, 104–5, 106, 130–1, 413,
  415, 416;
 others, 413
Hobbes, 35, 100 n., 104, 355, 420, 479
Holland, H. S., 401, 409
Hooker, 63 n.
Hort, 26 n.
Hume, Reid against, 65–8, 72–3; 75,
 78, 80, 129, 139, 142, 166, 175 n.,
 219 n., 332, 333–4
Hutcheson, F., 79, 84, 86, 99, 104, 107,
 175 n., 211
Hutton, R. H., 183–4, 185, 186 n.,
 375–6
Huxley, 18, 386
Huygens, 106

Idealism, 6, 384, 392, 395, 399, 401,
 402–3, 404–5, 408–9
Indefinable concepts, Reid, 66, 68;
 A. Smith, 83, 87; Coleridge, 93–5;
 Maurice, 100; Whewell, 109,
 111–12, 168; Grote, 118, 181–2;
 Paley, 127; Macaulay, 131;
 McCosh, 181; Ward, 182–3;
 Davies, 183; Martineau, 241;
 Spencer, 388;
 S and, 204, 206, 215; arguments,
  217–19; 221–6, 232–7, 317, 389,
  417, 419;
 see Basic moral notion
Ingleby, 14 n.
Intention, 138, 244; S on, 248, 249,
 257–8, 266
Intuition, in Reid, 64, 76; Coleridge,

93, 95; Maurice, 98–9; Whewell,
 102–3, 106–7, 112–13; Grote, 118;
 Paley, 124; Bentham, 133–4; James
 Mill, 143–4; Cobbe, 173; Martineau,
 174, 238; J. S. Mill, 178–9; Spencer,
 175, 387–8; S, 43–4, 48, 56–60, 61,
 205, 222; fallibility of, 232, 319;
 266–7, 272, 280–1, 286, 304, 312;
 and pleasure, 319, 324, 326; and
 empiricism, 57–8, 59–60, 98, 134,
 179, 302
Intuitionism, 2–3, 63, 409; proponents,
 Reid, 64–5, 67–8, 72; 75–7;
 Brown, 79–80, and A. Smith, 82–3,
 separate epistemology and morals,
 84, 87–8; cf. 201; at Cambridge,
 89–90, 95 ff.; Coleridge, 92–4;
 Maurice, 98–100; Whewell, and
 progressive intuition, 102–3, 115–
 17, 169; and nature of intuition,
 106–7, 113; Grote, 118–19;
 Martineau, 173–4, 238, 240–1;
 Spencer, 387;
 criticized, Paley, 123; 127–8; Bentham, 133–4; Austin, 156; James
  Mill, 159–60; Bain, 177; J. S.
  Mill, 178–9, 187;
 S and, early views, 41–2, 43–4, 63;
  and common sense, 193, 260–2,
  and see Dependence argument,
  Systematization argument; 349–
  51; three phases, 200; how connected, 201; perceptional, dismissed, 202, 265, 313, 400;
  dogmatic, 202–4, 265–6, 282, 306;
  philosophical, 289, 306, 329; and
  genesis, 206; and basic notion,
  215, 218–19;
 reconciled with utilitarianism, A.
  Smith, 82, 84; Coleridge, 91,
  94–5; Maurice, 99; Grote, 118–19;
  122, 139–40, 150; Mackintosh,
  152; Cobbe, 173; Spencer, 176–7;
  S, 26–7, 43–4, 201, 262–3, 336–7,
  349, 352, 370, 420–1

Jacobi, 91
James, D. G., 15 n., 379, 393 n.
James, William, 14
Jeffrey, 75 n., 153 n.
Jevons, 128, 129
Jones, 175 n.
Jouffroy, 129 n., 157 n.

Jowett, 20
Justice, 7, 41, 66, 72–3, 76, 80, 84, 110–11, 113, 115, 119, 135, 142, 150, 157–8, 176, 199, 212; in S, 271, 273–7, 333–5, 407; axiom, 291–3; obtained, 298; 300–2, 305, 330, 360–1; 407; *see* Universalizability

Kant, 2, 43–4, 45, 47, 48, 55 n., 63, 90, 91–2, 107, 113, 173, 222, 227, 238, 274, 286, 287, 291, 384, 392, 412; S criticizes, 208, 250, 251–2, 269, 270, 271, 281, 302–3, 310, 313–14, 318–19, 353–4, 371–2, 375; compared with S, 419–20, 422
Kepler, 106
Kirkus, 187
Krug, 129 n.

Lacey, A. R., 290 n., 305
Laurie, S. S., 185, 186 n.
Leckey, W. E. H., 18–19, 30, 33 n., 180, 181, 184, 185, 186, 332, 387
Leibniz, 80
Leslie, T. Cliffe, 185, 186 n.
Lightfoot, 33 n.
Little, I. M. D., 322
Locke, 89, 95, 104
Love, 41, 42, 43, 46, 48, 100, 167, 241, 270
Lyell, 18
Lyons, D., 131 n.

Macaulay, T. B., 5, 130, 131, 140, 147–8, 149 n., 158, 166
McCosh, 63 n., 181, 184, 186
Mackie, J., 147 n.
Mackintosh, Sir J., 129–30, 147, 152; James Mill's attack, 158 f.; 413, 472
McTaggart, 16, 290 n.
Mansel, 98, 181 n., 185, 186 n.
Marshall, A., 47
Martineau, James, 91, 95, 108 n.; against J. S. Mill, 173–4, 178; life, 237; and God, 238; free will and morals, 239, 246; scale of motives, 240–2, 244–5; religion and, 243 ff., 258; S on, 247 ff., 252 ff.; reply, 255–6; error, 257–8
Marxism, 193 n.
Masson, 75 n.
Maurice, F. D., 14, 90, 95; theology,

98 f.; order, 99–100; morality, 100; on Bentham, 130 n., 166
Mayor, J. B., 185
Mazzini, 402
Merit, 72, 79, 81, 210–12, 239–41, 243, 257, 333, 360
Method, 23–4, 25, 47, 49, 51, 55, 58, 61; importance, 191–3, 415–16; defined, 194–5; and principle, 195–7, 204, 213, 332; division, 198–204; intuitional, 200–4, 265, 281–2, 284, 289, 306, 351; utilitarian, 198, 336, 339–40, 342–8, 351, 359–60; egoistic, 198, 228, 353–4, 358, 359–60, 369; and Spencer, 391; and Green, 410–11
Methods of Ethics, The, vii, viii, xv, 1–3, 13, 15, 17, 25, 36, 40, 51, 61, 63, 83, 112, 122, 191, 303–4, 384, 392, 400, 402 n.; various editions cited, 36, 63, 191, 192, 195, 199, 203, 204, 205, 208, 209, 211, 214, 226, 227, 233–6, 248 n., 268, 269, 274, 275, 281, 290–1, 300, 301, 303, 306, 311, 314, 318, 321, 324, 326, 336–7, 352–3, 355, 365, 367, 369, 370, 371–2, 396, 397, 412, 414
Metz, 2
Mill, James, 36; and associationism, 143–4; against Mackintosh, 158; and rules, 158–60, 161, 187; 165 n., 175 n., 177, 243
Mill, John Stuart, 2, 3, 5, 20, 21, 23, 26, 34, 36; writes to S, 37–8; 41, 42, 43, 45, 47, 48, 57–8, 90 n., 117; and Bentham, 130–1, 134, 149, 150, 153, 171–2; role of philosophy, 163–6, 167–8, 169; and rules, 172, 179, 186–7, 261, 335, 336; criticized, 173–4, 180–8; 175, 177, 347, 366, 386; *Utilitarianism*, 178–9; S on, 194, 205, 262, 315–16, 320, 336–7, 338–9, 342
Monro, D. M., 134 n., 145 n.
Moore, G. E., 4, 16, 205, 365 n.
Moral code, 8, 45, 125, 152, 176, 275, 283, 284, 329, 336, 338–40, 348–9, 391–2, 399–400; *see also* Rules; Common sense morality
Moral order, in Butler, 7–8; Reid, 69, 73–4, 76–7; Brown, 80; Coleridge, 94–5, 376; Maurice, 99–100; Whewell, 108, 111–12, 114–15; Grote, 119–20; T. Belsham, 128; Bentham, 132; Godwin, 135; Bradley, 397–8;

Moral order (*cont.*):
Green, 407–8; in S, 213–14; 'Dualism of Practical Reason', 352, 366, 369, 370–4, 375–9, 405, 418; *see* God and moral order
Moral sense, 42, 43, 65, 67–8, 77–8, 85–6, 87–8, 107, 123–4, 128, 133, 141, 152, 156, 175, 234, 385; *see* Conscience
More, 45
Morell, 60 n., 413
Morley, John, 185–6
Motive, 7–8, 65–6, 72, 75, 109–10, 138–40, 143, 206; and consequences, in Martineau, 241 f., 244 f., 247–50, 252–5, 257–9; reason as, 65–6, 136, 206, 207, 208, 216–18, 221–3, 226, 229, 232, 234–5, 315, 370, 419
Muirhead, 91 n.

Neville, 150
Newman, 18
Newnham College, 16
Newton, 104, 106
Noel, 30, 45, 230

Obedience to law, 110–11, 113, 126, 273, 275, 277, 334–5
Obligation, 79, 84, 94, 124–5, 128, 138, 160–1, 168, 181, 184, 222, 255
Ogden, C. K., 133 n.
Ought, 68, 85, 118, 131, 161, 168, 181, 183, 211, 215–18; ethical sense, 222–3, 228, 233; 226, 228, 235, 354, 403–5; *see* Right
Owen, 139, 140, 148

Paley, 3, 7, 63 n., 78, 81, 82, 89, 94, 95; 101, 122; aim of ethics, 123; on moral sense, 123–4; obligation, 124–5; moral view, 125–7; rules, 127, 336; 128, 129, 130 n., 134, 137, 140; Gisborne's attack, 141–3; 144, 146; defended, 149–51; 152, 154, 160, 168, 241
Park, R., 144 n., 149 n.
Parr, Dr. S., 145 n., 152
Pattison, M., 20
Paul, St., 46
Payne, 81
Peirce, 60 n.
Perfection, 46, 199, 200, 202–4, 209, 212, 312, 323

Philosophy, in nineteenth century, 3–6; and religion, 32–5, 36, 41–2; S's view of, 52–5, 61–2, 191; J. S. Mill on, 163–6, 167–9, 178; Martineau, 238; Bradley on, 398–400; S's reply, 409–11; *see also* Theology
Plato, 34, 40, 90 n., 117, 357, 420
Pleasure, 111, 119–20, 128, 133, 135, 139, 149, 167; J. S. Mill on, 179; criticized, 181, 185–6, 320; S on, 316–17, 320–2; and good, 223, 226, 227, 310–11, 317–20, 322–8, 330; 354–5, 358–60, 364, 388; Bradley on, 392, 394–7; 403, 407
Plumptre, 90 n.
Pollin, B. R., 134 n.
Price, 127 n.
Priestley, 127
Principles, and analyticity, 64, 85, 87, 127, 131, 181–3, 226–7, 270, 272, 279, 286, 293, 308, 388–9; rationality of, 7–8, 65–7, 77, 82–3, 86, 107, 108–9, 133–4, 169, 261–2, 280, 311, 418–20, 421–2; rationality denied, 78–80; conflict of, *see* Moral order;
stated, Reid, 70–2, 74; Brown, 80; A. Smith, 84; Coleridge, 93; Maurice denies need for, 100; Whewell, 108–11; Grote, 119; Paley, 124; Bentham, 131; Godwin, 135; Martineau, 240–2, 255; S, *see* Axioms; Spencer, 389;
as 'first', 64, 67–8, 74; requirements for, in Whewell, 108–9; in Bentham, 133–4; in Godwin, 139–40; in Stewart, 142; in J. S. Mill, 172; in S, 194–6; self-evident, 267–9; no arbitrary limits, 272, 276–7, 278, 279–81, 287, *see* Dependence argument; determine actual rightness, 282–3, *see* Rightness; systematize common sense, 331, 411, *see* Systematization argument;
support for, 68–9, 72, 77–8, 112–13, 118–19, 124–5, 132–3, 135, 154, 171, 173, 176–7; against J. S. Mill, 183–5; in S, 260, 262–5, 280–4, 287–9, 310–11, 364–6, 417–18; *see* God;
and method, 195–8;
and axioms, 70, 76, 103, 106–7; in S, 289, 304–9, 363–4, 419–20

Priority, logical, 287–8; and good, 366–70

Progress, 21, 26–7, 28, 30–2, 37, 39–40, 44, 46, 94–5, 96–8, 100–3, 106–7, 111–12, 116–17, 176, 211, 213–14, 281, 332, 375–8

Promising, 113, 137, 277–8

Prudence, 7–8, 66, 76, 77, 80, 93, 112, 119–20, 149, 158, 176, 240, 242, 250, 407, 418; axiom, *see* Egoism, ethical

Ramsay, Sir G., 175 n.

Rands, W. B., 185, 186 n.

Raphael, D. D., 63 n.

Rashdall, H., 290 n., 304, 305 n.

Rawls, J., 2, 261 n.

Reason, 64–6, 68, 72, 75, 85–6, 93, 97, 107, 109–10, 112–13, 118; in S, 25, 34–5, 39, 40, 207–8, 216–17, 219, 221–2, 229–30, 233–5, 280; demands of, central, 303–4, 417–18; 328, 350–1, 353–4, 358, 365, 369, 370–4, 378–9, 393, 416, 419; dictation of, 208, 229, 315, 330, 370; *see* Basic moral notion; Motive

Received opinion, 261, 284, and *see* Common sense morality

Reeve, H., 186

Reid, vii, 3, 4, 5, 63; epistemology, 64–5; moral psychology, 65–6; moral theory, 66–9; will, 69–70; principles, 70–4; common sense, 74; 75, 76–7, 79, 80, 82–3, 84, 86, 91, 105, 107, 109, 115, 132, 142, 144, 166, 219, 267 n., 279

Religion, 17–21; miracles, 29–31, 42; and clergy, 48–51; 55, 74, 78, 127, 165–6, 168, 230, 385, 407, 414–16; and philosophy, 4–6, 19, 23, 32–6, 90–1, 104–5, 163–6, 402; and utilitarianism, 6, 95–6, 140, 142, 144–5, 149–51, 152, 154–6, 167, 179, 186; and intuitionism, 7–8, 64, 84, 91–5, 97, 237–8, 245–7; S and, 14, 21–5; on prayer, 27–8; 37–8; and Bible, 38–40; 42, 51–2, 60, 352, 371–9, 401; and morality, 19–20, 24, 28, 31, 32, 36–7, 42–3, 45–7, 75, 81, 105, 112, 120, 124–5, 127–8, 258, 325–6, 354, 356, 407, 409, 413, 414–16; *see* God; Retrospective judgement

Renan, 24, 39

Retrospective judgement, 46, 68, 210, 212, 243, 245–7, 252, 256–8

Right, meaning, 66, 79, 83, 84, 94, 181–2, 215–16, 217–18; and moral feeling, 220; and rationality, 221–2, 303–4, *see* Reason; and good, 223, 226, 235–6; 227–9, 233, 242, 249, 256, 259; and rules or principles, 46–7, 71, 111–12, 124, 252–3, 261, 270, 312, 329–30, 341, 345, 346–7, 348, 387; and S's axioms, 291–3, 295, 297–8, 299–300, 302, 306–8, 318, 362–3, 373–4; formal, 250–1; objective, 236, 251–2, 257, 302, 313–14; 341; putative and actual, 279–83, 285, 349, 360; relative to method and principle, 194–5, 196–7, 199–203, 204, 318

Ross, W. D., 205

Rothblatt, S., 14 n.

Rowell, G., 127 n., 214 n.

Rules, 49, 108, 110–12, 113–14; in utilitarianism, Paley, 125–7, 149–50, 160, 168–9, 336; Godwin, 137–8, 146, 152; Gisborne, 141; Jeffrey, 153 n.; Austin, 153–7; James Mill, 158–60; A. Smith, 160–3, 170–1; J. S. Mill, 171–2, 173, 177, 179, 186–7, 335–7; Spencer, 176, 390–1; Whewell criticizes, 168–70; in Martineau, 252–4, 259; Bradley, 398–9; conflict of, and exceptions to, in Reid, 73–4, 76; in Whewell, 115–16; Bentham on, 132–3, 161–2; J. S. Mill, 179; in S, 41, 234–5, 252–4, 266, 269, 272, 274, 277, 278, 282, 284, 314, 331–2, 335, 341, 344–6, 348–9; *see also* Validity

Russell, B., 16, 219 n.

Saint-Simonianism, 21, 163, 178

Scepticism, 23, 55–6, 64, 70, 165, 230–2

Schelling, 91

Schopenhauer, 413

Schurman, J. G., 386

Sedgwick, A., 89, 95, 150, 163, 172

Seeley, J. R., S's critique, 28–35, 45–6

Self-evidence, 21, 77, 84, 108, 264; needed for knowledge, 64, 67–8, 76, 107, 132–3, 173, 193, 286, 350; tests or criteria of, 61, 64, 103, 267–9, 272,

Self-evidence (*cont.*):
279, 282–3, 289, 297; recognition of, 65, 103, 265–6, 279, 286–9, 308, 391; element, 305–6, 364
Self-love, *see* Egoism; Prudence
Sen, A. K., 322 n.
Seth, J., 304, 305 n.
Sexual Purity, 41, 105, 110–11, 113, 278
Shakespeare, 15
Sidgwick, Arthur, 13
Sidgwick, E., 13, 16
Sidgwick, Henry, vii, viii, 1, 3, 6, 9, 87, 90, 113, 121, 188, 237, 383, 384–6, 392, 401–2; life, 13–17; early religious belief, 21–4; development, 25–8; writing on religion, 28–34, 36–40, 45–6, 48–51; later views, 374 ff., 378–9; and psychic research, 16, 30–1, 375; and reason, 25, 35–6, 379;
early ethics, 40–3; develops theory, 43–4, 45–7, 48, 51–2, 61; epistemology, 52, 55–60, 63, 205, 287–8, 302, 377–8; on philosophy, 34–6, 43, 52–5, 61, 191, 192, 213–14
Simon, W., 23 n.
Singer, M., 194 n.
Smedley, E. A., 245–6
Smith, Alexander, 5, 64; life, 82 n.; epistemology, 82–4; principles, 84; on moral sense, 85–6; rationality, 86–8, 107; praises Paley, 150, 160; on rules, 160–3, 335; 219, 286
Smith, Sidney, 75 n.
Smith, Dr. S., 129
Smith, William, 150–1, 163 n., 177
Social facts, 338–9
Socrates, 32–3, 55, 90 n., 414
Sparrow, 5 n.
Spencer, 3, 4, 6, 19; Mill on, 175; early ethics, 175–7; 237, 274, 316, 383, 384; and evolution, 386–7; S's criticisms, 388–92; 402 n.
Spinoza, 35
Spiritualism, 30, 31 n.
Stanley, 90 n.
Stephen, L., 384
Sterling, 90 n., 166
Stewart, D., 63 n., 75, 78, 80, 86, 107; on Paley, 142, 143, 149, 150
Stoicism, 33 n., 34, 35, 145, 250, 317–18, 414

Subjectivism, Reid, 67, 83; Brown, 78–81; A. Smith, 81–4, 85, 88, 107; S, 219–21, 229, 233
Symonds, J. A., 372, 376
Systematization, S on, 3, 25, 44, 53, 54–5, 59–60, 61, 76, 186, 198, 213–14, 221–2, 231–2, 252, 277, 310–11, 312, 361, 383, 415–16, 419, 422; Whewell, 103–4, 109–11, 112–13, 116, 171; Grote, 117, 191; 122; J. S. Mill, 172; argument, 264–5, 283, 328; outlined, 331–2; developed, 332 ff.; 342, 350–1; and egoism, 359–60

Taylor, J., 104
Tennyson, 5, 54 n., 378–9
Thales, 53, 54
Thayer, 184 n., 187
Theology, 23–4, 28, 39, 48–9, 55, 204, 212, 325, 375–6, 379, 398, 405
Thirwall, 90
Todhunter, 101 n.
de Tocqueville, 36–7
Torquemada, 256
Turner, F., 374 n.
Tylor, 18

Universalizability, 71, 73, 77, 92–3, 126, 135–6, 154, 160–1, 230, 251–2, 280–1, 292, 301, 302–3, 304, 318, 344–5
Utilitarianism, 2–3, 5, 6, 8–9, 38, 76, 77–8, 89–90, 121, 122, 261, 417–18, 422;
act and rule, 341, 348–9, *see* Rules
'unconscious', 157, 332
critics, 6; Reid, 72–3, 76; Brown, 80; Coleridge, 93–5; J. Hare, 97; Whewell, 105–6, 111–12, 115–17, 130–1, 157, 168–71, 172; Grote, 117–19, 181–2, 184–5; Gisborne, 141–2, 146; T. Green, 145–6; Hazlitt, 148–9; Sedgwick, 150; Carlyle, 164, 166–8; Cobbe, 173; Martineau, 173–4, 237, 241, 243; Ward, 182–3; Bradley, 392; T. H. Green, 403; minor, 140–51, 181–4;
proponents, A. Smith, 82, 84, 87–8, 160–3; Paley, 123–7; minor, 127–9; Bentham, 131–4; Godwin, 134–40; Austin, 153–7, 160; James Mill, 158–60; J. S. Mill, 163, 171, 178–80, 194; Spencer, 175–7, 387–9; Bain, 177; *see* Rules

S, early views, 41–4, 45, 47–8, 51; his own view, 192, 213–14, 262–3, 329, 352, 361, 399; method, 198–9, 336, 338–40, 342–6, 348–9; and determinism, 210–11, 213–14; formulated, 329–30; and basic concept, 226–7; argument for, 260, 264–5, 283–5, 288–9, 299–300, 304–9, 310–11, 314–15, 318–19, 322 ff., 327–8, 331–2, 420–1; *see* Common sense; on objections, 332–5, 349; and secrecy, 346–7; and egoism, 355–6, 359–61, 363–5, 367–9, 370–4; and intuitionism, 201–2, 262–3, 283–4, 294–5, 304–9, 336–7, 349, 352, 370;
limits to, 8–9, 111–12, 142, 147, 154, 161, 169–70, 172, 186, 331, 335–6, 340, 341–2, 348–9, 359;
as 'low', 90, 94, 95–7, 105–6, 115–16, 140–1, 145–51, 166–7, 186;
see Axioms; Benevolence; Dependence argument; Systematization

Validity, 263–4, 266, 268, 279–80, 282–4, 319–20, 326, 349; *see* Right, putative and actual
Venn, John, 60 n.
Veracity, 7, 48, 51, 76, 84, 110–11, 113, 138, 142, 199, 277, 278
Vico, 96
Victoria, Queen, 13

Virtue, 42, 65–6, 69, 71, 76, 79–80, 84, 105, 110, 111, 115, 124, 128, 139, 164, 167, 179, 227, 269, 270, 272, 273, 278; as ultimate good, 311–16

Wainewright, on Paley, 143–4, 149–50
Ward, James, 16, 58–9
Ward, W. G., criticisms of Mill, 182–3; criteria of self-evidence, 267 n.
Wardlaw, 80–1, 142 n.
Watts, Rev. R., 186
Welch, C., 17 n., 91 n.
Whately, 151
Whewell, 3, 5, 41, 42, 63, 64, 89–90, 95, 96, 98; his philosophy of science and ethics, 101–4; history of ethics, 104–6, 413, 415; intuition, 106–7, 112–13; system, 108–12; 113–15; anti-utilitarianism, 115–17, 119–20; and Bentham, 130–1, 134, 152–3, 157, 169–71; and Paley, 168–9; 150, 163, 172, 174, 177, 178, 179 n., 186, 194, 208, 237, 266, 273, 277, 278, 279, 286, 289 n., 332, 409, 416, 419
Whitehead, 16
Willey, B., 91 n.
Williams, B., ix, 228 n.
Winstanley, D., 14 n.
Wisdom, 6, 66, 72, 269–70, 272
Wollaston, 79
Worsley, 90 n.
Wren, 141